TIME SPENT AWAY

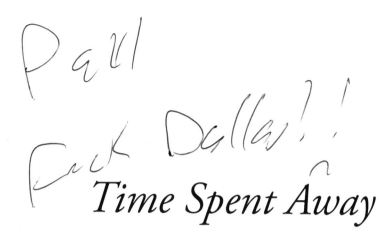

Time Spent Away

A novel

by

ANDREW MITIN

BOOKS

Adelaide Books
New York / Lisbon
2019

TIME SPENT AWAY
A novel
By Andrew Mitin

Published by Adelaide Books, New York / Lisbon
adelaidebooks.org

Editor-in-Chief
Stevan V. Nikolic

For any information, please address Adelaide Books
at info@adelaidebooks.org
or write to:
Adelaide Books
244 Fifth Ave. Suite D27
New York, NY, 10001

ISBN-10: 1-951214-58-7
ISBN-13: 978-1-951214-58-6

Printed in the United States of America

For Dad

Contents

PART ONE

After Dad died I sold the farm and moved to Chicago. I had worked the land four months and I couldn't any longer. The corn was doing well and a neighbor had agreed to take it off for me, the chickens in their silver ark were fed and producing as they always had and the machines were well-cared for. The buyers were a young family who wanted to relocate back to Huron County and raise their children and some hogs. I gladly yielded.

I asked Mr. Weurtzel to drive me to Bad Axe where I picked up a small rental truck. It was too big for the little I would take away with me, but it was all they offered for a one-way trip. Mr. Weurtzel offered to stay and help me load, but I told him I could manage.

"I wouldn't mind staying a bit longer, Joshua."

We carried twelve boxes of books, five for the kitchen, three suitcases of clothes, the leather chair and ottoman, two bookshelves and Mom's ironing board from the garage. We only spoke about our grips, watching our step and the surprising weight of the novels. I brought the door down and locked it, then gave him the keys to the house.

"It's hard to think about a new family living here," he said looking at the white two story home where he and his friend had shared theirs with one another.

"They seem like good people," I said. "The mother's excited to garden and pick the cherries. She's going to use the old canning room again."

"We're going to miss you, Joshua." He held me in a long embrace before slapping my back. "If you need anything at all, Karen and I are always here for you."

Mr. Weurtzel drove away and I stood beside the truck in the silence of the front yard. The July heat stilled the air. Nothing moved and I lingered in that moment trying to remember and feel all I had experienced there, knowing I would never have it again. Of course it was impossible, and anyway I was too excited thinking of my future to properly grieve my loss.

I watched the farmhouse and out-buildings in the side view mirrors until they were obscured by the green-standing fields then hidden by distance and woods. It was difficult to think of other voices filling our rooms and other hands opening the doors and windows. I imagined the loneliness of the painted walls and the carpeted stairs, the fireplace stones' bewilderment at the stark living room as they wondered what had happened to Dad and I. I saw the windows that had watched me run around the house and swing from the vines of the weeping willow and disappear into and out of the chicken house and the barn well up. I saw them see Dad trekking toward the shed to sharpen blades or wire new time clocks, toward the barn to change the tractor's oil or tinker with the old Ford's engine. When he emerged it was to stand in the front yard near the road and look across the fields and into the darkening evening before coming inside to have dinner with me.

Not yet two miles from home and I had to pull over until it passed.

I drove upon those cemetery roads in silence, alternately overcome with heartache and anticipation; by turns afraid yet anxious to have a few years to myself in which to discover the rest of my life, its capacity, both in terms of my ability and how much I could fill it with. Then there were times I didn't think about anything at all. I passed through familiar towns and made turns by rote without witnessing them and when I joined with the freeway heading south a dozen mile markers would pass in a moment. But however quick the distance separated me from my past and however grandiose I imagined my future in Chicago those windows remained, staring dark and empty in the stillness.

I first saw a glimpse of the skyline at 95th Street. It poked above the horizon in a small cluster of dark rectangles and I wondered if it would be big enough for my dreams. Then, as I-90 took me further west then north, the city opened up. What before had been an insignificant blot on the windshield now rose ominous around me. I was awed beneath it. Taken together the steel and glass, the concrete and ornamentation proved too much to take in. The history and the intentionality that pointed to their being man-made did not hinder my impression that these obelisks had always been and would always keep their watch along the shore. I was approaching an understanding of the city on par with those Dutch explorers landing on Easter Island or with those who stumbled upon Stonehenge years after its meaning had been lost.

A warning blast brought me out of this revery and I jerked the truck back within the limits of my lane. All around me were semi-trailers and speeding mid-size sedans, construction barrels and detour warnings, pick-ups and SUVS changing lanes and accelerating then breaking, causing me to react too strenuously then struggling to regain the communal speed again. In the chaos of the freeway I forgot about the cityscape. I had wanted to ease upon it, to take each change of perspective as it came and to chart the sun's reflection off the glass and ask if it would acquiesce to me and my intentions. Instead, I was pressed on all sides by speeding metal and the vulgar blatting of car horns. I glimpsed the Ohio Street exit sign above white knuckles. I mumbled a prayer and checked my side view. I pressed the blinker stalk but it wouldn't move and I panicked before realizing it had been on for some time. Traffic was not going to let me in without insistence and I decided to press my will. I nosed in behind an F-150 and a semi, whose company name and logo *MS Carriers: We deliver your future* seemed a portent of calamity.

Driving inside the city completely obscured it. Concrete walls rose up on either side and the broad shoulders I had read about had to be retrieved from memory. I sped into and out of sunlight as first Halsted then Hubbard passed overhead and while I was marveling at the concrete pillars and the grooved under carriage of top-side routes, the exit curve demanded deceleration, which I noticed in time to avoid rear ending a slow-moving Mazda. Traffic was slowed to a drifting pace and I crossed the Chicago River for the first time. I made out a brown sliver of water before the Northwestern Railway Bridge, with its zig-zag iron works pointing toward the sky as if in preparation for an ariel raid or else in the collection of celestial data, interrupted the view. Then the whole of it vanished behind condominiums.

I turned onto LaSalle toward Division. The four blocks to State, though bewildering to me then, would quickly become as familiar to me as the two main streets of my small home town, one of which was dominated by the municipal parking lot and the other by the grain elevator. Here there were multi-purpose buildings of brown brick with ten foot panes of glass that allowed natural light to illuminate rental spaces. Colorful awnings covered the darkened entrances of the bars and their patrons, who were sipping at sidewalk rails in the middle of the day. American flags, green shamrocks, Mother's heart marquee, FedEx, US Bank and, at State Street, two stories of grey orioles ornamented with diamonds and pin wheels and designed to appear like the shuttle used in the pneumatic tubes at Thumb National Bank, where Dad's legacy rested.

Restaurants lined the shaded side of the street and I parked outside Canterbury Court Apartments. The heat wasn't so different from what I had left only six hours earlier and I stood beside the truck, stretched my back in the sun and looked. The narrow facade began as smoothed, dense concrete and seemed like a vault through which a large chisel had scored lines for window placements. The Southeast corner appeared to have been sliced off revealing windows that I hoped to gaze out of soon. The building's growth was amended at the third floor by an abundance of tan bricks and the whole structure seemed to taper against the blue sky that seemed affixed to the affluent neighborhood.

Inside, a disinterested man looked my name up on his computer. He checked my ID against the leasee's name and confirmed that I had paid the first month's rent plus deposit.

He opened a box mounted on the wall and took out a small key ring.

"Yours will be 702. That's on the seventh floor. Laundry is through there. You'll pick up your mail here. Bring your ID for the first week or so until my staff recognizes you. You got furniture you need to move in? Take your vehicle to the end of the block, turn left, left again down the alley. I'll have a guy meet you."

There was a mere foot on either side of me in the narrow lane and because of the truck's height I had to steer away from fire escapes while keeping an eye on the corner bumpers to avoid hitting refuse and recycling containers. When I saw brick that resembled the front of my new home, I stopped. The truck's door couldn't open fully and I squeezed out. A maintenance man appeared with a dolly and showed me the freight elevator. I thanked him, but he had already seen to me and couldn't be bothered anymore.

When I opened the overhead door and saw that everything was where Mr. Weurtzel and I had put it, I felt the pang of heartache. It had given me some comfort that he knew where those boxes were and that he could conjure up my place within the truck and on the road. But when I loaded my boxes on to the dolly, the boxes Mr. Weurtel had last touched and that Dad had not seen me pack, I felt the beginnings of what it meant to be alone.

The elevator doors opened on Seven and I wheeled my first load of boxes down the dim hallway. It was quiet on the floor and smelled of carpet cleaner. 702 opened into a small hall leading to the bathroom. On the right was a built-in closet and drawers, natural light from the left laid across the grey carpet. I pulled the dolly into the single room. It was long and narrow with a double mattress I would use as a couch. The kitchenette was fit into a closet and there was a desk situated beneath the middle window. When I saw I had the corner apartment the sadness I had carried with me dissipated. I was filled again with optimism as I remembered what I had come here to do.

I opened an unscreened window and leaned out, extending my arms to embrace all of State Street, from Lincoln Park to Trump Tower, the parking garage opposite my building, the green ash trees below me, the Gold Coast as far as Lake Michigan, and all the possibilities my future could birth, before gathering to me all I had in the world.

The size of my apartment — my cell — appealed to the aesthete in me and when I stumbled upon Le Corbusier and his golden ratio in one of the many deserted aisles of the Harold Washington Library I knew I couldn't have lived anywhere else. Not that my cell had any architectural affinity with *Saint Marie de la Tourette*, but I used the space in similar ways.

I woke while it was still dark and in the silence of my space I hummed a hymn from my youth and read from the Psalms; I looked at a passage from the gospels before turning to one of Paul's letters, which was Romans at the time of my arrival in Chicago and is perhaps the most difficult book in the New Testament, not because its subject matter is so mystifying, but because it takes the believer to the very beginning of faith, as if, were the message of that letter not realized and adhered to by a Christian's life, it could be said not to have yet begun. I followed these readings with prayer: a litany of thanksgiving then intercessions, both for my old community and my new one, followed by a request for wisdom. I would put on music on, either Berlioz or Mozart, Dvorjak or Hayden, and disappear into the world of a novel. I sat content in those quiet mornings and wondered at how perfect it all was. I had a comfortable bed, a solid writing desk with a view I believed I would never weary of, drawers full of notebooks eager to be filled and bookshelves loaded down with odes to my enthusiasm for literary work.

I had only a vague idea about what a literary life looked like, but I dedicated my time to writing stories and whatever followed from that would make such a life clear. I submitted my work and was rejected by innumerable literary magazines, college reviews and writing contests. Anonymity and assured dismissal gave me confidence and I reveled in the freedom to experiment; my indifference toward being published, feigned early on except in moments of great optimism that often accompanied me on lengthy walks throughout the city, allowed my writing to play. I wanted only to send my little birds out and if one should return with an olive branch, so much the better. I amassed a healthy portfolio of rejection letters, all of the stock variety, neither condemning my work nor encouraging it. That tone suited me.

When I had finished with the day's pages and the city's morning rustle became too much to ignore, I took up my weatherworn satchel and stepped out. I had an idea of which streets I wanted to walk, ones that would take me to a new museum or a different bookstore or another stately architectural achievement, or at least where one had once stood in Chicago, but most days I didn't care. Inevitably I would saunter upon something.

Proponents of the walk may object to my choice of wilderness. They may wonder why I left the idyllic country with its isolated terrain, its lake shores and the stone quarry, to meander through an urban labyrinth of civilization and culture, the very aspects of our humanity early enthusiasts of the walk had sought to escape. Those men and women declaimed such vulgar apparitions and instead, ensconced in a serene environment, they looked inward for unadulterated impressions of meaning and truth. Well, the city has triumphed and enough time has passed that we are better equipped to stave off the noise and speed of modern life than our forefathers.

When I wrote that I saunter through the city, I had a specific idea in mind that I meditated on while I wandered. Some time ago in France, beggars would seek alms claiming they were going to the Holy Land, the *sainte-terrer*. It was a ruse for sure, more elegant and ironic than beggars' stories today, but it betrays a time in history when we really did aspire to have peace with God, or spiritual fulfillment. The saunterer walks to the Holy Land and I took great pleasure in the idea that my life would be a perpetual pilgrimage. Though I was not tramping across swaths of dangerous terrain with hundreds of other devotees to reach a city packed with religious meaning, nevertheless I felt I was on a spiritual quest. I had indeed taken to the city; I was waiting only for fellowship.

I woke at six on my first morning in Chicago. It was a clean fifty-nine degrees and there was a promise of sun in the clear dawn sky. I made coffee and sat down with some psalms accredited to King David and Proverbs 8 that is accredited to his son. I positioned my leather chair in such a way as to see Hancock Tower through one window and the impression of Willis Tower in the other. The lights of each were aglow in the early between-time and I raised my cup to the tireless sentinels. After a time of meditation and a quick prayer I ate a banana and watched Rush Street separate from State, the divorce having been commemorated with the planting of trees in the Viagra Triangle. I tied on my running shoes and was on the pavement before the newspaper kiosks had opened their shutters.

By the time I was in the midst of the Magnificent Mile, I was out of breath and clutching my sides, spitting foul mocha-stained phlegm near the entrances of Burberry and Cartier. I had to stop again on DuSable Bridge, compelled equally by the frailty of my lungs and the beauty I saw from there. It was as though the wind had planed the steel and glass and, through a millennium of insistence, created a unique landscape, like the

Wave in Arizona or the entrance to Keya Cave Island. I walked beneath the monoliths to North Wabash then lingered on Irv Kupcinet Bridge. The sun had risen over the lake and its light played upon the stone walls of the Wrigley Building. Beneath me the Chicago River lolled inland. I felt understanding, beauty and artistic expression beckon all around me. The fact of the city, its enormity and influence, took my breath away. I leaned over the rail inhaling the air of the metropolis, the scent of the river and the hum of roused activity. How different from a land suffused with green acres and where the nearest light illuminated a neighbor's yard a mile away. I had felt that I would be in for a painful assimilation; that the difference between the two environments would necessitate a kind of decompression chamber where my blood could calm down and my mind acclimate to the glut and speed of sensory perceptions. However, I found I could live in such a state of excitement with some ease and that I could ignore the city's impulsiveness for substantial parts of the day, if only by reading the slow lines of a novel or a work of fragments, taken in whatever order I chose whenever I chose it.

So I was encouraged to make my way and Wordsworth spoke of my time: *Dear Liberty! Days of sweet leisure, taxed with patient thought.*

I strolled beneath old oak trees that lined the streets of the Gold Coast. I walked in concentric circles, first around my block, then in ever increasing orbits until all the streets enveloped by the latitude lines of Division and North Avenue and the longitude lines of LaSalle Drive and Lakefront Trail became my new county. There was not a street I didn't grow to appreciate for its hidden qualities, made more precious by a general lack of attention; that a few of them were named after poets delighted me and I read those signposts from the great tradition as lights from the winking heavens.

Returning home via Goethe Street one evening I happened to pass under the first floor window of a brownstone. From a distance I had heard the low strings of a violin solo and when I looked to see where the music was coming from I saw a young girl in an upper window. Her eyes were intent on the sheet music and that intensity opposed the languid way her delicate chin rested on the lower bout. The music was lovely and I leaned against the rough brick of the walk-up and watched the street. There was a wakening bustle; a few cars had already abandoned their spots by the curb and an arrhythmic closing of doors punctuated my thoughts at least effective moments. The life of the morning street is not unlike my own life, I thought; even my own self. There is an aura of preparation about it, a beginning of what, to my limited point of view relating to the strange lives of others, I knew not what. Like the rising sun, shining ever brighter until the fullness of day, my own strange life was just beginning and where I would be at that sun's apex I had no idea. Indeed, I was also ignorant of what I would be in only a moment's time; which poet would become a beacon, which lines I would recite like an incantation either chasing away doubt and fear or beckoning hope and wisdom. Pessoa had written the men and objects share an equally insignificant destiny in the mystery of life's algebra. However magisterial I thought that idea to seem, I knew there was nothing insignificant about my destiny or the destiny of the street, and even the destiny of the child serenading her own becoming.

After three weeks of living alone in Chicago I was still understanding how deep a grief could be. I was walking around the river at night admiring Wacker Drive and the dark water that forever washed against its retaining walls. I descended the ornate steps to the river's edge looking for a place that would allow me to lay hands in the eternal stream. None existed and I sat against the wall and listened to the traffic above me. I stretched my legs and looked for constellations through the city's incandescent veneer — Andromeda, Cassiopeia, Perseus — but there weren't enough stars in the firmament to connect the images. I attempted to outline my own story in the deep dark, but the earth-bound illuminators obscured their awesome forebears and I was no closer to understanding the Why.

Across the river a Wendella sightseeing boat was waiting to disembark. Awed chatter carried across the water and I saw camera flashes going off in passengers' hands. What they were pointing at and exclaiming about I had made a point to see every day since arriving in Chicago. Modern obelisks of varying shades of gray, together with glassed steel frames rose behind a cream, concave stone spotted with squares of blue that reflected the sky's demeanor. I could see it without looking and while families laughed and captured one of their unforgettable moments with each other, I saw it.

The tourists soon disappeared around the South bend, and about the time they would become enthralled with the sheer wall of Insull's Civic Opera House, which had given me the impression of approaching Petra, I climbed away from the Riverwalk. I was crossing DuSable Bridge when a white light like a horseshoe or *omega* caught my eye. I was drawn to it because I had to see if it announced a more fortunate day or the end of all days. Before I reached Pioneer Plaza I realized it wouldn't be either of these. Instead it was J. Seward Johnson's larger-than-life installation of Grant Wood's *American Gothic*. Tourists mingled around the plaza taking pictures and consulting maps, asking other sight-seers if they would take their picture and asking how to get to Oak Street, was it far or should they get a taxi and how much would that cost. I told them I didn't know, but if they caught the lights right and didn't stop along the Mile it would be a fifteen minute walk.

When I finally had space to myself I was standing opposite the father's shins. I looked up at his long face, his dead eyes and thin spectacles. The expressions on the face of the farmer and his daughter were exact, at least from what I could remember from the original painting, but what the painting may have concealed and what was now present was the daughter's suitcase resting beside her muddy clogs. It was plastered with Southeast Asian hotel labels and still the eyes of the farmer and his daughter were disheartened, as though not even escape to the other side of the world could alleviate the pain of existence. Their hands, omitted by the original artist, were represented by the travails of fieldwork. They were rough and scratched and scarred over; dirt was embedded beneath the fingernails, which were shorn and asymmetrical; the daughter's were close to wringing.

I thought, If the demands of a motherless farm had rescued the daughter from Eve's curse, she could not escape Adam's. The vibrancy of youth had been drained from her by the monotonous labor required to maintain healthy lands. A quiet fury hid within the tightness of her chin and her blue eyes refused to acknowledge the silver tines of her father's pitchfork. Instead, she would glare at the steel wall raised above Wacker Drive for as long as the installation would last.

In leaving my farm for the city I was determined to avoid both curses. That is not to say that either curse is without its own pleasures or peculiar fulfillments. Technological improvements assured that I did not suffer the same toiling with the land that Dad did, let alone Adam. I enjoyed working up ground on a spring afternoon beneath a warm sun, watching the damp earth spilling off the plow behind me, folding over itself, becoming a fertile maroon beneath a high blue sky. I often put my hands into the soft earth afterwards. There was no resistance in the soil; what before was cracked and caked had become light and rich. I pulled up fistfuls of healthy, wriggling worms coated with dark flecks. These worms, turned out of their winter homes by my steel blades, would surface to the delight of waiting seagulls that dove down upon them like a white sheet thrown over a bed. Those flocks mirrored the sporadic clouds that lazed between heaven and earth. I would lean against the large tractor tire and look at the clouds and eat my lunch and be happy with my life; that I knew it and would not fail in it.

I knew all too well I was the manifestation of the second curse. Though medical advancements have made labor more comfortable since our first mother cried out, not all of the suffering has been taken out of childbirth. And death, the fact of life that makes mankind's labors futile, has yet to be staunched by laboratory science. I would have been my mother's pain had she not slipped into a coma before I was quickly taken out of her. As it was, I believe, the fact of life's ultimate horror was delayed in her consciousness; she fell asleep believing her doctor would be able to keep her and I attached and that, one lovely day in the not distant future, she would swaddle me and sing to me and take great delight in me.

Through scattered conversations with Mrs. Weurtzel over time, and one especially enlightening dialogue during my Senior year that occurred on a cold February evening accompanied by fat flakes of snow that floated past her kitchen window, I learned that during the last month of her pregnancy my mother was diagnosed with pre-eclampsia and was relegated to a hospital bed until I had come to term. Dad worked the farm during the day and was with her in the evenings, staying well past visiting hours.

"What little sleep he got in that ill-fitting chair was sporadic and fitful, but he simply couldn't stay in that big old house by himself, let alone sleep in it," she said. "I can't imagine living in that drafty old thing by myself. I know how dark it gets out there, Joshua. Oh, I know it gets dark here too, but it's a different kind of dark. We have the woods around us and that helps me, but where you are with all those empty fields for miles around would just unsettle me. I imagine it unsettled your father too, because he never wanted to leave the hospital. He only wanted to be with her and they would talk some, but mostly she just rested and he would watch *Jeopardy* and the *Wheel* on mute. Just him awake, alone in the TV's blue light, listening to the room's beeps and sighs. And he would never clean up before coming either. He'd just come clomping in through the waiting area wearing those big ugly boots of his all caked with dirt and snow, and poop probably, but she didn't mind him smelling that way. She never did. That was her man and that's how he would provide for you guys. Then I or another nurse on duty would have to tell him to go home and he would kiss her on the forehead and squeeze her foot and stay over her a moment longer before returning to that big empty house. I don't know what he did there nights."

Mrs. Weurtzel was a small woman who had kept her black hair in a perm since the late-80s. Her job at the hospital gave her a certain authority in the town, as nearly every one of us has either had to ask her about our loved ones or been ourselves, in one degree or another, cared for by her.

"If he'd done then what he's done every night since I can remember, he stayed out working half the night."

"I don't doubt it, Joshua. Your father . . . You know he loves you."

"I do."

"That's good. It was just so difficult for him. And it was hard to watch him go through it. We helped all we could. Everyone did."

"I know and I'd have thanked you then if I could've."

"You did thank us then. We all just loved you. But somehow, our all being together only made her absence more painful. I really missed her and it was hard being with your father. He lost a good chunk of himself then. He never smiled the same way after and he was once so funny, teasing her like he did. And then he had all these voices he'd do for us. I say for us, but everything he did was for her. Without her he wouldn't have see the point."

"I like hearing you talk about them."

She took my hand and squeezed it. "It does me good, too, Joshua. Sometimes it still gets to me though."

I squeezed back as she reached into her pocket for a tissue.

Shortly after lunch on what my family would from then on celebrate as my birthday, Mrs. Weurtzel said my mother began to convulse and her blood pressure spiked. The doctor took appropriate measures to stabilize her, but the episode had occurred too quickly and he ordered Mrs. Thomas to be delivered. A nurse called the house, but our telephone's insistent rings went unanswered. Mrs. Weurtzel knew this would be the case. She abandoned her post at the nurse's station and raced to our farm. Dad remembered seeing the cloud of dust rising off the gravel road while he was planting corn.

"I cursed the maniac who would be speeding by the house like that. I stopped the tractor so I could get a good look at the make and model because if I ever saw that car again, at the hardware store or the football game or at church even, what I wouldn't do. I let my mind go thinking about that and I waited for him to come out from behind house, but he never did. I wondered what business he had pulling into the drive, or I thought maybe he put it in the ditch. And then I saw that small woman dressed in blinding white and racing across the yard then falling between the planted rows and I knew she had taken a terrible turn. I don't remember doing anything after thinking that, neither stopping the planter or getting out of the cab, whether I climbed down or jumped. And then she saw me coming at her and she stopped and said, Oh Daniel, hurry. I left her there between the rows and then I was the one spitting out gravel and dust praying, God in Your mercy have mercy. Sweet Jesus."

And while Dad was numbly offering interceding, nurses were pulling me free of my mother's belly. When he saw I was clear the doctor pressed her chest with the paddles. They determined the time of death occurred at 2:08 PM, and because no one had thought to look in all the chaos, they took off a few minutes when my birth was recorded on April 26th, 1987.

During especially restless moments after his own passing, I imagine Dad returning to the house that evening. He's quiet and I can hear the steady *ohm* of the Chevette engine beneath the whooshing of wind through the cracked windows. He hasn't eaten all day and his belly rumbles, he sniffs and downshifts. Pulling into the driveway I can hear the crackle of rubber depressing pea stone. Then there is darkness. The engine idles in the garage. He can't convince himself to turn the key, a movement whose action precipitates further action, and he can't think about that small future because the significant one has been taken from him. The awed father in dumb wonder, holding his wife's hand and marveling at their infant son warmly sleeping in the car seat, became a squalling, needy thing in the presence of his deep wails and the lamentations of a disappointed saint. His distraught hands pull the red-faced boy free from the tight straps and carries the burden into the silent house, taking him into the prepared room and laying him in the crib, suddenly at a loss as to what the child should eat. I imagine him responding to my inevitable cries in the night, waking him from oblivion to the terrible reminder, again and again, that there was none to revel with him in the joys and sorrows of childrearing. He comforted me as best he could while he himself was desperate and in the throes of fear and I've often wondered what it means that our first conversations were ones of wailing and tears.

Dad's parents lived down the road from us and they helped when they could. Grandma reminded everyone just what joy a newborn could be. She made a big deal of me and encouraged my serious face, delighting in the spasms that were beginning to pull at my limbs and voice. She was constantly smelling my head and kissing the tips of my fingers waiting for me to need changing. While Dad worked in the fields and picked the eggs and repaired equipment, or while he simply wandered around the property in a slow daze, Grandma swept the floors and dusted the furniture and prepared his lunch, which Dad took on the porch and studied before returning to work. I imagine him alone in the small cab of the tractor weeping and cursing, sometimes violently so, and if a car were to pass on its way into town or on a Sunday tour of the fields, they would only see a green planter rumbling over the earth at a leisurely pace, a flock of seagulls spread behind it like the train of a wedding gown.

I hadn't thought about being lonely in the city. However, without any substantial duty or responsibility, besides providing my own rigor toward a better understanding in the humanities, I often went days without speaking to anyone. I took my notebooks and novels to coffee shops, not only because I hadn't yet discovered the peace of writing alone in my room, but because I began to crave interaction, however scripted and trite. Those moments talking with a barista and the hours I spent scribbling and reading there, while also watching other students do the same, gave me a sense of community. But when I had finished my work and stepped back into the city, the illusion of meaningful fellowship was broken and I was just another solitary in the crowd.

To satisfy this longing I sought out places where I might meet people. I attended a few churches, but they were either too small and made me feel too much under an interrogation lamp, or else too large and I couldn't find anyone who acknowledged all I had left behind to be there. I stood when the congregation stood; I bowed my head when they bowed; and I made notes in the cramped margins, but still I would leave those places of worship unknown, made more aware of my strangeness in the city than when I had first arrived. Eventually I left off going altogether.

So I attended sermons of a different sort. I rode the Metra system and the CTA to lecterns scattered across the city eager to learn about an array of topics that would be helpful filling in the gaps of my aborted formal education. As it happened, Chicago was then celebrating the centennial of Daniel Burnham's *The Plan of Chicago* and opportunities to learn about the city's architectural past were abundant. On one such evening I listened to a distinguished professor discuss the history of the White City generally and Louis Sullivan's impact upon it specifically. The soft-spoken gentleman lingered on the Golden Doorway of the Transportation Building and suggested this was a tall, broad, brightly colored middle finger to the Neo-Classicism advocated by the World Exposition organizers. Sullivan, I was told, was also paying homage to the elegance of the Medici Palace and this curious relationship of old and new revealed, first to the gentleman and secondly to me, hidden aspects of each.

I was left with a curiosity for Sullivan and determined to learn about his work, which was then unknown to me but that populated Chicago to an astounding degree. When I learned the Auditorium Theater was Sullivan's, I reserved my tour spot for the following day.

The guide was a whirlwind of information, anecdotes and personal asides that to have remembered them all would be akin to knowing each ornamental plate in the place, which Felix Servo, no doubt, did. He was a small man with thinning hair; his nose appeared slightly big for his slender face and he wore dark glasses, whose frame he so continually found askew I decided his adjustment of them was a nervous tic. I wrote down what he said, whatever I could catch when I wasn't recording that is, but his excited torrents were merciless and I found it was easier to simply go limp and luxuriate in the rising flood.

Mr. Servo ushered his charges around the Auditorium with swift dexterity. He led us into a row of beige cushioned seats and pointed out the golden megaphone design "for which Dankmar Adler walked the length and breadth of Europe, searching for the secrets of perfect acoustics;" then up narrow leaning staircases to the box seats that Sullivan was "pressed to install, but who had loathed the idea of classes. This was the very antithesis of what Sullivan was attempting with his architecture. He believed the funders merely wanted to be seen, to be heard and applauded for their generosity, which of course they did. In the end Sullivan did what he was asked, but I think he rested easy knowing the best seats would of course be down there: center row, amidst the people. Only those not especially interested in the performance itself would sit here. And they did;" up still more staircases, making sure to mention the fireplace, the air conditioning system designed to accommodate Victorian fashions of the late nineteenth century, and lamenting our city functionaries whose job it was to make everything safe and well-lit, but who made "accurately representing the Auditorium as it was then impossible. It was the first electrified theater and the light bulbs of that time had exposed filament. Sullivan wanted to showcase that ornament as often as he could. And he did so approximately 3,500 times. Today only a few of those bulbs remain on display the rest are these blasphemous LED fixtures made to look like Sullivan's original intent;" still climbing stairs to what would be the ninth floor, and without a hint of exertion upon him, Mr. Servo delayed upon a landing for our benefit to say, "the elevator, too, was installed as a modern convenience. It seems our population cannot endure such a climb, even with so many lovely spots laid out to refresh ourselves in. Our forefathers were better equipped for the climb, I suppose. The seats you'll notice are fairly narrow up here as well."

He balanced the weight of his glasses and I saw the playfulness in his eyes.

From such a vantage point I saw more clearly the kinship between this auditorium and the Golden Doorway. While Mr. Servo answered questions, I pulled down a seat to keep myself from falling forward into him. He seemed used to such reactions for he smiled and clasped the iron railing behind him with both hands. "It can be a dizzying place, can't it?" he said to me. "If anyone would like more information about Sullivan or the Auditorium I can recommend some books, either for the novice or for the scholar. Of course, those texts will lead to others that will assuredly lead to still others and suddenly you'll find your life has been well-spent." His crooked smile belied the seriousness with which he was speaking and while the tour participants gathered their things I asked about those books.

I had found two titles at the Harold Washington Library and was sitting at a high table inside Intelligentsia leafing through them. Occasionally I looked up at the men and women in line or out the large windows at people hailing cabs and striding across the frame engaged with cell phones or the transporting of packages back to hotels, wrangling the confused desires of their children, which changed depending on what they heard and saw and smelled, each sensation a veritable chaos for them and a bane to their parents, who were just as inflamed by the city's possibilities as their children were, as I was.

When I looked up from the introduction to think about the author's premise, and also to consider using the restroom, I saw Mr. Servo ordering at the counter. He spoke softly, but in such a peculiar tone and with remarkable authority that I was instantly curious about what he was saying. Unable to pick up his words I watched the barista's facial expressions and gestures, which seemed genuine and were not meant to hasten the story's end and keep the growing line moving, but with sincere interest. Mr. Servo's hands fluttered about him and when they landed, either on the counter or beneath his arms when he crossed them or upon his dark frames, his fingers remained actively uncoiling, tapping and rolling.

I returned from the men's room in a far more comfortable state to read and to think and to watch, when I saw Mr. Servo handling the borrowed book I had used to reserve my seat.

"Mr. Servo?" I extended my hand to indicate that the book was mine, which he mistook for another kind of greeting. He shook it mechanically and laid the book down.

"I enjoyed the tour you gave earlier," I said. "At the Auditorium."

"It's not a good idea to leave your valuables unattended."

"Oh. Well, it was only for a moment."

"More than enough time for someone to relieve you of Professor Twombly's good work."

"I don't think too many would be interested in it." He was caught up in the weight of the pages, remembering his younger self perhaps, when its impact on him was new and his own influence was yet to be felt. The book was large, unusually rectangular with thick pages of architectural photographs. It would not be easily concealed beneath an arm or stuffed into a satchel. "I'll be more careful."

He pulled out a stool and we sat down together.

"I saw you abandon it for a greater calling and thought I'd watch over it for you. There are always those who will graciously keep an eye things for you."

"I feel awkward asking."

"One of those odd, unforeseen consequences to the life of study, isn't it? When you're not home, that is. The body feels neglected and throws its tantrums. And we must listen. But the library will not care about such problems and will levy an exorbitant fee for losing this."

He flipped through the pages, laying first the back cover, then the front upon the table to keep the spine tight, inhaling the musty odors as if it were incense and mumbling something — either the captions or a prayer, maybe — before happening upon an example of Sullivan's use of correspondence, nodding to himself, that tacit agreement between a man's thought and his experience, before finally closing the book. He kept his soft pink hand on the cover, blessing it or himself, or all of us.

"The wonderful thing about this book is the care Dr. Twombly takes in presenting Sullivan's artistic temperament. He was considered an impractical architect. Too idealistic they thought, and they may have been right because the man did not take easily to people. He may have been disappointed with them. And of course he didn't do houses. Not surprising then that he died a poor man. Obscure. Yet this city is nothing without his presence."

"I didn't know that. I see the Wainwright Building is a big deal."

"Yes, it is. But that one lives in St. Louis and is of little importance for our purposes here. How closely are you reading, Mr. Klein?"

I was surprised that he remembered my name. I was re-assured when I heard it, as though a tightness had slackened and I was once again in the company of those who knew me.

"I've only just started," I said.

"We are only given a few years upon this earth and only a few hours each day in which to do what we will. Have you chosen to spend them on a subject you have no interest in?"

"I've been skimming it before diving in."

Felix turned *The Poetry of Architecture* around to look at it again. He seemed appeased, but then he was never really accusatory. He closed the book and ran his hand over the cover, lightly fingering the spine. He sipped his coffee, loudly.

While Felix was familiar with the city's past and took great care to know its present, he didn't neglect the future. He had many friends stashed around the city's cultural centers and even organized an artist's colony in Dearborn Park, through which he was made aware of the latest movements. He never

said so, but I believe many of those directions had their origins in Felix's mind. He wrote reviews of artist's works for
neighborhood magazines and avant-garde art houses and acted
as mediator between artist and buyer, who were often young
couples looking to enhance the value of their homes, but who
were sometimes part of the city's elite. This held him in good
stead when he confronted zoning committees at judicial hear-
ings, defending Chicago's great forgotten buildings against the
tides of progress. In a brown suit, dated in cut and too long in
the sleeve, wide in the shoulders, Felix would canvas the city's
opinion on recent decisions effecting historical landmarks or
changes in policies that no longer benefited preservation efforts. He spoke at city council meetings and was an active
member of a few well-chosen societies, but he never felt so
good as after tramping across closeted neighborhoods gathering signatures with other grass roots devotees.

"When do you plan on diving in?" he said.

"As soon as I get home."

"I remember when I was beginning my own studies," he
said. He looked up at me and smiled. "You're in an enviable
position."

"I've had some college."

"Not all of it?"

"I didn't graduate, if that's what you mean."

"Did you study architecture at . . . Where did you attend?"

"Michigan State and no, I didn't."

"Ah. There's a lot of you Spartans around."

"I haven't seen any yet."

"You've not been paying attention."

"I'll do better."

"And what was your focus at Michigan State?"

"I declared English, with a philosophy cognate."

"Then you're at the beginning again. An enviable place, the beginning. Of course, the humanities do speak easily to one another."

I nodded my assent, both because I believed I was feeling that initial flush of belief and optimism that comes from a new course of study, and because I had no other recourse for confronting another's sadness at his own passing time.

"Did you begin with Twombly?" I said.

Felix grasped the edge of the wooden table and stretched his back. He slid off the high stool and stood with his arms extended over his head.

"Oh, no. This was published some ten years ago now and I've been at Sullivan for close to forty. Since the Seventies. Can you believe that? He actually began with Lloyd Wright. Twombly, that is."

The conversation was getting beyond me and I said, "Do you give other tours around the city?"

"I don't even give Auditorium tours. Today was a favor for a friend who had to tend to a personal matter, but I don't ever mind talking about Sullivan. Except now I'm curious about you. Moving here. Without a degree, no less." He reached inside his jacket pocket. "And what have you found to do?"

I gestured at the table, taking in my satchel, the book and our conversation. "This for now."

Felix took a pen and a business card from his pocket and scribbled two titles that would further my general knowledge of Chicago's architectural history. He believed everyone in the city should have a shared understanding of where they lived and since I was calling Chicago my home now, I was no different.

"I don't know what that means," he said, passing me his card.

"I suppose I'm here to finish my education. My dad recently passed away and I had to leave school. When I could finally go back, I found I didn't want to. I still have a desire to learn and the courses I've taken have prepared me to think critically about any number of things. So that's what I'm going to do."

His handwriting was tight and legible. The titles were among those he had already recommended at the Auditorium. His phone number was circled.

"I'm sorry about your father."

"Thank you. It caught us all by surprise."

"Yes, your mother. Is she here with you?"

"She's passed away as well. I don't remember her."

Felix nodded.

"Thank you for the help," I said holding up his card before slipping it between Twombly's pages.

"Yes, I've highlighted my number so if you'd like to meet again to discuss Sullivan or Chicago. I've lived here since before the Sears Tower was completed so, do take advantage."

Felix gripped his coffee cup and gave a salute or else it was a misplaced wave. I watched him exit and turn east toward Millennium Park, then stop, start again, mumble into his hands as he blew on them and about face into a three-piece suit's elbow, which was cocked out on a phone call. Felix reached for his face, bowed slightly, then stood still, gazing up, I presumed, at the elevated tracks as the Green Line crackled toward Cottage Grove. Felix check his palm, then vanished outside the window frame and out of sight.

I read the entirety of Twombly's essay that evening. The following morning I read Narcisco G. Menocal's accompanying piece and walked around the Auditorium before boarding the train to Hyde Park. I found Felix's recommendations at the

Seminary Co-op Bookstore and began them with a flourish. I kept his business card as a bookmark and after I had finished a treatise on the Chicago School, I dialed his number. He was amiable and we made plans for the following week.

After another evening of study, I walked the length of Rush Street and found myself at the river again. There was a small plaza between the buildings and I leaned against the railing and watched the buildings. When the earth had finally turned its cheek from the sun, I left my rail and sauntered beneath the Wrigley Building. Soft yellow lights burned overhead and painted the thick, concrete walls orange. Shadows stretched across the buried stanchions and collected in hidden corners. The wind blew angry through the subterranean enclave. I thought of God's Spirit racing across the expanse of the deep, before there was light, thinking of what he would create. I thought of Wisdom by his side, suggesting ideas, arguing her point and considering his counter-point. Then I thought of those intimate corners he created for us to discover, many remaining unseen and unfelt for thousands of years: the ocean floor, the top of Everest, the Appalachian caves, and the vast stretches of monotonous prairie. There are perhaps thousands of spaces yet to be seen, both near and far, right under our noses and at the very edge of the known universe, whose discovery would make us even more God's confidante.

I was thinking these things and making my way toward a far staircase lit by a streetlight, wondering if I would become an oceanographer or a park ranger, perhaps a travel writer or a monk, and having a private moment of wonder at the breadth of options available to me, when I was stopped by a signal. After the traffic cleared, but before I could step into the street,

I felt a pressure on my back and heard a rough voice demand my wallet.

"Who carries a wallet anymore?" I said.

I was too taken by pleasant thoughts to understand the peril I was in.

"Give me the cash then."

"That's even more of a stretch, sir."

The pressure released and I imagined my assailant was scratching his temple with the nose of his gun.

"I guess it'd be just as useless to take your credit cards?"

"I'd only cancel them once you'd gone."

"So then I'll take your phone."

"I don't carry one with me."

"What do you do in case of emergencies?"

"What's the likelihood of something bad happening?"

"Pretty good, I'd say."

I turned and saw the man had pocketed his weapon. He was a shorter than I was and thin, but filled out. He wore a tailored grey suit with a black tie, the silver bar of which caught every glance of light to be had below ground. He removed his fedora and rubbed a long white hand across his bald head. His eyes were aqua marine, liquid though sharp and sparkling with youth and playfulness in these Chicago catacombs. He could very well have been in legitimate finance and I thought for a moment that I would look behind him and see his fellow stockbrokers laughing it up in a parked car somewhere, or leering from behind one of the pillars, but we were alone and each of us were unsure how to proceed.

"Should I hit you, then? Knock you out for a bit?"

"What would be the point?" I said. "You haven't taken anything you would need time to escape with."

"There'd be no purpose to it. You're right."

He rubbed his chin, wondering if those were all his options, considering if I had anything at all that was worth the hassle.

"No, this ain't right. It doesn't leave me with the feeling I was hoping for."

"That's probably my fault."

"Everything you said would've been true whether you gave up your cards or not. It was never about the money anyway. Why're you walking around down here alone anyway? Don't you know how dangerous it is?"

He relaxed his shoulders and put his hand in his pocket.

"It's not so bad," I said.

"You're not convinced?" The man's jaw stiffened and he raised a fist.

"I am," I said raising my own in mock self-defense.

He smiled and patted me on the shoulder. "It was never about the money, man."

I kept my fists up and he laughed.

"Come on. Let me buy you a beer."

He put his arm around my shoulders and started walking. "I feel bad for putting you through this mess."

We went to the Billy Goat Tavern and Roland Charles bought me a beer. We touched glasses to our health and to distract myself from the strangeness of such a meeting I asked him what he did, since his life of crime seemed like an empty venture.

"That's presumptuous, Joshua." He leaned back in his green vinyl chair, which must have been original to the place. "I just didn't pull it off tonight. Who knows? I might make good on my threats after all. Leave you unconscious in a dark corner. Take your shoes, maybe. Or your jacket. Leave you for the birds. Maybe come back, finish the job. Dump you in the river. It hasn't given up a body in long time." He leaned forward and the table wobbled beneath his elbows. "It's a disgrace, really. This city used to be tough."

He was smiling through it all, clearly enjoying himself by enumerating the possibilities.

"Oh, well."

"Next time."

"You talked me out of it. That's what happened. You smooth son-of-a-bitch."

"If I'd known you were serious, I wouldn't have found any words to say."

"Yea. My heart wasn't really in it anyway."

He took a long swallow of ale.

"You don't seem the criminal type, Roland."

"Why do you say that?"

I demurred. I had offended him and didn't want to step in it too much. "I suppose the suit. Maybe."

"You're being disingenuous, Joshua.

"Why do you do it?"

Roland let a moment pass in which he decided not to press me. I was grateful for that.

"I was passing through when I saw you looking around all clueless, not watching where you were going, stumbling along the sidewalk and talking to yourself. So many of my days are exactly alike. Nothing separates them, Joshua. And if my days are all alike, what if my thoughts and emotions are just memories of yesterday's thoughts and emotions and I really haven't had an original thought or emotion in years? That's not living, that's habit. So I exploded my habitual evening. Spur of the moment, honest to god. If I took your money, cool. If you resisted with some hostility, I'd have gotten my knuckles bloodied. And if you really wanted to keep your shit, then we'd have had it out in a big way. Either way it would have been an evening to remember. And I was prepared for all of it. Except, I didn't figure you for a talker."

"I'm really not."

We had taken a seat beside the wall. Above our table was a poster of a movie I'd never heard of, or maybe it was a playbill from the 1970s.

"If you want a memorable day, try submerging yourself in the river," I said.

"Have you?"

"No. I thought about it though, and the thought alone made that day stand out."

"How so?"

"I think the unreality of it. I had only imagined it, but it was like a real baptism. When I came up, figuratively speaking, I wasn't able to see beyond this material world any more than when I went under, but I believed I was nearer the place where the veil is thinnest."

"You some kind of religious nut?"

"A nut? I don't think so."

"I guess we'll see."

"I find the idea of God going through the trouble for all this more compelling than chance or coincidence."

"What about tonight? Us being here, the way all that went down, that's no part of some divine plan."

"Maybe not. But then, maybe."

"Of all the marks bumbling through the city." He finished his beer in one long swallow. "I'm getting us another round."

I had only drank half of mine, but I didn't argue. He stood and worked his middle jacket button through the eye, then pulled at his shirt cuffs. There wasn't much to recommend the place except the collective memory of that old skit.

Formica tables gleamed beneath fluorescent lighting and resembled a cafeteria in their arrangement. One wall was papered over with Who's Who in a newspaper style. Another was painted in horizontal bars to resemble a rainbow overlaid with a large red goat in mid-leap. The bar resembled a diner from the soda fountain and paper hat days, rather than the gritty dive its location promised.

"Quit staring and finish it already," yelled Roland while the barman poured.

I lifted the pint and swallowed it down as Roland slapped the bar top in time.

He returned with two mugs and said, "You got a girl, Josh?"

When I didn't answer right away he said, "How long you been here?"

"Three months."

"So you know a few."

"I don't know any."

"Work taking up too much time?"

I shook my head.

"No? Why not, what do you do?"

"I'm not doing anything at the moment."

"You're not working?"

"Not in the conventional sense."

"So what, you got properties you're renting out? Residual income and all that?"

"I came into an inheritance."

"Rich uncle or something?"

"No."

"Fine, don't tell me. It's not important anyway. You got a problem with women?"

"Of course not."

"You queer? It's okay if you are."

"Thank you, but no."

"Then I don't get it, man. You're living in the world. Your body's craving the same things as any man's, right? So? What are you doing? Time and money and," he threw up his hands, exasperated.

I wasn't prepared to have that discussion. I didn't given my sexual instinct much thought, except for those occasions when it screamed for my attention. Maybe this is what men talk about, I thought. Maybe it devolves to this, and quickly, when they sit down for a beer together. I certainly couldn't imagine Dad and his friends discussing such things. I thought about what Rainer Marie Rilke would say or Thomas Merton, even Jesus Christ. I looked at the table and fidgeted. Those men were of no help to me with Roland Charles at the Billy Goat Tavern.

"It's not something that interests me. I'd be more intentional otherwise."

"What 'it'? We're talking about drinks and laughs. Quiet conversations and romantic walks by the lake."

Again, the smile refuted the sincerity of his speech.

"No we're not," I said.

"Then what are you talking about?"

"I'm gonna go."

"No you're not. Sit down. You have this whole other beer, which I bought for you rather than cracking your head open against the concrete. Now you have to accommodate me."

Roland studied my face, as if something about its make-up might be the key to solving something. "It's eight-thirty on a weekday and you're out walking around, underground, with a book bag and," he leaned over a get a view, "sneakers?" He sighed and shook his head. "Clearly you're not after women.

And okay, so we don't have to talk about that. But then what are you doing with here?"

It wasn't a question asked of me, but a thought spoken aloud. After a moment, Roland extended a long finger over the ketchup bottle.

"You're hoping life will find you. And judging by where you've chosen to put yourself tonight, it's life outside these restrictions of yours you're looking for.

"What restrictions?"

"How should I know?" He was jovial, sure he had hit upon the truth. "Clearly you deny yourself certain things. You spend all your time reading and alone probably, yeah? and you're getting tired of it. You need a little adventure. Why else did you come here with me? After what I did to you? Do something with your anonymity."

"I'll think about it."

"Do or don't, makes no difference to me."

"What do you do, then? Maybe I could take a cue from you?"

Roland snorted and folded his arms. He considered me.

"I'm an actor," he said. "Training in artifice. Making people believe things that are not, as though they were."

"And when you're not in class?"

"When I'm not in class I wait tables."

"Where?"

Roland was staring down the cook, who was wiping a hand on the front of his apron while the meat sizzled and smoked.

"It's all quite bohemian," he said. "Except I have a full stomach, good health and a cheerful disposition toward life."

Roland raised his glass, then left it half full.

"And a small caliber handgun."

Roland licked his lips and regarded the mug. "I like this brewery, Joshua. If you get the chance you should check them out. Half Acre Beer Company."

"Suddenly you're coy?"

"I got nothing to say."

"What was it then?"

He smiled. "It was what you say it is."

"I don't believe you."

"No, but you believed what your imagination and probability deduced it to be. It was a gun, then. That's all that matters. It could be a simple prop, too, I suppose. A fake gun, like on movie sets. Or a small piece of pipe, a simple bit of plastic. Does it really matter?"

"So you walk around all day with a piece of pipe in your suit coat?"

"Tell me about the first time you got laid and I'll show you what I have."

I had never had it put so bluntly to me before. In high school it was a given among my peers that I had no experience and so it never came up. When I got to college I didn't know anyone who would have cared. I kept mostly to myself and had abandoned any such socializing in favor of my studies, which I believed would bear more fruit than any friendships I could forge there would. I shook my head thinking about how to answer him.

"That's okay, Joshua, it was a trick question. I know you have to have a first time in order to tell somebody about it." He laughed. "You look so relieved. Why? You have, you haven't, who cares? Own your life, man. Shout it from the rooftops!"

I nodded and drank my beer, trying to recapture my ease, but his laughter was unmuzzled and I could feel the eyes of strange patrons bearing down on us.

"Now, if you were me you could have bullshit your way to a convincing answer. I can teach you if you wanted. That kind of thing comes naturally to me."

I had trouble determining his sincerity.

"For a small fee of course. Not a problem for a young man like you."

I had drunk more and quicker than I had thought. "What plays have you been in?"

"We call them 'productions,' Joshua. It can get quite pretentious sometimes. I played a spurned lover in a kabuki performance, that's a Japanese dancing drama with some sword play. I was all made up in white face paint with this bald wig and I chanted and threatened my rival, but the great thing about that genre is how it invites the audience to call out during the scenes. So my friends went crazy when I appeared, hollering and talking shit along with my character. And then they started flirting with the line of decorum. Then they delicately crossed it, then not so delicately. Then they profaned it and before intermission struck they were escorted out. Not all the good lines are said by actors. I was backstage reviewing the next scene and didn't know they'd been asked to leave, though I was confused about the applause that arrived earlier than planned."

"How many productions have you been in?"

"A few. The audition circuit is killing me, though."

"How so?"

"You know how it is. You get a call out of the blue and race to some random building you're not sure is right to sit with a bunch of guys you just know are more prepared than you and when you finally get in to say the lines you say them and you're back on the street without a word to say otherwise. It's no way to live."

"It's hard to get a regimen."

"It's loose for sure."

Roland finished his beer.

"Where do you go?"

"Where do I study? Roosevelt. Just down the Mile, there."

"I had a University, too. But I quit all that after . . ."

I tipped my mug. The beer was crisp and clean and I was feeling good about being in Chicago, about being at the Billy Goat, about meeting Roland, who was smirking at me.

"What?"

"After you got your inheritance, you mean? Sure. Who needs a piece of paper says you're trainable when the bills are already covered? Well, whatever you're doing with your self's gotta be better than serving people at Ditka's."

We finished our beers and I said, "Are you ready?"

"You faded quick on me," he said sliding his chair out. "Not much of a drinker are you?"

I opened the door at the top of the stairs and he gripped my shoulder.

"I like you, Joshua. I think we could have some times together. And hey, we got a great 'how we met' story."

"We sure do."

His grip reminded me of the pipe.

We walked to a bus stop on Michigan Avenue and shook hands. He gave me his number and said I should call him.

"I will," I said, but I had no intention of doing so.

"I'll be seeing you then."

Roland boarded the #26 and I walked home thinking about the evening's events and wondering if anyone back home could ever believe such a thing, when a new phenomenon appeared on the Mile. It was only a trickle at first, due to the side streets diverting people to their hotels and CTA stations or into cafes and bars, but the closer I walked to the source the more those delicate pink-striped bags proliferated.

Then I saw the crowd.

Victoria's Secret was celebrating its Grand Opening on the Magnificent Mile. Men and women were taking pictures of friends and beloved ones, who posed in various mock-ups of angel's wings. Men were sliding into them; elementary kids as well, two at a time; joy surrounded those little stands as if those wire frames, clothed over and feathered, were the very essence of the emotion. It was all smiles and whimsy outside, but inside the store, or what I could see of it through the windows as I passed, was emblazoned with large canvases of women sensually shadowed in draped hues of maroon and mustard and emerald. Hundreds of shoppers intently picked through tables of white silk and pink lace while others wandered aimlessly through the crush. The whole scene had something comical to it, as if there was a disconnect between the thing celebrated and the celebrants. Certainly we were not aflutter from the presence of another retail space, accustomed as we are now to the incitement of effervescent pop-beats to be so influenced by it; and certainly we had not been days or weeks without the thrill of sexual adventure, or at least from reveling in its representation in any myriad form, to be so roused. It was strange to see this odd pairing of commercialized sex, though it shouldn't have been. Still, only the most veteran aesthete would forgo such incitement and thrill.

I passed through the throng of laughter and camera flashes, careful not to run into oncoming pedestrian traffic, which was occupied with more pressing matters than whether they bumped into me or not.

Inevitably I thought of my own sexuality. Its peculiarity was exposed to me by my agrarian peers, and even my own religious cohort confessed their apprehension toward and fear of not accomplishing abstinence until marriage. I wasn't even thinking about marriage. I simply had other interests that consumed my time that I may otherwise have devoted to thinking about physical relationships with co-eds. Perhaps working the land exhausted me from thinking romantically about women; or maybe, because Dad and I lived rather spartan existences and he hadn't been convinced of the necessity of cable television or even internet access, my curiosity, when it was aroused, had no recourse to further titillation beyond my tepid imagination; it could just as easily be that I had no imagination for such things, that I was predisposed to this kind of non-behavior; or it could be there is already a kind of eroticism in what I choose to do, one that fulfills my needs in the way relations might for other men; or maybe, because I grew up without a mother, I lacked an essential balance in my person and had grown too used to a solitary life and its attendant joys, which precluded marital bliss, and thought, sub-consciously, that such eroticism would only distract me from achieving what I found truly worthy of my time. Away from the banal distractions of such a coupling, not to mention the euphoric distractions, I found myself with the time and peace required for me to conduct a well-lived day.

However, behind these hypothesis may lie the real reason for my celibacy.

The sidewalk maintained its weekend density and I turned at Pearson Street. While the Near North had a feeling of release, I felt I was being called back to work. The sensations evoked by my nearness to the secrets had translated themselves into desires for other hidden glories. At Rush Street I ordered a hot drink at Argo Tea and sat outside. I had stuffed a Penguin Great Ideas paperback in my jacket pocket and I took it out.

The air was cool and I watched the bustle of Loyola students loitering outside the library, smoking cigarettes and filling the sidewalks with their chatter about professors and parents, old friends and lovers, and milling beside garbage bins, sidewalk benches, sleek placards and other outdoor furniture. Each snippet I caught elided the previous one and I listened to the strange combinations as if I were reading an erasure of a text in which the subtext becomes emboldened.

After the snippets had become few and far between I opened my Seneca expecting an epiphany.

I finished a monograph on the Beaux Arts style the following week and I met Felix again. He was intent on showing me Sullivan's Chicago, what had come before and after the great man, and I would follow his lead on many occasions. The resulting conversations would constitute a friendship I was delighted to have found and on Labor Day, with the hot sun obscured by fast moving clouds and the trees ablaze in foliage, he took me to Graceland Cemetery.

"Now this is what we think about when we think about cemeteries," Felix said, spreading his arms across the green park as we walked the footpath. "But this was a grand departure from those usual squalid plots for the dearly departed. It was Queen Victoria who reimagined 'grave yards' as just the opposite. She wanted to reserve the best parcels of land to accommodate mausoleums and ornate head-stones with paths winding throughout, as you can see, and areas where mourners could picnic. We don't think to have light meals in such a place today — can you imagine headstones in Central Park? — but back then it was a matter of course. It was thought ponds and hills, manicured and well-cared for, would break up the landscape and make finding particular memorials easier."

And this was what we were here for. Not only was Louis Sullivan buried at Graceland, but a number of important memorials were designed by him. Felix was intent on showing me the Getty Tomb, which marked the beginning of Sullivan's involvement in the Chicago School style.

"But that phrase suggests an agreed upon aesthetic, which Chicago as a whole didn't have. It's also known as the Commercial style, which consists of three tiers. In office buildings, the base or ground floor, is ornamented and designed for retail and restaurants; the middle floors are offices and have little decoration besides the repetition of windows, or *oriels*, which are specific to Chicago, those three sided designs allow for optimum light and provide ventilation; and then the attic, topped by a cornice and heavily ornamented, houses the physical plant of the building. Where have you seen those examples before?"

"I've seen the Chicago Building. The Rookery and the . . . Monadnock?"

I wasn't questioning the style, but the pronunciation, which I must have spoken truly because Felix didn't correct me.

"And now you're seeing the Getty Tomb."

I looked and saw a terra cotta mausoleum. Wide, flat stones dominated the height of the entrance and culminated in highly ornamented bronze doors, which gave way to an arched design that seemed to represent a rising or declining illumination, depending on one's perspective. The top was capped by a sepulchral slab with a thin line of decoration at the bottom. The colorful exterior, the green doors and the bright sun deepened the sense of finality lying within the darkness.

I walked around the mausoleum pressing my palm against the smooth stones and feeling the ornamentation of a side window, its repeated columns and bronze lattice work. There was a simple geometry to the structure that did not tax the eye as it attempted to interpret the bas-relief. Inverted lemniscates chased themselves around the arched frame. I stepped back to admire the totality and rather than seeing the diminishing arches that fit inside that initial curving, I saw the fragments streaking through the curve, asserting the finality hidden just behind cut glass. I agreed that it's not that life is short, but that we waste so much of it; it is long enough and I believed I would see it lavished upon me if I invested it well. I thought then that if I were strong enough to do this, it would not matter when my heart gave out.

"It's a simple truth," I said after I'd had passed around it. "I could spend my life remembering it."

We considered the mausoleum a few moments more before continuing our tour. We passed beneath oak trees and maples trees, our shoes displacing crumbled stone. Felix pointed out Daniel Burnham's island and the sparkle of Lake Willowmere could be seen through the ebullient boughs. Then John Holmes and Edith Rockefeller McCormick; Charles Wacker and Potter Palmer; the Williams, Goodman and Kimball. Finally, we approached a modest headstone embedded in the dry lawn. A six-pointed design of Sullivan's own making blazed from the slab and we performed a moment of silence: Felix for Sullivan, myself for Dad.

The morning after his funeral, when it was too early to be up and I was alone and at odds with the searing change that had been created, I walked through the silent farmhouse. I haunted the kitchen and floated down the hall into the den to the threshold of Dad's bedroom. I crept into the basement canning rooms, which were first my mother's domain before it was ours, then mine alone before I signed it away. He had kept my mother's culinary habits as best he could, but he was never one for preparing meals. We made big pots in winter and scavenged in summer, but we never disregarded making her apple sauce. That had been a lunch box staple for me and as I outgrew my colorful tin and thermos, I never lost the taste for it. The ceremony of picking the apples, coring them, peeling then boiling the apples, adding the cinnamon and finally forcing the sweet slurry through a sieve, happened to be one Dad and I could do together, to honor my mother I had supposed, though neither of us said so outright. Looking back on those moments now, I believe they were the only times we were truly together as a family.

I wished he would have spoken to me about her then. We spent hours in the basement, he hunched over the smoothed and worn wooden table and me standing on a crate or sitting on a high stool, which was a covered trash can filled with useless cores and mounds of apple peels. He spoke vaguely about her, as I supposed only a man should about his son's young mother, but I wanted him to tell me so more about her and reveal to me, even more than the photographs and the old home movies did, just how beautiful she was. As it was we performed the rituals silently in the communal acknowledgment that we believed the same things about her.

I took a Mag light outside. I ransacked the brown shed emptying the wooden drawers of his workbench onto the ground. I hoped to find some kind of treasure comparable to the discovery of the Dead Sea Scrolls, riches that would deepen my understanding of her, of them, before she passed and validate what I had come to believe about him and what his grief had hindered. Maybe there was a manila envelope stashed away and stuffed with pages of his handwriting, or a collection of their letters to one another, if they ever found letter writing to be necessary, or even a final letter to me. However, all that was left behind were the tractors and plows, the bearings and the chains and the belts that efficiently moved chicken feed down the hundred yard stretch of chicken house; he left rusty hammer heads, dulled phillips screw-drivers and a multitude of wrenches that had lost their sharpness and slipped easily off bolt heads; he left his soiled coveralls and ratty t-shirts; two sagging pairs of high-topped work boots suffered their idleness.

When I had searched through all the sheds and scoured the barn, when I had sifted through all the drawers in the house and emptied all the closets, I crossed the threshold. I seldom went into his bedroom and when I did he was always with me. We never had to spend time in there because we were always together outside that space. If he were ever sick, and I don't recall but a few times when this was ever the case, he rested in his room while I was away at school, but remained on the couch when I was home.

I stood in the middle of the room, the backs of my knees pressing against the foot of their queen bed. The thin curtains were closed and the spring light that filtered through them cast a timeless aura throughout the room. For the first time, I noticed the smell: there was none. Neither was there a sound, either above or below me, and I believed I would never be as alone as I was that moment. I went through his desk; I opened his dresser and felt among his good t-shirts and socks, I touched his cufflinks and tie pins; I opened the bottom drawers and found them empty. I went into his closet. What I saw convinced me it was still their closet, it always had been. There were his suits and ties, his collared shirts and slacks. And on the other side were her things. Only a few items he could not bring himself to throw away. A wedding gown in a sealed bag, a paisley blouse. Cream slippers softly covered by a coat of dust. I don't know what ever happened with her jewelry.

I closed their closet door, then I closed his bedroom door. I had hoped to find something out about him, something hidden that, when revealed, would lessen my pity for him. I had come to believe that his life occurred without him. The circumstances that shaped it never relinquished their influence and I saw him, resigned and limp, floating in the consequences of cursed fate.

I sat in his recliner. I felt the frayed threads of his arm rests and turned my nose into the headrest. When I rose to go do something, anything, I looked over the side, between the chair and the wall, and saw his readers resting on his Bible. These were the artifacts of his longing and fulfillment, but I couldn't understand what they did for him. We were faithful on Sundays and every morning when I was passing through my own routine I could catch a glimpse of him reading from it, but we never discussed religious matters, not even in the car after church or at a diner after church, where we would sometimes go with other families and I would chatter with my friends before spending the afternoon watching football and taking naps, or else finishing up chores around the house.

I reached for his Bible.

It's hard cover had been smoothed and the binding was heavy. I had never looked through it before and the act of carefully lifting the worn spine, of touching the thin pages and seeing his small script in the margins of columned verses, had brought the fact of his death into my real life in a way the funeral hadn't. I struggled to read those lines he had underlined because of the unruly markings slashing at the letters and the hot tears that blurred my vision. Here were the phrases he paused over; here were the words that kept vibrant the sensitive dream of seeing his wife again and that sustained his love for God despite the poor life he had lived since her passing. In those pages I saw what he would have said to me had he been able. I began to read it in that way and in doing so the Bible became a source of joy for me, a text wherein my father's breath whispered hope and favor and I knew I was deeply loved, still.

"It was good of his friends to do this for him," said Felix. "Even if his buildings are more than enough memorial, it does me good to remember him here."

That evening I rested in my leather chair, unmoving except for the rhythmic turning of pages and the spastic marking with a pencil. I had given my hand free rein to pick from hordes of shelves whatever I saw fit. I thrilled over obscure titles I happened upon at the library or The Seminary Co-Op: *The Sickness Unto Death*, *The Alcoholic Republic*, *Entertaining Satan*, *Zong!*, *Boredom: The Literary History of a State of Mind*, *Information for Foreigners*, *Sonnets to Orpheus*, *Grave Robbing and the Search for Genius*. I sat with these texts both in my apartment and at random tables throughout the city. I sat in restaurants surrounded by men in tailored suits and women who offered their soft shoulders to the evening glow, bowing across small plates and sipping from glasses awash in brown, gold, pink and blue accents; I sat in cafes and coffeehouses lured by the aroma of baked bread and sweet glaze; I sat in museums and considered brush strokes, lines of marble, the arrangement of fabrics through the centuries; I sat on curbs and benches and leaned against storefronts; I walked this way and that. And lo! the sun that had risen from behind the lake had made its gallop across the firmament and took its meal of dry prairie grass before retiring yet again, leaving we citizens to provide our own light, whether from a Bic, from a novel, or from our own virtue.

What my hand found that evening was a treatise on grace written by Chinese pastor who was imprisoned after the 1949 Revolution and had spent his career thinking and writing about the person of Jesus Christ. I had discovered him on Dad's shelf while boxing up the books I would donate to our church or else throw away. I saw the title and though it was innocuous I was compelled to read the first lines, then the first chapter. I had never read anything quite like it. The author had set out to elucidate *A Normal Christian Life*, but had destroyed such a culturally prescribed notion in the first paragraph. What I actually held in my hands was a treatment of The New Testament I had grown up with, but written from the perspective "in Christ." That many believers had never heard of such a position reinforced Nee's impression that Christianity is such a life is scarcely lived.

As a child I was told about the blood shed for my sins; I was told each sin I committed was akin to crucifying Christ again and again and again; I was told the blood covered me, but that I needed to life a life worthy of keeping my salvation; I was told when the allure of sin captivated me to think about Christ on the cross, to hear his agony, to see his body broken and bruised, to see the blood drip from his limbs and pool among the stones, staining the earth maroon and to feel, if I could imagine such a thing, the searing pain he felt when he lifted his body upon the nails, a torment required to continue breathing. Of course, I couldn't imagine any of this. While the gruesome details of crucifixion captivated me, I could not reconcile that moment with the peculiar hostilities of my life that made such an execution necessary.

Nee's remarkable idea was that the blood of Christ, however important to men's salvation, is not meant for them. Instead, the blood is primarily for God. It is not for me to look at the bloodied Christ and cease my sinful ways, but for God to see the Son's blood upon me, as it were, and reconcile me to himself. It is for me to trust God's valuation of me through that blood. In fact, I am not meant to see the blood at all. The first Passover in Egypt required the captive Jews to mark their doorposts with lamb's blood. While the families were inside, the Spirit of Death hovered over the city heeding those homes with outward marks. That blood became the first instance of national atonement; it came before the Law and its attendant ceremonies, the performance of which would constitute righteousness before God for hundreds of years. Christ put an end to the performance. Like those ancient Jews, my only act was to accept the blood's redemptive character, to brush the lintels and rest inside.

I was coming into something special then. I believed a corner of the veil was being pulled back. I traversed some difficult terrain that had required me to abandon childish ideas and I was nearing a moment of revelation. But just as light from behind the veil was beginning to crawl across the cell's floor, I heard a knock at a door. I ignored it and followed the spreading light. Angels were leaning over the balcony. I was closing in . . .

. . . and someone pounded on my door.

"Joshua. Man, open up."

The veil fell heavy from its drawing back and the floor became and ordinary carpeted space. The only illumination came, not from holy candelabras, but from Hancock inside my window frame. I put down my texts and crept toward my door. I leaned into the peephole.

"If you're home man you gotta let me in," said Roland.

I looked again. He was pressing his palms against the door frame, head bowed. He raised it and I saw him smile at the small circle in my door.

"Let me in."

Had he seen my shadow beneath the door, my breath through the glass, my spirit against the wood? I struggled with his presence there. I couldn't rationalize how he'd found me, and not just my neighborhood either, but my street, then my building, the floor and now my door. That was too much for his intuition and I didn't know anyone in the city who would tell him. When good sense told me to remain still, curiosity would let me think of nothing but how he came to be there. I spun the dead bolt back.

Roland was beaming and rubbing his gloved hands together.

"You're not going to try that criminal thing again are you?"

"I have something new to mark my days. Come with me."

I considered this a moment.

"You got something better to do?"

Of course I did. There was hard work being done. There were tenuous attempts to get at the ephemeral realities of this world. There were revelations waiting for one who would only look for them, and not in the usual way, but in the way a star or a galaxy, the Pleiades for instance, looks brighter and becomes more substantial when your eye is trained upon another spot, that dark nothing between it and the next reflective rock. It was these revelations that would give me a clearer picture of who Christ is, of who I am in him.

I moved aside and Roland walked passed me and into my apartment. After all, revelations could occur any time. I followed him down the small hallway, passed my closet. He glanced into the bathroom and nodded at my home.

"Your place sucks."

He couldn't see what I saw. Or vise versa.

"Get dressed," he said.

"Yeah, right." He raised his eyebrows. "What for?"

"I'm taking you out. I owe you for that pipe in the back."

"How did you even find me?"

"Never mind, I found you. I've been feeling bad for days about what I did. It's tearing me up. You're a good sport and if I'd known you were that sort I never would've pressed you."

"That's all fine, but…"

"No it isn't. Now get ready."

"This is just a little too odd, Roland. Did you follow me home?"

"How much time do you think I have on my hands? It's a new age for keeping track of people, Joshua. I typed your name and got your address."

"You don't even know my last name."

Roland frowned.

"Yeah, okay. You're right. But don't think I'm some kind of nut, okay?"

Roland sat down in my chair. He rubbed the leather and fingered the gold rivets. He looked out the window and whistled.

"So after I got on the bus it just sat there. I could see the driver on her CB and shaking her head. Must have been some mechanical problem or else a delay at the next stop. I thought maybe the bus ahead of us got hi-jacked or the driver was assaulted. It happens. Had just happened, actually. I heard about this guy that was beaten then stabbed by two men who were furious their bus was late. Killed the only guy who could get them there on time. No one bothered to stop it. One passenger took out his phone and videotaped the whole thing, though. I suppose he's a hero, I don't know.

"So I got bored just sitting there. I can't be sitting still when there's still so much to do. There's too much going on,

Joshua. Everywhere you look is something and if I'm sitting I'm losing, getting further and further behind. I have to be moving. Movement is progress. So I got off and skipped over a few blocks. I had so much energy that must have come with thinking about what I had tried out on you and how that ended and then how we got on so well and I just felt so good. I think I scared a bunch of tourists laughing like I was. And then I saw you, or thought I did. I was hoping, you know? It wasn't intentional, but since I had nothing else going on I followed him, who turned to be you, here. Honestly, I didn't know it would really be you until you opened the door."

"And if I hadn't of answered?"

"I would've figured it wasn't your place or that you'd gone out. I'd have probably waited downstairs at the Zebra or Mc-Fadden's and tried again in a few hours. They really need to get a better doorman."

"I'll let them know."

"And get yourself another apartment. At least have the place furnished properly. You got nothing but bookshelves."

"It suits me."

"Whatever, man." Roland slapped his hands on the arm rests. He looked and saw the paperback, my Bible. He picked up my notebook and squinted at my handwriting before dropping it on the carpet. He stood up. "You got dough. Live a little. Flaunt yourself. Aw hell man, you got a double bed?"

I was beginning to see my life from another perspective. What had seemed a glorious space moments before had become sparse and a little ridiculous.

"Payback starts now." He pulled a cigar from his jacket pocket. "Let's go to the park."

"Pass."

"You gotta get up early or something? You gotta deadline you're up against? You got nothing. I got a whole hamper of dirty laundry needs tending to, but for you I make time."

He rolled the cigar in his fingers. He smelled the wrapper and smiled.

"Don't do me any favors," I said.

Roland put his arm around me.

"Don't have to be rude, Josh. We're becoming fast friends, I can tell. I'll humor you. Whatever you want to talk about, okay? Even if it's that God stuff I'll look interested, like I give a shit, maybe even ask some questions. It'll be good practice for my career."

I slouched out from under his arm.

I couldn't make sense of it all; how I could be on the cusp one moment and the next be swept away.

"It's all a bit of a shock, I know," he said. "In your place, not knowing what I know, I would react the same way. Fortunately, I'm in my place and I know what I know, and when this evening is over you'll shake your head at how stubborn you're being right now."

I thought about escorting Roland out, of closing my door and being left alone in my studio, quiet and still, to pray for experiences that would prove my stake in the divine nature. However, an opposite desire was revealing itself. The apartment seemed warmer, as though having new eyes upon it, even if critical, gave to it, to me, a kind of community in the world.

"Do you know how difficult this was for me to get?"

"Of course not," I said, taking my keys. "It may have been the easiest thing you've done all day."

"I knew it was a good idea to come here tonight."

Outside the wind coming off the lake was obstructed by stone and glass. It was a warm evening and people lingered on the sidewalk in front of the bars smoking and chatting about work, discussing how much they would drink and whether they could use a sick day tomorrow. Taxis crept by hoping to be flagged down before accelerating through yellows toward the next intersection.

We walked to Washington Park. The Newberry Library was lit behind us and I looked at the century old steps of Connecticut granite beneath concrete arches. Saul Bellow had worked here and I looked for his shadow leaping into the marvelous, with which he was so concerned. I was much taken by his novels then and had taken the tour as a means to get closer to the man. I was inspired by the idea that where he had thought of things both wonderful and mundane I was then thinking in. The political and cultural world about which he wrote had changed significantly, but the essentials of mankind were still quite similar, if not identical. I had followed my guide into the archives and the map room where surveys from the 1600s had misrepresented the North American continent and given the landmass a relevance only in so far as a chronology of error. They were correct in broad scopes, but the subtleties of the inlets and peninsulas, the too-severe rounding of Michigan's northwestern coast, created another world, an alternate reality that exposed the misfires of scientific measurements and reflected the familiar in a fun-house mirror.

"I suppose that's what people do who have nothing better to do," said Roland.

He pointed to the bench furthest away from the light where we quietly exchanged draws off the diminishing Corona Grande.

"I thought I'd have to twist your arm again," he said, taking the cigar from me.

I exhaled and watched the luxurious smoke, rich and deep in complexity, corkscrew around itself, taking long swimmer's strokes into the stillness above the park. We were shielded

from any breeze that may have found its way down East Delaware and from any passing eye by a row of shrubbery. I felt
the freedom, like a complicit brother, such seclusion provides.
An ink-ling of the marvelous and the grotesque steadily grew
more pronounced with each draw from Roland's cigar. Each
park feature manifested itself in these sensations: the cool of
the earth rising, caressing my stretched legs, the city lights
morphing into a swirl of confused astrological signs and the
words cascading off my tongue, spilling down my shirtfront in
hyperbolic nonsense and crazed confessions that fractured my
surface self and exposed the heart of the matter.

"It's the blood, you see? It's rest from works. But so many
people Roland, when they ever think of that blood, most
people only think of it coming from his wrists and ankles,
spilling down the wood and dripping into the dust. But
wouldn't it also have spilled out from the lashes on his back
as well? They whipped him thirty-nine times. Because forty
would have killed him, they say. So what about that blood?"

"What about it?"

"Well, that was for us, too. When Jesus was strapped to
the block and his arms were stretched and the flesh of his back
was pulled tight and then, ah, those bits of bone and iron tied
like lures lashed around his ribs and ripped the skin from his
bones. The blood then, too. Not just at the cross, Roland, but
there as well."

"It's something."

"And all that was after."

"After what?"

"Huh?"

"All that was after what?"

"After the garden. The blood from the garden he sweat out.
That blood, too. So much blood. The man must've been seven

feet tall with an unbelievable wingspan, don't you think? The Romans must've had to nail extensions on the crossbar, don't you think? To have all that blood cover us?"

"Surely."

"So he was not a small Jew, but a sprawling one. Even now he extends from thousands of years away to influence."

"He sure does."

Roland was chuckling and he put his arm around me. I noticed I'd been holding the cigar and I had the impression I'd been doing so for some time. I offered it, but Roland waved it away and I drew on it and watched the smoke.

I was living in the strange aspects of a Mannerist painting and I was both frightened and exhilarated. I thought perhaps the aged map makers had returned to prove they had not been mistaken, that they had indeed represented what truly was and it was myself, my time, that had distorted everything. I looked and saw waves rolling across Roland's face. His grin pulsed white, like a lighthouse beacon over an angry sea, and I swam for it.

"Take it easy Joshua," he said holding me up. "You're gonna be okay. Listen to me. I hand-rolled this cigar with tobacco leaves and some etcetera. This is normal. You're okay."

"I'm saying things I maybe shouldn't."

"Of course you are. But that doesn't mean you should stop."

I stared at the diminished cigar and said, "How did you manage it, Roland? I thought you'd need some kinda machine to get it so tight or else some kinda expert . . . to unroll the . . . coverings, they're called? . . . and roll everything back up again. What'd you say in this is, what?"

"Tobacco, other things."

"Things."

"Just rest, Joshua. Here's how it is," and he talked about the process of making the cigar, the rolling, bonding and heating and I must have enjoyed the repetition, the way the words sounded coming from him, their cadence or tone, because he kept repeating himself or else I asked him to say over and over because I didn't want the rhythm to stop. His voice was soothing and hearing about how such things were done consoled me. There was no label on the cigar that I could see or remember having seen and I abandoned myself to the good work of Roland's nimble hands.

The aroma from the cigar mingled with its milk-like vapor and dissipated in the evening boughs. The light from the city crashed into those same limbs and softened Roland's features. Everything became dulled and less sure of itself. My fingers grew light and I tried to clench my fists to keep them from floating off my palms. The fist wouldn't take, however, and I resigned myself to becoming ethereal, bit-by-bit, as if in a piecemeal rapture. I thought how wonderful it would be to live forever between the illuminated leaves and pungent air. I thought perhaps that was my soul's longing and I tried to meditate on the life inside that space and I thought, It must be infinite! and I thought, Man's belief tends toward guilt, first of others toward himself until maturity and its incumbent relationships with others compels him to believe the unthinkable: that he is guilty too; and with this guilt comes the prospect of punishment, either from another's hand, if we are profligate in the city's laws or, if we have transgressed a moral one that the civil code deems unworthy of sentence, adultery say, or lying, if such a lie is not professed as true while under oath, palm splayed across the Word, then punishment in the guise of divine wrath, righteous judgment or the natural tide of cause and effect, a kind of confused karma that reveals our neighbors to be just what we suspected all along. And this is our first introduction to the divine: guilt and fear. It is through these that the church, God's ambassador in the world, his emissary of good news, proclaims our standing before God and it is by explicating this relationship in these terms and finding within it such force to control an immature congregation that these spiritual leaders rarely dwell far afield from such common human feelings. There is no revelation here. Anyone who takes breath and has lived at least ten years knows what these are and begins to wriggle and squirm away from it. Why is the church here then? To make known our release from guilt and fear, what else? To teach the glory that will be gained through good standing with God, in his Son. It is these glories in which we are now living, the glories longed for by the Prophets who were writing for us who now see those glories, and that were anticipated by the angels who share God's delight in us and who marvel at the fact of salvation because they cannot fathom God's sacrifice, the blood of Jesus Christ, as a guarantor of peace and celebration. For what is man that God is mindful of him and what intrinsic value do we have to be called God's sons, co-heirs with Christ, in one brotherhood? The veil is parted, if only by the slightest breeze, the most fragile of breaths, to reveal, despite the frailty of our senses and the limits of our units of measurement, a modicum of revelation. The first glory is this justification of man so that we should be sons who share in God's divine nature. Oh, to be a son of God, to know peace and celebration with him; to see him as the father of the prodigal son, hoisting his robes off the earth, hitching his skirts as it were, and running — Oh, how unbecoming! — toward us; we, who decided to return to his house, in guilt and fear and in the guise of a servant, to offer our labor for water and fresh bread and vegetables, maybe a bit of cooked meat. Yet, before we can offer our work, the father embraces us. He hugs us so hard we do not have the breath to speak our plan of fearful return. He has wrapped us up in himself and has kept nothing of his kingdom from us. What does guilt and fear have with such a father? Where is it in this story? It is only in the prodigal's understanding of his relationship with his father. It is absent in the father's understanding. And this is our father. In the gospels Jesus spoke always of "my Father" or "the Father," but then his resurrection and suddenly it's "our Father." In this resurrection life the brotherhood established and our true parentage is revealed and this not from our plan or our ability to work our way back; it is the glory of God's grace, through Jesus Christ who hikes up his robes and runs to us, delighting in us. Ah, the glory of seeing ourselves through the eyes of the Almighty!

"Forget about all that," said Roland, enduring my runaway theology.

"When not profaned, Christ embarrasses men."

"Jesus, I know I said I would humor you, but you're all over the place with this nonsense. Is this what I took you away from? This what you get up to all alone in your cramped apartment? No wonder you spill your shit. Like a busted sewer main, you are."

I thought I had been peacefully marinating in spiritual matters and I was surprised to learn that Roland had heard the whole thing, or some facsimile of what I remembered of that night's monologue.

"Tell me something good, Joshua."

"I haven't been?"

"How do you live like this? You got no job, yet you live in the Gold Coast. Cheaply, I will say, even poorly. Still, even living cheap requires no small sum. What do you pay for your place?"

"Like, a grand."

"And no debt?"

"None." I drew on the cigar and felt like a master of the universe.

"And no bills to speak of. How much do you spend on food and entertainment, would you say? I'm serious. I want to know."

"What difference does it make?"

"Because you're a strange case, Joshua. Because I'm curious."

I told him a number I thought sounded right, but he wasn't satisfied until I gave it some thought.

"Five hundred," I said.

"So fifteen a month."

I shrugged and watched tree shadows expand and contract across the surface of the Newberry Library.

"I looked up what a guy could get for an acre of farmland. And you said you sold how many acres?"

"One fifty."

"One hundred fifty. Right."

I was slightly concerned by his smile. It had the effect of tracing a chill down my spine, of hinting at something formidable that had been set in motion and that I could not stop.

"Twenty years. You could live like this for twenty-some odd years."

A breeze began to throw the boughs across the Library.

"And you aren't doing anything with it."

"I'm learning how to spend the time," I said. "The ancient Greeks have some good things to say about it so that's where I'm starting."

Roland shook his head. He seemed put out by something.

"And what do they say?"

"That leisure isn't watching television or some other such waste of time. That one's leisure should be used to investigate, to explore, to challenge the mind in a deep way. It's a love for understanding that is seldom earned by a college degree."

"How do you get a hold of it?"

"Understanding is a process, like building a house. There's a lot of work before the foundation is poured, but it's important work. Day by day and a little at a time that one day exposes itself as a wisdom."

"Your money, Joshua. How do you get it?"

"It's in a fund I withdraw from every month."

"The same amount each time? Can you change it up?"

"I assume so. And Seneca says . . ."

"Yea yea, sure he does. But about your fund. IRA, 401K, mutual fund, stock options?"

"One of those, I think."

"Jesus, you don't even know. All this other nonsense you're all about, but the one thing of any value you have, you neglect. Angels don't know about these things, Joshua? I bet if that Bible of yours said so, you'd tell them all there was to know about it."

"Maybe it does. I haven't read it all yet."

"I'd love to hear about that when you do."

I put the cigar in my mouth and scribbled a note to myself in my pocket book.

"You let it sit too long. It won't draw now," said Roland.

I handed it to him and he tossed it over his shoulder.

"You ready? I got an appointment to keep."

I woke late the next morning and though I couldn't remember exactly what I had said I didn't have any regrets. Whatever Roland had packed inside those tobacco leaves had influenced my speech, at times jubilant, at others doleful, and left me feeling depleted the whole day. I laid about with the shades down and my eyes closed. I was fatigued in a strange way and I kept my books closed and enjoyed the languid pace of my mind, the spiritless pose in which I spent the day. In fact, I felt a strange relief, as if everything I was thinking about had been released. My spirit was lightened by such disclosure and I was happy to have someone in the city know at least some little thing about me. If I thought I hadn't missed such intimacy, I was lying to myself. I too had the primal urge to make myself heard, to proclaim and bark, to howl even.

Later, when I roused myself for a walk, I felt the notebook in my jacket *re: Rlnd and angl $$ wht it is & how its spnt.* I couldn't remember what it meant or why I had written it.

I was reading in my cell, legs stretched upon a leather ottoman, struggling with the words that had, until then, been so easy to consume. Outside my windows the familiar beacons were winking at airplanes flying overhead and I had to get out. I was restless; my heart was beating, my mind was engulfed in a high-pitched fever of discontent I hadn't experienced since before Dad had passed and that time, surrounded by laughing friends and cold soda in a Michigan basement, paled in comparison. I was alone and doing what I'd thought I always wanted to do. Of course, I couldn't be sure this was so until I actually took the steps to do it and now that I had I was beginning to see a downside to it all. It was possible such a life could not be maintained for long stretches without something else. That, or maybe my intellectual muscles needed to be strengthened.

I tossed my t-shirt aside and stepped out of my sweat pants. I finished the last of my Sherry. I had purchased three suits, black, navy and charcoal gray, and while I could have afforded to go to Ralph Lauren or Richard Bennett or Nicholas Joseph and have them made, tape stretched across shoulders around hips the infamous inseam my wingspan, tailoring fit for a tycoon or a socialite or a magnate of any sub-strata of society, I didn't trust myself to keep them up. I was not so used to nice things that I could start with these. I walked with too much distraction; I ate hurriedly and without much care, either of where I went — suits of such caliber were meant to frequent Gibson's and Alinea and Tru where I was sure to drip aioli on the lapels or spill caviar down my front — or in the preserving of my fabrics besides running them through a cold cycle once a week. But neither would I go to Mens' Warehouse or Joseph A Banks. Somewhere in the middle and with moderation; still pulling off the rack but grasping much finer material. I went to Banana Republic and because I opened a credit account at the register I walked away spending less than grand. I spent the difference on the complete works of W G Sebald (in English) and Nabokov's novels from his American years.

I rode the small elevator to the lobby. It was a great satisfaction to close the fragile metal curtain of the old box and during the smooth ride I observed myself in the fragmented mirrors. Clean cut and fitted out in navy, my white Oxford unbuttoned and widening at times too far, a crisp autumn scent on my neck and, unseen but felt, Wicked Bunnies against my toes sheltered by a patina of patent leather. I was a little intoxicated by Chicago and my image in it and too young to know such enthusiasm wouldn't last, that sooner or later the scoreless inning streak must end and when it does, it does fantastically.

McFadden's was wired that evening. I showed the bouncer my license. While he regarded it in his blue light I stood in the smoke blown over from the crowd of men on the curb, hollering and laughing and trying to catch a glimpse of female allure in the passenger sides of a stopped Lexus, an Escalade. Taxi cabs were in easy abundance, prowling for fares after bringing carousers to Division Street from across the city.

I paid the cover and went in. Lights taunted the dark mirror behind the bar, punching those seated at the rail with flashes of white light, orange red and green. I saw an empty stool and took the seat. Televisions were showing the Bull's post-game show until a bar manager found ESPN. I ordered a vodka tonic. I drank and watched. The loud chatter, the strobe lights bouncing off warmed flesh, the easy closeness between the sexes, palpable affability and the comfort with one's self to speak and do whatever one felt; how like an independent spirit is drunkenness!

And I too felt like talking. On my left was a waitress in a thin black tank showing hot pink straps on the shoulders, beneath the armpit, stretching arms across the well station and holding a tray being loaded with an array of black, amber and gold towers; squat pink, blue and green kiosks. She was straining from the weight and the crush of the crowd, fighting for tips and against the hands of life's more greedy enthusiasts. To my right sat a man with a shaved head and brown glasses holding a book opened against the bar, spinning the ice in his drink.

"Did the Cubs win?" I said.

"Hmm?"

"Do you know the score?"

"I'm sorry, I'm trying to read."

I sympathized. I wanted to have a book with me at all times as well, but even I thought it was strange. The type would be difficult to decipher beneath the shifting light; the tenor of his thoughts must be warped by the pounding bass, its fun-loving call to intimate embraces. Where was his pencil? and was that a library book?

"Okay. Sorry."

He ignored me, a good decision given my diminishing state, and I finished my drink. Zambrano had thrown a two hit shut out and drove in two. They had beat Lincecum 3-0. I lifted my glass and got a mouth full of soggy ice. A bartender pouring drinks asked if I wanted another.

"With something other than tonic, please," I shouted.

"Like what?" She was pouring liquor into the shaker, turning the bottles over with a quick twist of her wrists, drop stopping them then picking up fruit to be squeezed.

"I don't know."

She was getting impatient. "Moscow Mule. White Russian. I can make a Salty Dog."

She scrutinized the crowd behind me. I watched them in the mirror behind the bar, shaking and jocular, bawdy. She had wonderful blond hair and probing eyes that appeared put out by all of us distractions that kept her from her real labors. She began shaking, wrists dancing beside her ear, the soft bounce beneath her tank top, and I forgot what I had been thinking about. Acting as her echo I repeated the last thing I heard. "With Absolute," I said because I'd recently seen an advertisement. She nodded, poured the cocktail and presented it to a gentleman. I followed her humming bird movements behind the bar, reaching for the vodka, pulling down the glass, pausing mid-stretch while a bartender passed.

My thoughts ran from the probable to the definite to the unrealistic. Doubt, like a wave riding the contours of my shoulders, which I rolled to keep from capsizing, threatened my confidence of the future. What was I doing here? Why had I ordered another? The gentleman beside me personified my conscience, a reminder that greater deeds were being sacrificed for a night's debauchery. But boredom is as necessary to the active mind as sleep to the physical body. I could not expect myself to be always at the threshold of revelation. The mind, and also the body for that matter, are not strong enough for such ordeals. There must be something said for the common-places in life; for the purposefully wasted evening and the se-rious discussion of irrelevant matters; for world championships and the Hollywood blockbuster.

Still, even in this place and at this time of night, despite a ricocheting thought pattern, I would land upon literary ideas and the authors who had presented them to me. It was not such a stretch to think about the literary merits of drunken-ness, I supposed. Though I had seldom achieved such a state I had read extensively on the subject, as anyone might suppose given the propensity toward oblivion of those dealing in un-recognized matters, the soul and the spirit for example. There are only so many hours of the day in which to devote to such things before the body falters, until the mind is no longer in-terested and begins throwing up cynical responses to questions that only moments before had it in raptures. There needs to be hours in which to flop.

At first I was very hard on myself. Such a need to do-noth-ingness had surprised me and I condemned my decision to waste such valuable time and money to attempt a literary life; I berated my past self for its arrogance. Who was he to think he had the constitution for such things? Because after only three hours of work, with occasional sidebars into cyberspace and the necessary time leaning away from the page to reflect on their representations and observe the life traipsing through whatever coffee house or cafe I was in, I was spent. I thought to refresh myself through walking, and I did gain strength through this, but only enough to read those texts necessary for the next day's work. I did have some intoxicating moments beyond these routine days, however, just as I had very low days. During the former I was able to work twice as long, full of vigor and cheerfulness, like the runner who has caught his second wind and the ground beneath her feet evaporates; she is all spirit. On those days I longed to shout, to sprint down the Mile and announce myself. My eyes would dart around the tables to see if any observant fellow had detected the increased electrical charge that originated from my obscure corner of the place. None ever did, but no matter, the atmosphere had changed. I would hurry home to my desk to attempt a rational explanation for the creative outburst, the two towers silently nodding their approval. I had believed, on all such occasions, that I had turned a corner; that the muses had finally deigned to bequeath to me a style and tone exclusively my own and the stamina to finally put in the time necessary to garner the respect of those assuming I languished in the city.

Because I did do this as well. Some days the muses would not come. They flitted around my exertions, just out of reach of my strike, giggling and throwing out obstacles parading as distractions. I would rouse from my daydreams and realize twenty minutes had passed. I had sat staring at my notebook the whole time, tapping my pen, thinking God only knows what. I became frantic then and began filling lines with my scribbles, trying to capture an idea that would propel me into a fuller representation of life. However, those lines seldom survived the edits and the time I spent correcting them, forcing them into something readable, would have been better spent in a myriad other ways. Sometimes this day extended into the next and sometimes, not often, into a third day. On this day I stayed inside. I stayed beneath my blanket cursing the television even while I craved its company. It had no trouble finding content for the day and it had thousands of channels to concern itself with and millions of characters to see to with more on the way, in utero as it were. All while my child lay struggling in the drawer and shrouded in the darkness of my satchel. I didn't know then that this was a part of that literary life too, and it took me a fair amount of experience with such days to understand the healing properties of boredom and how good it was to fill those moments with something else; sometimes even with alcohol.

From Baudelaire I received: *O profound joys of wine . . . Whoever has had a remorse to appease, a memory to evoke, a sorrow to drown, a castle in the air to build, all, in short, have called on you, the mysterious god hidden in the fibres of the vine.* Yes yes yes; of course, yes. And how does he describe the workings of this mysterious god? Where does he set about his work? In *a throat parched by hard work. The breast of a decent man is a dwelling-place that I far prefer . . . and from there by invisible staircases I slip up to his brain where I perform my sublime dance.* Hidden fibers; invisible staircases; sublime dances! How could I not be carried away by such things? I was created to take such things to heart, to glory in them and pass them along, but who would deign listen to me? Who was I to do such things? Those marvelous phrases are like Andromeda in the night sky: those who would see must look away. And Baudelaire is notorious for grand impressions for which language is a poor tailor. And then there is this grand metamorphosis of which I had become greatly interested: *He will explain how and why certain drinks possess the ability of increasing immeasurably the personality of the thinking being, and of creating, so to speak, a third person — a mystical operation in which natural man and wine, the animal god and the vegetable god, play the roles of the Father and the Son in the Trinity; they engender a Holy Spirit who is the superior man who proceeds equally from the two of them.* I was just then enthusiastic about such mystical operations; they had become for me the thing of life, that for which all other pursuits must aid in capturing. If I work it is only so that I may earn the bread that supports my body and gives me strength to wonder . . . and also to buy books. And pens when the ink runs out. And paper when I've filled the spiraled bundle.

Putting aside the obvious complaints sure to be leveled against such a comparison considered this superior man. In Baudelaire's unique equation he is the Holy Spirit, too ethereal to be Christ and a too rambunctious to be God. This Spirit takes possession of Balaam's ass; it runs its finger across the wall of Belshazzar's banquet hall; it's power emanates from the apostles and destroys leprosy and paralysis and bleeding, even reversing the finality of death in some cases; it renews sight and returns understanding to men's minds. Mysterious operations, indeed! And so this superior man is not God, nor is he Christ, but they, according to my tinkering with Baudelaire's ideas, have invited the ordinary man, the normal man, the man who takes to wine without a remorse or a memory or a sorrow, the man compelled to chase visionary schemes, to take his share from them so that he becomes the superior man, and calls God his Father and Christ, brother.

I heard her gasp and thought it came from a place of desperation to be one with the Spirit, but in fact it was the response to my struggling to remain seated on the stool. Too many sensations were coming against me, from within and without, that I lost my aptitude for sitting. I felt a firm support on my back that helped steady me and with my palms squarely on the bar top I turned to see who had precipitated my falling and who had kept me from making an ass of myself at best, severe injury at worse.

"Someone's having a good night," she said.

"It's caught me off guard, for sure."

"I know you, don't I?"

I stared at the young woman's slender face, her pointed chin and black hair cut short like a boy's were beginning to align with an association. Her smirk widened to reveal lovely teeth, gleaming, and told me that her scornful attitude toward the rube who nearly collapsed on top of her had softened in the glow of reunion with an old classmate.

"And I know you."

"Malkim's class," we said.

She laughed at the coincidence. "And now you're in Chicago. At McFadden's of all places."

"Why, do you not come here often?"

"Rarely. I"m with some old friends tonight and they dragged me here. I had to get away from the table, though. A bunch of guys are getting annoying. My friends too, for that matter. They converged on us like a bunch of Neanderthals. And they're being encouraged."

"Oh no."

"Except none of them knows what to say. It was embarrassing. But I have a friend who's willing to play along tonight. So, is this your place?"

"I'm not out like this much."

"What's the occasion tonight?"

"I don't know exactly. It seemed like a good idea an hour ago. Something about my energy? I was feeling confident, maybe; hopeful, I think."

"Spur of the moment. I get it."

"And I live upstairs, so I didn't have time to change my mind before I sat down."

She suspected me. "Upstairs, sure. Why not? It's convenient."

"You're done with school?"

"Graduated in May. No one's hiring philosophy students, though. Surprise, surprise. The Dean handed me the diploma, you know that rolled up *blank* piece of paper tied with pretty green and white ribbons? I walked off the stage and into the waiting arms of debt collectors. So at their insistence I got a job working at a bank. Living at home for the time being. It's everything I imagined it would be."

"You don't want to teach?"

She was sipping her drink and her eyebrows jumped. "I'd love to teach. Are there Philosophy Departments hiring anywhere? I've been looking for months."

"I'm sorry."

She shrugged off my condolence.

"I knew there was a good chance of that when I started. And I may have been able to find a job had I been wiling to move. But I like this city too much. I can always go back for my PhD, too."

"But you don't want to."

"I told my dad if he ever hears me talking about that to hit me over the head with a two-by-four. We all think we're so smart, but it's got to be one of the dumbest things to get an advanced degree in the humanities. But it might just be the thing to do. Get me out of my old bedroom, defer the loans yet again, give my daily life some actual meaning. And I'd be able to study again. This nine to five really wears me out. I don't have any energy except to argue with my mom. And reading makes me sad these days."

"Sad? How come?"

"Because I remember all the other days of reading and where did that get me? I thought I was using my time well. All my favorite thinkers told me I was. My professors thought I was, too. My classmates and I all agreed we were being good stewards of our time. Now look at me. So intent on ethics and rightly understanding self-interest that I've completely ignored how to support my intellectual life. I'm useless to the consumer economy and nobody wants to hear about caves or magic rings unless you're talking about Peter Jackson."

It was upsetting to hear this. That Liz could become disheartened by such facts that she quit laboring under them terrified me. I had the luxury of not thinking about my endeavors in this way yet, and I wondered what other dark surprises lied in wait for one with aspirations like mine.

"But this is depressing conversation for a Friday night," she said. "What are you doing int he city? Must be something worthwhile if you're living in the Gold Coast."

I faltered. When I was alone with my books and pens or zipping around Chicago on the El or in taxi cabs, discovering new authors and wondering about canvases or attempting to grasp the foreign language of architecture, I had no problem rationalizing such elusive tasks to myself. I believed I had a special warrant to pursue such things. However, when I was asked to present that warrant to skeptical eyes it became loosed from my hands and dissolved in the wind.

"I'm still studying," I said.

"Graduate school?"

"No."

"Did you transfer, then?"

"No, I dropped out. I decided to work out my own program."

"Good for you. I haven't found the discipline to work full-time and still study toward any great project. In a few years though, when you have to get a real job and you only have your GED, you'll be fucked. But for now? No, good for you."

We were laughing, but I detected a partial note of sincerity from her.

"Here you are." I looked and saw the Salty Dog. "You have a tab started?"

"Yes."

"Is that what you're drinking?" said Liz.

"The last name," said the bartender.

"Thomas," I said.

I suffered a moment of anxiety saying the name, as though that quick syllable, packed with so much meaning and obligation for me, would prick the ear of someone in this crowded scene who would report my inebriation back home and I would be considered a fraud, a tourist in the literary world. I took out the red straws, shook them and laid them on the bar. I sipped. Liz pulled back, as though the drink had some inherent propensity to come spewing out of my mouth rather than enjoyed. It certainly had grapefruit juice in it.

Liz laughed at my face.

"Here," she took the glass away from me, "get rid of that. Hey!" She slapped the bar and caught the eye of the bartender, who was pouring beers. "This is no good. Fix him a… what do you like?"

I shrugged. "What do you have?"

"I'm a whiskey girl. Want a taste?"

It was delicious.

"Put two more of these on his tab," she said. "You would have offered to buy me a drink eventually."

The man beside me put a twenty on the bar and left. I managed to put my palm upon the vacated seat before an eager fellow fell into it. While he argued that I had no right to it I slid over, gesturing to Liz to take mine. He continued to argue, swaying a bit and losing focus, and when he saw I had been sitting there all along he apologized, offered to buy me a drink, then faded back into the crowd.

"That was smooth," said Liz getting comfortable at the bar.

We toasted to having discovered one another again and while she sipped I remembered those brief exchanges we had two years ago. She was as lovely then as now and I marveled at life's ability to grant second chances.

"I grew up in Wicker Park," she said when I asked about her. "My parents moved there from Oak Park to be closer to the city. They bought the house from a veteran who was moving in with his daughter after his wife died. My parents gave their condolences then bought the place cheap. Apparently he wanted to be rid of it and after the first month my parents knew why and wondered if they'd made a mistake."

"What happened?"

"Their neighbors gave them some trouble."

"What kind of trouble?"

"It was all long before I was born and I don't think it was ever as bad as they like to believe. They just tell stories to give themselves a bit of an edge, you know? To remind me and probably themselves that they weren't always so domesticated and middle class."

"Tell me one."

"Tell you a story?" She looked behind the bar and I saw the frantic hustle and heard the orders and laughter and shouts that had all blended into rushing wind while we were speaking.

"Unless you don't want to shout it."

"There isn't just one story, though. It's more like a collage of little events. My mom getting harassed at the corner market and Dad changing tires, gone flat from knife punctures. Broken windows and cars driving slow passed our house. But they were harmless threats."

"I bet he didn't think so then."

"A small price to pay then for the value of the place now, he says. The neighborhood was changing because the city wanted to invest in it, mostly because the El and Milwaukee lead straight to the Loop. And then the JFK, too. They enforced building codes and raised taxes so that businesses closed and long-time residents were forced out. Hundreds of properties were burned to the ground for the insurance money, then. Drugs became prevalent. Pimps and gangs. And then somebody got the great idea to transform the abandoned factories into loft spaces. Then the artists came. Then the businesses catering to that lifestyle and, for good or worse, it became a yuppy's paradise. Trendy boutiques, artisan cheeses, IT guys, music venues, and European cafes. Well, you've been there?"

"It's nice."

"Dad gets a kick out of it all. Every year our property value increases. We go for walks sometimes and he laughs about it. He likes to shop at these places just to keep them in business, then he'll make fun of his purchase at home, ask Mom if she's ever thought she needed something as ridiculous as a horse shoe for the wall or a mannequin's hand to display her rings."

"What does he do?"

"He's a defense lawyer in the Loop. Do you know the Monadnock Building?"

"I do. A friend of mine took me around there."

"I grew up in that place," she said as the decibel level rose. She leaned in and I turned my ear. "In the summer, Mom would take me downtown to shop or go to museums. We'd meet Dad at his office and have lunch somewhere, but sometimes he'd skip work and take me to the Cub's game. He's always been the one most full of energy and ideas. It's like the whole thing is recess to him. It's probably because he spends so much time cooped up in his office. I'd see him bent over his desk, writing and muttering to himself, shuffling through stacks of papers looking for that lost document. He's too tall for that kind of work, Joshua. He's in his element when he's striding."

"What about your mom?"

She sipped her drink and she shook her head. "I've been talking too much. Tell me about where you grew up."

"My dad and I were alone on our farm. The nearest neighbor was a mile away and that was my grandparents. When the corn came off in the fall, I could see their yard light across the field, like Venus low on the horizon. We worked mostly. Real busy in summer. Lots of down time in winter. I didn't mind it. We had friends and all, but mostly we worked and rested from working. We weren't that interested in being social, I guess."

"Sometimes you just want to lay around. Even his city can feel worn out and monotonous. I can't imagine an old farm town."

The bartender put down napkins and set two heavy tumblers of whiskey on them.

"Bored? In Chicago, Liz? I don't believe it," I said shaking the straws. "I'm taking you on a tour of your city. I'm going to show you the wonders of Chicago. Have you been to the Auditorium?"

"Which one?"

I nearly choked on my drink. "There's only Sullivan's."

"Sorry. I probably have, but I don't remember it."

"I'll never forget it," I said. "Especially at five in the morning. Empty and glowing."

"That's too early. Why do it?"

"Because even though the city is the same from a physical standpoint, its spirit is much different in the pre-dawn.

There are still some people about, either homeless or enduring insomnia, but they're quiet, for the most part, and slow, like they're trying not to wake the city up. As if the city itself needed rest from supporting all our pursuits. And then I can stop and stare at whatever catches my eye. During the day that's difficult to do. Any rounded stone or pane of glass, any shuttered kiosk or lighted lobby, even the slow meander of the Chicago River. All those still scenes . . ."

"I'll take your word on that."

I laughed at her teasing face. "Come with me one day. I'll show you."

I finished my drink and pointed at her half-full glass. She shook her head, but I wasn't sure which offer she was shaking away.

She said, "When you're done playing city-boy, what are you going to do? Your money won't last forever, will it?"

"Not forever, but not any time soon either."

I raised my empty glass and the bartender nodded.

"So?"

"I'm going to be here for a while, I think. I haven't come to any definite conclusions yet, but they're out there and with a little time and pressure, waiting for me. And who knows who I'll be when I reach them? And who can say what profit comes with pursuing such a life? Because there is profit, even if it can't be monetized. So I do the work I think will prepare me to receive those conclusions and let whatever importance it has for my future reveal itself then."

"That's really all you do, isn't it?"

"You don't think that's bad, do you?"

Liz mussed her hair and a silver ring winked in the bar light.

"As much as I like the idea of what you're doing, I know it's impossible to maintain that kind of concentration. For me, anyway," she said.

"Because you're accustomed to a broader social life?"

"Sure, that. And then I never enjoyed those thinkers so much that I'd devote my time solely to them. I used their thought to help me think about environmental ethics and how to think about just and unjust laws, or how much of an individual's life society should expect to use. If I had to read those books every day and related them only to my life now? I don't know, Joshua. It seems like a closed system."

Liz stirred her drink and sipped. She looked toward her friend's table.

"I don't think I'm being selfish in this," I said. "There are a lot of examples of people leaving life for a while to learn something great. There are countless monks and philosophers who thought there was more to life than the predictable plot markers. Kierkegaard broke off an engagement for the freedom to work out his salvation; Schopenhauer decided misery was the normal state of being for men and women and he went out of his way to avoid illusions of happiness like spouses, children, fulfilling work; even the apostle Paul left his society for a fourteen years to be taught by the Holy Spirit. And then they returned with something beneficial for society. The philosophers with their books and ideas that, without having eschewed a community, could never have been written and Paul with his revelations."

"So you have thought about life after?"

The bartender presented my drink.

"I want to return from this sojourn with something of value for myself first, then other people, if they'll have it."

"You want to write something like the Bible, or *The Seducer's Diary*."

"Why not? I have the precious gift of freedom; I have the time and the inclination; and I have a strong work ethic. I've been taught and I have seen and been convinced that hard work is rewarded. I have such expectations now."

"What is your grand idea, then?"

"I don't have one yet, but I've been thinking about God lately, what he thinks of us and how a relationship with him is possible. And I'm still working out my dad's life — what he taught me and what he believed — with his death. So many of the verses in Proverbs talk about long life being the reward for a righteous man and there's an unspoken expectation for all Christians that they will die of old age, peacefully in their sleep. So then if this isn't the case, if there is suffering or if there's a quick end, even violent, the man or woman must have had a secret sin that warranted their brutal end. Something only God saw and judged. And I believed that for a long time; I don't believe it anymore. But then what is righteousness in God's eyes? Can we even aspire toward it? Is it possible to obtain?"

"And you think this is what people want you to bring back?"

"It's what I'll have. And who can say how long I'll be seeking? Maybe after so much time people will be invested in my answers."

I was happy that Liz was there and I could speak aloud my intentions. I felt that, because she had heard of my plans and approved them, they had somehow been given a legitimacy in the world. Either that or else the house music was hitting its stride and I was sharing in a moment of optimism.

Her eyes were soft and the kaleidoscopic lights of the bar were stilled in them when loud roar ascended from the crowd. Liz gasped and I turned to see a young woman walking atop the bar. She wore white knee socks with two green stripes at the top, shorts and a tank top. Another woman similarly dressed was being helped up. Our bartender lifted two bottles.

They each took one and proceeded to pour shots directly into the eager mouths of grunting men.

"I can't believe this," said Liz readying herself to leave. I tried to move my chair so she could squeeze out, but the crowd had become thicker, actively pressing in on us.

"Lizzy," shouted a man. "Where'd you go?"

"Yea. We bought the table a round and you were gone. Alexa had to take your shot."

"Never mind. We'll get you this one coming."

"What's Alexa's story? She got a boyfriend?"

I managed to get out of my seat and behind Liz's chair. The shot girl was leaning out over the crowd. Helpful hands steadied her quads and shins.

"Another time fellas. We're just heading outside."

I pulled out Liz's chair and when she stood one of the men hopped in. The other scrambled for mine, forgetting Liz altogether, but another man had already taken it.

I pushed our way through the swarm, around the booths and toward the exit. The bouncer was watching the show and smiling. There was a huddle of men smoking on the sidewalk and yelling at one another in amiable camaraderie.

"That's why I don't come here. It's too much of a college bar."

"Is there another place you'd like to go?"

"Most of Division is like this, but Rush has some places that will make a proper drink for us."

"Have you ever been to the Zebra Lounge?"

"No. Where is that?"

I took Liz's hand and we walked toward Canterbury Court. I opened the front door for her and paid our cover. Inside the entertainer was thundering on the piano while the crowd sung along. His large brandy snifter was stuffed with crumpled bills and we had to fight our way to the bar. Liz found a crease in the crush and squeezed my hand. She led us toward a small gap beside the wall.

"I'll keep this spot for us."

"What do want to drink?" I said.

"An Old Fashioned, please."

I kissed her smooth hand. "You're so polite."

"If they have Four Roses, get that. Otherwise bartender's choice."

"Bartender's choice?"

"Of whiskey, dear."

I strained through the crowd, then fought my way to the rail. The bartender nodded, but I don't know how he understood me. Liz was swaying to the music and chatting up the people around her. She laughed and pushed her hair behind her ear before mussing it up again. In dark designer jeans and yellow heels she had an elegance I had not noticed in the classroom, a way of being that was casual and light and I grew anxious and excited. I began to have an inclination of what was happening, or what could happen, and I hoped the drinks would not arrive too soon. Whatever instinct I had for this kind of thing would not prove up to the task.

Within such a consciousness I sobered up.

"Did they have Four Roses?" said Liz.

"I think so," I said shaking the spilled liquor off my hands. "I asked for it and the guy made these."

"Then here's to meeting old friends," she said.

The whiskey kept getting better as the night went on.

"This is a real nice suit, by the way."

Liz was feeling the soft material of my jacket, then of my Oxford, the back pocket of my slacks. In the dark bar, surrounded by indifferent people and encouraging music, I kissed

Liz. We kissed again and I brought her close. I was drunk again, as if physical intimacy were an accelerant, and I had trouble doing anything except smile.

Conversation became easy and all-important. But now there arise significant gaps in my recall of time. I don't remember what had gotten us on to the subject of walking, though I can fairly assume I had something to do with it. Although it could have been Liz who started it. After all, Socrates and his friends would walk about while pondering the essence of Forms, which was the subject of her dissertation.

"I understood everything until you got to the agora. Then you lost me," said Liz.

"Two things we know about God from the beginning: one, he created and in the cool of the day and second, when his work was finished he took a walk. I witness the glory of God in those two acts and I can't contain myself. My breath catches in the heights! Sometimes I laugh like a lunatic alone in my quiet room."

"I can only imagine what your neighbors think."

"And they'd be right, Liz. Every one of them. Until they seek me out and ask about it. Then they'd shake their heads over how wrong they were."

"You've really taken to that drink."

I felt the warming ice knocking against my teeth and wondered who had been stealing sips.

"We met too late in the night, Joshua," she said. "But I'm going to give you my number," which she was putting on the back of a business card. "Call me and we'll catch up properly."

I took the card and met with a god's euphoria: the scent of fresh lake and sage softly warming my breast.

"Look at *Phaedrus*," I said. "There's a good walk in it."

"Okay, Joshua," she kissed my cheek. "Get home safe."

I laughed at her cleverness.

I don't know how long I stayed at the Zebra. I thought I had ordered another drink, but whether I sang or talked to anybody else, I couldn't say. I don't remember getting home, being buzzed in or taking the elevator.

I awoke from vivid dreams. The sun was shining in my windows and the traffic that seldom greeted me was insisting it be heard. My suit was crumpled on the floor and I checked the pockets. I found two receipts totally eight-seven dollars and Liz's card. I didn't know what kind of obligation I had now, whether I had to call her or not; and if I did want to what kinds of sorrows and joys were in store for me. I drank two glasses with water and I fell back on my bed. I wanted to go back to sleep, to delay such decisions and thoughts for another day, but I was wide awake now. I had slept for twelve hours.

I spent the rest of the day in bed, by turns chastising myself for spending too much money, for drinking too much and, mostly, for inviting a situation I either didn't want to deal with or wanted to very much but didn't know how to proceed in it. College football consoled me with its familiar voices and images. Between games and in the pink veneer of dusk I managed to walk to Chipotle. An hour later, still hungry, I got a burger to go from P J Clark's. Walking past McFadden's was a kind of hair shirt for me. I needed to feel an appropriate amount of shame, to show my guilt, if not to them then to God, whose face I felt turning away from me. Because McFadden's didn't care. They'd seen such things countless times before and weren't surprised. Then I thought, maybe, neither is God surprised. He's seen more of us than we could count. The earth is laden with the dust and ashes of billions of us who have behaved in a similar fashion throughout generations. Perhaps he is chuckling over my little drama? There, there, he says to me, nothing befalls you except what is common to man.

Upstairs I tried to read but I couldn't care less about Thoreau's nature thoughts or whether Phaedrus could actually remember such a speech from memory. I watched football and thought nothing of consequence for the rest of the night.

After a few days of recovery and emotional self-flagellation, I took the Red Line to Lake. The sun warmed the city streets, which were flowered in brightly colored apparel and easy smiles of Chicagoans. I stood in the shine of State and Madison looking at the rounded corner of the Sullivan Center. Originally the Carson Pirie Scott building, it opened twenty-eight years after the Great Fire in 1899, but looks as though it had survived it. The first twenty feet seemed to be sooted metal, as though the fire sweeping through the street had charred it to a point, leaving only the shadow of disaster. This building was the realization of a Mid-Western poet's dream. A monument to Louis Sullivan's belief in man's goodness, the Art Nouveau ornamentation was a fashioned from poetic ideals that spoke to our shared benevolent natures and the struggle to keep that other side under our thumbs.

I stood beside a street lamp and watched the movement of the designs. The spiraling and leafing of the iron left me with a sense of permanence and I understood that in the essence of change was return; that while my spirit was struggling with two persuasive desires, I would decide which prevailed and peace would be restored, either in solitude or with Liz. I approached the revolving doors and felt the softness of the corner as a man may well have done 110 years ago, amidst trolleys and gaslights, on the first day of business, the evening of which saw Carson put the last line through his ledger, drink a glass of Scotch with his Board, and turn out the light. Those thousands of doilies and baubles for sale then would soon be forgotten through myriad replacements, but their creation, manufacture and distribution funded the erection of this and so many other behemoths, strong and gleaming throughout the country. One could nearly see through the Sullivan Center, could gaze into the window down the corridors through the office and out onto Wabash. It must have given folks comfort that the light of day would be forever illuminating this place of business, that the golden eye of nature would be keeping watch over its darker side.

I stood against the building beneath the awning on State and watched the world pass through the intersection. I heard a shout rise above the din and through the crush of traffic I saw an outstretched arm holding still in the sun. The glowing hand lowered in salute and I recognized Roland's smiling face. He was leaning on the roof of a taxicab and he waved me over. I crossed the street and was surprised when Roland embraced me.

"Where are you going, Joshua? Let me give you a lift."

"I'm not going anywhere."

"Looking how best to put a dent in your golden pile? My advice? Don't be hanging around down here with the tourists at Macy's or Target and whatever else they got. Stay near where you live." He showed me his fingers, grabbing each one in quick succession, "Prada. Barney's. Hermes. Vera Wang, if you know someone needs something there? Graff Diamonds. You won't get much for quantity, but for quality," he kissed the tips of his fingers and shook the small cluster in the space between us, "you can't go wrong. And your pile will diminish for sure."

"I'm actually on my way to the library."

"What for?"

"Guidance, I suppose."

"You eat ideas like a fat man eats brats. Then you throw them up all over people, as if they thought about the same things you do and were just as curious about transubstantiation and which blood spilled where was best to drink. You went on and on the other night. I couldn't stop you."

"Your tobacco was a motivating factor."

"The least I could do. Besides, you did say some fascinating things."

A low chuckle came from inside the cab and I noticed a man reclining in the driver's seat, his thick arms folded across a barrel chest, chewing on a cigar of his own. The meter wasn't running.

"That thing must weigh twenty pounds," said Roland waving me over. "Come take a load off. Mikhail? I ever tell you how I met this guy?"

The cab driver seemed used to Roland's rhetorical style. He didn't attempt to answer, or if he had it was in a subtle way I didn't notice. Probably he just didn't care.

"It's a good story Mikhail, you could learn something from Joshua here."

Maybe Mikhail was deaf.

Roland smirked at his employee's audacity.

"Since you're not doing anything worthwhile at the moment, why don't you come with us?"

"I really do have to get to the library."

"I'm sure whatever books you want will be there tomorrow. I got class in an hour anyway. Come on."

"Where do you have to go?"

"I've got some business on the South Side. Have you been?"

He knew the answer to this question, just like he knew I wouldn't refuse being taken on a tour.

We pulled away from the curb and Roland patted Mikhail on the shoulder, who grumbled surly Slavic syllables while chewing his cigar.

"There's a seat belt if you want," he said disregarding his own.

Mikhail accelerated across the lanes with merely a show-glance into his mirrors and I pulled at the strap. We sped through the first light at Wabash. At Michigan Mikhail slammed the steering wheel and cursed at the town car in front of us. He laid on the horn when his first language wasn't enough. Horns blared behind us as well and I took comfort knowing we weren't the only maniacs on the road.

"This is the Bolshoi," cried Roland over the sudden riot of the street, clearly enjoying himself. "It's good theater being here."

"Does Mikhail always drive this angry?"

"He'd be useless if he didn't. Hey, Mikhail, can't you get around these assholes?"

Hard gutturals, like a shovel stabbed into a pile of rocks, attacked the windshield accompanied by more wheel slamming and horn blowing.

"Mikhail isn't one of God's patient creatures. Look at him. What's he going to do? He can't go anywhere, but he's furious all the same. I love it. All those years spent in the Gulag back in Siberia, eh, Mikhail? These close spaces remind you of unpleasant things?"

Mikhail took out his cigar to better wrap his tongue around discordant consonants. He wildly gesticulated with it, like a conductor's baton during "O Fortuna", trailing bits of loose ash and relying on other drivers to keep us safe. There was nothing to hold onto and the buckle wouldn't catch.

"This cab is a death trap," I shouted as Mikhail jerked the cab onto Michigan.

Roland gave me a thumb's up. "And it's all mine," he said. "Got it for next to nothing, can you believe it?" Roland was greatly amusement by my expression. He clapped his hands and howled and said, "How did such a young man scrape together the means to purchase his own cab and driver? Of what use could it possibly have for that young man? Oh, Joshua. In this world you can buy anything in this world. It's all for sale. A lesson you should learn quick. I don't have time to be wasting it in crowds waiting for trains and buses. Do you know how many screaming kids and senile people ride those things? All of 'em. Every single one of them. I made the mistake of getting some flashy wheels. A Mazda RX-7. Remember those? No? Well, I thought, look the part, you know? Impress the high-ups, and of course the ladies. Let the whole city hear me coming."

We were stopped again at Jackson and Mikhail was trying to wedge his way into the left lane, creeping closer to the bumper of an Escalade and putting me face to face with a passenger in a Lexus who mouthed an epithet. I shrugged and frowned. Roland put down his window and the sounds of the city rushed in.

"But I found out quick," he continued. "When such a magnificent vehicle was driven like I used to drive it, and especially the way Mikhail here drives it, we would spend all our time waiting for Chicago's finest to run our plates and write us tickets. Then afternoons in court contesting them, wasting money on fees and being looked for on a regular basis. No leniency.. But in a taxicab? When was the last time you saw one pulled over? And if we take a corner too quick or accelerate off the line too fast or stop too abruptly? So long as no one gets killed and we don't ride up on the sidewalk, eh Mikhail? Never again, right?"

Mikhail nosed his way into the left lane and sped up. He braked then blasted the horn, speeding forward again to retake the right lane, then turned onto Congress and sped through a gap in the traffic, ripping around a garbage truck, roaring beneath the elevated tracks and coming to rest at State.

Roland smacked the metal roof with his opened palm and caterwauled at two women pushing a stroller outside Panera

Bread. One bent to comfort the child while the other blazed contempt. Roland laughed more heartily and yelled out the window.

I pulled the seat belt across my chest and held it next to my pocket. The familiar constriction gave me some comfort.

"First you get used to it, then you enjoy it," said Roland.

We were off again and I was pressed back against the seat. We flew into and out of the reflected light that sliced through the interior, cutting across Roland's face, diving into the floor matts and scanning the yellow cab like a bar code. We tore through the city like an impossibility. Impressions of gold and glass and stone blurred in a swirl outside the window frame. Trash became disorganized in our wake and we caught the slightest air flying above the LaSalle Street Station. Mikhail took the ramp from 290 onto 90 at max speed and Roland put his hands on me to keep from being laid down.

We were shooting south on the Dan Ryan and Roland regained his posture.

"Good Lord! Has Mikhail ever killed anyone?" I said.

"Nothing confirmed," said Roland. "Where did you get your training, Mikhail?"

"KGB," he said.

"Putin wants you guys driving like this?"

"Sometimes is necessary."

"Not here though, Mikhail. Not in America?"

"Whatever Mr. Roland wants."

"What do you mean, *confirmed*?" I said.

Roland was all laughter. "Mikhail's driven me around this city for two years now. There isn't a street he doesn't know, an alley he hasn't been down, a straightaway that he hasn't timed the changing of the lights. He hits every green without decelerating. The guy's a genius. On ice and in rain, in the wind and fog, and never a scratch on her. Plenty of close calls, though. "

I looked for an alternate buckle to clip into.

"Do I seem like a guy who hates life?" said Roland, seeing me scramble for some kind of safety restraint. How much dark mischief can one smile conceal?

Mikhail got off on 35th and drove inside the shadow cast by US Cellular Field. We passed Armour Square Park and I was learning how to take the jerking speed. I was even beginning to find the beautiful rhythms inherent in Mikhail's Ukrainian or Slovenian, his Georgian or Czechnyan, vulgarity. It helped that traffic had thinned out.

We parked beside a vacant lot and Roland slapped my knee. "Hang tight."

He walked behind the cab and opened the trunk. When I saw him again he was carrying a small Adidas duffle bag down the sidewalk. I heard the snap of Mikhail's lighter and the buzz of the blue flame. Roland jogged across the vacant street and disappeared into the courtyard of an apartment complex.

"How long is he usually?" I said.

Mikhail spritzed the windshield and ran the wipers. If he didn't understand me he made no effort to try. I sat in the strange silence and watched the smoke fill the space between us, then mingle among us. I rolled my window down. Outside the sun was shining in a cloudless sky. A green tarpaulin was stretched across a chain-link fence that surrounded a vacant lot. It had been sliced with knives and hung limp beside the chatter of robins.

"Do you know what they're building here?"

If he did, he wouldn't say.

I thought about when the knives come out and wished I had been a better consumer of the metro news. However, that wouldn't have mattered then. Besides being on the South Side, I didn't know where we were and so any homicide I would have heard about could have been committed here as anywhere else. My life was in Roland's hands and I looked to see that no one was on the street behind us.

To calm myself, or at least give Mikhail the appearance of unconcern or total trust, I took out September's *Poetry* and read "At Thomas Merton's Grave." There are some words that strike me, regardless of where I am or how I got there, and become the tender memory that bathes the actual in a warm light. I read the poem again and stared out at the desolate landscape, wondering about Roland and about the knives, but thinking with the voice of the wood thrush,

I am marvelous alone!

Without the comma after marvelous, I did not read "alone" as signifying the Whitmanesque ego, but rather as a celebration of solitude. I read in it a validation of my chosen life and the positive possibilities inherent in such monkish ways. Being in a taxi with a stranger waiting for another stranger, a man who had attempted to rob me, to be finished with some shady task, I began to believe there was something important about my being alone. Jesus had something about this and I thought about the disciples' reaction saying, It's better not to be married and Jesus replying, Not everyone can accept this word and that those who can should accept it. I supposed the one who can accept it is the one who does not burn with passion, as Paul writes. For him, it is the burning that compels a man to marry. Today, that burning seems mollified by less radical solutions. I infrequently burned in this way and I wondered what Liz would say about that.

I chased away such unpleasant thoughts with more poetry. "How kind Time is . . . and light, / more new light, always arrives." I was so thankful for having stumbled upon this poem and I read it over and over. It became a kind of mantra that provided rich succor. It was this light that I truly burned for, and so I would never alone in my ludicrous beliefs.

In that moment and swaddled in those thoughts, Roland fell in beside me.

"See Joshua, owning this cab just saved me fifty bucks. Plus I don't have to be hassled with questions from the driver."

He smoothed the duffel bag and considered the neighborhood.

"What were you doing out there?"

Roland leaned forward to straighten his jacket. He leaned back and felt inside the pocket.

"Let's go."

Mikhail turned onto 31st. He was driving slowly and had even used his turn signal. Two and three story brick buildings lined the street. The front doors were barred with metal gates and many of the windows were covered on the inside with brown paper. What windows did allow me to see inside revealed empty hair salons and bare-shelved convenient stores.

"Is this where you grew up?" I said.

"Home sweet home."

Roland went into numerous apartment buildings and single family homes. Each time he took the duffle bag, which didn't seem to carry any weight either before he left or when he returned. He kept it close to him though, and while we were driving between places he treated it kindly. Whatever it carried was too much on his mind for him to act as though it wasn't.

Finally, Mikhail came to a stop at Wells. I began to get nervous about Roland's jacket pocket. He was staring at the Shell station on the corner, trying to see around the head rest and the cab's frame.

"What are we doing here?" I said.

"We're almost finished." He was intent on the Shell station. "Are you not having a good time, Joshua? Have I not been giving you the grand tour of Chicago?"

Mikhail by-passed the gas pumps and parked in a space near the Shell's front door.

"Roland?"

"Just a little fund raising," he said. "All on the up and up, Joshua. And quite dull. So much dullness. That's why I got this cab. That's why I met you the way I did. Can you imagine doing this all day without breaking a few laws? I need something to keep the heart rate up. For what you paid for the experience it's a real value."

"We'll talk about value if I end up in traction."

"You won't end up in traction."

"You're right, I probably won't survive."

"If I have it my way, you certainly will."

Roland's face grew hard and he felt inside his pocket again. Then he got out. The duffel bag hung limp from his hand. I couldn't decide which inefficient weight he took to or brought back from his connections, either drugs or money. I didn't have a sufficient imagination to think beyond those two sinister possibilities.

"Alone again," I said.

Mikhail chewed his cigar. One hand was wrapped tight around the wheel, the other was on the door handle.

I couldn't concentrate on the poems or the essays.

It was fifteen minutes before Roland was beside me again and we were heading back toward downtown.

We had turned so often and had made more stops that I wasn't sure we had left the South side. When we passed UIC from the West I knew I had a lot to learn about my new city. Roland enjoyed the chaos and I wondered if my being confused was half the point of all that jockeying.

Roland checked his watch.

"You're a genius, Mikhail. Time to spare." Roland turned to me, "Sorry we took a little longer than I promised."

"You're the only one here that's going to be late for anything," I said.

"We'll take Roosevelt to State, eh Mikhail? There's plenty of els to take you back North, Joshua. Or you can wait for me and we can grab a Happy Hour when I get out?"

"I really should be getting back."

"Joshua." He grabbed my arm and his voice was soft, almost heartfelt. "Just hang around for a bit. Go look at the pictures in the museum or read somewhere. Hell, pick up a Columbia girl."

He saw I could be convinced.

"Mikhail, tell him how nice those girls are."

Mikhail eyed me in the rearview mirror. "Very lovely. You'll like."

I had a sudden fear of what might happen if I refused.

"Two hours?" I said.

"Give or take."

Winslow Homer
American, 1836-1910
The Herring Net, 1885
oil on canvas
76.5 x 122.9cm
The Art Institute of Chicago

In 1884, after having spent only one summer with her son at Prout's Neck, roughly ten miles south of Portland, Maine, Henrietta Benson Homer died in Boston. Upon returning to the peninsula after the funeral and tiding up, a melancholy

Winslow wrote a letter to his brother: "I know that if possible she was with me." No doubt he felt alone, what with the sea surrounding him on three sides, its waves colliding with routine violence against the rocky cliffs, contemptuously spitting salt water into the air and onto the somber artist staring across the rough waters to the horizon where he hoped to find a sign from his departed mother; some kind of signal that she was safely ashore on the other side.

Winslow had moved to Portland after he failed to receive the acclaim he felt his canvases warranted in New York City. He fled the business and flippancy of the metropolis to ensconce himself in the unforgiving environment of the oceanside. His was like the retreat of those Greek soldier's who followed Cyrus on his quest to seize the throne of Persia only to be left behind upon strange sands, abandoned to the whims of the rightful King until Xenophon led them North to Trebizond on the coast of the Black Sea in present day Turkey. "The sea! The sea!" The song of the redeemed; the howl of the saved. In such a privileged state of solitude Homer surveyed the shoreline and he watched the fisherman whose lives were dependent upon the ambivalent tides. He felt a strange peace in the savage elements; at home in a landscape untouched by the hands of men and breathing the honesty of the dark woodlands, enlivened by the sights from mountain peaks and the strains of labor.

The years spent in Prout's Neck removed the tenderness from his canvases. Gone were the representations of women sweetly sitting, of children softly playing. Instead, he populated his late work with a masculine strain: the pressure to provide in an environment continually throwing him off. He job-shadowed the fishermen and while they struggled keeping their dory's afloat and their lines taut, Homer sat, detached, sketching their movements with charcoal, documenting the play of light in the sky and upon the water, memorizing the jagged shapes of the waves, how they came at the small vessel and the effect of the sudden contact on the balance of the men and how they appeared after the encounter. He considered the fish he caught.

The canvas that attracted my notice that particular day represented two men working the nets. One face is looking down and a hat obscures his eyes, but reveals thick facial hair damp with salt-glisten and a pink nose. The other man is turned, too busy to accommodate the artist, who is also at work on the sea. I found great characterization in the first man's left hand, the energy moving up from the clenched fist, animating the wrist through the elbow, pulled back with common heroism, and into the shoulder. All of it caught in stasis. It is the strain of labor, the heroism of work and also its tragedy. The men have ventured out in a dory — their solitude made more explicit by the presence on the canvas of distant schooners — to risk their lives for a few pounds of fish. And those fish! Silver flesh depicted with burnished delicacy and flecks of red life peppered across the expanse of netting, that transparent thing whose simplicity belies an awesome system of logistics behind and before it. Had the herring known his existence made possible an entire economy dependent on its destruction? Across the length and breadth of those United States were men and women who had designed the boat, chopped the wood, planed the planks, invented sealants, crafted the oars, picked the cotton to clothe the men, mass-produced the hats and overcoats, which needed the Industrial Revolution and all that entailed, knitted the nets, created the recipes, invented refrigeration, economized distribution, introduced marketing, created a desire for herring and, finally, mixed the paints used by artists to represent all this on a small frame.

Ah, the herring!

Perhaps today's moment, captured by a quick snapshot aboard a fishing vessel, would not be so different. Taken from the ship's bow, the image shows three men in various states of struggle: the man center frame and with his back to us is grasping at the net, pulling it into his chest; the man to the right is yelling, the veins in his neck are as visible as his collar bone and he is pointing at a crate, though his index finger appears to be tracing the horizon line that bisects the image in half and with great steadiness; the final man is stretched to full height, nearly on tip-toe, arms extended over his head, elbows bent, gloved fists clutching a baton that has already reached its apex, paused and is just now, in the image, reacting to the transfer of momentum downward, between his feet, where a drowning yellowish tuna gasps, mouth agape, sucking in quick droughts of useless air. There is no time for guilt on these waters; there is no hesitation in the gestures of the men. Were the eyes of the one dealing the death blows (quickly, so the blood hasn't time to settle and rob the beautiful creature of its shine) not shadowed by his red baseball cap they would reveal his ambivalence toward the task, the affect of having done this day after day and for years, thanking God so many demand such fare.

Instead of herring, cans of tuna decorated in varied palettes and signified by as many fonts line millions of shelves throughout hundreds of thousands of aisles in as many stores from the Portlands of Maine and Oregon and the peninsulas from Michigan to Florida. Every day the shelves are stocked and though this fact should be marveled at as a world wonder, we would be more horrified and shocked and brought to our knees were these cans absent from our weekly shopping trips. And how much thought and planning goes into the simple appearance of the tuna can! This object, like the herring or the fishing net, has behind and before it an entire system of economy, hundreds of thousands of men and women working around the clock in nearly all time zones to bring this nutritious, yet bland, meat option. And for $0.79 a can! Take this can; follow its journey backwards: stocked on the shelf, unloaded off the truck, loaded onto that truck from off another truck that received this can from a jumbo jet that landed at a major hub, Atlanta say, or Memphis, from an airport in England or Canada after being caught in Nova Scotia or Venice, Louisiana or the Reviilagigedos Archipelago by local fishermen like the ones Winslow Homer followed and lifted up for the country's adoration. Perhaps our snapshots should capture those men and women working inside the nondescript distribution centers; those heroic labors that go unmentioned for fear of attracting too many laurels and too much attention and that would, should someone decide to terrorize them, threaten the abundance of our shelves.

I thought, This would be meaningful labor; I could be happy doing this. Alone and struggling in a necessary and inherently valued chore, even if it went unnoticed by those distracted by more acknowledged pursuits. The fatigue of the shoulders, the lacerations of the hands, the constant taste of salt upon the lips would stay with them after their labors, would share their rest and be reward enough for the effort expended. What do the men tell themselves about their work? How do they justify their sea-soaked lives to worried wives? Because of their efforts, men and women dine in opulence on the luxurious fare of the herring. In crowded markets their lithe, translucent bodies draw a crowd and in display cases throughout the world they are presented with eyes wide open until they go bad and are thrown into the gutters. And do these men in the painting survive the night's ordeal? Do they return to shore and the embrace of their wives and families, or do they suffer in the chopping waves that eventually splinter their insignificant dory and toss them into its gaping maw, filling their lungs with salt water? What happens to their nets full of herring, then? How would the artist make his escape in order to finish his painting?

The painting doesn't answer. It hangs silently on a low-lit wall of the museum unconcerned with those who pass before it or their multitudinous questions, content merely to have supplied the occasion to think about them. Homer leaves it to the objective eye of the beholder. Whether the observer has an optimistic outlook or if he succumbs too quickly to a fatalistic interpretation, the bent of belief will go a long way toward predicting a warm hearth or a cold descent to the ocean floor. His ideas about work will also play a part in the fishermen's fate. To wish them a safe return into the folds of their home, surrounded by good will and a heavy tumbler of whiskey, is to actually send them out into the unforgiving sea again. Each return means a future departure. On and on; unceasing. The herring will continue to populate the ocean and, unless the demand for their luxurious flesh weakens, catching them will mean financial security for men in villages and in large economies. On and on until the day the ship does not return, in which case the labor has ceased, the men are at peace, either in limbo or in oblivion or at God's banquet table, depending upon the viewer's worldview and the strength of his pessimism.

Two hours after I had left Roland at Columbia, I was standing in line at Starbucks a few doors down from that college's library. I wasn't certain that Roland actually was what he claimed to be. I had seen him enter the front doors of Columbia, but I couldn't be sure he had taken the elevator to his classroom or if he'd simply used the restroom until he was sure I'd left, then came out immediately after. While he did know his Ibsen he didn't seem to have the curiosity or exuberance for academic studies that he clearly had for other things. And even if he were deceiving me for his own mercurial ends, Anna could have called him out on it. He did have a special vision, though, one that gave him a glimpse of how the world worked beyond the Ivory Tower. Roland moved through it without any trouble and I believed this was because he didn't submit easily to self-consciousness. Everything he did he did with complete self-confidence and with blinders. His plans did not suffer contrarians and if you didn't like the slapdash way he careened about the city, well, he wasn't going to stop to hear you out; he'd sooner bounce onto a curb or swing wildly across the lanes or simply run you over as listen to negative criticism, what others would call reason. He had stepped into the fissure between social convention and personal freedom, despite the risk to pedestrians or himself, and having found such a loophole he wasn't about to show his head for someone's personal qualms.

I knew that Roland was training in artifice. He was learning set design and how to arrange the lighting to give the best effect. He was arguing stage positioning and the techniques and affects of first appearance as well as vocal inflection — how to show kindness in one instance then personify vengeance the next, perfecting his adeptness at performing each, eliminating the time it would take a regular person racked with a bi-polar disorder to transition between the two with verisimilitude. But while I was considering how Roland was spending his class time I was actually diverting myself from more relevant questions, questions I should have been thinking about when I was thinking about the herring. I wondered if I had been some kind of accessory to racketeering or if some illegal medical aids were being exchanged for money or influence or simply to stay quiet. This was Chicago after all, and because all the great heroes of American crime have been dead for eighty years doesn't mean more nefarious one's today will have their own bio-pics released by Miramax or Pixar in the next twenty years.

I was stirring a drop of skim milk into my coffee when I saw Roland walking north back to Columbia. In my surprise (I hadn't expected to see him returning to the place I assumed he already was) I brought the stir stick out to quickly and knocked the cup over with my finger. Coffee soaked the condiments bar and splashed the backs of chairs and the floor. None were surprised and only a few acknowledged my clumsiness with wry smiles. It took the last of the already-diminished stock of napkins to soak up the mess. I tossed the sopping wad into the trash and left. Roland was standing outside Columbia's main entrance when I caught up with him.

"How long have you been waiting?" I said.

Roland stretched and yawned. "Just got out. I thought you went at the museum."

"I was, but then I got some coffee." He saw my hands were empty and I said, "I bought coffee then spilled it all over myself when I saw you go by."

"I went by? Where were you?"

I thumbed over my shoulder.

"When I didn't see you outside I walked around the block looking for you. I should've known you'd be there though, nose in a book, missing the feminine parade passing your table."

He put his arm around my shoulder and walked me up Michigan Avenue, cajoling all the while in the way my old school friends did back on the farm.

To change the subject — and to push back a little — I asked him how his class went.

"Same old, Joshua. The anticipation of learning something new is always more thrilling than actually learning it. Sitting in a classroom robs the material of its pulse, you know? It's only on the street that learning has any value."

Roland indeed looked drained, like he'd suddenly become lethargic after playing the same role too many nights without a break. His exclusive *joi de vivre* had ebbed during his time enclosed within the cell of academia and I thought he must have bolted early in order to recharge in the energy of the street. However, in Chicago, the city wide boulevards and sunlight imbuing building fronts with a haloed patina that eradicates all shadows beneath a wide blue expanse of sky, he wasn't getting the kind of bounce he normally received.

"Yes," I said, and he looked at me with fatigued skepticism.

"Oh yes, you have some experience with that, don't you. Being a dropout and all."

I took this as a kind of vetting, as if my delinquency, such that it was, was a currency he valued.

We stood on the corner in silence. I had always taken my cues from his leading. His personality carried our relationship and I drifted in it as a man reclining in an inner tube, letting the river's current do what it will, no matter how near to shore or how tangled he gets in the briars.

"Where are we going go?"

"Just give me a minute here."

He turned his face into the city. I heard him breathe deeply through his nose and saw his jaw clench and relax. Then nothing. We stood still at an intersection and I watched the light change multiple times while he meditated, or else pretended to. We were an impediment to the crowd streaming past us and the subject of curses, both spoken under breaths and non-verbally conveyed through murderous eyes and distinct scowls. Then Roland nodded slightly, resolved. He turned, squinting up at me in the sun. His teeth shone white and he lifted a pink palm to see me better.

"Damn, Joshua. Is that your future shining down on us or mine?"

"Why can't it be both?"

"The only thing the world offers to everyone in kind is mutual destruction." He took me by the arm and led us against the light across Harrison. "There's not enough good in the world to go around. We act like that's not so," he showed a finger to a put-out driver who had manifested his displeasure with the bleat of a horn, "and we feign shock and disappointment when we hear about the lengths some people will go to to get their own, but we all know it's kill or be killed. No matter how civilized we become, we never forget our animal nature, Joshua. That's the first thing I learned in class."

"Whose theory was that?"

"Theory? No, I had to figure that out on my own. No university-sanctioned course would ever teach such things But those lessons are the ones most worth learning. And it's only through sitting through hours of bullshit to know where the disconnect is. Because they teach you one thing, but that one thing is only valid in the context in which it's taught. As soon as you take it out of its iron lung it dies. So many of our classroom discussions end up talking about the minutia of motivation. They're all so interested in the subtle differences between one character's motivation and another. 'Well, this one loves her to this degree and so this, while this other one loves her only this far and so blah blah blah, you know? Well, I say there are only so many factors that determine a man's actions. And they're all simple because they stem from self-interest. But when I bring this up my peers scoff and tell me I'm not serious about my craft and that I don't want to put in the work. 'We aren't studying opera here. Those broad strokes won't cut it on the small stage.' Whatever. I rely on my skills for a helluva lot more than getting a glowing review in some neighborhood rag."

We were in the crush of the Congress Hotel and I had to move aside countless times to let people pass and Roland was getting frustrated.

"Keep up, Joshua. You'll miss something important. What was I saying just now?"

He didn't ask because he had lost his train of thought, but was offended that my politeness had taken away his proximity to my ear. His bubble and bounce had returned and his thoughts were branching off in too many directions for him, let alone me, to follow. I did the best I could.

"You were talking about your approach to acting. How you adhere to the bestial method."

At Congress Parkway the stone arches of the Auditorium Theater created the impression of cave entrances. Inside were men and women convinced of the reality of shadows and here we were, Roland and I, freed from those bonds and outside in the sun, still struggling with the reality of things, how best to emote and perceive actuality.

"You're half right, but it's not completely without reason. For being nothing but make-believe this acting racket has really been dissected. The bits and pieces have been separated from the whole and studied, turned over, handled until it's known absolutely. Except instead of lungs and hearts, we analyze gesture and tone and the effects of facial expression upon an audience's perception of character. It's very much like mathematics or brain manipulation: incredulous look plus wave of the hand elicits from the crowd an understanding that this character is more sympathetic to the one making the speech; in comedy it's the opposite. So we study these things, the *why* of our emotional response to scenes. It makes for good theater."

"How do you keep the response genuine? There must be something more to it."

"Of course there is. This class is only interested in the method."

"And within that method how do you find spontaneity?"

"Spontaneity comes from knowing what's supposed to happen next and forgetting that you know it. That's the real act on stage. Even the audience knows what's going to happen, especially if it's Shakespeare or Beckett. They suspend their clairvoyance just like those actors who know their character is going to die or be blinded, or if they're just going to sit on a bench for two hours. The actors still have to feign surprise when things don't go their way. It's all quite ridiculous, isn't it?"

"So that's what it is in the end? A communal forgetting? You're not caught up in the truth of the play, the belief in or merit of the subject matter?"

I looked at Roland and across the street was the Paris Metro Entryway replica. I could see the green metal stylized in Art Nouveau surrounded by a crowd. People disappeared below ground while more emerged; others took snapshots.

Echoes of laughter in exaggerated French dialect.

"Ideally. But I've never been a part of live theater. I don't want to be. I'm doing this strictly for the theory. I'll put it into practice how I see fit and not how some overpaid make-believe artist wants me to. Do you know the jesters from the Middle Ages?"

"About as much as the next guy."

"They performed for the king and other nobles, right? And if they didn't please the audience, what then? Banishment or death: the medieval cancellation. All clowns, man. Even those kids back there, wanting so desperately to be famous, to live in California or be discovered off Broadway, to drive fast cars and fuck beautiful people . . . what do they care about the genuine response? Why should they care? Okay, maybe for five years they'll care, and maybe they'll do good work. Win some awards, become highlighted in obscure magazines, but sooner or later they'll be headlining a Michael Bay movie, or Ridley Scott maybe, parading around in a green jumpsuit with electrodes pasted all over their bodies and attached to ropes and gurneys, letting the special effects department handle the awe of the spectacle. When the end of the world is being played out in 3D, who is paying attention to subtle expressions or meaningful gestures? They simply aren't there. So I don't take it too seriously."

We crossed Jackson Drive and Roland had yelled this last speech over his shoulder, jogging across the lanes to avoid getting hit by a garbage truck that was creeping off Michigan Avenue into our crosswalk. Outside the Santa Fe Building Roland and I were divided by a group of tourists who stood in a semi-circle around their tour guide, a thin man in an oversized baseball cap whose voice was amplified by a small speaker he had clipped to his belt. He was describing the historic features of its steel frame and the classical ornamentation evidenced by the dentils and baluster, it's column capitals, which none could see from the street with the naked eye, a fact the guide was not ignorant of since he finished his speech by alerting the suddenly curious tourists of the texts available for purchase at the Foundation's store. "Beautiful photographs," he said. "Wonderful essays."

Up ahead I saw the bronze lions, elegant, noses in the air — Defiance and Prowl, since 1893 — and I couldn't conceive how many of us had passed between them, up the steps and into the cathedral to art history, the evolution of humanity's vision. I wondered if they, like the tides, like the being of God or the person of Christ — *He did not need anyone to testify concerning man, for He Himself knew what was in a man* — could ever be surprised by any of us. Perhaps this is also a grace for we mortals: the ability to be surprised, the capacity for ignorance. And this not just in joyful ways, but in ways that produce shock and disappointment, fear even, the rush toward solitude.

I had seen a sculpture at the AIC. I was walking out of the American Wing when I saw a large marble block out of which protruded, in bas relief, four figures, two men, two women, in various states of sorrow and melancholy. A heightened sense of loss, an aura of inaccessibility, dominated the piece. Although touch linked the figures together it was not enough. One figure, head bowed, left hand grasping his right triceps, leaned his forearm across the shoulders of a woman, whose right index finger could not be said to comfort the man and who gazed with closed eyes at a present that could have been, but was not. Her left hand gripped the next man's right at a corner of the squared piece. Neither figure saw the other and the clasped hands could almost be read as a phantom memory. The closeness of the figures belied the statement of the whole: we are all unknown to each other.

And so I discovered a paradox within the relations of men and the beginnings of a solution in the belief in the beloved of God, the only son, the first among brothers, in whom we can be known by one another.

The Russian Tea Time was busier than I would have guessed, being four hours after the lunch rush and another four before the curtain rose on the evening's theater performances. It was also occupied by a much younger demographic than I would have thought. A few large tables were taken by a group of coeds dressed according to which school they belonged to: DePaul, Columbia, Loyola. A solitary man sat in the rear corner holding a fragile teacup and looking over an orchestral score. A woman was lost in thought behind the bar gazing into the darkness that was magnified by what little light was reflected by the liquor bottles and glassware. Service people dressed in black slacks and collared shirts stood in the back looking at their respective tables, sizing up the new customers.

The hostess walked us to a table in the middle of the room, but Roland insisted we sit in a half-moon booth. The young woman demurred, but he told her it would be all right, that there would surely be no large parties that would need the room, and slid in where he could watch the door. She told us Anna would be by shortly.

After she'd left to attend her podium at the entrance, Roland said, "Anna's who you want here. Over there we'd have gotten some old guy. I don't know his name. Had him once and that was enough of that. Something just don't feel right getting served tea and little sandwiches by a guy smells like Ben Gay, you know?"

"Do you have a tea to recommend?" I said.

"I've had them all. You can't go wrong. Try the Black Russian and we'll share the service."

The menu explicitly prohibited this.

"I don't think we can."

"Are you serious?"

I was, but then he'd been here many times and probably knew all about the policies; had probably disregarded them all before, too. Not the worst thing in the world. I had just witnessed some shady undertakings on the South Side after all, and though I couldn't testify in a court of law precisely what I had witnessed any number of objects could have been concealed within those paper bags and any number of people — journeymen, professors, fellow students, athletes, single moms, aldermen, physicists, congressmen — could have lived at or had interests seen too in those neglected homes outside of which I sat. Though a mere feeling of illegality and a presentiment of felonious activity would not be enough to convince a jury of our peers, it is more than enough to convince oneself and I smiled it off as a bad joke.

Anna appeared at our table and asked what we'd like. She was an attractive woman with a nearly too-full face and clear skin. Her accent was a fitting touch to the exotic feel of the room and I thought, if I were an ambassador's assistant I would eat in places like this with minarets on the skyline and a bazaar around the corner. I wondered if she was from Odessa or St. Petersburg; maybe she knew some of my long lost family making their lives beside the Volga beneath Putin's thumb, in the wake of Chernobyl, the terror of the Stalin years; perhaps she had taken a train across the steppes and seen the telegraph poles Chekov wrote about or had escaped across the Ural Mountains for the chance to be the American wife of a wealthy businessman.

"Where are you from again, Anna?" said Roland.

"Oak Park."

"What are you studying?" I said.

"Fashion design."

"No kidding. Where?"

"Columbia."

"You're schoolmates," I said.

"No class today?" said Roland, ignoring my remark.

"Not today. Do you need more time?"

"I'll have the tea service. And we're both fine with black currant."

I attempted to introduce myself in Russian, but Anna shook her head and walked away. "I must not have said it right."

Roland was watching her leave. "Or at all. Were those words?"

"I thought I was telling her my name."

"More than enough to a girl off. You can't blame a woman's first instinct, Joshua."

"I won't pursue her then," I said so Roland would know I hadn't planned on doing so anyway.

"Nonsense. I'll put in a good word for you. She was in a class with me last semester, but I've known her for a year or so."

"So. Fashion design."

"It was Costume Design, asshole. 'The Elements of Style.' I told you many facets of the theater, not just the acting, goes into perfecting the illusion. Stage design, lighting and specially the clothes. Even the settings the play takes place in, how the two-dimensional environment looks, how your character behaves in such settings, goes a long way toward revealing that character. Hell Joshua, more truth is said in non-verbal moments than when a man's mouth is open."

"So what about this place? Why do you come here? What do you reveal by begin here now?"

"Now you're starting to get it. Mikhail's family is connected to this place in one way or another. I can't remember how. I've been here too many times to count. Everyone knows me, including the lovely Anna. Dark hair, dark complexion, great body."

"Angry eyes."

"All part of her charm."

The way he said this and immediately picked up the menu, even though we'd already ordered and he was familiar with the fare, made me wary about his informal attitude toward our waitress.

"Did you have any other classes with her?"

Roland laid aside the menu. "Naturalism in the Theater. I think she was in that. The theories of Stanislavski, too. We worked from memories to convey emotions. Some of those kids were too young to have any memories. At least nothing they could use to depict *artistic truth*. The professor loved that phrase and now I'll never be able to forget it. It draws its own lines within truth itself and marks off its own boundaries so that it can easily be a lie."

"Well, sure. When I go to an opera I know that what's being depicted on the stage isn't really happening. Only a fool would try to start a fire to warm Mimi up or bring her some soup."

"And that's what Stanislavski was trying to eliminate: the illusion. So he designed these three-dimensional sets and used simple language and did away with Hamlet's father. We studied a few plays, but the only one I remember is *A Doll's House* because we got to slam a door. I don't think that sound had ever been heard from the stage until Ibsen wrote it."

"As significant as Aristophanes' hiccups."

"Sure," he frowned. "Anna there got to slam the door. She was good and I teased her that old Stan was her great uncle and that she was a natural born Naturalist. Didn't I?"

I was confused by his change of tone until an arm appeared and set down two miniature beer steins and a kettle between Roland and I.

"He was quite oppressive," said Anna.

"Oh, come on. A Russian can't throw that word around. Not with Putin always leering over your shoulder."

"Always he is like this?" Anna's question was tired and short. Whether she was annoyed before our arrival or if our presence precipitated her mood, I couldn't say.

"The best part about that class, though," he said after Anna had gone, "was the hysterics some of those kids worked themselves into. Big emotions, loud voices, arms flailing. It was ridiculous and completely contrary to the Naturalist method. Now, since I have had some experiences, I was able to contain myself and give a powerful performance. At least that's what my official transcript says."

"What are you going to do with this degree?" I was curious about this because even though he was taking classes and spoke about them as if they had a high level of importance for his future — as if he believed he was being trained to make valuable contributions to our country's economic growth as well as his own financial well-being — Roland behaved as though the university was just something one did, like stopping at red lights or buying groceries when the refrigerator was empty. But of course, there are always other options.

Roland filled my stein, then his own.

"I'm taking them for my own edification, my own self-improvement. Just like you. One never knows when an emotion, portrayed at just the right moment, can sway a situation in one's favor."

"You're taking the stage into the street?"

"Of course. You're not writing for academics, are you? You're writing for the real people."

"I haven't thought about an audience yet."

"You'd better. Otherwise you won't be studying for long." He lifted the stein to his mouth. "I'm sorry. Of course you will be, and for quite some time."

"How do you see the real world application to Stanislovski?"

"I'm glad you asked. For example: a married man is at home fucking a woman, who is not his wife, on the couch. The front door opens and the wife cries out. She drops the bags of groceries on the threshold, spilling milk, cracking eggs, the whole clichéd scene. The woman caught in adultery lifts herself off the man and runs into the kitchen with an arm covering her breasts. The man is caught, defeated. He will lose his wife and pay out is ass in a court of law."

"Kids?"

The tea was hot and had some flavor, but I felt I had either drank it before it cooled sufficiently or else Roland had ordered the wrong type because it didn't taste like currants.

"Who cares? All is lost. But is it though? Is it really?"

"I imagine not, though I can't see how."

"Where only a second before he was in the throes, full of forgetting and disoriented by his mistress's breath on his neck, the feel of her thighs in his hands, her soft rise and fall, now he is chilled with terror similar to being caught by your mother in a similar throe, ridiculously naked on his recliner, hands suddenly empty, bereft of the erotic charge he undoubtedly lives to experience. His old lady is berating him, screaming at him. She's unsure whether to pummel him or chase after the tart and in her uncertainty she stands rooted to the threshold, unbelieving what she has just interrupted. With the appearance of calm, because he isn't calm; because the man's heart is racing and his mind is fragmented with possible escape scenarios, the man rises. He doesn't cover himself and his movements are controlled, affecting her perceptions I suppose, as if his deliberateness means he isn't really moving at all. He slides passed her and goes into the bedroom. She's cursing him out, sobbing, grabbing at her hair."

"Hysterical."

Roland laughed and slapped the table, jostling the kettle and his mug, rattling the silverware and bringing a familiar silence to the place. "Exactly." He shifted in his seat and leaned into the center of the table to better present the climax. "The man comes out of their bedroom wearing jeans and a t-shirt. He walks past his wife who continues threatening him, condemning him to the hell of the life he has chosen with that thing who just escaped out the back door and was running down the street struggling to put on her dress.

"Really?"

"Why not? She's not the main focus here. You can follow her later if you want to. Anyway, says she's leaving him this time, for sure. Going to stay at her mom's in Des Moines. Her eyes are darting all over the place, looking for a weapon maybe or way to return to when she didn't know, to when she had never seen him with that other woman. The man sits back in his recliner with a newspaper and starts reading. She soon tires out from all her hollering. She's panting and exasperated by his demeanor, that he's not insisting in his innocence, and in the ringing silence he puts the paper down, looks up at the bulging eyes and tear-stained cheeks of his crazed wife and says, 'Hello honey, I didn't hear you come in.'"

Roland threw himself against the red cushions of the booth and laughed. I looked and saw Anna scowl. I followed her gaze toward the manager who was deciding whether or not to say something to us.

Hopeful I said, "That's it?"

"Oh no. Not by a long shot."

"So what happened?"

"The wife is adamant; he looks perplexed. She tells him she caught him with some other woman, that she saw her bare ass flee out the back, that she watched him go into the bedroom to put some clothes on and come back and that she's going to call a lawyer or her father. That she's going to call both. 'But I've been sitting her all evening, dear. I fixed myself a ham sandwich with carrots and apple sauce because I know we're trying to eat better; I put the game on and I've been waiting for you to get home. How was work? Was Mrs. Lewis impressed with your presentation?' Now she's incensed, says 'How dare you lie to me. I saw you, Earl. I saw you! You just got changed. You just sat back down. You only turned the TV on just now!' 'Honey, that's crazy. There's nobody here. Are you hungry? Can I make you something? Come here. Follow me. See, there's no one in the kitchen; no one running away through our back yard. Everything is peaceful outside: the birds are chirping away, the sun is shining, there aren't any neighbors shrieking at a naked woman hurrying away. It's a normal afternoon. Do you want cibatta or plain bread for your sandwich?' She goes out into the yard and sees he's right. The neighborhood is still. He's getting out the mayo. The cibatta is toasting. 'Do you want iced tea?' he says. 'Okay,' she says. She's still suspicious, but he sees she can be convinced and he laughs at her drama, hugs her and kisses her cheek. He convinces his wife that she's only imagined the whole thing. Suggests the stress of her job made her nervous and the anxiety had manifested itself in the hallucination of a woman straddling him on the Laz-y-Boy. 'Sure we have problems,' he tells her, 'but they're no different from what our neighbors are getting up to.' "Then, in a stroke of good thinking she looks around the sofa, behind the cushions, feeling the cushions for dampness, under the coffee table looking for panties or a purse or a bracelet. Anything that may have been tossed aside and forgotten. Her husband chuckles at her there on all fours swinging her arm under the couch, rifling through the magazines on the coffee table, picking through the long strands of shag for the back of an earring or the thin braid of a necklace. The husband is not sweating nor is he breathing hard. He appears unconcerned about his wife's allegations or if she has bought his lie. She mutters to herself in the middle of the living room, trying to remember if she had seen what she believes she has seen, wanting to believe her husband, wanting more to keep her life on an even keel and avoid a nasty divorce and starting over and anyway she still loves him. Like a good man he picks up the broken bags of groceries, saves the food that can be saved and mops up the yolks and the milk. He kisses her on the top of the head and tells her to relax, that he'll bring her the sandwich, and turns to a program she might enjoy."

"Unbelievable."

"Acting Joshua."

"And she bought it?"

"Apparently. I haven't heard any different."

"Are you that good?"

"We'll see when I get the test."

Anna brought a tower of small sandwiches and cakes to the table.

"Wait, did that really happen?" I said.

"Perfect timing, Anna."

"Do you need me to explain or do you remember?"

"Better give us the layout. Joshua's new to the experience."

Anna pointed to the savories and the sweets laid out on a four tiered tower. Salmon and cream cheese bites, potato piroshky bites, assorted quiches, crunchy crepes in a peanut sauce; napoleon tarts, apricot plum strudel, rugalah and lemon cakes, some cookies. I understood the presentation was most of the allure of the place. The morsels were laid out on white lace doilies the exact size of its tier and as Anna described them she rested her palm in the air directly above them. I got lost in her accent, prolonged as it was in describing, as though outside weren't Chicago and my search for a literary career of some sort, but a small town on the steppes or a cozy neighborhood in the suburbs of Eastern Europe, and I wondered if such imaginings could be fashioned into a novel, if they had the meat to satisfy large appetites or if they were merely small bites to tide one over until the main course.

Anna pushed a gold bracelet further up her right arm and her freckled flesh rose slightly around the band, powder blue nails tracked down her arm and rested on her hip, disappeared inside her apron.

"It looks delicious," I said.

"Enjoy."

Roland took a quiche off the tower.

"What have you been doing since last time?"

I thought of my time in terms of pages written and books read. I had to think what had filled my days since Newberry Park.

"Don't hold back on my account. I know you get up to some unusual ideas."

I chose the salmon. "You won't think I'm vomiting on you?"

"Don't be mad. I was giving you a hard time." Roland wiped his mouth with a cloth napkin. "Look, if I didn't want to hear your nonsense I wouldn't keep coming around."

I didn't have many interlocutors and I was beginning to come to some conclusions, so I said, "I want to know the good a man should do while he's here. I don't believe those answers can be found behind ivy-covered walls, though I was under that impression. And maybe it was, years ago, when it was the safe haven for men and women who wanted to question assumed knowledge, but now it doesn't seem interested in questions."

Roland had popped the quiche whole into his mouth and I watched his jaw work it down. He was looking at me and I said, "Instead, we're pushed through a four-year program, which require many classes that are useless to those concerns and are taught by unqualified, inexperienced MA candidates or disinterested PhDs who begrudge their undergrads for one, bothering them about the elementary questions in their field and two, keeping them from progressing in their own understanding and three, from making a name for themselves and acquiring more funding for their own particular research. If all we're expected to learn is a specialized skill that makes us marketable, then why bother with the first two years studying Aborigines' culture or deforestation? What's the point of knowing who Harriet Monroe is or Jane Addams? And even if you do know who these women are good luck finding someone else who does and then further luck if they think such knowledge makes you employable.

"And the students, Roland. So happy to be free, they spend their weekends with alcohol and coeds. The one chance independent thought has to get at these kids, that fleeting moment between the adolescence of high school and the banality of the looming nine to five, and it cowers before the strength of our culture, ever-changing, always looking for relief from the violent winds of fate and satisfied with artificial paradises. Those four years shouldn't be wasted. But the ones who are earnestly seeking an education get lampooned while those who wile away the years, declaring a major their third year, then applying to graduate school to delay inevitable unemployment and the payment of student loans, are lifted up as having had the model college experience." Roland cleared his throat to say something, but I kept going. "Now I'm no saint. I dabbled in some foolishness and I can see the benefit of forgetting life and yelling nonsense in a back alley and flirting with another guy's girl." My performance wasn't of Roland's caliber and he knew I was getting carried away. Nevertheless, I continued, "It's good to feel one's burgeoning power, to howl and strut. But look around. Those kids grow up to become fifty-year-olds who go to bars to forget their jobs and families and wish to God they could go back to where it all started to go wrong, but they can't see that moment and they don't understand how doing what was expected of them could bring such unhappiness. Well, those college years might be a good place to start. Little attention is paid to the powerful influence of habit, Roland. And a lot of bad ones are condoned under the watchful eye of Education."

Roland leaned back with a lemon cake.

"Been holding that in a while?"

"I guess so."

"What are the other option?"

"Immediate employment in a dead-end job because you're not qualified for anything else. Or a two-year trade school where they don't have the pretentious illusion of giving their students anything but a qualification."

"Is that where you see yourself in two years? Entering a skilled trade?"

"Why not? That we'll love we do is an illusion in our culture as deeply engrained as having to go to college to have a good life. Only a small few love their work. I'm thinking about life from a different point of view: from my leisure rather than my occupation. I want to use my job, whatever that may be, to sustain that time before nine and after five. That's where life resides, outside the chasm of duty, and if I use those hours wisely, then I'll love my job. I'm guessing."

"So you've decided to just read your whole life. Why not? You got the dough."

"Not just reading, Roland. Studying. Attempting to answer that all-important question about what is good to do on the Earth. I think I'll go on a Great Book tour: Flaubert's *bon mot*, Mann's theory of Culture, Tolstoy's praise of the farmer, Proust and the motivations of Albertine, Dostoevsky's noble sinners. Large, challenging books that believe in one thing to the exclusion of all others. Kierkegaard's purity of heart. Woolf's simultaneity. Literature that makes value judgments; that eschews relativism and embraces judgement, perhaps. Because we all make judgements, Roland. The thing to be refused is the condemnation that often follows someone making decisions I would not make. I can think someone is living poorly without chucking stones at them or brow-beating them on some internet site."

"Okay."

"What do you think?"

"I think you should do what you do."

"No, about using time wisely."

"I'm all for it."

"What do you think is the good we should do?"

"This is your thing, Joshua. I don't think about it. I go after mine so I don't have to struggle so much, so my girl can rely on my, so my neighborhood will respect me. It's really not that complicated."

I wondered if it could it be so simple.

Roland reached for the last salmon bite and folded his arms upon the table.

"You don't like my answer," he said.

"It makes sense. And it may be further in answering the big question than I've gotten."

"Which is?"

"I think we're here to learn how to die well."

Roland dropped his head and moaned. "What the hell does that mean?"

He was a good sport and I said, "I'm not sure, but I think courage and moderation are important to it. Moderation because in order to discover the good life, all lives may have to be tried. That's the lesson of Ecclesiastes, anyway. And it may be the remedy for condemnation."

"And courage?"

"Courage is necessary for attempting moderation."

"Thought of that all on your own?"

"Not all, but most. Sixty-thousand well spent."

"And do you still have that debt?"

"I took care of that with my dad's life insurance."

"You haven't touched the acreage money?"

Acreage money? "Not so far."

"Or from the house?"

I was reticent. I shook my head.

"Looks like you're paying for this one," he said and beckoned with the tea stein. "Then we'll discuss business."

So I had told him.

He lifted his hand and Anna came over.

"You see, Joshua? Gesture eliciting response, but everyone must agree on the translation. Yes Anna, we would like two glasses of Russian Standard, please. Neat. Three glasses if you need a break."

Anna smirked and said, "Will that be all?"

"Joshua wanted something from you. What was it again?"

Anna turned to me and I looked away.

"He wanted to order off the menu, I think."

She seemed ready for such comments and I wondered if she were used to Roland's harassment or if such things were understood to occur in the service industry. Maybe Roland had a special dispensation.

"Mikhail turned me on to this place," he said when she'd gone. "It's nice, right?"

"What did you need to talk to me about?"

"Let's wait for our drinks."

"Does it have something to do with your errands this morning?"

"Here, finish these cookies."

"You want me to be your emergency contact, then? You have no next of kin so you need me to memorize your incisors for easy identification?"

Roland leaned into the table. "It's more like an investment."

"Oh."

"Besides, I already have someone to identify my body."

"Do you have a brown sack for me? Should I start buying envelopes?" Maybe he needed a part-time employee to watch his currency exchange booth; maybe he wanted me to become certified in pest control, extermination rackets are profitable in a city this size.

"Joshua, you don't know what you're talking about. I already told you you can't come on board that one. You wouldn't want to."

Anna was holding a tray supporting two glasses. She turned her right hip toward our table and, back straight, bent her knees and set our vodkas in front of us.

"Your break is later, then?" said Roland. "We may be here awhile, Joshua."

He watched Anna's retreating form and said, "To women who know better,".

The glass was heavy and flared at the rim.

"It's the only place in the city to get a proper vodka. I mean, it's the same vodka you'd get anywhere else, but the atmosphere, being among vodka's appropriate *milieu*, gives it a special flavor. You see, Joshua? Much depends on setting."

"What do we have to discuss?" I said.

"All the time in the world and none for enjoying the finer things."

"One thing that hinders setting is anticipation. When one is waiting for something unknown the flora can rot off the earth."

Roland threw up his hands.

"Just ask me what you want to ask me," I said. That the business he had to discuss came up in relation to my inheritance made me anxious. I was too concerned with what I had told him to notice the vodka's charm, nor was I in a state of repose to consider the *milieu*.

Roland took my hand. I tried to wrench it free, but he held on tight.

"Joshua. Will you go to a basketball game with me?"

"A what?"

"Friday at Crane. There's someone there you need to see."

"A basketball game. Are you kidding?" I jerked my hand away. Roland feigned shock, then laughed. "You had me believing you really needed something."

"Quit being so dramatic. High school ball is quite the thing in this town. You should see a game, that's all it is. It's nothing."

"Why couldn't you have just asked in the cab? I would have spent the last three hours doing something productive with my time."

"The museum? Not productive? Just come to the basket-ball game. You'll see a remarkable talent, I promise." Roland inspected the bill then lifted his glass. "Come on. We can't drink until you agree."

He believed I was a passive observer of life, that I was hap-pily idling away my time until fate or coincidence should drop an opportunity at my feet. But I was active in other things, unobservable to one trained in performing and interpreting gestures. I was burrowing deep into ignorance and grace, Pas-cal's Wager and Nee's remarkable thoughts about the blood of Christ and man's powerlessness to influence to any degree its worth, what that means to believers regarding guilt and shame. "A basketball game."

The vodka was crisp and clean and when Roland had finished his eyes were illuminated. He waved Anna over and ordered another round. I had never experienced straight li-quor before and was apprehensive. Those old agrarian stric-tures creeping up to tap me on the conscience, the patient dripping of proverbs into my spirit. I was afraid that I would take to it and see my life reduced to a mere pining for the malevolent fermentation. But if it was disposed to wreaking so many lives, lives I had seen washed out and collected in shallow puddles even in my small community, it began with cheering and hearty humanitarianism, easy embraces and if not pure joy, joy nonetheless. The first swallow stung, the second was clear; while my mind battled on the field of pros and cons and while prudent habit clashed with perilous exuberance, the third an-nulled my doubts. Meanwhile, Roland had been talking about some kid.

"The papers are all over him; scouts at every game. I swear, it's as if ESPN were doing a red carpet show, you know? All the celebrity coaches, former Chicago stars coming back to pitch their alma maters, the talking heads of the sports world . . . It's a crazy show, Joshua. And the Kid's right in the center of it, the eye of the hurricane. The shine coming off him buffers a lot of the chaos and mischief swirling all around him. The recruiters and boosters and various other interested parties are all colliding just outside of the Kid's perception and their 'associates' are one remove away from them, getting their hands dirty and playing rough, talking with folks from Nike and Reebok, Adidas and Puma who're all ear-marking significant sums in the hopes that he'll pay off. They all think this one's a can't miss."

"Great percentage shooter, is he?"

"The climate isn't right for skepticism, Joshua. Everyone's riding the wave of optimism, hopeful that it's this time for sure. And with what Rose did at the United Center last year and the expectations for him this year . . . all that hometown euphoria is mixing with the Kid's fortune. There's an overwhelming wave of prosperity coming to the South Side and everyone wants it to land squarely on their homes. I can see it coming, too, but I'm not losing my head to grandiose visions of trickle-down economics or so fond of the Kid that to be a part of his entourage would fulfill my life's dreams. But that doesn't mean I don't have my own plans. I'm not a schemer, Joshua, but I've put myself in a position to profit from his hard work and sacrifice. And what's wrong with that? How many people invested in Microsoft who don't know what a circuit board is or still, to this day, have never gone surfing? It's the same thing. I've been . . ."

Anna set our drinks down. Roland leaned away from the table, taking no notice of her. " . . . I've been running my ass off with an eye to future payoffs. What you saw today was nothing, it was like a day off, a sight-seeing drive through the less visited parts of the city. And there was no danger to this one, either. I've been in some scraps with rival parties, all doing the same things we're doing and doing them at the same place, same time, and it got real, man. One time I was making the rounds at the Kid's AAU game, shaking his uncle's hands, asking after his little cousins, I kiss his aunts on the cheek whenever I see them. I've been in his life for some time now, since he was thirteen years old in fact, right before his growth spurt that launched his notoriety; when he went from handling the point to muscling in the paint. Muscling hard, Joshua, hurting kids, but only because he was learning the force and power of his new body. And now both skills have united in his 6'8" frame to create one of the fiercest ballers in the country. And I been with him from the beginning, on the sidelines mostly, but I aim to change all that. "

He reached across the table with his glass. I swallowed it with some effort.

"But that's just one of the things I got going on right now, Joshua." He was looking over my shoulder, eyeing the front door. "While you're wasting your days with books by dead guys I'm working toward a better future, collecting accolades and favors from all kinds of people, getting my name out there, accomplishing tasks with gusto and with expertise so when the time comes for me to reap what's been sewn these last five years my sack won't be nearly big enough." He slammed his empty glass down for emphasis and smiled through me toward his bright Tomorrow.

"All for one high school student?"

"Joshua, you spend all your time learning about life, but you don't have the least idea about it. Your teachers are all old guys who lock themselves in their rooms pining after the elusive meaning of it all. Let me save you the trouble: get yours.

Get yours. Ain't nobody gonna care one way or the other about you unless you hit it big or destroy yourself getting there. That middle ground is full of the dead, Joshua, the cowardly, the passive, the good men, Joshua. Good men lie in the mass grave of the good life. And that's what you're studying about. Don't you see? You're just lying down. The things I'd get up to if I were you . . . I'd be unstoppable."

For all his candor about my life being lived in the clouds I was certain he had a house next door to mine. Roland shook his head and stared through the interior of Russian Tea Time and toward that palace, white and gleaming in the City Beautiful, surrounded by shade trees and verdant lawns, copulating with the sun's rays, radiating golden beams outward, into Arcadian fields where his flocks thrive and his crops yield magnificence. I must have the same look when an author alerts me to esoteric facts and ethereal notions, when my heart becomes convinced of things my mind knows better of. We were not so different, Roland and I. Each of us were using the materials at hand to procure a meaningful life in the future. He had a knack for intrigues and a schemer's enthusiasm, the energy to move about in the world with confidence, the love for people that comes from ulterior motives; but maybe that's not right, perhaps his love was simply that of an actor in character toward other characters, reciting lines that progress the play to its denouement. He did carry himself like a stage actor, as if he knew the outcome of his actions, good and bad, but the consequences would not be suffered if he could only get off the stage in time. Myself on the other hand had too much to think about. What radiated out from my palatial doorsteps were the consequences of any and all actions I could think of doing; they were hypothetical shots of illumination or revelation, a golden wisdom that saw the ill I could perpetrate and convinced me to remain ensconced in my cell collecting the sayings of wise men and living a moral life safely secluded from any conflict that would challenge my perception of the self.

"Where is it and what time should I be there?"

"We'll pick you up at six. And about this morning . . . I appreciate you being a good sport. It's on the up and up and if it weren't I wouldn't have brought you along. Besides, you needed to meet Mikhail. I think everybody should."

At Oak Street I had the opportunity to think about coincidence, an aspect of Chicago unknown in smaller towns, full of mystery concerning its relationship to fate or chance. In the town I grew up in it was no coincidence to see your banker or green grocer or coach at church or the football game or the town festivals. Where else would either of you be? In the summer you ran into your algebra teacher buying bolts at the hardware store where your father was having his lawn mower blades sharpened, but even this is not a coincidence. The four square miles where life was lived was small enough to accommodate such homogeneity of routines. Therefore, everyone you saw was an expected encounter. I never ran across the street, shouting and waving my arms, to embrace a schoolmate or to catch up with a friend's mother. I never thought such encounters were worthy of wild animation or the effort to tell friends I'd just run into So-and-So. "What luck!", I never said. "I haven't spoken to him or her in weeks. S/he's doing good and we're going to have coffee and reminisce."

Never.

But in Chicago, where People Known outnumbers People Unknown by a 1:750,000 ratio, the opportunity of running into an acquaintance is the same as getting struck by lightning. It would be a stunning thing. So I hoped he wouldn't hold it against me when I saw Felix across the street and shouted his name. I had grown accustomed to floating through the streets like a gas or a shade, unconcerned with such run-ins or wary of begin spotted by people I wanted to evade. I embraced my anonymity like the most precious grace and there was nothing I would exchange for such a treasure. But when I saw Felix emerge in rush I embraced the deviation from habit and crossed the street.

He shook my hand and said, "The Twombly? Have you finished it?"

Felix had no time for social niceties, those presumed lines one recites before getting to the meat of the conversation, and I thought this strange until I grew accustomed to his habit of speaking. Often he would just start in on whatever it was he was thinking about, and this way of his didn't only include moments like this one, but those briefer moments in company when he had gone to use the restroom or had spaced out for a bit. He brought back subjects so far afield that you had to be on your toes with him, to have some knowledge of what he thought about to anticipate what he was speaking of.

I had read the Twombly and so the number of texts had been diminished by one.

"Yes, I managed it okay. I visited his building on Madison a week or so ago."

"The Carson Pirie. Did you get inside?"

"No. I was unexpectedly taken away before I could."

"You wouldn't have got in anyway. Their tours are sporadic at best. But make that a top priority, Joshua."

"I will."

"What are you doing tonight?"

"I thought I'd check out Big John, see what happens around there when no one's looking."

"Fantastic. I'm waiting for an associate to finish up at Best Buy. I'll walk with you."

We walked down Oak to Michigan and headed north. Felix thought it was wonderful I had finished the Twombly and was excited to talk about it. What had most struck me about the book wasn't so much Sullivan's ideas about architecture and I admitted to him that I hadn't yet appreciated form following function in his buildings. Instead, I had been caught up his enthusiasm for Chicago, of his arriving in the charred city and claiming it for himself. From the ashes, the City Beautiful; from soot-bearing limbs, new buds. It was indeed a garden. And I was again made aware of the significance of the city I inhabited. According to Sullivan it had all the potential to create life: earth, wind, fire and air. This last I had intuited already, but that a mind as sharp and concentrated on such things as Sullivan's had seen the same thing and had confidence enough in his perceptions to document them encouraged me to do likewise. Upon the wide open spaces of the prairie and in the expansive sky above the Lake were the potential for great ideas and noble impulses.

"Do you have time to see something?"

We were walking up Lake Shore Drive now and the across the median and through the trees the lake was darkening with the sky. City lights glowed all around us, giving evidence of the hidden qualities of disparate lives. And over the lake, where the space appeared content and still, the colors of the known world swirled in the vortex of the setting sun. Whatever accounted for the conflict — gases colliding and cooling then heating millions of miles away, leaving behind stellar remnants like arrow heads in a field of beets; and all of this having occurred millions of years ago, their light mere echoes or a rerun, as though the universe had already happened and we were late to the party — it was beautiful to see. I strained to find the square of Pegasus, though, and Andromeda would be invisible then, but still I looked. I knew it was there and seeing the galaxy before it became visible suddenly had some import on the ideas of faith I was developing.

"I want to show you what this area used to look like before the shore was built up and the only parks the city had were called forests."

Felix led us into the semi-circle drive of an apartment building. He held the front door open for me with the flourished gesture of a half bow. For a moment I was alone in the lobby. It was dimly lit and furnished in deep maroons. Elegant framings of a Lentulof and a Matiushin hung on the wall behind the security desk. The wall behind me was glass and on the far right wall was an enormous picture in faded sepia.

An imposing voice asked if I needed help and I saw the broad-shouldered man behind desk begin to rise. Felix brushed by me and the image of the security guard lightened. His teeth shone warmhearted and a deep chuckle softened the already luxurious space.

"Hello Rodger. Just looking at the print again."

"Take your time, Mr. Servo."

We stood in front of a large print, whose solid wood frame looked like a burden to hang, that captured North Lake Shore Drive immediately following its completion. Potter Palmer had convinced the city, in the enchanting ways that Chicago real estate barons convince of such things, to build the road next to the coast in order to increase his own land's value. Cobb and Frost completed this Norman Gothic mansion, his castle really, complete with stately turrets and minarets, an eighty foot spiral staircase, elevators, a conservatory and dummy knobs on the front doors, unusable, requiring entrance from the side only, in 1885 (only two blocks from where Felix and I were now contemplating this aerial photograph). The home was razed in 1950 to make room for apartments, an ironic consequence of the high property values Palmer so desperately wanted.

"Palmer's home had rooms designed after Indian and Ottoman styles. He had a Renaissance library and a Spanish music room. Some of the best examples of Impressionist art-work were displayed in his salon and were later bequeathed to the Art Institute, but Gabriel Ferrier's mural is lost forever. Many of the homes that are shown here have been destroyed by developers or converted into apartment buildings as well. Some have been brothels, others were speakeasies, depart-ment stores, even notorious hideouts. All historical sites, Joshua. All lost. Gone forever except in these stark echoes. Can you find the building we're standing in right now? Look closely."

I looked for John Hancock, then laughed at the powerful hold habit had on me. I lifted a vague finger toward the wall and said, "There?"

"We're actually further north than you'd suspect."

He exaggerated the angle of my arm.

"It's unrecognizable today. There was an elegance to the city it just doesn't have anymore. Of course, I now this isn't strictly true. Nostalgia remembers more fondly that which we didn't experience ourselves. It's in the old construction mate-rials they used; it's the lack of color in the print, the absence of clear shapes and sharp forms, that allows our imagination to press upon it; to pretend the past didn't have those things that harass us today."

"There wasn't any traffic then."

"True. There are no motor vehicles. And the promenade is still a part of the landscape architecture, rather than devoid of it. There is a slowness inherent in these old photographs. Maybe that's what we miss?"

"It's too bad."

"It is too bad. The speed at which our cities change dispatches tragedies being all across our city. There are countless casualties in the war of progress, Joshua. I'm not saying these things shouldn't be; of course the city breathes. It flexes and relaxes, reinventing itself over time and if land once used for a single family can be repurposed to accommodate two hundred then it should be done. That's the world we live in. But couldn't we take our time destroying it? Couldn't we extract some of the architectural wonders of the era and be precise in removing the artwork? Couldn't Ferrier's mural have been preserved, touched up maybe, and reinstalled? Wouldn't that be time spent to good benefit? I've worked on such projects for twenty-five years now and I'll never be convinced that the print preferred the fire."

Having never seen the mural or even hearing about Ferrier until that evening I can't say that I mourned its absence. In this practical matter I was mute, but theoretically I agreed with Felix. The energy it takes to manifest a hypothetical design, no matter how small, whether it be the ironworks of the front gate or the door knobs used throughout the house, should be respected. Saved, if possible. However, when time is money concern for the safety and fair treatment of artistic representations can't be assumed. I would take an altruistic person, a community made up of such people, to devote themselves to venerating that assumption. So I was not surprised to discover this was what Felix did with his time.

"How did you get involved with historical preservation?" I said.

"I was a few years out of high school when I met a man named Richard Nickel. Have you ever heard of him?"

I said that I hadn't.

"He was a remarkable person, Joshua, and it's not a stretch to say that I loved him. He was a beautiful man. He began it all. What we called then 'preservation' and what is now called 'urban renewal' didn't have a name, so to speak, when Richard started. He didn't have such banners to parade under. He simply loved Sullivan's old buildings. He could see their souls. Sure, Sullivan was one of the first practitioners of the steel frame and he was interested in this new material for creating office buildings, for launching a man's work space high above the street, but he was just as interested in the ornamentation. He loved working in terra cotta panels, molding whatever design the building called out to him. He believed that just as a leaf is the direct outgrowth of the tree, so to the ornament. A certain design followed from its column, a vine weave followed in harmony with the cornice.

"Richard didn't have the luxury of celebrity cachè behind him when he started. It was not a cause for the black-tie fund-raising scene then. There was hardly a thought for saving buildings. And there probably wouldn't have been had not Mayor Daley — he would be the father of our current mayor — started razing entire neighborhoods to build new ones. Around 1955 this would have been. Indiscriminately it seemed. One of Richard's first attempts was a Sullivan residence building in the Near West. While the bureaucrats had him going through the proper channels to secure permits — filling out applications, describing the appearance of the ornaments, the materials of the railings and the doors, justifying their value, not just for architectural history, but for Chicago and mankind itself, and proving other entities such as institutions, museums and private collectors with some clout wanted these things — they tore the poor things down. One day Richard was taking photographs of the panels he wanted to save and the next they had been ground to dust and scattered atop a pile of rubble.

"Mayor Daley brought destruction to the city of Chicago not seen since the Great Fire. What that disaster did in two days, consuming some 17,000 buildings, Daley did methodically, using a slow burn; 6,000 in three years. The Prudential Building was razed to make room for corporate headquarters and parking lots. Forty blocks of rubble and exposed wire and pipes and precious ornamentation followed. Richard received some notoriety when he began picketing the destruction of the Garrick Theater. This was in 1960. 'Do we dare squander Chicago's great architectural heritage?' he asked. The answer was, *yes, of course we do!* These buildings were not making a profit any longer. They were slowing progress and had to go. The theater was destroyed and Richard was devastated, depressed even. He had been shown what millions of men knew before him and what millions will know after, that the presence of one man is insignificant against the tide of progress. This was ten years before I met him, in 1970 it was. I was sixteen years old then, scuttling about Chicago, bored and eager to start doing something."

Felix looked away from the photograph and up at me, to gage my interest, I supposed, which he had, but also to get a feeling for my sense of history; to see whether I could listen to his story while also keeping in mind the state of our country. We were then beginning troop withdrawals in Vietnam after six years of escalation and Nixon had rushed a squadron of B-52s armed with nuclear weapons to the Soviet border. For three days the bombs were airborne, suspended just above the drop doors, and the administration was projecting its madman theory of diplomacy in which they attempted to make Krushchev think Nixon was a lunatic; that he was obsessed with Communism and subject to violent rages while he was near the button. Americans knew nothing of this, of course, and while protestors chanted slogans and got high on thoughts of Mutually Assured Destruction in each other's naked arms, the policies remained immune. Once the power has been unleashed how do you hide the Fat Boy?

Not knowing what to say I said, "Those were radical times."

Felix looked again at the picture. "Yes, they were," he said.

I didn't know how to redeem myself, so I did nothing.

"Richard turned to guerrilla preservation," Felix said. "He eschewed legal protocol and reclaimed all he could. Technically this was theft, but since it would all be broken and ground to dust and eventually hauled away to Lake Calumet, he didn't give a damn. If anything, he thought if someone were to bring charges against him these people would have to prove the worth of the things he stole. And he loved this idea. Being imprisoned for stealing items of historic significance would go a long way toward justifying his beliefs about architecture. So, he donned army fatigues and t-shirts and trespassed onto the sites, which were guarded by saw horses and rope. He took a camera with him — he was a gifted photographer, Joshua. It's how he made his name initially. He documented the buildings in what he called their 'rape phase.' He captured undefended buildings crying out in their nakedness while siege-works were being built, walls broken down, interiors stripped, all to the amusement of a board of directors somewhere planning their own building and spending the projected profits with little thought that it too would be similarly raped in fifty years by another board with the same thoughts. I preferred to call it 'the death phase' and even Richard called his theme *death before its time*, but the other moniker is much more visceral and brings more sympathy from the crowd that wants to help such a victim rather than attend a funeral. His photographs actually had a show at the Art Institute and are on permanent display at Southern Illinois University. They bring to mind Nadar's photographs of Haussmann's destruction of Paris — ." Felix paused in his reminiscence and nodded to himself before remembering his place in the story. "So yes, his camera and basic tools needed for such reclaiming: a wrecking bar, penetrating oil, some wrenches. He had done his recon and knew what he wanted. He took whatever original design work he could, even those ornaments that were bolted down, so to speak: doors, ironwork, atlas books, picture frames, office stationery, limestone panels, bay windows, the woodwork, sinks. I even saw what looked like a penny, five feet in diameter, with the carved face of a composer upon it, leaning against his lawnmower once. He had pieces of buildings lying around his home, in his car and hidden in woods throughout the prairie.

"I have some of his photographs in my home, actually; but you should take a few days and see the originals. There's beauty in ruins, Joshua. It's always been this way. And the camera is the perfect instrument to capture it. Those stark images hearken back to another time that's disappeared. Go look at pictures of Chicago after the Great Fire. It looks war-torn. And from a distance of nearly 150 years we can be thankful, in some respects, to Mrs. O'Leary. Who knows what would have become of Chicago without her clumsy cow. But even more remarkable, and perhaps more lamentable, are Richard's photographs of intact buildings before their deaths. There's a fallen majesty in them; in their sighs. Richard never knew why buildings had to be destroyed . . . well, he knew why, of course; I mean why they had to be destroyed so thoroughly.

Two hundred feet above the oblivious crowd carved stone cornices had watched; artistic details, time consuming work both on site and in the studio, never meant to be seen by those on the street. They were troubled over, expertly conceived and achieved, a beauty to behold for the artist alone. I have always found something heroic in such hidden art, even in the failed artist. It's one of the many reasons I was drawn to Richard, just as he was drawn to Sullivan. He was unappreciated, even within his own circle and especially within historical societies around the city. They never joined him in his nocturnal excavations, but they were always ready to take the pieces."

We lingered a moment longer before the remnant of passed time. Photographs like these had gotten to me lately. Before when I'd see them, in school textbooks mostly but sometimes on my own, in the obscure archives room beneath Conrad Hall at Michigan State or in the Historical Library in Lansing, I'd view them as an historian of sorts. I was looking for something in those by-gone days; a permanence maybe, or a building that would connect me to my university town. It was something to do and I enjoyed the excursions. However, since Dad had passed, I developed a sensitivity to such things. My eyes were opened to the transitory nature of all life, which was something I'd never had the opportunity to think about, or if I did it was with a cavalier attitude, the same way I learned about the law of gravity without really knowing its greater importance.

Dad and my life with him would only ever be a part of those by-gone years now. And those years would only ebb further and further from me as I made whatever mark upon the world I would make.

"We should getting along, Joshua. I don't want to keep Stephanie waiting."

"Thank you for showing this to me," I said. "I'd have never know it was here."

"There are pockets of these historical rarities hidden all around Chicago."

"I'll see all of them you're willing to show me."

"Good. I hoped that would be the case. Thank you for humoring us, Roger."

"Any time, Mr. Servo," said Roger.

I walked with Felix back down Lakeshore Drive. The wind was cold coming off the lake and with more intensity than usual.

"I remember one night at Richard's home," Felix continued. "He lived in a bungalow south of Hyde Park next to the lake and we were in the garage winterizing his boat. He was oiling the engine and he rose too quickly, forgetting the low-hanging light he was working by, knocking his head into it. It started swinging back and forth and we were chuckling at his clumsiness when the light happened to illuminate the back of the shed. He tells me to hold the direct the light for him and I shined a light on a grown man crawling over bits of junk toward some other junk and when he moved out of the light, I saw he was rubbing a piece of stone, angling it so the light caught it just so. Apparently he'e had never seen that piece in such a way before. It was taken from the Republic Building; a cornice ornament. No one had ever seen it from a garage perspective before. And very few had ever seen Richard in that same garage perspective."

"What happened to that piece?"

"Oh . . . who knows? He had so much of it."

We hit the Mile and I saw the Hancock, like a solitary temple column.

"What happened to him?" I said.

"To Richard? A heroic end, I'm afraid. They were tearing down Sullivan's Stock Exchange. This was back in '72. I was eighteen years old at the time and was anticipating my number being called while beginning my own career in preservation. The tactics were changing and we were being pulled more and more into the boardrooms and court systems, making more calls to wealthy philanthropists and any organization, however small, in the hopes of drumming up support. It took Richard away from the sites where his pulse quickened; from where he felt he was actually doing something. What would a Savior of Buildings need a suit for? The idea was preposterous to him. He couldn't see the point of the committees and there was no way to strain muscles in a three-piece suit. Such a beautiful man. So Richard retired. He was worn out with caring. And also a woman finally saw him as we all did and he got engaged, another reason to hang up that dangerous work of scouring across unreliable floors and climbing detached beams for art nouveau hardware. Still, the Stock Exchange was too much of a siren and he took to it with his ropes and hard hat. If he wasn't dragging those heavy ropes and going home with dirt all over his face and dust from the buildings under his fingernails, he felt he was wasting his time. He had to sit one last time with his dying friend.

"Well . . . So he went to cannibalize the Stock Exchange. It was already a mess by then. The interior was a pile of debris and pipes sticking out every which way. Two walls had been collapsed and the two that remained looked like it was full of cubbyholes. Eerily similar to those old shots of war-torn Europe, those lost cities of Cologne and Dresden. What had been the workspace for propelling a growing economy toward Super Power status, whose Trading Floor had been the glory of the region — you should have seen the steelwork and the sun pouring in through the skylights reflecting off the dust motes that buzzed and flittered above the din of frenzied hands — had been reduced to a treacherous landscape. It was no longer safe for any of us to be scaling around inside it, let alone by ourselves.

"I got the call the next day. The same day he was going to introduce his fiancé to his brother, actually. His inner circle had been searching the site all night and came up with nothing. We still had not found him a week later. People began to suggest he had run off from fear of being married or that he had faked the whole thing to generate sympathy for his cause; one person suggested we should look on the shores of Lake Calumet, as if he'd pulled a Thoreau on everybody. But then we found the stair stringer he had gone in search of, this was in what would have been the basement. You see Joshua, steel doesn't make a sound before it gives under weight. I imagine the floor collapsed suddenly and pray he was killed instantly."

"That's awful, Felix."

"He had been buried for four weeks and the dogs hadn't caught the scent. We had been walking on top of him, the machinery scooped the debris four inches from his crushed body. One beam had fallen across his shoulder and another had fallen perpendicular like, over his legs. But he was perfectly preserved, Joshua. Something about the coarse sand and dust, maybe the asbestos or other toxic compounds mixed with cold water, I don't know. There was no death odor. His fingertips gave pristine prints. The whole thing was just incredible. And then there was the sorrow and the suffering . . ."

"And you've been carrying his legacy," I said after a time.

"I've been trying. We did save the Chicago Theater. People still seem to enjoy that space. But that took the suits. I don't think Richard would be disappointed, though. We've come to realize that to fight the razing, we have to go where those proposals are being discussed; try to needle our way in to where the deals are struck. Not an easy task in this city. They don't just let anyone to the table and the table is always moving. The battle's not on street level, but high above it, in the clouds, on the fortieth floor. Truth be told, I prefer that kind of preservation. I'm getting to old to go digging into foundations and anyway, their on to us now; security is a lot tighter."

We were walking through the large square beneath the Hancock and because Felix didn't see his friend we took up positions at the rail looking into the submerged courtyard.

"Developers don't care about the past or art. And quite frankly they've been winning in America since the dedication of Sullivan's Auditorium. They see these beautiful buildings as obstacles on prestigious acres and lament that they weren't born a hundred years earlier; they see out-dated models of architecture furnished in an obsolete aesthetic and reason that because the Model-T no longer dominates the streets, neither should Henry Ford's homes besmirch our shoreline. What's ironic is that the time and money necessary to preserve these buildings equals the time and money it originally cost to create them. In preserving them it's almost as if the Historical Society is contracting them all over again."

Felix turned from the bustle beneath us and watched the bustle behind.

"If developers saw it this way, maybe the art of preservation would have a few more practitioners. There she is," he said, waving to the young woman walking toward him.

"This is Joshua. Joshua, Stephanie Willis."

"Like the Tower," I said, shaking her hand.

"If that helps you."

Stephanie was a slender woman with blond hair cut just below her shoulders. She wore dark glasses that gave depth to her eyes and complimented the severe lips that she held firm from expressing too much. In one gloved hand she carried a little blue bag, she concealed the other in a pocket of her black pea coat.

"Stephanie is an artist working in collage. There isn't a medium she doesn't incorporate into her pieces. All in an attempt to illuminate the unifying principle behind art."

"Behind all human discovery, actually," she said. "It's an attempt to integrate the world through a common understanding. In my generation alone there have been countless abuses of human rights, invasions of privacy, leaps in technological uses, cracks in our market systems, implosions really, racial divides economic divides religious divides. Our society is in flux; there's a palpable anxiety on the streets and in the air that hasn't been seen before. New discoveries are constantly subverting our way of life and we, as a society, can't possibly process them fast enough. So even as we create the future we are living in archaic times. It's a great strain on everyone and requires a grand scale to give our battles perspective."

"Stephanie's work is marvelous, Joshua. She's beginning to expand the scope of her ideas and with it the size of her canvases."

I nodded my approval, though I didn't understand the implication behind his meaning.

"Well, when I talk about a grand scale I'm not talking about the size of the surface, but something else."

"Of course," said Felix. "I didn't mean to imply . . . well, I'm sorry. Go ahead."

"On my last visit to New York I saw Fernand Leger's *Mural Painting*. It was simple and elegant and it shocked me out of my usual sensibilities, which had been in love with chaos and disruption, but was becoming too much for me. It wasn't providing release for my anger and fear so that I wanted to destroy everything. Including the work I was doing. I began screaming at the television until I threw a brick into it. And that alone brought some much needed calm to my life. So much so that I attributed that moment of violence to preparing my mind to see Purism for the saving force it could be."

"I'm not familiar with that," I said.

"It was a short-lived movement in the early twenties, as they all were back then. Le Corbusier and Ozenfant thought Cubism had become too decorative, which they believed was at the bottom of the artistic hierarchy. Like landscape or still-life in the early nineteenth century. And they thought conception was the thing. Style, technique and method, they thought, were all subservient to this."

"And what is conception?"

"It's where life begins," she said and laughed. "Of course not in the way the right wingers believe, but in that sense. Just as the fetus is unaffected by culture or history so my art attempts a return to the moment before these things. Earlier even."

"You have an ambitious project," I said. "Have you had exhibitions?"

"Not yet." She looked at Felix in fervid accusation. "But Felix is working on getting a space for the group."

"I have a space in mind. I'm just waiting to hear back from our donors."

"It's that bastard Eric."

"Stephanie," Felix said.

"He's had two exhibitions, Felix. Solo exhibitions. He's sold four paintings and one of his ironic lawn ornaments went for eight hundred. To someone who doesn't understand irony and lives on the 44th floor."

"Six, actually," said Felix, ashamed.

"What?"

"He's sold six paintings now."

"Six, then. Perfect. And there he sits there congratulating himself on making it while the rest of us rub our dimes together to pay for heat. How is he still living with us anyway?"

"He's paying what you all agreed to and you know he's not obligated to pay any more just because he's the first to have success. The same as if you . . ."

"What? Sold a piece?"

Stephanie had taken a cigarette from a silver case and was tapping the filter on it's embossed surface. She spoke in an even voice, free of escalating emotion, almost monotone, which unnerved me.

"It's my fault Stephanie," said Felix. "Of course it is. Once I procure a space, you and everybody else will see your work appreciated."

"They can show their appreciation with a check, Felix." She inhaled and before Felix could defend the masses who hadn't the slightest idea of her work yet she said, "You're doing your best. I know, I know." She blew smoke into the high air, lifting her face to the constellations, obscuring the angels' view. Felix was staring at his shoes, nodding. I tried to hear this championing as a positive statement from Stephanie.

"I'm sorry, Joshua," she said. "This probably isn't the best time to be having the same old discussion. Do you and Felix have plans now?"

Her voice affected a jovial lilt.

"Not really. We just bumped into each other on the street," I said.

"Would you like to have a look at our work? Maybe you need an investment opportunity or know people who do."

This was meant to hurt Felix and judging from his weakened smile Stephanie had hit him hard. I was fond of the man; I thought well of him and it was difficult to see how easily he could be chastised. As much to not leave him without a companion as to see something I'd never seen before I said, "I'd love to see the studio."

Stephanie smiled. "It's not exactly Montmartre."

"I think there are wonderful artistic statements being made there."

Stephanie blew smoke into Felix's step. "You're sweet," she said.

The artist colony was a two-story apartment building in the shape of an "L" with a dis-repaired landscaped courtyard in back. The bottom floor was made up of nine high-ceilinged lofts where the artists worked. Fourteen apartments made up the second floor. Only half were occupied. Though Felix had lease notices advertised in a plethora of outlets none were connecting with suitable tenants.

We approached the main entrance and the I heard the familiar riff of Def Leopard's sticky-sweet hit, a popular song during my first year on the farm. Then I saw that some artists had covered their large windows with plastic bags, either to keep out prying eyes or to eliminate natural light. One window was clean enough to seem invisible and the space was powerfully lit, the better to manipulate the small shadows of her work. Rods and cones listed, individually and in union, invitingly upon pedestals of varying heights while recumbent undulations bowed at their master's feet. The sculptor was plying two strands of wet clay.

"That would be Eric," said Stephanie, who assumed I'd been drawn to a different window. "He can't work without that racket. You can imagine how sophisticated his work is." "That's not fair, Stephanie," Felix said.

Stephanie mumbled and unlocked the front door. She led us away from the noise and into a back corner where she unlocked a second door and flipped on the light. I was introduced to a white space with clean floors. Light tan shelves adorned the far wall where clusters of color spotted the levels like a painter's palette. Next to this was a bench filled with larger objects that seemed to spill over the sides an onto the floor around it. A besotted cloth covered another workbench where brushes soaked in jars of putrid water and stacked cans of paint leaked color like cascading champagne. A gray cloth veiled a canvas that towered beside the bench. On the opposite side were still more canvases, whose width and height spoke to Stephanie's ambition. I only saw the thin strips of wood that held the surface taut against the rectangular frame. They seemed fragile but I imagined they supported great depth of feeling. Because their faces were turned I began to imagine the possible representations they bespoke.

"A working studio," Felix said. The *Tada!* in his voice was not out of place. I tried to hide my feelings of wonder at seeing it, but Felix knew I was thrilled.

In my studies outside the purview of the university I had stumbled upon Rilke and it was through him that I became conscious Rodin. His sculptures had been meticulously prepared in sketchbooks; minuscule rough drafts had been formed before the large blocks of stone and marble were beaten down, chiseled into and smoothed over to reveal the anguished torso and the benevolent hand; the blinding forehead of *Idea*, like the curvature of Earth seen from an Apollo's window, gave me pause as I considered what omniscience had crafted it and just how was it achieved. These wonderful works were conceived in such a studio; the kind of studio Rembrandt and Courbet allowed their viewers to witness, albeit with different subjects and through separate points of view.

Stephanie lit another cigarette. I imagined she needed the nicotine to calm down from being in the presence of her creative space or to relieve the anxiety of having a stranger naively criticize her work, or else she needed one every twenty minutes regardless of her surroundings or company.

I proceeded to the large shelves and saw that the clusters were small sculptures of abstract objects, figurines and small-scale menagerie of everyday household items, plants and animals I saw that the landscapes were terrariums enclosed in glass globes and shadowboxes of miscellanea that coalesced to define occupations, cityscapes and historical time periods. One that immediately struck me mimicked the green triangle of park from which State and Rush diverged. These streets had more curve to them than they actually had and the entrance to Gibson's had been placed on East Bellevue Place. I had to look again. Hugo's had been razed in order to complete the effect.

"Would you like to see what I'm working on now?" Stephanie held the cigarette loosely between her lips. "Take that corner, will you? Carefully."

I helped her disrobe the piece. Large brush strokes of black, white and grey with blue wisps of various shades dominated the otherwise black canvas. As I looked closer though, I realized something peculiar. It was indeed a canvas, rough-grained and ready to accept oil or acrylic, however the canvas itself was already painted on. But that wasn't right; no it was something else: a photograph, perhaps. The center of the piece was blinding white and of the same texture as the black spaces. I stepped back and saw in the dark spaces specks of light and wisps of green, orange and pink.

"It's not finished, obviously," said Stephanie. She was folding the veil and watching me. Felix was silent, arms folded, delighting in my looking.

I stood back from the piece. I didn't know how to read the subject of a canvas already overlaid with a subject. This was a celestial photograph; a picture of the heavens; a hidden burst of celebration millions of miles from Earth and taking place, or having already taken place, millions of years ago without any knowledge of our spying. It was a vision of untold majesty. Whose awe was such a joyous dance meant to elicit so long ago? Or was such a dance done then so that we would see it now, today? I couldn't speak to that design and I would not have been able to speak at all were it not for the streaks of paint that Stephanie contributed to the piece. They were sluggish right angles that slowed the momentum of the piece; that had relaxed the violent nature of destruction, or else creation. I couldn't be sure which.

"There's just the outline here. I'll add the details as they come to me."

"I can't understand what the canvas is trying to say. As a whole, I mean. I have an idea about the untouched canvas. Is the right way to talk about it? It's glorious."

I was trying to see through the steaks, mindfully scraping away the oils to unmuffle it; I was trying to see it with the streaks fully intact, projecting oils that would enunciate it.

"Maybe because it's not finished," I said.

"Do you recognize the image?" she said.

"I don't."

"It's the Butterfly Nebula. It was taken by the Hubbel Telescope, maybe five years ago? I found an enhanced picture of it and sent it to a company in California that specializes in turning photographs into canvases. It was not a cheap endeavor at this size and the first couple attempts were awful. I couldn't use them. They finally got it right a few months ago and I've been thinking about what I wanted to say on it for weeks. First,

I felt drawn to make a pro-woman statement given the center's energy; then I saw that Matrix movie and they'd already done it. With the woman in the restaurant? Eating the cake? Nevermind. It'd been done before. So then I thought about Abstract Expressionism. It was just such a pompous movement in art history. There's no subject, and whatever meaning it may have was meant to be understood by artists and intellectuals, not the public. Still, I'm really drawn to that center."

"It's incredible," I said. The photograph was sharp and the colors were truly otherworldly; I was amazed by the dreadful details, overwhelmed by the majesty of the image.

After a time I said, "What will you distill from it? What do you want to bring to the public lives?"

"Stephanie is an artist, Joshua," said Felix. "She dabbles in mysticism and necromancy; she communes with curative forces and the black arts. To reveal any more would be cheating you."

"Actually I . . ."

"No, no! Do not reveal your secrets," Felix said, waving his arms and laughing. "Else the spell be broken and . . ."

Stephanie frowned at him and invited me to look at her finished pieces.

They were of varying sizes but the premise was the same in each and I began longing for the original photograph to stand out. The whole composition hid itself from me; it would not surrender its message. I kept returning to the original photographs, which I later found on-line for my own purposes: Orion Nebula, Carina Nebula, NGC 2074, Mystic Mountain, Pillars of Creation. The adornment was unnecessary, I thought; her oils served only to obscure the revelation at best, disparage it at worst. I looked away from the infinite and realized Felix had left. I stumbled about the room. I didn't know what to do with my hands; if I should be saying something, if

Stephanie expected me to be speaking or if she was anticipating my speech. I didn't have anything for her.

"Are there any untouched canvases you'd be willing to sell?"

"Untouched? You mean just the photograph?"

"I'm sorry. No, that's not what I meant."

"What did you mean?"

"There's something in those photographs that . . ."

I looked for Felix again, but was just the two of us.

"They're like hearing Stravinsky for the first time," I said. "They're difficult to find the melody in; their harmony is cacophony. Between the photograph and your steaks, I mean. They're musicians from around the world playing whatever they want together in a field, waiting for a common language to present itself. I feel like these canvases are what these musicians play before the language coincides and relates each to the other. Beauty is somewhere off the edge of the canvases, but it's not represented on them. I'm sorry, I don't mean to . . ."

"You think they're shit." She twisted a cigarette butt on the wall and folded her arms.

"I'm not trained to see what you're going for, Stephanie."

"No kidding? And here I thought . . . Stupid; of course he wouldn't think like that."

Stephanie was mumbling to herself; she turned the canvases around, concealing their subjects with as much firmness of purpose as she'd revealed them. I wrung my hands. I wanted to dive into the photograph, to swim into the nebula and be forgotten.

Felix came back holding two Solo cups. "I brought some drinks to toast . . . What's happened?" said Felix.

"Your friend offered to take a canvas off my hands before I ruined it."

"No, that's not . . ."

"Joshua?"

"Felix, that's not what I was trying to do."

"He says I don't know what beauty is. Like you got any idea."

She tugged at a cigarette, crushing it in her hand. She took out another and turned her back on us.

"Stephanie, please. Not in here."

"Suck my . . . He's not even a real buyer, Felix."

"Joshua? No, he's not."

"I thought maybe tonight you were finally making good on your promises. Why did you bring him here then?"

"Because he would appreciate it."

"That's just great. Parade the tourists around our sacred spaces. That's what they are, right? Aren't you always telling us? And then here he comes."

She glared at me as though I were a representation she abhorred.

"The photographs speak to me. Those gases illumined by the center; they must be thousands of light years across and the explosion must have occurred thousands of years ago. Millions, even. The past is present here. I find that comforting, somehow."

"Aren't you a lucky one."

"The marvelous isn't illuminated, Felix. It's scoffed."

"So you do get it?" said Stephanie.

"Okay you two, let's try to remain calm."

"Get him out of here, Felix. I swear to god . . ."

"Will you tell her I'm sorry?" I said. We were walking up Wells to Division and I was mortified. "Tell her I don't know what I'm talking about; that I'm . . ."

"Joshua, it's all right. She'll be furious for a while, but she'll get over it. That's how she is. In the morning she'll have forgotten all about it and her work will continue."

I didn't believe him, but I appreciated what he was trying to do.

"Still, I don't know what you were thinking telling her she was destroying the marvelous."

"I don't know either. It was terrible, wasn't it?"

Felix smiled. "Yes, it was. But you're enthusiastic, Joshua. It's good to see, even if it hasn't been disciplined yet."

"Do you think I'll be welcomed back?"

"You can come with me whenever you like. It won't kill Stephanie to hear unpleasant opinions of her work. I don't think she was prepared to hear one tonight, though."

"She thought I was a potential buyer. I didn't consider how offering to buy the canvas she hadn't touched would make her feel."

"She's from a rich family, Joshua. She hasn't had to struggle, and she lacks the hardness needed to pursue the kind of life she wants right now. Or thinks she wants. This whole experience may very well be just a layover of sorts until she figures out what she really wants to do. I don't think she expected to create so long in obscurity. She's still a child, in that sense; she's irritated by her desired deferred. Eric's success doesn't help matters, there."

We passed Mother's and Landshark, whose ping-pong table prominently displayed in the front window was occupied by twenty-somethings swaying and yelling and laughing.

"Maybe she'll always will be childish when it comes to her art. Money has the effect of keeping some people in perpetual adolescence."

I nodded, but I was suddenly anxious that he had seen something in me. After all, I was not beholden to a job just then and I was entertaining the idea of a life of letters, the scholar's life, a life of seeking out the best way to live or, which comes to the same thing, how best to die. Infantile stuff, actually; a babe on his blanket kicking his feet and staring at the ceiling, waiting to be lifted.

We turned the corner and I invited Felix for a drink at the Zebra Lounge. He held up his hand and said he would be returning to Stephanie. I apologized again.

"It didn't affect our friendship, Joshua."

I went upstairs instead. I opened the first volume of Patrick Leigh Fermor's trek across Europe and stared at the same page for twenty minutes thinking about Dad and life on the farm, as it was then, when we were together, and as it is now, enjoyed by my friends who would be fellowshipping in one another's basements and living rooms or touring the Liphart's apple orchard, communing around their cider and donuts, or else, because it was Friday night, taking in our high school's football game, bundled in the chill and feeling nostalgic for the past, happy it was where it was in our lives. Such memories made me feel lonely, like I was missing out on what life actually is; instead, I had decided to pursue a life in the company of strangers I very well might never fully understand.

I continued reading until I couldn't anymore and I went to bed wondering if this was really what I was to do with the lifetime remaining to me.

I had a dream I was walking along the Danube. There were dark forests and green hills all around; wild flowers had grown up among the trenches and craters. Farmers were milking their cows and working the ground, concerned, they told me, but not overly, about the euro and Merkel's decision to bail out Greece. Somehow the hamlets and villages nestled in those valleys I'd created and in the castles built among the hills seemed better able to withstand the tides of history than our precarious pillars of steel and glass. Its force had consistently beaten against them, yet they remained. We will survive this, too, one farmer told me. He had put my mind at ease. I waved good-bye and made my way by foot across Westphalia. It's landscape was familiar to me. I knew where I was and my dream-self rebelled against it. I began pleading with whoever had placed me here to return me to Chicago. I had not finished what I'd intended when I left. I needed more time.

Then I woke up.

It took me some minutes to realize I was not on Dad's farm, but in a small studio apartment on Clark. I laid back down and sighed, thankful it had just been a dream. Later that morning, while I was reading and drinking coffee, a presence from that dream emerged from the shadows and I was left with the impression that it was Dad whom I'd been pleading with. I wondered why I thought Dad would have wanted me to remain on his farm; in all my time with him he'd encouraged me in whatever I found to do, or not to do. When I made the decision to sell and even during the grueling process of it all, I had never wavered in my resolve to go through with it or that it was the wrong thing to do. Perhaps the best decisions carry with them some aspect of regret that won't manifest itself until much later.

That had been the case when Dad returned to farm his father's acres. Across the dirt road beside Dad's farm was a patch of over-growth surrounded by a field. Small trees had taken root and untended shrubbery grew wild around half-buried stones that, after I had dug around them, revealed an architectural intent. I had uncovered ancient ruins. Subsequent investigations never failed to unearth something of interest to my developing imagination: glass beer bottles filled with mud,

bits of wrappers and pencil stubs, shotgun casings and a ragged
burlap bag I cleaned as best I could. I freed it of sod clumps
by whacking it against the low wall and left it on the bank of
a deep ditch to dry int he sun. The markings on it had faded,
but I was certain the faded smudges had once clearly defined a
skull and crossbones. Bay Port had once been the fishing cap-
ital of the world, so we were told, and the marina was only five
miles away. On the playgrounds at recess we would entertain
one another with macabre tales of pillaging and plundering
while waiting to be selected for kickball games and dodgeball
games. I kept this old hideout to myself, however, believing
if I told Billy or Mike, and especially if I told Norman, they
would ransack it or make fun of me for actually believing what
our parents and teachers told me. So to keep my imaginings
in the realm of the possible for as long as I could I kept things
to myself. I never doubted that pirates had portaged inland to
bury their booty on Dad's property and though I never found
a Spanish coin or an old map sketched out on leathery paper,
an eye-patch or peg legs, the absence of such proof only made
the case for their reality that much more persuasive to me.

As time went on though, and I became accustomed to the
presence of those ruins, I had to acknowledge that it was merely
an old hovel. No descendants of marine marauders would be
attempting to kidnap me for the land deed and neither would
robbers be returning to find I had looted their storehouse. I
accepted this and forgot about it for a time; the fact it had once
been a home was what drew me to it again.

I seldom crossed over the culvert then. Having outgrown
my adventurous play I no longer had reason to scramble about
within its dilapidated floor plan. I had begun a life of reflection
and so I thought about it; at my desk, staring out my bedroom
window at the tufts of straggly foliage there in that fertile field,

I considered it. No longer was it populated by those benevolent rascals that had fired my imagination seven years earlier; instead there was a father and a mother; there was a young boy and sometimes his little brother was there, sometimes it was his little sister. The little family was warm and close, both in its emotional intimacy and its physical proximity. Because there were only four rooms there was no place inside one could go where another was not already there. So the young boy and his sometimes-brother-sometimes-sister grew up in a home that nurtured their growing egos, that asked them what they thought and preferred and reveled in their silliness, in their lavish interpretations of the town's machinations. The young boy was safe and the young boy was celebrated; so it would always be.

"Your grandpa was born there," Dad said when I asked him.

We were inspecting the property at dusk. The gravel of our drive glowed a nocturnal blue and the soles of our shoes pressed and skipped the fledgling stones in that pleasant way. We would be picking the apples soon; soon the garden would need harvesting.

"But you weren't born there, right?"

"No, I was born in the house your grandparents live in now. I remember when they tore that building down, though. We forgot to paint the porch this summer."

"Again? Next year for sure then."

"I'm serious."

"I am too."

"Next year then."

"I'll get some friends."

"Get that big one. What's-his-name."

"Obviously we'll get Norman to help."

Dad took a knee beside the landscaping and pulled thin weeds up through the mulch.

"I don't think that black out matt did a dang thing."

"We spent all day doing that, though."

"Sold us a faulty product." He tossed the green wisps into a French lilac and brushed his hands.

"Why did they bring it down?" I said.

"The old place? Your grandpa was determined it should be cleared. The roof had collapsed and the walls would be going next. It was getting dangerous so we leveled it. Started clearing the stones, but then the work stopped. I didn't care much why at the time. I had a lot to do then and was glad to be finished with it. Don't know why he went through all the trouble for a few hundred square feet of unusable field soil only to quit before he got what he wanted. I always figured it was the whim of an aging man. To keep a remnant after all. But one evening I heard his car come into the drive. When I didn't hear him knock I looked for him in the front yard, then in the chicken house, the sheds. I had you with me. You were no more than three years old then, running around and picking up bits of this or that, catching bugs. I gave you free reign in the yards. Let you do whatever you willed out there. And you would run away from me and squat down somewhere. I never knew what could so suddenly demand you attention like that. Then up you'd spring with your little arm in the air. Naming whatever it was you'd found like it was the first ever of its kind. Those groundhogs are gonna eat every last one of our peaches."

There were gnawed pits scattered across the yard beneath the tree. Dad walked to the edge of the lawn and into the ditch where he suspected the varmints had taken shelter in a drain pipe.

"We've already tried with live traps."

"Those rascals know their way back. Got any bright ideas?"

"We could wrap the trunk. Trim the low-hanging branches."

"Except it's in the front yard."

He rubbed his chin and folded his arms. "We'll think of something," he said moving on.

"Where did you end up finding him?"

"He was out in the field there. I'd gone to the mailbox even though I collected it earlier. Just a thing to do while we were doing nothing. And I saw him sitting on the ledge of that old wall. I picked you up and went over to him. You saw your grandpa and hollered. Kept squirming so and I let you go. You ran through the tall grass to him. Arms over your head because you'd run into a parcel of stinging nettles that time. He patted your little head and I heard him call you, 'Danny.' Whatever he'd been thinking about had taken place years ago and I supposed he thought you were me. When I was that age, I mean. Then he started talking. Talking to you like you were me then. And so I listened. I felt like I'd died and been allowed to return to see my dad and I together."

"What did he tell you? Do you remember?"

Dad shook his head and chuckled. "It was so long ago. And it doesn't matter much anyway."

"But you're glad you got to see it."

"I suppose so. It's the only good memory I have of the two of us."

And what did I have now except a pile of money? And who knows about the fate of grandpa's first remnants or the house his brother had built and that Dad later improved, or the chicken house Dad constructed, whose management I was bequeathed on my fourteenth birthday? I heard it'd been refurbished by the new owners to raise hogs with or else to store hay in. I believe it's being put to better use in their hands than it ever would have been in mine. And when I think about a family living there, the walls warming in their kind words, like kisses, I am given a reprieve.

In the end the farm was a memorial to Dad's grief over losing her. It was meant to capture the loose hours of his day, beloved for the hassles and the upkeep; those first three years of financial losses distracted him from how much he missed her, from how much he was yet to miss. It occurred to me that I hindered his forgetfulness at that time. I was the constant reminder of his loss, often a persistent one, and more than my cries and needs, it was the memory of her that chased him into the fields and sheds, into ever-more laborious projects to ensure our fiscal independence, but that kept him from grieving too passionately. He may have thought such expression, if given too much slack, would never abate and he would truly be at his wits end.

Apparently such a life is better lived than never having loved at all, but I wasn't convinced.

There is nothing better in all the world than Michigan Avenue. It is the destination of everyone every day in Chicago, and because the world converges upon this city, hemmed in by the lake on one side and the prairie on the other, there is not a type, a past or a circumstance that is not seen here, invisible perhaps to the multitudes, but known to the spirit of the street. City officials at a brisk pace carrying critical papers in their briefcases blindly pass city workers diving below ground to investigate, estimate and repair damage, decay and oversight. Young men on holiday bounce from Apple and Nike to Tiffany's and Zara with small packages and large, curiously eyeing the young women in wool boots or heels, black Brancusi tights and cashmere tops who laugh at desire, having never experienced its other side. Foreign dignitaries and the shapers of skylines sweep by in black town cars with tinted windows. King's carriages. Affluence has never been more prevalent than it is here and the many who have attempted a closer look in the hopes of seeing Donald or Blagojevich have been disappointed by the unfamiliar faces of strangers, whose scale of influence would boggle the mind for how obscure they seem. These too must pass along Michigan Avenue. It is the great equalizer, traversed even by the beggars walking to the king's gates, those down-and-outs who are equally ignored by all social stratums, even as the beggars themselves ignore those native to the street and sing only for the foreigner's dime and for the tourist's dime, putting on their best act while showing disdain for the familiar faces who give nothing day after day. On that street, contempt is not solely the boon of conquerors; the conquered too are free to ridicule, shout down, shoo away and blaspheme.

Still, smiles are in great quantity on the Mile. Everyone is aware, as if suddenly, of their place upon it. In the entire world, it is magnificence. The sun itself deigns to tread with mortals along the breadth between the Wrigley Building and the John Hancock Center. Pedestrians could not be more surprised at suddenly being present here than if they were somehow transported to Babylon and the table of Nebuchadnezzar, seated with the seers, diviners, magicians and furnace stokers. One hundred years ago, men who reversed the flow of the Chicago River walked where we now walk and sighed where we too sigh. Weren't they magicians in their own right? Magic concealed by science, as if the masses would not tolerate such expenditures from a mystic. Yet despite this opulence, it is only for a time. There will come a time when we will see the original perfection, perhaps in Plato's Forms or in the Hebrew Bible's Garden or the Christian idea of the the Second Heaven. Because art is used by capitalism doesn't eliminate the Hyperion from which it came. I know I am one of the few who think this way. I have a peculiar spirit. To take the soul seriously one must look forward to its dominion over the body, which means looking forward to death. "What you are now, so once were we," say the Arcadians. This, too, is a reason to celebrate. So both time and not-time have a special place. In this time, however, I am a poor vessel for the mystical business; I am not able to recapture my future essence, perhaps the original essence. There is an exile within me. I discovered poetry is the means to assimilation; God speaks through poetry.

It is no coincidence that our comfort with poetry is on the outs. The wombs of our gods have dried up. What do our wools and aluminums and leathers beget if they lack the ability to perpetuate the beautiful? And then, what is the beautiful? Baudelaire wrecked it or broadened it, depending on how powerful your optimism is, with one poem about a reeking corpse. If rot is beautiful, then life is not a struggle; if rot is repugnant, what effort is required for men to wait for something better that may not materialize. What a blessing, this Magnificent Mile, where all is materialized! What need to wait? The greatest goods in every window, glowing under soft lights in wood paneled rooms beneath finely woven rugs. These sumptuous decors that fold you in and stroke your hair and whisper how everything will be all right. In those spaces you don't have to worry about rotting.

What was I doing, walking around this on my mind?

I dropped a couple poems off at Poetry Magazine and bought leather boots for the coming season at Columbia. I was carrying my Seneca and found the Starbucks where Liz had agreed to meet me. I arrived early because I was nervous, but also because I was deciding, and deciding is a terrible burden.

Every decision reached necessarily means the demise of competing options. Every man is an executioner; he is responsible for his own deaths. What matter if he is born in the metropolis of possibility or the jungles of determinism? There is sorrow in free will even as we know life would be repugnant without it. I was searching for that life which would yield the fewest aches. Once decided, it is essential to never look back. The backward glance at one's tombs will evoke the desire to dress the stone and pick a bouquet and lay fragrances on the sepulcher to mourn the positive moment in favor of an unrealized negative. That man is not alive who laments; he walks a tepid path, never embracing, but always watching the lives he could have lived. And they are Legion. He is exiled from his own heart, a perpetual voyeur. The streetlight that shines upon dense foliage will soon pass through naked boughs and when next the pedals bud, he will have departed. Who will mourn for him, the pathetic man of indecision?

Reading over the noise inside, a conglomeration of lengthy relaxed tracks and the lull of sanctioned conversation at the register, I didn't look up immediately at my name being uttered. A woman was standing at my side. She smiled and sat in the soft chair opposite mine. Liz took the top of her cup off and pulled at the string of the tea bag.

"How are you?" she said.

I was suddenly excited to see her. There is an erotic charge inherent to study, I think. Socrates was the first to note this, though probably he borrowed it from someone else. My mind was being fired by ideas and their import to the life I was currently living; that energy was manifesting itself physically.

"I'm doing good."

"I've seen you a few times since McFadden's, you know? Walking around town or sitting in a window reading."

She set her tea aside to cool and removed the plaid cap she'd been wearing. She smoothed her mussed hair and made herself comfortable. She had delicate features that unified around her striking eyes. Those imposing observers gave me pause before I ventured too far in imagining myself stroking her hair, kissing her lips. She wore dark jeans and soft brown boots; a small white collar peeked out from the neck of her teal blue sweater. She hadn't removed her name tag.

"You can always tap on the glass. These guys aren't so interesting that I would hate a break." I put down the ancient philosopher, scrambling for something to say to her. Perhaps I should have been thinking about Liz and why it was that I had called her, why I had felt the need for her company.

"Why do you spend so much time with them then?" She took the slim volume from my hands and flipped through its pages; light flickered upon her face as they flashed past.

"What else am I going to do?"

"You could get a job. Make money, live for the weekends, pray for early retirement." She laid the book aside like a child's drawing that, once the little guy leaves the room, no longer needs to be fawned over.

"Sounds like fun," I said. "I think maybe these old guys have something to tell me. Something that we knew once, but have forgotten, either intentionally or because that's our nature. There are unpleasant facts to be faced."

"Such as?"

I looked at the book in her hands. "Our idol's wombs are barren."

"Proof one that you need a job. A job would give you things to think about instead of powerless wombs. Also, you find common enemies in the office and bond with people through mutual disregard."

"Sounds delightful."

"And fatigue," she said, enumerating the penultimate proof. "Fatigue will keep you from laughing it up with guys like these."

Liz was having fun with me.

She returned my book. I smoothed its cover and felt the sharp corners.

"I'll look for one tomorrow."

"You're such a liar."

"No, I promise, Liz. But part-time at first. I need time to get re-acclimated."

"Not about that. About your love for old books. If I'd tapped on the window just now you'd have kept on reading."

"I sure wouldn't have."

Of course I would have. The trance those old thinkers put me in had become too strong for a pathetic knuckle on glass. And even if all their thoughts and ideas and logic were a noble nothing in the end, at least in the here and now those ascensions allowed for the world to hold within it unlimited potential, esoteric grasping and the skill to turn ordinary objects into symbols representing greater truths. History tied to fact; music tied to scale; words tethered to other words tethered to other words tethered to other words to become nonsense, or freedom.

"I said your name three times just now and you didn't budge." She was teasing, but I saw some disappointment behind her wry smile.

"I was thinking about this line. He says that living is the least important business of the busy man, yet it's the hardest to learn. He says we're all longing for the future and weary of the present.

"But not you?"

"Of course, me too."

"What are you tired of? Never mind; I can't listen to you complain about your life."

"I didn't complain before?"

"We talked about everything else."

"Oh no, what did I say?"

"You told me to read *Phaedrus*."

"That's a relief. Did you?"

"Hmm . . . "

Liz sipped her tea. She looked out the large window beside our chairs. The wind was gray against the brown bareness in the street's planters.

"You said before that it was just you and your dad?"

I nodded.

"What about your mom?"

"My mom passed away after I was born."

"Oh Joshua. I'm sorry."

I shook my head and smiled. I usually had something ready to say to the person I was having this kind of conversation with; something encouraging, a pretty phrase intended to exonerate them from unintentionally bringing up a painful memory, or lack thereof. But I couldn't ply those rote lines with Liz and without that memorized speech I lacked the words to placate her.

"How old were you?"

"About three minutes," I said. "Or she may have passed just before I was born. There was a lot of chaos at the time and we don't really know."

"Your poor father."

"I've often thought how he must have felt then. To have his future taken from him in such a way. To leave him alone with a little burden. I wouldn't wish that on anyone."

"I'm sure he loved you."

"I know he did, even if he wasn't always easy to be with. Since I've grown to understand him better I can't possibly complain about how I was raised. There are just some things he couldn't provide. In fact, I was never aware of any lack until I was eight or nine and started going to friends' houses. I never saw their dads, but their moms were there, chatting with us and fixing our snacks. There homes smelled different from my own, like lemons, and care was taken with the furniture arrangements, what was put upon the walls and how wonderfully the curtains billowed in the opened windows."

"And he never remarried?"

"No."

"Ever dated?"

"There was no one to date. The Thumb is no siren song for single professionals."

"So it really was yard lights and distant noises for you."

"And my books, don't forget."

"Of course, those. You never had a chance, did you?"

I was really starting to like this woman.

"How is your *Seducer* coming?" she said.

"Ah, yes. My inspired concoction. I'm thinking it will be a serious farce about boredom. The first three hundred pages will follow an unnamed protagonist through city as he walks its streets, sits in its parks, eats in its restaurants and drinks in its bars. Told in the third person, using plain language. There will be a lot about the weather in it."

"I'm already hooked."

"Oh, it gets better. The next five hundred pages will be narrated by a friend of the unnamed protagonist in an unrelenting monologue that may or may not be one sentence. I haven't decided that yet. The friend names him — possibly about four hundred times, maybe once per page — in the same unrelenting manner: *said Heinsohn to me then* and *so said Heinsohn* and *thus Heinsohn thought while he considered the droplet whisked from the wave's crest, subsumed* or something like that. And it will begin with a thirty page consideration of staring."

"And who's going to publish this monstrosity?"

"You're right. I'll probably need references."

"Not it."

To my mind, I had two viable witnesses for the kind of life I was living: William Henry Davies wrote

> *A poor life this if, full of care,*
> *We have no time to stand and stare*

while Walt Whitman enjoyed nothing better than to

> *lean and loaf and invite my soul*
> *observing a spear of summer grass*

Two poets proclaiming the strange splendor of self-examination. Very important work because there are so few who do it. Except to the initiated, those who see a grown man sitting in the grass or craning his neck to watch the clouds think him a nutcase, a King Baby, a man at odds with this world. Who but an idiot would watch the grass? Who but a child would find excitement in cloud flights or in the movement of pigeons ducking and wobbling after crumbs on a busy sidewalk? Who but one without the cares of the adult world can find time to loaf? Who could respect such a man? And what if more and more of us are content to watch the grass, to stand and stare? What if we were to become a society of men who fall into holes from contemplating the stars? What then?

"It's merit will have to vouch for itself, then."

"I'm sure it will. Just don't get too accustomed to all your free time. I'd hate for your work ethic to suffer in favor of your inspirations."

"Is that what you think I have? Free time?"

"What else would you call it?"

"Leisure."

"What's the difference?"

"I would hate to be misrepresented because our definitions of my life aren't in sync." Liz smiled and I was encouraged. "When I think of free time, I have a picture of crowded malls and movie theaters, softball games and Church picnics. It's the time we use when we're not working, when we need to occupy ourselves with nothing of consequence. Watching television, browsing the Internet and chatting on-line; none of it requires real effort. Leisure, on the other hand, involves effort directed toward an end for itself. It's not a distraction from time, but of making that time a gift to mankind."

"A 'gift to mankind.' You have some lofty expectations of yourself."

"I'm convinced there's no better way to live."

"Would you say these things to the men who worked the lines in Detroit? Or would you tell this to the men in Gary who work for U.S. Steel? They could say they give gifts to mankind as well. They worked to raise the standard of living for all of us and built the fortunes of this century. Their methods destroyed the Third Reich and enabled America to become the only superpower on the planet for the last thirty years."

"True, but their lives were consumed by those factories and mills, with production and the pockets of the owners. None of this should be condemned, of course. A man must find something to do. But what do the workers do when they have washed off the soot of labor? They take in a ball game, go for a drive, or crack open a beer and wile away their eight hours."

"It sounds like a good situation."

"Except, in most cases, free time is spent buying goods and services. It's made up of consuming what others have produced: cars and fashion and decor, entertainments. It's an unspoken contract we have with our consumer economy. We have to make time to purchase. Remember when the towers fell? We were told to continue life, to go to movies, to go out to eat otherwise the terrorists win. There's not a lot of room for the pursuit of personal excellence in it, especially if that involves a distancing from the economy. Leisure is time used apart from material concerns. There is a spiritual pursuit inherent in it, be it in meditation or prayer or the study of such concerns, the criticism of political economy or Church orthodoxy. It isn't idleness because it requires intellectual rigor. And that work has the potential to be the true gift to mankind."

"So you've decided to be a cultural critic."

"If the culture will have me? Sure."

"What have you found to say to it?"

"Nothing new, I suppose. Lay up your treasures where rust and moths can't get them; produce fruit in keeping with goodness; do unto others, et cetera."

"You sound as bored saying it as I am hearing it."

"It's all too familiar, isn't it?"

"Yes."

"Let's make an agreement, then. Let's agree to look into a mystery and tell each other what we've found."

I felt myself going out on a limb here, but I was confident the branch would hold, and I did nothing to stop myself.

"This is what we should do with our leisure time?"

"What else?"

"So when you laughed off your interest in old writers before, that was bullshit? You really do love them."

I was found out.

"You're quite absurd," she said.

"I defend myself against the perception of the world with laughter. I know it's not for everybody and I can see the foolishness of it. I do take it seriously, though. It's the one thing I've found worthwhile to do with my hands."

I was happy to have met Liz. Sitting at Starbucks I would steal glances at her wrists, soft and white, running out from cotton sleeves extending to her slender fingers that maneuvered her bracelet and the coffee cozy, all dancing with elegance and grace. My heart skipped when she dabbed her lips with the thin napkin. I believed her fingers had found the good she would do and that her life, the blood pulsing beneath her skin, had been the prime mover, the animating principle of her discovery. How could I not gaze at them? Her fragrance was to me then like the offerings presented to divine nostrils. I delighted in Liz and I was eager to share with her what I found important; to hear the same from her. So I decided to forge ahead with her, if she would like, and took stock of the ideas I'd sequestered to the furthest rooms of my mind, considering which ones I should bring out to meet her first.

"Is that how your books tell you to defend yourself?"

"That, and keep like company."

We walked to the Red Line on Grand Avenue. I held her hand; she closed her eyes and smiled in the sun.

We hugged then, and I watched her descend the steps wondering if I'd botched our farewell.

I'd given Felix my cell number, a sort of *open sesame* to the walls I had built around my literary life, and he contacted me about a writing opportunity.

He hadn't simply thought of me. I'd asked if he wouldn't mind looking over a piece or two I'd written and he said he'd be glad to. I didn't know if the stories were any good and needed a second opinion. My habit until then had been to write whatever came to me, look it over once or twice, send it to a few local magazines and a few national, then put it in a drawer, so to speak. But since I'd become convinced this was what I wanted to do with the better part of my life, I needed to know where I stood and how much further I needed to go to consistently create publishable work. He said I showed some talent and asked if I'd be amiable toward other genres.

I walked to Felix's artist community, but not to meet with him or to consult with Stephanie about more financial opportunities. Instead, I had been persuaded by Felix to try my hand at art criticism. He had arranged for me to meet with Eric Masur, tour his pieces, and give a thoughtful critique of them. If Felix thought my impressions warranted publication as a valuable insight or a good character study, he had some pull in the city and I was eager to try my hand.

"What kind of artist is he? How should I prepare for meeting him?"

"I think going in cold is the best thing to do," he said, grinning.

On that wet morning I passed beneath black limbs and limp leaves. Wet-stamped paper advertisements seemed glued to the sidewalk, introducing a new marketing space for just these kind of watch-your-step days. I dodged the deeper puddles and reveled in the irony of this kind of day being the sort to lead me toward my bright, beautiful Tomorrow.

Eric greeted me inside his studio. He had a skeptical twist of the lip and shaggy blond hair. He was average height and build and possessed an unassuming air, given the recent trajectory of his career. An all-consuming color spectrum was scattered and dried into the thick weave of his forest green corduroy pants. He wore a gray Henley over a white tank top and when he smoothed his hair it became knotted together from wet paint that had smeared into the creases of his hands. He apologized when he shook my hand and told me I could take the paint off with some thinner.

Eric led me to the large sink where he uncapped a large tin canister and poured its tangy aroma over my hands. I thought if ever there should be a gallery representation of the artist's studio this would be it. I saw a work-in-progress on the floor beside me surrounded by used tubes of red paint. Black and white daubs commingled with chestnut, jasper, maroon and dark sienna smudges to stain the weathered hardwood. Thin brushes lay about, crisscrossing one another in various angles. They seemed hardened to the floor.

"Felix tells me you've recently moved here," he said.

"Just over four months."

I applied more thinner. A work station was positioned in the center of the space. It too was weathered and covered in dried paint that one could decipher, like tree lines, the growth of the artist. I saw it was on wheels so Eric could move it around to any number of canvases he was currently engaged with. A sofa lined one wall in such a way that all the works could be considered from its position. Large books were piled upon a repurposed door that he used for a coffee table. Decanters and various glasses and mugs were left there, but whether they contained drinkable fluids or the remnants from polyester bristles, hog hair or badger, I couldn't know.

"And you've been with the *Art Journal* the whole time?"

"The journal? No. I'm not associated with any magazine."

"Really? Felix gave me the impression . . . well, never mind."

He offered me a rag, and I dried my hands. There was a small work-out bench near the entrance. An array of dumbbells were scattered around it and a pair of large speakers from which issued the annoyance Stephanie spoke of. Straddling that was a solid frame construction from which two cuffs hung. Eric later told me that hanging upside down helped him see clearly.

"This is a nice space," I said.

"Yea?"

"It's like kindergarden."

Eric chuckled and said, "Wherever you want to start, Joshua. Those are my previous attempts," he said brushing away a trove of canvases. "And those are my sales. I was going to say successes, but that's not really the same thing, is it?"

"Isn't it?"

"I guess it depends on your idea of success."

I thought this was rhetorical, but he was waiting.

"I suppose money has a part to play in it."

"But by which means: noble or base?"

I immediately felt comfortable. "Noble. Base means would taint the success and make a regret of it. I think."

"But money can be won through each, can't it?"

"Maybe less through nobility."

"So, through base means success becomes a curse and through noble means, one's pile becomes smaller. There must be a companion piece to that kind of nobility that makes it good."

"It appears so."

"And this . . . I don't know what; virtue, we'll call it . . . If one has it he will be content with a smaller pile if it means he has it with peace?"

"Of course."

"Then success in the form of dollar bills is of little consequence to him. But whatever this virtue is, he will chase after it and long for it and give all he has for it?"

"It hardly seems so."

"Then I'll let you chase after your chimeras and I will hold fast to my virtue."

Felix hadn't prepared me for this kind of dialogue. I anticipated a soft beginning, a round of pleasantries; but Eric immediately tested me, not out of malice, I believe, but to see what kind of material I was made of and if I would be suitable to bring his vision into the realm of language or theory. Eric, it turned out, despised theory.

"For most people, I mean."

Eric tightened the cap and set the thinner down.

"You're a kind of celebrity around here, Joshua. Stephanie's been on the warpath since she met you. It's all she talks about."

I thought he was taking too much amusement from my ignorance.

"I wish she hadn't brought that up around here."

"She's only being loud for my benefit, getting her digs in without seeming to be petty. I've had some success lately and that naturally comes with resentment. I try to be encouraging, but that comes off as condescension. So I remain quiet and am thought to be arrogant. I won't say I haven't enjoyed seeing her in a huff these past few days, though."

"You can't help how you appear to others."

"Do you think so?"

"Probably."

"I hope this piece you're writing will have more strength behind its opinions, Joshua."

Eric slapped me on the shoulder when I frowned.

"Anyway, the truth hurts. Let me show you the things."

He uncovered his successes and displayed them around the space. Six canvases had been purchased and they seemed to be part of a sequence. While the main thrust of the compositions stood on their own, their edges appeared to connect, but whether on a linear plane or else stacked side-by-side three high I couldn't determined. Though each was a singular achievement I spent this introduction attempting to put them together.

"I can't win with her, so I don't try to bother myself with how she feels about this or that. And anyway, she doesn't understand the spirit of an artist."

"And what is that, do you think?" I took out my pen and a small moleskin notebook.

"To judge impartially the reality of our world."

Eric watched me make notes and I felt conscious of my brushed silver pen and the eighteen-dollar book of blank paper.

"And Stephanie is too partial?" I said.

"Her work is adamant and I'm drawn to poking that kind of assurance. But that's not what you're here for."

I nodded and looked at his work. My experience living in Chicago had taught me that there are two factors at work in the world and in the souls of men: preservation and destruction. I thought that moderation should inform the extent of each, but that something else must be ahead of them. There are those who preserve wicked things and those who destroy good things. And shouldn't this be? A fire destroys a forest, but it is necessary for good growth; a child destroys a woman's body, but preserves the race of men; and a volcano may destroy an entire city only to preserve its ancient way of life for a future civilization's benefit. Not everyone should purge a woody ecosystem; not just any man should impregnate a woman; and perhaps we shouldn't build cities on volcano sites or fault lines; but all these things are done. Foolish smokers, careless couplings and valuable ports make all of it inevitable. And this city — Chicago: that somber city; Chicago: the big shouldered hog butcher — what beautiful benefit came from O'Leary's cow on DeKoven Street! Pictures of the corner of Dearborn and Monroe in 1871 would tell a different tale, one of war-torn, bombed-out buildings, streets lined with rubble, the stench of defeat before the brawling, half-naked Youth arrived. My kind of town.

Eric seemed to eliminate the idea of Time by combining these two factors. Geometric fragments swirled about, as if they'd been ripped from a fullness and tossed out of hand. The artist had then collected these bits to piece together some kind of meaning about the Whole. The overall effect was pleasing; there was a symmetry amidst the chaos that presented itself through sustained attention and I was getting somewhere . . .

The truth is I had no idea what I was doing.

"Whenever you're ready," said Eric, collapsing onto a decrepit couch.

"I noticed you referred to reality in its singular form. Do you believe there is only one?"

"Are you asking because you heard it in my speech, or do the paintings somehow reveal this?"

"You said it."

"If it doesn't come from the work I ask you don't discuss it. All of my opinions and judgments, if I am any kind of artist, will be present and accessible."

"There's a lightness to your work. And not only because of its lack of heft, of substantiality, although it does have some of that, especially at the edges of this one where these dark forms here funnel the sightline to the heart, here. But there is . . . illumination?"

I wanted to continue in this vein, but I grew self-conscious at my voice bouncing off the walls. I made the uncomfortable transition from dialogue to embarrassed contemplation, hoping Eric wouldn't notice my hesitation to tell him that his work, at least what I saw in it, was hopeful. The lines and color, the borders of his medium, were drawn in pleasant places. He didn't change the style that had been in vogue since the 1950s, but he attacked the main interest of those artists, sociologists, sexologists, psychologists, and theologians that was concerned with how bad a man can be, why he is so and for how long.

"Light is the dominant impression I get of your work," I said, confident about this line of critique. "There is a transformative quality to it. Do you believe this is the reality of the world? Or is the purpose of your art to reveal this reality?"

"Light is the central quality of the human experience," Eric said.

"Why is that, do you think? Darkness seems to have a greater hold on the imagination. It seems to have more to say to us. It's at least of more interest. Even Milton suffered from this knowledge when he made a hero out of the Satan and failed to convince us that heaven and God should be loved more."

"That seems like a perfect reason to aspire to light. To achieve what Milton couldn't; to produce what the history of mankind has failed to. Perhaps that could give us a new drama."

"Have you always been interested in painting?" I asked.

"Before I came to Chicago I was studying economics. I was interested in it for its overwhelming relevance to our world, our politics and laws, and in the simple illustration regarding the two great symbols of economic thought: guns and butter. Over winter break my sophomore year I gave myself a break from studying all that. The snow was piled up outside our door and it was cold and I wanted to stay in with some wine and a good book. So I pulled a novel from my dad's bookshelf. *Robinson Crusoe*. If you've read it, you know that it's not long before the poor guy is shipwrecked. And when he nearly drowns trying to bring up that chest of gold, I laughed out loud. What a ridiculous thing to have on a deserted island! But then I suffered. In that moment I felt a sense of gloom over my choice of career. I had decided to spend my life studying, analyzing, and worrying about an aspect of humanity that has no relevance to my original nature. And because I saw that in myself, I saw it everywhere. In all things. Our running after baubles and trinkets had obscured the essentials of life. And that is primarily what economics is. It's the study of how the marketing and producing and selling of baubles bestow great power on individuals and countries. So I became interested in what life actually is when it's not influenced by such things. And since I couldn't write I decided to devote myself to this other medium.

"I sketched as a kid. My mom took me to museums and showed me art books in the library. They were big, musty smelling things in grey cloth with yellowed pages coming away from their abused spines. I was enthralled by them and abhorred. They were such imposing tomes and I couldn't understand any of the pictures. But I kept trying and so she enrolled me in a watercolors class. I took to it easily. When I had exhausted all the art classes I could take, I taught myself from home. I spent a lot of hours in the basement drawing and in the summer I worked to be able to buy paints and canvases and quality brushes, but growing up outside Fort Wayne I never saw painting as a viable option for my life. I didn't see anyone doing it and thought only men from France could be artists or else eccentrics whose parents had ignored them or beaten them or had died too soon, or men who had suffered from depression and had tried to kill themselves. Really serious men, you know, with great internal strife."

"Your life doesn't have that?"

"I won't say that. Sorrows and disappointments are the common run of things. No one is exempt. Still, something needs to be a little off about a person who pursues representing ideals through abstraction. It has a mischievous element to it, a kind of disingenuousness, don't you think? But what am I going to do? Not paint? I'd go crazy."

"Tell me about these ideals."

"I already have," he said nodding to his canvases. "Like I said, I'm not adamant."

"Who are your influences?" I said.

"Well, the Impressionists attempted to represent light. They filtered their study through the visible world. I'm concerned with light in the invisible, the unseen, where light behaves according to itself and not in relation to things it bounces off or or corners it cannot bend into. Obviously, we can understand many complex things by thinking about its opposite so there will be some of that too, but only in so far as it shows the work I've made to reach a conclusion about light."

I wasn't the most adept thinker of abstract paintings. Much of it felt like an intimate conversation within the artist's consciousness and I could never fully understand the inside jokes or the bizarre associations that make up an individual's understanding. The conclusions relied on chance, chaos, dream, a world without space or consequences and if I asked Eric what those conclusions were, he would usher me out of his studio as simply another tourist visiting serious intent.

I worried that my piece would be just another post card effort.

I looked at Eric's pieces while he leaned more canvases against the walls. I thought the best way to proceed would be to take in all of his work, not with a critical mind, but with my eyes and ears spiritually attuned to what the canvases were saying to me. I relied on my intuition, trained by my study of other artists in the Chicago museums, both contemporary and classical, to speak to me about Eric's place in their history: what he was coming out of, where he was divergent. I knelt down to inspect a piece that drew my curiosity. I made a few notes. I had been on my tour for twenty minutes before I realized I was alone.

When Eric returned, I had drawn a few conclusions about his work and felt I could write about its aims and expressions without proposing a theory or connecting him with one. It had worked in my favor that he didn't pledge himself to any -*ism*. Of course he was in the midst of one, though, but as a tributary of its larger stream.

"How's it coming?" he said. "I have greater expectations for your ideas than what you shared with Stephanie."

I faltered beneath his stare, but I believed I had some solid footing and I said, "I can see why you're having solo shows. Optimism doesn't have a long history in the world of art and people are curious."

"Is that so?"

"I do have one question, though. How do you see darkness?"

"I think about myself. I think about all of the things I would do if no one could ever know about them, and then I look into my actual actions to see if there are similarities of kind, if not degree. Through this exercise, I know how what I'm capable of."

"And you do the same with light?"

"That gets tricky. I don't use the fantasy that whatever I do with all the lights on everybody sees. That's theater. It's not a spontaneous action of the soul then, but performance. It has no truth to tell regarding my virtue. In this case, I see a paradox: virtue must be performed in darkness as well. Otherwise it's performance. Make-up."

"So darkness is tolerated only so far as it illuminates virtue and light is pursued for its own sake?"

"And everyone's conscience is a separate factor. It's a constantly changing variable determined by many outside factors. I think the more light one captures in life the more sure the virtue is, though that's not certain. A constantly changing morality is no morality at all, but a response to a poor meal maybe, or an unexplained check in the mail or unrequited love. It becomes a mere feeling whose only reference to the good is alleviating a hurt or acknowledging an undeserved blessing. There needs to be a belief about light and dark that isn't susceptible to the vagaries of emotion or circumstance. Something beyond feeling."

"And these paintings are those spiritual beliefs?"

"I think so. In the beginning God created light. Good is given by God to a people whose nature is darkness."

"Optimism is a gift from God, then?"

"All good things, Joshua. There's a line I like from a Rios poem about light. 'In light, something is lifted' and then 'You are not where you were but you have not moved.' I hope that my work articulates this idea as well as his words do."

I wrote this down.

"What do you think is lifted?"

"Obviously it isn't a physical lifting, since your place in space remains constant. It is a spiritual lifting, a raising of your vision to see the heavens as well as the gutters and to meditate on that elevation."

"And that is where you reside?"

"I am where my art says I am."

"So you're a landscape painter," I said. "Of the spiritual realm."

Eric sat up. His elbows rested on residue from the infinite.

"As I work and wander around Chicago, my physical presence is felt along the streets and benches, my shadow is cast long across State Street and foreshortened on Navy Pier. In the winter my breath is exhaled to mingle with the steam escaping from beneath the streets or the water evaporating off the river. But in spite of all the evidence that my place and being are within this material world, I have another place. One that shows me the ephemeral quality of my essential substances. I have seen that my blood and breath are not mine, but have been borrowed from another and only for a time. Then I was shown that if these things are not me, why do I believe my affections and ambitions belong to me? What about my emotions? My vengeance? My rights? My force? And in that sense I am creating a new landscape, a new picture of what the world looks like."

I looked at his lines and forms and imagined what could be written if I saw these elemental figures as *Pieta* or *The Calling of St. Matthew*. Eric was attempting a new form for the Holy Family, a new way to depict Christ on the cross.

"It could be called Resurrection Art," he said. "I've been toying with a new moniker, though."

"That's the first step towards establishing a school."

Eric cringed. He shook his finger:

"Yes, but the thing about this school is that it's always empty. These paintings could be seen as empty tombs. Life without death. I believe this is what abundant light looks like. That's just what it is." He said this last bit to himself. "It's like

. . . how does that story go? About the women at the tomb? And the being of pure light tells them Jesus is gone. That light. What would it do in the cave? It would blind the women and eradicate all shadow and come bursting out of it into the the garden, Jerusalem, all the way to Caesar's Rome. And then Chapter Eight."

"What's chapter eight?"

Eric was staring at the wall. His lips were moving quickly around a thought that had taken him away from the present moment.

After a time I asked if he had ever read Plato's *Republic*. He shook his head. "Should I?"

"Of course. Whenever I hear talk about caves and shadows, I immediately return to what he said about them."

"Tell me."

"Just that men are chained in this cave, forced to stare at the back wall while other men parade fashioned shapes — art, I suppose — in front of a fire. Shadows of these representations are cast upon the walls: horses, pigs, trees. They make noises, too, these men do. And all those chained believe these are actual creatures living in the world. But then a man escapes and climbs out of the cave and into actual light and he sees things for what they truly are. He sees actual shadows. To him this is a revelation. He even marvels at actual shadows. When he returns to tell those in the cave, of course no one believes him."

"What happened to him?"

"He may have been killed by those who made the false images. I can't remember."

"When was this written?"

"400 BCE. Thereabouts."

"You read a lot?"

"It's my exclusive pursuit."

"'In the beginning God read?' No, Joshua. Don't merely consume, create something."

On Rush Street, between Walton and Delaware, I paused at Saint James Chapel. It had a façade of stone and an arched entrance that opened into a large courtyard. It was under construction or being cleaned, and tonight the iron gate was closed. Scaffolding climbed the walls, yellow fingers planked with wood. Hadn't Jesus talked about a cup being clean on the outside, but filthy on the inside? Then I thought that was too easy and decided he wasn't talking about buildings; he didn't care for them actually, but then his words proved difficult. A pure heart; looking beyond the veil; clean on the inside; all of it seemed too abstract and helpless without outside control, some sort of guidelines for behavior that helped men to be good. But what are they and whence the power? If the eye cannot observe itself, how can the conscience judge itself? Others it sees, no problem. But ourselves? We are too close to the perpetrator to find him guilty. His defenses are always prepared. Which leaves men between two poles: love and hate; preservation and destruction. All else is moral ambiguity and too confounding for men to understand. And from what corner of the world will agreement come?

No answers came from the clouds and none were written by an invisible hand upon the stone walls of Saint James. Still, it was good to think of these things and I imagined I was heard. Internal monologues are prayers, too. Or else it's madness, just the babbling from the rag-picker. Maybe closeness to God is necessarily madness. Abraham. Noah. Moses. The Baptist. Jesus. The throes of Eros. Perhaps any thought that disregards the world and its rationale is mad. The poets were possessed;

the prophets were inspired. They ate bugs and lived in septic tanks. And the poets? But how far can one go with all of this?

I turned from the chapel and headed home.

The last religious building I had such serious thoughts in was the United Methodist Church where I grew up. It was a funeral ceremony like any other of that sort, except it was Dad's. The spoken words were taken from the back of the hymnal and were just vague enough to apply to any recently deceased.

It had snowed the night before his interment. There was no wind and the flakes, full to bursting, weighed the earth down with its elegant burden. I was alone in the big farmhouse watching the snow in the yard light and listening to the furnace click on and off. Three miles away was a hole, the dirt of which was piled beneath a green tarpaulin. It was filling with snow while my father's body chilled at the morgue. Drained of its former vitality and replaced with preserving chemicals, it waited to be fitted into the oak coffin. I had him dressed from the waist up in his gray suit. It was the only one he wore. Always to church.

I don't know what's become of the slacks.

I stalked around the two stories of Dad's house by turns silent, then sobbing. I found myself in the basement, opening doors I hadn't been curious about for years. In one sequestered space stood hundreds of old canning jars placed there by my mom some twenty years ago. They had turned brown from dust and neglect and I could only stare at them. I pictured her lining them up, imagining what she intended for the beets and onions, the asparagus and tomatoes, her apple sauce. I was told she hummed to herself when she thought no one was around .

In another room were coffee cans of old nuts and bolts, all sizes of screws, washers, locknuts, wing nuts, carriage bolts, lengths of chain, rusted nails, buckets of oil, tubes of grease.

Drawers of wrenches and screwdrivers; a toolbox loaded down with hammers. A saw with blunt teeth hung by the door. Dad's worn boots. The tongues were smooth like water and creased with lace marks. The soles were worn out of them, of course, and the toes were beat up, dented, pierced, and crushed. They seemed to be waiting, at rest before animation, like dogs re-signed to sit by the fire until their master lets them outside.

I went into his bedroom. He hadn't thrown all of mom's clothes away. In his closet, hanging among his shirts, was a white blouse, yellowing and thin. In the drawers, I found a pair of her socks balled up and mingling among his loose pairs. I saw myself in the mirror — the same full-length mirror that had captured the reflections of my now-dead parents — and thought if I looked long enough and hard I would see them. Shouldn't mirrors have memories? It is we who forget what we look like after all; the mirror never does. Instead, I saw a boy's face streaked with tears and crumpled on the shag carpeting of an empty bedroom. The next day a team of movers would take everything out of the house to either sell at auction or be scrapped. They told me it was the right thing to do and since I was busy at the university, I wouldn't have time to sort everything out.

I still haven't finished sorting.

I may never be. I see his boots at night. In my dreams their eyelets stare up at me, their leather ripples like muscles twitching for a challenge, like there is more work to do. I lift them in my hands and question them. "What are you waiting for? Why are you looking at me? How do I know what to do?" But the tongues just lay over themselves, crazed and weary. Dad's feet were the lightning bolts that shocked them to life. It was his energy that kept the farm going; it was his vitality that worked the ground in the fall, planted in the spring and reaped in the summer; it was his hands that scraped and bled against hardened machinery, that burned upon steam pipes; it was his ingenuity that found ways of saving money on repairs and upgrades to the equipment and that ark of a chicken house, which ran him into the ground.

They found my father late in the afternoon. When he didn't show up at the Lamp Lighter to talk shop with other farmers, they simply shrugged and mumbled about land prices, the worthlessness of the Almanac, the forecasted rainfall and the possibility of a brighter outlook that would produce a better yield. While they discussed these things, Dad lay partly on a concrete aisle beneath thousands of caged birds that clucked and squawked over the whir of fans and the rattle of the conveyor belts that brought feed to their beaks. The other part of him was lying in the offal.

Mr. Weurtzel had stopped over to chat about this and that. He entered the breezeway and hollered for Dad. When he was answered by silence, he followed the well-tread path through the snow to the chicken house. The afternoon light raced into the ark's opened door and the birds grew silent, as they will do whenever a sudden change, like light or a thunderclap or a sudden scream, interrupts their routine. He found Dad, a lump of dirty clothes with a pocket full of water cups he'd been replacing. One red cup had fallen out of his hand and was resting in a puddle of my father's vomit, soaking into the shit.

An ambulance was called and despite the paramedic's best efforts he was pronounced dead at the hospital. I was informed at the university within the hour and was home that night. It was a whirlwind of regrets and memories; of condolences; of young girls' tears and the handshakes of men. Decisions had to be made and it was agreed, with some trepidation, that I would take over the farm. Dad had left it to me and because I was of age the decision was mine alone. I was advised against such a decision, but I was adamant. The farm belonged to my father. It belonged to me now and to my offspring after me. I was angry then. Somehow I was getting even.

The spring semester had just begun and I withdrew from my classes without penalty.

Gravestones were buried in four inches of new and heavy snow; the boughs of the trees drooped, as if paying their respects. Black vehicles lined the somber driveway beside the site and Dad's friends and my own stood quietly as the minister said a few words. Soon enough they lowered him into the ground and when his casket could no longer be seen, I decided he was somewhere in the blue sky taking marvelous flight and no longer concerned with the traditions and institutions — mere shadows after all — of this world. Somewhere he was being introduced to a new vision of what life is: the soul-life, I thought then. And if the soul doesn't perish but is eternal, then preparation for that soul-life had taken place in him while he was physically alive. In his menial day-to-day, trudging to and from the chicken house in winter and summer, in twilight and dusk, his thoughts were fashioning his soul's apparel; his tongue speaking out what his soul was becoming. I didn't think of all this then, but only recently, since I've been in the city alone with strange books and the city's affects. Had I remained on the farm, diligently working the earth's dust amid the shit of our animals and blood of our animals until fatigue collapsed me, where would these inspirations have come from? Did Did have ideas about this soul-life, or of what eternity must be made of? Did he wonder if Mom was waiting for him or if she had expanded forever beyond his means of understanding? Would he be alone in eternity like he was on the earth?

"Gather again into your bosom, Oh, Lord, those that are Yours. Grant those of us left behind your comfort as we struggle through the meaning of Your will in this difficult time. You are a gracious God. Quick to save and to hear the cries of Your children. Daniel Thomas was one of these. Never were two Sundays joined that didn't see him gazing after the altar. His insights into Your Word were those of a man who cherished the Scriptures. Often I would return home puzzled over what he had shared with me. And often he would be proved correct after my own careful examination. But right and wrong are no longer words that can be used to describe his position with God now. There is only the light from our Savior's radiance and the worship pouring forth from Daniel's lips. In his life, Daniel prepared for death. Let the angels rejoice and be glad in this, even as they scratch their heads in awe."

So said the old minister covered in a dark trench coat, leather gloves, his loose neck skin shaking with the words he read, small dark circles protecting his ears from the chill. I had known him for ten years, but he remained a stranger to me. He was not the mediator between heaven and earth that I would choose for myself. The picture he drew of my father left me wondering about whom he was talking. Habit had taken us to church and I never saw him in conversations with the pastor. He read the Bible every morning and I believe he took comfort from it, even enjoyment, but when we were sitting in the wooden pews on Sunday morning altar-gazing was what he did in order to organize his work week. He jotted notes and calculated costs on the reverse side of attendance cards and in the bulletin's margins. When I was small, he drew pictures of houses and trucks and football players to my great amusement. When I would forget where I was in my excitement and talk about the backstory of the athlete or the destination of the trucks in a too-loud voice, he would grip my small leg and squeeze me back into line.

But perhaps he did speak to the minister about such things. He must have thought about Mom constantly. He was alone on the farm, after all. From inside, doing my homework, I would watch him lingering in the yard, disappearing into our dilapidated sheds and the frail standing barn. At night I would watch his shadow move across the illuminated lawn while his body moved among the branches of our weeping willow. His memory of her was draped over the entire place. They must have held hands and walked the dusty roads crisscrossing the fields, talking about their future, about beginning their own family and about so many other exceptional matters that I, to this point, am ignorant of.

Across the lake from the Gold Coast there are two plots of precious ground that I see every night upon falling asleep and every morning while I read from my own Bible. One is being worked upon by hands with no special feeling for who developed it; the other holds only the bones of my father wrapped in gray wool. That plot is not meant to hold anything more. Of what use to the soil is a spirit freed from its own dust? He is concerned with another world; its ways and means occupy him now. By seeking out what those are, I tell myself, I did not abandon his legacy. By striving for that greater radiance, by catching glimpses of the invisible world and embracing spiritual matters, I am coming into the true inheritance Dad left me. Someday I will reach the fruition of my age. My bones will be wrapped in gray wool and I will possess what he has taught me to build. This is what I tell myself and it's all the explanation I can give for the life I've chosen. Plato said beauty is knowing the good and having it forever. Jesus said to invest in those things that will not suffer decay. These things cannot be material, but spiritual. The spirit does not recoil from the city.

PART TWO

Midway through October the city turned cold. Tables and chairs were taken in one night and never returned; doors that had been opened onto the sidewalks were now shut tight and the night sky arrived earlier in the day than it had the day before. I took a table at PJ Clarke's near the window and ordered a Scotch. The space was long and narrow with a floor of alternating black and white tiles. The elegant bar had soaked the laughter and tears of Chicago's past into its grain and the black-vested bartenders gave the impression they had been there to hear it all. Late afternoon light came through the windows and reflected off the mirrors and bottles, illuminating fine dust mites. I felt I was breathing gold.

I saw a silhouette that resembled Stephanie seated at the bar. I couldn't be certain it was her, however, as many women in Chicago subscribed to her fashion aesthetic and just as many are slender and well kept. She wore a black knit sweater tight against her body and dark jeans. Her yellow shoes matched the gloves she had laid inside her hat that rested on the bar. She was putting her up in a ponytail and had arched away from the bartender, who was wiping down a section of mahogany and smiling at whatever she was saying.

I took a table looking onto the street traffic, the covered pedestrians and the leaves shaken from their boughs and cartwheeling down North Clark. I ordered a drink and opened my Pessoa. The quick sections skipped by. I read the words but their meaning eluded me. I couldn't connect with his train of thought, by turns glorious and vulgar, and though I believed him to be an important thinker for what I was then attempting I couldn't explain why. I had emptied my glass some time earlier and because service was not forthcoming I thought I would get a drink at the bar.

Stephanie, or who I thought was Stephanie, was alone and stirring a rum and coke with a thin red straw. I touched her elbow and said hello.

"Joshua? Give a girl some warning." Her hand was on her heart and she took a deep breath.

"I'm sorry." I grabbed some napkins and dabbed at the spilled drink.

"I got it," she said, licking her fingers. "Thanks. I didn't see you when I came in."

"I just got here a bit ago. I was doing some work when I noticed you."

She laughed with some malice and said, "Alone with a book."

She wiped her hands with a napkin.

The bartender emerged from the kitchen with a plate of nachos for the couple sitting along the far wall. He set it down and approached us.

"I wanted to apologize again for my rudeness the other day. I didn't know what I was talking about."

"It's all right, Joshua. I'm so over it."

"Can I get you something?"

I ordered an IPA and asked to have the spilled drink put on my tab.

"It's already been taken care of," he said.

"Then let me get you the next one."

"Okay."

She took out the straws and finished the drink. The bartender smiled and took the empty glass away.

"The canvas is finished, by the way."

"Congratulations!"

"You may even like it. Who knows?"

"I'm sure I will. How's the work going?"

"Progressing."

"Still listening for the regularity in the chaos?"

It was a poorly phrased question. It sounded mocking, disingenuous. Stephanie was holding back, no doubt wondering why I was bothering her; why I had chanced into the same bar she had. It was a massive city after all. And here I came bumbling into her time and consciousness with awkwardness and biting quips. I began to apologize again, but Stephanie held her hand.

The bartender brought over a fresh drink.

"Mark, this is Joshua. I don't think you two have met."

"Hello."

Mark nodded. He was a sturdy man made more impressive by his tightly rolled shirtsleeves. His hair was cut short and he had small eyes that didn't miss anything happening in his bar. "I've seen you in here a few times," he said.

"Joshua does . . . what is it you do, Joshua? I never asked the other night."

There was a challenging tone in her voice and a joy in her eyes that came from putting me on the spot in front of her friend. I thought she was making me pay for my earlier sin and wondered if I should step into the trap to smooth that over, or sidestep it and never speak to her again.

"I'm doing some personal research at the moment. Finding answers to some questions I have."

"Felix said you consider yourself a . . . what was the word he used? A romancier? What is that exactly?"

"He said that, huh?"

"I couldn't possibly make it up."

Mark snorted and returned to more pressing matters.

"A *romancier*, yes. I told him that. Nelson Algren was one. Saul Bellow was another. But without putting a fancy name to it . . . and it feels, I don't know . . . talking about it now."

I was not stepping easily into the trap.

"What?"

"It feels kind of silly."

"That's on you. I just asked what you're working on."

"What's your question?" said Mark, who had finished aligning the liquor labels to square with the room. "I may have an answer for you."

"Mark meets all kinds in here. It's amazing the conversations he overhears or is sucked into."

Stephanie was not easily satisfied. Blood was in the water and she was circling.

"At the moment, I'm wondering what is good for a man to do with his life. In these fleeting moments, what lasting difference can he make?"

"The meaning of life? That's your question?"

I had to smile, too.

"I know, but I mean it in all seriousness. It's an easy question to answer if you believe man has only one essence; if he is only his body, then the best way to live would be for its pleasure and well-being. But if he is two parts, say you believe in the soul or the spirit, then the body isn't our only consideration. The soul desires those things that are not of the body — knowledge, wisdom, virtue — and those desires will trump the body's. So while some will eat, drink and are merry, others will abstain; while one passes life as an aesthete, another will be immune to such sympathies. One will have a celibate desire and another will possess a hundred lovers. Is one way better? Is the good life found in the middle of these extremes? Or does any way really matter?"

"The soul, huh?" Mark sighed and looked for a glass to clean.

"Death is it, I think," said Stephanie. "There's nothing after all of this and even this isn't so much to get worked up about."

"But what if that's not true? What if life's simply become so familiar that nothing distinguishes one day from the next, and in that comfort or boredom we've stopped looking for what could last or even seeking out alternatives to that point of view?"

"Like what?" said Stephanie.

"Like your canvases, for instance. The fact that such scenes as you've highlighted exist and have existed for millions of years, exploding and swirling hundreds of light years away, never seen before by man until now, but possibly seen by someone or something who's been delighting in it all for eons."

"No such one; no such thing," Mark said draping the towel over his shoulder.

"No imagination for the eternal?"

Mark rolled his eyes and I returned to Stephanie.

"I read once that what we call acquiring knowledge is simply remembering. Meaning we already knew what we've learned. That must mean we were once a knowing being we were alive, in the sense of being ourselves in this world. There was a mathematical formula used thousands of years ago that convinced many learned men of this. So we existed before, either as separate parts, or else all of us within a whole. I don't know which, but a part of me hopes it was in a whole and so I mentioned God."

"Why not as individuals?" said Stephanie.

"If we all come from the same source, then there is hope that all of the ideals we have of peace, love, friendship, etcetera, are true because we would basically be loving ourselves, which is quite normal. If we have always been single beings, then self-ishness and avarice and hatred may indeed be our true nature."

"But then where did the ideals come from?" said Mark.

"I don't know. But I think time and thought can offer a convincing hypothesis, if not an entertaining one."

"Have fun with that," said Mark quitting the conversation.

"And who pays you for this, Joshua?" said Stephanie.

"Nobody."

"He doesn't care about his body, Stephanie," said Mark over his shoulder. "What does he need money for?"

Stephanie took a drink and checked her watch. "Felix is going to meet me at the studio in an hour to discuss some exhibition possibilities. Has he mentioned these places to you?"

"We haven't talked about it."

"I'm surprised he's not involving you."

"As far as I'm concerned, I've done all I can do."

"I know you won't like the finished piece," she said setting the gloves aside and putting on her hat, "but if you want to come by, you're welcome to."

We stepped into the afternoon chill. I had survived my penance and we strode together like old friends. Autumn-burnt leaves clung to the wet boughs of elm trees catching the wind in their leathery skin. Their siblings had been swept off the sidewalk and were gathered in the gutters or pressed against the buildings, like thieves avoiding the dull shop lights of hardware stores, car dealerships and CVS. Thick clouds surveyed the land below, preparing their snowfall, the five month siege of cold and wet and dark.

But I was walking in Chicago with an artist in a yellow woolen hat who was concerned with the infinite stretches of space, even if that concern was represented by cynicism. She smelled like patchouli and looked like Bird in Space.

Before when I'd think of an artist, I thought about their being conduits to some kind of spiritual life, a seer of sorts, whose vision would guide those with the time to seek for themselves and to convince those who couldn't believe such things as the marvelous, the genuine; things relating to our essential natures. That these people had a share in the secret things gave them a mystical appeal in my eyes to that whenever I thought about becoming one of their number, I shooed such a notion away. I believed that searching out such matters would be an essential good for the rest of my life, but that I could be one to represent such things artistically; that I could somehow clothe ideas in convincing scenes and characters or in streaks and daubs of paint, or even within the confines or architectural dimensions seemed too starry-eyed, even for me. But now that I was communing with them, walking their routes and becoming friendly with them, even at the most beginning of intimacies, I became aware that I was not so different from them. The thing that made them artists and myself only an aspiring one was that they believed that's what they were, while I believed I couldn't be that. Even though I was currently writing and reading and thinking about the city and its inhabitants and the traditions that informed my beliefs about such things I could not openly declare my intention to live the artist's life.

Even as I was doing just that, I didn't believe I knew how to do it.

"I'm sorry for how heated I got the other day," she said.

"No, don't apologize Stephanie. Please. I was out of line."

"No, you didn't deserve that. I've just been promised some things by our mutual friend that he's failed to make good on and I lost patience. I actually thought you were a prospective buyer. Can you believe that? Only because Felix said he'd be able to accommodate private viewings of our work, which he has yet to provide. So when I realized you weren't a buyer and then what you wanted to buy had nothing to do with my . . . Well, I'm sorry."

"Thank you. And I am to."

"Good. Hell of a way to meet, though," she said lighting a cigarette. She offered the opened silver case.

"No thank you," I said.

She shrugged and exhaled.

"Are you trying to get into the art scene?"

"Not intentionally. But I've been thinking now that I'd like to hang some originals on my walls. Kind of a memento of my time here."

She nodded and I regretted the phrase; the way I denigrated those canvases by equating them with souvenirs.

"Well, if you bought one of mine you'd have a great story to go with it."

I chuckled.

"Of course, if you were interested in something more than stories . . . I mean, really getting into the scene. Effecting influence?"

I didn't know where she was going with this. She concealed her exasperation behind a tense smile.

"There's an opportunity for you to act as a benefactor. Not just for me, but for the entire community there. Even Eric."

"How so?"

"There are some gallery spaces that we could show our work in, but Felix is dragging his feet. He tells me the spaces aren't right, that not everyone is ready to show their work, or willing for that matter. Then there's the cost."

She turned from me and inhaled. She blew smoke over her left shoulder into Blue Agave's facade. When I didn't respond she said,

"There's the gallery fee and the rental vans for transporting the work. Some of us have to crate them, so there's that. Then there's advertising; we'd have to create artist bios and decide on a unifying theme to giver our pieces context with one another. And Felix said he would do all that, but so far . . ."

"He hasn't."

"Not so far. So I figure we farm all that out."

"I could write something up for everyone."

"Sure. Yea, that would be a great help. But I was thinking, if you could . . . well, I don't know how much something like this costs to put together, but."

I had caught on. "Ah."

"Unless I'm overstepping."

"No, I see."

"Come on. It's not such a terrible thing to ask."

I was reconciling what I knew about Felix with his taking such liberties with my circumstances.

"Besides, you'd be helping Eric out as well. And Felix would be grateful. Anyway, talk it over with him. I'm sure he could give you some accurate numbers. It's probably not as much as you think."

She chatted about insignificant topics then, laughing and overemphasizing the stakes of light dramas then happening in her building. She exalted the work of her peers and when I asked about the sculptor I'd seen that first night, she had nothing but high praise for her energy, the way she eschewed tradition for the freedom to discover a new form and also for her physical appearance and character; how jealous she, Stephanie, was that one woman could embody such beauty along with deep intellectual concerns.

"And she's such a sweetheart, too. I'll introduce you. She might still be working, actually."

We approached the studio. The chords of "November Rain" knocked Stephanie off balance.

"Eric." The name on Stephanie's lips sounded like an obscenity. "That damn music. I can't work like this much longer. I'm constantly annoyed and it will come out in my work. It has come out. They're going to say it's a polemic against art or that it represents a snobby reaction against our culture when it's simply saturated with his bullshit music."

She stabbed her key into the lock and twisted it to breaking before colliding her shoulder into the door and ushering me inside. She was muttering under her breath and walking at a brisk pace to her studio. When I was safely inside she slammed the door and howled.

"It's just reaching that point, you know?" she said.

I didn't know what to do with myself. Other than getting out of there as fast as I could, I was bereft of ideas.

"It's over there," she said.

The finished canvas appeared like the others. I tried to find moments in it that had moved me before, but they had been covered over with blunt colors and shapes that left my imagination with no space to freely think in. It seemed that everything Stephanie knew was in this piece; the work was a monologue she had spoken before. This one was louder, though.

"It's very good," I said.

"My vision's a bit more complicated than that first draft conveyed."

"Yes."

"You can understand why I was so upset before."

"I can. I don't think Eric's music influences your work as much as you think."

"I admit, it is hopeful to see someone here have an impact out there. It makes what I'm doing seem real, like I am going to break through. It's just, why does it have to be Eric?"

She began a mock sob, pouting her lips and shaking up and down. I didn't know what to say to her.

"I think his work has a special merit."

" . . . Of course you do."

I was going to say more when Felix knocked on the opened door. He wore baggy jeans and white tennis shoes; a tongue of fire rose from the acronym of his UIC sweatshirt. I had never seen him look so unofficial. He was grinning childishly.

Stephanie's eyes lit up. "Did you get it?" she said. "Tell me you got it."

Felix inhaled and bit his breath. "Not yet."

"Damn it, Felix. What's it going to take to get that place?"

"We may have to let that venue go. I'm in talks with other spaces, however."

"What's the hold up with Tuesday's? You know the owner. She's in love with Eric. We can afford her place and we'd have it for ten days. That's two weekends, Felix."

"There have been some developments."

Felix shifted his weight and rubbed his hands together. He was looking at the wall behind Stephanie, avoiding her furious eyes. His gaze settled on me and he said, "I think it would be better to discuss these matters privately. There's no need to involve people who don't already have a stake in it."

"Just say what you're going to say, Felix."

"Mrs. Khouri was all set to support us. She's very excited about what everyone is doing here. Everyone, Stephanie, but after Eric's solo show . . . He has to be given more consideration."

"My god. What does that mean?"

"She feels he should be given more space in her gallery. I bigger font on the marquee, as it were."

"So . . . okay, then the rest of us, what do we do? Stand in the back rooms? Maybe set up in the loading dock?"

"I'm just the messenger here. His newfound notoriety has lent his name a bit of cultural currency, especially in Linda's circle, which means she can ask a higher price."

"How does that make sense?"

"There's an expectation that he will sell. Because of that the price goes up. A kind of finder's fee."

"And if he doesn't sell?"

"Look, Mrs. Khouri wants to do the show. That's good news."

"So what's the hold-up?"

"Without Eric the deal is dead."

"I don't understand. Where's Eric going? Of course he'll be there."

"He hasn't decided yet."

Stephanie released an exclamation into the air that sounded more animal than a woman.

"Unless we can come up with another five thousand dollars, Eric will not participate. And Mrs. Khouri will pass."

"That arrogant prick! He's going to hold us all back unless he gets paid five thousand dollars? Fuck that, Felix. That's not the purpose of this community. You made it quite clear to us when we signed on with you that . . ."

"Yes, but I didn't know . . ."

"What? That one of us might actually have some talent? Jesus, Felix, you should have assumed all of us would be big deals."

"I can get the money."

"How?"

Felix couldn't say how. Stephanie shook her head.

Felix said, "Mitchell's and the Bravo Galleries will have us. 7/10 Split, as well."

"They're too small, Felix. You shouldn't have even wasted your time with them. They're apartments for Christ's sake. Studio apartments. You better talk to Eric, Felix. Get his ass on board this thing."

"He's adamant, Stephanie."

"Fuck him, Felix, so am I. This is about all of us. I've seen what you can do with buildings and monuments. You're a capable guy. But somehow raising money for this little endeavor of yours may be beyond your expertise."

"Selling the idea of a person or an artistic movement is more difficult than the idea of a historic landmark," he said. "People can get behind a solid structure more than they can an abstract idea. But I can do it, Stephanie. I have done it."

"One time, Felix. You did it one time. Wasn't he a real good friend of yours, too?"

They stared at one another. Stephanie was not going easy on Felix's efforts and I couldn't be certain she was out of line. Felix absorbed the impact of her words, they ricocheted off all his sensitive feelings. His shoulders slumped as he acquiesced in her perception of things. Eric's music continued to burst onto Stephanie's wall like paint hurled from a bucket. The longer we stood listening to it the more it mediated between their moods, displaying them, tearing Felix up and stoking Stephanie's contempt.

She turned away, exasperated. Felix raised his eyes. I wondered how many times he had been so chastised; if he took it hard as a matter of course, but would in no way be persuaded by such outbursts.

"I have a solution," Stephanie said. "We need to get someone with the money to finance this thing, right?"

She turned toward me and I froze. Felix saw and waited.

"What do you say, Joshua? Do you want to help out some starving artists? We'll put your name on the posters and everything. Maybe even get it in the papers? Definitely in *Art News*. Hell, you could even write about it."

"Stephanie, this is not the time. If it were strictly about money then . . ."

"Then what? Your correctness has gotten us to this moment where we've got nothing. A bit of madness might be just the thing. Besides, I've already talked to him about it."

Stephanie had laid down the challenge. She was all sharp edges. Felix held my elbow and quietly apologized; he said I wasn't obligated to make any decision just then.

"The hell he isn't. How much time do we have until Tuesday's gets booked? How many openings does she have in the next year?"

"We are under the gun a bit," said Felix.

"Exactly. I know you wanted more time to think it over Joshua, but there's been a lot of foot-dragging lately and we don't have that luxury anymore."

Felix's position had drifted toward her point of view. She was not wrong and from the look on his face I knew he could not be counted on to present an alternative.

"Well, like I said earlier . . . It's not that I'm . . ."

"I could go over the details with you if you'd like," said Felix. "There are some interesting aspects to such expenditures. And then, if it's not something you're comfortable with we'll move on from this unpleasantness."

"For god's sake, Felix. What's so uncomfortable? You said he's got the money, we give him some status and he gets the write-off. Pay-for-play, right?"

"That's enough, Stephanie."

This time it was Stephanie who relented. She held her hands up in surrender.

"Do have a few moments to discuss the details?"

His sudden formality unnerved me.

"By all means, discuss," said Stephanie. "Talk it all out. Talk talk talk."

Felix led me into the hallway and down the corridor. He gave stuttered directions to his office even though he was leading. It was obvious he didn't want to talk about money. That wasn't his way. Money was too impersonal, too much associated with privileges. It was an easy key that unlocked too many doors, none of which opened into a worthwhile room. I was saddened by Stephanie's infatuation of my financial situation, that she had invited that fact, rather than me, back to her studio. But I was more hurt that Felix would have plotted this scenario with her in the first place. He was too delicate to broach the subject with me outright. He needed her gruffness, her impersonal matter-of-fact approach, to bring it up. Whether he planned such an evening with Stephanie beforehand seemed unlikely. I believe he had told Stephanie what she needed to know to get the ball rolling. He knew her that well.

I let him struggle in the net he had cast.

"I'm sorry to have to drag this into this Joshua. I have fought Stephanie on this point for days."

"I'm not completely blind-sided, Felix. She brought this up earlier today."

"It's not the way things are done, Joshua. At least, not how I'd prefer it anyway. She suggests using your tragic profit for her own benefit."

I didn't see it quite like that. From my perspective, many people would reap some reward from this showing; including Felix.

"When I saved this property and began this endeavor, it was with certain promises that I was able to fill the studios. In exchange for rent, not only would they get living and work-spaces, but I would also act as their manager. I've booked a few venues and managed to get some of their smaller works hung in coffee houses, but it hasn't been anything they couldn't have done themselves. The rest of the artists don't mind. The set-up affords them time to work they wouldn't have otherwise. They know I'm busy with other efforts and are content to work on their own and, frankly, they would prefer to meet art dealers and promoters and museum curators on their own. It's part of the world they've dedicated their lives to. But Stephanie is some-thing else. It's not that she isn't an artist. She simply demands that I make good on my promises, which is a quality I admire in her, but technically I have made good. No lawyer would pros-ecute me for not abiding by the contract. It's just, the results haven't lived up to her expectations. She hasn't broken through yet. I've tried to manage her expectations, but now, with Eric's success, she's even more insistent I make things happen."

"Why not let her leave if she doesn't appreciate what this situation is, or if she's unhappy with you? Can't you dissolve the contract or buy her out?"

"Because she isn't wrong. If I released her from the con-tract that would be seen as my failing to satisfy it. I would be in breach then. That's what her lawyer tells me."

"She's contacted a lawyer?"

"It's her father's lawyer. The family's. They've promised to take the property if I don't make available a certain level of recognition for their daughter."

"What does that mean?"

"They're not being unreasonable, Joshua. They know her work will be the eventual arbiter of her success. But they believe that it's my job to get her exposure. I've agreed to get everyone here seen, of course, but she's the one pushing most for it. I can't fault her for that."

"Does her family decide when she's been adequately seen or have they left that up to you, or to her? Do they know the places where she should be shown? And for how long?"

Felix rubbed his hands together as if he were washing away the stains of these matters. It was the affluent family of a vengeful artist that wanted my money now. I wished he would get rid of the pretense and approach me as a prospective bene-factor of an artistic movement.

"They know who reviews art for the *Sun Times* and the *Tribune* and they would like to read about their daughter in those papers. They'd like their friends to read about her. I've told them those critics aren't the final word; that they're merely describing exhibits coming to Chicago, preparing buyers and motivating an exploration into another culture. But they know a vast and mostly anonymous group of taste-makers are be-hind artists' success. Not unlike families like Stephanie's. Quite frankly, not even Eric's work is prepared for that kind of notice."

I won't pretend not to know the value of five thousand dollars in the art world, but at that time in my life I could part with such a sum. I had to consider my ease of giving, though. I didn't believe Felix would ever ask me again — he was taking this pretty hard — but I couldn't know for sure. To agree too quickly could set an annoying precedent and inundate me with all manner of requests. Stephanie's litigious instincts gave me pause, as well. Also, I felt Felix wasn't giving it to me straight. For a lawyer to become involved hinted at a misplacement of justice; maybe Felix played down his promise of managing the artists to me; maybe Stephanie was so insecure of her artistic standing or disgusted by the idea of returning home that she would succeed by any and all means; perhaps the building had more structural damage than Felix originally suspected and he and Stephanie were in cahoots to have me pay for the repairs. I entertained all these notions, an annoying little trip into the myriad motivations any one person could have and multiplied by a factor of a thousand when another person's were involved. I told Felix I would have to check with my accountant. I was about to say attorney, but I thought Felix would have a stroke if too many of that sort were brought into his circle. Maybe I couldn't withdraw such a sum at one time, I said. Maybe the bank wouldn't approve of my reason for needing it. There were many strictures tied into the fund my money was attached to, I told him. All lies of course. The existence of an accountant or a board was as substantial as my attorney. As in all things, I was alone in this venture.

"How soon?" Felix said.

"A couple of days."

"I'll tell Stephanie. What more can she expect? I appreciate you thinking about it at least."

"What kind of return could I expect? The board likes that question."

I had heard something of that sort on a television drama and thought it would give credence to my hesitancy.

"Oh, Joshua, it's art," he said. "You could claim a charitable deduction, I suppose."

Three days later I gave Felix a check. I had decided that helping a friend with such little sacrifice on my part was very altruistic of me. I felt good about myself. I washed my hands of their calculations and maneuverings, if there were any malicious forms of either, and told myself it would be worse for them if they had taken advantage of me. I would have time to practice shrewdness later in life. For now I was young, adventurous, excitable and a little dizzy from the opportunity taking shape. I never would have thought myself a patron of the arts, but now that I was I couldn't have been more thrilled.

I hadn't botched the farewell after all.

When I called Liz said she was running errands in the Loop. She had taken the afternoon off and agreed to meet me for a late lunch. I couldn't believe my luck: that such a woman, an intellectual with a proud bearing and a quick mind, would think enough of my company to desire it again only intensified my affection for her.

I bought the newest issue of *Poetry* and waited for Liz inside Chiptle. I lifted the satchel off my shoulder and regarded the cover art. An upright canine was smoking a cigarette and stalking down a sidewalk, fists clenched; the poet seemed to be on a mission of grave import. This attitude certainly didn't mimic my own as I preferred a slow saunter and had nothing so intense to tend to at the walk's end. However, I was beginning to feel Chicago in the soles of my feet, along my hamstrings and quads; it was tugging at my heels and creeping into my knee joints. Even the small of my back was beginning to speak with the streets and I wondered, if the intensity wasn't there then the quantity of my walks would compel me either to find their end or their purpose.

Liz was crossing the street and I watched her mouth curl and pucker against the wind. I didn't yet know how to decipher such twitches, if they were tells of some kind, and I wondered if, over time, I would be able to decipher what she was thinking by interpreting such signs.

I met her at the door and we stood in line. I was happy she had come and she was happy that I had called and her optimism made me giddy, which made her smile and falter before the register. We were both a bit awkward in our enjoyment in one another and while we waited for our order I asked what she'd been thinking about.

"When?"

"Well, in general I'm always interested, but just now. When you were crossing the street."

"I don't know, Joshua. Nothing really. The afternoon, I guess."

"What happened?"

"Nothing. I had to pick up the dry cleaning and I took some papers to my dad's office."

"How was that visit?"

"He wasn't in. I just left them with his secretary."

"Do you like going to his office?"

"Sure. I don't get into the Loop very often any more. I miss it, I think."

"What do you miss?"

Liz smirked and squinted her eyes at me.

"What's gotten into you?"

"What do you mean?"

"You're very inquisitive."

"Well, I mean to be. Tell me what you miss."

"'Miss' isn't the right word. I remember it then, or I remember myself then. Like today. I walked up the spiral staircase and I was holding on to the banister and when I reached the landing I felt the ironwork. Something about the texture or the gaps in the design, I had felt it before. And for a brief moment I was a little girl again, holding Mom's hand as we climbed to see Dad. Then I saw the old mail box in the hallway. I was insistent that Dad give me letters to put in it and I could hardly reach the slot, but I knew it was important that I do that. I don't know; it made me sad."

"Why?"

"Because Dad isn't there when I come by now. Maybe I've been there so much over the years that the novelty of having me visit has worn off or maybe because I don't react to the world in the same way. How can I? I thought those letters were essential to him, that the place would fall down if his communications weren't sent. I haven't done anything as important since."

"That's not true."

"I'm kidding, of course. But now those things I find important to do are mostly for my benefit. What I write . . . if no one receives it, nothing will crumble. Yea. That's what I was thinking."

"There's some freedom in that, though. You can write about whatever you want."

Our order came up and I took the tray with a burrito and bowl to the table. Liz got us napkins and asked how much heat I wanted in my salsa. I told her mild and she said she'd surprise me.

"There is one benefit of time passing, though," she said handing me the salsa. "There was no Intelligentsia back then."

"We're living in halcyon days."

We dug in. I tried not to smear my face with sour cream and guacamole; I believed such a sight would diminish the implications of whatever came out of my mouth and I wanted Liz to delight in my ideas as I did.

"How's your novel coming?" she said.

"Fits and starts. When I think I have enough to material to make some progress it turns out to be a dead end. My ideas about it are more thrilling than its actuality, I think. I get more enjoyment thinking about the novel than writing it."

"Oh no."

"How about your work? What's been taking up your time?"

"I've taken my thesis out of the drawer. I've even looked at it a bit. I think there are a few chapters I could reconfigure. There's a call for papers to explore the relationship between Socrates and Athens that I will submit something to. I've already done much of the work in my study of *Phaedrus*. It's the only dialogue that takes place outside of the city and so what Plato says Socrates discusses there clarifies what the city means to him."

"How so?"

"It seems that in the country humanity is more free, at least in terms of how they think about certain things. The ideas of justice and regimes that takes up Plato's *Republic* have no place in this work. Instead, Socrates talks about madness and the immortality of the soul, about beauty and what a lover is. These ideas are important for the city insofar as its citizens' beliefs about such things shape the character of the city, but they are far more important for the individual. And Plato seems to be saying these things are best discussed in nature, away from the civility of society, who would find such ideas as the chariot and the soul-mate infantile, if not ludicrous. Outside the city, nymphs and spirits roam; the muses seem to hold sway. Where before Socrates says all he needs to learn he can learn from men, now he pays special attention to the hum of the cicadas."

"Sounds like it's filled with potential."

"I think so. It's the closest Plato comes to something like *A Midsummer Night's Dream*."

"Do you think I made a mistake coming to Chicago for literature? Maybe the farm would have been better?"

"I could answer that for you if I thought you'd seriously consider what I thought."

"Of course I'd consider it."

"I think you're in the right place."

Liz held her gaze on me. I stayed fixed upon her.

"What about you?" she said. "What mystery have you set out to solve today?"

I told her about Seneca's belief that time is not short if we use it well and in that in keeping with that idea I'd decided to look into the idea of beauty as it pertains to God; that I'd begun with the creation myths of Genesis 1 and 2 and believed I'd found something.

Liz wiped her mouth and said, "What?"

"I don't know for sure . . . who does? . . . but I think we might be living in the seventh day. If you read the creation passage the phrase that's repeated is "and there was evening and there was morning." This happens the first day, the second, every day until the seventh day. By the seventh day God had finished and so he rested. There's no mention of an evening on the seventh day."

"Neither is there an eighth day."

"Right."

"What do you think that means?"

"Well, for the literalists it might cause some problems with their time line. But those for whom such literal interpretations have caused some distress I think this might allow them to think about earth's age in the context of millions of years, rather than thousands."

"Did you just reconcile science and religion?"

That teasing voice; those winking eyes. How could I not fall for this woman?

"It's what I do, Liz. Then it makes me think the eighth day is what happens after Revelation. The New Jerusalem, a new creation in which we live on earth as we were meant to: in God's rest. I don't know. Something to think further about."

"It sounds like a return to Eden."

"Yes."

"They didn't plant seeds or harvest the crops; springs watered everything; they ate from trees. There was no work for them to do. Nothing but rest."

"Then it makes me wonder, if it was so perfect for Adam, why he needed a companion."

"Probably because a life without work is boring. Imagine, alone all; laying around or walking through a garden, thinking about God and being and wondering how much longer this life thing lasts."

"That would be terrible."

"Because how can you have a conversation with God? He'd always be right."

"Not unlike a dialogue with Socrates."

We finished our lunch and when Liz asked to see my apartment we went upstairs. We talked about some things and she looked at the titles I had chosen for my shelves. She stepped up to my window and commented on the view. I put my arm around her waist and told her about the different lights that illumined the building depending on the season. She asked what color they were today. I said I didn't know and kissed her.

We spent the afternoon between comments and silences. We talked about what we wanted to do in the city, in life, with each other. We sealed each plan with a kiss, the duration and intensity of which spoke to our affirmation of the other's hope.

It was getting late and the sky was darkening. I had been struggling with how I could best spend the evening, but decided I should keep my date. I told Liz I was meeting Roland on the corner in half and hour and that I should get ready. She understood and twenty-five minutes later we were both waiting on the curb outside CVS.

Roland called to say he would be at my corner in five minutes; then he called ten minutes later to say he'd be late. We didn't mind. Delay only provided an opportunity for us to learn something about the other we wound't otherwise have learned.

When Liz asked, I said, "I'm attracted to his exuberance, the faith he had in his unique vision, clipping his heels through life because he knows what he wants."

That kind of certainty had eluded me in Chicago and it was good to be subjected to it. In that same vein, I received a certain amount of pleasure in our adventures. This is difficult to admit since most of what I experienced with him had been shrouded in mystery and violence, but I had an instinct toward the hiddenness of life and thought that ideas of right and wrong, good and evil could be subsumed under the banner of knowledge. Also, I was afraid of him. I didn't know what Roland was actually capable of and since he knew how to find me I stayed up nights wondering just who the real Roland was: the amiable actor talking shop or a swift terror streaking through the night wielding a crow bar. And so I thought it would just be easier, and safer maybe, to join him as planned.

I heard him coming before I saw him. Rather, I heard Mikhail urging the cab to make up time. The tires gripped what pavement they could while turning off LaSalle onto Division. He cut a Mercedes off to get around a bus and stopped in the turning lane forty feet from us. I waved toward him.

"I thought you were meeting him here?"

She thought I was hailing the cab, which I guess I was, in a way.

The street suddenly exploded in a dissonance of horns and flashing lights as Mikhail calmly waited out the green arrow. At a gap in the eastbound traffic he accelerated through — tires screaming at a witless pedestrian who thought himself safe by following agreed upon signals — cutting off more cars until after a reckless u-turn they were idling beside me.

Roland was all smiles. He leaned across the seat and opened my door.

"Let's go, Joshua. We're late."

"Are we in a hurry?"

"Couldn't you tell? Who is this?" Roland slid across the seat and extended his hand. "I'm Roland."

"Liz."

"So nice to meet you. You're with this guy?"

I hadn't seen her blush before.

"Are you coming with us? You should come."

"I can't tonight."

"Well, meet us after. Where will you be at nine?"

"In bed."

"You work?"

She nodded.

"Good. Somebody should do something productive in this city."

I kissed Liz good-bye and knew I was making a terrible mistake leaving her. Still, I closed the door with conviction.

"What are you doing, Mikhail? Don't take Lake Shore now. Back streets, man. He's earning his stripes tonight."

"You got a nice one there, Joshua. Been holding out on me."

"It's only started to get serious."

"How long?"

"Today."

"You hear that Mikhail? The boy's growing up."

I buckled the seat belt and listened to Roland tell me about the star I was risking my life to see. Six-foot-seven and two hundred twenty-six pounds: handles, posts, rebounds and never breaks a sweat.

"The Kid's amazing. The papers love him. Colleges are burying his poor grandmother in letters and unofficial apparel. Promises and phone calls every day. He floats above it all, same as on the court. He simply floats. He's like water when he rushes to the rim and an orgasm when he comes down on it."

Roland was very excited.

"Why do you care so much about him?" I said.

"Why shouldn't I? He's from my neighborhood. I know his family. Had dinner with them last week, in fact. Everybody sees the glamorous side of being a McDonald's All-American, but the secret reality shouldn't be wished on an enemy. All these old white guys flirting with him, telling him they love him, that their lives will be complete only when he signs with them. Even if only for one year. They promise how they can make him the happiest boy in the country if only he'd commit to them. Then they bad-mouth his other suitors, tell him what a bunch of pricks the whole lot is, how they're all crooked and in bed with some vile characters, everyone except whoever's making the accusations, of course. And all this in his grandma's presence with language better suited to the gutter than her cozy living room. It gets nasty, Joshua, I'm telling you."

"He's a regular Penelope."

"I don't know who that is, but it'd be a sweet relief to see them all together when a madman with an axe and a grudge decided to nix 'em all."

"Exactly."

"Mikhail! How much longer, comrade? Tip's in twenty minutes."

Mikhail was unconcerned and a few tight turns and sharp stops later he pulled into a large parking lot. The school appeared from among rows of winter-worn houses, broken streetlights, and grassless parks. Cars lined the streets until they faded into the darkness. Groups of men in Sox and Bulls coats converged on the building from all sides. The Kid's name was on countless tongues and in the course of the evening I heard so many stories of his exploits that he would have needed to play basketball every evening for the last twenty years and at the highest level to have achieved half of what was said about him.

When I saw him I didn't have to be told who he was.

Roland shoved his way through the narrow gym doors stuffed by men looking for a vacant seat in the stands. The gym was filled to ensure no one's safety. Men stood five rows deep beneath the baskets; they seemed upset by that fact, or else their game faces were for a different event. A referee nervously checked that their feet weren't encroaching on the playing area. To kick people out at this point would have been beyond irresponsible.

On the spacious hardwood, twenty-five boys ran lay-up drills. Many still hadn't lost their baby fat and most lacked any sign of muscle development. The Kid was warming up on the far rim. Buoyant, already seeming like a college junior, he unconcerned by the upheaval. I watched him glide through the lines, his head and shoulders never leaving a level plane. The crowd was agog when he leaped for a rebound and he teased the crowd with near-dunks. A wry smile for how pliant we all were. He seemed bored by his own ability and ambivalent to the attention it brought him. He never fully smiled, but neither did he scowl. His teammates ignored him, offering low fives while turning their faces away from him. The Kid kept himself subdued.

At center court during the captain's meeting, he looked over the heads of the refs and his opponents. He shook their hands, but he didn't see them.

"It looks like he just has to show up and that's that," I yelled to Roland.

Roland winked and pointed to the Kid's team huddle. His coaches were standing at the scorer's table talking to themselves. The players stood apart in a small huddle waiting. The Kid broke from center court and began a chant that the other boys responded to, clapping hands and stomping feet, hopping up and down, until they roared, which brought spectators to their feet, clapping and yelling in turn. The starting five swaggered to center court where the other team was waiting. The Kid was like a man insulted; a man ready to remove five trespassers from his home; a man protecting his woman's honor against aggressive pawing.

He controlled the jump ball and streaked toward the far rim guarded by two boys. The point lobbed the ball and in an instant The Kid had exploded through four arms, the collective gasp of fifteen hundred people, scouts, official visitors, envelopes of money and family pleas to grab the ball with both hands and send it through, quick and powerful, to the floor where it may have splintered the hardwood.

The crowd finally achieved release. The noise was deafening.

For the next forty minutes I watched The Kid run and shoot his team to a seventeen-point lead. At halftime his team didn't go to the locker room. Instead, they stayed on the court and did more lay up drills. The Kid was jawing with his teammates, broad smiling shoulder rolling head dipping to the joy of the crowd. Everyone was watching everything he did.

The Kid played six minutes of the third then sat for the rest of the quarter. Roland grabbed my arm and said, "He's done for the night. Let's go."

He led me into the cafeteria.

"Tell me I was wrong," said Roland.

"You weren't wrong."

"Hasn't been anyone like him in years. He's better than Wade ever was."

"How does he do against competition?"

Roland looked shocked, then threw his arm around my shoulder. "Don't say that too loud, man or I'll be carrying your beat-ass out of here."

I followed him through the crowd and popcorn lines to a relatively deserted corner of the high school. We walked own a hall where a metal gate barred further exploration. School spirit banners hung above the lockers and Roland assumed an interested demeanor in them.

"I have to meet a guy here. When he shows up you stand behind me and look hard."

"What are we looking for?"

"No, Joshua. Look hard." Roland narrowed his eyes and scowled. "Like you ain't gonna put up with any shit tonight, okay?"

In the gymnasium the crowd sent a roar to the ceiling that filled the space and came crashing through the small doors like a tidal wave pushing Roland and me further from the bright lights and into the shadows. Two men had been swept away by it as well. One was a tall, heavy-set man made thicker by a Blackhawks jacket. He wore Oakley frames and had a thin goatee. I wasn't sure he would buy my toughness act and wondered how he could see to protect his friend who was smaller only by weight. He wore a cream camel hair trench coat that made him seem long and slender, powerful even, and when Roland reached into his back pocket, he stayed Blackhawk's hand from reaching too deep into his jacket. Roland frowned at my clueless immobility and brought out an envelope. Camel Hair reached out his gloved hand and Roland handed it over. The thickness of it clearly impressed him.

"If there isn't enough there to suit your boys up your uniform guy is taking advantage of you," Roland said.

As if thinking of something else, Camel Hair said, "You're doing good work, just don't push it. Any hassles?"

"I don't like to kiss and tell, Mr. Smith," said Roland.

Mr. Smith looked me over. "Who's this guy?"

"Yeah, he's here for moral support. He finds the righteousness in all I do."

He was amused for a moment then said, "Don't give us a reason to let you go, Jack."

"No way, Mr. Smith. I'm having too much fun with ya'll."

Mr. Smith nodded and handed the envelope to Blackhawk.

"We haven't seen our West Siders in a while. They still owe us a bit, too. You hear anything?"

"Not a thing. I don't make it my business to keep up with those guys."

"That's interesting. Because as light as they were this week, you appear to be heavy."

"I'm just putting in the work Mr. Smith. Nose to the ground."

He was expressionless or else just out of the light enough to conceal his thoughts.

"If you happen to hear anything we'd be very interested to find them."

"Of course, Mr. Smith. I'm not here to hinder anything."

Camel Hair walked away. Blackhawk stood his ground a moment, presumably threatening us, but I couldn't see his eyes, then followed his boss. Before he was lost in the crowd I saw Camel Hair answer his phone and stare back down the dark corridor at us. Roland turned toward me like we were having a conversation, but he was just breathing. A bit too quickly, perhaps. When they disappeared, he exhaled and laid his hand on my shoulder.

"That one took something out of me, Joshua."

"Who was that?"

"I asked one thing from you tonight, Joshua. Remember what that was?"

"I'm here, aren't I?"

"Not that. Look hard, man? Where were you?"

"When?"

"When? When the heavy fucker was reaching for his gun. Didn't you see that?"

"I didn't see anything."

"Man, it happened right in front of you. I needed you to step forward or something, do something that would cause me to hold you back. Something."

"You knew I was out of my element here."

He sighed. "Yea, okay. That guy just works me up. You did all right, I guess. Considering it's you. Let's get a drink. I know just the place."

"Why did he call you Jack?"

"He just always has. I think he thinks he's punking me."

Mikhail sped down Eisenhower and into the city while Roland told me about The Kid and his own involvement in the young man's recruitment, especially on the family front. What I'd been privy to earlier, the worn down porches and all those brown paper bags, was money collection for The Kid's AAU team. Camel Hair was an assistant coach of some kind, though not officially. He initiated meetings for his players with boosters from Division One college programs. Not the top tier, maybe not even the third, but he was real friendly with programs that have emphatically danced in March and even a couple programs that had begun to take steps to being

Madness fixtures. With The Kid, those schools could dream of building palaces to rival those of North Carolina, Kansas and Michigan State. However, with the extended success of those programs it proved difficult to get a seat at the table. Camel Hair, Roland said, was a new player in a game with thousands of players. He wasn't trusted yet. He hadn't delivered anything. Those top programs already had their favorite front men who had served well in previous recruiting wars and had proven capable of keeping secrets and hiding evidence of improprieties. With millions of dollars at stake they weren't enthusiastic about taking chances on upstarts; not when their personal integrity was on the line, and certainly not with the prospect of unemployment and the loss of kick-backs to supplement an already substantial salary were these rookies found wanting. Unless, that is, those upstarts had a rare talent to bring with them.

It's amazing how much risk some will take for even one year with a Blue Chip.

Roland chose a bar near the LaSalle Street Station. Inside the bar was dark and people stared into their glasses and the light of televisions mounted from the ceiling. He chose a secluded booth and a tattooed woman took our order without enthusiasm.

"Granted, Crane didn't play a rival tonight or even one of the top twenty schools in the city," Roland said. "But you saw how easy the game comes to him. Didn't break a sweat. Intense, too. That swagger. His frame. Hell, The Kid already looks the part."

He leaned in and whispered, "He looks like Benji."

He leaned back as though the name meant something to me.

"Benji? Ben Wilson. Man, Benji man."

I shook my head.

"Whatever, Josh, I'm feeling good tonight. Better than I have a right to maybe, but when you have one success it topples onto the next thing, and that onto the next one and so on. I'm going to be on a roll soon. If I were traded on NASDAQ you'd be a fool not to buy up a shit-ton of shares."

"Who would broker that deal?"

"I will personally take as much as you wanted to invest."

The waitress brought two whiskey shots and two beers.

"To the future meteoric rise of Roland Charles," he said.

We touched glasses and I swallowed my shot hard. It wasn't the kind of stuff I normally drank, especially without a prior lubricant. Roland saw my squint and shake and, like all things that night, he got a kick out of it.

"I feel like getting into a fight," he said. "Nothing menacing, but one where we each leave the field bloodied and tired and licking each other's wounds."

I wasn't surprised to hear this, considering how we met.

"Have you ever been in a fight, Joshua? Do you know what one is?"

"Do you really have to ask that?"

"You could be holding out on me."

"No, I haven't."

"A fight is how men fuck. The initial insult is the flirtation, the time between that remark and the first blow is foreplay and the coming to blows is, well . . . It's not talked about that way, but that's what it is. The good fights, anyway. A fight between equals. I've beaten my share of scrubs, you know? little guys with no guts, drunk and proud, thinking they're really up to something. The kind of guys who talk shit to waitresses and slap women. That ain't fuckin'. Not the way I'm talking about. And it definitely ain't jumping a guy with three of my friends. No, the best fighting, the purest fighting that mimics a good fuck is the kind you get into without knowing if you're going to win or not. There's trepidation in that and that 'holy shit' moment when you realize this is going to hurt and when you each hold your own, when you're both left wallowing in your own blood on the curb, there's a feeling of release and a gladness of heart. You're happy to have met and grateful you'll never see each other again. And then the scars you're left with. Proud of those things."

"Where are your scars?"

"Whoa, Josh. Too personal, man. Didn't you just hear what I was saying? Mikhail, take this piece of shit out of here."

Mikhail folded his arms and I drank my beer. I'd been around Roland long enough to know his hyperbole. That was comforting and also a bit frightening.

"Had our first meeting gone differently, would you have fought me?" he said.

"No. I would have rolled over pretty easily."

"I get that about you."

"Why? Would you have fought me?"

"You're an attractive guy, Joshua, but let's take it easy. Seriously, I would have pounded the shit out of you. I told Mikhail that I'd never been so put off from being a scoundrel as I was that night. You touched me, Joshua. Here. And here."

Mikhail shook the booth with amused grunts.

"That night could have been much worse for you, though. If it wasn't me who was after your dollars but someone else, maybe a guy high out of his mind or desperate for a score, we wouldn't be talking tonight."

"Is that common in the city?"

"Not so much where we were, but the South Side is notorious for it. It's creeping north, too, the scoundrel element. A couple of years ago a man and his woman were walking home from a show at the Green Mill. It was late. He was drunk. Three guys jumped 'em a block from their apartment. They beat the woman unconscious and stole the man's suit before shooting him in the head. Didn't want to get blood on the material, I suppose. Smart, actually. Despite the gun shot in the middle of the night, the cops weren't called until three hours later when people started leaving for work."

"That's terrible. Did the woman survive?"

"Doubtful. She wasn't killed or nothing, but the memory and the fact of her dead boyfriend or husband, whatever he was to her would have wreaked her head, I'm sure. So you get that from time to time. Roving gangs moving in the shadows of up-and-coming neighborhoods looking for some quick loot, a little adventure, some respect and BAM! Good-bye charmed life. What did they call themselves, Mikhail? I'm terrible with names."

"The Envies."

"The Envies, that's right."

"All for a suit?"

"It ain't one of the seven deadlies for nothing."

"Would you care so much about another person's stuff that you'd kill him for it, Roland?"

"It's more fun to deal and dive and fix things so I don't have to kill anyone."

"Would you ever fight the guy we met tonight?"

"He's on to us, Mikhail."

Roland drank half his beer and waved the waitress over.

"Only in my wildest dreams would I think of fighting him. He's the right hand of the guy who's the right hand of The Guy. If The Kid rolls onto an elite campus, The Guy will be set. He won't be an assistant coach or anything, but he'll be on the AD's payroll. He'll have an office and a paycheck for a few years, and the only one he'll use is the check. Interns and road trips, all costs compensated, connections made, opportunities presented. See, I know all this," Roland waved his palms around his face and torso, "is a means to that end. I got to put on this little performance for that guy so he recommends me to The Guy. I gotta play the lackey for a bit. But the payoff, Joshua. The payoff is huge. And tonight was a big step."

It didn't seem so momentous to me, but then I didn't have the right eyes to see what was really happening in that dark hallway. Nor was I privy to the months of manipulating by Roland before I entered that gym with him. He saw that I was trying to piece the whole thing together so that I could celebrate with some sincerity.

"I made sure he was getting more from me than from any of his other lackeys tonight. And he noticed."

"Jack does good work," I said.

Roland laughed and slapped the table just as the waitress was setting down our second round.

I swallowed the rest of my beer, to Roland's great pleasure. We threw back another round of shots, which went down agreeably, and collided the mugs against each other, spilling beer on the table and down the cold sides of glass.

"You just bought a hundred shares, Joshua.

The next morning passed in the same lethargy I had begun to experience after my nights with Roland accompanied by condemnation and the all too familiar promise never to drink so much again. Really, it was getting to be too much, if only for the work lost during my day of penance. The next day I returned to my walks. The Archdiocese on Rush Street was being cleaned. Scaffolding scaled the outer walls and men wearing insulated coats and thick gloves were taking tools and material out of dark vans and dusty trucks. They had power washed the bricks before the October chill could numb their fingers, and now they were winterizing the windows. Earlier in the year, while the weather was still and comforting, I had watched the work from Argo Tea's sidewalk. However, the sidewalk tables and chairs had been put away as the cold and wind settled upon the urban landscape. City workers had uprooted the potted plants in the dark of night and I contemplated such labors in the warmth of the comforting interior.

I had a great appreciation for my studies; they were a labor I could perform in cold weather and warm and its nature was such that I could pursue them rain or shine, from my youth into old age, and its pleasures would not be dampened, I hoped, if I employed the material in an acceptable way. I saw the audience for a writer's work was dwindling and too frequently their words fell before blind eyes. I became obsessive about being those eyes for them, of somehow continuing the conversations they had contributed to. While I read one book, I had tens of others on my desk and stacked on my floor and I imagined what I might find in the next one and wondered about the men and women slumped over their desks right now, at this moment, frantically finding just the right word to express an idea or wildly filling their notebooks with a story's energy. I decided their discipline and concerns would be rewarded in my hands. I took all their seriousness with me when I read them, pencil in hand, dictionary at the ready and always scribbling notes, commenting for myself on what I had just read, if what they wrote seemed correct to me or if there was still work left to do. In this way I trained myself to see the world through a literary lens.

All the while baristas steamed milk, prepared scones, laughed with customers, scanned frequency cards debit cards credit cards, accommodated special orders, clinked mugs onto saucers, wiped down tables and greeted the steady stream of customers. I was surrounded by all of it and before my eyes and in my mind floated the ideas of Plato, Seneca, Saint Paul, Walter Benjamin, Roland Barthes, Saul Bellow, and the Poets. Inside such coffeehouses and cafes and bars I escaped the persistent shadows of life for a few hours and forgot that man has a limited number of days upon this earth in which to accomplish all that his hands find fit to do.

Still, I enjoyed myself. I even sent a few of my commentaries to local newspapers and magazines in hopes of getting them published and beginning the writer's life and the life of an ambassador for the speeches and stories of those long silent.

My pursuit of the contemplative life: to sit beneath the stones and listen; to wait.

Stones can remain silent a long time.

And so I came to stand on the opposite corner of the Monadnock Building. I was looking at the Gilded Age structure with its uneven red brick and imposing weight and I heard its stones sighing. At one time, its grand opening was the event in Chicago. Its architects were the Fathers of the Chicago School and had been the luminaries of this city then. Once the largest office building in the world and an architectural marvel resting on a floating foundation, the Monadnock is lost amidst the lightness of the modern business aesthetic. It rises silent and narrow, catching the sun upon its rough façade and returning it to the city through blue windows. It seems as if it would be more comfortable at sea; as if its purpose was meant for a different life. Unfortunately, that life had passed it by and it was too late to remember what it had been; it no longer had the energy to chase it down.

Looking at the Monadnock Building, I fell into sadness at the inevitability of life's fleeting quality; I heard the Arcadian's

What you are now we once were, like a mantra the venerable stones repeated during the day and throughout the night. They sat like conquered heroes, swallowed up in the shadows of the new heroes. I thought of Milton's Samson blinded, atrophied, bald and resting near a rock taking the abuse of Harapha from Gath. But maybe there is still glory in their future? I walked around the noble structure. Though I couldn't see from the sidewalk, I knew the external warehouse appearance concealed open staircases bathed in elegant light, clean and stately, and oak framed offices of frosted windows and heavy doors. Materials and design to promulgate ideas of simplicity, meditation and honor.

From Jackson Boulevard I walked down State Street, following the Red Line's small pavilions that sheltered the descending stairs, to the Harold Washington Library. I needed their copy of *The Cambridge Companion to Milton* to better my understanding of poetics and the epic mindset shared by Cicero and the Apostle Paul. The Samson poem had begun to work on me. I hadn't given much thought to the story outside the parameters of the ordained text. But in Milton's hands, the two-dimensional presentation I'd grown accustomed to suddenly exploded in possibilities and conjecture.

After some time I set Dr. Bennett's essay aside and read over what I'd written down. There was life in those dry bones and I thought I could do something similar. I wondered which ancient story I could possibly modernize; which one had the most in common with today's world and would speak the most to it.

It was nearly five-thirty. I hadn't noticed the sky darken and I quickly packed up my things. I checked out the volumes I thought would be most helpful to me and abandoned the others on the table. I skipped down the escalators and burst onto Congress Parkway. I was meeting Liz at DePaul's Barnes and Noble before deciding on a place for dinner.

I lingered on the corner waiting for the light to change. A gray wind swept strange leaves through the labyrinth and I thought I would eschew the audience for the time being and choose whichever ancient story I most enjoyed and that would challenge my skill as a dramatist. I crossed the street with the light, passing dozens of weary workers returning to their homes or to their chosen rails. Chances were good there would never be an audience for my little endeavor, anyway.

I pushed through the revolving doors of the bookseller's and saw Liz right away. She wore a yellow sweater out of which escaped the light blue cuffs and collar of a cotton blouse. Her slacks were pinstriped with ghostly lines and she held a red coat in the crook of her arm.

She saw me and smiled.

She kissed me.

"What have you been up to?"

"Finding my next thing."

She looked at my book, twisted my wrist to read the title.

"Nurturing strange ideas, more like," she said.

My satchel was packed to bursting and I couldn't fit this last one in. "Why? Do you think it's ridiculous?"

She took it out of my hands and showed me the title: *The Intimacy and Solitude Self-Therapy Book.*

"Well, that's unfortunate."

"Do you have a few minutes? I'd like to look for something else," she said.

"Take all the time you need."

"Oh, right. Forgot who I was talking to."

She squeezed my arm and I followed her through the aisles, distractedly pulling titles off the shelves so as not to appear so utterly taken with being so near her. I felt impressive, substantial; because Liz felt being with me was time well spent I believed I was in the midst of doing something marvelous. Likewise, being with her created in me a sense that I could do whatever my hands found fit to do. I found confidence to indulge my peculiar habits and to discuss these things openly. I had great hopes that she would be my audience. What I didn't know yet was what I would be for her, and this gave me some pause.

We made our way downstairs. She was browsing the art books, looking for a study on Chicago architecture.

"So I can keep up with you," she said, a wink in her voice.

I wanted to return with something witty, but I faltered, overwhelmed by the ease with which she could disorient me.

"How's Roland?" she said with a casual flip through a heavy title.

"He's doing well. I think he's coming in to something big."

"Oh yea? What does he do?"

"I couldn't say, really. Taking classes."

"You haven't talked about it?"

"We kind of stick to things we've already talked about. I guess those sorts of things are unimportant to us."

"Okay."

She put the book back and walked away from me, toward the monographs of painters.

"He's made an impression on you," I said.

"Not at all. I'm trying to make a judgment about you by the company you keep."

"I haven't seen much of him lately. He has odd jobs that keep him busy and with me pounding the pavement . . ."

"Your hands look real bruised and battered."

"I may have carpal tunnel," I said mimicking my typing style. "Or arthritis from holding the pen wrong."

"They didn't teach you that in your little town?"

"I never caught on."

Liz smiled and lifted a book about Modigliani. Then her face soured. I thought she was expressing her opinion of the artist's style and I was preparing my rebuttal when she said, "I saw him the other day," she said. "That's why I wondered."

She looked at me like she had just threatened my King with her knight and waited for my move so she could topple me.

"You saw Roland? Where?"

I was suddenly frightened and hoped she hadn't seen me with him.

"I met some friends after work. We went to a sushi place in Wicker Park, then walked to The Violet Hour. We were feeling good I remember, and because it was a Tuesday we got right in. Beautiful place; great drinks. After two rounds we wanted to go somewhere else. Someplace cheaper. We hadn't planned on making a night of it, but one thing led to another and, we were off. Scott went into 7-Eleven to buy cigarettes and I waited in the parking lot with Louise and Sam. You don't know them; it doesn't matter. Anyway, we were laughing about something dumb when a man yelled, *Shut your fucking mouth, you fucking* blah blah blah. Clear as day from the lot behind the 7-Eleven. Then a woman screamed, *I don't care about* whatever it was, I couldn't understand it. *You promised! You worthless liar!* Sam made this face then that just cracked Louise and I up. We were real buzzed and things were just funny then and we got the brilliant idea that we'd have a look, right? So we crept around the building, all stealthy and giggling, and I saw the man pulling her through the lot by her arm. *Let me go! I'm not coming with you!* She was clawing at his hand and digging her feet in the ground. Then she bit him. Hard. Because he yelped and let go of her. She must have drawn blood and he was pissed. He yanked on her arm and took her to the ground. He was holding his hand and when she looked up at him he slapped her. Well, that sobered us up quick. Louise walked away, but I couldn't move. He picked her up and she wasn't fighting anymore. They walked right passed me, Joshua. She was holding her face and he was mumbling at her, calling her names and blaming her for what he'd done. Their car was parked next to where I was standing and I had to move out of their way. He opened the door and pushed her inside. When he turned back toward me his face was lit up beneath the streetlight. *The fuck you looking at?* Of course I just stood there. Of all the suddenness of the event, recognizing that monster was the most chilling."

"Are you sure it was him? You only saw him the one time."

She looked astonished, either that I would doubt her memory or that I would try and defend such a man. "It was him, Joshua."

"I believe you."

"Does he have a girlfriend?"

"I don't know. Maybe."

"Then I hope she has enough sense to get out while she can. If he's doing that to her in public, God knows what's going on where no one can see."

I couldn't imagine Roland behaving in such a way, but then I really didn't know him or what he was capable of. Somehow I remembered our first interaction as being playful rather than menacing.

"No one should be treated like that," said Liz. "What a . . ."

There wasn't an epithet strong enough for her.

The book was shaking in her hands and put my arm around her.

"You understand my concern, right?"

"I don't keep regular company with him, Liz."

"Irregular, though."

I began to think about Roland's behavior. He had explained how he first found my building, but not how he got buzzed through or how he knew which floor and apartment were mine. I assumed trial and error, but I was uneasy about the meaning of his persistence. Then there was the joy he took at humiliating those businessmen, the readiness he summoned when a there was a fight to be had. It hadn't proven to be much of a confrontation and I didn't press him on it, given that any disagreement on my part could possibly have put me on the receiving end of his large fist.

"He's so untroubled, though. I can't think of what would set him off."

"You can't always point out a violent man on the sidewalk, Joshua. They're not wearing a red *V* on their chests."

"I know that."

"And what difference does it make what set him off? You don't resort to that kind of behavior. Ever."

"Of course. I just meant . . ."

"Men are capable of everything. And I saw him, Joshua. It was him. I got a real good look at him while he was cursing me out. And I was twenty feet from where them when he hit her. I've never heard a person yelp like he did. She got him good, the bastard."

"I'll ask him about it when I see him."

"You're still making plans with him?"

"Not plans exactly. But we somehow manage to run into each other now and again."

"You don't find that odd?"

I hadn't, until then.

"Which old lady? What are you talking about?" said Roland when I asked him.

We were having drinks at McCormick and Schmick's on Chestnut at two in the afternoon. I decided to keep the questioning innocent. I didn't want to accuse him of anything straight off in hopes that Liz was mistaken.

"She saw you in last week in Wicker Park. Said you were with a woman."

"Liz, huh? Have I met her?"

"You met her when you picked me up. For the game?"

He didn't seem interested in either acknowledging that or debating it.

"Are you hooking up with her?"

"No."

"What's the problem?"

"We're still too . . . it's way to early for . . . Anyway, she's sweet and I like her and that's plenty for now."

"Poor Joshua," Roland put his hand on my shoulder. "They're all sweet, man. And all of 'em are full of secrets and lies. The best thing is love 'em and leave 'em."

"Do you think so?"

"I wouldn't have said it otherwise."

He saw I was unconvinced. He put his beer down and said, "Look. I've had my share of heartbreak. Who hasn't? Some people power through it, convinced there's someone out there just for them and all that and then they settle for someone who's not quite right, but if the other option is more waiting and more wondering and the constant barrage of hope unfulfilled they take the plunge. I decided to forgo all that nonsense and take life as it gives it. The way it's supposed to happen didn't work out for me; now I wing it. And Joshua, I'm winging it well."

He raised his glass.

"But I can see how you'd still be caught up in all that traditional shit. You don't strike me as a guy who's had the rug pulled out from under him. More like a doe in headlights. You're still in awe of them and think they occupy some kind of special space in the world when they're really just walking through your hazy expectations. Then Wham! your blood's all over the hood of the car and you're taking your last breath in a ditch somewhere thinking it's the first time anything's ever been struck so hard."

"So that wasn't you, then?"

"Hell man, it might have been. I do eat out, you know. Sometimes I take a woman with me."

I was getting nowhere with him and regretted having to get more specific.

"Well, she thins she saw you. Said you even spoke to her."

"Did I? What did I say?"

"Nothing kind."

He looked confused.

"You asked what she was looking at."

"Did I? And what did she say?"

"If it wasn't you then it's not important."

"No no, Joshua. You thought enough of it to bring it up. Probably have to go back and report to this Liz person so come out with it. What does she say she saw?"

"Roland . . ."

"I can't very well defend myself if you're gonna be cagey with her accusations."

"She saw you hit a woman."

"That I . . . Liz says she saw me hit? Well, that wasn't me. Do I look like a guy who would let a woman get into him that far?"

I had told Liz as much.

"Believe what you want," said Liz when we met for drinks the next day. She was irritated and angry. This was not the kind of mystery I had in mind when I suggested we each tackle one. "I know what I saw."

We were seated next to a window in Morton's barroom. The place was filled and the wall space was taken up with people waiting for tables, sipping drinks and talking about the day's events and the night's prospects. Liz sipped her martini.

"It's not that I don't believe you, Liz. I can't very well convince him that he did what you're saying he did. He says he didn't, and if you're right then . . . I'm afraid of what you think of me, knowing I hang out with someone like that."

"If I thought you resembled him at all we wouldn't be discussing it now."

"How do you know I'm any different?"

"Woman's intuition."

I drank my Scotch to that. There are less valid reasons why a woman would spend time with a man, and since I believed she was right about the disparities between my character and Roland's, I trusted her even more.

"How do you train this intuition of yours?" I said.

"Frequent use. I'm in the habit of consulting my spirit when it comes to people. I read about this or heard about it a long time ago. I don't remember where or from whom, or even if it's true, but they say the world spins in the key of C. So if that energy has a musical equivalent, we as people could possibly live on a similar scale of notes. I don't know if a note emanates from us as we walk around or if it's as natural to us as our scent or our hair color or what, but I like that as an explanation for why we get along with some people and not with others. Why there's harmony with some and discord with others."

"And when you're with me you hear harmony?"

The Scotch was finding its way to my innermost parts and the joy I felt simply being with Liz was giving me a brashness I wouldn't normally have had with a woman. I felt powerful, immune from crushing defeat, sure that whatever I said and however I said it would be welcomed and enjoyed.

Liz looked down at her drink; she may have blushed. "I think so. It's easy to talk to you. You don't seem to have a problem being open about yourself. And you have enough sense to laugh at how absurd your life is right now. That's enough evidence for a harmonious relationship."

"So, where does the note come from? Does it come from the blood circulating in our systems or from our heart beat pumping it around, or from someplace else? Maybe from the thoughts we think? Or maybe it comes from a combination of all of it to produce these musical auras?"

"I think it's more spiritually speaking. Aura sounds good, though. It makes me wonder if we are the notes or maybe the instruments that make the notes possible. Like wind blowing across the top of a jar. Who is the performer then? And for whom is this human concert if we can't distinguish the symphony?"

I was astonished by these ideas. I reached across the table and squeezed her hand.

"You already have some ideas about that, don't you?"

People were crowded all around us and their voices were the orchestral pit warming up before the concert. Perhaps we were both a bit wary of our voices carrying to the next table. Neither of us were unaware of the peculiarity of our conversations. If there was one developing harmony in our friendship it was this shared love of the peculiar and the absurd; in our own versions of them. That we had stumbled upon each other and could give voice to such things was a miracle to me, but then I was eager to find such things wherever I could.

"Nothing I'd go on record about." She covered my hand with her own. It was warm and she smiled in that way she had: brazenly coy.

"Do you think it's God?" I said.

"You mean who the concert is for?"

"Sure. Or even if it's his spirit that's shared in common. Maybe the prevalence of him in us is what draws people together."

"Or its opposite."

"That is also a harmony, of sorts."

"It could be."

"But you're not convinced?"

"It's hard to be convinced about something like that. It's all theoretical, isn't it? I mean, there's no proof for any of it and I can't even remember where I heard that silly little thing about the C note."

"But I like that idea. It reminds me of something I'd heard all my life sitting in the hard pews of the Methodist church Dad took me to. I've heard it said that when we die, when our souls are finally released from these bodies, and we're finally able to do all we were created to do, the thing we'll do most is sing."

"About what exactly?"

"I guess about how great God is. Sing his praises, I guess. His goodness. The excellencies. That was the theme in church, but I don't know. But maybe we all get one shot to sing a dirge and lament our lives here and bemoan the shortness of it and how brutish it is, how nobody gave a damn and how we spent all our time trying to protect ourselves from each other and mistrusting our friends and families. Or maybe all of that will be forgotten in a flash and all we'll have is reality itself, truth itself, justice itself: God in all his goodness. If that's the case then perhaps, to go back to your idea, we are all individual notes in the supreme opus created by him, for him, about him."

"I can't go that far. It sounds wonderful I suppose, but then all of this," she motioned to the buzz surrounding our small table, "is some cosmic concert for a beam of light? A kind of entertainment for a callous deity?"

"Callous?"

"If one could find enjoyment in our pain and suffering, what else could you call it?"

"I think He delights in us, regardless of the songs we sing.
"Hmm."

She had meant for such characterization to be evidence about the futility of the playing, but I was convinced it weighted the scales in my favor.

"Maybe all of this is our rehearsal, then? Maybe we need all this time, thought, bitterness, joy, flailing, resting, smiling suffering loving and giving to perfect our one note; that one note that's ours and that we have to play in order to bring the piece He wrote to its ultimate perfection?"

"You've thought about this more than I have." Liz released my hand.

"Not at all. I'm only riffing on your theme." She was un-convinced. "The Scotch gives me a little oomph."

"We do get along, don't we?" she said.

"I think we can blame Plato."

"You really are struck by the philosopher's life."

"I don't know what else there is."

In the days that followed I read and wrote and walked. Liz and I saw each other often enough to be considered official.

She told me people don't say such things anymore, but I didn't care if my vocabulary for such things ever escaped the sixth grade. Evenings spent with her had the opposite affect of those with Roland. I was able to unburden myself of all I had been thinking about and puzzling over — except of course my precarious involvement with Roland — and she also took advantage of a sympathetic ear. We each expressed ourselves to the other, even laughing at our particular struggles to understand it all.

I received rejection letters from prestigious publishing companies and magazines for whom my stories and essays were not a good fit. It was always the same form letter relating the unfortunate circumstances of their rejection. I submitted to every writing contest I was aware of and had so many pieces out that I lost track of them and when I received notice that such-and-such hadn't won I struggled to remember which piece had been found wanting. In the end, they all were. Whatever thought I had about any topic, whatever curiosity and care I had about a building or a poem or a park bench, I followed through with pen and paper. There was nothing else to do but this.

Meanwhile, Felix suggested I re-work my failed profile about Eric's emerging role in the city. Since I was in the habit then of denying myself nothing in terms of subject and because Eric was amiable, I went.

When I arrived at his studio, Eric was outside waiting for me. He wore the same uniform I had seen him in earlier and his hair had grown longer, though he kept it tied back while he worked. It was down now and when he saw me approach beneath the linden trees, he smiled through the cold afternoon and waved me inside.

"Do you want something to eat or drink?"

"No. Thank you, though."

Eric slouched into the sofa's deep softness and sighed. I sat as straight as I could in the love seat.

"Felix said you wanted to flesh some things out."

"There are some things I wanted to explore further with you."

"I hope this one goes over better with the Powers That Be."

"You and me both."

"Felix seems to have confidence in you."

I tried to hear a note of encouragement in this, but whatever he may have meant I was already taking out my pen, ready to do good work.

"In both of us I think. Although in your case it's warranted."

"I don't mean to seem apprehensive, Joshua. It's good to have a benefactor like Felix. He's a good man, I think. I'm just getting too used to his promises, you know?"

I uncapped the pen.

"Shoot," he said.

"I want to ask you about something you said in passing the last time we met. You mentioned a chapter eight and I'm not sure what you meant by it."

"Chapter Eight is the culmination of all I'm searching for in my art, in what I want to represent on canvas with oils and inks and charcoal. It comes from a letter Paul wrote to the Romans. It starts with 'There is now no condemnation' — a wonderful way to begin — and this toward man from God through Jesus. It's freedom from Law; freedom from those church requirements of weekly and faithful attendance, the ten percent tithe, the prohibition on drinking and smoking and gambling and pre-marital sex and the even more stringent laws for church membership. The Law and its subsidiaries had finally become obsolete. What the prophets had been talking about for a thousand years had finally reached it fulfillment. The conscience of the congregation was free to express its relationship with God in new, revolutionary terms. But those men who rattled the chains and chanted just the right words looked into the theological ramifications of that freedom and found there's more to be feared from it than there is to embrace. Chapter Eight flips that around. It corrects it and views God as the deity we can call Abba, Father; the man racing out to embrace his prodigal son. Those Churches will only and ever call him "God" and they'll say it deep and soft, with the downcast eyes of guilty men, of condemned men, Joshua. Their self-imposed position is contrary to Paul's letter. And so their spirits are contrary to the Spirit and they walk accordingly, attempting righteousness through their own acts, and they fail accordingly."

"How is it that they fail exactly?"

"From their position as condemned men. We are only as successful as the place we begin in. As men trying to gain a pardon through working hard, keeping their noses clean, not getting into fights, being docile sheep. Meek, is the term they like to use. They see themselves on a spiritual plantation working for an Overseer afraid of the whip, rather than as sons who can sleep late, laugh at whatever suits them, slaughter fattened calves whenever the urge strikes, drink wine from the cup and hug their Father who loves them and who has declared nothing would hinder his children from coming near him. The difference in perspective is everything."

"In what ways did you discover the means to depict such things?"

"I paint as my spirit directs me. I spend every morning meditating on these things . . ."

"Upside down?"

Eric laughed. "Of course. I hang there, suspended, and remind myself of their truth and validity and of my impression that, one, the ideas are not universally accepted and two, they are not locally known. Nobody knows these things, Joshua. We can understand those not initiated in the doctrine of grace not knowing, but it's those people in the church who are ignorant of these things. So, in my own creative way I attempt to get grace and righteousness into the cultural conversation. God has a bad rap, but the God they're talking about is not the one I know. If that God everyone so confidently chides existed, I would be on the front lines beside them with my torch and pitchfork. But that God is simply one from their imagination, taken from obsolete scriptures."

"So your art attempts to introduce the viewer to a new understanding of God?"

"Art should be directed toward a new understanding if it wants to be effective. But I'm not claiming anything new. All my representations have been known for thousands of years, since 70 AD or CE, whichever moniker you like. The God that people have such a problem with did have a long reign, but that all ended when Jesus was put to the cross. Then a new covenant was revealed; through a torn veil and a resurrection we have new life. There is now no need for a mediator, no need for priests and hence, no need for the Law, which was never put in place to bring righteousness before God. It was meant to make us aware of sin and to bring Death, which is the culmination of our body's weakness, its futile energy to bring about anything good. Now, in Jesus we have direct access to God. There's no need for animal sacrifices or purification rituals; no need to go into exile for ten days after a wet dream, or to kill a dove because we forgot to wash our hands properly.

There is only the call to know Him, which may very well be the harder of the two."

I tried to find God in the dabs and smears and streaks of paint, the disjointed patterns, the cacophony of Eric's spiritual landscape.

"Of course we're accustomed to seeing Jesus in Western Art," he said. "He may be the most depicted man in our culture. The *pieta* has been done to death. After my European Tour — through the art books, mind you — I decided I wouldn't add my take to the genre. Mary's serene face, the fat little guy on her lap, the doe-eyed supplicants huddled around a pristine manger with chiseled angels playing harps . . . I got sick of that stuff early on. Who cares? Let Christmas go to the dogs. Give me Easter! So my pieces represent Christ after the cross and death. 'The glories that follow.' The excellencies. There is no limp body laid out on stone or draped, weak and ineffectual, in the apostle's arms. I want to bring the vibrancy of life back into a corpse."

I thought of the scaffolding erected outside the church beside Argo Tea and jotted down a note, an impression for a larger text. I got up to have a closer look at the canvases. They were like shoots of light streaked across the landscape of burgundy and orange; emergent buds on dripping wet boughs; illuminated corners enveloped by dark hallways.

"What are your impressions?" he said.

"I may not be too eager to know this Jesus."

"Why do you say that?"

"Because he may not be the man I think he is, which is an idealized version of myself; a man who has the same lifestyle and ideas and relationships with the world as I, in my mind, have. That I would meet him and find I don't like him and he doesn't like me. The same fear I have that other great men wouldn't find me worth their time to discuss questions with; that I would be a poor interlocutor."

"Do you think He would ask you to do something you couldn't or wouldn't do?"

"Probably. He's been known to make remarkable requests of men."

"What would that be, do you think?"

"I don't know. I don't know him well enough to venture a guess."

"What frightens you about Him? Whatever it is, you can be sure that it's not from God. Fear has no place in a correct knowledge of Him."

The conversation had quickly turned into a therapy session that reminded me of my Youth For Christ days on the farm. I felt like I was a kid being talked down to, as if I couldn't be expected to understand the realities of life and had to be convinced of childish things. And yet this was exactly the kind of thing I wanted to hear about and absorb: new ideas; new views of man's harrowing existence, a new take on the shortness and brutality of it; a building of light in which to endure the dark history. Still, it was hard to listen to Eric talk about Jesus and crosses and love in a sincere manner, outside church walls and between young men. That talk had always been reserved for the pulpit and the elderly. It was only with cynicism and anger that Jesus was mentioned on the streets and in the clubs and between the sheets. A candid reappraisal of that good man in this century, starting from the belief that He was who He said He was, was a curious thing.

"Rilke said that beauty is the beginning of terror. I don't know what that means for God, but I suspect that in understanding His beauty there comes a cost. A loss of something, as all beauty demands one thing or another from the beholder."

"Rightly so. I mentioned the excellencies before."

"Yes, what comes after the cross."

"What do remember that being?"

"The resurrection . . . "

"Of course."

"Pentecost."

"The descending of the Spirit in fired tongues. Yep."

"That's all I got."

"And the ascension."

"Right."

"Christ ascended to make room for the Spirit, who enables us to know Him, who convicts us of our righteousness. That's one of them. The other is a bit more esoteric. It comes in Ephesians. When Christ ascended He was seated at the right hand of God. That's in the first chapter, but in the second chapter we're given more insight into what this really means. Along with Christ, we also have been raised up in Him. And if we have been raised with Him, then God has also seated us with Him at His own right hand. Will God condemn Christ?"

"No."

"And if we are in Him, will He condemn us?"

"I shouldn't think so."

"There is now no condemnation. This is what the Spirit convicts us of. Excellent."

I moved away from the theological underpinnings of Eric's work to the nuts and bolts aspects: form and color, composition and the figures in space. He didn't give anything away; he responded to most of my questions with questions of me, which I did my best to answer. Whether these were in keeping with his aims I didn't know. He seemed quite content to let me defend my own analysis of his work.

When I had reread my notes and had nothing further to ask Eric suggested I take a closer look at Paul's letter, which I told him I would.

Those last days in October were alike in their make-up and I walked with greater frequency in the dark and cold and rain. City lights, once so crisp and clear, fought through the misting and downpours and diffused their illumination, blurring into each other and weakening their affects. In the puddles that collected beside the curbs and in the sheen upon the streets neon storefronts reflected their persuasive exclamations. The crowds that had gathered upon the bridges to watch the river's flow and marvel at the skyline had dwindled in the harsh climatic turn. I was often alone to traipse where I would and my thoughts were free to contemplate the landscape without the intrusions of pedestrians. Those moments of repose and silence were a great boon for me then. I had much to consider; many disparate themes had collided around me and within myself the justifications for keeping relationships and terminating the same, howled and swirled like Dante's condemned adulterers, ever-touching yet never consummating.

This was becoming Liz's complaint.

Indeed, I was softening toward her; I didn't hesitate to answer her calls or to propose certain excursions together. However, I didn't consider the sexual component of such a relationship. I had resolved to live a certain kind of life in Chicago and the prospect of further complicating it, of heaping further duties and responsibilities upon it, of detracting time from my pressing investigations in order to commiserate encourage and explain myself, made me recoil and chased me from my warm apartment and my phone's proximity to the canopies of leafless trees and the play of light upon soft bark. I didn't know my own mind fully, or else I lacked the confidence to pursue my ideal life; perhaps I was still taking applications for such a thing. Either way, I was unprepared to answer her when she called late one evening and our conversation led to,

"How do I fit into all that?"

Her voice was soft and a bit muffled, her words spoken with a care reserved for those conscious of how much they've drunk and attempting to circumvent their interlocutor's skepticism.

"The way we're getting along now."

"So we do get along then?"

"Quite well, I think."

I waited for her; I heard her sigh. I could see her brow furrowed, her nose squinting in exasperation at my contribution to this strange dialogue.

"Don't you think I'm pretty?"

"Of course I do."

"Do you even think about me?"

"Yes, of course. Much of the time."

"Much of the . . . "

"Every day, Liz."

"I shouldn't have called you. Just forget it. Forget I called. Forget everything."

Perhaps I should have called her back, but I decided to do as she asked. Then I took my hat and coat and ventured off into the dark and cold and wet.

Two nights later I still hadn't heard from her. I called and left a message. I called again and didn't. Another night and no word. I sent a text without avail. She had told me to forget and I grew sad thinking of what I had lost.

The next night my phone rang. I clamored after it, thinking it could only be one person, but when I answered

TIME SPENT AWAY

the voice on the other varied significantly from Liz's melodious tenor. At first I thought what I had heard was a joke. Roland was quite capable of such a grand jest. But then there was panic in his voice that even he could not have sustained. There was a short circuit somewhere that caused him to speak in dots and dashes so that he had to repeat the story, which I still couldn't decipher.

"It's Melanie," he finally blurted. "Those fuckers!"

I agreed to meet him at the hospital.

It was Halloween and the streets were bright with the aura of the fantastic. From every corner of Division and Rush came costumed ethereals, freaks and ghouls. It was a stage performance of a dream world where anything and anyone was possible. In my shocked state, numb and dulled to the city's debris and atmosphere, I sensed the fantastic event that had occurred just minutes and yards from my own time and space, like a half-forgotten dream. The half I remembered was being played out in front of me. The buildings were slanted and shortened and the curbs weren't where they should be. Realities were colliding and the fabric of the actual was being stretched. Grisly and abscessed faces wielding butcher knives, zombies and imps who squealed or yelped in striking jocularity, while the stuff of wet dreams paraded through the carnage flaunting the lace of garter belts, the taste of a hip's curve.

I waved at a taxi that had already stopped to let out a group of witches wearing matching black bustiers and boy shorts, leather boots to their knees. The last one out raised a dildo over my head and said, "bippity-boppity-boo".

I slammed the door on their laughter.

Inside the hospital was colored in bland softness that allowed the striking greenscapes to emit their therapeutic aid. The reception area was like that of a church apse. High

265

ceilinged and ornate due to the three stories of windows populated by still more plants and people waiting, praying, festering.
The information desk was like the altar, where we supplicants
softly spoke the names of those suffering; itself a prayer, a hope
that their names are written in some kind book in the end.
The illusion that this was such a place would have been perfect
had it not been for the aged men in hospital gowns shuffling
across the upper window's frames and those ladies breathing
oxygen from tanks and the few people exhausted from sorrow,
stoic and speaking without blood and in hushed tones on the
phone, to each other.

"I'm sorry sir. There's no one here with that name."

"Can you check again?"

"No. No one by the name of Charles. Are you sure she's
here?"

"Saint Joseph. This is where I was told to come."

"I'm sorry. I'm not showing anyone with that name who's
been admitted."

"My friend is here, though. This is where he is. He called me
thirty minutes ago. Check patients admitted within the last half
hour. Do you have a way to search by time rather than by name?"

"There is no one here with the name you're giving me."

I thanked the gentleman and walked through the lobby
area that stretched a hundred yards and had a multitude
of doors exiting and entering long hallways visible behind
panes of glass. Red and white lights burst from the walls an-
nouncing arrivals and departures of elevators whisking people
to the heavens, to the depths. Amid the rush and hesitancy,
I saw a man walking toward me with his hand raised. Our
eyes met and having performed his last duty of the long night,
he slumped into the nearest chair. Roland was pale; the color
had been drained of its vibrancy and even his limbs, once so

flamboyant, lethal and sure, were atrophied and hanging off him like an Irish leine. He seemed thinner and when he spoke his voice sounded as if it were coming from the large end of a megaphone, small and uncertain, lacking its usual mischief.

"What's happened?" I said.

"It's Melanie. Someone sliced her up bad tonight. Some goon out on the street hiding in the crowd."

"She was attacked?"

Roland struggled to vocalize what had happened. "She was stabbed." He looked at me for the first time to judge by my reaction if such a thing could be possible.

"Roland, that's terrible. Is she going to be all right?"

"The doctors think so. The knife missed her major arteries, although her left shoulder is badly hurt and she has lacerations on her hands and arms. They think it was quick, only three or four swipes before her screams sent him running."

"Where was this?"

"Near our home, I guess. She can't remember exactly. The cops said that was normal in such cases; because of shock, I guess? Melanie said she didn't even know she'd been . . . hurt. She only remembers a costumed man lunging at her and then fighting him off. Well, fighting isn't the word. Scrambling backwards, flailing her arms and screaming. Eyes closed, disbeliev-ing. It wasn't until she got home that she felt her wounds and noticed the blood. She called me and I cleaned her and our place up as best I could before the ambulance came. I was in a state, too. We were both in a panic. I could hardly remember 9-1-1; all I wanted was the fucker to still be hanging around so I could tear him up and spread him across the neighborhood. But I don't know who it was, or where to even begin looking. But he's out there, that sick son-of-a-bitch and I can't do anything about him."

Roland leaped off his chair and stalked the small, empty area in front of us. He raised his fists and considered striking a thick pillar beside him or tossing a chair through the window. I stood and comforted him as best I could. I put my hand on his shoulder; I told him she'd be all right, that the cops would find who did this. He sat back down again.

"Anyway, they're stitching her up. They want to keep her a few hours more. Maybe the rest of the night. She did lose a bit of blood."

"This is terrible. What do you need? Have you eaten?"

"I'm not hungry."

"Do you want me to call anyone for you?"

"No. I don't know why I called you. I guess I just didn't want to be alone tonight. The police may have more questions for me. I don't know. Melanie was pretty rattled and I don't think they're satisfied with her story."

I waited with Roland. We found a television and watched a basketball game. I had never seen him so inside himself. It was as if all the energy he projected upon the world — his smile, his jokes, his fragrant gestures had been sucked back inside him for purposes of self-preservation in order to survive this ordeal. Perhaps it was the energy that kept him from sobbing at the terrors at the door or raging out at the insidious carnival, seeking revenge on someone, anyone.

By the game's end, an officer had taken Roland to the police station to document his story with videotape and signatures. Maybe to confirm its validity with a polygraph. As calm as Roland was, I was sure he would be found speaking the truth. I asked if he wanted me to come with him, or if I should stay with Melanie.

"No, Joshua. Thank you."

"If you need anything . . ."

"I know, Joshua. Thanks."

So I was surprised to hear from him three hours later, talking fast and laughing as easily as if one of his brothers had just signed a Nike deal. When I asked what the police had told him, his smile nearly broke his cell phone.

"Nothing to worry about, Joshua. Nothing to worry about. Melanie is home with me now. She's resting and I'm cooking her some chicken and garden fresh vegetables . . . garden fresh, Joshua. It's November! And whatever this is . . . ?"

"I don't know, Roland. Can't really see it."

"What is this other stuff Mel? She says it's couscous. Some kind of pellety mush, but she likes it so what the hell? She's been a real saint through all this. I'm thrilled to have her back."

"You sound great, Roland, and if she's . . . "

"Yeah, yeah. No, she's fantastic. Listen. How fast can you get over here?"

"Over where?"

"My place. What are you, sleeping?"

"It's one in the morning."

"Shut-up. What do you have to do tomorrow? Lincoln Park on Clark and Arlington. I'll reimburse you. And bring wine."

Roland was waiting for me on the corner. He took the bottle from my hand and put his arm around me.

"Is this good stuff? We're celebrating tonight."

"The guy recommended it," I said.

"You should have brought a couple more then. Hey, let's invite Liz. You still seeing her?"

"Yes, but it's too late to call her now."

"Sure sure sure. I know. I'm busting, Joshua. She's still with me. She's still here. You have no idea. She's a princess. She really is and I ain't taking her for granted no more. She's up there right now."

"She's real fortunate, Roland. Do the cops have any leads or suspects or anything?"

"They don't have shit. And never will. The guy was all masked up. It's Halloween, man. What are they going to do, put out an APB on Bozo the Clown? They'd have to arrest a thousand jackasses tonight."

"So what did you tell them?"

"They wanted to know where I was, what I'd been doing all night; if I knew anyone that might want to be threatening me with this. They said if someone had wanted to kill Melanie they would have and they reasoned that whoever did this didn't want her dead and further reasoned it must be a threat. Something left half-done so I'd know how easy it would be to do it all the way next time."

"Is there someone you know who would do that?"

"Hell, Joshua, maybe. Sure; but I'm not into anything that serious now. I've got my interests, but nothing worth killing her or me for. I told them it was just a Halloween whack-job who'd seen too many movies this week, took some bad drugs and tried to go Michael Myers on a girl. Give me that bottle."

He twisted the cap.

"I'll never get used to these cork-less things," he said taking a long drink.

"It tastes like asparagus. It's good."

He passed it to me. I swallowed the wine and agreed.

"Wet earth, too."

Roland took another kiss from the bottle, long and passionate. "I don't get the wet part."

I laughed at his smile, but it soon turned thoughtful. He pointed the bottle to the sidewalk.

"This is where she was attacked."

"Right here?"

"This is where it happened."

We were silent. It was an unconvincing spot: plain, pedestrian, not a setting for horrors. Trash had collected around the trees and gated walkways. Potholes and cars lined the street. It was like any stretch of any street in any city in America. Now it had tragedy. But Oedipus kills his father on a lonely road and *Equis* takes place in a routine stable.

"He was walking toward Melanie. From this direction. He held the knife behind his back and when he neared her, he stuck it into her shoulder. She fell against this fence and he struck out a few more times, cutting her across the arms and hands. Right here, Joshua. Right here."

Neither of us could bring ourselves to believe it. It couldn't happen to someone he knew so well.

"Terrible," I said.

"It is. But now I have wine and a good friend. My girl;s upstairs with a healthy pulse. Obviously, she's still rattled. She's going to have nightmares of that man for the rest of her life, possibly. Probably she won't want to go out for a while. She'll even flinch when she meets people, maybe cathartically." He paused and thought about this. "But that man isn't here anymore. Only this man and I got my shit together here."

He lifted the bottle at me and drank.

Their apartment was full with the smell of a fresh meal. A card table with worn edges was set for dinner. Roland took my jacket and brought out a third folding chair. A television filled one corner and a couch sat against the opposite wall. A recliner was pushed away to make room for the table, which Roland must tear down after every meal. Or else they eat on the couch most nights. Frameless posters were tacked to the wall: Jordan in '88, Monet's water lilies. The kitchen was off the living room, concealed from the rest of the one bedroom design. Roland told me to get comfortable and went to Melanie, who was long in coming despite Roland's soft calling. She was visibly shaken, and I could see bandages on her hands and forearms despite the extra-large sweatshirt. I stood to introduce myself.

"I'm so sorry for what happened," I said.

"It wasn't your fault, was it? Did you bring that bottle?"

Before I could answer she had taken it from me. I wondered about the drugs she was on, if the wine would throw her equilibrium off further.

"Joshua and I had a drink outside."

"Figures." Melanie wiped off the lip and had a drink.

I credited the silence and the clumsy way we occupied the room to the shock of it all.

I pointed to the water lilies and said, "Have you been to the Art Institute to see them?" Melanie wasn't listening. "I just saw them last week. Impressionism was a terrific revolution. Even people who don't like art know about Impressionism. It's funny that a group of men interested in prostitutes, light, and adolescent dancers could carry so much cultural weight one hundred and fifty years later. And yet no one knows who Whistler is."

"Who's ready to eat?" said Roland.

Melanie sat down and Roland put a large pot on the card table and spooned out portions.

"I know who Whistler is," said Roland. "He's the guy I hear from across the street when Mel and I are out for a walk."

I smiled at his effort, but Melanie was oblivious.

"Isn't that right, sweetheart? You should eat something."

Melanie stared at her plate while Roland and I talked about nothing in particular. When she'd finished staring at the meal she left her full plate and disappeared into the bedroom and closed the door.

"I'm sorry for the oddness of the evening," said Roland.

"Don't be ridiculous."

"I thought the wine might have loosened her up. I hate to see her so quiet. You should have seen her before all this. I was afraid of her sometimes. Swear to God. She'll get going about something and if I'm not giving her my whole attention she'll let me have it. Like you sometimes, on and on about whatever she was into just then. Quite the spitfire in a tight little package. I was hers instantly. She can put me in my place, you know?"

He poured another glass for me and then finished the bottle. I thought it couldn't have gone to better use.

"She doesn't want to be with me right now, though. I got the couch indefinitely. She's going to keep the bedroom door locked; keeping a loaded gun on the nightstand next to her. Asked me to load it for her. Now she wants to board up the window, but I told her that criminals wouldn't climb to the second floor on the street-side of a building. I took her outside and showed her it was physically impossible. So she made me move the bed and we put a lamp in front of the window. It's always on now."

"She wouldn't feel safer with you?"

"You would think so, but no. She doesn't trust anyone at the moment."

"It'll be fresh for a while, I imagine. Thank God there isn't more sorrow here. Things could have gone very bad."

"I'm lucky, aren't I?" said Roland.

"Very lucky."

"Yea."

Roland wiped his eyes and I thought how sensitivity takes great pains to conceal itself. I loved my friend. It may have occurred at that moment. It could have been lying dormant for some time, unsure if there was anything else to this man other than shady business deals and an aggressive hunger for life. But with the concern for Melanie and the tears shed in sympathy for the terror she surely felt in that moment, I saw a man able to converse with the deeper needs of his soul.

Roland was sullen and somber, sitting in a fragile folding chair with his hands on his knees staring through the table and Melanie's untouched plate.

"Is there any way you can find out who did this? Anyone you know who can ask around for you?"

"Not first hand." He was thinking about something else, another aspect of the crime, perhaps. Maybe he was going over what he had told the police in case he may have forgotten something vital. Maybe he was wondering what Melanie had told them and how their oral testimonies of the evening may have differed; what she could have told them that would bring the matter to a swift conclusion. Roland was far away from the living room and I stood up to go.

"I'm here for you and Melanie if you need me, Roland."

"It's not going to be easy for us, Joshua. Making it, I mean. I don't see how we can."

"It's only just happened. Of course it will take time, but you guys will be all right. Right?"

Roland didn't move his gaze from the table. His hands looked like wax resting on his brown slacks. They looked like the smell of carnations.

It was too late to call Liz.

The stars were obscured behind winter clouds that sauntered over the lake. Through the naked boughs, the disjointed transparency of the heavenly filament sparkled, and I dialed her number.

Dan Goodwin had climbed John Hancock Tower almost twenty-nine years ago to the day. Disguised as Spider-Man, he had to avoid firemen repelling toward him on a win-dow-washing plank. He suffered their attempts to knock him off with high pressure water; he maneuvered past grappling hooks attached to poles; the firemen had even broken win-dows to reach him, the shattered glass plummeting earthward, spraying the sidewalk with specks and slivers of the pane. Having failed to swat the public nuisance, the mayor conceded the ascent. It was done, Goodwin had said, to demonstrate the fire department's inability to rescue people from a burning high-rise. Rescue? They couldn't even destroy Goodwin! And that's the simpler of the two.

I thought of Goodwin looking for a foothold upon the sheer glass and in the November frost. I looked out my window to the Tower and wondered at his struggled and strain to reach the top, fighting his muscles and the civil servants. I wonder if they were kind or if they cursed him out as they fired their water cannons and blasted out heavy sheets of glass. It's dif-ficult for such actions to be accompanied by pleasant speech offered in sincerity. And all he wanted was to do something marvelous. I imagine there are few shadows one hundred sto-ries high, but man is not permitted to live in the Himalayan zone. At least not on that side of the glass.

I poured a cup of coffee and sat down with a book in the pre-dawn. I thought about Liz, who had been reading Pascal, a mathematician and philosopher that her father had enjoyed during his college days. I wanted her to know that I was able to live quietly in my own room, too. I was theorizing, I had told her, but wouldn't know if any of the things I thought were true until I had stubbed my toe on the city streets or been hit by a bus. Maybe the proof of truth comes from the wet end of a fire hose, I said. Goodwin, civil rights, Palestinians breaching the sand walls of Israeli defenses. But more than that I wanted to see her, to hold her, to test the reliability of the foothold I was beginning to have with her. I hoped I was the same for her — her father admired a theorist, after all — and that I wasn't just a man off whom she repelled or used to swing to the next one.

I had met Liz for dinner and gallery tours and walks by the river and through downtown bookstores and retail clothiers. We took day trips to Evanston and Hyde Park. We caught a few lectures and had a few drinks. Through it all, I managed to stay in my apartment some, keeping pen to the page. Soon I had a passable critique of Eric's Resurrection Art. I showed it to Felix who returned it a few days later with comments. He didn't return it the second time, but called to tell me he had given it to an editor who was interested in publishing it. I was excited and Felix shook my hand when we met for a late dinner of tapas and Rioja on Ohio Street. He kissed Liz's hand with a flourish I had not seen from him. As optimistic as I was about what this publication might mean as a proof for the decision I had made, Felix was more so. His hope came from the fact that he had discovered Eric; that he had seen the evidence of his great talent in the amateurish prints and collages of the young artist before anyone else. The same talent Felix had of remembering the glory of Chicago's architectural wonders and bringing that remembrance to the community in an effort to preserve the memory had been coupled with a second sight in the other direction. From the purging mish-mash of enthusiastic streaks of paint, Felix was able to see, in this case, the prospect of an artist, of a man with a unique vision of the world and the means to create that vision in a culturally relevant way. That the other residents of Felix's community hadn't yet created anything to hold the city's attention, or that they spent most of their time smoking in the courtyard and arguing about abstraction and the relative mediocrity of the current schools, didn't deter Felix from telling Liz and I what a person has to have, and what he had presumably seen in all of them, before he or she becomes an artist.

"Vision, of course. That goes without saying. He has a wonder about everything that surrounds him. Nothing is left off his palette. As various as a box of crayons, as many colors that mingle in the arch of a rainbow, are the opportunities afforded to an artist with vision and wonder. But with these two qualities the young artist must have a firm lack of self. He must understand that his vision is not his own, but was given to him. Whether that be from his upbringing or the effect of the sun upon his skin, how he endures the night, or what he truly thinks of human nature. If this vision, given by other forces, is correct, then it is always correct and rather than read into objects for evidence of his vision, every object will contain that vision and needs only the artist's confidence to bring it out. It was this assurance that I caught in Eric's canvases when I interviewed him for the space."

I said that sounded right and Liz nodded and picked at the remaining *banderillas*, moving around the olives and red peppers, regretting the last bit of *gambas al ajillo*.

Felix raised his glass of sherry. "And we have placed him upon the altar of the city."

I drank to that, but was at a loss for what he meant by such a martyred image. However, the concerns brought on by our strange presentation were steadily dulled by euphoria and the dark blood swirling in my glass and clinging to the sides, the easy laughter coming from Felix's side of the table, and the excitement emanating from Liz's eyes, given voice through her exclamations and congratulations. It was good to celebrate and to be celebrated, and I became drunk on hope and wine and love.

Outside a sharp wind blew snow between the buildings and unheeded down the boulevard. Liz and I huddled together as we walked. I hailed a cab and we all climbed in.

"Let me take you both to my place for a night cap," said Felix. "I have some things that might interest to you, Joshua."

"What kinds of things?" I looked at Liz to make sure she was okay with another stop.

"Things you could never guess," said Felix.

Liz was blowing on to her gloved hands and shivering. Despite the weather there was an aura of whimsy in the cab and the sense that, like a summer night releasing its abundant fragrances, we were a rare company that would benefit from staying out late.

It was a short drive to the Newberry Plaza Condominiums, where Felix lived on the 17th floor. The building's concierge gave him a package that he casually put under his arm. Liz was clearly impressed by the elevator, by the luxury of its materials, its smoothness and silence, and the way Felix, who picked at the box's packing tape, took such opulence as a matter of course. She told me later that she had never thought of Versailles as seeming mundane to its occupants until that moment.

"By way of preamble to the evening," said Felix, who stood fixedly by the light switch, keeping us in the dark, "have you ever looked closely at the Tribune Tower? Not just glanced at it as you rushed by. Have you noticed more than the statue of Nathan Hale? There are stones embedded into the façade that have no right to be there." Felix smiled and put his hand on the switch. "Keep that in mind."

At Felix's insistence, Liz and I walked down the dark hallway that opened into a large space bathed in blue light. The entire east wall was made of glass and the vivacious city winked and glinted in the cold stillness. Below us was the park and on our left we could see where State and Rush became one. We watched the cars jammed up outside Gibson's and Hugo's, circling the Triangle, looking for space or opportunity. Big John dominated the left side and beyond the last light was the dark expanse of Lake Michigan stretching toward Grand Haven, rushing toward its lighthouse atop the substantial pier of green lights, washing upon its shore in the monstrous rhythm of eternal patience.

I held Liz's hand and we looked.

Then a sudden light vaporized the cityscape and only our reflections shone in the glass. We were a kind of American Gothic.

I turned toward Felix's interior. There was not a barren spot on the wall. Every square inch was covered in original art work, framed or situated on pedestals. He was a master of coordinating space to fit such a disparity of rectangles and squares, of colors and forms, portraiture and landscape and the grotesque, in a way that didn't disorient a first-time viewer. It was like a Parisian salon. The floors were cluttered with sculptures and totems. Some were being used as end tables that supported early twentieth century lamps. Globes and chess tables, glassware and plates, carpets and fabrics; empty ornate frames worth the price of a mid-size hybrid, Japanese prints and old papyrus scrolls; swords and shields and urns leaned against each other in an amiable family reunion.

"Where did you get all of this?" said Liz, looking at a faded water color.

"It's all around us if you know where to look. Mostly estate sales. Bazaars overseas. It sounds cliché now, but I actually found this Matisse at a garage sale in Lakeview. I paid fifty dollars for it. It's worth a bit more than that, of course. I told the seller I liked the artist's palette. He shrugged and took my money."

"But you knew what it was worth?" said Liz.

"I had a good idea. And if it was a knock-off, I was only out fifty bucks."

"But you knew it wasn't."

"Of course."

"How many works of art have you acquired like that?"

"Most of them. If those people I bought from don't sell them, they wind up in a junk heap or worse. Come over here." Felix moved a number of canvases away from the wall. "Do you know what this is?"

"No." Liz wasn't looking at the object, but at Felix. I was suddenly annoyed by her thinking of preservation in terms of fairness when the loss of such works, if they were destroyed by ignorant owners, would be a detriment to future genera-tions, to our own cultural understanding, to the knowledge of ourselves as a species. It was the first time I had seen her stern judgment in the face of the world and seeing her frown at Felix, who, for his part, was feeling strong in his power to captivate a young woman with the validity of his pursuits, was unaware of the daggers coming from her eyes.

"What does it look like to you?"

"I don't know. A block of cement."

"But nothing too original or worthwhile?"

"Not really. Although I suppose it is since it's in your house."

"If it were yours what would you do with it?"

"Is it art?"

Felix shrugged.

"I would have it appraised then."

"You would spend a couple hundred dollars to have someone tell you that you have a piece of plaster from the inte-rior of a 1970s era building that holds no value, except maybe of the sentimental kind and to a man who has no reservations about filling his home with dusty old junk."

"It's worthless?"

"Absolutely. But you couldn't have known that unless you spent a good amount of money. Now what about this one?"

Felix pointed to a rough-edged chunk of rock. There were books piled on top of it and a heap of faded newspaper beneath it to keep the edges from burrowing into the smooth oak floor.

"I don't know," said Liz.

"I'll give you fifty bucks for it." he said.

"What is it?" said Liz.

Felix smirked and knelt beside the stone, rubbing it, thinking about it, waiting.

"Fine," she said. "Fifty bucks. What's your point?"

"It's a deal." He stood up with some difficulty, hands on his quads, straightening slowly. It was the first time I saw age in him. "I found this at an estate sale in a little town south of Florence, Italy. I gave the gentleman seventy-five Euros. He took it with gusto and I shipped it back here for five hundred dollars."

"What is it?" Despite herself, Liz was getting curious.

Felix paused for effect. "This is a piece of façade from a Roman temple. I approximate circa 280 BC. That's just after Alexander the Great was killed thousands of miles from home. Tragic for him, but a blessing for us today. It's illegal to own a piece like this, I'm sure. It should be in a museum."

"How much could you get for it?"

"Nothing. It's priceless. Quite literally, I'm afraid. But it's no different from any number of fragments I have, including that piece from the seventies, depending on your ideas of time. On the eternal time line, Chicago is no different from Rome. But what if you could separate yourself from each city equally? Great landmarks have been razed here, too. Works by the founders of the Chicago School, who poured all their theories and spirit into the masonry and ornamentation, have been reduced to rubble. Wouldn't that rubble, those fragments of *art nouveau* vitalized by Sullivan's fingers, be worth as much as a cornice from the Coliseum?"

"You mean priceless?" said Liz, skeptical.

"Exactly. Taken from that view, I shouldn't have half the objects I do. Taken from that view, we should not be destroying our heritage to construct more landmarks that we will then destroy in thirty years."

Liz moved around the apartment with more care and thought, but with less enthusiasm than when she first entered. I could see her wandering about the stones, the rusted daggers and scraps of salvaged metals, the African idols and small obelisks. Even the rugs on which she stood could have been culled from the palaces of Persia, tread upon by Xerxes himself, or Darius; they were possibly brought back by Xenophon from his retreat to the sea. Probably not. But the presence of these objects made all fantasies possible. The objects themselves stood mute and satisfied in themselves, yet words and voices, the clash of metal and cries of despair and ecstasy surrounded them. The aura of the objects filled the room with heaviness. It was now a sacred space and I wanted to take my shoes off.

Despite Liz's moral objection toward the way Felix obtained these objects, she was just as enthralled as I was. She hesitated before statuettes; any wooden, metal, or plastic item she came across would cause her to look at Felix's benevolent nod before touching it, lifting it from its constraints, like an aunt with her infant niece, to indulge in a form of time travel or wish fulfillment. Each piece was silent and indifferent to the brief thoughts a mere mortal had about it; they were ambivalent toward the dreams we nurtured about their origins, purposes and meanings.

"That's just an ashtray from a Mexican restaurant in Greece," said Felix to Liz's raised eyebrows. "I stole it for its sheer absurdity. If it were a Warhol, maybe its mass produced quality would have some value. Or a Duchamp. As it is, its significance comes from how it received its individual markings and chips rather than itself. See that potted plant in the corner. The stones in the soil came from the Acropolis. I bent down to tie my shoes ten or fifteen times and some gravel bits got into the cuff of my pants."

The strangeness I felt in Felix's apartment was akin to that of standing on the Thames trying to grasp the enormous significance of the London Tower while trying to ignore City Hall on the opposite bank, then trying to reconcile the time that lay between their erections and the heavy-handedness of the Thames flowing listlessly by. Liz held an ancient stone in her hand; she smoothed the contours of its rough shape and thought of the thousands of miles it had traveled to be here, thousands of years removed from its birth, millions even, while outside the window, seventeen stories above Chicago, with a view of similar dimensions to the ancient temple site, thousands of lights sprinkled the air beneath our feet before giving way to the perpetual lake.

"These would have to be illegal here," said Liz.

"They're just stones, officer," said Felix in mock protest. He was right. Who could possibly convict him? Who would care to bring a case against him?

Liz smiled and knelt to replace the stones in the fern's pot. She wiped her hands together and scanned the living room. "It's all a bit much, isn't it?" she said and sat on the couch.

"I think so," said Felix. I couldn't tell if he was happy with all the paintings and sculptures speaking to him all day and night, or if his sighing signified an acceptance of his fate to be surrounded by these artifacts. I imagined it had to be both ways. A reward and punishment: the rub of the blessing.

"Do you think Pascal could have imagined a room like this?" I asked Liz.

"He would have had to change his theology," she said and rubbed her eyes.

I continued to look around Felix's apartment. When I was halfway down the narrow hallway that led to the front door, I stopped in front of a peculiar piece. Framed waist high was a charcoal print of a resurrection. It was not the Christ's; nor did it represent Lazarus' emergence from the grave and the stripping of those incumbent clothes. In fact, there was not a resurrected body in the entire composition. Instead, there was sorrow and lamenting. The faces of the mourners were like masks, eyes closed and mouths open in silent sobs. A downcast woman tended to the corpse's feet, another rested the dead man's head on her lap. The light behind the Christ-figure was like a halo, but was merely an erased cloud, as if the light were able to eradicate nature. And the most significant eradication of nature would be death. The print anticipated that.

I asked Felix about the artist. He told me the man had painted murals for the Works Progress Administration, contracted tuberculosis, and died in Colorado. He didn't know where the sketch had originated, only that he had found it at yet another estate sale. There were getting to be a lot of these kinds of sales and began to wonder if Felix didn't have a bit of Roland in him.

"It might be worth six-hundred. He was known during his lifetime."

"Do you think this guy will be brought back to life?"

"According to the Biblical records, Jesus had that power. Common sense and human experience tend to disagree with that ancient account, though. There's a lot of doubt in this work. And really, what does it matter? Do good to your neighbor — what do we need miracles for?"

"Maybe that is the miracle," I said. "Maybe selflessness is part of the divine spark. Acknowledging the needs of others. I read somewhere that that's the beginning of mature love. If Jesus was divine, then wouldn't this be the ultimate love: to take seriously the sorrows and joys of mortals? Too often we hear about Noah's flood, but we never advance through the years to see how our world was preserved. How we are preserved in it."

"How is that?"

"Possibly through that divine spark. Have you read Wilde? *The Picture of Dorian Gray*? The ugliness of his life was manifested on the painted face; and then the actual destruction of his body represented his invisible spirit. Maybe we're preserved in the same way; through the divine spark of selflessness."

"You've been talking to Eric."

"Of course."

"You left that idea out of your essay."

"Yes, well . . . That idea didn't seem likely to find a soft reception. Somehow it does seem childish to put in print and I'd like my first published piece to be taken seriously."

"Well, good luck to you. Doubt and pessimism are the dominant indicators of sensibility today. The rest is naïveté and juvenilia. And we are too far along as a species to venture back to our primitive ways."

"But then who, if not our artists, will look behind the veil of accepted opinions and remind us of what could be?"

My father would be able to tell me. After the clots had starved his heart of blood and he had fallen into the chicken dirt, life continued. While his body lay still in the filth, his neighbor's were with their wives and children. While they ate and talked about their days my father was looking into the face of Eternity. While men squabbled over the bill at the Dutch Kettle, my father's spirit had entered eternal preservation. Mr. Weurtzel had found Dad, and in the painting, I saw him cradling my father's head in his lap, lifting it out of the offal and cleaning it off, checking for a pulse, perhaps crying for the loss he would be made more aware of later, after the shock had passed, and then the rest of his life. Through the silent ambulance ride to the morgue, Dad would have known what was infinite and what was rational. He would have been experiencing for the first time in life the existence of his spirit without its body. Freedom and the exquisite release from its concerns. Perhaps Dad even saw Mr. Weurtzel cradling him? Maybe Dad had laughed and howled, in fear and in joy, and shot across the fields and lakes in his exuberance, returning to the chicken coop full of life and wonder, trying to explain to his weeping friend how foolish he looked hunched over the least consequential matter in the universe! How easy it would be then to leave, to get away; faster than light, even . . . as quick as thought. How long at such speeds until the entirety of space is known? Dad may know. How long would he have spent within the Orion Nebula, dispersed among the dust and ash of forming stars had he wondered at seeing his late body's material used for such glorious purposes? Had he somersaulted down the Horsehead Nebula? or climbed the Mystic Mountain, dodging, as though it were necessary, the blasts of radiation carried along by streams of charged particles? And even in the empty nothing were marvels lurking, wonders to be seen? Had he found hidden glories in death?

I like to think he has. Such thoughts send me peacefully into sleep.

I took Liz by the hand and raised her off Felix's couch. She yawned and we said our good-byes. We marched through the park, holding hands and talking about all we'd just seen, our teeth chattering and our shoulders rolling with the wind. I led her away from the late dinner crowds toward my apartment. She let me lead her into my elevator and I kissed her. My throat was dry and we became quiet, holding hands and listening to the rumble of gears.

After, I held Liz in my arms and watched the snow swirling outside my windows.

"Is that all?" she said.

"Isn't that enough?"

"Yes."

Later:

"I'm sorry there wasn't more," I said.

"I didn't say there should be."

"That's as much as I've ever allowed myself."

"It was wonderful."

"We won't regret it."

"No."

Then:

"Was it really alright?"

"You can do that whenever you want."

"I want to," I said.

In the morning we took an early breakfast at the Corner Bakery. My head felt heavy, but the air was light and clean, like a saline flush or a dive into the lake after a long run, and I thought I'd be on the mend shortly. The heavy smell of the city at night had been driven from the avenues by the prairie wind and deposited over the lake. Liz walked beside me and

I thought about how close we had been last night. I could tell Liz was disappointed, even agitated; she'd gone into the bathroom upon waking and I didn't hear or see her for twenty minutes. I was feeling sheepish that I had indulged in that aspect of our relationship. I was not used to such evenings and when I realized what we'd begun I became inhibited. Such fear and trembling had never descended upon me in such fury as it had then. I was not reduced to a tightly cowering ball rolling around on the floor; I still had the wherewithal to speak and move my limbs as I desired, but I did not have full control over other aspects of my anatomy. I shrank from the too-great mystery; I recoiled from the enormous responsibilities I perceived lurking in tomorrow's shadows. I was too afraid of the one great thing and rather than finish what we'd started I made a declaration.

Liz had guessed my inexperience soon after we started. Perhaps my hesitancy, my lingering foreplay and the unfamiliarity I showed regarding the female body told her all she needed to know about my neophyte status. Perhaps she had been used to a more straight-forward man, a man determined to get to the point, no turning aside, not stalling to articulate the spiritual components hidden within the physical acts. The last was a tactic I used to hide the fact I was too scared to perform.

I told her that I intended to keep it for a while longer, and we agreed that my peculiar desire shouldn't bring our pleasant evening to an end. Perhaps I wanted to keep that knowledge far from the actual, to leave it, undisturbed, in the aesthetic realm. I had many more texts to read on the matter. Besides, I had heard the ribald talk and I wanted to preserve the mystery just a bit longer.

"I think it's sweet," she had said. "I'm a little jealous that you still get to have a first time."

It was exactly what I needed to hear and I loved her for it, but sitting inside the bakery, as we made small talk, careful and light, in the fresh light of morning, I wondered just what she thought of me. Of course, I couldn't just ask her; her downcast eyes and eerie stillness were all the cues I needed to keep to such questions to myself. The pigeons were coming around, bobbing their heads and cooing, looking for crumbs. Brilliant burgundy breasts and emerald necks, orange eyes that hinted toward the maniacal. I asked if Liz would like to take a slow walk through the city and see Sullivan's theater.

"I need to get home, actually," she said. "I'll see it when we go."

"That's a week away. Can you stand not seeing it that long?"

"I'll manage."

I tucked my feet under the chair and watched the pigeons.

"What are you going to do today?"

"I have to do laundry and clean up a bit. My parents are having a dinner party and I told them I would help set up. Just a lot of errands to run for that."

"Can I help you then?"

"No. It's nothing I can't manage; just time consuming."

"I can run a vacuum. I can put salt on the drive. I have a lot of indispensable skills."

I didn't know if I wanted to be with her or if being alone was what I most needed.

Liz shook her head.

"You're sure? I could talk about T.S. Eliot's objective correlative while I clean your blinds."

Liz finished the last of her bagel and wiped the cream cheese from her mouth. I sat twisting my napkin, trying to seem natural, but she was distant, cold even. I was anxious to know just what it all meant, but she wasn't indicating any desire to tell me. Perhaps she didn't know, either. At the time,

I didn't give this possibility any thought; it never occurred to me that she could be confused by it all as well. But then I've always felt most comfortable as the student.

I gathered up Liz's trash and disposed of it.

On the curb Liz hugged me. She told me she'd walk toward Michigan Avenue and find a cab home.

"Okay."

"You look so sad," Liz said, pouting.

"No, it's just . . . I just thought I'd be with you today."

"I told you I have things to do."

"I know." Liz looked up at me and smiled faintly. I moved to kiss her, but she turned and I brushed her cheek instead.

I watched her hurry away. I decided it was to get out of the cold sooner, rather than away from me. Grey clouds had descended upon the city and the sky scrapers had to hunch their shoulders so as not to pierce the atmosphere. I spent the rest of the day walking the streets, absently venturing into shops and riding escalators, sitting on benches to watch the human activity of a Saturday afternoon. By evening, despite my messages, I still hadn't heard from Liz. I had dinner at PJ Clark's and watched a football game. Maybe the vacuum had been too loud for her to hear my ringing? Maybe she had washed her phone by mistake? I thought about her body, her soft skin and warm hair and how she moved and smelled, and I wished I'd had more experiences so that she would think kindly of me as well.

But then, I was being ridiculous. She called around ten that evening and we talked until eleven. I asked her about the dinner party, but she wanted to hear about Eliot.

I was spending more time with Liz. She had taken two weeks off to celebrate the holiday and we began a bought of leisure together. Because of this new complication, I was free to neglect Roland. I felt he would understand how a woman can make a man forgo all his usual habits and procedures for the sake of her voice, her skin and the soft flow of her hips, the strange turns of her mind that took me by surprise. I needed all my energy to understand her and what was left behind I considered useless. I forgot about my solitary walks and dinners alone; I forgot those electric evenings in my chair or at a coffee house reading the poets and essays, drinking at the bars and making small talk with bartenders before the evening rush for a more dynamic charge.

Seeing *La Boheme* proved memorable. The set was wonderful and the singing was the best I'd ever heard. Liz wiped her eyes and leaned against my shoulder when Rodolpho held his dying beloved in his arms. The anguish with which he bellowed Mimi's name, the love and despair, kept us in silence as we watched the crowd in the low-ceilinged foyer of Sullivan's Auditorium Building. After the show we had drinks at Carmine's, then walked to my place.

Upstairs, in my bed, I was overwhelmed with her yet again. Though our relationship was never, in the modern tradition, consummated, I was breathless with her. Perhaps it was because I didn't know what I was missing that I felt this way. It all seemed so momentous; holding her, listening to her talk; watching her eyes close and open with a slow voluptuousness. How could I possibly take anymore?

"Is that all we're ever going to do?" said Liz. Her head was on my chest and I was holding her.

"What do you mean? It's all I can do to keep myself coherent with you now. Any more and I would go crazy."

"It's fine that you're getting what you want, then. We'll just continue keeping you happy."

"Liz, what's wrong?"

"You make me bad."

"How?"

"Because I want more than just . . . "

"Just what?"

"Are you really so dumb, Joshua? Do you really not understand what I'm asking? You take me out and we talk and we laugh and then you take me to the opera and hope I'll have a powerful experience and when I do and I want to express those things with you here you lie there with a dumb look on your face, like you didn't know what's happening. And I feel like I'm taking advantage of a boy."

"Does that matter so much?"

"My God, Joshua. Where do you live? Are you here with me or are you stuck in some backwards ideas of, I don't know what? Joshua, I don't know what this is."

"Is all this about . . . ?"

"Of course it is. Do you even want to, with me I mean? Am I not pretty enough for you? Are you gay? I mean, if you don't want to be with me that's fine, but I need to know what you're doing.."

She was crying now, not like how she teared up and rested on my shoulder in the soft seats of Sullivan's Auditorium when Mimi died or how she pressed soft against me as we stood looking at the lights reflected in the Chicago River, but from frustration. I didn't know how I could possibly answer her question. Why wouldn't I make love with her? What could possibly be the reason? I hadn't wanted to complicate my life; to add burdens to an already heavy load. It seemed foolish to say that I wanted to keep my life free in case I should happen to be a writer of any gifts at all; that I believed I would resent her if she took time away from that purpose, that if I didn't achieve what I believed I could I would blame these very nights for keeping me from my desk. Even that would be scoffed at; Liz could count any number of writers, all of them found on my shelves, for whom sex was a profitable Muse.

"You should be excited, Joshua. There's a woman in your bed, throwing herself at you and God only knows what you're thinking. It's not that complicated." She crossed her arms over her breasts and stared at the ceiling.

"But it is. I don't want to have that experience yet. I don't know what will happen to me if I do."

She turned toward me. "What do you think will happen?"

"Maybe nothing good."

"Tell me."

I wanted to take issue with this line. Whatever instincts I had screamed at me to preserve my self. But that wasn't fair to her, or me. I'd waxed enthusiastic over inconsequential matters and now, when such explanations were truly warranted, was I going to demur? In order to come out with it I opened wide the valve.

"What if sex is my sleeping dragon? If I poke it and enflame it and arouse it, it will know that it's been hungry for a long time. And once it's awake, what if all it wants to do is eat? What if I lose all my peace and comfort for the sake of that one appetite? What if I decide that the woman I'm with isn't enough and I need to make up for lost time, that I want two at a time, that I want some from every walk of life and every corner of the earth? Where will my searches for a good lay end? How many women is enough? 'The eye never has enough of seeing or the ear of hearing', Liz. When will the mad monster be satisfied? I'm not strong enough to keep the lake at bay if I know how pleasurable the swim is.

"And what if it's not? What if it's as manageable as a bottle of wine? What if you're giving too much power to it? You're like the child who refuses to play on the jungle gym because then the slide won't be as fun, or because you'll be sad at home with only a tire swing."

"Those aren't legitimate reasons?"

"No. They're all just theories you have about yourself."

"And don't I know myself."

"Maybe not. You're a man, too. Men do this every day. They're constantly looking for women; they spend every waking moment they have trying to get a woman to consent to going home with them. And look, here I am. What more do I have to do?"

"How can it be both the immeasurable experience I think it is and a mundane act on par with drinking or eating? I hardly expect myself to be good for anything for days after being with you as it is."

"It is both, Joshua. Of course it is."

"Then why should I desire to grab hold of it so much? I'd much rather spend time with you doing these other things. It's been wonderful, Liz. But you see how much this is tearing me up just talking about it. I can't trust myself with that knowledge, and I don't want it."

Liz spun out of bed and collected her clothes that had been hastily removed and tossed about the small space. I turned my head to give her the privacy I would want if I were in her place. She was mumbling to herself and slipping the green sweater over her head, smoothing out the fabric and searching for her pinstriped pants, her orange socks. I saw all this in my mind and berated my decision to continue within celibate parameters. Wouldn't I curse this moment when bouts of loneliness descended upon me? When I was left alone in my dark room surrounded by books and papers and plans to be some kind of literary success, wouldn't I condemn myself for considering that prize worthy of this sacrifice?

"I am not a trap, Joshua. I want you to be a success and I think we can help each other in whatever we decide to do. But I need more. And if we want different things we need to be honest about that."

"I want to be with you."

She buttoned her jeans and said, "I have to go."

"This is ridiculous, Liz."

She shrugged. "This is your decision, Joshua. I've been very compliant so far."

"You're not deciding any of this? That's convenient."

"We're both deciding. Now we have to find a common ground."

"I thought we'd already found it, Liz. This is the common ground."

"It's not enough."

"I'm not going to rush into what could be a life-changing event because you think it's no big deal. And if it is a big deal, then admit that, too, and give me some credit for hesitating.

"I have waited with you, Joshua. It's been six weeks. How long does a woman have to wait with you?"

"I don't know."

"That's right. You don't."

Liz stalked into the bathroom and slammed the door. I sat on the edge of the bed shivering from what had just happened. I felt hollow and metallic. She hadn't left, so I felt that we weren't done and that there was still time left to salvage whatever this night had become. It was all too much for me. What I thought had been honesty was heartless and what I thought would legitimize my position had been selfish. I shook my head wondering how my sexual decisions could be thought to disparage another's. Hadn't I been accused of prudery growing up on the farm, of having a fondness for livestock and cornstalks?

I could take a joke, but it didn't matter much what those boys thought of me. I laughed thinking about how much my sexuality mattered to them that they would take the time to belittle me for it. But this was different. I loved Liz and I didn't know how badly I had hurt her or if I could lessen that hurt; then a part of me wondered if this would end us and I could be free again. How these relations can assail one!

I knocked on the door and I heard her blow her nose. I knocked again and said her name. She opened the door and held me. I thought then that it was an embrace of understanding. Now I know it was one of farewell. Time serves to bring correct definitions to life's ambiguities.

I anticipated that my invitation to the McCormick Thanksgiving would be rescinded, but Liz never withdrew it. In fact, she called to confirm that I would still be coming. I expressed my surprise that she still wanted me there and she laughed.

I did wonder what she had told her parents about me. I had met them all for lunch at Caffe de Luca and we walked around Wicker Park. Darren told us all what the neighborhood used to look like, which businesses had once been where now there was a artisanal bakery, a gastro-pub or else a trendy boutique. I showed them where Nelson Algren had lived and wrote his dark novels; we admired the Flat Iron Building. I liked them and wanted them to think highly of me, so I was a bit anxious upon entering their home, whether I'd be seen as a serious candidate for their daughter or merely a tourist.

I was hoping their expectations would direct me in which role I wanted to play.

The McCormicks lived on Honore Street in Wicker Park. They had moved there in the mid-eighties from Near North

Side. Mr. McCormick had caught wind of the proposed developments then being discussed and made an educated gamble.

Darren McCormick was nearly sixty and worked in the Loop as a consultant, after having spent his productive years in sales. He was a tall man with broad shoulders that had begun to drop without preamble and, because he smiled and found life an easy maze to maneuver, a youthful face. He proved Liz's description of him: full of convention and confident that whatever the topic, he could convince you that he had the final word. His choice of career did not happen by mere coincidence. He was a born convincer and because he was handsome and walked without haste or surprise, he was able to expand his employer's market. He did this so well that he was able to cut himself free from the corporate world and support his family simply by consulting with firms. No matter the size, Mr. McCormick was able to increase their sales and line the pockets of shareholders, CEOs and partners.

His wife, Sharon, was eight years younger than her husband and had recently chosen to allow the State of Illinois to buy her out rather than spend another five years teaching grade school children how to multiply fractions. She had enjoyed her job and the children she helped prepare for the world, but enough was enough. In the summers, she had been able to devote all her energy toward Liz, a duty she gladly welcomed, not just because Liz was her very special girl, but it gave her something to focus on in the strange place Darren had moved his family to. The difficult years of raising their only daughter in a neighborhood bourgeoning on affluence, but still haunted by shadowy figures, had fatigued her with worry over her daughter's, and her own, safety. Then as the neighborhood crime rate dwindled and more and more upwardly mobile residents moved out of the city and into those enclaves, corporations followed them, setting up shops on what were once dirty street corners, crumbling buildings and barred windows. Overnight, it seemed to Sharon, Wicker Park became a place of *bonhomie*. Even the architecture began taking on her sensibilities; glass and openness created an inviting atmosphere and gave her the courage to, once again, make her way in the city.

Mother and daughter would walk up and down the Mile with colorful bags and museum souvenirs, or they would ride the train into distant neighborhoods, to a cafe Sharon had heard about or a park where forgotten moments of cultural shifts were said to have happened. She chatted with Liz about what she had seen and what she wanted to see next. Sharon never tired of stoking her daughter's curiosity. On these excursions into the city and other official communities, while her husband was holed up in conference rooms high above the city streets, Sharon directed her child and the day. It was her own agenda that the two of them followed, her own plan, and she took advantage of her husband's absence to investigate the city's obscure corners. Otherwise, she was quiet and deferred to Darren on most matters.

The kitchen was filled with the sights and smells of Thanksgiving. There was a turkey in the oven and cranberry sauce would be served in a festive bowl on the dining room table beside a tray of rolls and a butter dish; the green bean casserole was cooling on the stove and Darren was whipping the potatoes, adding sour cream and chives to the pot as he went.

Liz made a general greeting then set about basting the bird.

"Joshua, good to see you again," said Mr. McCormick shaking my hand. "Help us out with that bottle, would you? Sharon took it out a bit early, but it should still be cool. Corkscrew's in the drawer there. Hi, Liz. You're looking splendid. How's the money behaving?"

"Same as always, Dad," she lowered her head beneath her father's lips.

"That's good. Keep a close eye on it. Those idiots in DC will do anything to stall everything."

"Yes, Dad."

"Don't leave any of that cork in the wine. I won't have our table sullied by a strainer."

"No, sir."

"Did you hear that, Sharon? 'Sir' he calls me. Takes me back to my days in Financial Place. The action days, I mean. Back when we were moving millions of dollars around like they were spices on the rack. Those days flew by. Too quick. Too quick."

"Yes, Dad, we've all heard your stories hundreds of times."

"Not all of you. Does Joshua know how I reversed the flow of the Chicago River?"

"You did no such thing, Darren. Don't listen to him, Joshua."

"Oh, let me expand my girth of influence for one day. What's it going to hurt if I credit myself with a feat achieved fifty years before my birth?"

"Why don't you tell him about your real experience with the river, Dad?"

"The truth, huh? That could be interesting, I suppose. You probably don't know about this one, Joshua, but long about twenty years ago has it been that long already . . . " The swirling potatoes could give no explanation. He looked into the slurry as if the jumble of chive flecks would give him an acceptable rationale for the passing of time and the destruction of bodies, the forgetfulness of past deeds; " . . . the city of Chicago flooded. Pilings for the Kinzie Street Bridge punctured an abandoned tunnel below the city and after a few weeks, we had forty feet of water in the basement of the Chicago Board of Trade. There were fish swimming in Merchandise Mart. At topside, all was normal. Never a drop on the streets, but below ground, in the storehouses of furniture stores, wine cellars and government buildings, a miniature reckoning was at hand. Crazy days. I took out my fishing pole and caught the staff lunch one day."

"Oh, Darren."

"Lame."

"I can laugh about it now, but my company took a rough hit when the insurance claims began to inundate some of our investment responsibilities. My poor girls didn't see much of me then. The Great Chicago Flood."

He took the beaters out of the potatoes and licked one.

"Can you think of anything as fantastic as a department store flooding at its foundations with river water, mingling its cut glass and bed frames and oven mitts with that ungodly assortment of river trash while thousands of people, over weeks and weeks, walked about as if nothing unusual were happening?"

"It makes me wonder what other catastrophes are lying just out of our view to suddenly became all we think about," I said.

"Nothing so extraordinary as the flood. The Towers going down for sure. But for the individual, those catastrophes happen every day. A heart attack, a domestic dispute, a broken condom." He paused and put on a stern look for me. Liz snorted. "You shrug your shoulders when you hear about them, tell yourself that those sufferers are fools to have had those things happen to them. The Towers, though, and the flood, too, are like a collective heart attack. I saw a picture of a man sobbing in his car when he heard about those terrorists. And he was driving around in Montana or some such nowhere place. But that speaks to the American character nowadays. Do you think serfs toiling in Siberia wept for the flames of Moscow when Napoleon arrived? Did people in that same Montana territory sob when they heard Sherman had burned his way through to Savannah?"

"That's enough now, Darren. Do we have to talk about disasters today?"

"It's the perfect day, Honey. How can we be thankful unless we know what miseries await us and have already enveloped others?" Darren took his wife in his arms and kissed the top of her head. "Besides, our Misery lurks in the corner while we stand with our wine and smile at each other thinking, 'It will always be like this.' He's so close we should set a place for him and whenever he no-shows, we can be thankful all over again."

"And when he does finally show?" said Liz picking a fried onion off the casserole.

"Then we'll thank him for all his delays and learn to live with him. Maybe he won't be such a sour houseguest? Of course Old Job would have something to say about that. You know about Old Job? Good for you; yes, Liz told us you were a bit into that kind of thing. Then you know 'The rain falls on the wicked and the righteous.' I never knew who was getting the bum deal there. Do the wicked benefit or are the righteous flooded out of their homes?"

Darren seemed to want my opinion, so I said that the rain fell where it did to the benefit of some and the distress of others and that sometimes the benefit and distress are reversed.

"You have a wonderful way of saying nothing, Joshua."

"Daddy."

"He knows I'm only teasing, Sweetie."

"Anyway, nobody thinks of God like that anymore," I said. "A deity making bets, throwing disasters on us poor mortals, bending down to lift us out of our own filth. The allegory of

Him taking a newborn Israel out of his own afterbirth, kicking and screaming and weeping, wiping him off and raising him up hasn't been thought about in hundreds of years. Our modernity has done away with all that."

"Now we're talking about religion? Really, you two need to go in the other room and let us girls work."

"Let the young man speak, Honey. We'll gauge his worth by what he says."

"No pressure," said Liz.

"I just mean that God is no longer in the equation. Our technologies are matching his gifts and miracles in the same way Pharaoh's magicians could mimic Moses' right hand. And as for the curses, we've eliminated those, too. We still work the fields, but we do it in air-conditioned comfort and spray pesticides that know the difference between what makes a farmer money and what chokes his yield. We still suffer during childbirth, but there are drugs for that as well, and if you don't want to get pregnant, there are still more precautions. And what about the flood? Thousands of years ago one destroyed the world; twenty years ago it wasn't noticeable to the people eating and drinking and buying land and getting married."

"You sound like a cynic," said Mr. McCormick. He glanced at Liz who was taking rolls out of the oven.

"Not at all. I'm just wondering where God is to be found today. If He isn't in the curses or the blessings, then He's in the living room watching television waiting to be called for dinner."

"Which is now ready everyone," said Liz.

We each took an armful of trays and bowls and set them on the white linen Mrs. McCormick had laid on the table. Mr. McCormick invoked God to bless our dinner and we spooned and forked the holiday fare onto our plates with the rattle of silver and easy conversation.

After dinner, Mr. McCormick poured me a glass of Sherry while the women cleared the plates and talked in the kitchen. The Sherry was sweet and thick and the thimble glass forced me to savor it. I held it in my hand like an egg and swirled the brown tint while Mr. McCormick reclined in his chair.

"I prefer this to Port, Joshua. Have you ever been to Spain?"

"I haven't."

"Make that a priority. The Spaniards are a brave and crass people who easily mix the vulgar and the sublime in their character. It's a remarkable commingling. It's only Sherry if it comes from Jerez, Spain. That's in Andalusia in the south whose symbol is the mighty Hercules. When you drink this, do you think of that brute of a man clearing out the Augean stables? That's one example of what I mean."

"I didn't think Hercules was Spanish."

"Oh, he's not. Have you read the Greeks?"

"I'm making my way through them."

"I honeymooned with the Mrs. in Andalusia. It's a beautiful country."

"I'll make a priority of that, as well."

"Of marriage or Spain?"

I coughed in my Sherry and smiled at the large man leaning back in his dining room chair. He had a wry smile, like he had just moved his bishop atop a pivotal square that only then revealed its importance.

"What are your plans, Mr. Thomas?"

Check.

The question made me shift in my chair in an obvious attempt to get a clearer picture of the board. I put my elbows on the table and stared at the crumbs on the white linen. Mr. McCormick was calmly holding his glass. He appeared unconcerned about my answer, whether it was too forward or too casual, but I was not under the impression that this question had suddenly just occurred to him. I cursed myself for not having thought of an appropriate answer ahead of time. Why else would a family invite a young man into their home if not to understand his interest in one of their own, their only in fact, and to see if his expectations of himself were valid in their eyes?

"Regarding?"

"Oh," he put his glass down and leaned over the table, the better to observe my squirming, I supposed. "Your life, goals you have. You've been spending a lot of time with Liz and I'm curious."

"Well, I have thought about it. All of it. And, I suppose . . . at the moment I'm just figuring those things out. Nothing established yet, I'm afraid."

"I'm sorry, Joshua. Even while I was asking I was wondering why this old man was bothering his guest."

"Not at all."

"I was thinking about Spain and my honeymoon and you said you wanted to go there as well. I associate the place with my particular experience and there you have the blunt question." Having come to some conclusion about me, whether to my advantage or not I couldn't tell, he leaned back in his chair. "Liz tells me you're currently, how shall I put it, living the life of the mind?"

I was put off by his incredulous tone. It veiled a subtle contempt or maybe just a smirch of an adult watching a child do childish things, waiting until he should grow out of such juvenile things and become useful.

"That's true."

Mr. McCormick waited.

"Well, I mean, I don't claim to have any great ambitions about discovering new ways of thinking about any particular subject or anything. In fact, right now I'm filling in the blanks of my education, reading all the works that I believe a young man should read, or at least I should read, since I have the inclination. And I do. So I am."

"Joshua, there's no need to be nervous. I'm curious about you. That's a good thing. You may not know this, but I had a bout with the intellectual life while I was in college. That was the late sixties when there were pressing matters to be discussed and we were attempting to install a new American Dream, a movement away from the domesticated lives of our parents and toward an ideal bohemia. In the end, we all just wanted to get laid and become rich and many of us did, most from the inheritance of our hard-working parents who had disgusted us so much."

"Our cultural circumstances aren't that similar."

"They're miles apart, Joshua. There is no comparison. So why do you do it? What pressing question drives you to live the life you're leading?"

"No one question, I suppose. There's death, of course."

"Yes. Liz told us about your father. I am sorry about that."

"Thank you. It was last winter. Almost a year ago, now. Anyway, I've never had a more definite feeling that I am going to die than I do now. And the seed of my death was planted at my conception; the heartbeat my mom never heard, or heard only a few times, during those routine examinations, and that my dad moaned over so many years ago, was the first grains of finite sand escaping down the tiny neck of the hourglass. One day my heart will stop, the sand will run out, as it has with everyone, as it must with me, too, and so I want to be prepared. I want to die well and I have no idea how or even what that means."

"I'm no help to you there."

"My first step was to think of someone I admired and emulate what it was I admired about him. My dad was the first to come to mind, obviously. I was impressed by his work ethic actually, and the skill he had with the farm, of running it, even though it ended up burying him. Though we didn't talk about God much, we sang together during the church services and I saw him reading his old battered and stretched Bible every morning. So that's where I started, too. It's been a number of years ago now, but I read it through and thought 'okay this is alright, I can read this.' It does take some getting used to, though, the turns of phrase and the poems that seem to say the same thing over and over."

"Interesting." Mr. McCormick finished his Sherry and looked over my shoulder into the kitchen where I could hear the women passing dishes and talking in light voices about pleasant things.

"So I developed a passion for reading and I dove into Dickens and then one winter, Dostoevsky and Tolstoy, then the modern Americans, then the French, the Germans. That summer I tackled Shakespeare and in the fall discovered philosophy and Montaigne's essays. A lot of different lives are examined and presented as idols or examples in literature and all of them deal in some way or another with death, the supposed tragedy of it all."

"You don't believe it's tragic?"

"Some instances are, of course. Dying before one's parents or in senseless accidents or in drawn-out suffering. But old age, I think, falls into this last category as well. So even a long life, a blessing to be sure, becomes a burden, something not to be desired because of the limitations and perhaps the menial care, the absence of family and friends. Poor food delivered in single serving Styrofoam."

"So dying young is out and dying old is no better. What age should it be?"

"It's not the when so much as the how. I think."

"That's not exactly a choice we get to make."

"But I think it is."

"Do you?"

"Every day we decide how we'll die, I think, by choosing to live in certain ways. Just men die in their justice; thankful men die in their thankfulness; arrogant men die in their arrogance. Their spirits become a sort of amniotic fluid in which they live and breathe. We all know the way to live life: selfless, caring, loving without conditions, humble; but these are difficult ways to live up to. I think if a man is proud or lustful or envious his life becomes a hell of jealousies and envies and that's what he dies in. The man who avoids these things will live and die in peace. Anyway, this is what I think about now and I'm trying to find ways to train my spirit so that when I am confronted by my own passions, I can tame them."

"That's a nice way to think about life, Joshua. I'd say it's a view perfectly in keeping with your way of life now. You have separated yourself from the ways of the world, from people with whom you don't get along, from a job you detest; you have no family, which would challenge your pretty ideas about selflessness and love. I don't mean to sound harsh, but the theories of life aren't mysterious and it's easy enough to idealize them when you're living in the clouds and away from the mud and dust we all have to breathe in."

"I've been thinking about that, too. Your daughter brought that to my attention when we first met. She thinks I need to get a job."

"What would you do?"

"I don't know."

"Maybe you should spend some time contemplating that, too."

"I will."

"Good. I like you, Joshua. I hope you don't think I'm a hard man. I'm only trying to see what inspired Liz to bring you to our family and if you're up to snuff."

He winked at me and I said he was being a perfect host.

"Let me pour you another glass." I hadn't finished my first yet. With all of my talk, I had only taken one sip. Mr. McCormick lifted himself out of his chair and turned toward the cabinet behind him. I downed the remaining Sherry and squinted at the sweetness.

"Tell me what made you agree to meet us. In my day, this was a big step and I imagine it still is, though this generation has a tendency to downplay momentous events such as this. You two have been seeing each other for a few months now?" He pulled the glass stopper from the decanter and splashed a shot into his glass. I held my glass above the table and a drop of brown liqueur ran down the square body and fell into the white cloth. "I'm going to catch hell for that, young man. You'll see what I mean."

"Six weeks, I believe."

"You kids today. Need all the time in the world to figure out how you feel at any one particular time. After six weeks, I had declared my intentions to Sharon's dad and it was expected we would marry soon after."

"I believe Liz enjoys her freedom. She has more of her mother in her, I'm told. She's strong and sure like you, but not given to bouts of imagining."

"Is that a fact?"

"Those aren't my words. I spend a lot of time with my imagination as well. I think she likes that about me."

We drank our Sherry and processed the likelihood that Liz had found a bit of her father in me. To break the silence I said, "In fact, I did tell her that I loved her."

"And?"

"She laughed at me."

"Is that right? Ha ha. I'm not surprised."

"I can't blame her. I don't have any solid plans or prospects for work. I have no idea what kind of career awaits me or even if I want one. I don't think about the future except when I think about seeing Liz and what we'll do and say to each other. I'm trying my hand at writing."

"How's that going?"

"I'm getting a piece published. I hope. It has some good ideas in it, but I see it's not finished yet. I need to take a risk with it and that may temper a publisher's enthusiasm for it."

"You're a theoretical man, then."

"I suppose so."

"Another Rimbaud."

"Oh, no. I can have my art with my reality, I think. I could never really read him or the other Symbolists because of their personal abstraction. For art or anything to be relevant I think it has to mingle with reality, with the shouts of the street, the joys and miseries of the people."

"Young Joshua. What do you know of misery?"

In all of us there is a feeling that we understand the truth better than most. There is a pocket of experience that we will not allow to be trumped and I had stumbled upon Mr. McCormick's. He grew serious and pensive and sipped his Sherry. It's difficult to imagine what kinds of miseries another has suffered. He sat in his life like he did in his leather chair, surrounded by success and a beautiful family, but then perhaps money does something to a man that can only be understood by another man with money. I didn't think my sum put me on his level yet, but I wondered what it was he swallowed with his amber drink and if he would teach it to me one day.

I asked Liz about it on the train into the city.

"He was probably just tired from work. Or maybe he was hoping for a nap during the football game. You didn't stop talking about one thing or another."

"Your mom looked bored sitting on the couch. Why was she so far away from the rest of us?"

"It was sweet of you to look through the albums with her. She hasn't thought about those early years in quite a while."

"She remembered an awful lot. I bet they're on her mind more than you think."

Liz nodded and looked out the window.

"Your dad asked what my intentions are with you," I said.

"He did? What did you say?"

"Just that I'm infatuated with you and spend all my time thinking about when I'll see you next."

"You're sweet."

"And that I didn't know how you felt about me exactly."

She turned her head to look at me. "You know I like being with you."

"Obviously. But you did laugh at me when I told you I loved you."

"I remember. And I apologized if I'm not mistaken."

"It's not as if you spilled beer on me or dog-eared a page in one of my books, Liz."

"Why can't we just enjoy this now?"

"Because 'now' will last forever until we discuss 'then.'"

"Don't be mean. We'll have plenty of time to figure all that out. Of course, it will have to be when I get back from Florida."

"Florida? You didn't mention you were going away."

"I'm sure I did. I always go away with my girlfriends after Thanksgiving. We started the tradition back in college as a way to blow off steam after the holidays and blow off a couple days of classes."

"So we have a few days left."

We said good-bye at Lake Street, I to return to my studies and she to "decompress." When the yellow light and the metallic rumble of the Green Line emerged from around the bend, she let me go and adjusted her purse and the buttons of her jacket. She cocked her hat just right and boarded the train. She didn't wave to me from the seat and after she pulled away I stood amidst the current of returning revelers until the platform was empty and silent and only my footfalls echoed in the chamber.

A month after Melanie's attack, Roland invited me to their apartment. The wind cut through my layers of clothing and pinched at my ears. The change of seasons had always had the affect of fanning a renewed enthusiasm toward my intellectual endeavors, and that autumn had been no different. I reworked the essay about Eric's subject matter. He encouraged me to write about what we had talked about in his studio, though I was still apprehensive about getting specific, spiritually speaking. However comfortable it is to discuss the idea God in an atmosphere of good will and tolerance, the name of Jesus has within it a tendency toward vitriol and defense. There are specific words and ideas associated with that name that "God" doesn't have. We can speak about God as though we were talking about the same thing, even though we are not; "Jesus" doesn't allow for such confusion. So it seemed better to keep Eric's ideas in the abstract realm. Too much detail about his beliefs could deter prospective buyers from attending his shows and slow his momentum. But Eric was not concerned about that and I became the first man in the history of modern art to analyze abstraction through the lens of Jesus Christ, so far as I knew.

I got off the bus and walked to Roland's apartment. Snow covered the leaves that had fallen weeks ago and gave the impression of future drifts pushed out of the street by that most necessary, though seldom appreciated, civic expenditure: the snow plow. Roland met me on the stoop. He wore a derby and a large wool pea coat buttoned to the throat; a thick scarf spilled over its collar. He thrust his hands in his pockets and I followed him into Lincoln Park.

"I wanted to tell you upstairs the other night, but I thought a better opportunity would present itself. Then I realized there is no better opportunity to tell you this. They are all equally poor."

"Tell me what?"

"It's Melanie. I found out a few months ago and I thought it was over. She told me it was over. But . . . She's been seeing another man, Joshua. I don't know, maybe more. It's been off and on with this one for a few months now. At least that's what she's told me then. Or else it's been off and on with me. I can't tell anymore. Anyway, it's on again."

"Why?"

"Who knows? I've begged her to stop and she told me it was over between them, but now she's . . . Oh, she's not happy with her life, what I'm providing. The money is too sporadic, the jobs too obscure. She says she never knows where I am at any time and that worries her. She's suspicious, you know? Thinks I'm getting up to no good with other women or with less than reputable guys. But we always have enough money. I have a proven record of getting what we need and I've told her my plan hundreds of times; that it takes time; that everything is progressing how I want it to, it's just taking a bit longer. Hell, I get it. But she gets these panic attacks; wakes up at night gasping for air, imagines all kinds of awful things about me, about us. Thinks men will come at her trying to get at me. She's convinced they're going to kill her one day. I tell her that's crazy; that no one wants my ass so much they'd off her to get it. So I got her pills to take and she ignores them. They're sitting in a plastic baggie beneath the sink like poison.

"So then she meets an old friend one day last year who's carried a torch for her since their college days. He's in advertising; has an office near Willis. Silk ties and gold watches. I followed Mel when my suspicions became too great for me. She met him for lunch, but I never saw thcm come out. After two hours, I went inside and walked through the restaurant. They were gone. The exit on the other side of the place entered into a hotel lobby.

"I was furious and demanded the front desk tell me where she was. Of course they had no idea and when they called the cops, I bolted. That night I accused her and she denied it, but I knew she had fucked him because she listened to my accusation without passion. She didn't raise her voice or call me a son-of-a-bitch or slap me or run into the bathroom to cry. She leaned her hip against the kitchen counter with a carrot in one hand and a peeler in the other, waiting for the conversation to be over so she could get back to making soup.

"After that we started arguing about all this little shit. Just nonsense. Everything next to the big issue, either her infidelity or my jealousy. I hit her a few times and she threatened to call the police. The neighbors grew suspicious; they side-stepped me on the sidewalk and avoided my eye, but they never did anything before and I didn't expect them to start. And then things would calm down and we'd have a few days of love and trust before it began all over again. Every criticism she had of me, innocent or otherwise, I heard as if it were coming from his mouth filtered through Melanie's voice. Some financial hot-shot wearing thousand dollar shoes through the slush and muck and dragging my name into it while his shoes remain clean? I couldn't believe how she had been so manipulated to say such things. And I work my ass off, Joshua. For that guy to come into my home, my business, and pry away the love and respect of my woman from me was an invitation to war.

"So I went to his office. I stalked his lobby and when I was told to leave, I hung around on the sidewalks. But I never saw him. At every predictable hour I was there waiting for him. He does work, right? They do have to arrive at a certain time and leave after they've put in their eight hours, right? Or have they changed all that? Anyway, I think Melanie tipped him off. At least that's what I thought then. But she would've had to tip him off every day. And she didn't know when I was there."

"How did she even know you were doing this?"

"Oh, I told her. I threatened her with it; told her I what I was going to do to this boy-friend of hers. Got real specific, too. She was shaking 'cause she knows I don't just say shit to hear myself talk. But you're right; she wouldn't have known when I was down there . . . She probably told him I'd be around, just a vague warning, you know? He probably took a vacation; maybe decided to work from home.

"Then things went to hell between Mel and me. I came home after a long day of odds and ends. I'd neglected certain responsibilities toward my people with all my attentions directed at Mel and what I should do to him. So that day had been particularly rough. I saw him all over the city. There wasn't a corner I passed that he wasn't on it reading a paper, talking on the phone or holding hands with his woman, who I believed was Mel. I saw the two of them together so many times, Joshua. So when I came home tired from thoughts about this man being with Mel and condemning myself for the line of work I'd chosen, I was ready to lash out. I'm not one prone to self-doubt and I was angry that this fucker was getting to me. And then I saw him. He was getting into a Lexus parked outside my apartment. Melanie denied it, though, and now I wonder myself. I don't even know what he looks like, for Christ's sake. But why, on that night, was there a well-dressed man so close to my place getting into a luxury car I'd never seen before? And if I was so sure it was him why didn't I bring misfortune upon his head instead of . . . Well, when I saw that man coming down my steps and heard the engine rumbling its challenge, I believed it was me. For a split second I was confident that I was driving away, leaving my trustworthy wife well provided for, off to take care of some legitimate business. I don't know enough about the human brain to know what this phenomenon is called, or if there's even a name for it; if it's something that's even diagnosable, but I swear the truth of what I'm saying. And if I were him, driving away, then I wasn't myself.

"And I knew exactly what I would do to her. I saw it all ten minutes before I did it. But I don't remember it clearly. It's the premonition that I recall. I was driving out of the neighborhood. That's what I remember."

"What did you do, Roland?"

"It was me, Joshua. I attacked her."

I didn't understand what he was saying. I stared at him, waiting for him to finish with words that made sense. His face was heavy with sorrow; it pressed upon his cheeks and the weight of it made his eyes water. He slumped onto a wet bench facing North Pond. I brushed off the snow and sat beside him and waited.

I remained quiet during his confession. I couldn't move and I was getting sick with the thought that I had spent so much time and developed an affection for a man capable of such brutality. When he composed himself I prayed he would begin again; that he would focus his mind upon himself and leave me free from having to give advice or pledge an oath of silence, a pact sealed in the spilled blood of an unfortunate woman.

"I love her so much. But at the time it was the only thing I could do to return balance."

I didn't know how such a thing could return anything to a normal state. I didn't ask him about this either. I thought it prudent to not interject into things I knew nothing about.

"The police don't know it was me. They were suspicious, of course, and I answered the same questions fifty times. After the first hour at the station, I knew they didn't have anything on me except those suspicions. Melanie hadn't told them anything, either. Because she'd kept to the mugging story they had to let me go. There was no blood on the street, though. I couldn't account for that. I think that's why they kept me so long; they were waiting for Melanie to flip on me or for me to slip in the re-telling. The story has holes, but there's no one involved who will admit this or press charges."

Roland looked at me in a meaningful way that I'd been preparing for.

"I'm not going to say anything," I said.

"I know you won't. But I'm worried that Melanie will tell this guy what I've just told you. In fact, I know she already has."

I could tell Roland had decided on a course of action and I leaned away from him, subconsciously distancing myself from whatever further act of violence he had concocted.

"He would have suspected me anyway, so I can't really blame her. Hell, he may have knocked her around a bit to get it out of her. She doesn't have no bruises, but that don't mean shit: phone books, bags of oranges; hell, even a padded baseball bat will do."

"Why a knife, Roland? Why couldn't you just slap her or toss her around?"

That I was discussing these heinous acts as viable options to what he'd done proved I wasn't thinking right.

"We'll be haunted by it forever. Together."

He was deep in thought now, far away from the cold and the dark of Lincoln Park, and living in myriad of other scenarios. He shook his head and clenched his jaw.

"He wants to be paid, Joshua." He looked at me. Anger and desperation were in his eyes; a pleading he was not used to. "He told her if he doesn't get forty-thousand dollars he'll go to the police."

I thought for sure he wouldn't pay this man. It was easier to just get rid of him. This time there would be no need for brass knuckles or a small bit of pipe; either way, there wouldn't be a bag of money in Roland's hands when next they met. But I wasn't thinking right.

"Joshua. Help me. Can you help me?"

I shook my head, more in disbelief than in refusal.

"I'm not going to kill this man, Joshua. I've thought about it and there's too much heat on me right now. I wouldn't get away with it. And it kills me to have to give in to this guy. I just don't see any other way at the moment."

"You want me to pay him off?"

317

"You won't have to meet him. I just need the cash. No check, Joshua; cash. In a briefcase or a lunchbox, or . . ."

"A paper bag?"

"Or a paper bag. I give it to him and we're clear."

"I can't get that kind of money, Roland."

"Now, I've come up with a way to pay you back. It'll take a few years and you'll get a good interest rate, not a fair one, though — I can't afford to be fair right now — but I won't forget that I owe you."

"Roland, this is . . . "

"If we don't pay him, he'll go to the cops; if we don't pay him, I will kill him. So, either way I'll go to prison, Joshua. One day you'll read about this guy going missing, then a few days later he'll be found on the shore or in a sewer, disfigured, mutilated; or else lying in some vacant lot full of holes, skull beat in; or else inside a construction site, embedded in the ground after a hundred foot fall. And all the evidence will point to me. These are my options if you don't come through for me."

"I can't . . . "

"It's him or me, Joshua. And I won't go away and let this guy have his way with Melanie. Not while I'm alive, anyway."

"You're asking me to pay for this man's life? You want me to buy the life of the man Melanie . . . "

"Be careful here, Joshua. I told you what I'm going to do. You have to decide what you're going to do."

I walked to the Red Line at Fullerton and rode it to Division where I ascended to street level. The wind pierced through every chink of my winter armor, battering all my soft spots with shards of darkness. I spent the next few hours walking up and down once familiar streets considering my spiritual

318

sickness. How easily I'd been blinded to the world's actuality, to its true nature. I wondered just what help were all those dead men and women who had been alive and thought such wonderful things and who I mistook for brilliant instructors. They were embarrassingly quiet now; I was embarrassed for them. For I had no idea the depths to which human beings are capable of plunging without thoughts toward consequences or another's legitimacy overwhelmed me. I thought of Roland's sinister optimism; of how he believed himself to be a kind of knight who had ridden to his lover's aid and expecting to be rewarded with renewed ardor; of the mania blazing from his eyes, the eyes of my friend, as he attacked a young woman with a blade, a perverted penetration whose scars would forever serve as a memorial to whom Melanie truly belonged.

While I was speeding below ground in a swaying car crowded with somber faces coming to terms with their own tragedies, Melanie was shaking under the covers in a dark room hidden away from the life she once lived there. She was locked away from her attacker, her lover, on the second floor; her only way out was to expose herself again to his hands as she crept through the living room and passed the couch where Roland slept like a dragon, then out the door and down the steps into street. From there she could go wherever she willed and without a trace.

The world became a dangerous place that night. Before, in my innocence, I had walked the dark streets thinking of the aesthetics of city corners and elevator shafts; the Chicago River's new current and the violent magnificence of Lake Michigan; the cause for building, for destroying, and the cost of preserving; meditating on the elegance of Baudelaire's "Hymn to Beauty", puzzling over *Four Quartets*. Roland had now put his unlikely face upon the capability of men and women to veer into the maniacal. If he was capable of such an act, then whomever I met or bumped into or cut off on the sidewalk could be wielding a weapon of some sort with which to manifest his or her justice. I recalled our first meeting and wondered how close I had come to lying in my own blood if I'd had cash on me. I should have known better.

"You were right," I told Liz when I called the next morning. "Roland is capable of terrible things."

"So he admitted to hitting that woman?"

"What? No. He . . ."

"Joshua, what's happened?"

I hadn't considered the ramifications, if indeed there would be any, of my telling someone else about Roland's confession. I was under no obligation to remain silent; I was not a therapist or a priest, neither was I a lawyer and had no non-disclosure agreements to respect. Still, I was bound by some kind of law, one I had neglected to observe and that I was on the precipice of breaking, that I would break shortly. After all, Roland didn't know who Liz was. He'd only met her the one time and, as far as I knew, wasn't interested in her. Surly I was allowed to unburden myself, to seek advice regarding this unhinged circumstance.

"Melanie was taken to the hospital a few weeks ago. On Halloween. She'd been officially mugged, according to police documents, I mean. She suffered a stab wound and numerous lacerations."

"Who's Melanie?"

"Roland's girlfriend. I assume she's who you saw with him that time. Maybe not. I don't know anything about him, Liz."

"Where was this?"

"Outside their apartment."

"Is she going to be all right?"

"She's home now. With Roland."

"Joshua, did he do this?"

"He told me he didn't. He said she'd been mugged. But now . . . "

"You have to tell the police. Joshua. You can't leave her alone with him."

"I'd be surprised if she isn't gone already."

"How could you not have reported him the second he told you?"

"Liz, I don't condone it."

"Of course you don't. Who would?"

"Melanie went out of her way not to bring charges against him. She had hours by herself while Roland was at the station to leave or to file an honest report. The cops had been at the hospital with her for hours. The were waiting for Melanie to tell them the truth because without her testimony they don't have anything. She helped him clean the blood off their kitchen floor."

"This is sick. This is your friend?"

"I've asked myself the same question."

"That poor woman. You have to get her away from him. Tell the police what you know. Let them handle it."

"She's a grown woman, Liz. With more than enough reason to leave if that's what she wants."

"Do you know how difficult it is for a woman to leave an abusive relationship?"

"Of course not."

"Very. That's why so many of them don't. Most of them stay, Joshua. Many abuses don't even get reported. And the man doesn't change. He gets worse. The violence becomes more frequent, Joshua, and then you have a body on your hands. Why do I have to tell you this?"

"I haven't slept all night, Liz. You make the right thing sound so simple, but there are other factors involved."

"Like what?" Liz was incredulous.

"Like the fact that Melanie didn't tell the police."

"She never would."

"How are you so certain?"

"Joshua . . . Are you a coward?"

That question, put to me by a woman for whom I had great affection, filled me with shame. I didn't want to appear weak or scared when it came to doing good. I also didn't want to seem passive, since my life took on that aspect in her eyes already. I believe Liz was enduring my life as I chose to live it. That such a decision, how I would act in this grotesque circumstance, could affect my relationship with Liz; that what I chose to do could facilitate its end or worse, could drive her to report what I'd said and turn me in as an accomplice as well, was too much for me. My mind burned with all the possibilities, on all sides, and my blood chilled thinking of all the consequences. Among them, I had to consider the fact that I was indeed a coward.

I told her I had been up most of the night thinking about this situation without coming to any certainty, that I was scared about the responsibility Roland's confidence put upon me and that I needed her to understand I wasn't going to act spuriously on such a matter.

"I don't know what I'm doing and I need you to be patient until I can figure this out."

"I don't understand. You hardly know the guy and what you do know isn't good. And you're still hesitating?"

"Liz, Melanie didn't leave . . . "

"Then go see if she's okay. Or I'll call 9-1-1 and report a domestic disturbance."

"You don't know where they live, Liz."

In the silence that followed I had to think if she did know; in the silence she was waiting for me to tell her.

"Thanks for letting me know about all this. Real good timing."

"I'm sorry, Liz. I'd forgotten. I'll call you . . . " but she'd hung up before I finished.

I put on my boots but remained sitting in my chair. I couldn't go to Roland's, but neither could I stay in my apartment. My conscience was worrying me and I was scared to make an aggressive move. Melanie was trapped in with Roland, I was being coughed up into the street and Liz was lamenting the burden I'd place on her, cursing me for bringing such things to bear on her time of frolic in the sun.

I boarded the 22 bus and headed north. I bought some coffee from Einstein Bakery near their stop and tried to read Pessoa, who was inept at distracting me from more urgent matters. I ordered some bagel sandwiches to go and I paced up and down side streets telling myself I could leave, that I didn't have to do anything. But I knew how that would play in Liz's mind. I rang the bell. No one answered and I waited. I rang again. With every toll I grew more optimistic that Melanie had left. I thought of her sitting in the ladies room at Union Station until the last possible moment before boarding the California Zephyr. I offered a prayer of thanks, but as my conscience was acclimating to the relief of an empty apartment the speaker crackled and I heard Roland's fatigued and disjointed voice.

He looked miserable and while I tried to give the impression that I was there for him I looked for any signs that Melanie had gone. There was a throw pillow outside their bedroom's closed door and my spirit fell.

"Yea, that's where I sleep now. I lay there on the floor talking to her through the crack under the door. She never says anything to me. I never hear her moving around. She may have gone out the window for all I know."

"Do you think so?"

He detected a note of hope in my voice and shook his head. I handed him the bag, which he took without comment.

"I mean, does she have family around here? Some place to stay for a while?"

"She's staying here."

"I know, Roland. But maybe some place she can go to heal for a bit?"

"Away from me, you mean? That's not what she wants."

"Has she told you that?"

His mouth was full of bread and egg and ham. "The only reason I'm still here is because she wants me here. She loves me, Joshua. I should be in jail, sitting in a cell and waiting for a twenty year sentence."

I knocked on the door.

"It's Joshua. I brought breakfast. Roland and I are going to go out for a bit, okay?"

I knocked again; there was no response.

"Where are we going?"

I led him outside and we stood beneath Melanie's window. I kept watch on the blinds, hoping not to see signs of movement. I got my wish, but it didn't have the calming effect I believed it would. I started down the street and he followed. If she was going to leave she would do it when he couldn't see to stop it.

"It's too cold for this," said Roland lighting a cigarette.

"They're calling for snow this weekend."

"I like when it snows in the city."

He smoked and we circled the block. I asked how Melanie was doing and what their plans were; if she'd had second thoughts about pressing charges.

"Your sympathy is overwhelming."

When we returned red and near frostbit, the bag and coffee remained where I had left them. I was disappointed because it didn't prove if Melanie was there or not, not like the missing bag would have or seeing evidence of its consumption, and I hoped she'd escaped during the night.

Roland collapsed on the couch and resigned himself to waiting. He was quiet and my attempts to draw him out were fruitless.

"I don't think it's a good idea for you to be here with Melanie," I said.

"You said that already. Look, are you with us on this one or you going to be difficult?"

"I'm trying to help you."

"No, you're not. You obviously have a problem with our still being together. We don't have to fit easily into your farmer's morality. And it's not our job to convince you about what's right for us. This is how we're going to live now and that's that."

"What about the next time, Roland? God forbid you suddenly aren't so convinced she can keep silent or that she . . . "

"We're not capable of hurting each other."

He was tired. His eyes were closed and there was no life in his voice. I believed this was the only true thing he'd ever told me.

I didn't know how to proceed. Roland was in a place I had no comprehension of. It was like talking to a man who had found the secret of time jumping and could no longer be surprised at anything, having knowledge of the future and thus understanding the present. He was morose and stoic, incredulous at my uncertainty. Gone was the man who had rocked in the taxi cab with me, who had raced up and down driveways chasing a promotion in a youth basketball hustle, who laughed as easily as catching raindrops in a wide palm. Now that palm was closed, his fingers wrapped around an invisible object, either the life he couldn't do without or the weapon he'd use on the one who would try to pry it away from him.

"Can I trust you, Joshua? I would be disappointed if I couldn't."

I hesitated, thinking of my loyalty to him — a fact I was surprised to have discovered — and my desire to do good for Liz.

"However you're feeling about all this, I need to know you're with me," he said. "I need to have an assurance that it won't be you who pulls the rug out. If I don't have that . . . "

His eyes were opened now and stern as he bored into me. I could sense his fist flexing and knew it could easily be unleashed upon me.

"If Melanie hasn't . . ."

"I need to know that Liz won't talk either." Roland's voice was crisp and sure.

I didn't know what to say. That he had asked about her showed he knew she knew. I didn't play innocent.

"She's not happy about it."

"I could give a shit about her happiness."

"She's adamant that I do something."

"What could you possibly do about it?"

I shrugged. Roland looked at me hard then rubbed his face, smacked his cheeks.

"Joshua. Forget about Liz a minute. Think about me and Mel. Hasn't she had opportunities to do what she wants? She could've turned me in or had her boyfriend take her away from me; hell, she could have left on her own. At any time she can call the police and change her story."

"I told Liz all those things."

"And?"

"She wants Melanie to be safe, Roland. We both do." "She is. Tell her you know she is."

"Would you let me talk to her? Just to ease our minds."

Roland stared at Melanie's door. "Such an errand boy. Sure, talk to her. I got no problem with that."

I knocked again.

"Melanie. It's Joshua. Do you need anything? I brought you some breakfast." There was silence. Then I heard movement, a rustling of covers, the creak of springs. "Melanie, can I call somebody for you? Do you need anything?"

"No," she said. "Got everything I need."

"Melanie? Melanie, will you open the door? Melanie."

"I said I'm fine."

I was taken aback by the vehemence in her voice.

Roland put his hand on my shoulder. "That's enough, man. Let her rest."

"Is that her?"

"Who else would it be?"

I decided to walk back to the Gold Coast. I let Liz's calls go to voice mail. I could have easily tell her I'd been out and didn't take it with me. After all, I never took it with me. I stopped at cafes to escape the cold and I filled my notebooks with indecipherable lines. I couldn't hold on a thought for long without it returning to themes of guilt and cowardice. I'd done all I could do, short of reporting what he'd told me to the police, and it was this that I worried over. Liz would tell me it was the logical step to take and so I avoided speaking to her.

What had Sullivan to say to me now? What was the example of Judah's great King David? How would a man on the 78th floor deal with this? I could imagine, but none of it helped me and I realized that only action would save me from anxious days.

I called Liz that evening.

"So she's still there."

"Someone is there."

"You don't believe it's her?"

"I don't know what to believe with him."

"It's not that complicated."

"I never saw her, Liz. I took her breakfast, but it was never touched. I took him out for a bit and nothing. Roland sounded sure, though."

"Did you try the door?"

"It locks from the inside."

"So break it down."

"Break it down?"

"Yes."

"Are you crazy?"

"Are you? Why didn't you think of that yourself? Why wouldn't you do whatever you had to do to get that woman out of there?"

"The only reason I think I should is because you keep saying so. Otherwise, based on the actions of each of them, they're doing exactly what they want to do. And who am I to involve myself?"

"Who are you, is right."

I immediately called back but was sent to voice mail. I was terrified that she was calling the police herself. When I tried again ten, then twenty minutes later it was the same story and I believed then she was only avoiding me. I was in the same position I'd been in that morning. The only way I would have peace was to know that I'd done everything I could do and hope that in the eyes of the law it was enough.

Roland let me in and I stormed by him. I banged on their bedroom door and demanded she let me in. Roland grabbed at my arms and pulled me away, but I flung free and pounded some more. I pleaded with her as though she were Peace itself.

"Is she even in there, Roland? You didn't put some other girl behind this door, did you?"

"Liz really has your head spinning."

Roland was holding his lip. He spit blood into his hand.

"Did you?"

"Calm down. This is all getting way too serious."

He left to tend to his wound.

"Please."

I heard the dead bolt click and when the door opened Melanie was incredulous. She unleashed a torrent of curses and blame at me, hands thrown up in exasperation and wild eyes that convinced me I'd trespassed upon their lives. I wish Liz could have felt those eyes; they were meant for her, after all.

"Where the fuck do you think are?" she demanded.

I stammered something. Her eyes blazed at my incoherence.

"Roland! Roland, what's this guy doing here? Get him out of here!"

His hands were immediately on my shoulders and I was dragged into the living room and tossed into the couch like a flimsy pillow. When I righted myself Melanie stood behind Roland, hands on her hips, glaring first at me then at Roland. I saw the bandages on her arms and shoulder.

"Fucking idiots. What the hell do you think you're doing?"

I couldn't summon my reason. I had valid reasons for being there, I was sure of it, but in that moment I truly did not belong.

"It's your fault," she said.

Roland tried to explain my being there, that I was only looking out for her.

"Give me a break."

"It's good to see you up and around," he said.

Melanie groaned and went back into her bedroom.

Roland brushed by me, pleased with how things had turned out.

"You need a drink?" he said.

I couldn't say anything. He fixed two whiskey sodas.

Melanie returned dressed and putting a phone in her purse, checking her pockets.

"I'm going out. When I come back, you don't need to be here."

"Is she going to be okay out there?" I said when she'd left.

"She's meeting friends."

"For drinks? How will that go with her pain meds?"

"You didn't even hear her, did you?"

Roland was coming out of his timelessness. He smiled freely and cracked wise; an aura of simplicity and a confidence in the nature of the whole human experiment oozed out of him.

I couldn't have been more at a loss.

Roland gave me a glass. "Thank you," he said.

"For what?"

"For giving us a common enemy."

"But I'm not you're enemy."

"For a critical moment, you were. Before you came tonight, it was her versus me. I held her infidelity against her and she held my vengeance against me."

"The stabbing, you mean."

I thought that Roland wasn't taking that seriously enough and I wanted to hurt him and his idea of the world by bringing it out of the shadows.

"Damn Joshua. Of course the stabbing. But who can claim which is worse? That's why she's staying with me. She understands that and I understand that she understands it. The question then became one of time, and brother, you accelerated it with all your do-goodery. It gave us common cause. By declaring she wasn't safe you insulted me, you cast doubt on the strength we have together. Do you see?"

"Not even a little bit."

"Well, don't worry about that."

He swallowed his drink and suggested I do the same and get out of there in case Melanie decided to come back.

I was reassured. Not as to the good character of my friend, that was still in doubt and had probably always been so, but in the ability of people, of couples together, finding their own peculiar way. Hadn't I just been told and become convinced that an entire spectrum of possibilities exists in that realm? Was I now going to disallow this one, however brutal the violence and infidelity, simply because I didn't understand it? I felt a closeness with humanity then, which may have been simply a chemical release in my brain from having such tensions resolved and the hope that Liz will be pleased.

"I haven't forgotten what you asked about earlier, Roland," I said before leaving.

"And?"

"I have to run it by my accountant. Sums in that amount aren't easily withdrawn. I need to write up a reasonable cause for withdrawing it. It's a simple process, really. I'll just say I need a vacation or that I've decided to go back to school. Just something on record. But it takes time to get approval."

"How long?"

"A week. Ten days, tops."

"Thank you, Joshua."

I called Liz and left her an enthusiastic message.

For days afterward I stumbled around the city. I would have felt less like a foreigner in Europe than I did in this strange American city. I questioned the capacity of my spirit to live and work among the ambitions and affections of an urban populace. I saw everyone as either a victim or a perpetrator, and though I doubted the event of a knife in every case I was ruling it out less and less. The old proverb about heaven, where the spears will be pounded into plows, gave me an unsettling sense that this case with the knife was not an isolated event, but that knives and spears and sickles and every imaginable blade exists to sever the tenuous hold we have on life. Granted, we were not in heaven yet, but it had become difficult to believe in such a place given recent events.

I hadn't heard from Liz and I wondered, if she ever had knives for me, would she be willing to work them into a more useful shape, with a more noble purpose? I had once read an old French philosopher who said a fallow ground of weeds is unprofitable and that we are to cultivate the land with seeds proper to our service. I wondered then what fruit could be of service to me? Courage, moderation, and justice all came to mind. But shouldn't courage be used in war and justice in peace? And moderation in all things? Doesn't that allow us to be immoderate, and hence unjust and cowardly, at times? Self-justification is an arduous task.

I was struggling with my ideas of the good and reading *Poetry* when I came upon Fernando Pessoa's notebook:

How often, in the age-old trajectory of the worlds, a stray comet must have brought an Earth to its end! A catastrophe so utterly material will determine the fate of countless mental and spiritual projects. Death spies on us, like a sister of the spirit.

I had thought of my chance meetings with men and women as planets traveling in their determined orbits, and that is still true. However, not all celestial bodies are benevolent, not all coincidences are trite; sometimes a mad comet comes crashing into our plans and turns all of our previous life into a dream. It's then that we see how besmirched the City Beautiful is.

PART THREE

My contact with Roland Charles decreased significantly. I made it a point at first to answer only a small percentage of his incoming calls. I returned even fewer, then none at all. However, the frequency of his calls never wavered. I kept close to the buildings when I walked through the city, preferring the shadowy side of the streets and Avenue, and I was always accompanied by the crowd. I stayed away from Columbia University, the Monadnock Building and even the Institute, and when I couldn't do without an influential work of criticism about an artist or a poet, or a scholarly treatment of a historical event, I took the train to Hyde Park and walked to Chicago University's Seminary Bookstore. I rarely hailed a taxi, and on those evenings when it couldn't be prevented I suffered a moment of trepidation, of trembling, of sweats and chills, in case Mikhail should be at the wheel with Roland in the back seat eager to hear the explanation for my deliberate absence, but not to forgive.

Whenever I thought of Roland, which was more often than I care to admit, it was during those anxious moments or else in my daily thanksgiving to God that I was no longer embroiled in his schemes and small-time hijinks and attempted murders (at worst) and assaults (at best). I felt I had escaped my brief association with him unharmed, even while a small part of me missed the adventures I had in his tow and the confidence he had in his attempt to strangle a lucrative life from the city's grip. I never told Liz about this part of me that waxed nostalgic. She would have scoffed at my lack of moral fortitude and the weakness I had for his exuberance. I knew the story of Lot and his wife, who suffered the same predilection as myself, and became a pillar of salt because of it. But why wouldn't you look back? For me, such moments with him were so far beyond the pale that I couldn't believe they had happened. Even if his affect on my life and on the lives of those around me had not resulted in a fiery apocalypse, I was spellbound by the memories as Lot's wife was by the liquid inferno crashing upon her friends and neighbors. Don't we try to understand Dresden? Aren't we still perplexed by Sherman's March? Didn't those in the lifeboats watch the Titanic disappear beneath the frigid water? If the technology had existed we'd have those videos as well as that of planes colliding with the World Trade Center. Look away from that absurd moment; do not wonder at the city in ruins, at those sleeping on the sidewalks and park benches, at the man scaling the side of a building and those trying to wash him off. Impossible! Destruction will always have a special place in our imagination, examples of how awesome mankind can be even if they're on the wrong end of the scale. It reminds us just how fragile all of this really is and may even teach us to loosen our grip a bit.

After spending the Holiday weekend by myself and then the next one alone, I decided it would be best to let Liz be. I had sent texts and left messages on her phone, I e-mailed her a few times and sent quips to her other social media outlets, but they all disappeared at the end of the electronic superhighway, piled up and disregarded. I wondered that someone I had grown so fond of suddenly disregard my company. At first

I blamed her own shortcomings for this: her idea of friendship was too narrowly defined, she had become impatient with my sexuality, or else she didn't have the enthusiasm to discuss ideas that she had pretended at first. Then I had to relent and see my character and its peculiar leanings as someone not entirely fit for commingling. My own desires were not easily integrated into a healthy relationship, at least not one that Liz may have wanted. But then I didn't know what she wanted. I lacked the experience to divine such a thing and, I suppose, she was under no obligation to tell me.

Her absence had shaken me. I had my share of ghosts and now I had Liz in the same way. I looked out my apartment window and down State Street, knowing that whenever I walked through the city I would see Liz on her walks as well or else sitting at café tables reading, or looking out the windows of the CTA in the same way I saw Roland; perhaps the same way Roland saw Melanie's man everywhere he looked. Chicago was filled with such shadows.

It was a cold December morning when just such a shadow crossed my path.

Argo Tea was pressed to its capacity with Loyola students cramming for the final time of the year and there was no room for me to work. I walked down Chicago Avenue and thought about the prospect of losing a day's work if I couldn't find familiar repose. I supposed it would be all right. I had a number of such days left to me and if the world would not bow to greet my day's consistency, I would simply put my hands in my pockets and wait for the next one.

I was in just such a frame of mind later at Third Coast Café contemplating the usefulness of writing with a pen and carafe of wine. After two hours I still hadn't arrived at any profitable conclusions and I left feeling bit deflated and a little drunk. It was four-thirty and nearly dark so when I heard a gruff voice thick with a Muscovite accent bellow out syllables vaguely resembling my name I didn't acknowledge the connection. Then I caught the familiar scent of a pungent cigar as I strolled past a rust colored sedan and saw Mikhail climbing out from behind the wheel. He stood beside the car and laid his hands on the roof.

"Where's the taxi?" I said.

"It's warmer inside. You wait there."

"He's around, then?"

"Get inside. You will see."

I thought about what the alternative might be and got in. The windows were rolled up and the interior was filled with the smell of sharp tobacco. My eyes burned and when I tried to roll the window down, there were no handles and the button had been disabled or else Mikhail had the child locks engaged. We sat in the ambiance of Indian music that came softly from the speakers and tussled with the smoke so that when the melody came to my ear it was tired from the effort.

I took *Humboldt's Gift* out of my bag and after seven pages of fitful reading that I hoped gave off a care-free demeanor, I felt the cold Chicago winter on my face and heard the familiar jocularity of my friend.

"What a pleasant surprise. How are you, Joshua? Still kicking around, I see."

"You to. I almost didn't recognize Mikhail sitting here."

"Good thing he recognized you, then." Roland's easy smile was at odds with his eyes; they told me not to take his humorous nature at face value. "We had to upgrade our ride. Getting to be a big deal in the game now."

I doubted this very much. The interior was falling apart. There were rips in the upholstery, the ceiling cloth was frayed and there were impossible stains on the headrests. What little

I saw of the outside was enough to convince me that the body would rust out before the lake froze over. I decided much of what recommended it lay hidden under the hood.

"So I guess you and Liz are getting serious."

"Why do you say that?"

"Haven't seen you around lately. Or heard much from you. Figured it was that girl taking all your free time away."

"That's how it goes when you're in love, I guess. Time gets consumed in that one person and the rest are . . . "

"Forgotten. But not gone, Joshua. But I don't think that girl's doing much consuming. At least not with you. Here you are milling about in your usual spot, all depressed and shit. So sad and lonely you couldn't think of a reason not to wait for me. You didn't even think to say you had a date. So I think what happened is Liz got wise and split. Am I right?"

It wasn't a question, though. He knew.

"No."

He mocked surprise, "No?"

"You're wrong, Roland."

"I'm glad to hear it, then."

Roland stared through the haze into my eyes. His smile hardened into his jaw. I kept his gaze fearing that if I dropped it, he would jump me or break my nose.

"What's this about, Roland?"

"I wouldn't believe it, would I Mikhail? Everyone I talked to told me that it was you. That you were behind it. That no one other than you could have pointed the finger at me. But I told them that was impossible. Not Joshua. It couldn't have been. He has too much respect for the overall point of view, I told them. He can see it from all angles, which exempts you from acting. You're a coward, Joshua. I don't say that to belittle you. Hell, you know it's true. So I came to the only rational conclusion: your girl gave the police a call. Obviously, you told her. How could you not? She pushed you to act in the first place. Probably she couldn't stand to look at you anymore because of how scared you were. All shut up in your room scribbling into notebooks, thinking about pictures and what's good to do, but you don't know and even if you did you couldn't do it. Well, I know the good, Joshua. It's my business to know."

Mikhail pulled away from the curb.

"Anonymous tip. Someone told the police to look closer at my involvement in Melanie's attack. I'm told this person said some incriminating things. I'm told that I'm a person of interest now. Did she think I didn't have friends over there? I've made a lot of people a lot of money. Even a few on that side of the badge."

Roland never broke eye contact with me or loosened his jaw. My mouth had gone dry and I was wondering if I'd ever get to walk away from this smoking tomb. Is this why I hadn't heard from Liz? My God!

"But I'm a smart man, Joshua, and I can elude questioning for a little while. But I'm also smart enough to know that they'll get me sooner or later if I don't leave town. And if I leave town, I have no living. Everything I have is here. So I'm not going anywhere."

Now he waited for me. I heard him speaking, but my mind was occupied with thoughts of Liz, the last words I said to her and the last I saw of her deep below the city.

"You want the money? I'm your bail out?"

"That would be fine, Joshua."

"But if Melanie doesn't press charges, how can they take you in?"

"It's aggravated assault, domestic violence, testimony of the neighbors, and I'll be looking at three to five. Maybe more.

Probably more, unless I talk. Do you think they give a shit about my girl? Hell, I've got seven just like her all over the city. You know, for all your talk about vision, you don't see anything. I showed it to you one day, remember? Basketball game; countless stops; man in a fur coat? Had nothing to do with some little shit with a jump shot. He's small change. A distraction from the real action. A hundred thousand changed hands that day. With all your dough you've never seen it live before, in action, on center stage. You don't know what it can do, what it's capable of. If you did you wouldn't be wasting your time here."

"Then why do you need me?"

"'Because all my money's tied up at the moment and I can't get at it. Because I'd rather not use my stash on this annoyance. Because you brought this upon me and you're going to fix it so that it doesn't crush me. Take your pick man, I'm not going to explain it to you. I'm telling you this so that when you get my one phone call, you'll know why. And if you find yourself struggling between what's right and what's comfortable, Mikhail will be more than happy to convince you about what's good. Maybe even convince Liz to tell you what's good. She seems to be good at that."

I hoped this meant they hadn't gotten to her yet.

"So I pay your bail and you split? What happens to Melanie?"

"What do I care? I told you, I got seven more just like her."

I was speechless.

"Chicago's my town, Joshua. If I start going down here then I'm going to go all the way down in it. Melanie will fend for herself. You don't know a thing about her and it's about time you learned what kind of world you're actually living in. You have mixed up ideas about what kind of life you can live by . . . 'purity of feelings', you once said. And what was it that other time? How the sunset is God winking at you or some shit. Hell, Joshua, who can remember half the stuff you go on about? Well, he's not winking at you. God's winking at me. And then he disappears beneath the prairie and lets me do as I please. He's on my side, Joshua. Because when he finally peeks up from beneath the lake, it's only to survey the damage I've done and to see if I've allowed his special ones to have their coffee and take their morning runs. When they read the papers, it's my exploits they're curious about. My hands shape the world. Don't you see? It's my will you're fighting against."

"When God makes a bet with the devil it's to show him that he's wrong about the world. Men will their lives and not find a flaw in your way, but when one mind is renewed and it's given another line of sight, your proofs crumble and what remains is something else."

"What's that?"

"Thankfulness."

Roland laughed.

"A thankful man is the one who sees all that's good in the world and can endure all that's not," I said. "Of course, that comes across as naive to you because you don't have it and your life is filled with people you don't care about and who don't care about you. It's why you can give Melanie up so easily and why you're afraid I've turned on you."

"You're embarrassing yourself, Joshua. Be ready when I call."

Mikhail pulled the car into an alley. As I was getting out of the arid sedan, Roland grabbed my arm.

"If you don't pay Mikhail will beat your ass. Then he'll pay a visit to your little friends."

The car tore away from the curb. The acrid smoke clung to me and I was frantic. Why had he pluralized it? I fumbled with the buttons of my phone. I had to warn Liz and probably her family. But what could I say? How could I say it? She was only in danger if I didn't come through. But how could I let such a man go free? And how difficult would it be for me to disappear? I could easily relocate. Pay the remaining balance on my apartment and take off for California or Europe or buy another place in the country. Take Liz with me. Tell her family to be mindful. Take a description of Mikhail to the police; have him picked up as an accomplice of any one of Roland's schemes. But then how did Roland know Liz and I were through? The word was out about him, but any number of people could have turned: neighbors, mothers of ballplayers, another one of his girls who was finally fed up with sharing him. Unless he had someone on the subway with us who had heard everything, who knew where the McCormick's lived and where Liz lived. Roland was right, I didn't know the half of what he was. How many men worked for him? How far up was he in organized crime? How many plans had he devised in which to use my inheritance that I had innocently told him about?

Voice mail. I closed my phone. Of all the conversations I needed to have with Liz, this was the most fearful. I had to tell her that a man whose friendship I defended had threatened her life. I needed to reevaluate everything I had experienced with Roland. This new information changed the roles; it illuminated the actor he was, the wonderful props he used to portray a man at odds with the world struggling to gain an economic foothold. Perhaps Melanie herself was a prop. How did I know she was admitted to the hospital except that Roland told me? Hadn't they been unable to find her in the database? He could have easily met me at the hospital without having Melanie admitted . . .

I was easily persuaded, an eager audience, ready to assume the good in people.

I was too distressed to find any comfort in my apartment. I stepped back into the city and found myself in front of St. James Chapel. The church façade was still being cleaned and was covered by three stories of rusted yellow scaffolding. The driveway was open and I walked into the cobbled courtyard surrounded by stone and concrete walls with stained glass that caught what light there was and translated it into a kind of Holy Writ. Though for the most part muted or dull, when once a white beam struck the technicolor panes the window exploded in new light, the possibility of revelation. I considered the kaleidoscopic affect of the windows and wondered how the transcendental aspects of God could help me in this moment. I stared: at the spires, once the beacons of 1919 Chicago architecture, now themselves muted; into the late large gray afternoon; through that thick veneer into the black of infinite space; and passed the wonders of gas and rock to the very end of the cosmos before my imagination failed me. I remained chilled on the sidewalk. It was quiet and still. The stones didn't speak, either from stoicism or from boredom, which may be the same in the end. I asked if they had ever seen through all of us; if all our scurrying about made sense to them or if the absence of one from our vast number ever gave them pause.

Outside the walls I heard a delivery truck sigh.

Wasn't this the epicenter of resurrection? Where had such an idea originated if not from within these walls? Who would have the audacity to come up with such a thing? And I don't mean the raising of the dead. This hope and fear, depending upon your state of mind, has been with us since we first lost a friend or a beloved. No, I mean the idea that our natures, its desires and instincts, could be bettered, and this not from our own effort, the skillful management of vices or from living alone to hide one's flaws from himself, but through the belief that, through some peculiar transformation that has no reality at a molecular level, Christ's nature becomes our own. Sometimes overnight, sometimes not. This is not to say perfection comes to the man or woman; far from it. It simply means that when God looks at them, he sees his son, his daughter as co-heirs with Christ. Of course, this is not saying anything so great to those who haven't the time to consider what Christ has or who he is, and of course there are varying degrees of awe in which such things are discussed, both in oratory, in sanctuaries and in bars, and in writings, both secular and spiritual, as e-books or found in caves marked upon scrolls. *Through him all things were made; without him nothing was made* writes the one Christ loved. I do not claim to know what any of this means; I feel it, though. Another idea has been added to this, thanks to my discussions with Eric. I read Ephesians and we discussed the relevance of our lives *in Christ* in this world. We are His glory, he had said. According to His pleasure and good will and just like the Prodigal Son we have, each of us, the extent of his riches. Ephesians lays out what these riches are, because obviously they're not rubies or real estate or handsome features, but things of eternal value and not just valuable in our time; therefore these things — because their value exceeds our understanding of time — must be taken on faith. The long line of time removes Beauty from a man's body because it crumbles; in the same way plots divided on the lakeshore lose their value; wealth too becomes something else. I asked him what this *something else* was and he said, Verse three of Chapter One says: Praise God who has blessed us in the heavenly realms with every spiritual blessing . . . I had remained silent, thinking he was preparing to enumerate them. But that time he remained seated on his couch sipping his whiskey and nodding. A mischievous line of a smile hidden behind the rim of his glass. Subsequently, I have discovered *something else* on my own. I puzzled over it, fought against it, tried to understand it, then accepted it and thank God for it.

The courtyard of St. James Chapel had the aura of an empty tomb and I stared out from it onto Rush Street. I saw the entire city of Chicago stretch out into the prairie in one direction and dip into Gary, Indiana in the other; and I saw its highways reach into the fertile farmland of southeastern Michigan, stretch across the palm and into the Thumb where GE has, since my departure, erected a multitude of windmills, which stick out of the earth like acupuncture needles and eased the pain of some landowners; and I saw the narrow two-lane road that fed into my home town and led me past my elementary school turned retirement home turned apartment complex that has littered my kickball diamond with automobile frames and spare tires, rusted scrap metal and tattered patio furniture, around the bend to the cemetery where Dad's tombstone, beside my mother's, sticks out of the frozen ground like a thumbnail attached to a buried hand, ready to pull Earth away and show us what death really is, and I found rest from my mind's wandering. To this day I meditate in such a way before bed or when the traditional prayers aren't adequate and I sit or I lay upon the green grass and I wonder about them: where they are, what they're doing together, how they think of me, if they know how soon I'll see them again, if I'm doing okay here.

A Chapel attendant laid his hand on my shoulder and told me this was not an appropriate place to loiter. I was about to say I was praying, but I felt I had already said my piece and apologized to the gentleman.

I left Liz another message and walked home. I holed up in my room for a few days thinking about these things and not caring to stem the grief. Then I wanted to talk about them, so I put on my boots and went to see Eric.

I had been expecting a certain amount of flurry at the commune: hints of conversation, a stirring in the hallways, the faint scratching or smoothing of paint upon pliable canvases or other surfaces. None of this could be heard from the street of course, but the aura of artistic labor has its own strain, registered by the spirit and applauded. Instead, there was silence. A stillness had pervaded the complex, as if things had been settled.

and I took flight to Felix's building.

The doorman set aside his phone and buzzed me through to the elevator, inside which I had time to wonder if my donation had been for naught, or if the funds had been mismanaged resulting in the building's abandonment. After a moment taken to orient the sudden appearance of my face, Felix greeted me warmly and showed me in. I was surprised to see Eric standing in the living room observing Felix's collection. We shook hands, though Eric was not so cheerful as I; nevertheless, a sense of relief warmed my limbs as I found myself high above the city surrounded by objects and artifacts, anticipating the conversation I hadn't thought existed as I hurried along the frigid streets.

"I just came from your studio," I said. "Has something happened?"

"We were just discussing it," said Eric. He sat on the sofa, hunched over, pressing his palms together. "It seems a Situationist has emerged. A lover of the spectacle."

I couldn't see the connection and Felix said, "A man has been invited into the space by a fellow artist . . ."

"Stephanie invited him, Joshua."

"I've personally met with all the residents. I've seen their work and have visited them at their studios; I've made inquiries of people who know them personally and who vouch for them; I make sure the space I provide is not upset by more radical influences. I'm not afraid of dissent or of heated discussions about subject or expression, but I cannot allow anarchists to gain a foothold in the space."

"And now she's done it," said Eric. "I suppose it was inevitable."

"I don't understand."

"Stephanie has taken up with an artistic movement. She's abandoning the community."

"I don't know why you just don't let her go, Felix. Dissolve the contract and let her go on her merry way."

"Because I owe her the benefit of the doubt."

"Because you're afraid of her."

"Because it's my fault she's taken this action."

"She's a fool."

"She's looking out for herself," I said. "She believed you were abandoning them just as the community was beginning to work."

"That was never the case," said Eric. "At least, that was not my intention. I held out of one show in order to secure more funds for the building. To keep it going. I told Felix not to tell anyone about that because I felt uncomfortable about the whole thing and when the offer was rescinded word got around that I was holding out."

"But then it should have been a dead point," I said to Felix. "The show could have gone on. I would think."

Felix didn't understand, or he pretended not to. He said, "Eric was a scapegoat."

"Now that was my idea, said in a moment of insecurity or sensitivity."

"How's that?" I said.

Eric shook his head, not from regret but from self-doubt. He was as uncertain of other people's motivation as anyone.

"Stephanie's frustration resulted from her artistic expectations not aligning with reality. She needed something or someone to blame for her inability to translate her ideas onto canvas. Enter Felix; easy enough, I suppose. It was his fault that she wasn't selling. But she wasn't putting the work in. She wasn't ruthless enough toward her endeavors. When she was faced with struggling with her subject, of acknowledging her lack and striving that much more, she quit. This man she invited, Cornelius, encouraged her in this and has made surrender seem like a viable artistic choice."

"Surrender? In what way?" I said.

"We don't know for certain what they're planning," said Felix. "It could all be posturing . . ."

"They've taken their canvases to the beach to burn. It's an old idea from the Surrealist period that's been recycled to suit the eccentric whims of a bored sycophant."

"Eric."

"Let's call it what it is, Felix."

"We don't know that's what they're doing," Felix pleaded.

"He's attempting to capture chaos," said Eric. "Chaos is his only interest. He's very charismatic, speaks with passion and some authority and with that conviction, feigned or otherwise, he can convince many people to do what he wants. And all he wants, I believe, is to belittle conviction, to ridicule beliefs and condemn stances in art."

"And that has its place," said Felix.

"Not when those he leads to the bonfire can't see his real intention."

"Which is?" I said.

"I had better hopes for her," said Eric, who thought Cornelius was more of an open book than he let on. "She has talent as an artist, and her ideas are interesting, but her passion was never in expression. I think she merely wanted to appear to be an artist. That it could be a struggle was never something she entertained. Now with Cornelius, she's found exactly that."

"Do you grudge her finding happiness with him?" said Felix. "Maybe his ideas are just the thing to spur her on."

Eric shrugged. "It's not a good start if she's losing her own artistic sensibilities within his peculiar vision. And if she really has abandoned her art, we need to find someone else to take her studio space."

"I'm not going to do anything about that until I hear from her," said Felix.

"I have some people in mind, Felix. Artists who will lend this project validity."

"Cornelius's methods may be contrary to our traditional ones, Eric, but that's no reason to cast him off," said Felix. "Have you spoken to him?"

"I've met him a few times. We had an engaging conversation once, when we were alone, and one not-so-good conversation in Stephanie's presence."

"What's your impression?" said Felix.

"He's a contrarian," said Eric. "He was interested in my work and its ideas only as a foil to his own. He needs an Other from which to work. His vision is to paint sarcasm onto seriousness. That has its place, and God forbid we artists become too serious, but when it's all you've got it will dry up fast and you'll starve. Artistically, I mean. I don't know how long he'll last, Felix."

"And Stephanie?" I said.

"Stephanie never cared for my work. I am too moralistic for her taste. Too high-minded maybe; a Holy Roller and a 'Jesus Crispy' she once said. She's doubtful of her talents and desires. I challenged her to really engage with her art, to struggle with it and seek it out at all hours of the day and in all manner of perfecting. She preferred Cornelius's situations. Automatic painting. Get into a state, set the clock in motion, and *voila!* It seems like a séance for dead auras to me."

Felix was intent on Eric's tone. In my brief knowledge of him I had never heard Eric speak so vehemently.

"I told her about the Spirit once. She heard 'true being', but that's not what I was talking about. If the Spirit is what I think it is, then everything we see, touch, hear, and taste are all shadows of it. That includes art. This world that come at us from all sides, whose very air seeps into our skins and penetrates our systems are representations of some greater truth already. They serve as reminders of the Spirit if we use them carefully. And this is the new path my art will travel on: to become a reminder of the mysteries we already know."

Felix was nodding his head, surrounded by his artifacts and paintings, and I wondered what Eric already knew and how he was reminded that he knew. His ideas had left me behind and I became merely a willing listener.

"I think I'm on the right path, though" said Eric playfully, retuning to his more familiar tone, perhaps knowing he had spoken too freely about things only he understood. "Stephanie thinks I'm mad, of course. You look a bit confused as well, Joshua. 'Since he is remote from human concerns and close to divinity, his is criticized', though he be possessed by a god.

That's Plato. Phaedrus. The things I think of are peaceful, stable, perfect. I spend a good part of my day in blissful meditation upon these mysteries, and the fullness I have in them gives me strength to endure my loneliness here. I hope to meet others who think like I do, who know these mysteries and have traveled in that life further than I have. I have spent many hours in my room alone with fevers from seeing, however briefly, those reminders of 'the plain of truth'; in my walks around the city or within the pages of forgotten books. I will catch a glance from a beautiful woman or hear an encouraging word from the mouths of men, or witness an act of kindness in our harried world and know that I have seen something strange yet familiar. I look for these reminders everywhere now. Every day the veil is drawn back further and further and my spirit longs for the day when it will be completely removed and I will dwell within those mysteries forever."

There was no suitable place to respond after this statement. I feared that further questions — a first question, really — would slap the cherub-like innocence and fascination of the unseen off Eric's serene face. In fact, Eric had been somewhere else during his soliloquy and when Felix cleared his throat to speak, Eric smiled sheepishly.

"The world of art is able to embrace all methods, Eric. Your idea, tentative perhaps, happens to be one. Cornelius happens to have another. It's all very exciting."

Eric was stung and Felix turned to me, "Cornelius has had numerous showings."

"Where?" said Eric.

"In Nebraska. He had quite a following there, I'm told. In fact, his current pieces are going to be displayed at a restaurant opening. I believe the manager has the right of first refusal after the opening. Perhaps they will remain permanently on the walls."

This idea kept Felix in a peculiar state, envisioning a success for his own endeavor that eluded Eric.

"Cornelius represents a hedonism that people are too cowardly or ashamed to admit in their daily lives," said Eric. "They're nothing but wish-fulfillment pieces. Life is destroyed if those fantasies come down off the walls and mingle with real people."

"Poor Stephanie," I said.

Eric shook his head. "Stephanie is doing exactly what she wants. She never wanted to be an artist. That was a pretext toward independence. A way to gain some cultural clout, even. But she doesn't have the discipline to continue with the hard work of creation nor the strength to look deep within herself and reveal what she finds. With Cornelius, she disappears into his importance, into mere act. It's a way to dissolve her vision, or to deflect the fact that she doesn't have one."

"All the more reason why we should talk to her," I said.

"She's a grown woman, Joshua," said Eric. "She'll only resent you. Let the logical consequences of her decisions play the part of the parent."

"What's happened to the exhibit that I helped fund? Has that gone up in flames, too?" I said.

"It's been set up, Joshua," said Felix. "Except Eric has pulled out. It seems it will primarily be the collaboration of Stephanie and Cornelius's art."

"I can't be a part of that," Eric said. "Cornelius thrives on satire. He doesn't hold any serious beliefs. He simply ridicules others. If I'm presented by his side, then his art has some power to persuade some people. I can't risk that. I don't want my art to be a springboard to something opposed to my meaning. Let Cornelius's art speak on its own, if it can."

The evening grew tired and I left them to their concerns. I was not ashamed in my heart to desire the meaning and importance of a resurrected life. The disappointment I carried with me was not in that search, but rather that my search had thus far, that night, led to dead ends. But the more I walked those dark, cold Chicago streets, the more I became aware that everything in this world is a shadow of the mysteries, like Eric said: indistinct, multi-formed, casting out from a house, dragging behind a cockroach, flitting across a building from a bird, a plane, a cloud, a particle of water falling off a window-washer's scaffolding and shattering upon the sidewalk or onto a scalp and into a million other particles again, each with its own shadow, etcetera.

Where are the mysteries not found?

And I was even hopeful of Cornelius' exploration. Strong opinions, even those expressed with a smirk, are necessary of course, but only because options, however repugnant to some, must be available in order to understand desire. However, I couldn't help feeling that Stephanie's canvases deserved better than the flames.

Walking home, with digressions and the free flow of associations the city presented me, beneath darkened buildings and through the steam exhaling from the tunnels, I felt I had secured a solid hold from which to continue climbing through this treacherous life. I was convinced this idea was the first real grasp I had toward living with the mysteries inherent in resurrection. Within this revelation, I re-evaluated my relationships and my ambitions, what I hoped for myself and the world I would one day inhabit, and fell asleep in my chair, holding a pen.

The next morning, I reread what I had written and found I'd vastly overrated my control of language. I had only written my thoughts, not what had been between them. I hadn't captured any of the euphoria or the fear and my revelation read like juvenilia, something to not bother adults with or those more attuned to what this world actually is. My wish for a miracle, for some kind of mystical experience in the flesh — to see Dad's face in a shop window or to feel my mother's hand in mine as we waited to cross the street — was scolded by the morning light, which revealed the banality of my room.

I sat in my chair with another book and imagined it was not too late to expect a call from out of the silent expanse. I was primed for a validation of some kind from the inroads I had made in the city. My spirit had grown. It had escaped its ties to childish ways and, I hoped, was having its effect, if not yet upon those men and women I had become conscious of, then on the waves of the lake and the grass on the prairie. Instead, I lived through that day and the next in silence and doubt. I was not incapable of reaching out; I had phone numbers that would connect me to my loved ones back home and those scattered throughout the city. I had addresses I could speak into the ears of taxi drivers who would take me to their thresholds. But I was tired, and it was only with difficulty and in brief stages that I could read anything of note. Nothing from the past reached out its hand to aid me. These desires were not common to men and the mystical life, I was realizing — that inward vision of resurrection and its attendant mysteries could not easily be transferred to works of fiction.

Not having any expectations towards strengthening my spirit or educating my soul then, I watched television. I left it on continuously and when I returned with a bag of food, it was to its easy glow and comforting noise and easy drama that I returned.

I have since come to see days such as those as the natural affect of serious literary work. I was engaging then with

heady things and a corrective was bound to become necessary. I found boredom was just the thing and when my mind
needed to rest I felt no guilt or remorse for having spent an
entire afternoon at the movies or laying on my bed watching
football and napping, ordering in and keeping myself from
those daily hygienic rituals that can become so bothersome.
I began needing such days twice a week, whether from habit
or because my mind could only sustain concentration or even
interest in its various projects that long. My attitude toward
such days of rest — longed for and embraced in the morning
hours, unthought of in the afternoon and dispensed with by
evening when my ambitions began urging me again toward
the next morning's work — evolved from one of scorn to one
of satisfaction. I was not wasteful of my time; I was putting in
work the only way I knew how and believed, with the appearance of such unproductive days, that I had turned a corner in
my pursuit as a writer.

The next day I again set myself to my task. What caught
my attention in John this particular day holed up in my apartment above the snow-covered streets licking my many-faceted
wounds was his description of Jesus' interaction with the crowd.
No one had to tell him about men; he knew what was in a man.
And then I thought how understanding is the beginning of
love. And I thought, if God knows all of us and still loves us,
then we must all be of great and rich value. For God sees all
that is not seen and calls things that aren't as though they were.

I became convinced that I needed new eyes; eyes that saw
beyond the constructs of the world of men and into the spiritual and mystical realities of the world of God, his perspective,
his point of view. Somehow I needed to destroy my vision in
order to resurrect a new sight. I needed mud on my face. And
strength, of course, for my courage balked when I thought of

how the blind man, once healed, saw men who appeared as trees. The miraculous has never been entirely freed from the ridiculous, I suppose.

This is what I had wanted to talk to Eric about the night I stumbled upon the Situationists.

I walked through the Viagra Triangle, down the broad avenue of the Magnificent Mile and among the denizens caught up Chicago's golden apples and its fleeces, its industrial capabilities and logistical solutions, its well-oiled system of private trade and, yes, in each other: ad executives poets substance abusers stock traders sycophants pastors adolescents oil tycoons Moms cattle rustlers architects adulterers number crunchers hypocrites engineers ball players receptionists the unemployed the unemployable federal postal employees artists professors criminals graphic designers and philosophers all pacing toward or away from DuSable Bridge, while the black water ran silently between concrete shores. I was awash in strange and intoxicating humanity, their voices and exclamations, their sly nose picks and strap adjustments, their confusion and laughter, trips and stumbles, pushing when they should pull, walking when they should stay on the curb, bumping into caroming off of halting mid-stride blowing breath smoke words into faces of friends and strangers, whose desires brushed against motivations, whose wills were constantly being challenged as the city attempted to corral everyone from every side or itself be razed in the crush.

Eric wasn't at his studio and when I knocked on Felix's door he hesitated to allow me entry. When he finally opened the door I was ushered into yet another nightmare.

Felix stood battered and small before me. His right arm was in a sling and his head was bandaged. I saw his left eye was swollen and it looked as though his nose had been shattered.

The apartment was in shambles, as well. Furniture was flipped, its upholstery torn with knives; statues had toppled and broken; ribbons of canvases were strewn about, ripped from their frames, hanging off the ceiling fan and covering lamps. The large concrete block sat inside the coffee table surrounded by broken glass.

"Felix? What happened?"

"I was robbed. Or maybe not robbed. Vandalized. And I got jumped."

"Who would do this?"

"Friends of yours. Or, I don't know; one of them said he was your friend. I didn't ask any questions. When I opened the door he struck my head. While I was on the ground, his friends kicked me and hit me. They took some things, I think. I haven't been able to assess the damage. They destroyed what they couldn't carry."

"Felix . . . "

"Who were they, Joshua? Who would do these things in your name?"

The obvious answer screamed through the carnage and my fear of Roland's destructive nature deepened. I remembered how Roland had come to my apartment that first night, uninvited, full of pep and a mouth full of teeth, the smile of a devil already hinting at what he really was, enjoying the foolishness of his prey. He had followed me here, too.

"Eric is in the hospital. He's in critical condition, Joshua."

"You can't believe I had anything to do with this."

He lowered his eyes, but said he didn't.

"But I can't say I'm completely innocent, either," I said. "I think the man was a . . . I may know the man. He needs money. He's already asked me for twenty-five thousand and when I tried to evade him he found me and threatened me. He must have followed me here. But I have no idea how he would know your name or which apartment you were in or how he could get that information. How reliable is your doorman?"

"You know him?"

"If it's who I think it is, yes. Believe me, if I thought this guy was going to be any kind of threat to you, I would have warned you."

I thought how imperative it was for me to know Liz had received my messages, that she was taking them seriously.

"I know, Joshua," he said and slowly lowered himself into a chair. "If you wouldn't mind, I could use some help cleaning up. I have an obvious deficiency in hoisting pillars and hanging canvases."

I helped Felix as best I could. He was groggy from the pain medication and when he fell asleep I returned his relics to the best of my memory. When I was finally at a loss, I called the police and told them a man named Roland Charles had assaulted my friends and stolen some valuable art. Felix would be alarmed at my mentioning his collection, but there needed to be some clarity about whom we were now dealing with. Clearly Roland was losing the grasp of his many operations. Art had never been among his interests, so far as I knew them. He was not discriminating in what he chose to take, either. His only criteria seemed to be size, but even in this he failed to lift the 7"x10" Picasso sketch that Felix had framed on the kitchen wall. Apparently, Roland believed real art would never be so diminutive nor be found in such a pedestrian space.

I left another message for Liz. I told her I believed Roland had attacked Felix, that I was at his apartment cleaning up the damage and was certain something similar could happen to her and her family. I held nothing back from her.

I cleaned the floors and picked up the glass. I piled busted frames by the door and draped salvageable canvases over the couch and on his spare bed until replacement frames could be found. The resurrection piece I had admired was torn down the center and trampled, ripped and twisted where a heel had spun upon it.

When Felix woke up I warmed up some soup and we ate at his table. I told him what I'd told the police and he shrugged. He told me stories about how and why he had purchased the works and the frames; how the two separate pieces, both worthy of admiration in their different rights, were gathered from the width and breadth of the world to fuse into what he had proudly displayed. He reminisced and I listened and when the effort became too difficult for him or when he could no longer caress his memories with a steady voice, he sat on his and talked about his life that had nothing to do with his art collection or that world.

"I grew up here, you know. The city right out there . . . It has never disappointed me, Joshua. It's always been there for me, even after Richard died and I was convinced it would destroy us all, if not with pleasure then with indifference. But I have felt its enfolding arms around my dreams since I was a small boy. I've always endured. I saw a lot of life back then, some of it strange. Most of it, in fact. And I knew that I wasn't any more strange than the rest of it, and if Chicago could find happiness for all those millions of people then surely it would have room for me, too.

"And I have lived in that embrace. I am good at what I do, Joshua. I have found favor with powerful men and with kind men. I have butted heads with some ruthless characters and been encouraged by saints. Through it all I was allowed to follow my peculiar path and see my dreams materialize. That's what all this art is. Or was. They were my dreams materialized. I followed their call throughout the world, but it was always only those pursuits that I salvaged. The art was just souvenirs of what I had found within myself. Even after all of this," he waved his good arm over the remaining ruins, "after looking around and cleaning up the debris and taking an inventory of all that has been taken, I believe nothing of true value was disturbed."

"That man is a lunatic, Felix."

"And yet Chicago holds him, too. Even his way of life will be preserved in the arms of the metropolis. Perhaps it could only be so in the city."

"Is Eric allowed visitors?"

"Yes."

We finished cleaning up the aftermath of his ordeal. I wiped down the kitchen while he emptied the bathroom trashcan and tied the refuse bags in a knots before seeing me out.

"There's a shoot at the end of the hall," he said. "I appreciate all you've done today."

"Felix, I wish I'd never met that man."

"But you have met him. Be careful."

I listened to the dead bolt slide and disposed of the trash. The city was abuzz in its familiar energy, but I couldn't retrieve my exuberance of the fact. I took a cab to the hospital where I recognized the gentleman at the reception desk. To him I was just another in a long string of unremarkable, sorrow-streaked faces.

Eric's room had a chapel feel to it, dim and somber. A low light buzzed from the television on the wall and a speaker spoke softly beside his ear. His face was swollen and covered in bandages. His nose had been broken and his left cheekbone was shattered. The blankets concealed a snapped clavicle, his shoulder was separated, five ribs were bruised and three were cracked; a lung had been punctured and there was severe bruising on his legs that made them numb and unusable for the next few weeks, maybe longer, depending on the severity of the muscle damage.

I knocked on the wall to announce myself and said his name. The one eye I could see in the low light rolled toward me. His face didn't betray any feelings he may have had toward me and I was thankful for the medication that impaired his ability to express himself. I did not care to hear him condemn me for being mercilessly beaten by three hoodlums chanting my name and laughing while he hugged a pedestal, anticipating he'd be thrown out Felix's large window onto the street below.

"Who's there?" he said timidly.

"It's Joshua. Eric, I am so sorry."

He winced as he turned toward me.

"Don't move. Here." I pulled a chair around and sat next to him.

"How is Felix?"

"He's home. I just came from there."

"We need to have a talk with that doorman of his," Eric said.

"We thought the same thing."

Eric clenched his eyes and groaned.

"What can I do for you?"

"The nurses are doing all anyone can do for me at the moment."

"It's all my fault, Eric. Those men would never have had the opportunity to do this to you if I hadn't led them to Felix's door. I should have paid attention to all the red flags."

"They only turn colors after the fact. Until then, they're always white. Anyway, Felix was a fool to let them in. Your name brought his guard down. I was on the couch when the crew burst in. I heard a loud crash and Felix yelped, then screamed. By the time I was able to appreciate the situation two men were upon me and, well. I blacked out, of course, and came to here. The doctor told me what had happened. 'Joshua says hello.' That's the last thing I remember hearing."

I bowed my head.

"You said you went to the studio that night? Did those men go there too? Was anyone else hurt?"

"I don't know. I don't think so. Roland doesn't see the value in contemporary art."

"I would think with his appreciation for destruction he's enjoy Cornelius's *oeuvre*." I was surprised by his ability to crack jokes in his state, but then laughter is not entirely barred from tragedy. "Maybe what Roland did to us was his performance piece, eh? I don't recall having seen any cameras, though. Then again it happened so fast."

A nurse came in and checked Eric's vitals and the dosage rate on his intravenous. He scratched on the chart and smiled before quietly closing the door.

"They're like little spirits," said Eric. "They flutter in to make sure nature still has its way with me and when they see that it does, they fly away until I'm better suited to serve the world. I have Stephanie's number if you wouldn't mind calling her. Just in case he . . . gets any ideas . . ." I had tired him out and the pain medication was keeping his mind in a fog.

"I will."

Eric's lips continued to move, but the room was silent except for the beeping and clicking of machines. I stepped into the hall and called her, but there was no response. I was beginning to think cell phones would prove as useful in an evening emergency as smoke signals.

After some casual scrutiny I got into a cab. The studio was dark and sullen and I told the driver to sit tight a moment. This time the doors were locked and I couldn't be sure the place hadn't been ransacked from peering into the window. No one was there and I was unsure what that meant for Stephanie's safety. There was no police tape or signs of a task force investigation so I paid the cabbie and walked back to my building.

I stepped into the Zebra Lounge for a drink. It was empty except for the barman and the television showing the local news. There was no mention of Roland or the theft of ancient artifacts, or that someone in Chicago would actually have the things Felix had. It was too dark to be this early, I thought. I dialed Liz again. A man's voice answered.

"Is Liz there?" I said, straightening up.

"This is her father. To whom am I speaking?"

So she'd lifted me from her contacts.

"This is Joshua Thomas. I had dinner with your family last weekend."

"Oh, Joshua. You've put our family in a bad way, young man."

"I was hoping he didn't know about you all."

"We had the pleasure an hour ago. My wife is inconsolable. What have you gotten us into over here?"

"I'm not exactly sure, sir. I think a man I know is desperate. He's already been to my friend's apartment, maybe a second friend as well, I don't know. He's threatened me, too. I called the police and they are aware of him and may already have him in custody."

"Have they called you to identify him?"

"No."

"Then he's still out there."

"Can I talk to Liz?"

"She would prefer not to."

"Is she okay?"

"Of course she's not okay. He came right up to our door and rang the bell like it was

some kind of social call. When my wife answered it, the brute shoved her to the ground and demanded to speak with me. I was at the office at the time and the maniac went berserk, shouting all kinds of things about how reliable a working man's schedule should be and that I should be having dinner with my family in the evening. It'd almost be comical if he hadn't struck my wife and thrown over our China cabinet. He demanded a hundred thousand dollars, Joshua. On the spot."

"Mr. McCormick I . . . "

"I'll bet you are."

"Did he say if he'd be back? Are you protected over there?"

"Until I know more about this situation and feel confident that you're not playing a part in it, I'm not going to answer any of your questions. I've called the police and suggested they have a talk with you."

"I understand, sir. I'll be happy to talk to them. I should have . . . "

Mr. McCormick cursed my name and hung up.

There was nothing else for me to do. I rested in my room and watched the city sparkle under the winter sky. The lights were clear and sharp in the early darkness, as if the cold had frozen their illumination. Events had proven too powerful for me. My duty to my friends had been completed, such as they were, and I marveled at just how little one man can do for another. Ever hopeful, I picked up a book and tried to read. I put it down and started another one at random. I passed considerable time with this game and it was still early evening. I called the police and was told someone would be getting back to me. I thought my reaching out to them would speak to my innocence in all of this.

I was wakened by soft knocking at my door and a gentle whistling, an Irish tune perhaps. I thought I dreaming and saw what appeared to be an orchestra, a dark and rolling figure swallowing winks of light reflected off polished winds, backed by a maroon-draped choral group swaying to the solitary wind instrument off-stage. I grew anxious for the symphony to rise and crash over me and when that didn't happen, when the knocking became persistent and the voice less cooing, I roused myself and had a look through the peek hole. Until I saw him, I held out hope that it would only be a neighbor, or maybe Liz had come to assuage the horror I felt at bringing Roland into their lives . . .

"Open the door, Joshua. I can hear you sniffling."

"Are you alone?"

"What are you worried about?"

"You put my friends in the hospital."

"Did I?"

'You robbed him of valuable things."

"Is that right?"

"Yes. It is."

"Do you have valuable things in your room, Joshua?" I looked around, then cursed myself for being instinctively accommodating. "I've been in your place. You got nothing I want, so don't worry about it. As for the other, if I wanted to beat the shit out of you I'd have brought some of my friends along. And we wouldn't have waited for you to answer, either."

"And you threatened Liz."

"Let me in, Joshua."

"What are you planning with her?"

"Let me in. I'm not going to explain every goddamn thing through a fucking door."

I hoped for any foresight I may have had earlier in obtaining a weapon or two, but of course I hadn't. I could hear Eric and Felix shouting in my ear as I twisted the deadbolt; I could see Liz throwing up her hands in exasperation as I turned the knob; and I saw Roland grinning up at me, fists pressed into the frame as I opened the door. He wore a dark fitted suit and a brown bowler hat pulled low over his eyes. I couldn't see the bulge of a weapon anywhere on him, nor did I notice any metal surrounding his knuckles. I didn't rule out the pipe concealed in a closed fist.

"Now invite me in."

I moved aside and he took off his hat and walked down my small hallway. He frowned when there was no hook and dropped the felt hat on my bed before sitting in my leather chair.

"Got anything to drink?"

"Whiskey."

"Two fingers, then."

I poured it for him.

"You're not joining me?"

I didn't move. I pressed my back against the wall stunned at my inability to keep the wolves from my sanctuary. Roland swirled the auburn liquid and swallowed half of it. He grimaced and shook a bit. "You drink strong shit."

"I usually cut it."

"Of course you do."

I waited.

"I want to apologize to you, Joshua. I haven't been forthright with you lately. Or at all, for that matter. For instance,

I remember telling you that I would call you for bail money if I should be picked up, but . . . do you mind sitting down, please? You're making me nervous . . . as it turns out I need to get the cash from you now. I'm sorry I told you I would need bail money in the first place. That must have worried you and you already have so much on your mind as it is. I told you that hoping you would be more apt to fork over some of your idle dough if a friend were really in trouble. Now I see, hell I've seen it for some time, we were never really friends."

Roland swallowed the remaining whiskey. He took it much better.

"It's always been about the money with you, hasn't it?" I said.

"I don't want all of your money, Joshua. Just a fraction."

"There are millions of fractions, Roland."

"Probably more."

"And when you don't get it, you'll hurt Liz."

"I've got a man on her, yes; and though I would hate to green light him I won't hesitate. He'll do it right now. Hell, we can be sure to have her on the phone so you can hear her and not miss any of his work, which is quite good. And when that's done we'll still be sitting right here and I'll dial another number. I noticed only one of your friends was hospitalized overnight."

I looked out the window and down State Street illuminated by the behemoth Hancock. The world carried on as it usually did.

"I don't want to deal unfairly with you, Joshua," he said. "It's a heartless bastard who strong-arms a hundred thousand out of a defenseless man so I'll make you a better deal. You give me what I want and not only do I call off the dogs, but I return all that man's worthless shit to him."

"You don't know what to do with it all, do you? You saw his apartment and thought you'd hit it rich. Thought your camel hair and Blackhawk buddies would be proud of you and give you money or respect or let you in on some new scheme simply because you beat a kind man and took his blocks and sketches."

"Yea, well I overestimated their appreciation for beautiful objects."

"And you don't know anybody in that world who could move it for you. Your sitting on priceless artifacts that are worthless in your hands. A man adrift on the Atlantic, dying of thirst."

"You're doing a lot of teasing for a man this close to hearing the screams of the woman he loves."

"How can you threaten such things after what Melanie's suffered? It tore you up to see her afterward and yet you're still capable of . . ."

While the question was still being worked out in my mind I had my answer. Training in artifice, Roland had been adept at creating uncanny situations and had some skill at convincing the audience it was probable. Roland's sinister smile came slow, like a sunrise, and like a man sitting on a beach, it dawned on me.

Roland raised his glass in salute. I sighed and collapsed on my bed.

"The moans of enlightenment," he said, laughing.

That's why the nurse couldn't tell me which room Melanie was in; it's why Roland was waiting for me in the lobby instead of with her in the ICU or the waiting room; it's why I never got a clear look at Melanie's injury and why she left as soon as I insisted. What was that about the wise man falling into a pit from looking at the heavens? I had been ideally dumb.

"From the start, Roland?"

"From day one. But to be honest with you, I had good intentions at first. The way you talked me out of mugging you was priceless. I'll never have that experience again and while it was happening I kept yelling at myself, 'Crack him open already!' Stupid asshole alone down there and I didn't take advantage, but what the hell. You were oblivious. Anyway, we had a nice drink, some laughs. But you say all kinds of interesting things when you're high Joshua, and it got my wheels turning."

My head was swimming from the evening's revelations. In this world it seems the cruelty of a man is as difficult to discover as the machinations of the divine spark. Both need a stern resolve to find them.

"A hundred thousand dollars, Joshua. It would really help me out." He got out of my chair and smoothed down his pants, adjusted his lapels. "And if I don't get what I want I'm going to drop the man's shit into the Chicago River, maybe send him in after it. Then if I still don't get what I want, I'll introduce myself to your girlfriend and her parents. After that, your connections to this city become less substantial, but I'll do away with them as well."

He reached into his jacket pocket and pulled out a piece of paper. He unfolded it and showed me a sketch that I remembered from Felix's hallway depicting a brown inked cityscape of an Indian bazaar. He took a lighter from his other pocket and set it on fire. He turned the print up and down, guiding the flame as it devoured, watching the flame pulse, inhale exhale, until, satisfied, it shrank into the last corner and he dropped it onto my carpet, pressing a burgundy wingtip into char, embedding the ash.

"I don't know what that was or who drew it or when or how much it might be worth," he said. "To me it's worth exactly what it is now. To others it may be worth more. I don't give a damn about the sacks of shit I have holding countless junk just like it. I'd just as soon drown it all."

He took out his phone and dialed. "You still on her? We're leaving now. I'll be in touch." He dropped the phone into his breast pocket and said, "Let's go."

"Where are we going?"

"To get my money."

"How do I know your guy is anywhere near Liz? How do I know you were even talking to somebody just now?"

"The time for playing is over, Joshua. Everyone's off the stage now and this is really happening." He took out his phone. "You see this? Recent calls, see? Press it and listen."

I waited until Mikhail picked up then gave it back.

"What does that prove?" I said.

"What's our girl wearing, Mikhail? Uh-huh… Oh, nice. Looks good, huh? Alright, that's enough. Don't go falling in love, Comrade." The call ended. "Now call her. She's wearing green pants and a brown coat. White hat. Some other shit, too, but I stopped listening to him. I think he's quite taken with her. Maybe he hopes you don't come through."

"Liz, this is going to sound ridiculous, but I need you to call me back. I need to know . . . and I know it's not going to sound good . . . I need to know what you're wearing. Roland has . . ."

Roland took my phone.

"Alright, that's enough. If she calls back you'll see I'm right and even if she doesn't you know Mikhail's keeping a close eye. If I was lying I would've never let you make that call. So, let's go."

"To the bank?"

"Where else?"

"I can't just withdrawal a hundred grand."

"Did you know if you take out ten grand the bank has to report it to the IRS, who will come around asking questions that I'm afraid you can't answer responsibly. But sums less than that don't attract attention. Now you can't be a dick and take out $9,990. Bankers are smart people and shouldn't be trifled with. So we come in every couple of weeks, take out eight or nine at a time . . . Should be okay."

"And you're going to follow Liz the whole time?"

"Why not? Mikhail's got nothing to do and all the time to do it in. You two actually have a lot in common."

Roland was getting what he wanted and he was giddy at the prospect.

I was sick thinking about these maniacs stalking my friends, extorting my inheritance.

"Or I tell them I'm going to Northwestern. Live on campus, finish my undergraduate degree. That should cover what you want."

"And when you endorse the check to cash? What do you think they'll do? Alarm bells, man. No, I'm afraid you're going to have to have the cash on you when I come calling."

"In a little brown sack?"

"Oh Joshua, all the signs were there and still you kept hanging on."

The teller but the bills inside a small manilla sleeve and I signed the receipt. Roland had waited on the corner outside. Said he wasn't looking his best to be on so many cameras. I gave him the money and he slapped my shoulder.

"It's too bad it has to be this way, Joshua. I really do like you, in spite of this, I mean," he said thumbing the wad of hundreds, music to his ears, the sensual fragrance. "But I have an opportunity that requires me to forego the luxury of friendship.

It's too bad you weren't looking for investment opportunities. We could have been partners."

The next day I walked to Felix's apartment. The still, gray air that surrounded the noise and the smell of the city created a substance through which I moved with some difficulty. The fact of this obstacle was almost imperceptible except that I felt it in my blood, in my faltering step, in the slow movement of my head as I took in the usual Gold Coast. There was not an object that opened itself up to me; there was not a sensation given to easy interpretation; and every face I passed on my slow walk to the bruised and battered man's home seemed to look away with more reason than before.

"Call the cops again," said Felix when I told him I didn't know what else to do. "They're trained in this sort of thing."

Felix wore a burgundy robe and had gone a few days without shaving or showering; his hair was thick and disheveled and he didn't conceal the fatigue he suffered as he fell into a chair, arms limp over the armrest, out-spread legs smooth and white. He wasn't as helpful as I had hoped. Granted, I woke him from much needed sleep and he was struggling through the fog of memory, trying to piece together actual events from those he experienced in his dreams, where he was presumably content to spend the remainder of his days. He offered this advice in a direct, common sense tone that had run out of patience with me even though I was offering a chance to retrieve his life's work.

"And then what further complication could be expected if they were involved?" I said. "Will they put a watch on Liz's apartment and her parent's house? On you and Eric? Roland has people on her and if they happen to spot the cops or if the cops spot them, if there's a shoot-out on the street or Roland's people get taken in, or if he doesn't get his money, he'll kill Liz before the cops can even get the paperwork through."

"He's not going to kill her," said Felix. I was surprised to hear him say this given his current situation.

"I believe he will."

"You believe quite a bit of what this fellow tells you. Perhaps you should think how well that's served you."

"What should I do then?"

Felix shruggd.

"You really don't want your pieces back?"

"Joshua, art has a separate life after it has been created. It has its own destiny, its own fate. It's either granted with permanent exhibition, thankful residents and inspired citizenry, or else it remains secluded, unappreciated except by a few, covered in volcanic ash or floodwaters, leveled by a demolitioner's explosive, sunk to the ocean's floor or shelved with countless others in one of our libraries. Like men, we don't know how art will live out its days or when its time to die is. Did Rushdie know how many years of his life would be sacrificed by the publication of the *Verses*? Did he know his work would come to kill its translators and that his publishers' houses and the stores that sold the novel would be bombed? Art has this effect, too. It's an eventuality that all men and women should consider after the Muse has left them with something beautiful."

I couldn't believe how easily he was acquiescing to destruction. "But we can stop this, Felix."

"No, we can't. Only you can. You can decide what you're going to do, Joshua. I've given my advice and I'm coming to terms with losing those pieces. I'll be okay and the world will be okay without them, too. That man will not destroy my love for the beauty of higher things. He'll merely burn paper or sink stone."

"But you loved them."

"I did, but representations aren't meant to last forever. They do for a time and then that time passes and another representation is needed. It's the evolution of an idea that art as a whole represents. Past works, present efforts, are merely the steps toward a final art. They're postcards from the stages of that journey, which will never be completed. If I hadn't intervened in rescuing them, someone else would have or else they'd have perished then. Who's to say in which time it was better to have died in? And who's to say that one rescue won't require a second, a third? On and on and on . . . Do you want coffee?"

"If you do."

Felix rose, grimacing off his chair. He waved away my efforts to help and disappeared into the kitchen. Familiar noises of domestic ease filtered into the living room with a melancholy drip. On and on and on, he had said, and it occurred to me that once Roland had a piece of my inheritance he would not stop until he had all of it. If he could watch Liz for two months, why not for six? It would be another thing after this thing; it would be another threat, another home invasion, another ruse. Who would he stab next? Who would pretend to have been stabbed? What even greater lengths would people go with the promise of residual income? And why wouldn't Roland gather his friends, track me down and threaten my life with real intent? Could I refuse then?

Felix returned with two cups. Steam rose from them like spirits of the departed and disappeared into a better existence.

"He's threatened you again, Felix. Said he knows you were discharged."

He blew on his cup. "What else can he take?"

"I don't think he's messing around now."

"Do what you think you should do."

This was all too much and I pulled out my phone.

"Who are you calling?"

"The police. I can't do this on my own."

This time I was passed on to the man in charge of the investigation. I gave him a description of Roland Charles and Mikhail (surname unknown) as well as the make and model of the sedan. I hadn't thought to look at the plate. The detective took my information as well and told me that if no one had contacted me yet someone would soon.

"I can't imagine your friend being too upset by our going to the police if that was the only result we could muster," said Felix.

"Maybe it's just something Roland likes to say. Maybe criminals know it's a pointless move for their victims, but they pretend it means something to give their victims a sense of hope and power, if only to heighten their despair and drive them deeper into a state of dependence on the thief's honor. There's a part of me that wishes that were so."

"What will you do now?"

"Maybe I'll destroy my phone."

"What good will that do?"

"He can't call me to collect. He'll have to run into me at my apartment."

"He can do that fairly easily."

"I'll stay downtown for a while."

"Are you sure that's wise? What about the man following Liz?"

I still hadn't heard from her, but Mr. McCormick was a man used to the city and had had experiences with it at its worst. I decided that under his care Liz would be the safest person in Chicago. If she wasn't then I'd have heard about it already, either from him or from the detective come to book me as an accessory.

"My instinct tells me it's the right move."

"Instinct? Even that gives you a choice. Fight or flight, Joshua. They're both natural. Interesting that you choose flight."

"Liz called me a coward, too."

"Did she?"

"If you have a course of action you'd like me to follow just say so. I've given you plenty of opportunity."

"Giving such a man that much money makes me sick," said Felix. "It's nearly the stipend for a McArthur Genius Grant, for God's sake. Do you think he'll stop after you deliver the last check or the briefcase or whatever it is money goes into?"

"A manila envelope . . . "

"You're his golden goose, Joshua. He'll keep feeding you lines to keep you laying your bits of gold and when you've been drained he'll lop off your head, stuff you with Stovetop and feast on his good fortune. I'm sorry, Joshua, I don't see a happy ending if you keep paying him."

"Do you see one if I don't?"

Felix sipped his coffee. I saw it was getting late and I thanked him for his time, even if all we did was talk in circles.

"I'll call you directly before I come over from now on. I don't trust your doorman."

We shook hands and I walked into the late afternoon and down Rush Street. When I reached the Wrigley Building I avoided the dark sub-streets and climbed up to State then crossed the river. It was a simple maneuver, one that could have saved me a lot of grief had I decided on such a course three months ago, and I wondered at the little decisions fate uses to destroy us.

I walked to Grant Park and over the soft red gravel beside Buckingham Fountain before crossing South Lake Shore Drive to sit beneath the columns of Queens' Landing. The lake was black and still and the evening sky that passed overhead was obscured by the city lights, unmindful of the struggles of harried people left alone to suffer their lives. It was content with managing its own birthing and death to let us find our own way through such things. How many of us they had seen? Perhaps in the beginning the spirits marveled at us; maybe in our original appearance we had been celebrated by the heavens and sung in angel's choirs. But all our comings and goings must give them no pause now. We were merely generations passing ever on to be followed by another and then another, like tides collapsing on a beachhead. The incessant waves never diminish the vast supply from which they come; mired in constancy they lack originality, save for events of wind or flood that carry them to the shore and onward, swift, intent and with more violence. Perhaps only then will the angels lean over the balcony.

Perhaps not.

Felix preferred to keep his love of beauty within him. He was beginning to distance himself from the importance of having representations and artifacts detailing those beliefs. As I reflected on this change of attitude, I thought he was on to something. After all, artists, once they have achieved their art, continue to challenge themselves and explore ancillary themes and desires. Why not those people who ponder these higher things in their hearts? Taking one's ideals off the walls, out of their frames and into the streets, seems a better way, though it is rife with complications and hypocrisies. Ideals cannot be kept pure when they contact the city street, the gutters; they are imperiled by falling detritus beneath the El, the brown water from the window washers platform. They must morph, necessarily, through compromise and our inability to keep our shoes clean.

Then from out of my melancholic reverie, I shook with joy. I had Roland's address. I thought if they hadn't put him in custody by now then perhaps Roland Charles wasn't his real name. Of course it wasn't. I didn't stop to consider what this meant, but released my excitement onto the buttons of my cell phone, which put my voice to the ear of a man who could bring finality to all of this. I told the detective what I knew. He thanked me without betraying his opinion of the new information and I hung up.

In the weeks that followed I was decidedly out of the loop. Rather than take a room in Evanston near the University as I had originally planned and even booked, I decided to remain where I was. I acquired a new phone number and waited. I never heard from Roland again; neither did I ever see him, in the months that followed, being whisked along the streets of Chicago, however hard I strained my eyes. I thought perhaps the police had tracked him down, arrested him, and put him away for any number of misdemeanors and felonies that would have accumulated over the years and added up to a long stretch of prison time. But I was never called in to identify him. Felix was never called to give an account, either. He kept to himself mostly, healing, processing and deciding what exactly this city was and where his place would be in it moving forward.

I decided that Roland and Melanie had left the city. They had ten thousand of my dollars and that would be enough to set them up somewhere else for a little while. It was more likely that Roland was on his own, however. Melanie may have been exactly who he said she was.

The line leading to Liz was similarly silent. I no longer called her and as the days passed I thought of her less and less, though I googled her father's name often as a way to keep my conscience at ease. I did see her once, though. It was after the New Year and the fourth day I had emerged with confidence back onto the street. She hadn't seen me standing in the court-yard outside Tribune Tower on a surprisingly pleasant after-noon. The warm sun was rejoicing on the facade stones and I took the opportunity to expose my hands to the elements, rub-bing them over the bricks that had been recovered or stolen or bought from the edifices of passed centuries. I touched China's Great Wall, Lincoln's tomb and the Alamo, Notre-Dame and Hagia Sophia . . . After my capacity to understand the immor-tality of stone had been filled, I sat on the steps eerily content with my own life — its brevity and the course I had decided for it — when I saw her walking quickly on the periphery of the crowded sidewalk. I don't know if she saw me, but her mouth puckered and curled the way it did when the past made her sad. She was holding the hand of a young man and I watched them disappear together behind the Tower wall.

When they had vanished from my sight and jealous thoughts and magnanimous thoughts slowly gave way to other, more pressing ones, I thanked God for whatever experience I had had with Liz and for all that it would teach me, even if those lessons wouldn't be apparent until much later. Who knows why our personal orbits cross with some and not with others? And what a fertile playground exists in thinking these remarkable meetings are the result of divine intervention rather than chance?

My essay about Eric and his work ended up being re-jected by Felix's friend. The content was far too religious for the publication, though I was simply told it would not fit with the tone of the issue. I had not been encouraged to send more of my work. I had felt, while writing the piece, that Jesus had been discussed far too openly. It's one thing to talk about God in the vague, universal sense, the one where we're all talking about the same God, but when Jesus is brought up God becomes too specific: ideas of hatred and prejudice and judgment overshadow the glory he has worked in the lives of those who believe He was God's son. I was not entirely surprised. I had a fear that something of the sort would happen, but the subject demanded such treatment and I was happy to have obliged, or else I had placed such ideas in the text to guarantee the failure was in that and not in my ability to think critically.

Eric was released from the hospital four days after being admitted. I helped him back to his studio and arranged his space so he could live his life with some convenience. He was still in pain and taking medication and I talked with him while he lay on the couch. He had liked my essay, but could see where it had fallen short, and not just because of the Jesus talk. We spoke of many things and when he slept I cleaned his kitchenette and tidied up a bit. I made baked spaghetti and a big pot of chili that he could warm up when he wanted. I did his laundry. He wouldn't let me clean his brushes, though. He said I didn't have to perform any penance for him to obtain his forgiveness, but I thought he was just saying that. I had much to make up for.

So publication eluded me then, and I redoubled my efforts, validating my belief that how to find what one wants to do in life is simply by doing it.

In February I received a call from Country Gardens back home telling me that my grandfather had passed away. He had the foresight to make all of the funeral arrangements ahead of time and the call was only to inform me that services would be held in three days. I spent the rest of the evening looking at John Hancock through the snowflakes dropping softly out of the sky, preparing myself for the journey home and the reacquaintance with death.

The next day I called a couple of friends and made preparations to stay with each one of them for a few nights. They were happy to hear from me and though I was looking forward to seeing them, I couldn't reconcile the person who was returning with the one who had left. Perhaps the two would meet, in Dowagiac or Durand, and everything would be okay.

I reserved a seat on Amtrak's Blue Water leaving out of Union Station that afternoon and made a list of everything I would need. I bought a new suit when the stores on Michigan Avenue opened, a black wool three piece that was cut to fit off the rack and didn't make me look too misshapen. I picked out a white Oxford shirt, a black tie, and socks from Ralph Lauren. My shoes would suffice to pull the outfit together, but I found a pair I liked at Mark Jacobs and bought those, too. At Barney's, I bought a garment bag and a weekend duffle. And a watch. I toted my apparel home through a stiff wind that stung my eyes and made me tear up.

I packed and took *Austerlitz* to the Third Coast Café where, despite the early hour, I ordered a bottle and brie and failed to escape from the permanence of death with ideas that had once given me hope of regaining some semblance of normalcy. My choice of novel was not particularly uplifting, either.

The afternoon passed slowly and rather than wait in my apartment until a proper time, by two o'clock I had paid for the cab ride to Union Station and was sitting the Great Hall. I watched the people and listened to conversations faintly echoing around the space. A man was snoring on the opposite bench. After a time I took my luggage to the waiting room. It was filled with fatigued travelers, those on their phones making plans, watching the weather and others struggling with crying children, rambunctious children, children angelically dreaming in their carriers. Amtrak attendants kept order to the lines that were forming near the gates and stretching in odd jerks and turns throughout the space and through which people would pass on their way to Peoria, Indianapolis, Madison and San Francisco.

When the time came, I too fell into line. On the platform I saw where the tracks either ended or commenced, depending on your point of view and general attitude. Or, if you're looking at a phone or trying to maneuver a suitcase and a stroller across the narrow walkway and around pillars, trying to heed the directions of the stewards placed at various doors to the train, you're not thinking about these things at all, but on simply boarding. For my part, I felt the tracks represented my own lifespan accurately. I was forever moving backward and forward on the same track, my future taking place beneath the steel shadows of the metropolis, ever connected to my past where my thoughts emerged from and tended toward: the fertile fields and wind turbines of Huron County.

I had six hours of evening to think about what had happened over the previous months. I gazed at my reflection in the dark window and cupped my hands around the glass to see the lights of Kalamazoo, Battle Creek, and East Lansing. Between stops, I rested my mind in the pages of my book and when that failed to remove me from life's principle fact, I bought a beer and reread John's account of the life of Jesus. It was a refreshing change of pace from the dense narrative of a boy forgotten in the apocalypse of war. In the silence of the dining car that gently rocked along the steel tracks, I found a glimpse of what my father was experiencing. It was a mere shadow in the pages, one that flitted by like a bird's shadow across the edge of a building or a cloud obscuring the sun for a time. Yet for all of its quietness, the suddenness I felt would trail beside me for the rest of my life.

It was simply this: Thomas, that doubting disciple, for all that he had seen and found unbelievable in his time with the God-man — the lepers cleansed, the blind seeing the face of God, the deaf hearing God's voice, the lame leaping at new strength, the dead coming out of their grave clothes, the water turned to wine, the words, like kisses, landing soft and pleasant on the hearts of men who longed to be kissed — was not convinced of Jesus Christ's resurrection. And when he suddenly appears in their midst and tells Thomas to finger his wrists and penetrate the spear wound with his own hand; when he tells him to become intimate with the means of salvation and righteousness, I believe Thomas sees Jesus Christ for the first time in eleven days, but maybe in three years. To such a revelation he says: *O kurios mon kai o theos mon*; "My Lord and my God."

What else could he say? What else can Dad say? And how long is too long to be able to do this? To endure the presence of God requires a body, not of bone and pulse, but of something akin to his spirit; the duration of his presence is such that time must be shattered and forgotten; no longer will the heartbeat remind us of our time's end, nor the waves, nor the passing of shadows across the land. I thought then that when my time on the earth is fulfilled and my spirit becomes whatever it must become when it is no longer affected by my senses and nerves, and I meet with the Holy Trinity, Dad will run to me and hug me and guide me into the celebration as if he had not gone an hour without seeing me, but an hour that has been too long. It is then, I hope, that all of my suffering on this earth wrought by others — the suffering of simply living, of taking breath, that which is inherent in our predicament here, between these buildings and from these other people and their suffering caused by me, will vanish from memory and the thoughts of earth and the tears shed at loss and our failures to meet our needs, one to the other, will be overwhelmed by the chorus of that phrase . . .

I hope.

We had just stopped in Flint and I was anxious to return to Chicago and discuss these things with Eric.

The train rocked across the tracks through empty the snow-covered acreage. I turned off the reading light and stared out at the frozen land and the yard light-spotted farmhouses. In the mirror of the darkened window I saw my face hovering behind and before those dots of light. They came out of the evening landscape as if from behind a veil, a peculiar reality that had been poked at through the ages by clandestine fingers to show us the light, if we only cared to look for it.

Acknowledgments

The author would like to thank Dan DeWeese, Sean Hennessey, Suman Malick and Delores Schnaar for their mindfulness.

Photo by Steve Barnard

About the Author

Andrew Mitin lives in Michigan. This is his first novel

YO-CPX-083

SCOTT

1989 U.S. POCKET
Stamp
CATALOGUE
& CHECKLIST

ALL NEW PRICES

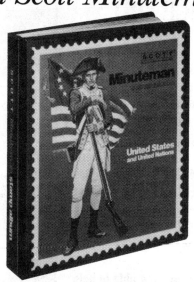

SCOTT

CONTENTS

INTRODUCTION TO STAMP COLLECTING

A fascinating hobby, an engrossing avocation and a universal pastime, stamp collecting is pursued by millions. Young and old, rich and poor, cultured and uncultured, they are all involved in that king of indoor sport, "the paper chase."

It was 148 years ago that Rowland Hill's far-reaching postal reforms became a reality and the world's first adhesive postage stamp was put on sale throughout the post offices of Great Britain. The date was May 6, 1840. Not too long after, the world's first stamp collector came into being and a hobby was born that has continued to grow ever since.

Although for the next seven years there were only three stamps in England, the 1p black, 2p blue and 1p red, there were people who saved them. One apocryphal story has it that a stylish Victorian lady had a room papered with the ebon-hued "Penny Black." In 1850 there were reportedly collectors who were even more rabid. The Illustrated London

4

News for May 8th of that year reports the dire tale of another Victorian damsel, this one in desperate need of help. Her collector father declared he would place her in a convent if she did not amass one million used postage stamps within a certain time. The story aroused concern and sympathy and the stamps poured in, "...many from persons of the highest rank, expressing the most kindly feeling." Shades of Rumpelstiltskin! Fortunately, few collectors have risen to the aberrative heights of those fabled fanatics. Stamp collecting, however, continued to spread, and as country after country began to issue stamps the fraternity flourished. Today, their numbers are legion, as are the number of stamp issuing countries.

Specialization can take many forms. There are those that collect the stamps of a single country. There are those that collect a single issue and those that collect a single stamp in all its nuances and variations. Some collect a particular type of postage stamp such as air mails, commemoratives, etc. Others specialize in cancellations and postmarks and collect their stamps on "cover" that is on the entire envelope. Most popular, however, is collecting by country-especially one's own country. The catalogue you now hold is designed to aid in forming just such a collection; it lists the stamps of the United States. A simplified edition of the 1988 Scott Standard Postage Stamp Catalogue, it has many uses. We will go into them later. First let us briefly discuss some of the ways of forming a collection.

Although the methods of collecting postage stamps are varied and many, anyone can enjoy them. One may begin by attempting to gather a single specimen of every stamp issued by a country. As one becomes more experienced, the collection may be enlarged to include the different types of each stamp such as perforation varieties, watermark varieties, different printings and color changes. The stamps may be collected on cover complete with all postal markings. Thus, the postal rates, cancellations and postmarks and any other postal information that helps speed a letter to its destination may be studied.

A very popular form of collecting practiced today is called "topical" collecting. Here, the subject depicted on the stamp is the paramount attraction. The topics or themes from which to choose are myriad. Animals, flowers, music and musicians, ships, birds and famous people on stamps make interesting collections as do transportation, exploration of space, artists and famous paintings. The list is endless.

Building such a collection is simple. Pick a topic that interests you, check it out on one of the many available lists of stamps dealing with that subject and begin. If your subject is broad enough, forming an interesting and meaningful collection should not be difficult.

Let us not forget another very popular form of collecting, the "First Day Cover." These are envelopes franked with a new stamp and canceled on the first day of use, usually at a specially designated location. The envelope ordinarily contains a cachet commemorating the event or persons for which the stamp was issued.

Collections may be limited to types of stamps. The postage stamps issued by most countries are divided into such categories as definitives, commemoratives, air mail stamps, special delivery stamps, postage due stamps, etc. Any of those groups provide the means for building a good collection.

5

Definitive stamps are those regular issues used on most of the mail sent out on a daily basis. Issued in a rising series of values that allows a mailer to meet any current postal rate, they range in the U.S. from one cent to five dollars. Printed in huge quantities, they are kept in service by the post office for long periods of time.

Commemoratives meet another need. They are stamps issued to celebrate an important event, honor a famous person or promote a special project. Such stamps are issued on a limited basis for a limited time. They are usually more colorful and of a larger size than the definitives, making them of special interest to the collector.

Although few air mail stamps are issued by the United States they remain highly popular among collectors. They, too, are subject to several ways of collecting. Besides amassing the actual stamps, enthusiasts eagerly pursue "First Flight Covers," "Airport Dedications" and even "Crash Covers."

Not as important, but often collected as a unit are the special delivery stamps which secure speedier delivery of a letter and postage due stamps which indicate that a letter did not carry enough postage to pay for its delivery, subjecting the recipient to a fee to make up the difference.

Let us move on to the tools of collecting. They are not many, but they are both useful and necessary. First, a home for your collection is needed.

THE ALBUM

Stamps, to display them at their best, should be properly housed. A good album not only achieves this, but gives protection from dirt, loss

and damage. When choosing one, however, make sure of three things. That the album is within your means, meets your special interests and is the best you can afford. There are many on the market and they are geared to fit every taste and pocketbook.

Loose-leaf albums are recommended. Not only will they allow for expansion of a collection, but the pages may be removed for mounting and for display. A special advantage of the loose-leaf album is that in a good many cases it may be kept up-to-date with supplements that are published annually on matching pages and are available at your stamp dealer.

MOUNTS AND HINGES

Along with the album one must have mounts and hinges. Let us consider the mount first. These days, when the never-hinged stamp has assumed some importance, the mount has become a necessary accessory. It is a must for mint stamps.

Most mounts consist of a pre-glued, clear plastic container that holds a stamp safely and can be affixed to an album page with minimum effort. They are available in sizes to fit any stamp, block or even whole envelopes.

Although the mount is important, the hinge is equally so. Many a stamp in the old days was ruined beyond redemption by being glued to an album page. Hinges are cheap and effective. The best ones are peelable and may be removed from a stamp or album page without leaving an unsightly mark or causing damage. They are perfect for less expensive stamps, used stamps and stamps that have previously been hinged. Using them is simple. Merely fold back about a quarter of the hinge, adhesive side out. Moisten the folded part and affix it to the back of the stamp. Then, holding the stamp with a pair of tongs, moisten the bottom part and place it and the stamp in its proper place on the album page.

STAMP TONGS

We mentioned tongs above. This simple, but important, accessory should always be used when handling a stamp. They cost little and will quickly pay for themselves. The ones with round ends are preferable, those with sharp ends may damage a stamp. Once you get used to using them you will find them easier to work with than your fingers. What's more, your stamps will be the better for it.

MAGNIFYING GLASS

A good magnifying glass for scrutinizing stamps in detail is another extremely useful philatelic tool. It lets you see flaws that are otherwise

7

invisible to the naked eye. It makes minute parts of a design large enough to see. It saves wear and tear on the eyesight. It too pays for itself.

PERFORATION GAUGE AND WATERMARK DETECTOR

As one becomes familiar with stamps he will discover that although many stamps appear to be exactly alike, they are not. The color and design may be identical, but there is a difference. The perforations around the edge of the stamp are not the same, nor is the watermark. To determine these differences a perforation gauge and a watermark detector are needed. Often, the perforations or the watermark found in the paper on which a stamp is printed are the only ways to classify it properly.

The perforation gauge, printed on plastic or cardboard, contains a graded scale that measures the size of the perforations used for most stamps. Placing the stamp on the gauge and moving it up or down until the dots on the gauge and the teeth of the perforation mesh gives one the size of the perforation. Most gauges also contain a small millimeter rule that allows one to accurately determine the dimensions of the stamps.

Watermarks are not quite so easy to detect. They are a design or device impressed into the paper on which the stamp is printed. Occasionally a watermark may be seen by holding a stamp up to the light, but normally a watermark detector is necessary to bring it out. Many types of detectors exist, but the simplest and most useful is that old standby, the small black tray. The stamp is placed face down in it, some lighter fluid is poured over the stamp causing the watermark to become visible.

CONDITION

As collectors and stamp collecting become more sophisticated, "condition" becomes more and more important. "Condition," speaking philatelically, means the state of a stamp - superb, mediocre or below average. Like anything else, a stamp in fine condition will always bring more than the same item in poor condition.

A stamp when added to a collection should be the best obtainable. If it is unused, it should be well-centered and have a clean, fresh look. The gum should be intact. Stamps that have been hinged sell for less than those with pristine gum and stamps with part gum sell for much less.

Used stamps should be well-centered and lightly canceled. They should not be faded or dirty. They should not have any thinning.

When buying a stamp labeled "superb," it should be of top quality, perfectly centered, brilliant in color and have perfect gum. Used copies should be fresh, lightly canceled and sound in every respect.

When buying a stamp labeled "fine," it should be without flaws, but with average centering. The gum may have light hinge marks. Used copies are not quite as fresh as "superb," centering is average and the cancels are heavier.

A stamp listed as "good" or "average" is usually off-center, but attractive. It may have minor defects such as disturbed gum, tiny thins or heavy hinge marks. Used copies, except for the gum, fall into the same classification. Stamps that fall below these standards should be ignored.

THE CATALOGUE

The catalogue is one of the collector's most valued tools. Without it he is liable to be as lost as a sailor at sea without a compass. An illustrated and priced list of the postage stamps issued by every country of the world, it is a prime source of basic information pertaining to stamps and

stamp collecting. Issued annually, it is the chief and handiest guide to what postage stamps exist. Its illustrations make it easy to identify one's stamps and are a guide to the fundamental elements of the hobby.

Scott's Standard Postage Stamp Catalogue is the leading general catalogue in the United States. It identifies every stamp and its major varieties by color, design and denomination. It gives the date of issue, the printing method, perforation size and watermark, if any, of each stamp where possible and the reasons for its issuance. Every stamp is priced used and unused. In addition, every stamp has an identifying number. These are used by dealers and collectors as a quick method of identifying stamps they wish to buy or sell.

This pocket edition of the "Standard Catalogue" which you hold in your hand is a simplified version of the parent volume. Limited to the United States, it does not go into the massive detail that the larger one does. Nevertheless, it is a valuable and useful tool containing the basic information needed to identify and assign the stamps to your collection. Besides giving the current market value of each stamp it gives their philatelic details as well. As in the parent catalogue, the following style of listing is used.

The number in the first column is its Scott number or identifying number. The letter and number that come next (A41) indicate the design and refer to the illustration so designated. Following that is the denomination of the stamp and its color. Finally, the price, unused and used is shown.

Especially useful in this catalogue is the provision for making your own inventory and checklist. It allows one to keep a complete record of his holdings with a minimum of effort.

Above the columns of boxes are spaces in which a collector may indicate such designations as, "Mint," "Used," "Block," "Plate Block," "First Day Cover," or any other classification he desires. A mark in any of the boxes below makes a quickly visible checklist that instantly shows the status of his collection. A handy pocket inventory, it eliminates such chores as the compiling of buying lists.

HOW TO USE THIS BOOK

The number (1811) in the first column is the stamp's identifying Scott number. The letter-number combination (A984) indicates the design and refers to the illustration having this same (A984) designation. Following that is the denomination of the stamp and its color or description along with the color of the paper in italics if other than white. Finally, the price, unused and used is shown.

Scott Number	Illustration Design No.	Denomination	Color or Description	Color of the stamp paper	Prices Unused	Prices Used
1811	A984	1c	dk blue, *greenish*		.05	.05

COLOR ABBREVIATIONS

amb	amber	ind	indigo
anil	aniline	int	intense
ap	apple	lav	lavender
aqua	aquamarine	lem	lemon
az	azure	lil	lilac
bis	bister	lt	light
bl	blue	mag	magenta
bld	blood	man	manila
blk	black	mar	maroon
bril	brilliant	mlky	milky
brn	brown	multi	multicolored
brnsh	brownish	mv	mauve
brnt	burnt	myr	myrtle
brnz	bronze	ol	olive
brt	bright	olvn	olivine
car	carmine	org	orange
cer	cerise	pck	peacock
cham	chamois	pnksh	pinkish
chlky	chalky	Prus	Prussian
chnt	chestnut	pur	purple
choc	chocolate	redsh	reddish
chr	chrome	res	reseda
cit	citron	ros	rosine
cl	claret	ryl	royal
cob	cobalt	sal	salmon
cop	copper	saph	sapphire
crim	crimson	scar	scarlet
cr	cream	sep	sepia
db	drab	sien	sienna
dk	dark	sil	silver
dl	dull	sl	slate
dp	deep	stl	steel
emer	emerald	turq	turquoise
gldn	golden	ultra	ultramarine
grn	green	ven	Venetian
grnsh	greenish	ver	vermilion
grysh	grayish	vio	violet
hel	heliotrope	yel	yellow
hn	henna	yelsh	yellowish

Benjamin
Franklin
A1

A3

George
Washington
A2

A4

Reproductions. The letters R. W. H. & E. at the bottom of each stamp are less distinct on the reproductions than on the originals.

5c. On the originals the left side of the white shirt frill touches the oval on a level with the top of the "F" of "Five." On the reproductions it touches the oval about on a level with the top of the figure "5."

10c. On the reproductions, line of coat at left points to right tip of "X" and line of coat at right points to center of "S" of CENTS. On the originals, line of coat points to "T" of TEN and between "T" and "S" of CENTS. On the reproductions the eyes have a sleepy look, the line of the mouth is straighter, and in the curl of hair near the left cheek is a strong black dot, while the originals have only a faint one.

Franklin
A5

A5

ONE CENT.

Type I. Has complete curved lines outside the labels with "U.S. Postage" and "One Cent." The scrolls below the lower label are turned under, forming little balls. The ornaments at top are substantially complete.

Type Ib. Same as I but balls below the bottom label are not so clear. The plume-like scrolls at bottom are not complete.

A6

Type Ia. Same as I at bottom but top ornaments and outer line at top are partly cut away.

A7

Type II. The little balls of the bottom scrolls and the bottoms of the lower plume ornaments are missing. The side ornaments are complete.

A8

Type III. The top and bottom curved lines outside the labels are broken in the middle. The side ornaments are complete.

Type IIIa. Similar to type III with the outer line broken at top or bottom but not both.

A9

Type IV. Similar to type II, but with the curved lines outside the labels recut at top or bottom or both.

Prices for types I and III are for stamps showing the marked characteristics plainly. Copies of type I showing the balls indistinctly and of type III with the lines only slightly broken, sell for much lower prices.

UNITED STATES

Scott No.	Illus. No.	Description	Unused Price	Used Price	//////

1847 All issues from 1847 to 1894 are unwatermarked   *Imperf.*

1	A1	5c red brown, *bluish*	4500.00	700.00	☐☐☐☐☐
2	A2	10c black, *bluish*	*18500.00*	2000.00	☐☐☐☐☐

1875 REPRODUCTIONS   Bluish paper without gum   *Imperf.*

3	A3	5c red brown	1100.00		☐☐☐☐☐
4	A4	10c black	1500.00		☐☐☐☐☐

1851-56   *Imperf.*

5	A5	1c blue, Type I	*100000.00*	22500.00	☐☐☐☐☐
5A	A5	1c blue, Type Ib	*9500.00*	3750.00	☐☐☐☐☐
6	A6	1c blue, Type Ia	*16000.00*	5500.00	☐☐☐☐☐
7	A7	1c blue, Type II	450.00	85.00	☐☐☐☐☐
8	A8	1c blue, Type III	*5250.00*	1450.00	☐☐☐☐☐
8A	A8	1c blue, Type IIIa	1750.00	575.00	☐☐☐☐☐
9	A9	1c blue, Type IV ('52)	300.00	75.00	☐☐☐☐☐
10	A10	3c orange brown, Type I	1200.00	45.00	☐☐☐☐☐
11	A10	3c dl red, Type I	130.00	7.00	☐☐☐☐☐
12	A11	5c red brown, Type I ('56)	*9500.00*	1300.00	☐☐☐☐☐
13	A12	10c green, Type I ('55)	8500.00	700.00	☐☐☐☐☐
14	A13	10c green, Type II ('55)	1700.00	275.00	☐☐☐☐☐
15	A14	10c green, Type III ('55)	1750.00	285.00	☐☐☐☐☐
16	A15	10c green, Type IV ('55)	*10000.00*	1500.00	☐☐☐☐☐
17	A16	12c black	1850.00	250.00	☐☐☐☐☐

1857-61   *Perf. 15*

18	A5	1c blue, Type I ('61)	725.00	375.00	☐☐☐☐☐
19	A6	1c blue, Type Ia	*9500.00*	*2500.00*	☐☐☐☐☐
20	A7	1c blue, Type II	425.00	140.00	☐☐☐☐☐
21	A8	1c blue, Type III	4250.00	1250.00	☐☐☐☐☐
22	A8	1c blue, Type IIIa	650.00	250.00	☐☐☐☐☐
23	A9	1c blue, Type IV	1750.00	300.00	☐☐☐☐☐
24	A20	1c blue, Type V	110.00	22.50	☐☐☐☐☐
25	A10	3c rose, Type I	650.00	27.50	☐☐☐☐☐
26	A21	3c dl red, Type II	45.00	2.75	☐☐☐☐☐
26a		3c dl red, Type IIa	110.00	20.00	☐☐☐☐☐
27	A11	5c brick red, Type I ('58)	*7500.00*	1000.00	☐☐☐☐☐
28	A11	5c red brown, Type I	1350.00	285.00	☐☐☐☐☐
28A	A11	5c indian red, Type I ('58)	*9000.00*	1500.00	☐☐☐☐☐
29	A11	5c brown, Type I ('59)	750.00	225.00	☐☐☐☐☐
30	A22	5c orange brown, Type II ('61)	750.00	900.00	☐☐☐☐☐
30A	A22	5c brown, Type II ('60)	450.00	185.00	☐☐☐☐☐
31	A12	10c green, Type I	5000.00	525.00	☐☐☐☐☐
32	A13	10c green, Type II	1650.00	170.00	☐☐☐☐☐
33	A14	10c green, Type III	1750.00	185.00	☐☐☐☐☐
34	A15	10c green, Type IV	*15000.00*	1600.00	☐☐☐☐☐
35	A23	10c green, Type V ('59)	175.00	57.50	☐☐☐☐☐
36	A16	12c black, plate I	325.00	85.00	☐☐☐☐☐

Washington
A10

Thomas Jefferson
A11

A13

Type II. The design is complete at the top. The outer line at the bottom is broken in the middle. The shells are partly cut away.

A10

THREE CENTS.

Type I. There is an outer frame line at top and bottom.

A11

FIVE CENTS.

Type I. There are projections on all four sides.

A12

A12

TEN CENTS.

Type I. The "shells" at the lower corners are practically complete. The outer line below the label is very nearly complete. The outer lines are broken above the middle of the top label and the "X" in each upper corner.

A14

Type III. The outer lines are broken above the top label and the "X" numerals. The outer line at the bottom and the shells are partly cut away, as in Type II.

A15

Type IV. The outer lines have been recut at top or bottom or both.

Types I, II, III and IV have complete ornaments at the sides of the stamps and three pearls at each outer edge of the bottom panel.

A16

14

Franklin
A20

ONE CENT.

Type V. Similar to type III of 1851-56 but with side ornaments partly cut away.

A21

THREE CENTS.

Type II. The outer frame line has been removed at top and bottom. The side frame lines were recut so as to be continuous from the top to the bottom of the plate.

Type IIa. The side frame lines extend only to the top and bottom of the stamp design.

A22

A22

FIVE CENTS.

Type II. The projections at top and bottom are partly cut away.

A23
(Two typical examples).

TEN CENTS.

Type V. The side ornaments are slightly cut away. Usually only one pearl remains at each end of the lower label but some copies show two or three pearls at the right side. At the bottom the outer line is complete and the shells nearly so. The outer lines at top are complete except over the right "X".

A17   **A18**

A19

TWELVE CENTS.

Plate I. Outer frame lines complete.
Plate III. Outer frame lines noticeably uneven or broken, sometimes partly missing.

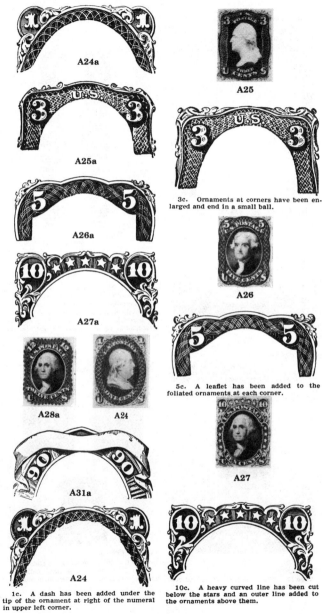

A24a

A25

A25a

3c. Ornaments at corners have been enlarged and end in a small ball.

A26a

A5 POSTAGE
A26

A27a

A28a   A24

5c. A leaflet has been added to the foliated ornaments at each corner.

A31a

A27

A24

1c. A dash has been added under the tip of the ornament at right of the numeral in upper left corner.

10c. A heavy curved line has been cut below the stars and an outer line added to the ornaments above them.

16

Scott No.	Illus. No.	Description	Unused Price	Used Price	//////
36b		12c black, plate III ('59)	250.00	100.00	☐☐☐☐☐
37	A17	24c gray lilac ('60)	600.00	220.00	☐☐☐☐☐
38	A18	30c orange ('60)	750.00	285.00	☐☐☐☐☐
39	A19	90c blue ('60)	1450.00	2750.00	☐☐☐☐☐

1875 GOVERNMENT REPRINTS Without gum *Perf. 12*

Scott No.	Illus. No.	Description	Unused Price	Used Price	//////
40	A5	1c bright blue	*550.00*		☐☐☐☐☐
41	A10	3c scarlet	*2850.00*		☐☐☐☐☐
42	A22	5c orange brown	*950.00*		☐☐☐☐☐
43	A12	10c blue green	*2250.00*		☐☐☐☐☐
44	A16	12c greenish black	*2600.00*		☐☐☐☐☐
45	A17	24c black violet	*2850.00*		☐☐☐☐☐
46	A18	30c yellow orange	*2850.00*		☐☐☐☐☐
47	A19	90c dp blue	*4250.00*		☐☐☐☐☐

1861

Scott No.	Illus. No.	Description	Unused Price	Used Price	//////
55	A24a	1c indigo	*17000.00*		☐☐☐☐☐
56	A25a	3c brown rose	*700.00*		☐☐☐☐☐
57	A26a	5c brown	*12500.00*		☐☐☐☐☐
58	A27a	10c dk green	*5500.00*		☐☐☐☐☐
59	A28a	12c black	*35000.00*		☐☐☐☐☐
60	A29	24c dk violet	*6000.00*		☐☐☐☐☐
61	A30	30c red orange	*16000.00*		☐☐☐☐☐
62	A31a	90c dl blue	*20000.00*		☐☐☐☐☐

The paper of Nos. 55-62 is thin and semitransparent. That of the following issues is thicker and more opaque, except Nos. 62B, 70c, and 70d. It is doubtful that Nos. 55-62 were regularly issued.

Scott No.	Illus. No.	Description	Unused Price	Used Price	//////
62B	A27a	10c dk green	*5500.00*	450.00	☐☐☐☐☐

No. 62B unused cannot be distinguished from No. 58 which does not exist used.

1861-62

Scott No.	Illus. No.	Description	Unused Price	Used Price	//////
63	A24	1c blue	110.00	17.50	☐☐☐☐☐
64	A25	3c pink	3500.00	250.00	☐☐☐☐☐
64a		3c pigeon blood pink	—	*1200.00*	☐☐☐☐☐
64b		3c rose pink	250.00	45.00	☐☐☐☐☐
65	A25	3c rose	50.00	1.10	☐☐☐☐☐
66	A25	3c lake	*1650.00*		☐☐☐☐☐
67	A26	5c buff	4000.00	375.00	☐☐☐☐☐
68	A27	10c yellow green	250.00	30.00	☐☐☐☐☐
69	A28	12c black	450.00	50.00	☐☐☐☐☐
70	A29	24c red lilac ('62)	550.00	77.50	☐☐☐☐☐
70a		24c brown lilac	450.00	67.50	☐☐☐☐☐
70b		24c steel blue	3500.00	275.00	☐☐☐☐☐
70c		24c violet	3500.00	550.00	☐☐☐☐☐
70d		24c grayish lilac	1100.00	275.00	☐☐☐☐☐
71	A30	30c orange	450.00	65.00	☐☐☐☐☐
72	A31	90c blue	1200.00	250.00	☐☐☐☐☐

Nos. 70c and 70d are on a thinner, harder and more transparent paper than Nos. 70, 70a, 70b, or the later No. 78.

A28

12c. Ovals and scrolls have been added to the corners.

A29   **A30**

A31   Grill

A31

90c. Parallel lines form an angle above the ribbon with "U. S. Postage"; between these lines a row of dashes has been added and a point of color to the apex of the lower pair.

A32   **A33**

A34   **A35**

A36   **A37**

A38   **A39**

A40   **A41**

A42   **A43**

A40

FIFTEEN CENTS. Type I. Picture unframed.

A40a

Type II. Picture framed.

Type III. Same as type I but without fringe of brown shading lines around central vignette.

18

Scott No.	Illus. No.	Description	Unused Price	Used Price	//////
1861-66					
73	A32	2c black ('63)	110.00	22.50	☐☐☐☐☐
74	A25	3c scarlet	*4500.00*		☐☐☐☐☐
75	A26	5c red brown ('62)	1200.00	210.00	☐☐☐☐☐
76	A26	5c brown ('63)	300.00	52.50	☐☐☐☐☐
77	A33	15c black ('66)	450.00	65.00	☐☐☐☐☐
78	A29	24c lilac ('63)	275.00	50.00	☐☐☐☐☐

Same as 1861-66 issues, embossed with grills of various sizes

GRILL WITH POINTS UP

1867   **A. Grill covering the entire stamp**   *Perf. 12*

79	A25	3c rose	1650.00	425.00	☐☐☐☐☐
80	A26	5c brown	*40000.00*	–	☐☐☐☐☐
80a		5c dk brown		*37500.00*	☐☐☐☐☐
81	A30	30c orange		*32500.00*	☐☐☐☐☐

  B. Grill about 18x15mm. (22 by 18 points)

82	A25	3c rose		*45000.00*	☐☐☐☐☐

  C. Grill about 13x16mm. (16 to 17 by 18 to 21 points)

83	A25	3c rose	1600.00	375.00	☐☐☐☐☐

  GRILL WITH POINTS DOWN

  D. Grill about 12x14mm. (15 by 17 to 18 points)

84	A32	2c black	3000.00	900.00	☐☐☐☐☐
85	A25	3c rose	1350.00	425.00	☐☐☐☐☐

  Z. Grill about 11x14mm. (13 to 14 by 17 to 18 points)

85A	A24	1c blue		–	☐☐☐☐☐
85B	A32	2c black	1200.00	350.00	☐☐☐☐☐
85C	A25	3c rose	3500.00	950.00	☐☐☐☐☐
85D	A27	10c green		*25000.00*	☐☐☐☐☐
85E	A28	12c black	1550.00	550.00	☐☐☐☐☐
85F	A33	15c black		–	☐☐☐☐☐

  E. Grill about 11x13mm. (14 by 15 to 17 points)

86	A24	1c blue	750.00	250.00	☐☐☐☐☐
87	A32	2c black	325.00	70.00	☐☐☐☐☐
88	A25	3c rose	225.00	10.00	☐☐☐☐☐
89	A27	10c green	1200.00	175.00	☐☐☐☐☐
90	A28	12c black	1400.00	190.00	☐☐☐☐☐
91	A33	15c black	3000.00	450.00	☐☐☐☐☐

  F. Grill about 9x13mm. (11 to 12 by 15 to 17 points)

92	A24	1c blue	325.00	100.00	☐☐☐☐☐
93	A32	2c black	120.00	25.00	☐☐☐☐☐
94	A25	3c red	85.00	2.50	☐☐☐☐☐
95	A26	5c brown	850.00	225.00	☐☐☐☐☐
96	A27	10c yellow green	650.00	110.00	☐☐☐☐☐
97	A28	12c black	675.00	115.00	☐☐☐☐☐
98	A33	15c black	675.00	125.00	☐☐☐☐☐
99	A29	24c gray lilac	1250.00	475.00	☐☐☐☐☐

A44

A45

A48

A49

A44

A48

A45

A49

A46

A50

A46

A51

A47

A51

20

Scott No.	Illus. No.	Description	Unused Price	Used Price	//////
100	A30	30c orange	1400.00	375.00	☐☐☐☐☐
101	A31	90c blue	4000.00	950.00	☐☐☐☐☐

1875 Re-issues Without grill *Perf. 12*

102	A24	1c blue	*500.00*	*800.00*	☐☐☐☐☐
103	A32	2c black	*2500.00*	*4000.00*	☐☐☐☐☐
104	A25	3c brown red	*3250.00*	*4250.00*	☐☐☐☐☐
105	A26	5c brown	*1800.00*	*2250.00*	☐☐☐☐☐
106	A27	10c green	*2100.00*	*3750.00*	☐☐☐☐☐
107	A28	12c black	*3000.00*	*4500.00*	☐☐☐☐☐
108	A33	15c black	*3000.00*	*4750.00*	☐☐☐☐☐
109	A29	24c dp violet	*4000.00*	*6000.00*	☐☐☐☐☐
110	A30	30c brownish orange	*4500.00*	*7000.00*	☐☐☐☐☐
111	A31	90c blue		*5750.00* *18500.00*	☐☐☐☐☐

These stamps can be distinguished from the 1861-66 issues by the shades and the paper which is hard and very white instead of yellowish. The gum is white and crackly.

1869 G. Grill measuring 9½x9 mm. (12 by 11 to 11½ points) *Perf. 12*

112	A34	1c buff	225.00	60.00	☐☐☐☐☐
113	A35	2c brown	160.00	25.00	☐☐☐☐☐
114	A36	3c ultra	135.00	5.50	☐☐☐☐☐
115	A37	6c ultra	775.00	95.00	☐☐☐☐☐
116	A38	10c yellow	850.00	95.00	☐☐☐☐☐
117	A39	12c green	750.00	90.00	☐☐☐☐☐
118	A40	15c brown & blue, Type I	1750.00	250.00	☐☐☐☐☐
119	A40a	15c brown & blue, Type II	850.00	125.00	☐☐☐☐☐
119b		Center inverted	*145000.00*	*17500.00*	☐☐☐☐☐
120	A41	24c green & violet	2500.00	450.00	☐☐☐☐☐
120b		Center invtd.	*125000.00*	*16500.00*	☐☐☐☐☐
121	A42	30c blue & carmine	2250.00	225.00	☐☐☐☐☐
121b		Flags invtd.	*120000.00*	*45000.00*	☐☐☐☐☐
122	A43	90c carmine & black	7000.00	1200.00	☐☐☐☐☐

1875 Re-issues Without grill Hard white paper *Perf. 12*

123	A34	1c buff	325.00	225.00	☐☐☐☐☐
124	A35	2c brown	375.00	325.00	☐☐☐☐☐
125	A36	3c blue	3000.00	1500.00	☐☐☐☐☐
126	A37	6c blue	850.00	550.00	☐☐☐☐☐
127	A38	10c yellow	1400.00	1200.00	☐☐☐☐☐
128	A39	12c green	1500.00	1200.00	☐☐☐☐☐
129	A40	15c brown & blue, Type III	1300.00	550.00	☐☐☐☐☐
130	A41	24 green & violet	1250.00	550.00	☐☐☐☐☐
131	A42	30c blue & carmine	1750.00	1000.00	☐☐☐☐☐
132	A43	90c carmine & black	5500.00	*6000.00*	☐☐☐☐☐

1880 Soft porous paper

133	A34	1c buff	200.00	135.00	☐☐☐☐☐
133a		1c brown orange	175.00	120.00	☐☐☐☐☐

A52

A46a

3c. The under part of the upper tail of the left ribbon is heavily shaded.

A53

A47a

6c. The first four vertical lines of the shading in the lower part of the left ribbon have been strengthened.

A54

A48a

7c. Two small semi-circles are drawn around the ends of the lines which outline the ball in the lower right hand corner.

A44a

1c. In pearl at left of numeral "1" is a small crescent.

A49a

10c. There is a small semi-circle in the scroll at the right end of the upper label.

A45a

2c. Under the scroll at the left of "U. S." there is a small diagonal line. This mark seldom shows clearly. The stamp, No. 157, can be distinguished by its color.

Scott No.	Illus. No.	Description	Unused Price	Used Price	//////

H. Grill about 10x12mm. (11 to 13 by 14 to 16 points).
On all values, 1c to 90c.
I. Grill about 8½x10 mm. (10 to 11 by 10 to 13 points).
On 1, 2, 3, 6, 7c.

Two varieties of grill are known on this issue. On the 1870-71 stamps the grill impressions are usually faint or incomplete. This is especially true of the H grill, which often shows only a few points. Prices are for stamps showing well defined grills.

1870-71 White wove paper *Perf. 12*

Scott No.	Illus. No.	Description	Unused Price	Used Price	
134	A44	1c ultra	475.00	55.00	☐☐☐☐☐
135	A45	2c red brown	325.00	37.50	☐☐☐☐☐
136	A46	3c green	265.00	10.00	☐☐☐☐☐
137	A47	6c carmine	1500.00	250.00	☐☐☐☐☐
138	A48	7c vermilion ('71)	1000.00	225.00	☐☐☐☐☐
139	A49	10c brown	1350.00	400.00	☐☐☐☐☐
140	A50	12c dl violet	*12000.00*	1500.00	☐☐☐☐☐
141	A51	15c orange	1700.00	700.00	☐☐☐☐☐
142	A52	24c purple	—	*10500.00*	☐☐☐☐☐
143	A53	30c black	4000.00	825.00	☐☐☐☐☐
144	A54	90c carmine	5500.00	750.00	☐☐☐☐☐

1870-71 Without grill White wove paper *Perf. 12*

Scott No.	Illus. No.	Description	Unused Price	Used Price	
145	A44	1c ultra	150.00	6.50	☐☐☐☐☐
146	A45	2c red brown	57.50	4.50	☐☐☐☐☐
147	A46	3c green	110.00	.50	☐☐☐☐☐
148	A47	6c carmine	210.00	12.00	☐☐☐☐☐
149	A48	7c vermilion ('71)	300.00	50.00	☐☐☐☐☐
150	A49	10c brown	210.00	12.00	☐☐☐☐☐
151	A50	12c dl violet	500.00	60.00	☐☐☐☐☐
152	A51	15c bright orange	475.00	60.00	☐☐☐☐☐
153	A52	24c purple	550.00	80.00	☐☐☐☐☐
154	A53	30c black	900.00	95.00	☐☐☐☐☐
155	A54	90c carmine	1200.00	175.00	☐☐☐☐☐

1873 Without grill* White wove paper, thin to thick *Perf. 12*

Scott No.	Illus. No.	Description	Unused Price	Used Price	
156	A44a	1c ultra	50.00	1.75	☐☐☐☐☐
157	A45a	2c brown	140.00	7.00	☐☐☐☐☐
158	A46a	3c green	45.00	.15	☐☐☐☐☐
159	A47a	6c dl pink	190.00	9.00	☐☐☐☐☐
160	A48a	7c orange vermilion	375.00	55.00	☐☐☐☐☐
161	A49a	10c brown	200.00	10.00	☐☐☐☐☐
162	A50a	12c black violet	550.00	65.00	☐☐☐☐☐
163	A51a	15c yellow orange	525.00	60.00	☐☐☐☐☐
165	A53	30c gray black	600.00	60.00	☐☐☐☐☐
166	A54	90c rose carmine	1250.00	185.00	☐☐☐☐☐

* All values except 90c exist with experimental J grill, about 7x9½mm.

A50a

12c. The balls of the figure "2" are crescent shaped.

A51a

15c. In the lower part of the triangle in the upper left corner two lines have been made heavier forming a "V". This mark can be found on some of the Continental and American (1879) printings, but not all stamps show it.

Secret marks were added to the dies of the 24c, 30c and 90c but new plates were not made from them. The various printings of these stamps can be distinguished only by the shades and paper.

A55   **A56**

A44b

1c. The vertical lines in the upper part of the stamp have been so deepened that the background often appears to be solid. Lines of shading have been added to the upper arabesques.

A46b

3c. The shading at the sides of the central oval appears only about one-half the previous width. A short horizontal dash has been cut about 1mm. below the "TS" of "CENTS."

A47b

6c. On the original stamps four vertical lines can be counted from the edge of the panel to the outside of the stamp. On the re-engraved stamps there are but three lines in the same place.

A49b

10c. On the original stamps there are five vertical lines between the left side of the oval and the edge of the shield. There are only four lines on the re-engraved stamps. In the lower part of the latter, also, the horizontal lines of the background have been strengthened.

Scott No.	Illus. No.	Description	Unused Price	Used Price	//////
1875	Special printing	Hard, white wove paper	Without gum	*Perf. 12*	
167	A44a	1c ultra	*7500.00*		☐☐☐☐☐
168	A45a	2c dk brown	*3500.00*		☐☐☐☐☐
169	A46a	3c blue green	*9500.00*	—	☐☐☐☐☐
170	A47a	6c dl rose	*8500.00*		☐☐☐☐☐
171	A48a	7c reddish vermilion	*2100.00*		☐☐☐☐☐
172	A49a	10c pale brown	*7750.00*		☐☐☐☐☐
173	A50a	12c dk violet	*2750.00*		☐☐☐☐☐
174	A51a	15c bright orange	*7750.00*		☐☐☐☐☐
175	A52	24c dl purple	*1850.00*	—	☐☐☐☐☐
176	A53	30c greenish black	*7000.00*		☐☐☐☐☐
177	A54	90c violet carmine	*7000.00*		☐☐☐☐☐
	Yellowish wove paper	*Perf. 12*			
178	A45a	2c vermilion	150.00	5.00	☐☐☐☐☐
179	A55	5c blue	165.00	9.00	☐☐☐☐☐
	Special printing	Hard, white wove paper	Without gum		
180	A45a	2c carmine vermilion	*17000.00*		☐☐☐☐☐
181	A55	5c bright blue	*32500.00*		☐☐☐☐☐
1879	Same as 1870-75 issues				
	Soft porous paper	Varying from thin to thick	*Perf. 12*		
182	A44a	1c dk ultra	110.00	1.20	☐☐☐☐☐
183	A45a	2c vermilion	50.00	1.20	☐☐☐☐☐
184	A46a	3c green	42.50	.10	☐☐☐☐☐
185	A55	5c blue	200.00	7.50	☐☐☐☐☐
186	A47a	6c pink	400.00	12.00	☐☐☐☐☐
187	A49	10c brown (w/o secret mark)	700.00	14.00	☐☐☐☐☐
188	A49a	10c brown (with secret mark)	425.00	15.00	☐☐☐☐☐
189	A51a	15c red orange	150.00	14.00	☐☐☐☐☐
190	A53	30c full black	475.00	30.00	☐☐☐☐☐
191	A54	90c carmine	1000.00	150.00	☐☐☐☐☐
1880	Special printing	Soft porous paper	Without gum	*Perf. 12*	
192	A44a	1c dk ultra	*9000.00*		☐☐☐☐☐
193	A45a	2c black brown	*5750.00*		☐☐☐☐☐
194	A46a	3c blue green	*13500.00*		☐☐☐☐☐
195	A47a	6c dl rose	*9500.00*		☐☐☐☐☐
196	A48a	7c scarlet vermilion	*2100.00*		☐☐☐☐☐
197	A49a	10c dp brown	*8750.00*		☐☐☐☐☐
198	A50a	12c black purple	*4000.00*		☐☐☐☐☐
199	A51a	15c orange	*8250.00*		☐☐☐☐☐
200	A52	24c dk violet	*2750.00*		☐☐☐☐☐
201	A53	30c greenish black	*7000.00*		☐☐☐☐☐
202	A54	90c dl carmine	*7000.00*		☐☐☐☐☐
203	A45a	2c scarlet vermilion	*16000.00*		☐☐☐☐☐
204	A55	5c dp blue	*28500.00*		☐☐☐☐☐

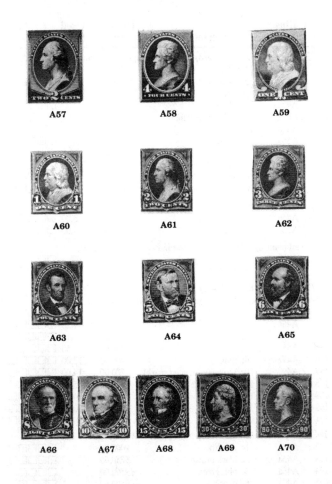

A57   A58   A59

A60   A61   A62

A63   A64   A65

A66   A67   A68   A69   A70

HOW TO USE THIS BOOK

The number in the first column is its Scott number or identifying number. The letter and number that come next (A41) indicate the design and refer to the illustration so designated. Following that is the denomination of the stamp and its color. Finally, the price, unused and used is shown.

Scott No.	Illus. No.	Description	Unused Price	Used Price	//////
1882	*Perf. 12*				
205	A56	5c yellow brown	100.00	4.00	☐☐☐☐☐
	Special printing	Soft porous paper	Without gum		
205C	A56	5c gray brown	*16500.00*		☐☐☐☐☐
1881-82					
206	A44b	1c gray blue	32.50	.40	☐☐☐☐☐
207	A46b	3c blue green	37.50	.12	☐☐☐☐☐
208	A47b	6c rose ('82)	225.00	45.00	☐☐☐☐☐
208a		6c brown red	200.00	55.00	☐☐☐☐☐
209	A49b	10c brown ('82)	70.00	2.50	☐☐☐☐☐
1883					
210	A57	2c red brown	30.00	.08	☐☐☐☐☐
211	A58	4c blue green	130.00	7.50	☐☐☐☐☐
	Special printing	Soft porous paper			
211B	A57	2c pale red brown	700.00	–	☐☐☐☐☐
211D	A58	4c dp blue green	*12500.00*		☐☐☐☐☐
1887-88					
212	A59	1c ultra	55.00	.65	☐☐☐☐☐
213	A57	2c green	22.50	.08	☐☐☐☐☐
214	A46b	3c vermilion	42.50	37.50	☐☐☐☐☐
215	A58	4c carmine	130.00	11.00	☐☐☐☐☐
216	A56	5c indigo	130.00	6.50	☐☐☐☐☐
217	A53	30c orange brown	300.00	70.00	☐☐☐☐☐
218	A54	90c purple	675.00	130.00	☐☐☐☐☐
1890-93					
219	A60	1c dl blue	18.50	.10	☐☐☐☐☐
219D	A61	2c lake	135.00	.45	☐☐☐☐☐
220	A61	2c carmine	15.00	.05	☐☐☐☐☐
220a		Cap on left "2"	35.00	1.00	☐☐☐☐☐
220c		Cap on both "2's"	110.00	8.00	☐☐☐☐☐
221	A62	3c purple	50.00	4.50	☐☐☐☐☐
222	A63	4c dk brown	50.00	1.50	☐☐☐☐☐
223	A64	5c chocolate	50.00	1.50	☐☐☐☐☐
224	A65	6c brown red	55.00	15.00	☐☐☐☐☐
225	A66	8c lilac ('93)	40.00	8.50	☐☐☐☐☐
226	A67	10c green	95.00	1.75	☐☐☐☐☐
227	A68	15c indigo	135.00	15.00	☐☐☐☐☐
228	A69	30c black	200.00	20.00	☐☐☐☐☐
229	A70	90c orange	325.00	90.00	☐☐☐☐☐
1893					
230	A71	1c dp blue	22.50	.30	☐☐☐☐☐
231	A72	2c brown violet	21.00	.06	☐☐☐☐☐
232	A73	3c green	50.00	15.00	☐☐☐☐☐
233	A74	4c ultra	70.00	6.00	☐☐☐☐☐
233a		4c blue (error)	*7000.00*	*2500.00*	☐☐☐☐☐

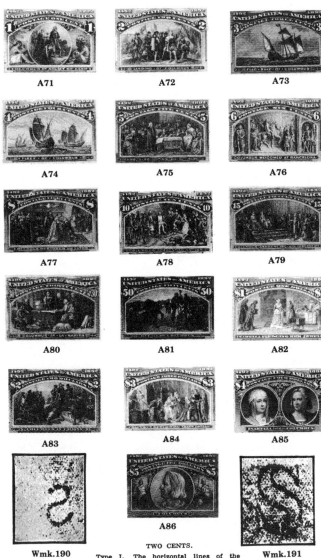

A71   A72   A73

A74   A75   A76

A77   A78   A79

A80   A81   A82

A83   A84   A85

A86

Wmk.190   Wmk.191

TWO CENTS.

Type I. The horizontal lines of the ground work run across the triangle and are of the same thickness within it as without.

Type II. The horizontal lines cross the triangle but are thinner within it than without.

Type III. The horizontal lines do not cross the double frame lines of the triangle. The lines within the triangle are thin, as in type II.

28

Scott No.	Illus. No.	Description	Unused Price	Used Price	//////
234	A75	5c chocolate	80.00	7.00	☐☐☐☐☐
235	A76	6c purple	70.00	20.00	☐☐☐☐☐
236	A77	8c magenta	55.00	8.00	☐☐☐☐☐
237	A78	10c black brown	120.00	6.50	☐☐☐☐☐
238	A79	15c dk green	200.00	65.00	☐☐☐☐☐
239	A80	30c orange brown	275.00	90.00	☐☐☐☐☐
240	A81	50c slate blue	325.00	140.00	☐☐☐☐☐
241	A82	$1 salmon	1150.00	550.00	☐☐☐☐☐
242	A83	$2 brown red	1250.00	500.00	☐☐☐☐☐
243	A84	$3 yellow green	2600.00	1100.00	☐☐☐☐☐
244	A85	$4 crimson lake	3400.00	1450.00	☐☐☐☐☐
245	A86	$5 black	3600.00	1700.00	☐☐☐☐☐

1894 Unwatermarked *Perf. 12*

Scott No.	Illus. No.	Description	Unused Price	Used Price	//////
246	A87	1c ultra	22.50	3.00	☐☐☐☐☐
247	A87	1c blue	55.00	1.25	☐☐☐☐☐
248	A88	2c pink, Type I	17.50	2.00	☐☐☐☐☐
249	A88	2c carmine lake, Type I	125.00	1.35	☐☐☐☐☐
250	A88	2c carmine, Type I	21.00	.25	☐☐☐☐☐
251	A88	2c carmine, Type II	175.00	2.50	☐☐☐☐☐
252	A88	2c carmine, Type III	100.00	3.25	☐☐☐☐☐
253	A89	3c purple	80.00	6.25	☐☐☐☐☐
254	A90	4c dk brown	90.00	2.50	☐☐☐☐☐
255	A91	5c chocolate	80.00	3.50	☐☐☐☐☐
256	A92	6c dl brown	140.00	15.00	☐☐☐☐☐
257	A93	8c violet brown ('95)	110.00	11.50	☐☐☐☐☐
258	A94	10c dk green	175.00	7.50	☐☐☐☐☐
259	A95	15c dk bluc	250.00	45.00	☐☐☐☐☐
260	A96	50c orange	325.00	75.00	☐☐☐☐☐
261	A97	$1 black, Type I	850.00	250.00	☐☐☐☐☐
261A	A97	$1 black, Type II	1850.00	475.00	☐☐☐☐☐
262	A98	$2 bright blue	2100.00	650.00	☐☐☐☐☐
263	A99	$5 dk green	3250.00	1150.00	☐☐☐☐☐

1895 Watermark 191 𝕌𝕊ℙ𝕊 in double lined capitals

Scott No.	Illus. No.	Description	Unused Price	Used Price	//////
264	A87	1c blue	5.00	.10	☐☐☐☐☐
265	A88	2c carmine, Type I	25.00	.65	☐☐☐☐☐
266	A88	2c carmine, Type II	20.00	2.50	☐☐☐☐☐
267	A88	2c carmine, Type III	4.50	.05	☐☐☐☐☐
268	A89	3c purple	35.00	1.00	☐☐☐☐☐
269	A90	4c dk brown	37.50	1.10	☐☐☐☐☐
270	A91	5c chocolate	35.00	1.75	☐☐☐☐☐
271	A92	6c dl brown	65.00	3.50	☐☐☐☐☐
271a		Wmkd. USIR	*1850.00*	350.00	☐☐☐☐☐
272	A93	8c violet brown	45.00	1.00	☐☐☐☐☐
272a		Wmkd. USIR	700.00	110.00	☐☐☐☐☐
273	A94	10c dk green	60.00	1.20	☐☐☐☐☐
274	A95	15c dk blue	160.00	8.25	☐☐☐☐☐

A87   A88   A89   A90

A91   A92   A93   A94

A95   A96   A97   A98

A99

ONE DOLLAR.

Type I. The circles enclosing "$1" are broken where they meet the curved line below "One Dollar." The fifteen left vertical rows of impressions from plate 76 are Type I, the balance being Type II.

Type II. The circles are complete.

TEN CENTS

Type I. Tips of foliate ornaments do not impinge on white curved line below "TEN CENTS".

Type II. Tips of ornaments break curved line below "E" of "TEN" and "T" of "CENTS".

A100   A101   A102

A103   A104   A105

A106   A107   A108

Scott No.	Illus. No.	Description	Unused Price	Used Price	//////
275	A96	50c orange	235.00	20.00	☐☐☐☐☐
276	A97	$1 black, Type I	550.00	70.00	☐☐☐☐☐
276A	A97	$1 black, Type II	1200.00	135.00	☐☐☐☐☐
277	A98	$2 bright blue	900.00	290.00	☐☐☐☐☐
278	A99	$5 dk green	2000.00	425.00	☐☐☐☐☐

1898

Scott No.	Illus. No.	Description	Unused Price	Used Price	//////
279	A87	1c dp green	10.00	.06	☐☐☐☐☐
279B	A88	2c red, Type III	9.00	.05	☐☐☐☐☐
279e		Bklt. pane of 6	350.00	*200.00*	☐☐☐☐☐
280	A90	4c rose brown	32.50	.70	☐☐☐☐☐
281	A91	5c dk blue	35.00	.65	☐☐☐☐☐
282	A92	6c lake	50.00	2.00	☐☐☐☐☐
282C	A94	10c brown, Type I	160.00	2.00	☐☐☐☐☐
283	A94	10c orange brown, Type II	95.00	1.75	☐☐☐☐☐
284	A95	15c olive green	125.00	7.50	☐☐☐☐☐
285	A100	1c dk yellow green	27.50	5.50	☐☐☐☐☐
286	A101	2c copper red	25.00	1.50	☐☐☐☐☐
287	A102	4c orange	140.00	22.50	☐☐☐☐☐
288	A103	5c dl blue	125.00	20.00	☐☐☐☐☐
289	A104	8c violet brown	165.00	40.00	☐☐☐☐☐
290	A105	10c gray violet	185.00	20.00	☐☐☐☐☐
291	A106	50c sage green	725.00	165.00	☐☐☐☐☐
292	A107	$1 black	1750.00	625.00	☐☐☐☐☐
293	A108	$2 orange brown	2650.00	875.00	☐☐☐☐☐

1901

Scott No.	Illus. No.	Description	Unused Price	Used Price	//////
294	A109	1c green & black	20.00	4.00	☐☐☐☐☐
294a		Center invtd.	*10000.00*	*4500.00*	☐☐☐☐☐
295	A110	2c carmine & black	20.00	1.10	☐☐☐☐☐
295a		Center invtd.	*45000.00*	*13500.00*	☐☐☐☐☐
296	A111	4c dp red brown & black	110.00	20.00	☐☐☐☐☐
296a		Center invtd.	*13000.00*		☐☐☐☐☐
297	A112	5c ultra & black	125.00	20.00	☐☐☐☐☐
298	A113	8c brown violet & black	150.00	75.00	☐☐☐☐☐
299	A114	10c yellow brown & black	225.00	35.00	☐☐☐☐☐

1902-03 *Perf. 12*

Scott No.	Illus. No.	Description	Unused Price	Used Price	//////
300	A115	1c blue green ('03)	10.00	.05	☐☐☐☐☐
300b		Bklt. pane of 6	500.00	*250.00*	☐☐☐☐☐
301	A116	2c carmine ('03)	12.50	.05	☐☐☐☐☐
301c		Bklt. pane of 6	425.00	*250.00*	☐☐☐☐☐
302	A117	3c bright violet ('03)	45.00	3.00	☐☐☐☐☐
303	A118	4c brown ('03)	45.00	1.00	☐☐☐☐☐
304	A119	5c blue ('03)	55.00	1.00	☐☐☐☐☐
305	A120	6c claret ('03)	60.00	2.25	☐☐☐☐☐
306	A121	8c violet black	40.00	2.00	☐☐☐☐☐
307	A122	10c pale red brown ('03)	60.00	1.50	☐☐☐☐☐
308	A123	13c purple black	40.00	8.50	☐☐☐☐☐
309	A124	15c olive green ('03)	135.00	6.00	☐☐☐☐☐

A109   A110   A111   A112

A113   A114

A115   A116   A117   A118

A119   A120   A121   A122

A123   A124   A125   A126

A127   A128   A129

32

Scott No.	Illus. No.	Description	Unused Price	Used Price	//////
310	A125	50c orange ('03)	400.00	27.50	☐☐☐☐☐
311	A126	$1 black ('03)	700.00	60.00	☐☐☐☐☐
312	A127	$2 dk blue ('03)	950.00	200.00	☐☐☐☐☐
313	A128	$5 dk green ('03)	2500.00	650.00	☐☐☐☐☐

1906-08 *Imperf.*

314	A115	1c blue green	30.00	21.00	☐☐☐☐☐
314A	A118	4c brown ('08)	*17500.00*	*9000.00*	☐☐☐☐☐
315	A119	5c blue ('08)	550.00	250.00	☐☐☐☐☐

1908 Coil stamps *Perf. 12 horizontally*

| 316 | A115 | 1c blue green, pair | *22500.00* | — | ☐☐☐☐☐ |
| 317 | A119 | 5c blue, pair | *5500.00* | — | ☐☐☐☐☐ |

Perf. 12 vertically

| 318 | A115 | 1c blue green, pair | *4250.00* | — | ☐☐☐☐☐ |

1903 *Perf. 12*

| 319 | A129 | 2c carmine | 6.00 | .05 | ☐☐☐☐☐ |
| 319g | | Bklt. pane of 6 | 110.00 | 20.00 | ☐☐☐☐☐ |

1906 *Imperf.*

| 320 | A129 | 2c carmine | 30.00 | 21.00 | ☐☐☐☐☐ |

1908 Coil stamps *Perf. 12 horizontally*

| 321 | A129 | 2c carmine, pair | *35000.00* | — | ☐☐☐☐☐ |

Perf. 12 vertically

| 322 | A129 | 2c carmine, pair | *5500.00* | — | ☐☐☐☐☐ |

1904

323	A130	1c green	27.50	5.00	☐☐☐☐☐
324	A131	2c carmine	25.00	1.50	☐☐☐☐☐
325	A132	3c violet	95.00	35.00	☐☐☐☐☐
326	A133	5c dk blue	110.00	25.00	☐☐☐☐☐
327	A134	10c red brown	185.00	35.00	☐☐☐☐☐

1907

328	A135	1c green	20.00	4.00	☐☐☐☐☐
329	A136	2c carmine	27.50	3.00	☐☐☐☐☐
330	A137	5c blue	110.00	30.00	☐☐☐☐☐

1908-09 Watermark 191 *Perf. 12*

331	A138	1c green	8.00	.05	☐☐☐☐☐
331a		Bklt. pane of 6	165.00	*35.00*	☐☐☐☐☐
332	A139	2c carmine	7.50	.05	☐☐☐☐☐
332a		Bklt. pane of 6	125.00	*35.00*	☐☐☐☐☐
333	A140	3c dp violet, Type I	32.50	3.00	☐☐☐☐☐
334	A140	4c orange brown	37.50	1.00	☐☐☐☐☐
335	A140	5c blue	50.00	2.00	☐☐☐☐☐
336	A140	6c red orange	60.00	4.50	☐☐☐☐☐
337	A140	8c olive green	42.50	2.50	☐☐☐☐☐
338	A140	10c yellow ('09)	70.00	1.50	☐☐☐☐☐

A130

A131

A132

A133

A134

A135

A136

A137

Franklin
A138

Washington
A139

Washington
A140

Franklin
A148

A141

HOW TO USE THIS BOOK

The number in the first column is its Scott number or identifying number. The letter and number that come next (A41) indicate the design and refer to the illustration so designated. Following that is the denomination of the stamp and its color. Finally, the price, unused and used is shown.

Scott No.	Illus. No.	Description	Unused Price	Used Price	//////
339	A140	13c blue green ('09)	40.00	25.00	☐☐☐☐☐
340	A140	15c pale ultra ('09)	65.00	5.75	☐☐☐☐☐
341	A140	50c violet ('09)	300.00	17.50	☐☐☐☐☐
342	A140	$1 violet brown ('09)	450.00	90.00	☐☐☐☐☐

Imperf.

343	A138	1c green	8.00	3.50	☐☐☐☐☐
344	A139	2c carmine	11.00	3.00	☐☐☐☐☐
345	A140	3c dp violet, Type I ('09)	25.00	13.50	☐☐☐☐☐
346	A140	4c orange brown ('09)	40.00	20.00	☐☐☐☐☐
347	A140	5c blue ('09)	60.00	35.00	☐☐☐☐☐

1908-10 Coil stamps *Perf. 12 horizontally*

348	A138	1c green	25.00	13.00	☐☐☐☐☐
349	A139	2c carmine ('09)	45.00	6.00	☐☐☐☐☐
350	A140	4c orange brown ('10)	110.00	75.00	☐☐☐☐☐
351	A140	5c blue ('09)	130.00	85.00	☐☐☐☐☐

1909 Coil stamps *Perf. 12 vertically*

352	A138	1c green	55.00	18.50	☐☐☐☐☐
353	A139	2c carmine	45.00	6.00	☐☐☐☐☐
354	A140	4c orange brown	120.00	50.00	☐☐☐☐☐
355	A140	5c blue	130.00	70.00	☐☐☐☐☐
356	A140	10c yellow	1300.00	400.00	☐☐☐☐☐

1909 Bluish paper *Perf. 12*

357	A138	1c green	110.00	100.00	☐☐☐☐☐
358	A139	2c carmine	100.00	75.00	☐☐☐☐☐
359	A140	3c dp violet, Type I	1650.00	1250.00	☐☐☐☐☐
360	A140	4c orange brown	*15000.00*		☐☐☐☐☐
361	A140	5c blue	3500.00	4000.00	☐☐☐☐☐
362	A140	6c red orange	1000.00	650.00	☐☐☐☐☐
363	A140	8c olive green	*15000.00*		☐☐☐☐☐
364	A140	10c yellow	1050.00	700.00	☐☐☐☐☐
365	A140	13c blue green	2100.00	1100.00	☐☐☐☐☐
366	A140	15c pale ultra	1000.00	700.00	☐☐☐☐☐

1909 *Perf. 12*

367	A141	2c carmine	7.00	2.75	☐☐☐☐☐

Imperf.

368	A141	2c carmine	30.00	25.00	☐☐☐☐☐

Bluish paper *Perf. 12*

369	A141	2c carmine	225.00	200.00	☐☐☐☐☐

Perf. 12

370	A142	2c carmine	12.00	2.25	☐☐☐☐☐

Imperf.

371	A142	2c carmine	45.00	30.00	☐☐☐☐☐

A142

A143

A144

A145

A146

A147

TYPE I

THREE CENTS.

Type I. The top line of the toga rope is weak and the rope shading lines are thin. The fifth line from the left is missing.

The line between the lips is thin.

Used on both flat plate and rotary press printings.

Scott No.	Illus. No.	Description	Unused Price	Used Price	//////
Perf. 12					
372	A143	2c carmine	16.00	4.75	□□□□□
Imperf.					
373	A143	2c carmine	50.00	30.00	□□□□□

1910-11 Watermark 190 USPS in single lined capitals *Perf. 12*

374	A138	1c green	7.50	.06	□□□□□
374a		Bklt. pane of 6	135.00	*30.00*	□□□□□
375	A139	2c carmine	7.00	.05	□□□□□
375a		Bklt. pane of 6	110.00	*25.00*	□□□□□
376	A140	3c dp violet, Type I ('11)	18.50	1.50	□□□□□
377	A140	2c brown ('11)	27.50	.50	□□□□□
378	A140	5c blue ('11)	27.50	.50	□□□□□
379	A140	6c red orange ('11)	37.50	.75	□□□□□
380	A140	8c olive green ('11)	115.00	13.50	□□□□□
381	A140	10c yellow ('11)	110.00	4.00	□□□□□
382	A140	15c pale ultra ('11)	275.00	15.00	□□□□□

1911 *Imperf.*

383	A138	1c green	4.00	3.00	□□□□□
384	A139	2c carmine	6.00	2.00	□□□□□

1910 Coil stamps *Perf. 12 horizontally*

385	A138	1c green	25.00	12.00	□□□□□
386	A139	2c carmine	45.00	11.00	□□□□□

1910-11 Coil stamps *Perf. 12 vertically*

387	A138	1c green	75.00	22.50	□□□□□
388	A139	2c carmine	550.00	75.00	□□□□□
389	A140	3c dp violet, Type I ('11)	*13000.00*	5500.00	□□□□□

1910 Coil stamps *Perf. 8½ horizontally*

390	A138	1c green	5.00	3.25	□□□□□
391	A139	2c carmine	32.50	8.50	□□□□□

1910-13 Coil stamps *Perf. 8½ vertically*

392	A138	1c green	20.00	15.00	□□□□□
393	A139	2c carmine	40.00	6.00	□□□□□
394	A140	3c dp violet, Type I ('11)	50.00	27.50	□□□□□
395	A140	4c brown ('12)	50.00	27.50	□□□□□
396	A140	5c blue ('13)	50.00	27.50	□□□□□

1913 *Perf. 12*

397	A144	1c green	17.50	1.75	□□□□□
398	A145	2c carmine	20.00	.50	□□□□□
399	A146	5c blue	80.00	11.00	□□□□□
400	A147	10c orange yellow	160.00	25.00	□□□□□
400A	A147	10c orange	250.00	20.00	□□□□□

TYPE I

TWO CENTS.
Type I. There is one shading line in the first curve of the ribbon above the left " 2 " and one in the second curve of the ribbon above the right " 2."

The button of the toga has a faint outline.

The top line of the toga rope, from the button to the front of the throat, is also very faint.

The shading lines at the face terminate in front of the ear with little or no joining, to form a lock of hair.

Used on both flat and rotary press printings.

TYPE II

TWO CENTS.
Type II. Shading lines in ribbons as on type I.

The toga button, rope, and shading lines are heavy.

The shading lines of the face at the lock of hair end in a strong vertical curved line.

Used on rotary press printings only.

TYPE III

TWO CENTS.
Type III. Two lines of shading in the curves of the ribbons.

Other characteristics similar to type II.

Used on rotary press printings only.

HOW TO USE THIS BOOK

The number in the first column is its Scott number or identifying number. The letter and number that come next (A41) indicate the design and refer to the illustration so designated. Following that is the denomination of the stamp and its color. Finally, the price, unused and used is shown.

Scott No.	Illus. No.	Description	Unused Price	Used Price	//////
1914-15 *Perf. 10*					
401	A144	1c green	27.50	6.50	□□□□□
402	A145	2c carmine ('15)	90.00	1.50	□□□□□
403	A146	5c blue ('15)	190.00	17.50	□□□□□
404	A147	10c orange ('15)	1250.00	75.00	□□□□□
1912-14 Watermark 190 *Perf. 12*					
405	A410	1c green	7.50	.06	□□□□□
405b		Bklt. pane of 6	65.00	*7.50*	□□□□□
406	A140	2c carmine, Type I	6.50	.05	□□□□□
406a		Bklt. pane of 6	70.00	*17.50*	□□□□□
407	A140	7c black ('14)	100.00	8.00	□□□□□
1912 *Imperf.*					
408	A140	1c green	1.50	.60	□□□□□
409	A140	2c carmine, Type I	1.65	.60	□□□□□
Coil stamps *Perf. 8½ horizontally*					
410	A140	1c green	6.25	3.50	□□□□□
411	A140	2c carmine, Type I	8.50	3.75	□□□□□
Perf. 8½ vertically					
412	A140	1c green	21.00	5.00	□□□□□
413	A140	2c carmine, Type I	35.00	.60	□□□□□
1912-14 *Perf. 12*					
414	A148	8c pale olive green	40.00	1.50	□□□□□
415	A148	9c salmon red ('14)	55.00	15.00	□□□□□
416	A148	10c orange yellow	40.00	.30	□□□□□
417	A148	12c claret brown ('14)	47.50	4.50	□□□□□
418	A148	15c gray	80.00	3.50	□□□□□
419	A148	20c ultra ('14)	175.00	16.00	□□□□□
420	A148	30c orange red ('14)	125.00	16.00	□□□□□
421	A148	50c violet ('14)	500.00	17.50	□□□□□
Watermark 191 *Perf. 12*					
422	A148	50c violet	250.00	17.50	□□□□□
423	A148	$1 violet brown	575.00	70.00	□□□□□
1914-15 Watermark 190 *Perf. 10*					
424	A140	1c green	2.75	.06	□□□□□
424a		Perf. 12x10	*300.00*	*250.00*	□□□□□
424b		Perf. 10x12		125.00	□□□□□
424d		Bklt. pane of 6	4.00	.75	□□□□□
425	A140	2c rose red, Type I	2.50	.05	□□□□□
425d		Perf. 12x10		250.00	□□□□□
425e		Bklt. pane of 6	15.00	*3.00*	□□□□□
426	A140	3c dp violet, Type I	13.50	1.25	□□□□□
427	A140	4c brown	35.00	.40	□□□□□
428	A140	5c blue	30.00	.40	□□□□□
428a		Perf. 12x10		*400.00*	□□□□□

TYPE Ia

TWO CENTS.

Type Ia. Design characteristics similar to type I except that all lines of design are stronger.

The toga button, toga rope and rope shading lines are heavy. The latter characteristics are those of type II, which, however, occur only on impressions from rotary plates.

Used only on flat plates 10208 and 10209.

TYPE II

THREE CENTS.

Type II. The top line of the toga rope is strong and the rope shading lines are heavy and complete.

The line between the lips is heavy.

Used on both flat plate and rotary press printings.

TYPE IV

TWO CENTS.

Type IV. Top line of toga rope is broken. Shading lines in toga button are so arranged that the curving of the first and last form "ᒌID".

Line of color in left "2" is very thin and usually broken.

Used on offset printings only.

Scott No.	Illus. No.	Description	Unused Price	Used Price	//////
429	A140	6c red orange	37.50	1.20	☐☐☐☐☐
430	A140	7c black	90.00	4.25	☐☐☐☐☐
431	A148	8c pale olive green	37.50	1.50	☐☐☐☐☐
432	A148	9c salmon red	50.00	8.50	☐☐☐☐☐
433	A148	10c orange yellow	47.50	.25	☐☐☐☐☐
434	A148	11c dk green ('15)	22.50	7.00	☐☐☐☐☐
435	A148	12c claret brown	25.00	4.50	☐☐☐☐☐
437	A148	15c gray	115.00	7.25	☐☐☐☐☐
438	A148	20c ultra	225.00	4.00	☐☐☐☐☐
439	A148	30c orange red	275.00	20.00	☐☐☐☐☐
440	A148	50c violet ('15)	800.00	20.00	☐☐☐☐☐

1914 Coil stamps *Perf. 10 horizontally*

441	A140	1c green	1.00	.90	☐☐☐☐☐
442	A140	2c carmine, Type I	10.00	7.50	☐☐☐☐☐

Perf. 10 vertically

443	A140	1c green	22.50	6.00	☐☐☐☐☐
444	A140	2c carmine, Type I	30.00	1.50	☐☐☐☐☐
445	A140	3c violet, Type I	225.00	110.00	☐☐☐☐☐
446	A140	4c brown	130.00	35.00	☐☐☐☐☐
447	A140	5c blue	45.00	22.50	☐☐☐☐☐

1915-16 Coil stamps Rotary press printing *Perf. 10 horizontally*

448	A140	1c green	8.50	3.00	☐☐☐☐☐
449	A140	2c red, Type I	1600.00	160.00	☐☐☐☐☐
450	A140	2c carmine, Type III ('16)	12.00	3.00	☐☐☐☐☐

1914-16 Coil stamps Rotary press printing *Perf. 10 vertically*

452	A140	1c green	12.00	1.75	☐☐☐☐☐
453	A140	2c carmine rose, Type I	120.00	4.50	☐☐☐☐☐
454	A140	2c red, Type II	115.00	13.50	☐☐☐☐☐
455	A140	2c carmine, Type III	10.00	1.00	☐☐☐☐☐
456	A140	3c violet, Type I ('16)	300.00	95.00	☐☐☐☐☐
457	A140	4c brown ('16)	30.00	18.00	☐☐☐☐☐
458	A140	5c blue ('16)	30.00	18.00	☐☐☐☐☐

1914 *Imperf.*

459	A140	2c carmine, Type I	450.00	600.00	☐☐☐☐☐

1915 Watermark 191 *Perf. 10*

460	A148	$1 violet black	975.00	95.00	☐☐☐☐☐

Watermark 190 *Perf. 11*

461	A140	2c pale carmine red, Type I	100.00	85.00	☐☐☐☐☐

1916-17 Unwatermarked *Perf. 10*

462	A140	1c green	8.50	.20	☐☐☐☐☐
462a		Bklt. pane of 6	12.00	*1.00*	☐☐☐☐☐
463	A140	2c carmine, Type I	5.00	.10	☐☐☐☐☐
463a		Bklt. pane of 6	85.00	*20.00*	☐☐☐☐☐
464	A140	3c violet, Type I	80.00	11.00	☐☐☐☐☐

TYPE V

TWO CENTS.

Type V. Top line of toga is complete. Five vertical shading lines in toga button.

Line of color in left "2" is very thin and usually broken.

Shading dots on the nose and lip are as indicated on the diagram.

Used on offset printings only.

TYPE Va

TWO CENTS.

Type Va. Characteristics same as type V, except in shading dots of nose. Third row from bottom has 4 dots instead of 6. Overall height of type Va is 1/3 mm. less than type V.

Used on offset printings only.

TYPE VI

TWO CENTS.

Type VI. General characteristics same as type V, except that line of color in left "2" is very heavy.

Used on offset printings only.

HOW TO USE THIS BOOK

The number in the first column is its Scott number or identifying number. The letter and number that come next (A41) indicate the design and refer to the illustration so designated. Following that is the denomination of the stamp and its color. Finally, the price, unused and used is shown.

Scott No.	Illus. No.	Description	Unused Price	Used Price	//////
465	A140	4c orange brown	45.00	1.75	☐☐☐☐☐
466	A140	5c blue	80.00	1.75	☐☐☐☐☐
467	A140	5c car (error in 2c plate, '17)	750.00	525.00	☐☐☐☐☐
468	A140	6c red orange	95.00	7.50	☐☐☐☐☐
469	A140	7c black	125.00	13.00	☐☐☐☐☐
470	A148	8c olive green	55.00	6.50	☐☐☐☐☐
471	A148	9c salmon red	60.00	16.00	☐☐☐☐☐
472	A148	10c orange yellow	120.00	1.00	☐☐☐☐☐
473	A148	11c dk green	32.50	17.50	☐☐☐☐☐
474	A148	12c claret brown	50.00	5.00	☐☐☐☐☐
475	A148	15c gray	175.00	12.00	☐☐☐☐☐
476	A148	20c lt ultra	250.00	12.50	☐☐☐☐☐
476A	A148	30c orange red	—	—	☐☐☐☐☐
477	A148	50c lt violet ('17)	1400.00	75.00	☐☐☐☐☐
478	A148	$1 violet black	950.00	22.50	☐☐☐☐☐
479	A127	$2 dk blue	500.00	45.00	☐☐☐☐☐
480	A128	$5 lt green	400.00	47.50	☐☐☐☐☐

Imperf.

481	A140	1c green	1.00	.75	☐☐☐☐☐
482	A140	2c carmine, Type I	1.25	1.25	☐☐☐☐☐
482A	A140	2c carmine, Type Ia		6000.00	☐☐☐☐☐
483	A140	3c violet, Type I ('17)	15.00	8.50	☐☐☐☐☐
484	A140	3c violet, Type II	11.00	4.00	☐☐☐☐☐
485	A140	5c car (error in 2c plate, '17)	13000.00		☐☐☐☐☐

1916-19 Coil stamps Rotary press printing *Perf. 10 horizontally*

486	A140	1c green ('18)	1.00	.15	☐☐☐☐☐
487	A140	2c carmine, Type II	18.00	2.50	☐☐☐☐☐
488	A140	2c carmine, Type III ('19)	3.00	1.50	☐☐☐☐☐
489	A140	3c violet, Type I ('17)	6.50	1.00	☐☐☐☐☐

1916-22 Coil stamps Rotary press printing *Perf. 10 vertically*

490	A140	1c green	.75	.15	☐☐☐☐☐
491	A140	2c carmine, Type II	1450.00	225.00	☐☐☐☐☐
492	A140	2c carmine, Type III	11.00	.15	☐☐☐☐☐
493	A140	3c violet, Type I ('17)	21.00	3.00	☐☐☐☐☐
494	A140	3c violet, Type II ('18)	11.50	.60	☐☐☐☐☐
495	A140	4c orange brown ('17)	12.50	3.50	☐☐☐☐☐
496	A140	5c blue ('19)	4.50	.60	☐☐☐☐☐
497	A148	10c orange yellow ('22)	26.50	8.50	☐☐☐☐☐

1917-19 *Perf. 11*

498	A140	1c green	.30	.05	☐☐☐☐☐
498e		Bklt. pane of 6	1.75	.35	☐☐☐☐☐
498f		Bklt. pane of 30	550.00		☐☐☐☐☐
499	A140	2c rose, Type I	.25	.05	☐☐☐☐☐
499e		Bklt. pane of 6	2.00	.50	☐☐☐☐☐
499f		Bklt. pane of 30	9000.00		☐☐☐☐☐
500	A140	2c dp rose, Type Ia	275.00	130.00	☐☐☐☐☐

TYPE VII

TYPE VII

TWO CENTS.

Type VII. Line of color in left "2" is invariably continuous, clearly defined, and heavier than in type V or Va, but not as heavy as in type VI.

Additional vertical row of dots has been added to the upper lip.

Numerous additional dots have been added to hair on top of head.

Used on offset printings only.

TYPE III

TYPE III

THREE CENTS.

Type III. The top line of the toga rope is strong but the fifth shading line is missing as in type I.

Center shading line of the toga button consists of two dashes with a central dot.

The "P" and "O" of "POSTAGE" are separated by a line of color.

The frame line at the bottom of the vignette is complete.

Used on offset printings only.

TYPE IV

TYPE IV

THREE CENTS.

Type IV. Shading lines of toga rope are complete.

Second and fourth shading lines in toga button are broken in the middle and the third line is continuous with a dot in the center.

"P" and "O" of "POSTAGE" are joined.

Frame line at bottom of vignette is broken.

Used on offset printings only.

Scott No.	Illus. No.	Description	Unused Price	Used Price	//////
501	A140	3c lt violet, Type I	17.50	.10	☐☐☐☐☐
501b		Bklt. pane of 6	75.00	*15.00*	☐☐☐☐☐
502	A140	3c dk violet, Type II	20.00	.25	☐☐☐☐☐
502b		Bklt. pane of 6	50.00	*10.00*	☐☐☐☐☐
503	A140	4c brown	13.00	.20	☐☐☐☐☐
504	A140	5c blue	11.00	.08	☐☐☐☐☐
505	A140	5c rose (error in 2c plate)	550.00	400.00	☐☐☐☐☐
506	A140	6c red orange	15.00	.30	☐☐☐☐☐
507	A140	7c black	32.50	1.50	☐☐☐☐☐
508	A148	8c olive bister	13.50	.70	☐☐☐☐☐
509	A148	9c salmon red	17.50	2.75	☐☐☐☐☐
510	A148	10c orange yellow	20.00	.10	☐☐☐☐☐
511	A148	11c lt green	10.00	3.75	☐☐☐☐☐
512	A148	12c claret brown	10.50	.45	☐☐☐☐☐
513	A148	13c apple green ('19)	12.00	7.00	☐☐☐☐☐
514	A148	15c gray	50.00	1.00	☐☐☐☐☐
515	A148	20c lt ultra	60.00	.30	☐☐☐☐☐
516	A148	30c orange red	50.00	.95	☐☐☐☐☐
517	A148	50c red violet	95.00	.65	☐☐☐☐☐
518	A148	$1 violet brown	75.00	1.75	☐☐☐☐☐

1917 Watermark 191 *Perf. 11*

519	A139	2c carmine	250.00	275.00	☐☐☐☐☐

1918 Unwatermarked

523	A149	$2 orange red & black	800.00	200.00	☐☐☐☐☐
524	A149	$5 dp green & black	350.00	30.00	☐☐☐☐☐

1918-20 Offset printing *Perf. 11*

525	A140	1c gray green	2.25	.60	☐☐☐☐☐
526	A140	2c carmine, Type IV ('20)	32.50	4.00	☐☐☐☐☐
527	A140	2c carmine, Type V	17.50	1.00	☐☐☐☐☐
528	A140	2c carmine, Type Va	8.00	.15	☐☐☐☐☐
528A	A140	2c carmine, Type VI	55.00	1.00	☐☐☐☐☐
528B	A140	2c carmine, Type VII	20.00	.12	☐☐☐☐☐
529	A140	3c violet, Type III	3.00	.10	☐☐☐☐☐
530	A140	3c purple, Type IV	.70	.06	☐☐☐☐☐

Offset printing *Imperf.*

531	A140	1c green ('19)	10.00	8.00	☐☐☐☐☐
532	A140	2c carmine rose, Type IV ('20)	47.50	27.50	☐☐☐☐☐
533	A140	2c carmine, Type V	235.00	70.00	☐☐☐☐☐
534	A140	2c carmine, Type Va	12.50	9.00	☐☐☐☐☐
534A	A140	2c carmine, Type VI	42.50	25.00	☐☐☐☐☐
534B	A140	2c carmine, Type VII	1550.00	425.00	☐☐☐☐☐
535	A140	3c violet, Type IV	8.50	6.50	☐☐☐☐☐

Offset printing *Perf. 12½*

536	A140	1c gray green	15.00	15.00	☐☐☐☐☐

A149

A150

A151

A152

A153

A154

A155

A156

A157

A158

A159

A160

A161

A162

A163

A164

A165

A166

A167

A168

A169

Scott No.	Illus. No.	Description	Unused Price	Used Price	//////
1919	*Perf. 11*				
537	A150	3c violet	11.00	4.25	☐☐☐☐☐
1919	*Perf. 11x10*				
538	A140	1c green	10.00	9.00	☐☐☐☐☐
539	A140	2c carmine rose, Type II	2350.00	750.00	☐☐☐☐☐
540	A140	2c carmine rose, Type III	11.00	9.00	☐☐☐☐☐
541	A140	3c violet, Type II	37.50	35.00	☐☐☐☐☐
1920	Size: 19x22½-22¾mm. *Perf. 10x11*				
542	A140	1c green	11.00	1.00	☐☐☐☐☐
1921	Size: 19x22½mm. *Perf. 10*				
543	A140	1c green	.60	.06	☐☐☐☐☐
1923	Size: 19x22½mm. *Perf. 11*				
544	A140	1c green	*6500.00*	*1750.00*	☐☐☐☐☐
1921	Size: 19½-20x22mm. *Perf. 11*				
545	A140	1c green	150.00	110.00	☐☐☐☐☐
546	A140	2c carmine rose, Type III	100.00	90.00	☐☐☐☐☐
1920	*Perf. 11*				
547	A149	$2 carmine & black	300.00	40.00	☐☐☐☐☐
548	A151	1c green	5.50	3.00	☐☐☐☐☐
549	A152	2c carmine rose	8.50	2.25	☐☐☐☐☐
550	A153	5c dp blue	52.50	18.50	☐☐☐☐☐
1922-25	*Perf. 11*				
551	A154	½c olive brown ('25)	.15	.06	☐☐☐☐☐
552	A155	1c dp green ('23)	2.25	.05	☐☐☐☐☐
552a		Bklt. pane of 6	5.50	*.50*	☐☐☐☐☐
553	A156	1½c yellow brown ('25)	3.50	.20	☐☐☐☐☐
554	A157	2c carmine ('23)	1.75	.05	☐☐☐☐☐
554c		Bklt. pane of 6	7.00	*1.00*	☐☐☐☐☐
555	A158	3c violet ('23)	21.00	1.25	☐☐☐☐☐
556	A159	4c yellow brown ('23)	22.50	.20	☐☐☐☐☐
557	A160	5c dk blue	22.50	.08	☐☐☐☐☐
558	A161	6c red orange	40.00	.85	☐☐☐☐☐
559	A162	7c black ('23)	10.00	.75	☐☐☐☐☐
560	A163	8c olive green ('23)	55.00	.85	☐☐☐☐☐
561	A164	9c rose ('23)	18.00	1.25	☐☐☐☐☐
562	A165	10c orange ('23)	24.00	.10	☐☐☐☐☐
563	A166	11c lt blue	2.00	.25	☐☐☐☐☐
564	A167	12c brown violet ('23)	8.50	.08	☐☐☐☐☐
565	A168	14c blue ('23)	5.00	.85	☐☐☐☐☐
566	A169	15c gray	27.50	.06	☐☐☐☐☐
567	A170	20c carmine rose ('23)	27.50	.06	☐☐☐☐☐
568	A171	25c yellow green	24.00	.50	☐☐☐☐☐
569	A172	30c olive brown ('23)	45.00	.35	☐☐☐☐☐
570	A173	50c lilac	75.00	.12	☐☐☐☐☐

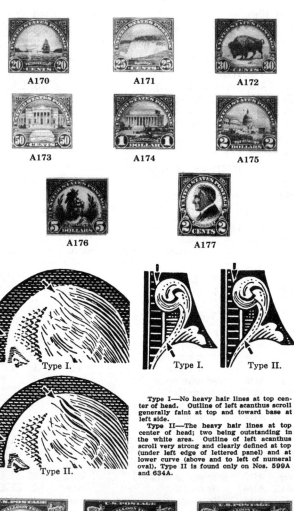

A170   A171   A172

A173   A174   A175

A176   A177

Type I.

Type I.   Type II.

Type II.

Type I—No heavy hair lines at top center of head. Outline of left acanthus scroll generally faint at top and toward base at left side.

Type II—The heavy hair lines at top center of head; two being outstanding in the white area. Outline of left acanthus scroll very strong and clearly defined at top (under left edge of lettered panel) and at lower curve (above and to left of numeral oval). Type II is found only on Nos. 599A and 634A.

A178

A179

A180

Scott No.	Illus. No.	Description	Unused Price	Used Price	//////
571	A174	$1 violet black ('23)	50.00	.45	☐☐☐☐☐
572	A175	$2 dp blue ('23)	120.00	11.00	☐☐☐☐☐
573	A176	$5 carmine & blue ('23)	300.00	15.00	☐☐☐☐☐

1923-26 *Imperf.*

575	A155	1c green	10.00	3.50	☐☐☐☐☐
576	A156	1½c yellow brown ('25)	2.25	1.75	☐☐☐☐☐
577	A157	2c carmine	2.50	2.00	☐☐☐☐☐

Perf. 11x10

578	A155	1c green	80.00	65.00	☐☐☐☐☐
579	A157	2c carmine	57.50	50.00	☐☐☐☐☐

Perf. 10

581	A155	1c green	10.00	.65	☐☐☐☐☐
582	A156	1½c brown ('25)	5.00	.60	☐☐☐☐☐
583	A157	2c carmine ('24)	2.50	.05	☐☐☐☐☐
583a		Bklt. pane of 6	75.00	*25.00*	☐☐☐☐☐
584	A158	3c violet ('25)	27.50	1.75	☐☐☐☐☐
585	A159	4c yellow brown ('25)	17.00	.40	☐☐☐☐☐
586	A160	5c blue ('25)	16.00	.18	☐☐☐☐☐
587	A161	6c red orange ('25)	7.50	.40	☐☐☐☐☐
588	A162	7c black ('26)	11.50	5.00	☐☐☐☐☐
589	A163	8c olive green ('26)	27.50	3.00	☐☐☐☐☐
590	A164	9c rose ('26)	5.00	2.25	☐☐☐☐☐
591	A165	10c orange ('25)	75.00	.10	☐☐☐☐☐

Perf. 11

594	A155	1c green	*7000.00*	*2500.00*	☐☐☐☐☐
595	A157	2c carmine	225.00	175.00	☐☐☐☐☐

Nos. 594-595 were made from coil waste of Nos. 597 and 599, and measure approximately 19¾x22¼mm.

596	A155	1c green		*13500.00*	☐☐☐☐☐

No. 596 measures approximately 19¼x22¾mm. Most copies carry the Bureau precancel "Kansas City, Mo."

1923-29 *Coil stamps* *Perf. 10 vertically*

597	A155	1c green	.35	.06	☐☐☐☐☐
598	A156	1½c brown ('25)	.75	.10	☐☐☐☐☐
599	A157	2c carmine, Type I ('23)	.30	.05	☐☐☐☐☐
599A	A157	2c carmine, Type II ('29)	140.00	12.00	☐☐☐☐☐
600	A158	3c violet ('24)	8.00	.08	☐☐☐☐☐
601	A159	4c yellow brown	4.50	.40	☐☐☐☐☐
602	A160	5c dk blue ('24)	2.00	.18	☐☐☐☐☐
603	A165	10c orange ('24)	4.00	.08	☐☐☐☐☐

Perf. 10 horizontally

604	A155	1c yellow green	.25	.08	☐☐☐☐☐
605	A156	1½c yellow brown ('25)	.30	.15	☐☐☐☐☐
606	A157	2c carmine	.30	.12	☐☐☐☐☐

A181

A182

A183

A184

A185

A186

A187

A188

A190

A189

A191

A192

A193

Scott No.	Illus. No.	Description	Unused Price	Used Price	//////
1923		Size: 19¼x22¼mm. *Perf. 11*			
610	A177	2c black	.75	.10	☐☐☐☐☐
Imperf.					
611	A177	2c black	11.00	6.00	☐☐☐☐☐
Perf. 10					
612	A177	2c black	25.00	2.50	☐☐☐☐☐
		Size: 19¼x22¾mm. *Perf. 11*			
613	A177	2c black		*13500.00*	☐☐☐☐☐
1924					
614	A178	1c dk green	4.50	4.50	☐☐☐☐☐
615	A179	2c carmine rose	7.50	3.50	☐☐☐☐☐
616	A180	5c dk blue	45.00	22.50	☐☐☐☐☐
1925					
617	A181	1c dp green	4.50	4.50	☐☐☐☐☐
618	A182	2c carmine rose	8.00	7.50	☐☐☐☐☐
619	A183	5c dk blue	40.00	20.00	☐☐☐☐☐
620	A184	2c carmine & black	7.00	5.00	☐☐☐☐☐
621	A185	5c dk blue & black	22.50	21.00	☐☐☐☐☐
1925-26 *Perf. 11*					
622	A186	13c green ('26)	17.50	.65	☐☐☐☐☐
623	A187	17c black	25.00	.35	☐☐☐☐☐
1926					
627	A188	2c carmine rose	4.00	.60	☐☐☐☐☐
628	A189	5c gray lilac	10.00	5.00	☐☐☐☐☐
629	A190	2c carmine rose	2.75	2.25	☐☐☐☐☐
630	A190	2c car rose, sheet of 25	500.00	425.00	☐☐☐☐☐
Imperf.					
631	A156	1½c yellow brown	2.25	2.10	☐☐☐☐☐
1926-34 *Perf. 11x10½*					
632	A155	1c green ('27)	.15	.05	☐☐☐☐☐
632a		Bklt. pane of 6	3.50	.25	☐☐☐☐☐
633	A156	1½c yellow brown ('27)	2.50	.08	☐☐☐☐☐
634	A157	2c carmine, Type I	.15	.05	☐☐☐☐☐
634d		Bklt. pane of 6	1.00	.15	☐☐☐☐☐
634A	A157	2c carmine, Type II ('28)	350.00	25.00	☐☐☐☐☐
635	A158	3c violet ('27)	.50	.05	☐☐☐☐☐
635a		3c bright violet ('34)	.30	.05	☐☐☐☐☐
636	A159	4c yellow brown ('27)	3.50	.08	☐☐☐☐☐
637	A160	5c dk blue ('27)	3.00	.05	☐☐☐☐☐
638	A161	6c red orange ('27)	3.00	.05	☐☐☐☐☐
639	A162	7c black ('27)	3.00	.08	☐☐☐☐☐
640	A163	8c olive green ('27)	3.00	.05	☐☐☐☐☐
641	A164	9c orange red ('31)	3.00	.05	☐☐☐☐☐
642	A165	10c orange ('27)	5.50	.05	☐☐☐☐☐

51

No. 634
Overprinted
MOLLY
PITCHER

SCOTT 646

Nos. 634 and 637
Overprinted
HAWAII
1778 - 1928

SCOTT 647-648

A194

A195

A196

A197

A198

A199

A200

A201

A202

A203

A204

A205

HOW TO USE THIS BOOK

The number in the first column is its Scott number or identifying number. The letter and number that come next (A41) indicate the design and refer to the illustration so designated. Following that is the denomination of the stamp and its color. Finally, the price, unused and used is shown.

Scott No.	Illus. No.	Description	Unused Price	Used Price	//////
1927					
643	A191	2c carmine rose	1.50	1.65	☐☐☐☐☐
644	A192	2c carmine rose	5.00	3.75	☐☐☐☐☐
1928					
645	A193	2c carmine rose	1.10	.65	☐☐☐☐☐
646	A157	2c Molly Pitcher ovpt.	1.50	1.50	☐☐☐☐☐
647	A157	2c Hawaii ovpt.	7.00	6.00	☐☐☐☐☐
648	A160	5c Hawaii ovpt.	20.00	17.50	☐☐☐☐☐
649	A194	2c carmine rose	1.50	1.40	☐☐☐☐☐
650	A195	5c blue	8.50	5.00	☐☐☐☐☐
1929					
651	A196	2c carmine & black	.85	.80	☐☐☐☐☐
653	A154	1½c olive brown	.05	.05	☐☐☐☐☐
654	A197	2c carmine rose, perf. 11	.90	1.00	☐☐☐☐☐
655	A197	2c carmine rose, perf. 11x10½	.85	.25	☐☐☐☐☐
Coil stamp		*Perf. 10 vertically*			
656	A197	2c carmine rose	20.00	2.00	☐☐☐☐☐
1929					
657	A198	2c carmine rose	1.00	.90	☐☐☐☐☐
Overprinted Kans.					
658	A155	1c green	2.00	1.65	☐☐☐☐☐
659	A156	1½c brown	3.00	3.00	☐☐☐☐☐
660	A157	2c carmine	3.00	.65	☐☐☐☐☐
661	A158	3c violet	17.50	12.00	☐☐☐☐☐
662	A159	4c yellow brown	17.50	7.50	☐☐☐☐☐
663	A160	5c dp blue	13.00	9.00	☐☐☐☐☐
664	A161	6c red orange	30.00	17.50	☐☐☐☐☐
665	A162	7c black	27.50	22.50	☐☐☐☐☐
666	A163	8c olive green	85.00	72.50	☐☐☐☐☐
667	A164	9c lt rose	13.00	11.00	☐☐☐☐☐
668	A165	10c orange yellow	22.50	11.00	☐☐☐☐☐
Overprinted Nebr.					
669	A155	1c green	2.00	2.00	☐☐☐☐☐
670	A156	1½c brown	3.00	2.25	☐☐☐☐☐
671	A157	2c carmine	2.00	.85	☐☐☐☐☐
672	A158	3c violet	12.00	8.75	☐☐☐☐☐
673	A159	4c yellow brown	17.50	11.00	☐☐☐☐☐
674	A160	5c dp blue	16.00	13.50	☐☐☐☐☐
675	A161	6c red orange	42.50	19.00	☐☐☐☐☐
676	A162	7c black	22.50	15.00	☐☐☐☐☐
677	A163	8c olive green	32.50	22.50	☐☐☐☐☐
678	A164	9c lt rose	37.50	25.00	☐☐☐☐☐
679	A165	10c orange yellow	110.00	17.50	☐☐☐☐☐

A206   A207   A208   A209

A210   A211   A212   A213

A214   A215   A216   A217

A218   A219   A220   A221

A222   A223   A224   A225

A226   A227   A228

Scott No.	Illus. No.	Description	Unused Price	Used Price	//////
1929					
680	A199	2c carmine rose	1.00	1.00	☐☐☐☐☐
681	A200	2c carmine rose	.80	.80	☐☐☐☐☐
1930					
682	A201	2c carmine rose	.80	.60	☐☐☐☐☐
683	A202	2c carmine rose	1.65	1.60	☐☐☐☐☐
Perf. 11x10½					
684	A203	1½c brown	.25	.05	☐☐☐☐☐
685	A204	4c brown	.75	.06	☐☐☐☐☐
Coil stamps *Perf. 10 vertically*					
686	A203	1½c brown	2.10	.07	☐☐☐☐☐
687	A204	4c brown	4.00	.50	☐☐☐☐☐
1930					
688	A205	2c carmine rose	1.40	1.40	☐☐☐☐☐
689	A206	2c carmine rose	.80	.75	☐☐☐☐☐
690	A207	2c carmine rose	.25	.18	☐☐☐☐☐
1931					
692	A166	11c lt blue	3.00	.10	☐☐☐☐☐
693	A167	12c brown violet	6.50	.06	☐☐☐☐☐
694	A186	13c yellow green	2.50	.10	☐☐☐☐☐
695	A168	14c dk blue	4.00	.30	☐☐☐☐☐
696	A169	15c gray	10.00	.06	☐☐☐☐☐
Perf. 10½x11					
697	A187	17c black	5.00	.25	☐☐☐☐☐
698	A170	20c carmine rose	12.00	.05	☐☐☐☐☐
699	A171	25c blue green	11.00	.08	☐☐☐☐☐
700	A172	30c brown	18.50	.07	☐☐☐☐☐
701	A173	50c lilac	55.00	.07	☐☐☐☐☐
1931					
702	A208	2c black & red	.15	.12	☐☐☐☐☐
703	A209	2c carmine rose & black	.40	.35	☐☐☐☐☐
1932					
704	A210	½c olive brown	.08	.05	☐☐☐☐☐
705	A211	1c green	.13	.05	☐☐☐☐☐
706	A212	1½c brown	.55	.08	☐☐☐☐☐
707	A213	2c carmine rose	.10	.05	☐☐☐☐☐
708	A214	3c dp violet	.60	.06	☐☐☐☐☐
709	A215	4c lt brown	.25	.06	☐☐☐☐☐
710	A216	5c blue	2.25	.10	☐☐☐☐☐
711	A217	6c red orange	6.00	.06	☐☐☐☐☐
712	A218	7c black	.30	.20	☐☐☐☐☐
713	A219	8c olive bister	4.50	.90	☐☐☐☐☐
714	A220	9c pale red	4.00	.25	☐☐☐☐☐
715	A221	10c orange yellow	15.00	.10	☐☐☐☐☐

A229

A230

A231

A232

A233

A234

A235

A236

A237

A238

Scott No.	Illus. No.	Description	Unused Price	Used Price	//////
716	A222	2c carmine rose	.50	.25 ☐☐☐☐☐	
717	A223	2c carmine rose	.18	.08 ☐☐☐☐☐	
718	A224	3c violet	2.25	.06 ☐☐☐☐☐	
719	A225	5c blue	3.50	.30 ☐☐☐☐☐	

Perf. 11x10½

720	A226	3c dp violet	.15	.05 ☐☐☐☐☐	
720b		Bklt. pane of 6	22.50	5.00 ☐☐☐☐☐	

Coil stamps   Perf. 10 vertically

721	A226	3c dp violet	3.00	.08 ☐☐☐☐☐	

Perf. 10 horizontally

722	A226	3c dp violet	1.85	.45 ☐☐☐☐☐	

Perf. 10 vertically

723	A161	6c dp orange	12.50	.25 ☐☐☐☐☐	
724	A227	3c violet	.35	.25 ☐☐☐☐☐	
725	A228	3c violet	.50	.40 ☐☐☐☐☐	

1933

726	A229	3c violet	.35	.25 ☐☐☐☐☐	
727	A230	3c violet	.15	.10 ☐☐☐☐☐	
728	A231	1c yellow green	.12	.06 ☐☐☐☐☐	
729	A232	3c violet	.18	.05 ☐☐☐☐☐	

Imperf.

730	A231	1c dp yel green, sheet of 25	30.00	35.00 ☐☐☐☐☐	
730a		Single stamp	1.00	.50 ☐☐☐☐☐	
731	A232	3c dp violet, sheet of 25	27.50	30.00 ☐☐☐☐☐	
731a		Single stamp	.85	.50 ☐☐☐☐☐	

1933

732	A233	3c violet	.14	.05 ☐☐☐☐☐	
733	A234	3c dk blue	.85	.85 ☐☐☐☐☐	
734	A235	5c blue	.85	.40 ☐☐☐☐☐	

1934   Imperf.

735	A235	3c dk blue, sheet of six	22.50	20.00 ☐☐☐☐☐	
735a		Single stamp	2.50	2.50 ☐☐☐☐☐	

1934

736	A236	3c carmine rose	.20	.20 ☐☐☐☐☐	

Perf. 11x10½

737	A237	3c dp violet	.15	.06 ☐☐☐☐☐	

Perf. 11

738	A237	3c dp violet	.20	.20 ☐☐☐☐☐	
739	A238	3c dp violet	.20	.12 ☐☐☐☐☐	
740	A239	1c green	.10	.06 ☐☐☐☐☐	
741	A240	2c red	.15	.06 ☐☐☐☐☐	
742	A241	3c dp violet	.20	.06 ☐☐☐☐☐	
743	A242	4c brown	.55	.50 ☐☐☐☐☐	

A240

A239

A241

A242

A243

A244

A245

A246

A247

A249

A248

A250

A252

A253

Scott No.	Illus. No.	Description	Unused Price	Used Price	//////
744	A243	5c blue	1.10	.90	☐☐☐☐☐
745	A244	6c dk blue	2.00	1.25	☐☐☐☐☐
746	A245	7c black	1.00	1.00	☐☐☐☐☐
747	A246	8c sage green	2.85	2.50	☐☐☐☐☐
748	A247	9c red orange	3.00	.90	☐☐☐☐☐
749	A248	10c gray black	5.00	1.35	☐☐☐☐☐

Imperf.

Scott No.	Illus. No.	Description	Unused Price	Used Price	//////
750	A248	3c dp violet, sheet of six	35.00	25.00	☐☐☐☐☐
750a		Single stamp	3.75	3.75	☐☐☐☐☐
751	A248	1c green, sheet of six	15.00	12.00	☐☐☐☐☐
751a		Single stamp	1.75	1.75	☐☐☐☐☐

1935

Scott No.	Illus. No.	Description	Unused Price	Used Price	//////
752	A230	3c violet	.15	.10	☐☐☐☐☐
753	A234	3c dk blue	.85	.85	☐☐☐☐☐

Without gum *Imperf.*

Scott No.	Illus. No.	Description	Unused Price	Used Price	//////
754	A237	3c dp violet	1.00	.60	☐☐☐☐☐
755	A238	3c dp violet	1.00	.60	☐☐☐☐☐
756	A239	1c green	.30	.20	☐☐☐☐☐
757	A240	2c red	.40	.35	☐☐☐☐☐
758	A241	3c dp violet	.75	.70	☐☐☐☐☐
759	A242	4c brown	2.00	2.00	☐☐☐☐☐
760	A243	5c blue	2.75	2.25	☐☐☐☐☐
761	A244	6c dk blue	4.00	2.75	☐☐☐☐☐
762	A245	7c black	3.00	2.50	☐☐☐☐☐
763	A246	8c sage green	3.50	2.75	☐☐☐☐☐
764	A247	9c red orange	3.75	2.75	☐☐☐☐☐
765	A248	10c gray black	6.25	5.50	☐☐☐☐☐
766	A231	1c yellow green, pane of 25	35.00	35.00	☐☐☐☐☐
766a		Single stamp	1.00	.50	☐☐☐☐☐
767	A232	3c violet, pane of 25	30.00	30.00	☐☐☐☐☐
767a		Single stamp	.85	.50	☐☐☐☐☐
768	A235	3c dk blue, pane of six	22.50	20.00	☐☐☐☐☐
768a		Single stamp	2.50	2.50	☐☐☐☐☐
769	A248	1c green, pane of six	15.00	12.00	☐☐☐☐☐
769a		Single stamp	1.75	1.75	☐☐☐☐☐
770	A248	3c dp violet, pane of six	35.00	25.00	☐☐☐☐☐
770a		Single stamp	3.75	3.75	☐☐☐☐☐
771	APSD1	16c dk blue	3.00	3.00	☐☐☐☐☐

Note: In 1940 the P.O. Department offered to and did gum full
sheets of Nos. 754 to 771 sent in by owners.

1935 *Perf. 11x10½, 11*

Scott No.	Illus. No.	Description	Unused Price	Used Price	//////
772	A249	3c violet	.15	.06	☐☐☐☐☐
773	A250	3c purple	.12	.06	☐☐☐☐☐
774	A251	3c purple	.12	.06	☐☐☐☐☐
775	A252	3c purple	.12	.06	☐☐☐☐☐

A251

A255

A254

A256

A257

A258

A259

A260

A261

A262

A263

A264

A265

A266

A267

A268

A269

A269a

A270

A272

A273

A274

A275

A271

A277

A276

A278

Thomas Jefferson
A279

James Madison
A280

White House
A281

James Monroe
A282

John Q. Adams
A283

Andrew Jackson
A284

Martin
Van Buren
A285

William H.
Harrison
A286

John Tyler
A287

James K. Polk
A288

Zachary Taylor
A289

Millard Fillmore
A290

Franklin Pierce
A291

James Buchanan
A292

Abraham Lincoln
A293

Andrew Johnson
A294

Ulysses S.
Grant
A295

Rutherford B.
Hayes
A296

James A. Garfield
A297

Chester A. Arthur
A298

Grover
Cleveland
A299

Benjamin
Harrison
A300

William
McKinley
A301

Theodore
Roosevelt
A302

Scott No.	Illus. No.	Description	Unused Price	Used Price	//////
1936					
776	A253	3c purple	.12	.06	☐☐☐☐☐
777	A254	3c purple	.15	.06	☐☐☐☐☐
778		Sheet of 4	3.00	3.50	☐☐☐☐☐
778a	A249	3c violet, imperf.	.60	.60	☐☐☐☐☐
778b	A250	3c violet, imperf.	.60	.60	☐☐☐☐☐
778c	A251	3c violet, imperf.	.60	.60	☐☐☐☐☐
778d	A252	3c violet, imperf.	.60	.60	☐☐☐☐☐
782	A255	3c purple	.12	.06	☐☐☐☐☐
783	A256	3c purple	.12	.06	☐☐☐☐☐
784	A257	3c dk violet	.10	.05	☐☐☐☐☐
1936-37					
785	A258	1c green	.10	.06	☐☐☐☐☐
786	A259	3c carmine ('37)	.15	.06	☐☐☐☐☐
787	A260	3c purple ('37)	.20	.08	☐☐☐☐☐
788	A261	4c gray ('37)	.65	.15	☐☐☐☐☐
789	A262	5c ultra ('37)	1.00	.15	☐☐☐☐☐
790	A263	1c green	.10	.06	☐☐☐☐☐
791	A264	2c carmine ('37)	.15	.06	☐☐☐☐☐
792	A265	3c purple ('37)	.20	.08	☐☐☐☐☐
793	A266	4c gray ('37)	.65	.15	☐☐☐☐☐
794	A267	5c ultra ('37)	1.00	.15	☐☐☐☐☐
1937					
795	A268	3c red violet	.12	.06	☐☐☐☐☐
796	A269	5c gray blue	.35	.25	☐☐☐☐☐
797	A269a	10c blue green	1.10	.85	☐☐☐☐☐
798	A270	3c bright red violet	.15	.07	☐☐☐☐☐
799	A271	3c violet	.15	.07	☐☐☐☐☐
800	A272	3c violet	.15	.07	☐☐☐☐☐
801	A273	3c bright violet	.15	.07	☐☐☐☐☐
802	A274	3c lt violet	.15	.07	☐☐☐☐☐
1938-54 *Perf. 11x10½, 11*					
803	A275	½c dp orange	.05	.05	☐☐☐☐☐
804	A276	1c green	.06	.05	☐☐☐☐☐
804b		Bklt. pane of 6	1.75	.20	☐☐☐☐☐
805	A277	1½c bister brown	.06	.05	☐☐☐☐☐
806	A278	2c rose carmine	.06	.05	☐☐☐☐☐
806b		Bklt. pane of 6	4.25	.50	☐☐☐☐☐
807	A279	3c dp violet	.10	.05	☐☐☐☐☐
807a		Bklt. pane of 6	8.50	.50	☐☐☐☐☐
808	A280	4c red violet	.60	.05	☐☐☐☐☐
809	A281	4½c dk gray	.20	.06	☐☐☐☐☐
810	A282	5c bright blue	.40	.05	☐☐☐☐☐
811	A283	6c red orange	.45	.05	☐☐☐☐☐
812	A284	7c sepia	.50	.05	☐☐☐☐☐
813	A285	8c olive green	.65	.05	☐☐☐☐☐

William
Howard Taft

A303

Woodrow
Wilson

A304

Warren G.
Harding

A305

Calvin
Coolidge

A306

A308

A307

A309

A311

A310

A312

A314

A313

A315

A316

A317

Scott No.	Illus. No.	Description	Unused Price	Used Price	//////
814	A286	9c rose pink	.70	.05	☐☐☐☐☐
815	A287	10c brown red	.50	.05	☐☐☐☐☐
816	A288	11c ultra	1.00	.08	☐☐☐☐☐
817	A289	12c bright violet	1.90	.06	☐☐☐☐☐
818	A290	13c blue green	2.00	.08	☐☐☐☐☐
819	A291	14c blue	1.75	.10	☐☐☐☐☐
820	A292	15c blue gray	.75	.05	☐☐☐☐☐
821	A293	16c black	1.75	.35	☐☐☐☐☐
822	A294	17c rose red	1.50	.12	☐☐☐☐☐
823	A295	18c brown carmine	3.25	.08	☐☐☐☐☐
824	A296	19c bright violet	2.00	.50	☐☐☐☐☐
825	A297	20c bright blue green	1.20	.05	☐☐☐☐☐
826	A298	21c dl blue	2.25	.10	☐☐☐☐☐
827	A299	22c vermilion	2.00	.50	☐☐☐☐☐
828	A300	24c gray black	6.00	.25	☐☐☐☐☐
829	A301	25c dp red lilac	1.40	.05	☐☐☐☐☐
830	A302	30c dp ultra	8.00	.05	☐☐☐☐☐
831	A303	50c lt red violet	11.00	.06	☐☐☐☐☐
832	A304	$1 purple & black	12.50	.10	☐☐☐☐☐
832b		Wmkd. USIR ('51)	350.00	90.00	☐☐☐☐☐
832c		$1 red violet & black ('54)	8.00	.15	☐☐☐☐☐
833	A305	$2 yellow green & black	32.50	6.00	☐☐☐☐☐
834	A306	$5 carmine & black	125.00	5.50	☐☐☐☐☐

1938

Scott No.	Illus. No.	Description	Unused Price	Used Price	//////
835	A307	3c dp violet	.25	.08	☐☐☐☐☐
836	A308	3c red violet	.25	.10	☐☐☐☐☐
837	A309	3c bright violet	.25	.08	☐☐☐☐☐
838	A310	3c violet	.25	.08	☐☐☐☐☐

1939   Coil stamps   *Perf. 10 vertically*

Scott No.	Illus. No.	Description	Unused Price	Used Price	//////
839	A276	1c green	.25	.06	☐☐☐☐☐
840	A277	1½c bister brown	.30	.06	☐☐☐☐☐
841	A278	2c rose carmine	.30	.05	☐☐☐☐☐
842	A279	3c dp violet	.75	.05	☐☐☐☐☐
843	A280	4c red violet	9.00	.35	☐☐☐☐☐
844	A281	4½c dk gray	.60	.45	☐☐☐☐☐
845	A282	5c bright blue	6.50	.35	☐☐☐☐☐
846	A283	6c red orange	1.40	.20	☐☐☐☐☐
847	A287	10c brown red	15.00	.40	☐☐☐☐☐

Perf. 10 horizontally

Scott No.	Illus. No.	Description	Unused Price	Used Price	//////
848	A276	1c green	1.00	.12	☐☐☐☐☐
849	A277	1½c bister brown	1.50	.40	☐☐☐☐☐
850	A278	2c rose carmine	3.50	.50	☐☐☐☐☐
851	A279	3c dp violet	2.75	.45	☐☐☐☐☐

Washington
Irving
A318

James Fenimore
Cooper
A319

Ralph Waldo
Emerson
A320

Louisa May
Alcott
A321

Samuel L. Clemens (Mark Twain)
A322

Henry W.
Longfellow
A323

John Greenleaf
Whittier
A324

James Russell
Lowell
A325

Walt
Whitman
A326

James Whitcomb Riley
A327

Horace Mann
A328

Mark Hopkins
A329

Charles W.
Eliot
A330

Frances E.
Willard
A331

Booker T. Washington
A332

John James
Audubon
A333

Dr. Crawford
W. Long
A334

Luther Burbank
A335

Dr. Walter Reed
A336

Jane Addams
A337

Stephen Collins
Foster
A338

John Philip
Sousa
A339

Victor
Herbert
A340

Edward
MacDowell
A341

Ethelbert Nevin
A342

Gilbert Charles
Stuart
A343

James A. McNeill
Whistler
A344

Augustus
Saint-Gaudens
A345

Daniel Chester
French
A346

Frederic Remington— **A347**

Eli Whitney
A348

Samuel F. B. Morse
A349

Cyrus Hall
McCormick
A350

Elias Howe
A351

A353

A352

A355

A356

A354

A361

A358

A357

A359

A362

A360

A363

A364

A366

A367

Scott No.	Illus. No.	Description	Unused Price	Used Price	//////
1939					
852	A311	3c bright purple	.12	.06 ☐☐☐☐☐
853	A312	3c dp purple	.15	.06 ☐☐☐☐☐
854	A313	2c bright red violet	.35	.10 ☐☐☐☐☐
855	A314	3c violet	.35	.08 ☐☐☐☐☐
856	A315	3c dp red violet	.30	.08 ☐☐☐☐☐
857	A316	3c violet	.15	.08 ☐☐☐☐☐
858	A317	3c rose violet	.15	.08 ☐☐☐☐☐
1940					
859	A318	1c bright blue green	.08	.06 ☐☐☐☐☐
860	A319	2c rose carmine	.10	.08 ☐☐☐☐☐
861	A320	3c bright red violet	.12	.06 ☐☐☐☐☐
862	A321	5c ultra	.35	.30 ☐☐☐☐☐
863	A322	10c dk brown	2.00	2.35 ☐☐☐☐☐
864	A323	1c bright blue green	.12	.08 ☐☐☐☐☐
865	A324	2c rose carmine	.10	.08 ☐☐☐☐☐
866	A325	3c bright red violet	.18	.06 ☐☐☐☐☐
867	A326	5c ultra	.35	.25 ☐☐☐☐☐
868	A327	10c dk brown	2.75	3.00 ☐☐☐☐☐
869	A328	1c bright blue green	.09	.08 ☐☐☐☐☐
870	A329	2c rose carmine	.10	.06 ☐☐☐☐☐
871	A330	3c bright red violet	.30	.06 ☐☐☐☐☐
872	A331	5c ultra	.50	.35 ☐☐☐☐☐
873	A332	10c dk brown	1.85	2.25 ☐☐☐☐☐
874	A333	1c bright blue green	.08	.06 ☐☐☐☐☐
875	A334	2c rose carmine	.10	.06 ☐☐☐☐☐
876	A335	3c bright red violet	.10	.06 ☐☐☐☐☐
877	A336	5c ultra	.30	.25 ☐☐☐☐☐
878	A337	10c dk brown	1.75	2.00 ☐☐☐☐☐
879	A338	1c bright blue green	.08	.06 ☐☐☐☐☐
880	A339	2c rose carmine	.10	.06 ☐☐☐☐☐
881	A340	3c bright red violet	.15	.06 ☐☐☐☐☐
882	A341	5c ultra	.60	.30 ☐☐☐☐☐
883	A342	10c dk brown	4.00	2.25 ☐☐☐☐☐
884	A343	1c bright blue green	.08	.06 ☐☐☐☐☐
885	A344	2c rose carmine	.10	.06 ☐☐☐☐☐
886	A345	3c bright red violet	.10	.06 ☐☐☐☐☐
887	A346	5c ultra	.40	.22 ☐☐☐☐☐
888	A347	10c dk brown	2.00	2.25 ☐☐☐☐☐
889	A348	1c bright blue green	.12	.08 ☐☐☐☐☐
890	A349	2c rose carmine	.10	.06 ☐☐☐☐☐
891	A350	3c bright red violet	.20	.06 ☐☐☐☐☐
892	A351	5c ultra	1.25	.40 ☐☐☐☐☐
893	A352	10c dk brown	10.00	3.25 ☐☐☐☐☐
894	A353	3c henna brown	.50	.15 ☐☐☐☐☐
895	A354	3c lt violet	.40	.12 ☐☐☐☐☐
896	A355	3c bright violet	.20	.08 ☐☐☐☐☐

A365

A368

A369

A370

A371

A372

A373

A374

A375

A377

A376

A378

A379

A380

A381

A382

A383

Scott No.	Illus. No.	Description	Unused Price	Used Price	//////
897	A356	3c brown violet	.20	.08 ☐☐☐☐☐	
898	A357	3c violet	.20	.08 ☐☐☐☐☐	
899	A358	1c bright blue green	.05	.05 ☐☐☐☐☐	
900	A359	2c rose carmine	.06	.05 ☐☐☐☐☐	
901	A360	3c bright violet	.12	.05 ☐☐☐☐☐	
902	A361	3c dp violet	.25	.15 ☐☐☐☐☐	

1941

Scott No.	Illus. No.	Description	Unused Price	Used Price	//////
903	A362	3c lt violet	.22	.10 ☐☐☐☐☐	

1942

Scott No.	Illus. No.	Description	Unused Price	Used Price	//////
904	A363	3c violet	.15	.12 ☐☐☐☐☐	
905	A364	3c violet	.10	.05 ☐☐☐☐☐	
906	A365	5c bright blue	.35	.30 ☐☐☐☐☐	

1943

Scott No.	Illus. No.	Description	Unused Price	Used Price	//////
907	A366	2c rose carmine	.08	.05 ☐☐☐☐☐	
908	A367	1c bright blue green	.06	.05 ☐☐☐☐☐	

1943-44

Scott No.	Illus. No.	Description	Unused Price	Used Price	//////
909	A368	5c Poland	.35	.20 ☐☐☐☐☐	
910	A368	5c Czechoslovakia	.30	.15 ☐☐☐☐☐	
911	A368	5c Norway	.25	.12 ☐☐☐☐☐	
912	A368	5c Luxembourg	.25	.12 ☐☐☐☐☐	
913	A368	5c Netherlands	.25	.12 ☐☐☐☐☐	
914	A368	5c Belgium	.25	.12 ☐☐☐☐☐	
915	A368	5c France	.25	.10 ☐☐☐☐☐	
916	A368	5c Greece	.85	.60 ☐☐☐☐☐	
917	A368	5c Yugoslavia	.50	.40 ☐☐☐☐☐	
918	A368	5c Albania	.50	.40 ☐☐☐☐☐	
919	A368	5c Austria	.30	.25 ☐☐☐☐☐	
920	A368	5c Denmark	.50	.50 ☐☐☐☐☐	
921	A368	5c Korea ('44)	.28	.25 ☐☐☐☐☐	

1944

Scott No.	Illus. No.	Description	Unused Price	Used Price	//////
922	A369	3c violet	.20	.15 ☐☐☐☐☐	
923	A370	3c violet	.15	.15 ☐☐☐☐☐	
924	A371	3c bright red violet	.12	.10 ☐☐☐☐☐	
925	A372	3c dp violet	.12	.12 ☐☐☐☐☐	
926	A373	3c dp violet	.12	.10 ☐☐☐☐☐	

1945

Scott No.	Illus. No.	Description	Unused Price	Used Price	//////
927	A374	3c bright red violet	.10	.08 ☐☐☐☐☐	
928	A375	5c ultra	.12	.08 ☐☐☐☐☐	
929	A376	3c yellow green	.10	.05 ☐☐☐☐☐	

1945-46

Scott No.	Illus. No.	Description	Unused Price	Used Price	//////
930	A377	1c blue green	.05	.05 ☐☐☐☐☐	
931	A378	2c carmine rose	.08	.08 ☐☐☐☐☐	
932	A379	3c purple	.10	.08 ☐☐☐☐☐	
933	A380	5c bright blue ('46)	.12	.08 ☐☐☐☐☐	

A384

A385

A386

A387

A388

A389

A390

A391

A392

A393

A394

A399

A395

A396

A397

A398

A401

A400

A402

A403

A404

A405

A406

A407

A408

A409

A410

A411

A412

A413

A414

A416

A415

A417

A418

A419

A420

A421

73

A422

A423

A424

A425

A426

A427

A428

A429

A430

A432

A433

A431

A434

A435

A436

74

Scott No.	Illus. No.	Description	Unused Price	Used Price	//////
1945					
934	A381	3c olive	.10	.05 ☐☐☐☐☐
935	A382	3c blue	.10	.05 ☐☐☐☐☐
936	A383	3c bright blue green	.10	.05 ☐☐☐☐☐
937	A384	3c purple	.10	.05 ☐☐☐☐☐
938	A385	3c dk blue	.10	.05 ☐☐☐☐☐
1946					
939	A386	3c blue green	.10	.05 ☐☐☐☐☐
940	A387	3c dk violet	.10	.05 ☐☐☐☐☐
941	A388	3c dk violet	.10	.05 ☐☐☐☐☐
942	A389	3c dp blue	.10	.05 ☐☐☐☐☐
943	A390	3c violet brown	.10	.05 ☐☐☐☐☐
944	A391	3c brown violet	.10	.05 ☐☐☐☐☐
1947					
945	A392	3c bright red violet	.10	.05 ☐☐☐☐☐
946	A393	3c purple	.10	.05 ☐☐☐☐☐
947	A394	3c dp blue	.10	.05 ☐☐☐☐☐
948	A395	Sheet of two, imperf.	1.10	1.00 ☐☐☐☐☐
948a	A1	5c blue	.30	.30 ☐☐☐☐☐
948b	A2	10c brown orange	.40	.30 ☐☐☐☐☐
949	A396	3c brown violet	.10	.05 ☐☐☐☐☐
950	A397	3c dk violet	.10	.05 ☐☐☐☐☐
951	A398	3c blue green	.10	.05 ☐☐☐☐☐
952	A399	3c bright green	.10	.05 ☐☐☐☐☐
1948					
953	A400	3c bright red violet	.10	.05 ☐☐☐☐☐
954	A401	3c dk violet	.10	.05 ☐☐☐☐☐
955	A402	3c brown violet	.10	.05 ☐☐☐☐☐
956	A403	3c gray black	.10	.05 ☐☐☐☐☐
957	A404	3c dk violet	.10	.05 ☐☐☐☐☐
958	A405	5c dp blue	.15	.10 ☐☐☐☐☐
959	A406	3c dk violet	.10	.05 ☐☐☐☐☐
960	A407	3c bright red violet	.10	.06 ☐☐☐☐☐
961	A408	3c blue	.10	.05 ☐☐☐☐☐
962	A409	3c rose pink	.10	.05 ☐☐☐☐☐
963	A410	3c dp blue	.10	.06 ☐☐☐☐☐
964	A411	3c brown red	.10	.10 ☐☐☐☐☐
965	A412	3c bright red violet	.10	.08 ☐☐☐☐☐
966	A413	3c blue	.12	.10 ☐☐☐☐☐
967	A414	3c rose pink	.10	.08 ☐☐☐☐☐
968	A415	3c sepia	.12	.08 ☐☐☐☐☐
969	A416	3c orange yellow	.12	.08 ☐☐☐☐☐
970	A417	3c violet	.12	.08 ☐☐☐☐☐
971	A418	3c bright rose carmine	.12	.08 ☐☐☐☐☐
972	A419	3c dk brown	.12	.08 ☐☐☐☐☐
973	A420	3c violet brown	.12	.10 ☐☐☐☐☐

A437 A438 A439

A440 A441 A442

A443 A444 A445

A446 A447 A448

A449 A450 A451

A452

A453

Scott No.	Illus. No.	Description	Unused Price	Used Price	//////
974	A421	3c blue green	.12	.08	☐☐☐☐☐
975	A422	3c bright red violet	.12	.08	☐☐☐☐☐
976	A423	3c henna brown	.15	.08	☐☐☐☐☐
977	A424	3c rose pink	.12	.08	☐☐☐☐☐
978	A425	3c bright blue	.12	.08	☐☐☐☐☐
979	A426	3c carmine	.12	.08	☐☐☐☐☐
980	A427	3c bright red violet	.12	.08	☐☐☐☐☐

1949

Scott No.	Illus. No.	Description	Unused Price	Used Price	//////
981	A428	3c blue green	.10	.05	☐☐☐☐☐
982	A429	3c ultra	.10	.05	☐☐☐☐☐
983	A430	3c green	.10	.05	☐☐☐☐☐
984	A431	3c aqua	.10	.05	☐☐☐☐☐
985	A432	3c bright rose carmine	.10	.05	☐☐☐☐☐
986	A433	3c bright red violet	.10	.05	☐☐☐☐☐

1950

Scott No.	Illus. No.	Description	Unused Price	Used Price	//////
987	A434	3c yellow green	.10	.05	☐☐☐☐☐
988	A435	3c bright red violet	.10	.05	☐☐☐☐☐
989	A436	3c bright blue	.10	.05	☐☐☐☐☐
990	A437	3c dp green	.10	.05	☐☐☐☐☐
991	A438	3c lt violet	.10	.05	☐☐☐☐☐
992	A439	3c bright red violet	.10	.05	☐☐☐☐☐
993	A440	3c violet brown	.10	.05	☐☐☐☐☐
994	A441	3c violet	.10	.05	☐☐☐☐☐
995	A442	3c sepia	.10	.06	☐☐☐☐☐
996	A443	3c bright blue	.10	.05	☐☐☐☐☐
997	A444	3c yellow orange	.10	.05	☐☐☐☐☐

1951

Scott No.	Illus. No.	Description	Unused Price	Used Price	//////
998	A445	3c gray	.10	.05	☐☐☐☐☐
999	A446	3c lt olive green	.10	.05	☐☐☐☐☐
1000	A447	3c blue	.10	.05	☐☐☐☐☐
1001	A448	3c blue violet	.10	.05	☐☐☐☐☐
1002	A449	3c violet brown	.10	.05	☐☐☐☐☐
1003	A450	3c violet	.10	.05	☐☐☐☐☐

1952

Scott No.	Illus. No.	Description	Unused Price	Used Price	//////
1004	A451	3c carmine rose	.10	.05	☐☐☐☐☐
1005	A452	3c blue green	.10	.05	☐☐☐☐☐
1006	A453	3c bright blue	.10	.05	☐☐☐☐☐
1007	A454	3c dp blue	.10	.05	☐☐☐☐☐
1008	A455	3c dp violet	.10	.05	☐☐☐☐☐
1009	A456	3c blue green	.10	.05	☐☐☐☐☐
1010	A457	3c bright blue	.10	.05	☐☐☐☐☐
1011	A458	3c blue green	.10	.05	☐☐☐☐☐
1012	A459	3c violet blue	.10	.05	☐☐☐☐☐
1013	A460	3c dp blue	.10	.05	☐☐☐☐☐
1014	A461	3c violet	.10	.05	☐☐☐☐☐

A454

A455

A456

A457

A458

A459

A460

A461

A462

A463

A464

A465

A466

A467

A468

A469

A470

A471

Scott No.	Illus. No.	Description	Unused Price	Used Price	//////
1015	A462	3c violet	.10	.05	□□□□□
1016	A463	3c dp blue & carmine	.10	.05	□□□□□

1953

Scott No.	Illus. No.	Description	Unused Price	Used Price	//////
1017	A464	3c bright blue	.10	.05	□□□□□
1018	A465	3c chocolate	.10	.05	□□□□□
1019	A466	3c green	.10	.05	□□□□□
1020	A467	3c violet brown	.10	.05	□□□□□
1021	A468	5c green	.15	.10	□□□□□
1022	A469	3c rose violet	.10	.05	□□□□□
1023	A470	3c yellow green	.10	.05	□□□□□
1024	A471	3c dp blue	.10	.05	□□□□□
1025	A472	3c violet	.10	.05	□□□□□
1026	A473	3c blue violet	.10	.05	□□□□□
1027	A474	3c bright red violet	.10	.05	□□□□□
1028	A475	3c copper brown	.10	.05	□□□□□

1954

Scott No.	Illus. No.	Description	Unused Price	Used Price	//////
1029	A476	3c blue	.10	.05	□□□□□

1954-68   *Perf. 11x10½, 10½x11, 11*

Scott No.	Illus. No.	Description	Unused Price	Used Price	//////
1030	A477	½c red orange ('55)	.05	.05	□□□□□
1031	A478	1c dk green	.05	.05	□□□□□
1031A	A478a	1¼c turquoise ('60)	.05	.05	□□□□□
1032	A479	1½c brown carmine ('56)	.08	.05	□□□□□
1033	A480	2c carmine rose	.05	.05	□□□□□
1034	A481	2½c gray blue ('59)	.08	.05	□□□□□
1035	A482	3c dp violet	.08	.05	□□□□□
1035a		Bklt. pane of 6	3.00	.50	□□□□□
1035b		Tagged ('66)	.25	.20	□□□□□
1036	A483	4c red violet	.10	.05	□□□□□
1036a		Bklt. pane of 6 ('58)	2.00	.50	□□□□□
1036b		Tagged ('63)	.75	.16	□□□□□
1037	A484	4½c blue green ('59)	.15	.08	□□□□□
1038	A485	5c dp blue	.17	.05	□□□□□
1039	A486	6c carmine ('55)	.40	.05	□□□□□
1040	A487	7c rose carmine ('56)	.25	.05	□□□□□
1041	A488	8c dk violet blue & carmine	.30	.06	□□□□□
1042	A489	8c dk vio bl & car rose ('58)	.30	.05	□□□□□
1042A	A489a	8c brown ('61)	.25	.05	□□□□□
1043	A490	9c rose lilac ('56)	.30	.05	□□□□□
1044	A491	10c rose lake ('56)	.35	.05	□□□□□
1044b		Tagged ('66)	1.50	1.25	□□□□□
1044A	A491a	11c car & dk vio blue ('61)	.30	.06	□□□□□
1044c		Tagged ('67)	2.00	1.60	□□□□□
1045	A492	12c red ('59)	.55	.05	□□□□□
1045a		Tagged ('68)	.55	.15	□□□□□
1046	A493	15c rose lake ('58)	.85	.05	□□□□□
1046a		Tagged ('66)	.90	.22	□□□□□

A472

A473

A474

A475

A476

A477

A478

A478a

A479

A480

A481

A482

A483

A484

A485

A486

A487

A488

A489

A489a

A490

A491

Scott No.	Illus. No.	Description	Unused Price	Used Price	//////
1047	A494	20c ultra ('56)	.90	.05	☐☐☐☐☐
1048	A495	25c green ('58)	2.75	.05	☐☐☐☐☐
1049	A496	30c black ('55)	2.00	.08	☐☐☐☐☐
1050	A497	40c brown red ('55)	3.50	.10	☐☐☐☐☐
1051	A498	50c bright purple ('55)	3.25	.05	☐☐☐☐☐
1052	A499	$1 purple ('55)	10.00	.06	☐☐☐☐☐
1053	A500	$5 black ('56)	100.00	8.00	☐☐☐☐☐

1954-73 Coil stamps *Perf. 10 vertically, horizontally*

Scott No.	Illus. No.	Description	Unused Price	Used Price	//////
1054	A478	1c dk green	.35	.12	☐☐☐☐☐
1054A	A478a	1¼c turquoise ('60)	.25	.20	☐☐☐☐☐
1055	A480	2c rose carmine	.10	.05	☐☐☐☐☐
1055a		Tagged ('68)	.10	.05	☐☐☐☐☐
1056	A481	2½c gray blue ('59)	.55	.35	☐☐☐☐☐
1057	A482	3c dp violet	.15	.05	☐☐☐☐☐
1057b		Tagged ('66)	.75	.25	☐☐☐☐☐
1058	A483	4c red violet ('58)	.15	.05	☐☐☐☐☐
1059	A484	4½c blue green ('59)	3.25	1.20	☐☐☐☐☐
1059A	A495	25c green ('65)	.70	.30	☐☐☐☐☐
1059b		Tagged ('73)	.50	.20	☐☐☐☐☐

1954

Scott No.	Illus. No.	Description	Unused Price	Used Price	//////
1060	A507	3c violet	.10	.05	☐☐☐☐☐
1061	A508	3c brown orange	.10	.05	☐☐☐☐☐
1062	A509	3c violet brown	.10	.05	☐☐☐☐☐
1063	A510	3c violet brown	.10	.05	☐☐☐☐☐

1955

Scott No.	Illus. No.	Description	Unused Price	Used Price	//////
1064	A511	3c violet brown	.10	.05	☐☐☐☐☐
1065	A512	3c green	.10	.05	☐☐☐☐☐
1066	A513	8c dp blue	.20	.12	☐☐☐☐☐
1067	A514	3c purple	.10	.05	☐☐☐☐☐
1068	A515	3c green	.10	.05	☐☐☐☐☐
1069	A516	3c blue	.10	.05	☐☐☐☐☐
1070	A517	3c dp blue	.12	.05	☐☐☐☐☐
1071	A518	3c lt brown	.10	.05	☐☐☐☐☐
1072	A519	3c rose carmine	.10	.05	☐☐☐☐☐

1956

Scott No.	Illus. No.	Description	Unused Price	Used Price	//////
1073	A520	3c bright carmine	.10	.05	☐☐☐☐☐
1074	A521	3c dp blue	.10	.05	☐☐☐☐☐
1075	A522	Sheet of two, imperf.	4.00	3.50	☐☐☐☐☐
1075a	A482	3c dp violet	1.35	1.10	☐☐☐☐☐
1075b	A488	8c dk vio blue & car	1.75	1.50	☐☐☐☐☐
1076	A523	3c dp violet	.10	.05	☐☐☐☐☐
1077	A524	3c rose lake	.12	.05	☐☐☐☐☐
1078	A525	3c brown	.12	.05	☐☐☐☐☐
1079	A526	3c blue green	.12	.05	☐☐☐☐☐
1080	A527	3c dk blue green	.10	.05	☐☐☐☐☐
1081	A528	3c black brown	.10	.05	☐☐☐☐☐

A491a

A492

A493

A494

A495

A496

A497

A498

A499

A500

A507

A509

A508

A510

A511

A512

A513

A514

Scott No.	Illus. No.	Description	Unused Price	Used Price	//////
1082	A529	3c dp blue	.10	.05 ☐☐☐☐☐
1083	A530	3c *orange*	.10	.05 ☐☐☐☐☐
1084	A531	3c violet	.10	.05 ☐☐☐☐☐
1085	A532	3c dk blue	.10	.05 ☐☐☐☐☐

1957

1086	A533	3c rose red	.10	.05 ☐☐☐☐☐
1087	A534	3c red lilac	.10	.05 ☐☐☐☐☐
1088	A535	3c dk blue	.10	.05 ☐☐☐☐☐
1089	A536	3c red lilac	.10	.05 ☐☐☐☐☐
1090	A537	3c bright ultra	.10	.05 ☐☐☐☐☐
1091	A538	3c blue green	.10	.05 ☐☐☐☐☐
1092	A539	3c dk blue	.10	.05 ☐☐☐☐☐
1093	A540	3c rose lake	.10	.05 ☐☐☐☐☐
1094	A541	4c dk blue & dp carmine	.10	.05 ☐☐☐☐☐
1095	A542	3c dp violet	.10	.05 ☐☐☐☐☐
1096	A543	8c carmine, ultra & ocher	.22	.15 ☐☐☐☐☐
1097	A544	3c rose lake	.10	.05 ☐☐☐☐☐
1098	A545	3c blue, ocher & green	.10	.05 ☐☐☐☐☐
1099	A546	3c black	.10	.05 ☐☐☐☐☐

1958

1100	A557	3c green	.10	.05 ☐☐☐☐☐
1104	A551	3c dp claret	.10	.05 ☐☐☐☐☐
1105	A552	3c purple	.10	.05 ☐☐☐☐☐
1106	A553	3c green	.10	.05 ☐☐☐☐☐
1107	A554	3c black & red orange	.10	.05 ☐☐☐☐☐
1108	A555	3c lt green	.10	.05 ☐☐☐☐☐
1109	A556	3c bright greenish blue	.10	.05 ☐☐☐☐☐
1110	A556	4c olive bister	.10	.05 ☐☐☐☐☐
1111	A557	8c carmine, ultra & ocher	.25	.15 ☐☐☐☐☐
1112	A558	4c reddish purple	.10	.05 ☐☐☐☐☐

1958-59

1113	A559	1c green ('59)	.05	.05 ☐☐☐☐☐
1114	A560	3c purple ('59)	.10	.06 ☐☐☐☐☐
1115	A561	4c sepia	.10	.05 ☐☐☐☐☐
1116	A562	4c dk blue ('59)	.10	.05 ☐☐☐☐☐

1958

1117	A563	4c green	.10	.05 ☐☐☐☐☐
1118	A563	8c carmine, ultra & ocher	.22	.12 ☐☐☐☐☐
1119	A564	4c black	.10	.05 ☐☐☐☐☐
1120	A565	4c crimson rose	.10	.05 ☐☐☐☐☐
1121	A566	4c dk carmine rose	.10	.05 ☐☐☐☐☐
1122	A567	4c green, yellow & brown	.10	.05 ☐☐☐☐☐
1123	A568	4c blue	.10	.05 ☐☐☐☐☐

A516

A515

A517

A518

A519

A520

A521

Souvenir Sheet.

A523

A522

A524

A525

A526

A527

A528

Scott No.	Illus. No.	Description	Unused Price	Used Price	//////
1959					
1124	A569	4c blue green	.10	.05	☐☐☐☐☐
1125	A570	4c blue	.10	.05	☐☐☐☐☐
1126	A570	8c carmine, ultra & ocher	.20	.12	☐☐☐☐☐
1127	A571	4c blue	.10	.05	☐☐☐☐☐
1128	A572	4c bright greenish blue	.13	.05	☐☐☐☐☐
1129	A573	8c rose lake	.20	.12	☐☐☐☐☐
1130	A574	4c black	.10	.05	☐☐☐☐☐
1131	A575	4c red & dk blue	.10	.05	☐☐☐☐☐
1132	A576	4c ocher, dk blue & dp car	.10	.05	☐☐☐☐☐
1133	A577	4c blue, green & ocher	.10	.05	☐☐☐☐☐
1134	A578	4c brown	.10	.05	☐☐☐☐☐
1135	A579	4c green	.10	.05	☐☐☐☐☐
1136	A580	4c gray	.10	.05	☐☐☐☐☐
1137	A580	8c carmine, ultra & ocher	.20	.12	☐☐☐☐☐
1138	A581	4c rose lake	.10	.05	☐☐☐☐☐
1960-61					
1139	A582	4c dk violet blue & carmine	.18	.05	☐☐☐☐☐
1140	A583	4c olive bister & green	.18	.05	☐☐☐☐☐
1141	A584	4c gray & vermilion	.18	.05	☐☐☐☐☐
1142	A585	4c carmine & dk blue	.18	.05	☐☐☐☐☐
1143	A586	4c magenta & green	.18	.05	☐☐☐☐☐
1144	A587	4c green & brown ('61)	.18	.05	☐☐☐☐☐
1960					
1145	A588	4c red, dk blue & dk bister	.10	.05	☐☐☐☐☐
1146	A589	4c dl blue	.10	.05	☐☐☐☐☐
1147	A590	4c blue	.10	.05	☐☐☐☐☐
1148	A590	8c carmine, ultra & ocher	.20	.12	☐☐☐☐☐
1149	A591	4c gray black	.10	.05	☐☐☐☐☐
1150	A592	4c dk bl, brn org & grn	.10	.05	☐☐☐☐☐
1151	A593	4c blue	.10	.05	☐☐☐☐☐
1152	A594	4c dp violet	.10	.05	☐☐☐☐☐
1153	A595	4c dk blue & red	.10	.05	☐☐☐☐☐
1154	A596	4c sepia	.10	.05	☐☐☐☐☐
1155	A597	4c dk blue	.10	.05	☐☐☐☐☐
1156	A598	4c green	.10	.05	☐☐☐☐☐
1157	A599	4c green & rose red	.10	.05	☐☐☐☐☐
1158	A600	4c blue & pink	.10	.05	☐☐☐☐☐
1159	A601	4c blue	.10	.05	☐☐☐☐☐
1160	A601	8c carmine, ultra & ocher	.20	.12	☐☐☐☐☐
1161	A602	4c dl violet	.10	.05	☐☐☐☐☐
1162	A603	4c dk blue	.10	.05	☐☐☐☐☐
1163	A604	4c indigo, slate & rose red	.10	.05	☐☐☐☐☐
1164	A605	4c dk blue & carmine	.10	.05	☐☐☐☐☐
1165	A606	4c blue	.10	.05	☐☐☐☐☐
1166	A606	8c carmine, ultra & ocher	.20	.12	☐☐☐☐☐
1167	A607	4c dk blue & bright red	.10	.05	☐☐☐☐☐

A529

A530

A531

A532

A534

A533

A535

A537

A536

A538

A539

A540

A541

A542

A543

A544

A545

A546

A547

A551

A552

A553

A554

A555

A556

A557

A558

A561

A559

A560

A562

A564

A563

A565

A566

A568

A567

A569

A570

A572

A571

A573

A574

A578

A575

A577

A576

A580

A579

A581

A582

A583

A584

A589

A585

A586

A587

A588

A590

A591

A592

A593

A594

A595

A596

A597

A598

A599

A600

A604

A608

A603

A601

A613

A605

A606

A602

A609

A610

A611

A612

A607

A614

Scott No.	Illus. No.	Description	Unused Price	Used Price	//////
1168	A608	4c green	.10	.05	☐☐☐☐☐
1169	A608	8c carmine, ultra & ocher	.20	.12	☐☐☐☐☐
1170	A609	4c dl violet	.10	.05	☐☐☐☐☐
1171	A610	4c dp claret	.10	.05	☐☐☐☐☐
1172	A611	4c dl violet	.10	.05	☐☐☐☐☐
1173	A612	4c dp violet	.35	.12	☐☐☐☐☐

1961

Scott No.	Illus. No.	Description	Unused Price	Used Price	//////
1174	A613	4c red orange	.10	.05	☐☐☐☐☐
1175	A613	8c carmine, ultra & ocher	.20	.12	☐☐☐☐☐
1176	A614	4c blue, slate & brown orange	.10	.05	☐☐☐☐☐
1177	A615	4c dl violet	.10	.05	☐☐☐☐☐

1961-65

Scott No.	Illus. No.	Description	Unused Price	Used Price	//////
1178	A616	4c lt green	.18	.05	☐☐☐☐☐
1179	A617	4c *peach blossom* ('62)	.15	.05	☐☐☐☐☐
1180	A618	5c gray & blue ('63)	.15	.05	☐☐☐☐☐
1181	A619	5c dk red & black ('64)	.15	.05	☐☐☐☐☐
1182	A620	5c Prussian blue & black ('65)	.15	.05	☐☐☐☐☐

1961

Scott No.	Illus. No.	Description	Unused Price	Used Price	//////
1183	A621	4c brown, dk red & green, *yel*	.10	.05	☐☐☐☐☐
1184	A622	4c blue green	.10	.05	☐☐☐☐☐
1185	A623	4c blue	.10	.05	☐☐☐☐☐
1186	A624	4c ultra, *grayish*	.10	.05	☐☐☐☐☐
1187	A625	4c multi	.12	.05	☐☐☐☐☐
1188	A626	4c blue	.10	.05	☐☐☐☐☐
1189	A627	4c brown	.10	.05	☐☐☐☐☐
1190	A628	4c blue, green, orange & black	.10	.05	☐☐☐☐☐

1962

Scott No.	Illus. No.	Description	Unused Price	Used Price	//////
1191	A629	4c lt bl, mar & bister	.10	.05	☐☐☐☐☐
1192	A630	4c car, violet blue & green	.10	.05	☐☐☐☐☐
1193	A631	4c dk blue & yellow	.10	.10	☐☐☐☐☐
1194	A632	4c blue & bister	.10	.05	☐☐☐☐☐
1195	A633	4c *buff*	.10	.05	☐☐☐☐☐
1196	A634	4c red & dk blue	.10	.05	☐☐☐☐☐
1197	A635	4c bl, dk slate green & red	.10	.05	☐☐☐☐☐
1198	A636	4c slate	.10	.05	☐☐☐☐☐
1199	A637	4c rose red	.10	.05	☐☐☐☐☐
1200	A638	4c violet	.10	.05	☐☐☐☐☐
1201	A639	4c *yellow bister*	.10	.05	☐☐☐☐☐
1202	A640	4c dk blue & red brown	.10	.05	☐☐☐☐☐
1203	A641	4c black, brown & yellow	.10	.05	☐☐☐☐☐
1204	A641	4c black, brown & yellow (yel inverted)	.12	.08	☐☐☐☐☐
1205	A642	4c green & red	.10	.05	☐☐☐☐☐
1206	A643	4c blue green & black	.10	.05	☐☐☐☐☐
1207	A644	4c multi	.15	.05	☐☐☐☐☐

A616

A615

A617

A618

A619

A621

A622

A620

A623

A624

A625

A626

A627

A628

A629

A631

A630

A633

A632

A637

A634

A636

A640

A638

A635

A639

A639

A642

A645

A663

A646

A650

A644

A643

A641

A662

A664

A665

A666

A667

A668

A669

A671

A670

A676

A675

A680

A672

A678

A679

A673

A677

A674

A681

A682

Scott No.	Illus. No.	Description	Unused Price	Used Price	//////
1963-66					
1208	A645	5c blue & red	.12	.05 ☐☐☐☐☐
1208a		Tagged ('66)	.25	.05 ☐☐☐☐☐
1962-66	*Perf. 11x10½*				
1209	A646	1c green ('63)	.05	.05 ☐☐☐☐☐
1209a		Tagged ('66)	.06	.05 ☐☐☐☐☐
1213	A650	5c dk blue gray	.12	.05 ☐☐☐☐☐
1213a		Bklt. pane 5 + label	2.00	.75 ☐☐☐☐☐
1213b		Tagged ('63)	.65	.30 ☐☐☐☐☐
1213c		As "a," tagged ('63)	1.25	.50 ☐☐☐☐☐
Coil stamps	*Perf. 10 vertically*				
1225	A646	1c green ('63)	.20	.05 ☐☐☐☐☐
1225a		Tagged ('66)	.12	.05 ☐☐☐☐☐
1229	A650	5c dk blue gray	1.75	.05 ☐☐☐☐☐
1229a		Tagged ('63)	1.25	.06 ☐☐☐☐☐
1963					
1230	A662	5c dk carmine & brown	.12	.05 ☐☐☐☐☐
1231	A663	5c green, buff & red	.12	.05 ☐☐☐☐☐
1232	A664	5c green, red & black	.12	.05 ☐☐☐☐☐
1233	A665	5c dk blue, black & red	.12	.05 ☐☐☐☐☐
1234	A666	5c ultra & green	.12	.05 ☐☐☐☐☐
1235	A667	5c blue green	.12	.05 ☐☐☐☐☐
1236	A668	5c bright purple	.12	.05 ☐☐☐☐☐
1237	A669	5c Prussian blue & black	.12	.05 ☐☐☐☐☐
1238	A670	5c gray, dk blue & red	.12	.05 ☐☐☐☐☐
1239	A671	5c bluish black & red	.12	.05 ☐☐☐☐☐
1240	A672	5c dk blue, bluish black & red	.12	.05 ☐☐☐☐☐
1240a		Tagged	1.00	.40 ☐☐☐☐☐
1241	A673	5c dk blue & multi	.12	.05 ☐☐☐☐☐
1964					
1242	A674	5c black	.12	.05 ☐☐☐☐☐
1243	A675	5c indigo, red brown & olive	.15	.05 ☐☐☐☐☐
1244	A676	5c blue green	.12	.05 ☐☐☐☐☐
1245	A677	5c brown, green, yellow green & olive	.12	.05 ☐☐☐☐☐
1246	A678	5c blue gray	.12	.05 ☐☐☐☐☐
1247	A679	5c bright ultra	.12	.05 ☐☐☐☐☐
1248	A680	5c red, yellow & blue	.12	.05 ☐☐☐☐☐
1249	A681	5c dk blue & red	.12	.05 ☐☐☐☐☐
1250	A682	5c black brown, *tan*	.12	.05 ☐☐☐☐☐
1251	A683	5c green	.12	.05 ☐☐☐☐☐
1252	A684	5c red, black & blue	.12	.05 ☐☐☐☐☐
1253	A685	5c multi	.12	.05 ☐☐☐☐☐
1254	A686	5c green, carmine & black	.50	.05 ☐☐☐☐☐
1254a		Tagged	1.50	.50 ☐☐☐☐☐

A684

A683

A685

A686

A687

A688

A689

A690

A691

A692

A696

A694

A695

A693

A697

A698

96

Scott No.	Illus. No.	Description	Unused Price	Used Price	//////
1255	A687	5c carmine, green & black	.50	.05	☐☐☐☐☐
1255a		Tagged	1.50	.50	☐☐☐☐☐
1256	A688	5c carmine, green & black	.50	.05	☐☐☐☐☐
1256a		Tagged	1.50	.50	☐☐☐☐☐
1257	A689	5c black, green & carmine	.50	.05	☐☐☐☐☐
1257a		Tagged	1.50	.50	☐☐☐☐☐
1257b		Block of 4, #1254-1257	2.75	1.25	☐☐☐☐☐
1257c		Block of 4, tagged	6.50	3.00	☐☐☐☐☐
1258	A690	5c blue green	.12	.05	☐☐☐☐☐
1259	A691	5c ultra, black & dl red	.12	.05	☐☐☐☐☐
1260	A692	5c red lilac	.12	.05	☐☐☐☐☐

1965

Scott No.	Illus. No.	Description	Unused Price	Used Price	//////
1261	A693	5c dp carmine, violet blue & gray	.12	.05	☐☐☐☐☐
1262	A694	5c maroon & black	.12	.05	☐☐☐☐☐
1263	A695	5c black, purple & red orange	.12	.05	☐☐☐☐☐
1264	A696	5c black	.12	.05	☐☐☐☐☐
1265	A697	5c black, yellow ocher & red lilac	.12	.05	☐☐☐☐☐
1266	A698	5c dl blue & black	.12	.05	☐☐☐☐☐
1267	A699	5c red, black & dk blue	.12	.05	☐☐☐☐☐
1268	A700	5c maroon, *tan*	.12	.05	☐☐☐☐☐
1269	A701	5c rose red	.12	.05	☐☐☐☐☐
1270	A702	5c black & blue	.12	.05	☐☐☐☐☐
1271	A703	5c red, yellow & black	.12	.05	☐☐☐☐☐
1272	A704	5c emerald, black & red	.12	.05	☐☐☐☐☐
1273	A705	5c black, brown & olive	.15	.05	☐☐☐☐☐
1274	A706	11c black, carmine & bister	.50	.25	☐☐☐☐☐
1275	A707	5c pale blue, black, carmine & violet blue	.12	.05	☐☐☐☐☐
1276	A708	5c car, dk olive green & bister	.12	.05	☐☐☐☐☐
1276a		Tagged	.50	.15	☐☐☐☐☐

1965-78 *Perf. 11x10½, 10½x11*

Scott No.	Illus. No.	Description	Unused Price	Used Price	//////
1278	A710	1c green, tagged ('68)	.05	.05	☐☐☐☐☐
1278a		Bklt. pane of 8 ('68)	1.00	.25	☐☐☐☐☐
1278b		Bklt. pane of 4 + 2 labels ('71)	.75	.20	☐☐☐☐☐
1278c		Untagged (Bureau prec.)		.07	☐☐☐☐☐
1279	A711	1¼c lt green ('67)	.10	.05	☐☐☐☐☐
1280	A712	2c dk bl gray, tagged ('66)	.05	.05	☐☐☐☐☐
1280a		Bklt. pane of 5 + label ('68)	1.20	.40	☐☐☐☐☐
1280b		Untagged (Bureau prec.)		.10	☐☐☐☐☐
1280c		Bklt. pane of 6 ('71)	1.00	.35	☐☐☐☐☐
1281	A713	3c violet, tagged ('67)	.06	.05	☐☐☐☐☐
1281a		Untagged (Bureau prec.)		.12	☐☐☐☐☐
1282	A714	4c black	.08	.05	☐☐☐☐☐
1282a		Tagged	.08	.05	☐☐☐☐☐

A700

A706

A701

A703

A702

A705

A704

A708

A707

A699

A710

A711

A712

A713

A714

A715

A715a
Redrawn

A716

A717

Scott No.	Illus. No.	Description	Unused Price	Used Price	/ / / / / /
1283	A715	5c blue ('66)	.10	.05	☐☐☐☐☐
1283a		Tagged ('66)	.10	.05	☐☐☐☐☐
1283B	A715a	5c blue, tagged ('67)	.12	.05	☐☐☐☐☐
1283d		Untagged (Bureau prec.)		.15	☐☐☐☐☐
1284	A716	6c gray brown ('66)	.18	.05	☐☐☐☐☐
1284a		Tagged ('66)	.12	.05	☐☐☐☐☐
1284b		Bklt. pane of 8 ('67)	1.50	.50	☐☐☐☐☐
1284c		Bklt. pane of 5 + label ('68)	1.25	.50	☐☐☐☐☐
1285	A717	8c violet ('66)	.30	.05	☐☐☐☐☐
1285a		Tagged ('66)	.16	.05	☐☐☐☐☐
1286	A718	10c lilac, tagged ('67)	.25	.05	☐☐☐☐☐
1286b		Untagged (Bureau prec.)		.20	☐☐☐☐☐
1286A	A718a	12c black, tagged ('68)	.35	.05	☐☐☐☐☐
1286c		Untagged (Bureau prec.)		.25	☐☐☐☐☐
1287	A719	13c brown, tagged ('67)	.30	.05	☐☐☐☐☐
1287a		Untagged (Bureau prec.)		.25	☐☐☐☐☐
1288	A720	15c rose claret, tagged ('68)	.30	.06	☐☐☐☐☐
1288a		Untagged (Bureau prec.)		.30	☐☐☐☐☐
1288d		Type II	.30	.06	☐☐☐☐☐

On No. 1288d, necktie does not touch coat at bottom.

Perf. 10

1288B	A720	15c dk rose claret ('78)	.30	.05	☐☐☐☐☐
1288c		Bklt. pane of 8	2.40	1.25	☐☐☐☐☐

Perf. 11x10½, 10½x11

1289	A721	20c dp olive ('67)	.60	.06	☐☐☐☐☐
1289a		Tagged ('73)	.40	.06	☐☐☐☐☐
1290	A722	25c rose lake ('67)	.70	.05	☐☐☐☐☐
1290a		Tagged ('73)	.50	.05	☐☐☐☐☐
1291	A723	30c red lilac ('68)	.85	.08	☐☐☐☐☐
1291a		Tagged ('73)	.60	.06	☐☐☐☐☐
1292	A724	40c blue black ('68)	1.10	.10	☐☐☐☐☐
1292a		Tagged ('73)	.80	.08	☐☐☐☐☐
1293	A725	50c rose magenta ('68)	1.00	.05	☐☐☐☐☐
1293a		Tagged ('73)	1.00	.05	☐☐☐☐☐
1294	A726	$1 dl purple ('67)	2.40	.08	☐☐☐☐☐
1294a		Tagged ('73)	2.00	.08	☐☐☐☐☐
1295	A727	$5 gray black ('66)	12.50	2.00	☐☐☐☐☐
1295a		Tagged ('73)	10.00	2.00	☐☐☐☐☐

1966-81 Coil stamps Tagged *Perf. 10 horizontally*

1297	A713	3c violet ('75)	.12	.05	☐☐☐☐☐
1297b		Untagged (Bureau prec.)		.12	☐☐☐☐☐
1298	A716	6c gray brown ('67)	.30	.05	☐☐☐☐☐

Perf. 10 vertically

1299	A710	1c green ('68)	.06	.05	☐☐☐☐☐
1299a		Untagged (Bureau prec.)		.07	☐☐☐☐☐

A718

A718a

A719

A720

A721

A723

A722

A724

A725

A726

A727

A727a

A730

A732

A731

A728

A729

A733

A734

A735

100

Scott No.	Illus. No.	Description	Unused Price	Used Price	//////
1303	A714	4c black	.15	.05	☐☐☐☐☐
1303a		Untagged (Bureau prec.)		.15	☐☐☐☐☐
1304	A715	5c blue	.15	.05	☐☐☐☐☐
1304a		Untagged (Bureau prec.)		.15	☐☐☐☐☐
1304C	A715a	5c blue ('81)	.15	.05	☐☐☐☐☐
1305	A727a	6c gray brown ('68)	.20	.05	☐☐☐☐☐
1305b		Untagged (Bureau prec.)		.20	☐☐☐☐☐
1305E	A720	15c rose claret ('78)	.30	.05	☐☐☐☐☐
1305f		Untagged (Bureau prec.)		.30	☐☐☐☐☐
1305C	A726	$1 dl purple ('73)	2.25	.20	☐☐☐☐☐

1966

Scott No.	Illus. No.	Description	Unused Price	Used Price	//////
1306	A728	5c black, crimson & dk blue	.12	.05	☐☐☐☐☐
1307	A729	5c orange brown & black	.12	.05	☐☐☐☐☐
1308	A730	5c yel, ocher & violet blue	.12	.05	☐☐☐☐☐
1309	A731	5c multi	.12	.05	☐☐☐☐☐
1310	A732	5c multi	.12	.05	☐☐☐☐☐
1311	A733	5c multi	.30	.15	☐☐☐☐☐
1312	A734	5c car, dk & lt blue	.12	.05	☐☐☐☐☐
1313	A735	5c red	.12	.05	☐☐☐☐☐
1314	A736	5c yellow, black & green	.12	.05	☐☐☐☐☐
1314a		Tagged	.30	.15	☐☐☐☐☐
1315	A737	5c black, bister, red & ultra	.12	.05	☐☐☐☐☐
1315a		Tagged	.30	.15	☐☐☐☐☐
1316	A738	5c black, pink & blue	.12	.05	☐☐☐☐☐
1316a		Tagged	.30	.15	☐☐☐☐☐
1317	A739	5c green, red & black	.12	.05	☐☐☐☐☐
1317a		Tagged	.30	.15	☐☐☐☐☐
1318	A740	5c emerald, pink & black	.12	.05	☐☐☐☐☐
1318a		Tagged	.30	.15	☐☐☐☐☐
1319	A741	5c vermilion, yel, bl & grn	.12	.05	☐☐☐☐☐
1319a		Tagged	.30	.15	☐☐☐☐☐
1320	A742	5c red, dk bl, lt bl & blk	.12	.05	☐☐☐☐☐
1320a		Tagged	.30	.15	☐☐☐☐☐
1321	A743	5c multi	.12	.05	☐☐☐☐☐
1321a		Tagged	.25	.10	☐☐☐☐☐
1322	A744	5c multi	.20	.05	☐☐☐☐☐
1322a		Tagged	.45	.15	☐☐☐☐☐

1967

Scott No.	Illus. No.	Description	Unused Price	Used Price	//////
1323	A745	5c multi	.12	.05	☐☐☐☐☐
1324	A746	5c multi	.12	.05	☐☐☐☐☐
1325	A747	5c multi	.12	.05	☐☐☐☐☐
1326	A748	5c blue, red & black	.12	.05	☐☐☐☐☐
1327	A749	5c red, black & green	.12	.05	☐☐☐☐☐
1328	A750	5c dk red brown, lemon & yel	.12	.05	☐☐☐☐☐
1329	A751	5c red, blue, black & carmine	.12	.05	☐☐☐☐☐
1330	A752	5c green, black & yellow	.12	.05	☐☐☐☐☐

A737

A736

A739

A738

A741

A743

A745

A747

A744

A740

A742

A746

A749

A748

A751

A750

A752

102

Scott No.	Illus. No.	Description	Unused Price	Used Price	//////
1331	A753	5c multi	.90	.25	☐☐☐☐☐
1331a		Pair, # 1331-1332	2.00	1.50	☐☐☐☐☐
1332	A754	5c multi	.90	.25	☐☐☐☐☐
1333	A755	5c dk blue, lt blue & black	.15	.05	☐☐☐☐☐
1334	A756	5c blue	.15	.05	☐☐☐☐☐
1335	A757	5c gold & multi	.18	.05	☐☐☐☐☐
1336	A758	5c multi	.12	.05	☐☐☐☐☐
1337	A759	5c bright greenish blue, green & red brown	.15	.05	☐☐☐☐☐

1968-71 *Perf. 11*

Scott No.	Illus. No.	Description	Unused Price	Used Price	//////
1338	A760	6c dk blue, red & green	.12	.05	☐☐☐☐☐

Perf. 11x10½

Scott No.	Illus. No.	Description	Unused Price	Used Price	//////
1338D	A760	6c dk blue, red & green ('70)	.20	.05	☐☐☐☐☐
1338F	A760	8c multi ('71)	.20	.05	☐☐☐☐☐

1969-71 *Coil stamps Perf. 10 vertically*

Scott No.	Illus. No.	Description	Unused Price	Used Price	//////
1338A	A760	6c dk blue, red & green	.20	.05	☐☐☐☐☐
1338G	A760	8c multi ('71)	.20	.05	☐☐☐☐☐

1968

Scott No.	Illus. No.	Description	Unused Price	Used Price	//////
1339	A761	6c multi	.18	.05	☐☐☐☐☐
1340	A762	6c blue, rose red & white	.18	.05	☐☐☐☐☐
1341	A763	$1 sepia, dk blue, ocher & brown red	5.00	3.00	☐☐☐☐☐
1342	A764	6c ultra & orange red	.18	.05	☐☐☐☐☐
1343	A765	6c chalky blue, black & red	.18	.05	☐☐☐☐☐
1344	A766	6c black, yellow & orange	.18	.05	☐☐☐☐☐
1345	A767	6c dk blue	1.00	.50	☐☐☐☐☐
1346	A768	6c dk blue & red	1.00	.50	☐☐☐☐☐
1347	A769	6c dk blue & olive green	.60	.50	☐☐☐☐☐
1348	A770	6c dk blue & red	.60	.40	☐☐☐☐☐
1349	A771	6c dk blue, yellow & red	.60	.45	☐☐☐☐☐
1350	A772	6c dk blue & red	.60	.35	☐☐☐☐☐
1351	A773	6c dk blue, ol grn & red	.60	.35	☐☐☐☐☐
1352	A774	6c dk blue & red	.60	.35	☐☐☐☐☐
1353	A775	6c dk blue, yellow & red	.80	.35	☐☐☐☐☐
1354	A776	6c dk blue, red & yellow	.80	.40	☐☐☐☐☐
1354a		Strip of 10, #1345-1354	8.25	7.50	☐☐☐☐☐
1355	A777	6c multi	.20	.05	☐☐☐☐☐
1356	A778	6c black, apple green & orange brown	.20	.05	☐☐☐☐☐
1357	A779	6c yellow, dp yellow, maroon & black	.20	.05	☐☐☐☐☐
1358	A780	6c bright blue, dk blue & black	.20	.05	☐☐☐☐☐
1359	A781	6c lt gray brown & black brown	.20	.05	☐☐☐☐☐
1360	A782	6c brown	.20	.05	☐☐☐☐☐

A753 A754

A755

A757

A756

A758

A759

A760

A761

A764

A762

A765

A769

A766

A767

A768

A770

A771

A772

A773

A774

A775

A776

A777

A778

A781

A779

A783

A780

A785

A782

A786

A784

PLANT for more BEAUTIFUL CITIES
A787

PLANT for more BEAUTIFUL PARKS
A788

PLANT for more BEAUTIFUL HIGHWAYS
A789

PLANT for more BEAUTIFUL STREETS
A790

A795

A791

A792

A793

A796

A794

A797

A798

A799

A800

A801

Scott No.	Illus. No.	Description	Unused Price	Used Price	//////
1361	A783	6c multi	.25	.05 ☐☐☐☐☐
1362	A784	6c black & multi	.25	.05 ☐☐☐☐☐
1363	A785	6c multi	.20	.05 ☐☐☐☐☐
1363a		Untagged	.20	.05 ☐☐☐☐☐
1364	A786	6c black & multi	.30	.05 ☐☐☐☐☐

1969

Scott No.	Illus. No.	Description	Unused Price	Used Price	//////
1365	A787	6c multi	.90	.15 ☐☐☐☐☐
1366	A788	6c multi	.90	.15 ☐☐☐☐☐
1367	A789	6c multi	.90	.15 ☐☐☐☐☐
1368	A790	6c multi	.90	.15 ☐☐☐☐☐
1368a		Block of 4, #1365-1368	4.50	3.50 ☐☐☐☐☐
1369	A791	6c red, blue & black	.20	.05 ☐☐☐☐☐
1370	A792	6c multi	.25	.05 ☐☐☐☐☐
1371	A793	6c black, blue & ocher	.30	.06 ☐☐☐☐☐
1372	A794	6c multi	.20	.05 ☐☐☐☐☐
1373	A795	6c multi	.20	.05 ☐☐☐☐☐
1374	A796	6c multi	.20	.05 ☐☐☐☐☐
1375	A797	6c multi	.20	.05 ☐☐☐☐☐
1376	A798	6c multi	1.10	.15 ☐☐☐☐☐
1377	A799	6c multi	1.10	.15 ☐☐☐☐☐
1378	A800	6c multi	1.10	.15 ☐☐☐☐☐
1379	A801	6c multi	1.10	.15 ☐☐☐☐☐
1379a		Block of 4, #1376-1379	5.50	5.00 ☐☐☐☐☐
1380	A802	6c green	.20	.05 ☐☐☐☐☐
1381	A803	6c yellow, red, black & green	.25	.05 ☐☐☐☐☐
1382	A804	6c red & green	.25	.05 ☐☐☐☐☐
1383	A805	6c blue, black & red	.20	.05 ☐☐☐☐☐
1384	A806	6c dk green & multi	.18	.05 ☐☐☐☐☐
1384a		Precanceled	.60	.06 ☐☐☐☐☐
1385	A807	6c multi	.18	.05 ☐☐☐☐☐
1386	A808	6c multi	.18	.05 ☐☐☐☐☐

1970

Scott No.	Illus. No.	Description	Unused Price	Used Price	//////
1387	A809	6c multi	.22	.12 ☐☐☐☐☐
1388	A810	6c multi	.22	.12 ☐☐☐☐☐
1389	A811	6c multi	.22	.12 ☐☐☐☐☐
1390	A812	6c multi	.22	.12 ☐☐☐☐☐
1390a		Block of 4, #1387-1390	1.00	1.00 ☐☐☐☐☐
1391	A813	6c black & multi	.18	.05 ☐☐☐☐☐
1392	A814	6c *lt brown*	.18	.05 ☐☐☐☐☐

1970-74   Tagged   *Perf. 11x10½, 10½x11, 11 (#1394)*

Scott No.	Illus. No.	Description	Unused Price	Used Price	//////
1393	A815	6c dk blue gray	.12	.05 ☐☐☐☐☐
1393a		Bklt. pane of 8	1.25	*.50* ☐☐☐☐☐
1393b		Bklt. pane of 5 + label	1.20	*.35* ☐☐☐☐☐
1393c		Untagged (Bureau prec.)		.10 ☐☐☐☐☐
1393D	A816	7c bright blue ('72)	.14	.05 ☐☐☐☐☐
1393e		Untagged (Bureau prec.)		.10 ☐☐☐☐☐

A802

A803

A806

A807

A805

A804

A808

A809

A810

A811

A812

A813

A814

EISENHOWER·USA
Dot between ''R''
and ''U''

A815

EISENHOWER USA
No dot between
''R'' and ''U''

A815a

A816

A817

A817a

A818

A818a

A818b

A820

A819

A821

A822

A823

A824

A825

A826

A827

A828

A829

A830

A831

A832

A835

A836

A833

A834

A837

A838

A839

A840

Scott No.	Illus. No.	Description	Unused Price	Used Price	//////
1394	A815a	8c black, red & blue gray ('71)	.16	.05	☐☐☐☐☐
1395	A815	8c dp claret ('71)	.16	.05	☐☐☐☐☐
1395a		Bklt. pane of 8	2.00	*1.25*	☐☐☐☐☐
1395b		Bklt. pane of 6	1.00	.75	☐☐☐☐☐
1395c		Bklt. pane of 4 + 2 labels ('72)	1.00	*.50*	☐☐☐☐☐
1395d		Bklt. pane of 7 + label ('72)	1.75	*1.00*	☐☐☐☐☐
1396	A817	8c multi ('71)	.25	.05	☐☐☐☐☐
1397	A817a	14c gray brown ('72)	.32	.05	☐☐☐☐☐
1397a		Untagged (Bureau prec.)		.25	☐☐☐☐☐
1398	A818	16c brown ('71)	.35	.05	☐☐☐☐☐
1398a		Untagged (Bureau prec.)		.25	☐☐☐☐☐
1399	A818a	18c violet ('74)	.40	.06	☐☐☐☐☐
1400	A818b	21c green ('73)	.45	.06	☐☐☐☐☐
Coil stamps	*Perf. 10 vertically*				
1401	A815	6c dk blue gray	.20	.05	☐☐☐☐☐
1401a		Untagged (Bureau prec.)		.10	☐☐☐☐☐
1402	A815	8c dp claret ('71)	.22	.05	☐☐☐☐☐
1402b		Untagged (Bureau prec.)		.20	☐☐☐☐☐
1970					
1405	A819	6c black & olive bister	.18	.05	☐☐☐☐☐
1406	A820	6c blue	.18	.05	☐☐☐☐☐
1407	A821	6c bister, black & red	.18	.05	☐☐☐☐☐
1408	A822	6c gray	.18	.05	☐☐☐☐☐
1409	A823	6c yellow & multi	.18	.05	☐☐☐☐☐
1410	A824	6c multi	.45	.13	☐☐☐☐☐
1411	A825	6c multi	.45	.13	☐☐☐☐☐
1412	A826	6c multi	.45	.13	☐☐☐☐☐
1413	A827	6c multi	.45	.13	☐☐☐☐☐
1413a		Block of 4, #1410-1413	2.50	2.00	☐☐☐☐☐
1414	A828	6c multi	.20	.05	☐☐☐☐☐
1414a		Precanceled	.35	.08	☐☐☐☐☐
1415	A829	6c multi	.85	.10	☐☐☐☐☐
1415a		Precanceled	2.00	.15	☐☐☐☐☐
1416	A830	6c multi	.85	.10	☐☐☐☐☐
1416a		Precanceled	2.00	.15	☐☐☐☐☐
1417	A831	6c multi	.85	.10	☐☐☐☐☐
1417a		Precanceled	2.00	.15	☐☐☐☐☐
1418	A832	6c multi	.85	.10	☐☐☐☐☐
1418a		Precanceled	2.00	.15	☐☐☐☐☐
1418b		Block of 4, #1415-1418	4.50	3.50	☐☐☐☐☐
1418c		As "b," precanceled	9.00	6.00	☐☐☐☐☐
1419	A833	6c black, vermilion & ultra	.18	.05	☐☐☐☐☐
1420	A834	6c black, orange, yellow, brown, magenta & blue	.18	.05	☐☐☐☐☐

A841

A842

A843

A844

A845

AMERICAN
REVOLUTION
BICENTENNIAL
1776-1976

A846

A847

A848

A849

A850

A851

A852

A853

112

Scott No.	Illus. No.	Description	Unused Price	Used Price	//////
1421	A835	6c multi	.20	.10 □□□□□
1421a		Pair, #1421-1422	.50	.65 □□□□□
1422	A836	6c dk blue, black & red	.20	.10 □□□□□
1971					
1423	A837	6c multi	.18	.05 □□□□□
1424	A838	6c black, red & dk blue	.18	.05 □□□□□
1425	A839	6c lt blue, scarlet & indigo	.18	.05 □□□□□
1426	A840	8c multi	.20	.05 □□□□□
1427	A841	8c multi	.30	.10 □□□□□
1428	A842	8c multi	.30	.10 □□□□□
1429	A843	8c multi	.30	.10 □□□□□
1430	A844	8c multi	.30	.10 □□□□□
1430a		Block of 4, #1427-1430	1.30	1.00 □□□□□
1431	A845	8c red & dk blue	.25	.05 □□□□□
1432	A846	8c red, blue, gray & black	.50	.05 □□□□□
1433	A847	8c multi	.20	.05 □□□□□
1434	A848	8c black, blue, yellow & red	.20	.10 □□□□□
1434a		Pair, #1434-1435	.50	.35 □□□□□
1435	A849	8c black, blue, yellow & red	.20	.10 □□□□□
1436	A850	8c multi, *greenish*	.18	.05 □□□□□
1437	A851	8c multi	.18	.05 □□□□□
1438	A852	8c blue, dp blue & black	.18	.05 □□□□□
1439	A853	8c multi	.18	.05 □□□□□
1440	A854	8c black brown & ocher	.25	.12 □□□□□
1441	A855	8c black brown & ocher	.25	.12 □□□□□
1442	A856	8c black brown & ocher	.25	.12 □□□□□
1443	A857	8c black brown & ocher	.25	.12 □□□□□
1443a		Block of 4, #1440-1443	1.20	1.20 □□□□□
1444	A858	8c gold & multi	.18	.05 □□□□□
1445	A859	8c dk green, red & multi	.18	.05 □□□□□
1972					
1446	A860	8c black, brown & lt blue	.18	.05 □□□□□
1447	A861	8c dk blue, lt blue & red	.18	.05 □□□□□
1448	A862	2c black & multi	.06	.06 □□□□□
1449	A863	2c black & multi	.06	.06 □□□□□
1450	A864	2c black & multi	.06	.06 □□□□□
1451	A865	2c black & multi	.06	.06 □□□□□
1451a		Block of 4, #1448-1451	.25	.30 □□□□□
1452	A866	6c black & multi	.16	.08 □□□□□
1453	A867	8c black, blue, brown & multi	.18	.05 □□□□□
1454	A868	15c black & multi	.35	.22 □□□□□
1455	A869	8c black & multi	.16	.05 □□□□□
1456	A870	8c dp brown	.30	.08 □□□□□
1457	A871	8c dp brown	.30	.08 □□□□□
1458	A872	8c dp brown	.30	.08 □□□□□
1459	A873	8c dp brown	.30	.08 □□□□□
1459a		Block of 4, #1456-1459	1.25	1.25 □□□□□

A854

A855

A856

A857

A862

A863

A864   A865

A858

A867

A860

A861

A859

A866

A868

114

Scott No.	Illus. No.	Description	Unused Price	Used Price	//////
1460	A874	6c multi	.16	.12	☐☐☐☐☐
1461	A875	8c multi	.16	.05	☐☐☐☐☐
1462	A876	15c multi	.35	.18	☐☐☐☐☐
1463	A877	8c yellow & black	.16	.05	☐☐☐☐☐
1464	A878	8c multi	.25	.08	☐☐☐☐☐
1465	A879	8c multi	.25	.08	☐☐☐☐☐
1466	A880	8c multi	.25	.08	☐☐☐☐☐
1467	A881	8c multi	.25	.08	☐☐☐☐☐
1467a		Block of 4, #1464-1467	1.10	.85	☐☐☐☐☐
1468	A882	8c multi	.16	.05	☐☐☐☐☐
1469	A883	8c yellow, orange & dk brown	.16	.05	☐☐☐☐☐
1470	A884	8c black & multi	.16	.05	☐☐☐☐☐
1471	A885	8c multi	.16	.05	☐☐☐☐☐
1472	A886	8c multi	.16	.05	☐☐☐☐☐
1473	A887	8c black & multi	.16	.05	☐☐☐☐☐
1474	A888	8c dk bl grn, black & brn	.16	.05	☐☐☐☐☐

1973

Scott No.	Illus. No.	Description	Unused Price	Used Price	//////
1475	A889	8c red, emerald & violet blue	.16	.05	☐☐☐☐☐
1476	A890	8c ultra, greenish black & red	.20	.05	☐☐☐☐☐
1477	A891	8c black, verm & ultra	.20	.05	☐☐☐☐☐
1478	A892	8c multi	.20	.05	☐☐☐☐☐
1479	A893	8c multi	.20	.05	☐☐☐☐☐
1480	A894	8c black & multi	.20	.10	☐☐☐☐☐
1481	A895	8c black & multi	.20	.10	☐☐☐☐☐
1482	A896	8c black & multi	.20	.10	☐☐☐☐☐
1483	A897	8c black & multi	.20	.10	☐☐☐☐☐
1483a		Block of 4, #1480-1483	.85	.80	☐☐☐☐☐
1484	A898	8c dp green & multi	.16	.05	☐☐☐☐☐
1485	A899	8c Prussian blue & multi	.16	.05	☐☐☐☐☐
1486	A900	8c yellow brown & multi	.16	.05	☐☐☐☐☐
1487	A901	8c dp brown & multi	.16	.05	☐☐☐☐☐
1488	A902	8c black & orange	.16	.05	☐☐☐☐☐
1489	A903	8c multi	.20	.12	☐☐☐☐☐
1490	A904	8c multi	.20	.12	☐☐☐☐☐
1491	A905	8c multi	.20	.12	☐☐☐☐☐
1492	A906	8c multi	.20	.12	☐☐☐☐☐
1493	A907	8c multi	.20	.12	☐☐☐☐☐
1494	A908	8c multi	.20	.12	☐☐☐☐☐
1495	A909	8c multi	.20	.12	☐☐☐☐☐
1496	A910	8c multi	.20	.12	☐☐☐☐☐
1497	A911	8c multi	.20	.12	☐☐☐☐☐
1498	A912	8c multi	.20	.12	☐☐☐☐☐
1498a		Strip of 10, Nos. 1489-1498	2.25	2.00	☐☐☐☐☐
1499	A913	8c car rose, black & blue	.16	.05	☐☐☐☐☐
1500	A914	6c lilac & multi	.12	.10	☐☐☐☐☐
1501	A915	8c tan & multi	.16	.05	☐☐☐☐☐
1502	A916	15c gray green & multi	.30	.20	☐☐☐☐☐
1503	A917	8c black & multi	.16	.05	☐☐☐☐☐

A869

A870

A871

A872

A873

A874

A875

A876

A877

A878

A879

A880

A881

116

A883

A882

A884

A885

A887

A886

A888

A889

A890

A891

A892

A893

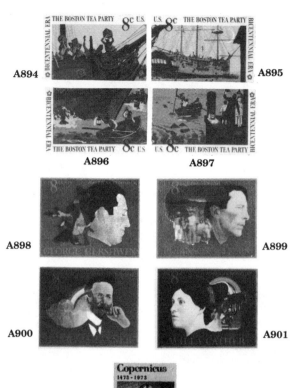

A894 A895 A896 A897 A898 A899 A900 A901

A902

HOW TO USE THIS BOOK
The number in the first column is its Scott number or identifying number. The letter and number that come next (A41) indicate the design and refer to the illustration so designated. Following that is the denomination of the stamp and its color. Finally, the price, unused and used is shown.

Scott No.	Illus. No.	Description	Unused Price	Used Price	//////
1973-74					
1504	A918	8c multi	.16	.05 ☐☐☐☐☐
1505	A919	10c multi ('74)	.20	.05 ☐☐☐☐☐
1506	A920	10c multi ('74)	.20	.05 ☐☐☐☐☐
1973					
1507	A921	8c tan & multi	.16	.05 ☐☐☐☐☐
1508	A922	8c green & multi	.16	.05 ☐☐☐☐☐
1973-74 Tagged *Perf. 11x10½*					
1509	A923	10c red & blue	.20	.05 ☐☐☐☐☐
1510	A924	10c blue	.20	.05 ☐☐☐☐☐
1510a		Untagged (Bureau prec.)		.20 ☐☐☐☐☐
1510b		Bklt. pane of 5 + label	1.50	*.30* ☐☐☐☐☐
1510c		Bklt. pane of 8	1.60	*.30* ☐☐☐☐☐
1510d		Bklt. pane of 6 ('74)	2.50	*.30* ☐☐☐☐☐
1511	A925	10c multi	.20	.05 ☐☐☐☐☐
Coil stamps *Perf. 10 vertically*					
1518	A926	6.3c brick red	.13	.07 ☐☐☐☐☐
1518a		Untagged (Bureau prec.)		.13 ☐☐☐☐☐
1519	A923	10c red & blue	.25	.05 ☐☐☐☐☐
1520	A924	10c blue	.20	.05 ☐☐☐☐☐
1520a		Untagged (Bureau prec.)		.25 ☐☐☐☐☐
1974					
1525	A928	10c red & dk blue	.20	.05 ☐☐☐☐☐
1526	A929	10c black	.20	.05 ☐☐☐☐☐
1527	A930	10c multi	.20	.05 ☐☐☐☐☐
1528	A931	10c yellow & multi	.20	.05 ☐☐☐☐☐
1529	A932	10c multi	.20	.05 ☐☐☐☐☐
1530	A933	10c multi	.20	.18 ☐☐☐☐☐
1531	A934	10c multi	.20	.18 ☐☐☐☐☐
1532	A935	10c multi	.20	.18 ☐☐☐☐☐
1533	A936	10c multi	.20	.18 ☐☐☐☐☐
1534	A937	10c multi	.20	.18 ☐☐☐☐☐
1535	A938	10c multi	.20	.18 ☐☐☐☐☐
1536	A939	10c multi	.20	.18 ☐☐☐☐☐
1537	A940	10c multi	.20	.18 ☐☐☐☐☐
1537a		Block or strip of 8, #1530-1537	1.60	2.00 ☐☐☐☐☐
1538	A941	10c lt blue & multi	.20	.10 ☐☐☐☐☐
1539	A942	10c lt blue & multi	.20	.10 ☐☐☐☐☐
1540	A943	10c lt blue & multi	.20	.10 ☐☐☐☐☐
1541	A944	10c lt blue & multi	.20	.10 ☐☐☐☐☐
1541a		Block of 4, #1538-1541	.80	.80 ☐☐☐☐☐
1542	A945	10c green & multi	.20	.05 ☐☐☐☐☐
1543	A946	10c dk blue & red	.20	.10 ☐☐☐☐☐
1544	A947	10c gray, dk blue & red	.20	.10 ☐☐☐☐☐
1545	A948	10c gray, dk blue & red	.20	.10 ☐☐☐☐☐

U.S. POSTAL SERVICE 8¢

A903

U.S. POSTAL SERVICE 8¢

A904

U.S. POSTAL SERVICE 8¢

A905

U.S. POSTAL SERVICE 8¢

A906

U.S. POSTAL SERVICE 8¢

A907

U.S. POSTAL SERVICE 8¢

A908

U.S. POSTAL SERVICE 8¢

A909

U.S. POSTAL SERVICE 8¢

A910

U.S. POSTAL SERVICE 8¢

A911

U.S. POSTAL SERVICE 8¢

A912

Harry S. Truman

U.S. Postage 8 cents A913

Marconi Spark Coil   Marconi Spark Gap

U.S. 6¢

Progress in Electronics

A914

Transistor   U.S. 8¢

Progress in Electronics

A915

Microphone   Radio Tube   Loudspeaker   TV Camera Tube

U.S. 15¢

Progress in Electronics

A916

A917

A918

A919

A920

A921

A922

A923

A924

A925

A926

A929

A928

A930

A931

A932

A933

A934

A935

A936

A937

A938

A939

A940

Scott No.	Illus. No.	Description	Unused Price	Used Price	//////
1546	A949	10c red & dk blue	.20	.10	□□□□□
1546a		Block of 4, #1543-1546	1.00	.80	□□□□□
1547	A950	10c multi	.20	.05	□□□□□
1548	A951	10c dk blue, black, orange			
		& yellow	.20	.05	□□□□□
1549	A952	10c brown red & dk brown	.20	.05	□□□□□
1550	A953	10c multi	.20	.05	□□□□□
1551	A954	10c multi	.20	.05	□□□□□
1552	A955	10c multi	.20	.08	□□□□□

Unused price of No. 1552 is for copy on rouletted paper backing as issued. Used price is for copy on piece, with or without postmark. Die cutting includes crossed slashes through dove, applied to prevent removal and re-use of stamp. The stamp will separate into layers if soaked. No. 1552 is untagged.

1975

Scott No.	Illus. No.	Description	Unused Price	Used Price	//////
1553	A956	10c multi	.20	.05	□□□□□
1554	A957	10c multi	.20	.05	□□□□□
1555	A958	10c multi	.20	.05	□□□□□
1556	A959	10c violet blue, yellow & red	.20	.05	□□□□□
1557	A960	10c black, red, ultra & bister	.20	.05	□□□□□
1558	A961	10c multi	.20	.05	□□□□□
1559	A962	8c multi	.16	.13	□□□□□
1560	A963	10c multi	.20	.05	□□□□□
1561	A964	10c multi	.20	.05	□□□□□
1562	A965	18c multi	.36	.20	□□□□□
1563	A966	10c multi	.20	.05	□□□□□
1564	A967	10c multi	.20	.05	□□□□□
1565	A968	10c multi	.20	.08	□□□□□
1566	A969	10c multi	.20	.08	□□□□□
1567	A970	10c multi	.20	.08	□□□□□
1568	A971	10c multi	.20	.08	□□□□□
1568a		Block of 4, #1565-1568	.80	.80	□□□□□
1569	A972	10c multi	.20	.10	□□□□□
1569a		Pair, #1569-1570	.40	.25	□□□□□
1570	A973	10c multi	.20	.10	□□□□□
1571	A974	10c blue, orange & dk blue	.20	.05	□□□□□
1572	A975	10c multi	.20	.08	□□□□□
1573	A976	10c multi	.20	.08	□□□□□
1574	A977	10c multi	.20	.08	□□□□□
1575	A978	10c multi	.20	.08	□□□□□
1575a		Block of 4, #1572-1575	1.00	.80	□□□□□
1576	A979	10c green, Prussian blue			
		& rose brown	.20	.05	□□□□□
1577	A980	10c multi	.20	.08	□□□□□
1577a		Pair, #1577-1578	.40	.20	□□□□□
1578	A981	10c multi	.20	.08	□□□□□
1579	A982	(10c) multi	.20	.05	□□□□□

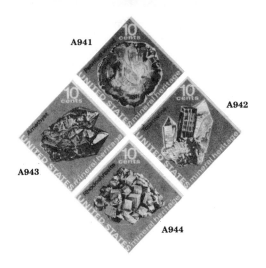

A941

A942

A943

A944

A946

A947

A948

A949

A945

A951

A950

Scott No.	Illus. No.	Description	Unused Price	Used Price	//////
1580	A983	(10c) multi	.20	.05	☐☐☐☐☐
1580b		Perf. 10½x11	.50	.05	☐☐☐☐☐

1973-81 *Perf. 11x10½*

Scott No.	Illus. No.	Description	Unused Price	Used Price	//////
1581	A984	1c dk blue, *greenish* ('77)	.05	.05	☐☐☐☐☐
1581a		Untagged (Bureau prec.)		.05	☐☐☐☐☐
1582	A985	2c red brown, *greenish* ('77)	.05	.05	☐☐☐☐☐
1582a		Untagged (Bureau prec.)		.06	☐☐☐☐☐
1582b		Cream paper ('81)	.05	.05	☐☐☐☐☐
1584	A987	3c olive, *greenish* ('77)	.06	.05	☐☐☐☐☐
1584a		Untagged (Bureau prec.)		.06	☐☐☐☐☐
1585	A988	4c rose magenta, *cream* ('77)	.08	.05	☐☐☐☐☐
1585a		Untagged (Bureau prec.)		.08	☐☐☐☐☐
1590	A994	9c slate green ('77)	1.00	.20	☐☐☐☐☐
1590a		Perf. 10	27.50	6.00	☐☐☐☐☐
1591	A994	9c slate green, *gray*	.18	.05	☐☐☐☐☐
1591a		Untagged (Bureau prec.)		.18	☐☐☐☐☐
1592	A995	10c violet, *gray* ('77)	.20	.05	☐☐☐☐☐
1592a		Untagged (Bureau prec.)		.25	☐☐☐☐☐
1593	A996	11c orange, *gray*	.22	.05	☐☐☐☐☐
1594	A997	12c brown red, *beige* ('81)	.24	.05	☐☐☐☐☐
1595	A998	13c brown	.26	.05	☐☐☐☐☐
1595a		Bklt. pane of 6	1.60	.50	☐☐☐☐☐
1595b		Bklt. pane of 7 + label	1.80	.50	☐☐☐☐☐
1595c		Bklt. pane of 8	2.10	.50	☐☐☐☐☐
1595d		Bklt. pane of 5 + label ('76)	1.30	.50	☐☐☐☐☐

Perf. 11

Scott No.	Illus. No.	Description	Unused Price	Used Price	//////
1596	A999	13c multi	.26	.05	☐☐☐☐☐
1597	A1001	15c gray, dk blue & red ('78)	.30	.05	☐☐☐☐☐

Perf. 11x10½

Scott No.	Illus. No.	Description	Unused Price	Used Price	//////
1598	A1001	15c gray, dl blue & red ('78)	.30	.05	☐☐☐☐☐
1598a		Bklt. pane of 8	4.25	.60	☐☐☐☐☐
1599	A1002	16c blue ('78)	.35	.05	☐☐☐☐☐
1603	A1006	24c red, *blue*	.60	.09	☐☐☐☐☐
1604	A1007	28c brown, *blue* ('78)	.70	.08	☐☐☐☐☐
1605	A1008	29c blue, *blue* ('78)	.70	.08	☐☐☐☐☐
1606	A1009	30c green, *blue* ('79)	.75	.08	☐☐☐☐☐

Perf. 11

Scott No.	Illus. No.	Description	Unused Price	Used Price	//////
1608	A1011	50c tan, black & orange ('79)	1.00	.25	☐☐☐☐☐
1610	A1013	$1 tan, brown, orange & yellow ('79)	2.00	.25	☐☐☐☐☐
1611	A1013a	$2 tan, dk green, orange & yellow ('78)	4.00	.50	☐☐☐☐☐
1612	A1014	$5 multi ('79)	10.00	2.00	☐☐☐☐☐

Coil stamp *Perf. 10 vertically*

Scott No.	Illus. No.	Description	Unused Price	Used Price	//////
1613	A1014a	3.1c brown, *yellow* ('79)	.20	.10	☐☐☐☐☐
1613a		Untagged (Bureau prec.)		.10	☐☐☐☐☐

A952

A953

A954

A955

A956

A958

A957

A959

A960

A962

A963

A964

A965

A961

US Bicentennial IOcents
A966

US Bicentennial IOc
A967

A968

A969

A970

A971

A972

A973

127

A974

A979

A975

A976

A977

A978

A980

A981

A982

A983

A984

A985

A987

A988

A994

A995

A996

A997

A998

A999

A1001

A1002

A1006

A1007

A1008

A1009

A1011

A1013

A1013a

A1014

A1014a

A1015

A1016

A1017

A1018

A1018a

A1019

A1020

A1021

A1022

HOW TO USE THIS BOOK

The number in the first column is its Scott number or identifying number. The letter and number that come next (A41) indicate the design and refer to the illustration so designated. Following that is the denomination of the stamp and its color. Finally, the price, unused and used is shown.

Scott No.	Illus. No.	Description	Unused Price	Used Price	//////
1614	A1015	7.7c brown, *bright yellow* ('76)	.20	.08 ☐☐☐☐☐
1614a		Untagged (Bureau prec.)		.16 ☐☐☐☐☐
1615	A1016	7.9c carmine, *yellow* ('76)	.20	.08 ☐☐☐☐☐
1615a		Untagged (Bureau prec.)		.16 ☐☐☐☐☐
1615C	A1017	8.4c dk blue, *yellow* ('78)	.25	.08 ☐☐☐☐☐
1615d		Untagged (Bureau prec.)		.16 ☐☐☐☐☐
1616	A994	9c slate green, *gray*	.22	.05 ☐☐☐☐☐
1616b		Untagged (Bureau prec.)		.18 ☐☐☐☐☐
1617	A995	10c violet, *gray* ('77)	.20	.05 ☐☐☐☐☐
1617a		Untagged (Bureau prec.)		.25 ☐☐☐☐☐
1618	A998	13c brown	.26	.05 ☐☐☐☐☐
1618a		Untagged (Bureau prec.)		.25 ☐☐☐☐☐
1618C	A1001	15c gray, dk blue & red ('78)	.40	.05 ☐☐☐☐☐
1619	A1002	16c blue ('78)	.32	.05 ☐☐☐☐☐

1975-77   *Perf. 11x10½*

Scott No.	Illus. No.	Description	Unused Price	Used Price	//////
1622	A1018	13c dk blue & red	.26	.05 ☐☐☐☐☐
1622c		Perf. 11	.30	.05 ☐☐☐☐☐
1623	A1018a	13c blue & red ('77)	.26	.05 ☐☐☐☐☐
1623a		Bklt. pane of 8 (1 #1590 and 7 #1623)	2.50	.60 ☐☐☐☐☐
1623b		Perf. 10	1.50	1.00 ☐☐☐☐☐
1623c		Bklt. pane of 8 (1 #1590a +7 #1623b)	40.00	– ☐☐☐☐☐

Coil stamp   *Perf. 10 vertically*

Scott No.	Illus. No.	Description	Unused Price	Used Price	//////
1625	A1018	13c dk blue & red	.30	.05 ☐☐☐☐☐

1976

Scott No.	Illus. No.	Description	Unused Price	Used Price	//////
1629	A1019	13c multi	.26	.08 ☐☐☐☐☐
1630	A1020	13c multi	.26	.08 ☐☐☐☐☐
1631	A1021	13c multi	.26	.08 ☐☐☐☐☐
1631a		Strip of 3, #1629-1631	.78	.60 ☐☐☐☐☐
1632	A1022	13c dk blue, red & ultra	.26	.05 ☐☐☐☐☐
1633	A1023	13c *Delaware*	.45	.30 ☐☐☐☐☐
1634	A1024	13c *Pennsylvania*	.45	.30 ☐☐☐☐☐
1635	A1025	13c *New Jersey*	.45	.30 ☐☐☐☐☐
1636	A1026	13c *Georgia*	.45	.30 ☐☐☐☐☐
1637	A1027	13c *Connecticut*	.45	.30 ☐☐☐☐☐
1638	A1028	13c *Massachusetts*	.45	.30 ☐☐☐☐☐
1639	A1029	13c *Maryland*	.45	.30 ☐☐☐☐☐
1640	A1030	13c *South Carolina*	.45	.30 ☐☐☐☐☐
1641	A1031	13c *New Hampshire*	.45	.30 ☐☐☐☐☐
1642	A1032	13c *Virginia*	.45	.30 ☐☐☐☐☐
1643	A1033	13c *New York*	.45	.30 ☐☐☐☐☐
1644	A1034	13c *North Carolina*	.45	.30 ☐☐☐☐☐
1645	A1035	13c *Rhode Island*	.45	.30 ☐☐☐☐☐
1646	A1036	13c *Vermont*	.45	.30 ☐☐☐☐☐
1647	A1037	13c *Kentucky*	.45	.30 ☐☐☐☐☐

State Flags A1023-A1072

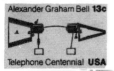

A1073

Commercial Aviation

A1074

A1075

132

Scott No.	Illus. No.	Description	Unused Price	Used Price	//////
1648	A1038	13c *Tennessee*	.45	.30	☐☐☐☐☐
1649	A1039	13c *Ohio*	.45	.30	☐☐☐☐☐
1650	A1040	13c *Louisiana*	.45	.30	☐☐☐☐☐
1651	A1041	13c *Indiana*	.45	.30	☐☐☐☐☐
1652	A1042	13c *Mississippi*	.45	.30	☐☐☐☐☐
1653	A1043	13c *Illinois*	.45	.30	☐☐☐☐☐
1654	A1044	13c *Alabama*	.45	.30	☐☐☐☐☐
1655	A1045	13c *Maine*	.45	.30	☐☐☐☐☐
1656	A1046	13c *Missouri*	.45	.30	☐☐☐☐☐
1657	A1047	13c *Arkansas*	.45	.30	☐☐☐☐☐
1658	A1048	13c *Michigan*	.45	.30	☐☐☐☐☐
1659	A1049	13c *Florida*	.45	.30	☐☐☐☐☐
1660	A1050	13c *Texas*	.45	.30	☐☐☐☐☐
1661	A1051	13c *Iowa*	.45	.30	☐☐☐☐☐
1662	A1052	13c *Wisconsin*	.45	.30	☐☐☐☐☐
1663	A1053	13c *California*	.45	.30	☐☐☐☐☐
1664	A1054	13c *Minnesota*	.45	.30	☐☐☐☐☐
1665	A1055	13c *Oregon*	.45	.30	☐☐☐☐☐
1666	A1056	13c *Kansas*	.45	.30	☐☐☐☐☐
1667	A1057	13c *West Virginia*	.45	.30	☐☐☐☐☐
1668	A1058	13c *Nevada*	.45	.30	☐☐☐☐☐
1669	A1059	13c *Nebraska*	.45	.30	☐☐☐☐☐
1670	A1060	13c *Colorado*	.45	.30	☐☐☐☐☐
1671	A1061	13c *North Dakota*	.45	.30	☐☐☐☐☐
1672	A1062	13c *South Dakota*	.45	.30	☐☐☐☐☐
1673	A1063	13c *Montana*	.45	.30	☐☐☐☐☐
1674	A1064	13c *Washington*	.45	.30	☐☐☐☐☐
1675	A1065	13c *Idaho*	.45	.30	☐☐☐☐☐
1676	A1066	13c *Wyoming*	.45	.30	☐☐☐☐☐
1677	A1067	13c *Utah*	.45	.30	☐☐☐☐☐
1678	A1068	13c *Oklahoma*	.45	.30	☐☐☐☐☐
1679	A1069	13c *New Mexico*	.45	.30	☐☐☐☐☐
1680	A1070	13c *Arizona*	.45	.30	☐☐☐☐☐
1681	A1071	13c *Alaska*	.45	.30	☐☐☐☐☐
1682	A1072	13c *Hawaii*	.45	.30	☐☐☐☐☐
1682a		Pane of 50	25.00	—	☐☐☐☐☐
1683	A1073	13c black, purple & red, *tan*	.26	.05	☐☐☐☐☐
1684	A1074	13c blue & multi	.26	.05	☐☐☐☐☐
1685	A1075	13c multi	.26	.05	☐☐☐☐☐
1686	A1076	13c sheet of 5	4.50	—	☐☐☐☐☐
1687	A1077	18c sheet of 5	6.00	—	☐☐☐☐☐
1688	A1078	24c sheet of 5	7.50	—	☐☐☐☐☐
1689	A1079	31c sheet of 5	9.00	—	☐☐☐☐☐
1690	A1080	13c ultra & multi	.26	.05	☐☐☐☐☐
1691	A1081	13c multi	.26	.08	☐☐☐☐☐
1692	A1082	13c multi	.26	.08	☐☐☐☐☐
1693	A1083	13c multi	.26	.08	☐☐☐☐☐

Surrender of Cornwallis at Yorktown, by John Trumbull– **A1076**

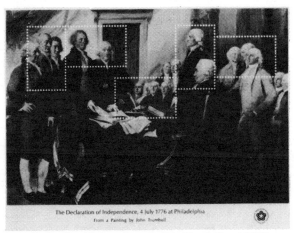

Declaration of Independence, by John Trumbull— **A1077**

Scott No.	Illus. No.	Description	Unused Price	Used Price	//////
1694	A1084	13c multi	.26	.08	☐☐☐☐☐
1694a		Strip of 4, #1691-1694	1.10	.75	☐☐☐☐☐
1695	A1085	13c multi	.26	.08	☐☐☐☐☐
1696	A1086	13c multi	.26	.08	☐☐☐☐☐
1697	A1087	13c multi	.26	.08	☐☐☐☐☐
1698	A1088	13c multi	.26	.08	☐☐☐☐☐
1698a		Block of 4, #1695-1698	1.10	1.00	☐☐☐☐☐
1699	A1089	13c multi	.26	.06	☐☐☐☐☐
1700	A1090	13c black & gray	.26	.05	☐☐☐☐☐
1701	A1091	13c multi	.26	.05	☐☐☐☐☐
1702	A1092	13c Overall tagging	.26	.05	☐☐☐☐☐
1703	A1092	13c Block tagging	.26	.05	☐☐☐☐☐

No. 1702 has overall tagging. Lettering at base is black and usually ½mm. below design. As a rule, no "snowflaking" in sky or pond. Pane of 50 has margins on 4 sides with slogans.
No. 1703 has block tagging the size of printed area. Lettering at base is gray black and usually ¾mm. below design. "Snowflaking" generally in sky and pond. Pane has margin only at right or left, and no slogans.

1977

Scott No.	Illus. No.	Description	Unused Price	Used Price	//////
1704	A1093	13c multi	.26	.05	☐☐☐☐☐
1705	A1094	13c black & multi	.26	.05	☐☐☐☐☐
1706	A1095	13c multi	.26	.08	☐☐☐☐☐
1707	A1096	13c multi	.26	.08	☐☐☐☐☐
1708	A1097	13c multi	.26	.08	☐☐☐☐☐
1709	A1098	13c multi	.26	.08	☐☐☐☐☐
1709a		Block or strip of 4	1.05	1.00	☐☐☐☐☐
1710	A1099	13c multi	.26	.05	☐☐☐☐☐
1711	A1100	13c multi	.26	.05	☐☐☐☐☐
1712	A1101	13c tan & multi	.26	.08	☐☐☐☐☐
1713	A1102	13c tan & multi	.26	.08	☐☐☐☐☐
1714	A1103	13c tan & multi	.26	.08	☐☐☐☐☐
1715	A1104	13c tan & multi	.26	.08	☐☐☐☐☐
1715a		Block of 4, #1712-1715	1.05	.90	☐☐☐☐☐
1716	A1105	13c blue, black & red	.26	.05	☐☐☐☐☐
1717	A1106	13c multi	.26	.08	☐☐☐☐☐
1718	A1107	13c multi	.26	.08	☐☐☐☐☐
1719	A1108	13c multi	.26	.08	☐☐☐☐☐
1720	A1109	13c multi	.26	.08	☐☐☐☐☐
1720a		Block of 4, #1717-1720	1.05	.90	☐☐☐☐☐
1721	A1110	13c blue	.26	.05	☐☐☐☐☐
1722	A1111	13c multi	.26	.05	☐☐☐☐☐
1723	A1112	13c multi	.26	.08	☐☐☐☐☐
1723a		Pair, #1723-1724	.60	.35	☐☐☐☐☐
1724	A1113	13c multi	.26	.08	☐☐☐☐☐
1725	A1114	13c black & multi	.26	.05	☐☐☐☐☐
1726	A1115	13c red & brown, *cream*	.26	.05	☐☐☐☐☐
1727	A1116	13c multi	.26	.05	☐☐☐☐☐

Washington Crossing the Delaware, by
Emanuel Leutze/Eastman Johnson— **A1078**

Washington Reviewing Army at Valley Forge,
by William T. Trego— **A1079**

A1080

136

JULY 4,1776: JULY 4,1776: JULY 4,1776: JULY 4,1776

Declaration of Independence, by John Trumbull

A1081   A1082   A1083   A1084

A1085

A1086

A1089

A1087

A1088

A1090

A1091

A1092

Washington at Princeton 1779 by Peale

US Bicentennial 13c

A1093   A1094

Zia Museum of New Mexico
Pueblo Art USA 13c

A1095

San Ildefonso Denver Art Museum
Pueblo Art USA 13c

A1096

Hopi Heard Museum Phoenix
Pueblo Art USA 13c

A1097

Acoma School of American Research
Pueblo Art USA 13c

A1098

A1099

COLORADO

13c
USA
THE CENTENNIAL STATE

A1100

Lafayette

US Bicentennial 13c

A1105

Swallowtail

USA 13c *Papilio oregonius*

A1101

Checkerspot

USA 13c *Euphydryas phaeton*

A1102

Dogface

USA 13c *Colias eurydice*

A1103

Orange-Tip

USA 13c *Anthocaris midea*

A1104

Scott No.	Illus. No.	Description	Unused Price	Used Price	//////
1728	A1117	13c multi	.26	.05 □□□□□
1729	A1118	13c multi	.35	.05 □□□□□
1730	A1119	13c multi	.26	.05 □□□□□

1978

1731	A1120	13c black & brown	.26	.05 □□□□□
1732	A1121	13c dk blue	.26	.08 □□□□□
1732a		Pair, #1732-1733	.55	.30 □□□□□
1733	A1122	13c green	.26	.08 □□□□□

1978-80

1734	A1123	13c brown & bl grn, *bister*	.26	.10 □□□□□
1735	A1124	(15c) orange, photo	.30	.05 □□□□□
1736	A1124	(15c) orange, engr.	.30	.05 □□□□□
1736a		Bklt. pane of 8	2.40	.60 □□□□□
1737	A1126	15c multi	.30	.06 □□□□□
1737a		Bklt. pane of 8	2.40	.60 □□□□□
1738	A1127	15c sepia, *yellow* ('80)	.30	.05 □□□□□
1739	A1128	15c sepia, *yellow* ('80)	.30	.05 □□□□□
1740	A1129	15c sepia, *yellow* ('80)	.30	.05 □□□□□
1741	A1130	15c sepia, *yellow* ('80)	.30	.05 □□□□□
1742	A1131	15c sepia, *yellow* ('80)	.30	.05 □□□□□
1742a		Bklt. pane of 10	4.00	.60 □□□□□

	Coil stamp	*Perf. 10 vertically*			
1743	A1124	(15c) orange	.30	.05 □□□□□

1978

1744	A1133	13c multi	.26	.05 □□□□□
1745	A1134	13c multi	.26	.08 □□□□□
1746	A1135	13c multi	.26	.08 □□□□□
1747	A1136	13c multi	.26	.08 □□□□□
1748	A1137	13c multi	.26	.08 □□□□□
1748a		Block of 4, #1745-1748	1.05	.75 □□□□□
1749	A1138	13c multi	.26	.08 □□□□□
1750	A1139	13c multi	.26	.08 □□□□□
1751	A1140	13c multi	.26	.08 □□□□□
1752	A1141	13c multi	.26	.08 □□□□□
1752a		Block of 4, #1749-1752	1.05	.75 □□□□□
1753	A1142	13c blue, black & red	.26	.05 □□□□□
1754	A1143	13c brown	.26	.05 □□□□□
1755	A1144	13c multi	.26	.05 □□□□□
1756	A1145	15c multi	.30	.05 □□□□□
1757	A1146	Block of 8, multi	2.10	2.10 □□□□□
1757a		13c *Cardinal*	.26	.10 □□□□□
1757b		13c *Mallard*	.26	.10 □□□□□
1757c		13c *Canada goose*	.26	.10 □□□□□
1757d		13c *Blue jay*	.26	.10 □□□□□
1757e		13c *Moose*	.26	.10 □□□□□
1757f		13c *Chipmunk*	.26	.10 □□□□□

A1106

A1107

A1108

A1109

A1110

A1112

A1111

A1114

A1113

A1115

A1116

A1117

A1118

A1120

A1119

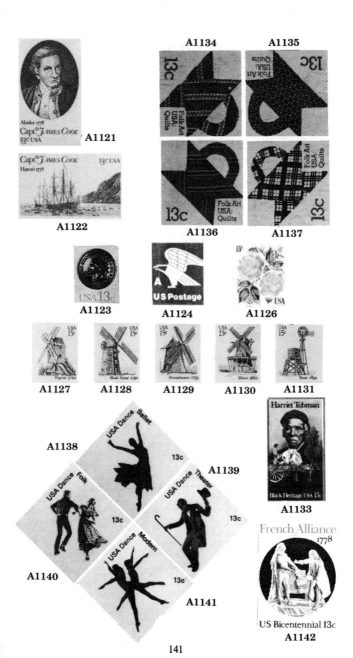

A1121

A1122

A1134 A1135

A1136 A1137

A1123 A1124 A1126

A1127 A1128 A1129 A1130 A1131

A1138 Ballet

A1139 Theater

A1140 Folk

A1141 Modern

A1133

A1142

A1143

A1146

A1144

A1149

A1150

A1145

A1151

A1152

A1147

A1153

A1154

A1155

A1156

142

A1148

A1157

A1158

A1159

A1161

A1160

A1162

A1163

A1164

A1165

A1166

A1167

143

A1168

Jefferson 1743-1826 · Virginia Rotunda
Architecture USA 15c

A1169

Latrobe 1764-1820 · Baltimore Cathedral
Architecture USA 15c

A1170

Bulfinch 1763-1844 · Boston State House
Architecture USA 15c

A1171

Strickland 1788-1854 · Philadelphia Exchange
Architecture USA 15c

A1172

A1173

A1174

A1175

USA 15c

Seeing For Me

A1176

I have not yet begun to fight

John Paul Jones
US Bicentennial 15c

A1178

Special Olympics

Skill·Sharing·Joy
USA 15c

A1177

Scott No.	Illus. No.	Description	Unused Price	Used Price	//////
1757g		13c *Red fox*	.26	.10 ☐☐☐☐☐
1757h		13c *Racoon*	.26	.10 ☐☐☐☐☐
1758	A1147	15c multi	.30	.05 ☐☐☐☐☐
1759	A1148	15c multi	.30	.05 ☐☐☐☐☐
1760	A1149	15c multi	.30	.08 ☐☐☐☐☐
1761	A1150	15c multi	.30	.08 ☐☐☐☐☐
1762	A1151	15c multi	.30	.08 ☐☐☐☐☐
1763	A1152	15c multi	.30	.08 ☐☐☐☐☐
1763a		Block of 4, #1760-1763	1.25	.85 ☐☐☐☐☐
1764	A1153	15c multi	.30	.08 ☐☐☐☐☐
1765	A1154	15c multi	.30	.08 ☐☐☐☐☐
1766	A1155	15c multi	.30	.08 ☐☐☐☐☐
1767	A1156	15c multi	.30	.08 ☐☐☐☐☐
1767a		Block of 4, #1764-1767	1.25	.85 ☐☐☐☐☐
1768	A1157	15c blue & multi	.30	.05 ☐☐☐☐☐
1769	A1158	15c red & multi	.30	.05 ☐☐☐☐☐

1979

Scott No.	Illus. No.	Description	Unused Price	Used Price	//////
1770	A1159	15c blue	.35	.05 ☐☐☐☐☐
1771	A1160	15c multi	.35	.05 ☐☐☐☐☐
1772	A1161	15c orange red	.30	.05 ☐☐☐☐☐
1773	A1162	15c dk blue	.30	.05 ☐☐☐☐☐
1774	A1163	15c chocolate	.30	.05 ☐☐☐☐☐
1775	A1164	15c multi	.30	.08 ☐☐☐☐☐
1776	A1165	15c multi	.30	.08 ☐☐☐☐☐
1777	A1166	15c multi	.30	.08 ☐☐☐☐☐
1778	A1167	15c multi	.30	.08 ☐☐☐☐☐
1778a		Block of 4, #1775-1778	1.25	.85 ☐☐☐☐☐
1779	A1168	15c black & brick red	.30	.08 ☐☐☐☐☐
1780	A1169	15c black & brick red	.30	.08 ☐☐☐☐☐
1781	A1170	15c black & brick red	.30	.08 ☐☐☐☐☐
1782	A1171	15c black & brick red	.30	.08 ☐☐☐☐☐
1782a		Block of 4, #1779-1782	1.50	.85 ☐☐☐☐☐
1783	A1172	15c multi	.30	.08 ☐☐☐☐☐
1784	A1173	15c multi	.30	.08 ☐☐☐☐☐
1785	A1174	15c multi	.30	.08 ☐☐☐☐☐
1786	A1175	15c multi	.30	.08 ☐☐☐☐☐
1786a		Block of 4, #1783-1786	1.25	.85 ☐☐☐☐☐
1787	A1176	15c multi	.30	.05 ☐☐☐☐☐
1788	A1177	15c multi	.30	.05 ☐☐☐☐☐
1789	A1178	15c multi	.30	.05 ☐☐☐☐☐

1979-80

Scott No.	Illus. No.	Description	Unused Price	Used Price	//////
1790	A1179	10c multi	.25	.22 ☐☐☐☐☐
1791	A1180	15c multi	.35	.08 ☐☐☐☐☐
1792	A1181	15c multi	.35	.08 ☐☐☐☐☐
1793	A1182	15c multi	.35	.08 ☐☐☐☐☐
1794	A1183	15c multi	.35	.08 ☐☐☐☐☐
1794a		Block of 4, #1791-1794	1.50	.85 ☐☐☐☐☐

A1179

A1180

A1181

A1182

A1183

A1184

A1185

A1186

A1187

A1188

A1191

A1189

Scott No.	Illus. No.	Description	Unused Price	Used Price	//////
1795	A1184	15c multi ('80)	.45	.08	☐☐☐☐☐
1796	A1185	15c multi ('80)	.45	.08	☐☐☐☐☐
1797	A1186	15c multi ('80)	.45	.08	☐☐☐☐☐
1798	A1187	15c multi ('80)	.45	.08	☐☐☐☐☐
1798b		Block of 4, #1795-1798	1.90	.85	☐☐☐☐☐

1979

1799	A1188	15c multi	.30	.05	☐☐☐☐☐
1800	A1189	15c multi	.30	.05	☐☐☐☐☐
1801	A1190	15c multi	.30	.05	☐☐☐☐☐
1802	A1191	15c multi	.30	.05	☐☐☐☐☐

1980

1803	A1192	15c multi	.30	.05	☐☐☐☐☐
1804	A1193	15c multi	.30	.05	☐☐☐☐☐
1805	A1194	15c multi	.35	.08	☐☐☐☐☐
1806	A1195	15c claret & multi	.35	.08	☐☐☐☐☐
1807	A1196	15c multi	.35	.08	☐☐☐☐☐
1808	A1195	15c green & multi	.35	.08	☐☐☐☐☐
1809	A1197	15c multi	.35	.08	☐☐☐☐☐
1810	A1195	15c red & multi	.35	.08	☐☐☐☐☐
1810a		Strip of 6 #1805-1810	2.75	1.25	☐☐☐☐☐

1980-81 Coil stamps *Perf. 10 vertically*

1811	A984	1c dk blue, *greenish*	.05	.05	☐☐☐☐☐
1813	A1199	3.5c purple, *yellow*	.08	.05	☐☐☐☐☐
1816	A997	12c brown red, *beige* ('81)	.24	.05	☐☐☐☐☐

1981

1818	A1207	(18c) violet, photo.	.36	.05	☐☐☐☐☐
1819	A1207	(18c) violet, engr.	.36	.05	☐☐☐☐☐
1819a		Bklt. pane of 8	4.50	*1.50*	☐☐☐☐☐

Coil stamp *Perf. 10 vertically*

1820	A1207	(18c) violet	.45	.05	☐☐☐☐☐

1980

1821	A1208	15c Prussian blue	.30	.05	☐☐☐☐☐
1822	A1209	15c red brown & sepia	.30	.05	☐☐☐☐☐
1823	A1210	15c black & red	.30	.05	☐☐☐☐☐
1824	A1211	15c multi	.30	.05	☐☐☐☐☐
1825	A1212	15c carmine & violet blue	.30	.05	☐☐☐☐☐
1826	A1213	15c multi	.30	.05	☐☐☐☐☐
1827	A1214	15c multi	.30	.08	☐☐☐☐☐
1828	A1215	15c multi	.30	.08	☐☐☐☐☐
1829	A1216	15c multi	.30	.08	☐☐☐☐☐
1830	A1217	15c multi	.30	.08	☐☐☐☐☐
1830a		Block of 4, #1827-1830	1.20	.85	☐☐☐☐☐
1831	A1218	15c multi	.30	.05	☐☐☐☐☐
1832	A1219	15c purple	.30	.05	☐☐☐☐☐
1833	A1220	15c multi	.30	.05	☐☐☐☐☐

A1190

A1192

A1193

A1194

A1196

A1197

A1195

A1208

A1209

A1210

A1211

A1212

A1213

Scott No.	Illus. No.	Description	Unused Price	Used Price	//////
1834	A1221	15c multi	.30	.08	☐☐☐☐☐
1835	A1222	15c multi	.30	.08	☐☐☐☐☐
1836	A1223	15c multi	.30	.08	☐☐☐☐☐
1837	A1224	15c multi	.30	.08	☐☐☐☐☐
1837a		Block of 4, #1834-1837	1.20	.85	☐☐☐☐☐
1838	A1225	15c black & brick red	.30	.08	☐☐☐☐☐
1839	A1226	15c black & brick red	.30	.08	☐☐☐☐☐
1840	A1227	15c black & brick red	.30	.08	☐☐☐☐☐
1841	A1228	15c black & brick red	.30	.08	☐☐☐☐☐
1841a		Block of 4, #1838-1841	1.50	.85	☐☐☐☐☐
1842	A1229	15c multi	.30	.05	☐☐☐☐☐
1843	A1230	15c multi	.30	.05	☐☐☐☐☐

1980-85

Scott No.	Illus. No.	Description	Unused Price	Used Price	//////
1844	A1231	1c black ('83)	.05	.05	☐☐☐☐☐
1845	A1232	2c brown black ('82)	.05	.05	☐☐☐☐☐
1846	A1233	3c olive green ('83)	.08	.05	☐☐☐☐☐
1847	A1234	4c violet ('83)	.10	.05	☐☐☐☐☐
1848	A1235	5c henna brown ('83)	.12	.05	☐☐☐☐☐
1849	A1236	6c orange vermilion ('85)	.12	.05	☐☐☐☐☐
1850	A1237	7c bright carmine ('85)	.14	.05	☐☐☐☐☐
1851	A1238	8c olive black ('85)	,16	.05	☐☐☐☐☐
1852	A1239	9c dark green ('85)	.18	.05	☐☐☐☐☐
1853	A1240	10c Prussian blue ('84)	.20	.05	☐☐☐☐☐
1854	A1241	11c dark blue ('85)	.22	.05	☐☐☐☐☐
1855	A1242	13c light maroon ('82)	.30	.05	☐☐☐☐☐
1856	A1243	14c slate green ('85)	.32	.05	☐☐☐☐☐
1857	A1244	17c green ('81)	.40	.05	☐☐☐☐☐
1858	A1245	18c dark blue ('81)	.44	.05	☐☐☐☐☐
1859	A1246	19c brown	.38	.07	☐☐☐☐☐
1860	A1247	20c claret ('82)	.50	.05	☐☐☐☐☐
1861	A1248	20c green ('83)	.50	.05	☐☐☐☐☐
1862	A1249	20c black ('84)	.40	.05	☐☐☐☐☐
1863	A1250	22c dark chalky blue ('85)	.44	.05	☐☐☐☐☐
1864	A1251	30c olive gray ('84)	.60	.08	☐☐☐☐☐
1865	A1252	35c gray ('81)	.70	.08	☐☐☐☐☐
1866	A1253	37c blue ('82)	.75	.05	☐☐☐☐☐
1867	A1254	39c rose lilac ('85)	.80	.08	☐☐☐☐☐
1868	A1255	40c dark green ('84)	.80	.10	☐☐☐☐☐
1869	A1256	50c brown ('85)	1.00	.10	☐☐☐☐☐

1981

Scott No.	Illus. No.	Description	Unused Price	Used Price	//////
1874	A1261	15c gray	.30	.05	☐☐☐☐☐
1875	A1262	15c multi	.30	.05	☐☐☐☐☐
1876	A1263	18c multi	.36	.08	☐☐☐☐☐
1877	A1264	18c multi	.36	.08	☐☐☐☐☐
1878	A1265	18c multi	.36	.08	☐☐☐☐☐
1879	A1266	18c multi	.36	.08	☐☐☐☐☐
1879a		Block of 4, #1876-1879	1.90	.85	☐☐☐☐☐

Coral Reefs USA 15c
Brain Coral; U.S. Virgin Islands
A1214

Coral Reefs USA 15c
Elkhorn Coral; Florida
A1215

Organized Labor
Proud and Free
USA 15c
A1218

Edith Wharton
USA 15c
A1219

Coral Reefs USA 15c
Chalice Coral; American Samoa
A1216

Coral Reefs USA 15c
Finger Coral; Hawaii
A1217

Glass by Josef Albers USA 15c
Learning
never ends
A1220

A1221 Heiltsuk, Bella Bella **Indian Art** USA 15c

Chilkat Tlingit **Indian Art** USA 15c A1222

A1223 Tlingit **Indian Art** USA 15c

Bella Coola **Indian Art** USA 15c A1224

HOW TO USE THIS BOOK

The number in the first column is its Scott number or identifying number. The letter and number that come next (A41) indicate the design and refer to the illustration so designated. Following that is the denomination of the stamp and its color. Finally, the price, unused and used is shown.

Scott No.	Illus. No.	Description	Unused Price	Used Price	//////
1981					
1880	A1267	18c *Bighorn*	.36	.05	☐☐☐☐☐
1881	A1268	18c *Puma*	.36	.05	☐☐☐☐☐
1882	A1269	18c *Harbor seal*	.36	.05	☐☐☐☐☐
1883	A1270	18c *Bison*	.36	.05	☐☐☐☐☐
1884	A1271	18c *Brown bear*	.36	.05	☐☐☐☐☐
1885	A1272	18c *Polar bear*	.36	.05	☐☐☐☐☐
1886	A1273	18c *Elk (wapiti)*	.36	.05	☐☐☐☐☐
1887	A1274	18c *Moose*	.36	.05	☐☐☐☐☐
1888	A1275	18c *White-tailed deer*	.36	.05	☐☐☐☐☐
1889	A1276	18c *Pronghorn*	.36	.05	☐☐☐☐☐
1889a		Bklt. pane of 10	7.50	–	☐☐☐☐☐
1890	A1277	18c multi	.36	.05	☐☐☐☐☐
	Coil stamp	*Perf. 10 vertically*			
1891	A1278	18c multi	.36	.05	☐☐☐☐☐
1892	A1279	6c multi	.50	.10	☐☐☐☐☐
1893	A1280	18c multi	.36	.05	☐☐☐☐☐
1893a		Bklt. pane of 8			
		(2 #1892, 6 #1893)	3.50	–	☐☐☐☐☐
1894	A1281	20c black, dk blue & red	.45	.05	☐☐☐☐☐
	Coil stamp	*Perf. 10 vertically*			
1895	A1281	20c black, dk blue & red	.40	.05	☐☐☐☐☐
1896	A1281	20c black, dk blue & red	.40	.05	☐☐☐☐☐
1896a		Bklt. pane of 6	2.50	–	☐☐☐☐☐
1896b		Bklt. pane of 10	4.25	–	☐☐☐☐☐
1981-84	**Coil stamps**	*Perf. 10 vertically*			
1897	A1283	1c violet ('83)	.05	.05	☐☐☐☐☐
1897A	A1284	2c black ('82)	.05	.05	☐☐☐☐☐
1898	A1284a	3c dark green ('83)	.15	.05	☐☐☐☐☐
1898A	A1285	4c reddish brown ('82)	.12	.05	☐☐☐☐☐
1898b		Untagged (Bureau prec.)		.12	☐☐☐☐☐
1899	A1286	5c gray green ('83)	.15	.05	☐☐☐☐☐
1900	A1287	5.2c carmine ('83)	.20	.05	☐☐☐☐☐
1900a		Untagged (Bureau prec.)		.20	☐☐☐☐☐
1901	A1288	5.9c blue ('82)	.20	.05	☐☐☐☐☐
1901a		Untagged (Bureau prec., lines only)		.20	☐☐☐☐☐
1902	A1288a	7.4c brown ('84)	.20	.08	☐☐☐☐☐
1902a		Untagged (Bureau prec.)		.20	☐☐☐☐☐
1903	A1289	9.3c carmine rose ('81)	.20	.08	☐☐☐☐☐
1903a		Untagged (Bureau prec., lines only)		.20	☐☐☐☐☐
1904	A1290	10.9c purple ('82)	.25	.05	☐☐☐☐☐
1904a		Untagged (Bureau prec., lines only)		.25	☐☐☐☐☐

A1225 Architecture USA 15c

Brunswick 1881 1875 Smithsonian Washington

Richardson 1838 1886 Trinity Church Boston

Architecture USA 15c A1226

A1227 Architecture USA 15c

Furness 1839 1912 Penn Academy Philadelphia

AJ Davis 1833 1892 Lyndhurst Tarrytown NY

Architecture USA 15c A1228

Christmas USA 15c

A1229

USA 15c
Season's Greetings

A1230

USA 15c
Everett Dirksen

A1261

Whitney Moore Young

Black Heritage USA 15c

A1262

A1263

Rose USA 18c

Camellia USA 18c

A1264

A1265

Dahlia USA 18c

Lily USA 18c

A1266

152

A1231

A1232

A1233

A1234

A1235

A1236

A1237

A1238

A1239

A1240

A1241

A1242

A1243

A1244

A1245

A1246

A1247

A1248

A1249

A1250

A1251

A1252

A1253

A1254

A1255

A1256

A1283

A1284

A1284a

A1285

A1286

A1287

A1288

A1288a

A1289

A1290

A1290a

A1291

A1292

A1294

A1296

A1207

A1281

A1267   A1268

A1269   A1270

A1271   A1272

A1273   A1274

A1275   A1276

A1277

A1278

A1279

A1280

A1332

A1333

A1334

A1390

A1299   A1300   A1301   A1302

Exploring the Moon — USA 18c
Benefiting Mankind — USA 18c
Benefiting Mankind — USA 18c
Understanding the Sun — USA 18c
Probing the Planets — USA 18c
USA 18c
USA 18c
Comprehending the Universe — USA 18c

A1303   A1304   A1305   A1306

The Gift of Self
USA 18c
American Red Cross
1881–1981

A1297

Save Wetland Habitats
USA 18c

A1308

Save Grassland Habitats
USA 18c

A1309

USA 18c

Save Mountain Habitats
A1310

USA 18c

Save Woodland Habitats
A1311

SAVINGS AND LOANS
SAVE
USA 18c

A1298

Scott No.	Illus. No.	Description	Unused Price	Used Price	//////
1905	A1290a	11c red ('84)	.25	.08	☐☐☐☐☐
1905a		Untagged (Bureau prec.)		.25	☐☐☐☐☐
1906	A1291	17c ultramarine ('81)	.34	.05	☐☐☐☐☐
1906a		Untagged (Bureau prec., Presorted First Class)		.35	☐☐☐☐☐
1907	A1292	18c dark brown ('81)	.36	.05	☐☐☐☐☐
1908	A1294	20c vermilion ('81)	.40	.05	☐☐☐☐☐
1983	**Bklt. stamp**	*Perf. 10 vertically*			
1909	A1296	$9.35 multi	25.00	6.00	☐☐☐☐☐
1909a		Bklt. pane of 3	77.50	–	☐☐☐☐☐
1981					
1910	A1297	18c multi	.36	.05	☐☐☐☐☐
1911	A1298	18c multi	.36	.05	☐☐☐☐☐
1912	A1299	18c multi	.36	.10	☐☐☐☐☐
1913	A1300	18c multi	.36	.10	☐☐☐☐☐
1914	A1301	18c multi	.36	.10	☐☐☐☐☐
1915	A1302	18c multi	.36	.10	☐☐☐☐☐
1916	A1303	18c multi	.36	.10	☐☐☐☐☐
1917	A1304	18c multi	.36	.10	☐☐☐☐☐
1918	A1305	18c multi	.36	.10	☐☐☐☐☐
1919	A1306	18c multi	.36	.10	☐☐☐☐☐
1919a		Block of 8, #1912-1919	3.75	2.25	☐☐☐☐☐
1920	A1307	18c blue & black	.36	.05	☐☐☐☐☐
1921	A1308	18c multi	.36	.08	☐☐☐☐☐
1922	A1309	18c multi	.36	.08	☐☐☐☐☐
1923	A1310	18c multi	.36	.08	☐☐☐☐☐
1924	A1311	18c multi	.36	.08	☐☐☐☐☐
1924a		Block of 4, #1921-1924	1.90	.85	☐☐☐☐☐
1925	A1312	18c multi	.36	.05	☐☐☐☐☐
1926	A1313	18c multi	.36	.05	☐☐☐☐☐
1927	A1314	18c blue & black	.45	.05	☐☐☐☐☐
1928	A1315	18c black & red	.36	.08	☐☐☐☐☐
1929	A1316	18c black & red	.36	.08	☐☐☐☐☐
1930	A1317	18c black & red	.36	.08	☐☐☐☐☐
1931	A1318	18c black & red	.36	.08	☐☐☐☐☐
1931a		Block of 4, #1928-1931	1.50	.85	☐☐☐☐☐
1932	A1319	18c purple	.36	.05	☐☐☐☐☐
1933	A1320	18c green	.36	.05	☐☐☐☐☐
1934	A1321	18c gray, green & brown	.36	.05	☐☐☐☐☐
1935	A1322	18c multi	.50	.25	☐☐☐☐☐
1936	A1322	20c multi	.40	.05	☐☐☐☐☐
1937	A1323	18c multi	.36	.06	☐☐☐☐☐
1938	A1324	18c multi	.36	.06	☐☐☐☐☐
1939	A1325	(20c) multi	.40	.05	☐☐☐☐☐
1940	A1326	(20c) multi	.40	.05	☐☐☐☐☐
1941	A1327	20c multi	.40	.05	☐☐☐☐☐
1942	A1328	20c multi	.40	.06	☐☐☐☐☐

A1307

 A1312

A1313

A1314

A1327

A1315

A1316

A1317

A1318

A1319

A1321

A1322

A1320

158

A1323

A1324

A1325

A1326

A1328

A1329

A1330

A1331

A1335

A1336

A1337

159

A1338-A1387—State Birds and Flowers

A1388   A1395   A1389

A1391   A1392

A1393   A1394

Scott No.	Illus. No.	Description	Unused Price	Used Price	//////
1943	A1329	20c multi	.40	.06 □□□□□
1944	A1330	20c multi	.40	.06 □□□□□
1945	A1331	20c multi	.40	.06 □□□□□
1945a		Block of 4, #1942-1945	1.90	.85 □□□□□
1946	A1332	(20c) brown	.45	.05 □□□□□
Coil stamp		***Perf. 10 vertically***		
1947	A1332	(20c) brown	.45	.05 □□□□□
1948	A1333	(20c) brown	.40	.05 □□□□□
1948a		Bklt. pane of 10	4.25	− □□□□□
1982				
1949	A1334	20c dk blue	.40	.05 □□□□□
1949a		Bklt. pane of 10	5.50	− □□□□□
1950	A1335	20c blue	.45	.05 □□□□□
1951	A1336	20c multi	.45	.05 □□□□□
1951a		Perf. 11	.50	.05 □□□□□
1952	A1337	20c multi	.45	.05 □□□□□
1953	A1338	20c *Alabama*	.45	.25 □□□□□
1954	A1339	20c *Alaska*	.45	.25 □□□□□
1955	A1340	20c *Arizona*	.45	.25 □□□□□
1956	A1341	20c *Arkansas*	.45	.25 □□□□□
1957	A1342	20c *California*	.45	.25 □□□□□
1958	A1343	20c *Colorado*	.45	.25 □□□□□
1959	A1344	20c *Connecticut*	.45	.25 □□□□□
1960	A1345	20c *Delaware*	.45	.25 □□□□□
1961	A1346	20c *Florida*	.45	.25 □□□□□
1962	A1347	20c *Georgia*	.45	.25 □□□□□
1963	A1348	20c *Hawaii*	.45	.25 □□□□□
1964	A1349	20c *Idaho*	.45	.25 □□□□□
1965	A1350	20c *Illinois*	.45	.25 □□□□□
1966	A1351	20c *Indiana*	.45	.25 □□□□□
1967	A1352	20c *Iowa*	.45	.25 □□□□□
1968	A1353	20c *Kansas*	.45	.25 □□□□□
1969	A1354	20c *Kentucky*	.45	.25 □□□□□
1970	A1355	20c *Louisiana*	.45	.25 □□□□□
1971	A1356	20c *Maine*	.45	.25 □□□□□
1972	A1357	20c *Maryland*	.45	.25 □□□□□
1973	A1358	20c *Massachusetts*	.45	.25 □□□□□
1974	A1359	20c *Michigan*	.45	.25 □□□□□
1975	A1360	20c *Minnesota*	.45	.25 □□□□□
1976	A1361	20c *Mississippi*	.45	.25 □□□□□
1977	A1362	20c *Missouri*	.45	.25 □□□□□
1978	A1363	20c *Montana*	.45	.25 □□□□□
1979	A1364	20c *Nebraska*	.45	.25 □□□□□
1980	A1365	20c *Nevada*	.45	.25 □□□□□
1981	A1366	20c *New Hampshire*	.45	.25 □□□□□
1982	A1367	20c *New Jersey*	.45	.25 □□□□□
1983	A1368	20c *New Mexico*	.45	.25 □□□□□

A1396

A1399

A1397

A1398

A1400

A1401

A1402

A1403

A1404

A1405

A1406

A1407

Scott No.	Illus. No.	Description	Unused Price	Used Price	//////
1984	A1369	20c *New York*	.45	.25	☐☐☐☐☐
1985	A1370	20c *North Carolina*	.45	.25	☐☐☐☐☐
1986	A1371	20c *North Dakota*	.45	.25	☐☐☐☐☐
1987	A1372	20c *Ohio*	.45	.25	☐☐☐☐☐
1988	A1373	20c *Oklahoma*	.45	.25	☐☐☐☐☐
1989	A1374	20c *Oregon*	.45	.25	☐☐☐☐☐
1990	A1375	20c *Pennsylvania*	.45	.25	☐☐☐☐☐
1991	A1376	20c *Rhode Island*	.45	.25	☐☐☐☐☐
1992	A1377	20c *South Carolina*	.45	.25	☐☐☐☐☐
1993	A1378	20c *South Dakota*	.45	.25	☐☐☐☐☐
1994	A1379	20c *Tennessee*	.45	.25	☐☐☐☐☐
1995	A1380	20c *Texas*	.45	.25	☐☐☐☐☐
1996	A1381	20c *Utah*	.45	.25	☐☐☐☐☐
1997	A1382	20c *Vermont*	.45	.25	☐☐☐☐☐
1998	A1383	20c *Virginia*	.45	.25	☐☐☐☐☐
1999	A1384	20c *Washington*	.45	.25	☐☐☐☐☐
2000	A1385	20c *West Virginia*	.45	.25	☐☐☐☐☐
2001	A1386	20c *Wisconsin*	.45	.25	☐☐☐☐☐
2002	A1387	20c *Wyoming*	.45	.25	☐☐☐☐☐
2002a		1953a-2002a, single, Perf. 11	.50	.30	☐☐☐☐☐
2002b		Pane of 50, Perf. 10½x11	22.50	–	☐☐☐☐☐
2002c		Pane of 50, Perf. 11	25.00	–	☐☐☐☐☐
2003	A1388	20c vermilion, bright blue & gray black	.45	.05	☐☐☐☐☐
2004	A1389	20c red & black	.40	.05	☐☐☐☐☐
Coil stamp		*Perf. 10 vertically*			
2005	A1390	20c sky blue	.50	.05	☐☐☐☐☐
2006	A1391	20c multi	.40	.08	☐☐☐☐☐
2007	A1392	20c multi	.40	.08	☐☐☐☐☐
2008	A1393	20c multi	.40	.08	☐☐☐☐☐
2009	A1394	20c multi	.40	.08	☐☐☐☐☐
2009a		Block of 4, #2006-2009	1.90	.85	☐☐☐☐☐
2010	A1395	20c red & black, *tan*	.40	.05	☐☐☐☐☐
2011	A1396	20c brown	.40	.05	☐☐☐☐☐
2012	A1397	20c multi	.40	.05	☐☐☐☐☐
2013	A1398	20c multi	.40	.05	☐☐☐☐☐
2014	A1399	20c multi	.40	.05	☐☐☐☐☐
2015	A1400	20c red & black	.40	.05	☐☐☐☐☐
2016	A1401	20c multi	.45	.05	☐☐☐☐☐
2017	A1402	20c multi	.45	.05	☐☐☐☐☐
2018	A1403	20c multi	.40	.05	☐☐☐☐☐
2019	A1404	20c black & brown	.40	.08	☐☐☐☐☐
2020	A1405	20c black & brown	.40	.08	☐☐☐☐☐
2021	A1406	20c black & brown	.40	.08	☐☐☐☐☐
2022	A1407	20c black & brown	.40	.08	☐☐☐☐☐
2022a		Block of 4, #2019-2022	1.90	.85	☐☐☐☐☐

A1408

A1409

A1411

A1410

A1416

A1412

A1413

A1414

A1415

A1421

A1422

A1418

A1417

A1419

A1420

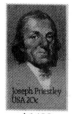

A1423

A1429

A1431

A1432

A1424

A1425

A1426

A1427

A1428

USA 20c
Medal of Honor
A1430

CIVIL
SERVICE
1883
1983
USA20c
A1438

Treaty of Paris 1783
US Bicentennial 20 cents
A1437

A1433

A1434

A1435

A1436

A1440

A1441

Charles Steinmetz

Edwin Armstrong

Nikola Tesla

Philo T. Farnsworth

A1442

A1443

Scott No.	Illus. No.	Description	Unused Price	Used Price	//////
2023	A1408	20c multi	.40	.05	☐☐☐☐☐
2024	A1409	20c multi	.45	.05	☐☐☐☐☐
2025	A1410	13c multi	.26	.05	☐☐☐☐☐
2026	A1411	20c multi	.40	.05	☐☐☐☐☐
2027	A1412	20c multi	.40	.05	☐☐☐☐☐
2028	A1413	20c multi	.40	.05	☐☐☐☐☐
2029	A1414	20c multi	.40	.05	☐☐☐☐☐
2030	A1415	20c multi	.40	.05	☐☐☐☐☐
2030a		Block of 4, #2027-2030	1.90	.85	☐☐☐☐☐
1983					
2031	A1416	20c multi	.40	.05	☐☐☐☐☐
2032	A1417	20c multi	.40	.08	☐☐☐☐☐
2033	A1418	20c multi	.40	.08	☐☐☐☐☐
2034	A1419	20c multi	.40	.08	☐☐☐☐☐
2035	A1420	20c multi	.40	.08	☐☐☐☐☐
2035a		Block of 4, #2032-2035	1.90	.85	☐☐☐☐☐
2036	A1421	20c multi	.40	.05	☐☐☐☐☐
2037	A1422	20c multi	.40	.05	☐☐☐☐☐
2038	A1423	20c multi	.40	.05	☐☐☐☐☐
2039	A1424	20c red & black	.40	.05	☐☐☐☐☐
2040	A1425	20c brown	.40	.05	☐☐☐☐☐
2041	A1426	20c blue	.40	.05	☐☐☐☐☐
2042	A1427	20c multi	.40	.05	☐☐☐☐☐
2043	A1428	20c multi	.40	.05	☐☐☐☐☐
2044	A1429	20c multi	.40	.05	☐☐☐☐☐
2045	A1430	20c multi	.40	.05	☐☐☐☐☐
2046	A1431	20c blue	.45	.05	☐☐☐☐☐
2047	A1432	20c multi	.40	.05	☐☐☐☐☐
2048	A1433	13c multi	.26	.05	☐☐☐☐☐
2049	A1434	13c multi	.26	.05	☐☐☐☐☐
2050	A1435	13c multi	.26	.05	☐☐☐☐☐
2051	A1436	13c multi	.26	.05	☐☐☐☐☐
2051a		Block of 4, #2048-2051	1.50	.65	☐☐☐☐☐
2052	A1437	20c multi	.40	.05	☐☐☐☐☐
2053	A1438	20c multi	.40	.05	☐☐☐☐☐
2054	A1439	20c yellow & maroon	.40	.05	☐☐☐☐☐
2055	A1440	20c orange & black	.40	.08	☐☐☐☐☐
2056	A1441	20c orange & black	.40	.08	☐☐☐☐☐
2057	A1442	20c orange & black	.40	.08	☐☐☐☐☐
2058	A1443	20c orange & black	.40	.08	☐☐☐☐☐
2058a		Block of 4, #2055-2058	1.60	.85	☐☐☐☐☐
2059	A1444	20c multi	.40	.08	☐☐☐☐☐
2060	A1445	20c multi	.40	.08	☐☐☐☐☐
2061	A1446	20c multi	.40	.08	☐☐☐☐☐
2062	A1447	20c multi	.40	.08	☐☐☐☐☐
2062a		Block of 4, #2059-2062	1.60	.85	☐☐☐☐☐
2063	A1448	20c multi	.40	.05	☐☐☐☐☐

A1439

A1448

A1449

A1444 **A1445**

A1446 **A1447**

A1450

A1452 **A1453**

A1451

A1456

A1454 **A1455**

A1457

A1458

A1461

A1462

A1459

A1463   A1464

A1460

A1467   A1468

A1466

A1473

A1469   A1470

A1474

A1465

A1471

A1472

169

A1475

A1476

A1477

A1478

A1479

A1480

A1481

A1482

A1483

A1484

A1485

A1486

Scott No.	Illus. No.	Description	Unused Price	Used Price	//////
2064	A1449	20c multi	.40	.05	☐☐☐☐☐
2065	A1450	20c multi	.40	.05	☐☐☐☐☐
1984					
2066	A1451	20c multi	.40	.05	☐☐☐☐☐
2067	A1452	20c multi	.40	.08	☐☐☐☐☐
2068	A1453	20c multi	.40	.08	☐☐☐☐☐
2069	A1454	20c multi	.40	.08	☐☐☐☐☐
2070	A1455	20c multi	.40	.08	☐☐☐☐☐
2070a		Block of 4, #2067-2070	1.90	.85	☐☐☐☐☐
2071	A1456	20c multi	.40	.05	☐☐☐☐☐
2072	A1457	20c multi	.45	.05	☐☐☐☐☐
2073	A1458	20c multi	.40	.05	☐☐☐☐☐
2074	A1459	20c multi	.40	.05	☐☐☐☐☐
2075	A1460	20c multi	.40	.05	☐☐☐☐☐
2076	A1461	20c multi	.40	.08	☐☐☐☐☐
2077	A1462	20c multi	.40	.08	☐☐☐☐☐
2078	A1463	20c multi	.40	.08	☐☐☐☐☐
2079	A1464	20c multi	.40	.08	☐☐☐☐☐
2079a		Block of 4, #2076-2079	1.60	.85	☐☐☐☐☐
2080	A1465	20c multi	.40	.05	☐☐☐☐☐
2081	A1466	20c multi	.40	.05	☐☐☐☐☐
2082	A1467	20c multi	.40	.08	☐☐☐☐☐
2083	A1468	20c multi	.40	.08	☐☐☐☐☐
2084	A1469	20c multi	.40	.08	☐☐☐☐☐
2085	A1470	20c multi	.40	.08	☐☐☐☐☐
2085a		Block of 4, #2082-2085	1.90	.85	☐☐☐☐☐
2086	A1471	20c multi	.40	.05	☐☐☐☐☐
2087	A1472	20c multi	.40	.05	☐☐☐☐☐
2088	A1473	20c multi	.40	.05	☐☐☐☐☐
2089	A1474	20c brown	.45	.05	☐☐☐☐☐
2090	A1475	20c multi	.40	.05	☐☐☐☐☐
2091	A1476	20c multi	.40	.05	☐☐☐☐☐
2092	A1477	20c blue	.40	.05	☐☐☐☐☐
2093	A1478	20c multi	.40	.05	☐☐☐☐☐
2094	A1479	20c sage green	.40	.05	☐☐☐☐☐
2095	A1480	20c orange & dark brown	.40	.05	☐☐☐☐☐
2096	A1481	20c multi	.40	.05	☐☐☐☐☐
2097	A1482	20c multi	.45	.05	☐☐☐☐☐
2098	A1483	20c multi	.40	.08	☐☐☐☐☐
2099	A1484	20c multi	.40	.08	☐☐☐☐☐
2100	A1485	20c multi	.40	.08	☐☐☐☐☐
2101	A1486	20c multi	.40	.08	☐☐☐☐☐
2101a		Block of 4, #2098-2101	1.90	.85	☐☐☐☐☐
2102	A1487	20c multi	.40	.05	☐☐☐☐☐
2103	A1488	20c multi	.40	.05	☐☐☐☐☐
2104	A1489	20c multi	.40	.05	☐☐☐☐☐
2105	A1490	20c multi	.40	.05	☐☐☐☐☐

A1487 A1488 A1489

A1490 A1494

A1491 A1492 A1493 A1495

A1496 A1497 A1498 A1499

HOW TO USE THIS BOOK

The number in the first column is its Scott number or identifying number. The letter and number that come next (A41) indicate the design and refer to the illustration so designated. Following that is the denomination of the stamp and its color. Finally, the price, unused and used is shown.

A1500

A1501

A1502

A1503

A1505

A1504

A1506

A1507

A1508

A1509

A1510

A1511

A1512

A1513

A1514

A1515

A1516

A1517

A1518

A1519

A1520

A1527

A1526

A1521

A1522

A1523

A1524

A1525

A1528

A1530

A1529

A1535

Scott No.	Illus. No.	Description	Unused Price	Used Price	//////
2106	A1491	20c brn & mar	.40	.05 □□□□□
2107	A1492	20c multi	.40	.05 □□□□□
2108	A1493	20c multi	.40	.05 □□□□□
2109	A1494	20c multi	.40	.05 □□□□□

1985

2110	A1495	22c multi	.44	.05 □□□□□
2111	A1496	(22c) green	.44	.05 □□□□□

Coil stamp *Perf. 10 vertically*

2112	A1496	(22c) green	.44	.05 □□□□□
2113	A1497	(22c) green	.44	.05 □□□□□
2113a		Bklt. pane of 10	5.50	— □□□□□
2114	A1498	22c blue, red & blk	.44	.05 □□□□□

Coil stamp *Perf. 10 vertically*

2115	A1498	22c blue, red & blk	.44	.05 □□□□□
2116	A1499	22c blue, red & blk	.44	.05 □□□□□
2116a		Bklt. pane of 5	2.20	— □□□□□
2117	A1500	22c blk & brn	.44	.05 □□□□□
2118	A1501	22c multi	.44	.05 □□□□□
2119	A1502	22c blk & brn	.44	.05 □□□□□
2120	A1503	22c blk & vio	.44	.05 □□□□□
2121	A1504	22c multi	.44	.05 □□□□□
2121a		Bklt. pane of 10	4.40	— □□□□□

Bklt. stamp *Perf. 10 vertically*

2122	A1505	$10.75 multi	22.00	— □□□□□
2122a		Bklt. pane of 3	67.50	— □□□□□

1985-87 Coil stamps *Perf. 10 vertically*

2123	A1506	3.4c dk blsh grn	.08	.05 □□□□□
2123a		Untagged (Bureau prec.)		— □□□□□
2124	A1507	4.9c brn blk	.10	.05 □□□□□
2124a		Untagged (Bureau prec.)		.10 □□□□□
2125	A1508	5.5c dp mag ('86)	.11	.05 □□□□□
2125a		Untagged (Bureau prec.)		.11 □□□□□
2126	A1509	6c red brown	.12	.05 □□□□□
2126a		Untagged (Bureau prec.)		.12 □□□□□
2127	A1510	7.1c Lake ('87)	.15	.05 □□□□□
2127a		Untagged (Bureau prec.)		.15 □□□□□
2128	A1511	8.3c green	.16	.05 □□□□□
2128a		Untagged (Bureau prec.)		.16 □□□□□
2129	A1512	8.5c dk prus grn ('87)	.18	.05 □□□□□
2129a		Untagged (Bureau prec.)		.18 □□□□□
2130	A1513	10.1c slate blue	.22	.05 □□□□□
2130a		Untagged (Bureau prec.)		.22 □□□□□
2131	A1514	11c dark green	.22	.05 □□□□□
2132	A1515	12c dark blue	.24	.05 □□□□□
2132a		Untagged (Bureau prec.)		.24 □□□□□

A1532

A1536

A1533

A1537

A1538

A1539

A1540

A1541

A1543

A1544

A1545

A1546

Scott No.	Illus. No.	Description	Unused Price	Used Price	//////
2133	A1516	12.5c olive green	.25	.05 ☐☐☐☐☐
2133a		Untagged (Bureau prec.)		.25 ☐☐☐☐☐
2134	A1517	14c sky blue	.28	.05 ☐☐☐☐☐
2135	A1518	17c brt bl ('86)	.34	.05 ☐☐☐☐☐
2136	A1519	25c org brn ('86)	.50	.05 ☐☐☐☐☐

1985

Scott No.	Illus. No.	Description	Unused Price	Used Price	//////
2137	A1520	22c multi	.44	.05 ☐☐☐☐☐
2138	A1521	22c multi	.44	.08 ☐☐☐☐☐
2139	A1522	22c multi	.44	.08 ☐☐☐☐☐
2140	A1523	22c multi	.44	.08 ☐☐☐☐☐
2141	A1524	22c multi	.44	.08 ☐☐☐☐☐
2141a		Block of 4, #2138-2141	2.00	1.00 ☐☐☐☐☐
2142	A1525	22c multi	.44	.05 ☐☐☐☐☐
2143	A1526	22c multi	.44	.05 ☐☐☐☐☐
2144	A1527	22c multi	.44	.05 ☐☐☐☐☐
2145	A1528	22c multi	.44	.05 ☐☐☐☐☐
2146	A1529	22c multi	.44	.05 ☐☐☐☐☐
2147	A1530	22c multi	.44	.05 ☐☐☐☐☐

Coil stamps		*Perf. 10 vertically*			
2149	A1532	18c multi	.36	.08 ☐☐☐☐☐
2149a		Untagged (Bureau prec.)		.36 ☐☐☐☐☐
2150	A1533	21.1c multi	.45	.08 ☐☐☐☐☐
2150a		Untagged (Bureau prec.)		.45 ☐☐☐☐☐

1985

Scott No.	Illus. No.	Description	Unused Price	Used Price	//////
2152	A1535	22c gray grn & rose red	.44	.05 ☐☐☐☐☐
2153	A1536	22c deep bl & lt bl	.44	.05 ☐☐☐☐☐
2154	A1537	22c gray grn & rose red	.44	.05 ☐☐☐☐☐
2155	A1538	22c multi	.44	.08 ☐☐☐☐☐
2156	A1539	22c multi	.44	.08 ☐☐☐☐☐
2157	A1540	22c multi	.44	.08 ☐☐☐☐☐
2158	A1541	22c multi	.44	.08 ☐☐☐☐☐
2158a		Block of 4, #2155-2158	2.00	1.00 ☐☐☐☐☐
2159	A1542	22c multi	.44	.05 ☐☐☐☐☐
2160	A1543	22c multi	.44	.08 ☐☐☐☐☐
2161	A1544	22c multi	.44	.08 ☐☐☐☐☐
2162	A1545	22c multi	.44	.08 ☐☐☐☐☐
2163	A1546	22c multi	.44	.08 ☐☐☐☐☐
2163a		Block of 4, #2160-2163	2.00	1.00 ☐☐☐☐☐
2164	A1547	22c multi	.44	.05 ☐☐☐☐☐
2165	A1548	22c multi	.44	.05 ☐☐☐☐☐
2166	A1549	22c multi	.44	.05 ☐☐☐☐☐

1986-87

Scott No.	Illus. No.	Description	Unused Price	Used Price	//////
2167	A1550	22c multi	.44	.05 ☐☐☐☐☐
2168	A1551	1c hen brn	.05	.05 ☐☐☐☐☐
2169	A1552	2c brt bl ('87)	.05	.05 ☐☐☐☐☐
2170	A1553	3c brt bl	.06	.05 ☐☐☐☐☐

A1542

A1549

A1548

A1547

A1550

A1552

A1559

A1579

A1581

A1582

A1583

A1584

A1585

A1586

A1604a

A1604b

Scott No.	Illus. No.	Description	Unused Price	Used Price	//////
2171	A1554	4c bl vio	.08	.05	□□□□□
2172	A1555	5c ryl bl	.10	.05	□□□□□
2176	A1559	10c lake ('87)	.20	.05	□□□□□
2177	A1560	14c crim ('87)	.28	.05	□□□□□
2179	A1562	17c dl bl grn	.34	.05	□□□□□
2183	A1566	25c blue	.50	.06	□□□□□
2191	A1574	56c scar	1.12	.08	□□□□□
2194	A1577	$1 dk prus grn	2.00	.50	□□□□□
2195	A1578	$2 brt vio	4.00	1.00	□□□□□
2196	A1579	$5 cop red ('87)	10.00	1.00	□□□□□

1986

Scott No.	Illus. No.	Description	Unused Price	Used Price	//////
2198	A1581	22c multi	.44	.05	□□□□□
2199	A1582	22c multi	.44	.05	□□□□□
2200	A1583	22c multi	.44	.05	□□□□□
2201	A1584	22c multi	.44	.05	□□□□□
2201a		Bklt. pane of 4 (#2198-2201)	1.80	—	□□□□□
2202	A1585	22c multi	.44	.05	□□□□□
2203	A1586	22c multi	.44	.05	□□□□□
2204	A1587	22c multi	.44	.05	□□□□□
2205	A1588	22c multi	.44	.05	□□□□□
2206	A1589	22c multi	.44	.05	□□□□□
2207	A1590	22c multi	.44	.05	□□□□□
2208	A1591	22c multi	.44	.05	□□□□□
2209	A1592	22c multi	.44	.05	□□□□□
2209a		Bklt. pane of 5 (#2205-2209)	2.25	.05	□□□□□
2210	A1593	22c multi	.44	.05	□□□□□
2211	A1594	22c multi	.44	.05	□□□□□
2216	A1599a	22c sheet of 9	4.00	—	☑□□□□
2216a		*George Washington*	.44	.20	□□□□□
2216b		*John Adams*	.44	.20	□□□□□
2216c		*Thomas Jefferson*	.44	.20	□□□□□
2216d		*James Madison*	.44	.20	□□□□□
2216e		*James Monroe*	.44	.20	□□□□□
2216f		*John Quincy Adams*	.44	.20	□□□□□
2216g		*Andrew Jackson*	.44	.20	□□□□□
2216h		*Martin Van Buren*	.44	.20	□□□□□
2216i		*William Henry Harrison*	.44	.20	□☑□□□
2217	A1599b	22c sheet of 9	4.00	—	☑□□□□
2217a		*John Tyler*	.44	.20	□□□□□
2217b		*James Knox Polk*	.44	.20	□□□□□
2217c		*Zachary Taylor*	.44	.20	□□□□□
2217d		*Millard Fillmore*	.44	.20	□□□□□
2217e		*Franklin Pierce*	.44	.20	□□□□□
2217f		*James Buchanan*	.44	.20	□□□□□
2217g		*Abraham Lincoln*	.44	.20	□□□□□
2217h		*Andrew Johnson*	.44	.20	□□□□□
2217i		*Ulysses S. Grant*	.44	.20	□□□□□

A1551

A1553

A1554

A1555

A1588

A1560

A1562

A1589

A1566

A1574

A1590

A1577

A1578

A1591

A1614

\ A1615

A1592

A1618

A1599a ✓

A1599b ✓

A1599c ✓

A1599d ✓

A1587   **A1594**   **A1604**

A1600   **A1601**

A1602   **A1603**

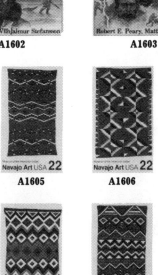

A1605   **A1606**

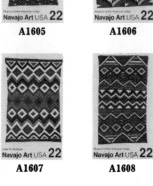

A1607   **A1608**

A1609

A1616

A1593

A1617

A1610

A1611

A1612

A1613

Scott No.	Illus. No.	Description	Unused Price	Used Price	//////
2218	A1599c	22c sheet of 9	4.00	—	☑☐☐☐☐
2218a		*Rutherford B. Hayes*	.44	.20	☐☐☐☐☐
2218b		*James A. Garfield*	.44	.20	☐☐☐☐☐
2218c		*Chester A. Arthur*	.44	.20	☐☐☐☐☐
2218d		*Grover Cleveland*	.44	.20	☐☐☐☐☐
2218e		*Benjamin Harrison*	.44	.20	☐☐☐☐☐
2218f		*William McKinley*	.44	.20	☐☐☐☐☐
2218g		*Theodore Roosevelt*	.44	.20	☐☐☐☐☐
2218h		*William H. Taft*	.44	.20	☐☐☐☐☐
2218i		*Woodrow Wilson*	.44	.20	☐☐☐☐☐
2219	A1599d	22c sheet of 9	4.00	—	☑☐☐☐☐
2219a		*Warren G. Harding*	.44	.20	☐☐☐☐☐
2219b		*Calvin Coolidge*	.44	.20	☐☐☐☐☐
2219c		*Herbert Hoover*	.44	.20	☐☐☐☐☐
2219d		*Franklin D. Roosevelt*	.44	.20	☐☐☐☐☐
2219e		*White House*	.44	.20	☐☐☐☐☐
2219f		*Harry S Truman*	.44	.20	☐☐☐☐☐
2219g		*Dwight D. Eisenhower*	.44	.20	☐☐☐☐☐
2219h		*John F. Kennedy*	.44	.20	☐☐☐☐☐
2219i		*Lyndon B. Johnson*	.44	.20	☐☐☐☐☐
2220	A1600	22c multi	.44	.08	☐☐☐☐☐
2221	A1601	22c multi	.44	.08	☐☐☐☐☐
2222	A1602	22c multi	.44	.08	☐☐☐☐☐
2223	A1603	22c multi	.44	.08	☐☐☐☐☐
2223a		Block of 4, #2220-2223	1.80	1.00	☐☐☐☐☐
2224	A1604	22c scar & dk bl	.44	.05	☐☐☐☐☐

1986-87 Coil stamps *Perf. 10 vertically*

2225	A1604a	1c vio	.05	.05	☐☐☐☐☐
2226	A1604b	2c blk ('87)	.05	.05	☐☐☐☐☐
2228	A1285	4c red brn	.08	.05	☐☐☐☐☐

1986

2235	A1605	22c multi	.44	.08	☐☐☐☐☐
2236	A1606	22c multi	.44	.08	☐☐☐☐☐
2237	A1607	22c multi	.44	.08	☐☐☐☐☐
2238	A1608	22c multi	.44	.08	☐☐☐☐☐
2238a		Block of 4, #2235-2238	1.80	1.00	☐☐☐☐☐
2239	A1609	22c cop red	.44	.05	☐☐☐☐☐
2240	A1610	22c multi	.44	.08	☐☐☐☐☐
2241	A1611	22c multi	.44	.08	☐☐☐☐☐
2242	A1612	22c multi	.44	.08	☐☐☐☐☐
2243	A1613	22c multi	.44	.08	☐☐☐☐☐
2243a		Block of 4, #2240-2243	1.80	1.00	☐☐☐☐☐
2244	A1614	22c multi	.44	.08	☐☐☐☐☐
2245	A1615	22c multi	.44	.08	☐☐☐☐☐

Scott No.	Illus. No.	Description	Unused Price	Used Price	//////
1987					
2246	A1616	22c multi	.44	.05 ☐☐☐☐☐	
2247	A1617	22c multi	.44	.05 ☐☐☐☐☐	
2248	A1618	22c multi	.44	.05 ☐☐☐☐☐	
2249	A1619	22c multi	.44	.05 ☐☐☐☐☐	
2250	A1620	22c multi	.44	.05 ☐☐☐☐☐	
2251	A1621	22c multi	.44	.05 ☐☐☐☐☐	
1987-88	**Coil stamps**	***Perf. 10 vertically***			
2253	A1623	3c ('88)	.06	.05 ☐☐☐☐☐	
2255	A1625	5c blk	.10	.05 ☐☐☐☐☐	
2259	A1629	10c sky bl	.20	.05 ☐☐☐☐☐	
2264	A1634	17.5c dk vio	.35	.05 ☐☐☐☐☐	
1987	***Perf. 10 on 1, 2 or 3 Sides***				
2267	A1637	22c multi	.44	.05 ☐☐☐☐☐	
2268	A1638	22c multi	.44	.05 ☐☐☐☐☐	
2269	A1639	22c multi	.44	.05 ☐☐☐☐☐	
2270	A1640	22c multi	.44	.05 ☐☐☐☐☐	
2271	A1641	22c multi	.44	.05 ☐☐☐☐☐	
2272	A1642	22c multi	.44	.05 ☐☐☐☐☐	
2273	A1643	22c multi	.44	.05 ☐☐☐☐☐	
2274	A1644	22c multi	.44	.05 ☐☐☐☐☐	
2274a		Bklt. pane of 10 (#2268-2271 2273-2274, 2 of each #2267, 2272)	4.50	– ☐☐☐☐☐	
2275	A1645	22c multi	.44	.05 ☐☐☐☐☐	
2276	A1646	22c multi	.44	.05 ☐☐☐☐☐	
2286	A1650	22c Barn swallow	.44	.15 ☐☐☐☐☐	
2287	A1651	22c Monarch butterfly	.44	.15 ☐☐☐☐☐	
2288	A1652	22c Bighorn sheep	.44	.15 ☐☐☐☐☐	
2289	A1653	22c Broad-tailed hummingbird	.44	.15 ☐☐☐☐☐	
2290	A1654	22c Cottontail	.44	.15 ☐☐☐☐☐	
2291	A1655	22c Osprey	.44	.15 ☐☐☐☐☐	
2292	A1656	22c Mountain lion	.44	.15 ☐☐☐☐☐	
2293	A1657	22c Luna moth	.44	.15 ☐☐☐☐☐	
2294	A1658	22c Mule deer	.44	.15 ☐☐☐☐☐	
2295	A1659	22c Gray squirrel	.44	.15 ☐☐☐☐☐	
2296	A1660	22c Armadillo	.44	.15 ☐☐☐☐☐	
2297	A1661	22c Eastern chipmunk	.44	.15 ☐☐☐☐☐	
2298	A1662	22c Moose	.44	.15 ☐☐☐☐☐	
2299	A1663	22c Black bear	.44	.15 ☐☐☐☐☐	
2300	A1664	22c Tiger swallowtail	.44	.15 ☐☐☐☐☐	
2301	A1665	22c Bobwhite	.44	.15 ☐☐☐☐☐	
2302	A1666	22c Ringtail	.44	.15 ☐☐☐☐☐	
2303	A1667	22c Red-winged blackbird	.44	.15 ☐☐☐☐☐	
2304	A1668	22c American lobster	.44	.15 ☐☐☐☐☐	

Scott No.	Illus. No.	Description	Unused Price	Used Price	//////
2305	A1669	22c Black-tailed jack rabbit	.44	.15	☐☐☐☐☐
2306	A1670	22c Scarlet tanager	.44	.15	☐☐☐☐☐
2307	A1671	22c Woodchuck	.44	.15	☐☐☐☐☐
2308	A1672	22c Roseate spoonbill	.44	.15	☐☐☐☐☐
2309	A1673	22c Bald eagle	.44	.15	☐☐☐☐☐
2310	A1674	22c Alaskan brown bear	.44	.15	☐☐☐☐☐
2311	A1675	22c Iiwi	.44	.15	☐☐☐☐☐
2312	A1676	22c Badger	.44	.15	☐☐☐☐☐
2313	A1677	22c Pronghorn	.44	.15	☐☐☐☐☐
2314	A1678	22c River otter	.44	.15	☐☐☐☐☐
2315	A1679	22c Ladybug	.44	.15	☐☐☐☐☐
2316	A1680	22c Beaver	.44	.15	☐☐☐☐☐
2317	A1681	22c White-tailed deer	.44	.15	☐☐☐☐☐
2318	A1682	22c Blue jay	.44	.15	☐☐☐☐☐
2319	A1683	22c Pika	.44	.15	☐☐☐☐☐
2320	A1684	22c Bison	.44	.15	☐☐☐☐☐
2321	A1685	22c Snowy egret	.44	.15	☐☐☐☐☐
2322	A1686	22c Gray wolf	.44	.15	☐☐☐☐☐
2323	A1687	22c Mountain goat	.44	.15	☐☐☐☐☐
2324	A1688	22c Deer mouse	.44	.15	☐☐☐☐☐
2325	A1689	22c Black-tailed prairie dog	.44	.15	☐☐☐☐☐
2326	A1690	22c Box turtle	.44	.15	☐☐☐☐☐
2327	A1691	22c Wolverine	.44	.15	☐☐☐☐☐
2328	A1692	22c American elk	.44	.15	☐☐☐☐☐
2329	A1693	22c California sea lion	.44	.15	☐☐☐☐☐
2330	A1694	22c Mockingbird	.44	.15	☐☐☐☐☐
2331	A1695	22c Raccoon	.44	.15	☐☐☐☐☐
2332	A1696	22c Bobcat	.44	.15	☐☐☐☐☐
2333	A1697	22c Black-footed ferret	.44	.15	☐☐☐☐☐
2334	A1698	22c Canada goose	.44	.15	☐☐☐☐☐
2335	A1699	22c Red fox	.44	.15	☐☐☐☐☐
2335a		Pane of 50 #2268-2335,			

1987-88

Scott No.	Illus. No.	Description	Unused Price	Used Price	//////
2336	A1700	22c multi	.44	.05	☐☐☐☐☐
2337	A1701	22c multi	.44	.05	☐☐☐☐☐
2338	A1702	22c multi	.44	.05	☐☐☐☐☐
2339	A1703	22c multi	.44	.05	☐☐☐☐☐
2340	A1704	22c multi	.44	.05	☐☐☐☐☐
2341	A1705	22c multi	.44	.05	☐☐☐☐☐
2342	A1706	22c multi	.44	.05	☐☐☐☐☐
2349	A1713	22c scar & blk	.44	.05	☐☐☐☐☐
2350	A1714	22c brt grn	.44	.05	☐☐☐☐☐
2351	A1715	22c ultra & wht	.44	.05	☐☐☐☐☐
2352	A1716	22c ultra & wht	.44	.05	☐☐☐☐☐
2353	A1717	22c ultra & wht	.44	.05	☐☐☐☐☐
2354	A1718	22c ultra & wht	.44	.05	☐☐☐☐☐
2354a		Block of 4, #2351-2354	1.80	1.00	☐☐☐☐☐

Scott No.	Illus. No.	Description	Unused Price	Used Price	//////
2355	A1719	22c multi	.44	.08	☐☐☐☐☐
2356	A1720	22c multi	.44	.08	☐☐☐☐☐
2357	A1721	22c multi	.44	.08	☐☐☐☐☐
2358	A1~22	22c multi	.44	.08	☐☐☐☐☐
2359	A1/23	22c multi	.44	.08	☐☐☐☐☐
2359a		Bklt. pane of 5	2.25	–	☐☐☐☐☐
2360	A1724	22c multi	.44	.05	☐☐☐☐☐
2361	A1725	22c multi	.44	.05	☐☐☐☐☐
2362	A1726	22c multi	.44	.08	☐☐☐☐☐
2363	A1727	22c multi	.44	.08	☐☐☐☐☐
2364	A1728	22c multi	.44	.08	☐☐☐☐☐
2365	A1729	22c multi	.44	.08	☐☐☐☐☐
2366	A1730	22c multi	.44	.08	☐☐☐☐☐
2366a		Bklt. pane of 5	2.25	–	☐☐☐☐☐
2367	A1731	22c multi	.44	.05	☐☐☐☐☐

1988

Scott No.	Illus. No.	Description	Unused Price	Used Price	//////
2368	A1732	22c multi	.44	.05	☐☐☐☐☐
2369	A1733	22c multi	.44	.05	☐☐☐☐☐
2370	A1734	22c multi	.44	.05	☐☐☐☐☐
2371	A1735	22c multi	.44	.05	☐☐☐☐☐
2372	A1736	22c multi	.44	.05	☐☐☐☐☐
2373	A1737	22c multi	.44	.05	☐☐☐☐☐
2374	A1738	22c multi	.44	.05	☐☐☐☐☐
2375	A1739	22c multi	.44	.05	☐☐☐☐☐
2375a		Block of 4, #2372-2375			
2376	A1740	22c multi	.44	.05	☐☐☐☐☐
		————————————	–		☐☐☐☐☐
		————————————	–		☐☐☐☐☐
		————————————	–		☐☐☐☐☐
		————————————	–		☐☐☐☐☐
		————————————	–		☐☐☐☐☐
		————————————	–		☐☐☐☐☐
		————————————	–		☐☐☐☐☐
		————————————	–		☐☐☐☐☐
		————————————	–		☐☐☐☐☐
		————————————	–		☐☐☐☐☐
		————————————	–		☐☐☐☐☐
		————————————	–		☐☐☐☐☐
		————————————	–		☐☐☐☐☐

A1619

A1620

A1621

A1637-44

A1623

A1625

A1629

A1634

A1645

A1646

188

A1650-99

Dec 7, 1787   USA
Delaware 22

A1700

Dec 12, 1787
Pennsylvania

A1701

Dec 18, 1787   USA
New Jersey 22

A1702

22
USA
January 2, 1788
Georgia

A1703

January 9, 1788
Connecticut

A1704

Feb 6, 1788
Massachusetts

A1705

April 28, 1788   USA
Maryland 22

A1706

A1713

A1714

A1724

A1725

A1715-1718

A1731

A1733

A1732

The Bicentennial
of the Constitution of
the United States
of America
1787-1987   USA 22

We the people
of the United States,
in order to form
a more perfect Union...
Preamble, U.S. Constitution   USA 22

Establish justice,
insure domestic tranquility,
provide for the common defense,
promote the general welfare...
Preamble, U.S. Constitution   USA 22

And secure
the blessings of liberty
to ourselves
and our posterity...
Preamble, U.S. Constitution   USA 22

Do ordain
and establish this
Constitution for the
United States of America.
Preamble, U.S. Constitution   USA 22

A1719-23

Stourbridge Lion 1829   USA 22

Best Friend of Charleston 1830   USA 22

John Bull 1831   USA 22

Brother Jonathan 1832   USA 22

Gowan & Marx 1839   USA 22

A1726-30

USA 22   Siamese Cat, Exotic Shorthair Cat

USA 22   Abyssinian Cat, Himalayan Cat

USA 22   Maine Coon Cat, Burmese Cat

USA 22   American Shorthair Cat, Persian Cat

A1736-39

A1735 **A1734** **A1740**

Scott No.	Illus. No.	Description	Unused Price	Used Price	//////
					☐☐☐☐☐
					☐☐☐☐☐
					☐☐☐☐☐
					☐☐☐☐☐
					☐☐☐☐☐
					☐☐☐☐☐
					☐☐☐☐☐
					☐☐☐☐☐
					☐☐☐☐☐
					☐☐☐☐☐
					☐☐☐☐☐
					☐☐☐☐☐
					☐☐☐☐☐
					☐☐☐☐☐
					☐☐☐☐☐
					☐☐☐☐☐
					☐☐☐☐☐
					☐☐☐☐☐
					☐☐☐☐☐
					☐☐☐☐☐
					☐☐☐☐☐
					☐☐☐☐☐
					☐☐☐☐☐
					☐☐☐☐☐
					☐☐☐☐☐
					☐☐☐☐☐
					☐☐☐☐☐
					☐☐☐☐☐
					☐☐☐☐☐
					☐☐☐☐☐
					☐☐☐☐☐
					☐☐☐☐☐
					☐☐☐☐☐
					☐☐☐☐☐
					☐☐☐☐☐

AP1

AP2

AP3

AP4

AP5

AP6

AP7

AP8

AP9

AP10

AP11

AP12

AP13

AP14

AP15

AIR POST STAMPS

For prepayment of postage on all mailable matter sent by airmail.

Scott No.	Illus. No.	Description	Unused Price	Used Price	//////
1918					
C1	AP1	6c orange	100.00	45.00	☐☐☐☐☐
C2	AP1	16c green	150.00	52.50	☐☐☐☐☐
C3	AP1	24c carmine rose & blue	145.00	65.00	☐☐☐☐☐
C3a		Center inverted	*120000.00*		☐☐☐☐☐
1923					
C4	AP2	8c dk green	40.00	20.00	☐☐☐☐☐
C5	AP3	16c dk blue	145.00	50.00	☐☐☐☐☐
C6	AP4	24c carmine	165.00	40.00	☐☐☐☐☐
1926-28 *Perf. 11*					
C7	AP5	10c dk blue	4.50	.50	☐☐☐☐☐
C8	AP5	15c olive brown	5.50	2.75	☐☐☐☐☐
C9	AP5	20c yellow green ('27)	14.00	2.25	☐☐☐☐☐
C10	AP6	10c dk blue	11.00.	3.00	☐☐☐☐☐
C10a		Bklt. pane of 3	110.00	*60.00*	☐☐☐☐☐
C11	AP7	5c carmine & blue	6.00	.65	☐☐☐☐☐
C12	AP8	5c violet	15.00	.45	☐☐☐☐☐
1930					
C13	AP9	65c green	450.00	275.00	☐☐☐☐☐
C14	AP10	$1.30 brown	1000.00	550.00	☐☐☐☐☐
C15	AP11	$2.60 blue	1600.00	800.00	☐☐☐☐☐
1931-32 *Perf. 10½x11*					
C16	AP8	5c violet	10.00	.50	☐☐☐☐☐
C17	AP8	8c olive bister ('32)	4.00	.30	☐☐☐☐☐
1933					
C18	AP12	50c green	115.00	90.00	☐☐☐☐☐
1934					
C19	AP8	6c dl orange	4.25	.12	☐☐☐☐☐
1935					
C20	AP13	25c blue	1.50	1.25	☐☐☐☐☐
1937					
C21	AP14	20c green	12.50	2.25	☐☐☐☐☐
C22	AP14	50c carmine	12.00	6.50	☐☐☐☐☐
1938					
C23	AP15	6c dk blue & carmine	.50	.06	☐☐☐☐☐
1939					
C24	AP16	30c dl blue	14.00	1.50	☐☐☐☐☐
1941-44					
C25	AP17	6c carmine	.15	.05	☐☐☐☐☐
C25a		Bklt. pane of 3 ('43)	6.50	*1.00*	☐☐☐☐☐

AP16

AP17

AP19

AP18

AP20

AP21

AP22

AP24

AP23

AP25

AP26

AP27

AP28

AP29

AP30

Scott No.	Illus. No.	Description	Unused Price	Used Price	//////
C26	AP17	8c olive green ('44)	.20	.05	□□□□□
C27	AP17	10c violet	1.65	.20	□□□□□
C28	AP17	15c brown carmine	3.75	.35	□□□□□
C29	AP17	20c bright green	2.75	.30	□□□□□
C30	AP17	30c blue	3.50	.30	□□□□□
C31	AP17	50c orange	16.00	4.00	□□□□□

1946

C32	AP18	5c carmine	.15	.05	□□□□□

1947 *Perf. 10½x11*

C33	AP19	5c carmine	.12	.05	□□□□□
C34	AP20	10c black	.30	.06	□□□□□
C35	AP21	15c bright blue green	.35	.05	□□□□□
C36	AP22	25c blue	1.60	.12	□□□□□

1948 Coil stamp *Perf. 10 horizontally*

C37	AP19	5c carmine	2.00	1.10	□□□□□

1948

C38	AP23	5c bright carmine	.18	.18	□□□□□

1949 *Perf. 10½x11*

C39	AP19	6c carmine	.18	.05	□□□□□
C39a		Bklt. pane of 6	12.00	5.00	□□□□□

1949

C40	AP24	6c carmine	.16	.10	□□□□□

Coil stamp *Perf. 10 horizontally*

C41	AP19	6c carmine	4.50	.05	□□□□□

1949

C42	AP25	10c violet	.35	.35	□□□□□
C43	AP26	15c ultra	.50	.50	□□□□□
C44	AP27	25c rose carmine	.85	.85	□□□□□
C45	AP28	6c magenta	.16	.10	□□□□□

1952-58

C46	AP29	80c bright red violet	11.00	1.50	□□□□□
C47	AP30	6c carmine	.16	.10	□□□□□
C48	AP31	4c bright blue	.12	.08	□□□□□
C49	AP32	6c blue	.16	.10	□□□□□
C50	AP31	5c rose red	.22	.15	□□□□□

Perf. 10½x11

C51	AP33	7c blue	.22	.05	□□□□□
C51a		Bklt. pane of 6	15.00	6.50	□□□□□

Coil stamp *Perf. 10 horizontally*

C52	AP33	7c blue	4.50	.20	□□□□□

1959

C53	AP34	7c dk blue	.25	.12	□□□□□
C54	AP35	7c dk blue & red	.25	.12	□□□□□

AP31

AP32

AP33

AP34

AP35

AP36

AP38

AP37

AP39

AP40

AP42

AP41-Redrawn

AP43

AP44

AP45

AP47

AP46

198

Scott No.	Illus. No.	Description	Unused Price	Used Price	//////
C55	AP36	7c rose red	.25	.12	☐☐☐☐☐
C56	AP37	10c violet blue & bright red	.40	.40	☐☐☐☐☐

1959-66

Scott No.	Illus. No.	Description	Unused Price	Used Price	//////
C57	AP38	10c black & green ('60)	3.00	1.00	☐☐☐☐☐
C58	AP39	15c black & orange	.75	.06	☐☐☐☐☐
C59	AP40	25c black & maroon ('60)	.75	.06	☐☐☐☐☐
C59a		Tagged ('66)	.75	.15	☐☐☐☐☐

Perf. 10½x11

Scott No.	Illus. No.	Description	Unused Price	Used Price	//////
C60	AP33	7c carmine	.30	.05	☐☐☐☐☐
C60a		Bklt. pane of 6	20.00	7.00	☐☐☐☐☐

Coil stamp *Perf. 10 horizontally*

Scott No.	Illus. No.	Description	Unused Price	Used Price	//////
C61	AP33	7c carmine	8.00	.25	☐☐☐☐☐

1961-67

Scott No.	Illus. No.	Description	Unused Price	Used Price	//////
C62	AP38	13c black & red	.65	.10	☐☐☐☐☐
C62a		Tagged ('67)	.80	.25	☐☐☐☐☐
C63	AP41	15c black & orange	.40	.08	☐☐☐☐☐
C63a		Tagged ('67)	.50	.12	☐☐☐☐☐

Perf. 10½x11

Scott No.	Illus. No.	Description	Unused Price	Used Price	//////
C64	AP42	8c carmine	.22	.05	☐☐☐☐☐
C64a		Tagged ('63)	.22	.05	☐☐☐☐☐
C64b		Bklt. pane 5 + label	7.50	1.25	☐☐☐☐☐
C64c		As "b," tagged ('64)	2.25	.50	☐☐☐☐☐

Coil stamp *Perf. 10 horizontally*

Scott No.	Illus. No.	Description	Unused Price	Used Price	//////
C65	AP42	8c carmine	.50	.08	☐☐☐☐☐
C65a		Tagged ('65)	.60	.10	☐☐☐☐☐

1963-67

Scott No.	Illus. No.	Description	Unused Price	Used Price	//////
C66	AP43	15c carmine, dp claret & blue	1.30	.75	☐☐☐☐☐
C67	AP44	6c red	.20	.15	☐☐☐☐☐
C67a		Tagged ('67)	3.00	.50	☐☐☐☐☐
C68	AP45	8c carmine & maroon	.30	.15	☐☐☐☐☐
C69	AP46	8c blue, red & bister	.90	.15	☐☐☐☐☐
C70	AP47	8c brown	.45	.20	☐☐☐☐☐
C71	AP48	20c multi	1.50	.15	☐☐☐☐☐

1968 *Perf. 11x10½*

Scott No.	Illus. No.	Description	Unused Price	Used Price	//////
C72	AP49	10c carmine	.30	.05	☐☐☐☐☐
C72b		Bklt. pane of 8	4.00	.75	☐☐☐☐☐
C72c		Bklt. pane of 5 + label	2.50	.75	☐☐☐☐☐

Coil stamp *Perf. 10 vertically*

Scott No.	Illus. No.	Description	Unused Price	Used Price	//////
C73	AP49	10c carmine	.65	.05	☐☐☐☐☐

1968

Scott No.	Illus. No.	Description	Unused Price	Used Price	//////
C74	AP50	10c blue, black & red	.60	.15	☐☐☐☐☐
C75	AP51	20c red, blue & black	.85	.06	☐☐☐☐☐

AP50

AP48

AP51

AP49

AP52

AP53

AP54

AP55

AP56

AP57

AP58

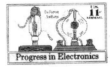

AP59

AP60

AP61

AP62

AP63

AP70

Scott No.	Illus. No.	Description	Unused Price	Used Price	//////
1969					
C76	AP52	10c multi	.30	.15 ☐☐☐☐☐
1971-73					
C77	AP53	9c red	.22	.15 ☐☐☐☐☐
C78	AP54	11c carmine, Perf. 11x10½	.30	.05 ☐☐☐☐☐
C78a		Bklt. pane of 4+2 labels	1.50	.40 ☐☐☐☐☐
C78b		Untagged (Bureau prec.)		.25 ☐☐☐☐☐
C79	AP55	13c carmine ('73)	.32	.10 ☐☐☐☐☐
C79a		Bklt. pane of 5+label ('73)	1.35	.70 ☐☐☐☐☐
C79b		Untagged (Bureau prec.)		.30 ☐☐☐☐☐
C80	AP56	17c bluish blk, red & dk grn	.55	.15 ☐☐☐☐☐
C81	AP51	21c red, blue & black	.55	.10 ☐☐☐☐☐
Coil stamps Perf. 10 vertically					
C82	AP54	11c carmine	.40	.06 ☐☐☐☐☐
C83	AP55	13c carmine ('73)	.40	.10 ☐☐☐☐☐
1972-74					
C84	AP57	11c orange & multi	.30	.15 ☐☐☐☐☐
C85	AP58	11c multi	.30	.15 ☐☐☐☐☐
C86	AP59	11c rose lilac & multi	.30	.15 ☐☐☐☐☐
C87	AP60	18c carmine, black & ultra ('74)	.45	.45 ☐☐☐☐☐
C88	AP61	26c ultra, black & carmine ('74)	.60	.15 ☐☐☐☐☐
1976					
C89	AP62	25c ultra, red & black	.60	.18 ☐☐☐☐☐
C90	AP63	31c ultra, red & black	.62	.10 ☐☐☐☐☐
1978					
C91	AP64	31c ultra & multi	.90	.15 ☐☐☐☐☐
C92	AP65	31c ultra & multi	.90	.15 ☐☐☐☐☐
C92a		Pair, #C91-C92	1.85	.65 ☐☐☐☐☐
1979					
C93	AP66	21c ultra & multi	1.25	.32 ☐☐☐☐☐
C94	AP67	21c ultra & multi	1.25	.32 ☐☐☐☐☐
C94a		Pair, #C93-C94	2.60	.75 ☐☐☐☐☐
C95	AP68	25c ultra & multi	1.50	.35 ☐☐☐☐☐
C96	AP69	25c ultra & multi	1.50	.35 ☐☐☐☐☐
C96a		Pair, #C95-C96	3.10	.85 ☐☐☐☐☐
C97	AP70	31c multi	.90	.30 ☐☐☐☐☐
1980					
C98	AP71	40c multi	.90	.30 ☐☐☐☐☐
C98a		Perf. 10½x11	2.00	– ☐☐☐☐☐
C99	AP72	28c multi	.70	.15 ☐☐☐☐☐
C100	AP73	35c multi	.75	.15 ☐☐☐☐☐
1983					
C101	AP74	28c multi	.56	.28 ☐☐☐☐☐
C102	AP75	28c multi	.56	.28 ☐☐☐☐☐

AP64

AP66

AP68

AP71

AP65

AP67

AP69

AP72

AP73

AP74

AP75

AP76

AP77

Scott No.	Illus. No.	Description	Unused Price	Used Price	//////
C103	AP76	28c multi	.56	.28	☐☐☐☐☐
C104	AP77	28c multi	.56	.28	☐☐☐☐☐
C104a		Block of 4, #C101-C104	2.75	1.75	☐☐☐☐☐
C105	AP78	40c multi	.80	.40	☐☐☐☐☐
C106	AP79	40c multi	.80	.40	☐☐☐☐☐
C107	AP80	40c multi	.80	.40	☐☐☐☐☐
C108	AP81	40c multi	.80	.40	☐☐☐☐☐
C108a		Block of 4, #C105-C108	3.75	2.00	☐☐☐☐☐
C109	AP82	35c multi	.70	.35	☐☐☐☐☐
C110	AP83	35c multi	.70	.35	☐☐☐☐☐
C111	AP84	35c multi	.70	.35	☐☐☐☐☐
C112	AP85	35c multi	.70	.35	☐☐☐☐☐
C112a		Block of 4, #C109-C112	3.25	1.85	☐☐☐☐☐

1985

Scott No.	Illus. No.	Description	Unused Price	Used Price	//////
C113	AP86	33c multi	.66	.20	☐☐☐☐☐
C114	AP87	39c multi	.78	.20	☐☐☐☐☐
C115	AP88	44c multi	.88	.20	☐☐☐☐☐
C116	AP89	44c multi	1.00	.20	☐☐☐☐☐

1988

Scott No.	Illus. No.	Description	Unused Price	Used Price	//////
C117	AP90	44c multi	.88	.20	☐☐☐☐☐
		_____			☐☐☐☐☐
		_____			☐☐☐☐☐
		_____			☐☐☐☐☐
		_____			☐☐☐☐☐
		_____			☐☐☐☐☐
		_____			☐☐☐☐☐
		_____			☐☐☐☐☐
		_____			☐☐☐☐☐
		_____			☐☐☐☐☐
		_____			☐☐☐☐☐
		_____			☐☐☐☐☐
		_____			☐☐☐☐☐
		_____			☐☐☐☐☐
		_____			☐☐☐☐☐
		_____			☐☐☐☐☐
		_____			☐☐☐☐☐
		_____			☐☐☐☐☐
		_____			☐☐☐☐☐
		_____			☐☐☐☐☐

AP78

AP79

AP80

AP81

AP82

AP83

AP84

AP85

AP86

AP87

AP88

AP89

AP90

Scott No.	Illus. No.	Description	Unused Price	Used Price	//////
					☐☐☐☐☐
					☐☐☐☐☐
					☐☐☐☐☐
					☐☐☐☐☐
					☐☐☐☐☐
					☐☐☐☐☐
					☐☐☐☐☐
					☐☐☐☐☐
					☐☐☐☐☐
					☐☐☐☐☐
					☐☐☐☐☐
					☐☐☐☐☐
					☐☐☐☐☐
					☐☐☐☐☐
					☐☐☐☐☐
					☐☐☐☐☐
					☐☐☐☐☐
					☐☐☐☐☐
					☐☐☐☐☐
					☐☐☐☐☐
					☐☐☐☐☐
					☐☐☐☐☐
					☐☐☐☐☐
					☐☐☐☐☐
					☐☐☐☐☐
					☐☐☐☐☐
					☐☐☐☐☐
					☐☐☐☐☐
					☐☐☐☐☐
					☐☐☐☐☐
					☐☐☐☐☐
					☐☐☐☐☐

ASPD1

SD1

SD2

SD3

SD4

SD5

SD6

SD7

SD8

SD9

HOW TO USE THIS BOOK

The number in the first column is its Scott number or identifying number. The letter and number that come next (A41) indicate the design and refer to the illustration so designated. Following that is the denomination of the stamp and its color. Finally, the price, unused and used is shown.

Scott No.	Illus. No.	Description	Unused Price	Used Price	/ / / / / /

AIR POSTAGE SPECIAL DELIVERY

1934

Scott No.	Illus. No.	Description	Unused Price	Used Price	/ / / / / /
CE1	APSD1	16c dk blue	.75	.85	☐☐☐☐☐
CE2	APSD1	16c red & blue	.40	.25	☐☐☐☐☐

SPECIAL DELIVERY STAMPS

1885-93

Scott No.	Illus. No.	Description	Unused Price	Used Price	/ / / / / /
E1	SD1	10c blue	275.00	30.00	☐☐☐☐☐
E2	SD2	10c blue	275.00	7.50	☐☐☐☐☐
E3	SD2	10c orange	175.00	14.00	☐☐☐☐☐

1894   Line under "Ten Cents"

Scott No.	Illus. No.	Description	Unused Price	Used Price	/ / / / / /
E4	SD3	10c blue	750.00	17.50	☐☐☐☐☐

1895   Watermark 191

Scott No.	Illus. No.	Description	Unused Price	Used Price	/ / / / / /
E5	SD3	10c blue	135.00	2.50	☐☐☐☐☐

1902

Scott No.	Illus. No.	Description	Unused Price	Used Price	/ / / / / /
E6	SD4	10c ultra	90.00	2.50	☐☐☐☐☐

1908

Scott No.	Illus. No.	Description	Unused Price	Used Price	/ / / / / /
E7	SD5	10c green	60.00	27.50	☐☐☐☐☐

1911   Watermark 190   *Perf. 12*

Scott No.	Illus. No.	Description	Unused Price	Used Price	/ / / / / /
E8	SD4	10c ultra	90.00	4.00	☐☐☐☐☐

1914   *Perf. 10*

Scott No.	Illus. No.	Description	Unused Price	Used Price	/ / / / / /
E9	SD4	10c ultra	175.00	5.25	☐☐☐☐☐

1916   Unwatermarked   *Perf. 10*

Scott No.	Illus. No.	Description	Unused Price	Used Price	/ / / / / /
E10	SD4	10c pale ultra	325.00	21.00	☐☐☐☐☐

1917-25   *Perf. 11*

Scott No.	Illus. No.	Description	Unused Price	Used Price	/ / / / / /
E11	SD4	10c ultra	15.00	.30	☐☐☐☐☐
E12	SD6	10c gray violet	22.50	.15	☐☐☐☐☐
E13	SD6	15c dp orange	24.00	.65	☐☐☐☐☐
E14	SD7	20c black	3.00	1.75	☐☐☐☐☐

1927-51   *Perf. 11x10½*

Scott No.	Illus. No.	Description	Unused Price	Used Price	/ / / / / /
E15	SD6	10c gray violet	.70	.05	☐☐☐☐☐
E16	SD6	15c orange	.80	.08	☐☐☐☐☐
E17	SD6	13c blue	.65	.06	☐☐☐☐☐
E18	SD6	17c orange yellow	5.00	2.25	☐☐☐☐☐
E19	SD7	20c black	2.00	.12	☐☐☐☐☐

1954-57

Scott No.	Illus. No.	Description	Unused Price	Used Price	/ / / / / /
E20	SD8	20c dp blue	.60	.08	☐☐☐☐☐
E21	SD8	30c lake ('57)	.90	.05	☐☐☐☐☐

1969-71

Scott No.	Illus. No.	Description	Unused Price	Used Price	/ / / / / /
E22	SD9	45c carmine & violet blue	2.25	.20	☐☐☐☐☐
E23	SD9	60c violet blue & car ('71)	1.20	.12	☐☐☐☐☐

RS1   CM1

Scott No.	Illus. No.	Description	Unused Price	Used Price	//////

REGISTRATION STAMP, CERTIFIED MAIL STAMP

1911 Watermark 190 Engraved

F1	RS1	10c ultra	75.00	4.50	☐☐☐☐☐

1955

FA1	CM1	15c red	.50	.30	☐☐☐☐☐

D1   D2   D3   D4   D5

Scott No.	Illus. No.	Description	Unused Price	Used Price	//////

POSTAGE DUE STAMPS

1879 *Perf. 12*

J1	D1	1c brown	30.00	5.00	☐☐☐☐☐
J2	D1	2c brown	175.00	4.00	☐☐☐☐☐
J3	D1	3c brown	20.00	2.50	☐☐☐☐☐
J4	D1	5c brown	275.00	25.00	☐☐☐☐☐
J5	D1	10c brown	325.00	12.50	☐☐☐☐☐
J6	D1	30c brown	165.00	20.00	☐☐☐☐☐
J7	D1	50c brown	210.00	30.00	☐☐☐☐☐

1879 Special printing

J8	D1	1c dp brown	*5750.00*		☐☐☐☐☐
J9	D1	2c dp brown	*3750.00*		☐☐☐☐☐
J10	D1	3c dp brown	*3500.00*		☐☐☐☐☐
J11	D1	5c dp brown	*3000.00*		☐☐☐☐☐
J12	D1	10c dp brown	*1850.00*		☐☐☐☐☐
J13	D1	30c dp brown	*1850.00*		☐☐☐☐☐
J14	D1	50c dp brown	*2000.00*		☐☐☐☐☐

Scott No.	Illus. No.	Description	Unused Price	Used Price	//////
1884-89					
J15	D1	1c red brown	25.00	2.50	☐☐☐☐☐
J16	D1	2c red brown	32.50	2.50	☐☐☐☐☐
J17	D1	3c red brown	475.00	100.00	☐☐☐☐☐
J18	D1	5c red brown	225.00	12.50	☐☐☐☐☐
J19	D1	10c red brown ('87)	185.00	7.00	☐☐☐☐☐
J20	D1	30c red brown	95.00	22.50	☐☐☐☐☐
J21	D1	50c red brown	900.00	125.00	☐☐☐☐☐
1891-93					
J22	D1	1c bright claret	10.00	.50	☐☐☐☐☐
J23	D1	2c bright claret	12.50	.45	☐☐☐☐☐
J24	D1	3c bright claret	27.50	4.00	☐☐☐☐☐
J25	D1	5c bright claret	30.00	4.00	☐☐☐☐☐
J26	D1	10c bright claret	60.00	10.00	☐☐☐☐☐
J27	D1	30c bright claret	225.00	85.00	☐☐☐☐☐
J28	D1	50c bright claret	250.00	85.00	☐☐☐☐☐
1894					
J29	D2	1c vermilion	500.00	100.00	☐☐☐☐☐
J30	D2	2c vermilion	225.00	50.00	☐☐☐☐☐
J31	D2	1c dp claret	17.50	3.00	☐☐☐☐☐
J32	D2	2c dp claret	15.00	1.75	☐☐☐☐☐
J33	D2	3c dp claret	75.00	20.00	☐☐☐☐☐
J34	D2	5c dp claret	80.00	22.50	☐☐☐☐☐
J35	D2	10c dp claret	85.00	17.50	☐☐☐☐☐
J36	D2	30c dp claret	185.00	50.00	☐☐☐☐☐
J36a		30c carmine	185.00	45.00	☐☐☐☐☐
J36b		30c pale rose	175.00	45.00	☐☐☐☐☐
J37	D2	50c dp claret	450.00	120.00	☐☐☐☐☐
J37a		50c pale rose	425.00	100.00	☐☐☐☐☐
1895 Watermark 191					
J38	D2	1c dp claret	5.00	.30	☐☐☐☐☐
J39	D2	2c dp claret	5.00	.20	☐☐☐☐☐
J40	D2	3c dp claret	32.50	1.00	☐☐☐☐☐
J41	D2	5c dp claret	35.00	1.00	☐☐☐☐☐
J42	D2	10c dp claret	37.50	2.00	☐☐☐☐☐
J43	D2	30c dp claret	250.00	22.50	☐☐☐☐☐
J44	D2	50c dp claret	185.00	20.00	☐☐☐☐☐
1910-12 Watermark 190					
J45	D2	1c dp claret	17.50	2.00	☐☐☐☐☐
J45a		1c rose carmine	16.00	1.75	☐☐☐☐☐
J46	D2	2c dp claret	17.50	.15	☐☐☐☐☐
J46a		2c rose carmine	16.00	.15	☐☐☐☐☐
J47	D2	3c dp claret	325.00	17.50	☐☐☐☐☐
J48	D2	5c dp claret	55.00	3.50	☐☐☐☐☐
J49	D2	10c dp claret	70.00	7.50	☐☐☐☐☐
J50	D2	50c dp claret ('12)	575.00	75.00	☐☐☐☐☐

Scott No.	Illus. No.	Description	Unused Price	Used Price	//////
1914-15	*Perf. 10*				
J52	D2	1c carmine lake	35.00	7.50 ☐☐☐☐☐	
J53	D2	2c carmine lake	27.50	.20 ☐☐☐☐☐	
J53a		2c dl rose	27.50	.20 ☐☐☐☐☐	
J53b		2c vermilion	27.50	.20 ☐☐☐☐☐	
J54	D2	3c carmine lake	375.00	20.00 ☐☐☐☐☐	
J55	D2	5c carmine lake	22.50	1.50 ☐☐☐☐☐	
J56	D2	10c carmine lake	37.50	1.00 ☐☐☐☐☐	
J56a		10c dl rose	35.00	1.00 ☐☐☐☐☐	
J57	D2	30c carmine lake	125.00	12.00 ☐☐☐☐☐	
J58	D2	50c carmine lake	*5000.00*	375.00 ☐☐☐☐☐	
1916	*Perf. 10*	**Unwatermarked**			
J59	D2	1c rose	900.00	150.00 ☐☐☐☐☐	
J60	D2	2c rose	80.00	8.00 ☐☐☐☐☐	
1917	**Perf. 11**				
J61	D2	1c carmine rose	1.75	.08 ☐☐☐☐☐	
J62	D2	2c carmine rose	1.50	.05 ☐☐☐☐☐	
J63	D2	3c carmine rose	8.50	.08 ☐☐☐☐☐	
J63a		3c rose red	8.50	.07 ☐☐☐☐☐	
J63b		3c dp claret	8.50	.25 ☐☐☐☐☐	
J64	D2	5c carmine	8.50	.08 ☐☐☐☐☐	
J64a		5c rose red	8.50	.08 ☐☐☐☐☐	
J64b		5c dp claret	8.50	.05 ☐☐☐☐☐	
J65	D2	10c carmine rose	12.50	.20 ☐☐☐☐☐	
J65a		10c rose red	12.50	.06 ☐☐☐☐☐	
J65b		10c dp claret	12.50	.06 ☐☐☐☐☐	
J66	D2	30c carmine rose	55.00	.40 ☐☐☐☐☐	
J66a		30c dp claret	55.00	.40 ☐☐☐☐☐	
J67	D2	50c carmine rose	70.00	.12 ☐☐☐☐☐	
J68	D2	½c dl red	.50	.06 ☐☐☐☐☐	
1930-31	*Perf. 11*				
J69	D3	½c carmine	3.50	.70 ☐☐☐☐☐	
J70	D3	1c carmine	2.50	.15 ☐☐☐☐☐	
J71	D3	2c carmine	3.50	.15 ☐☐☐☐☐	
J72	D3	3c carmine	27.50	1.00 ☐☐☐☐☐	
J73	D3	5c carmine	22.50	1.50 ☐☐☐☐☐	
J74	D3	10c carmine	47.50	.50 ☐☐☐☐☐	
J75	D3	30c carmine	125.00	1.00 ☐☐☐☐☐	
J76	D3	50c carmine	160.00	.30 ☐☐☐☐☐	
J77	D4	$1 carmine	30.00	.06 ☐☐☐☐☐	
J77a		$1 scarlet	25.00	.06 ☐☐☐☐☐	
J78	D4	$5 carmine	40.00	.12 ☐☐☐☐☐	
J78a		$5 scarlet	35.00	.12 ☐☐☐☐☐	

Scott No.	Illus. No.	Description	Unused Price	Used Price	//////
1931-56		*Perf. 11x10½, 10½x11*			
J79	D3	½c dl carmine	1.25	.08	☐☐☐☐☐
J80	D3	1c dl carmine	.15	.05	☐☐☐☐☐
J81	D3	2c dl carmine	.15	.05	☐☐☐☐☐
J82	D3	3c dl carmine	.25	.05	☐☐☐☐☐
J83	D3	5c dl carmine	.35	.05	☐☐☐☐☐
J84	D3	10c dl carmine	1.10	.05	☐☐☐☐☐
J85	D3	30c dl carmine	8.50	.08	☐☐☐☐☐
J86	D3	50c dl carmine	9.50	.06	☐☐☐☐☐
J87	D4	$1 scarlet ('56)	40.00	.20	☐☐☐☐☐
1959					
J88	D5	½c carmine rose	1.25	.85	☐☐☐☐☐
J89	D5	1c carmine rose	.05	.05	☐☐☐☐☐
J90	D5	2c carmine rose	.06	.05	☐☐☐☐☐
J91	D5	3c carmine rose	.07	.05	☐☐☐☐☐
J92	D5	4c carmine rose	.08	.05	☐☐☐☐☐
J93	D5	5c carmine rose	.10	.05	☐☐☐☐☐
J94	D5	6c carmine rose	.12	.05	☐☐☐☐☐
J95	D5	7c carmine rose	.14	.06	☐☐☐☐☐
J96	D5	8c carmine rose	.16	.05	☐☐☐☐☐
J97	D5	10c carmine rose	.20	.05	☐☐☐☐☐
J98	D5	30c carmine rose	.70	.05	☐☐☐☐☐
J99	D5	50c carmine rose	1.10	.05	☐☐☐☐☐
J100	D5	$1 carmine rose	2.00	.05	☐☐☐☐☐
J101	D5	$5 carmine rose	8.00	.15	☐☐☐☐☐
1978					
J102	D5	11c carmine rose	.22	.05	☐☐☐☐☐
J103	D5	13c carmine rose	.26	.05	☐☐☐☐☐
1985					
J104	D5	17c carmine rose	.34	.05	☐☐☐☐☐
		_____	___		☐☐☐☐☐
		_____	___		☐☐☐☐☐
		_____	___		☐☐☐☐☐
		_____	___		☐☐☐☐☐
		_____	___		☐☐☐☐☐
		_____	___		☐☐☐☐☐
		_____	___		☐☐☐☐☐
		_____	___		☐☐☐☐☐
		_____	___		☐☐☐☐☐
		_____	___		☐☐☐☐☐

Scott No.	Illus. No.	Description	Unused Price	Used Price	//////
					☐☐☐☐☐
					☐☐☐☐☐
					☐☐☐☐☐
					☐☐☐☐☐
					☐☐☐☐☐
					☐☐☐☐☐
					☐☐☐☐☐
					☐☐☐☐☐
					☐☐☐☐☐
					☐☐☐☐☐
					☐☐☐☐☐
					☐☐☐☐☐
					☐☐☐☐☐
					☐☐☐☐☐
					☐☐☐☐☐
					☐☐☐☐☐
					☐☐☐☐☐
					☐☐☐☐☐
					☐☐☐☐☐
					☐☐☐☐☐
					☐☐☐☐☐
					☐☐☐☐☐
					☐☐☐☐☐
					☐☐☐☐☐
					☐☐☐☐☐
					☐☐☐☐☐
					☐☐☐☐☐
					☐☐☐☐☐
					☐☐☐☐☐
					☐☐☐☐☐
					☐☐☐☐☐
					☐☐☐☐☐
					☐☐☐☐☐

Scott No.	Illus. No.	Description	Unused Price	Used Price	//////

U.S. OFFICES IN CHINA
1919

Scott No.	Illus. No.	Description	Unused Price	Used Price	//////
K1	A140	2c on 1c green	20.00	22.50	☐☐☐☐☐
K2	A140	4c on 2c rose	20.00	22.50	☐☐☐☐☐
K3	A140	6c on 3c violet	37.50	50.00	☐☐☐☐☐
K4	A140	8c on 4c brown	45.00	50.00	☐☐☐☐☐
K5	A140	10c on 5c blue	50.00	57.50	☐☐☐☐☐
K6	A410	12c on 6c red orange	60.00	72.50	☐☐☐☐☐
K7	A140	14c on 7c black	65.00	80.00	☐☐☐☐☐
K8	A148	16c on 8c olive bister	50.00	55.00	☐☐☐☐☐
K8a		16c on 8c olive green	45.00	47.50	☐☐☐☐☐
K9	A148	18c on 9c salmon red	50.00	60.00	☐☐☐☐☐
K10	A148	20c on 10c orange yellow	45.00	52.50	☐☐☐☐☐
K11	A148	24c on 12c brown carmine	52.50	62.50	☐☐☐☐☐
K12	A148	30c on 15c gray	65.00	80.00	☐☐☐☐☐
K13	A148	40c on 20c dp ultra	100.00	125.00	☐☐☐☐☐
K14	A148	60c on 30c orange red	90.00	110.00	☐☐☐☐☐
K15	A148	$1 on 50c lt violet	600.00	500.00	☐☐☐☐☐
K16	A148	$2 on $1 violet brown	425.00	425.00	☐☐☐☐☐

SHANGHAI

Nos. 498 and 528B
Surcharged

2 Cts.

1922

CHINA

Scott No.	Illus. No.	Description	Unused Price	Used Price	//////
K17	A140	2c on 1c green	90.00	75.00	☐☐☐☐☐
K18	A140	4c on 2c carmine, Type VII	80.00	70.00	☐☐☐☐☐

| | 01 | 06 | 08 | 011 | O12 |

Scott No.	Illus. No.	Description	Unused Price	Used Price	//////

OFFICIAL STAMPS
1873 DEPT. OF AGRICULTURE

Scott No.	Illus. No.	Description	Unused Price	Used Price	//////
O1	O1	1c yellow	60.00	30.00	☐☐☐☐☐
O2	O1	2c yellow	42.50	13.50	☐☐☐☐☐
O3	O1	3c yellow	35.00	3.50	☐☐☐☐☐
O4	O1	6c yellow	45.00	12.50	☐☐☐☐☐
O5	O1	10c yellow	100.00	47.50	☐☐☐☐☐
O6	O1	12c yellow	130.00	70.00	☐☐☐☐☐
O7	O1	15c yellow	100.00	47.50	☐☐☐☐☐
O8	O1	24c yellow	115.00	55.00	☐☐☐☐☐
O9	O1	30c yellow	150.00	85.00	☐☐☐☐☐

EXECUTIVE DEPT.

Scott No.	Illus. No.	Description	Unused Price	Used Price	//////
O10	O1	1c carmine	225.00	85.00	☐☐☐☐☐
O11	O1	2c carmine	150.00	70.00	☐☐☐☐☐
O12	O1	3c carmine	175.00	65.00	☐☐☐☐☐
O12a	O1	3c violet rose	150.00	65.00	☐☐☐☐☐
O13	O1	6c carmine	275.00	140.00	☐☐☐☐☐
O14	O1	10c carmine	250.00	150.00	☐☐☐☐☐

DEPT. OF THE INTERIOR

Scott No.	Illus. No.	Description	Unused Price	Used Price	//////
O15	O1	1c vermilion	17.50	3.50	☐☐☐☐☐
O16	O1	2c vermilion	15.00	2.00	☐☐☐☐☐
O17	O1	3c vermilion	22.50	2.00	☐☐☐☐☐
O18	O1	6c vermilion	17.50	2.00	☐☐☐☐☐
O19	O1	10c vermilion	16.00	5.00	☐☐☐☐☐
O20	O1	12c vermilion	25.00	4.00	☐☐☐☐☐
O21	O1	15c vermilion	40.00	10.00	☐☐☐☐☐
O22	O1	24c vermilion	30.00	7.00	☐☐☐☐☐
O23	O1	30c vermilion	40.00	8.00	☐☐☐☐☐
O24	O1	90c vermilion	90.00	15.00	☐☐☐☐☐

DEPT. OF JUSTICE

Scott No.	Illus. No.	Description	Unused Price	Used Price	//////
O25	O1	1c purple	40.00	17.50	☐☐☐☐☐
O26	O1	2c purple	60.00	20.00	☐☐☐☐☐
O27	O1	3c purple	60.00	8.00	☐☐☐☐☐
O28	O1	6c purple	55.00	11.00	☐☐☐☐☐
O29	O1	10c purple	65.00	25.00	☐☐☐☐☐

Scott No.	Illus. No.	Description	Unused Price	Used Price	//////
O30	O1	12c purple	47.50	14.00	☐☐☐☐☐
O31	O1	15c purple	100.00	47.50	☐☐☐☐☐
O32	O1	24c purple	275.00	120.00	☐☐☐☐☐
O33	O1	30c purple	250.00	85.00	☐☐☐☐☐
O34	O1	90c purple	375.00	175.00	☐☐☐☐☐

NAVY DEPT.

Scott No.	Illus. No.	Description	Unused Price	Used Price	//////
O35	O1	1c ultra	32.50	10.00	☐☐☐☐☐
O36	O1	2c ultra	22.50	9.00	☐☐☐☐☐
O37	O1	3c ultra	25.00	4.00	☐☐☐☐☐
O38	O1	6c ultra	22.50	6.00	☐☐☐☐☐
O39	O1	7c ultra	150.00	65.00	☐☐☐☐☐
O40	O1	10c ultra	32.50	11.00	☐☐☐☐☐
O41	O1	12c ultra	42.50	10.00	☐☐☐☐☐
O42	O1	15c ultra	75.00	25.00	☐☐☐☐☐
O43	O1	24c ultra	75.00	30.00	☐☐☐☐☐
O44	O1	30c ultra	60.00	15.00	☐☐☐☐☐
O45	O1	90c ultra	275.00	80.00	☐☐☐☐☐

POST OFFICE DEPT.

Scott No.	Illus. No.	Description	Unused Price	Used Price	//////
O47	O6	1c black	7.25	3.00	☐☐☐☐☐
O48	O6	2c black	7.00	2.50	☐☐☐☐☐
O49	O6	3c black	2.50	.75	☐☐☐☐☐
O50	O6	6c black	8.00	1.65	☐☐☐☐☐
O51	O6	10c black	37.50	16.50	☐☐☐☐☐
O52	O6	12c black	22.50	5.00	☐☐☐☐☐
O53	O6	15c black	25.00	8.50	☐☐☐☐☐
O54	O6	24c black	32.50	10.00	☐☐☐☐☐
O55	O6	30c black	32.50	9.00	☐☐☐☐☐
O56	O6	90c black	47.50	12.50	☐☐☐☐☐

DEPT. OF STATE

Scott No.	Illus. No.	Description	Unused Price	Used Price	//////
O57	O1	1c dk green	42.50	13.00	☐☐☐☐☐
O58	O1	2c dk green	85.00	25.00	☐☐☐☐☐
O59	O1	3c bright green	35.00	9.00	☐☐☐☐☐
O60	O1	6c bright green	32.50	9.00	☐☐☐☐☐
O61	O1	7c dk green	60.00	18.50	☐☐☐☐☐
O62	O1	10c dk green	47.50	15.00	☐☐☐☐☐
O63	O1	12c dk green	75.00	27.50	☐☐☐☐☐
O64	O1	15c dk green	67.50	20.00	☐☐☐☐☐
O65	O1	24c dk green	165.00	75.00	☐☐☐☐☐
O66	O1	30c dk green	150.00	60.00	☐☐☐☐☐
O67	O1	90c dk green	300.00	125.00	☐☐☐☐☐
O68	O8	$2 green & black	550.00	250.00	☐☐☐☐☐
O69	O8	$5 green & black	4250.00	2000.00	☐☐☐☐☐
O70	O8	$10 green & black	2750.00	1300.00	☐☐☐☐☐
O71	O8	$20 green & black	2250.00	1100.00	☐☐☐☐☐

Scott No.	Illus. No.	Description	Unused Price	Used Price	//////
TREASURY DEPT.					
O72	O1	1c brown	17.50	1.75	☐☐☐☐☐
O73	O1	2c brown	20.00	1.75	☐☐☐☐☐
O74	O1	3c brown	12.50	1.00	☐☐☐☐☐
O75	O1	6c brown	17.50	1.00	☐☐☐☐☐
O76	O1	7c brown	42.50	12.50	☐☐☐☐☐
O77	O1	10c brown	42.50	4.50	☐☐☐☐☐
O78	O1	12c brown	42.50	3.00	☐☐☐☐☐
O79	O1	15c brown	37.50	4.50	☐☐☐☐☐
O80	O1	24c brown	175.00	60.00	☐☐☐☐☐
O81	O1	30c brown	60.00	5.00	☐☐☐☐☐
O82	O1	90c brown	65.00	5.00	☐☐☐☐☐
WAR DEPT.					
O83	O1	1c rose	57.50	4.00	☐☐☐☐☐
O84	O1	2c rose	52.50	6.00	☐☐☐☐☐
O85	O1	3c rose	47.50	1.50	☐☐☐☐☐
O86	O1	6c rose	225.00	4.00	☐☐☐☐☐
O87	O1	7c rose	52.50	30.00	☐☐☐☐☐
O88	O1	10c rose	18.00	5.00	☐☐☐☐☐
O89	O1	12c rose	50.00	4.00	☐☐☐☐☐
O90	O1	15c rose	15.00	2.50	☐☐☐☐☐
O91	O1	24c rose	15.00	3.00	☐☐☐☐☐
O92	O1	30c rose	17.50	2.50	☐☐☐☐☐
O93	O1	90c rose	40.00	12.50	☐☐☐☐☐
1879	**DEPT. OF AGRICULTURE**				
O94	O1	1c yellow	1350.00		☐☐☐☐☐
O95	O1	3c yellow	175.00	37.50	☐☐☐☐☐
DEPT. OF THE INTERIOR					
O96	O1	1c vermilion	125.00	65.00	☐☐☐☐☐
O97	O1	2c vermilion	2.50	.75	☐☐☐☐☐
O98	O1	3c vermilion	2.00	.60	☐☐☐☐☐
O99	O1	6c vermilion	3.00	1.00	☐☐☐☐☐
O100	O1	10c vermilion	32.50	17.50	☐☐☐☐☐
O101	O1	12c vermilion	65.00	30.00	☐☐☐☐☐
O102	O1	15c vermilion	150.00	70.00	☐☐☐☐☐
O103	O1	24c vermilion	1100.00		☐☐☐☐☐
DEPT. OF JUSTICE					
O106	O1	3c bluish purple	45.00	17.50	☐☐☐☐☐
O107	O1	6c bluish purple	100.00	60.00	☐☐☐☐☐
POST OFFICE DEPT.					
O108	O6	3c black	8.50	1.40	☐☐☐☐☐
TREASURY DEPT.					
O109	O1	3c brown	25.00	3.50	☐☐☐☐☐
O110	O1	6c brown	45.00	17.50	☐☐☐☐☐
O111	O1	10c brown	60.00	15.00	☐☐☐☐☐

Scott No.	Illus. No.	Description	Unused Price	Used Price	//////
O112	O1	30c brown	700.00	135.00	☐☐☐☐☐
O113	O1	90c brown	725.00	135.00	☐☐☐☐☐

WAR DEPT.

Scott No.	Illus. No.	Description	Unused Price	Used Price	//////
O114	O1	1c rose red	2.00	.75	☐☐☐☐☐
O115	O1	2c rose red	3.00	1.00	☐☐☐☐☐
O116	O1	3c rose red	3.00	.65	☐☐☐☐☐
O117	O1	6c rose red	2.50	.70	☐☐☐☐☐
O118	O1	10c rose red	20.00	6.00	☐☐☐☐☐
O119	O1	12c rose red	15.00	3.00	☐☐☐☐☐
O120	O1	30c rose red	47.50	25.00	☐☐☐☐☐

OFFICIAL POSTAL SAVINGS MAIL

1911 Watermark 191

Scott No.	Illus. No.	Description	Unused Price	Used Price	//////
O121	O11	2c black	9.00	1.10	☐☐☐☐☐
O122	O11	50c dk green	110.00	32.50	☐☐☐☐☐
O123	O11	$1 ultra	100.00	9.50	☐☐☐☐☐

Watermark 190

Scott No.	Illus. No.	Description	Unused Price	Used Price	//////
O124	O11	1c dk violet	4.00	1.00	☐☐☐☐☐
O125	O11	2c black	30.00	3.50	☐☐☐☐☐
O126	O11	10c carmine	8.50	1.00	☐☐☐☐☐

1983-85

Scott No.	Illus. No.	Description	Unused Price	Used Price	//////
O127	O12	1c red, blue & black	.05	—	☐☐☐☐☐
O128	O12	4c red, blue & black	.08	—	☐☐☐☐☐
O129	O12	13c red, blue & black	.26	—	☐☐☐☐☐
O129A	O12	14c red, blue & black ('85)	.28	—	☐☐☐☐☐
O130	O12	17c red, blue & black	.34	—	☐☐☐☐☐
O132	O12	$1 red, blue & black	2.00	—	☐☐☐☐☐
O133	O12	$5 red, blue & black	10.00	—	☐☐☐☐☐

Coil stamps *Perf. 10 vertically*

Scott No.	Illus. No.	Description	Unused Price	Used Price	//////
O135	O12	20c red, blue & black	1.00	.40	☐☐☐☐☐
O136	O12	22c red, blue & black ('85)	.44	—	☐☐☐☐☐

1985

Scott No.	Illus. No.	Description	Unused Price	Used Price	//////
O138	O12	(14c) red, blue & black	3.50	—	☐☐☐☐☐

Coil stamp *Perf. 10 vertically*

Scott No.	Illus. No.	Description	Unused Price	Used Price	//////
O139	O12	(22c) red, blue & black	4.50	—	☐☐☐☐☐

Scott No.	Illus. No.	Description	Unused Price	Used Price	//////
					☐☐☐☐☐
					☐☐☐☐☐
					☐☐☐☐☐
					☐☐☐☐☐
					☐☐☐☐☐
					☐☐☐☐☐
					☐☐☐☐☐
					☐☐☐☐☐
					☐☐☐☐☐
					☐☐☐☐☐
					☐☐☐☐☐
					☐☐☐☐☐
					☐☐☐☐☐
					☐☐☐☐☐
					☐☐☐☐☐
					☐☐☐☐☐
					☐☐☐☐☐
					☐☐☐☐☐
					☐☐☐☐☐
					☐☐☐☐☐
					☐☐☐☐☐
					☐☐☐☐☐
					☐☐☐☐☐
					☐☐☐☐☐
					☐☐☐☐☐
					☐☐☐☐☐
					☐☐☐☐☐
					☐☐☐☐☐
					☐☐☐☐☐
					☐☐☐☐☐
					☐☐☐☐☐
					☐☐☐☐☐
					☐☐☐☐☐

N1　　　　　　N2　　　　　　N3

N4　　　N5　　　N6　　　N7

N8　　　N9　　　N10　　　N11

N12　　　N13　　　N14

Scott No.	Illus. No.	Description	Unused Price	Used Price	//////

NEWSPAPER STAMPS

1865 Thin hard paper, no gum

Scott No.	Illus. No.	Description	Unused Price	Used Price	//////
PR1	N1	5c dk blue	175.00	–	□□□□□
PR2	N2	10c blue green	85.00	–	□□□□□
PR3	N3	25c orange red	85.00	–	□□□□□

White border Yellowish paper

| PR4 | N1 | 5c lt blue | 50.00 | 30.00 | □□□□□ |

1875 Hard white paper, no gum

PR5	N1	5c dl blue	75.00		□□□□□
PR6	N2	10c dk bluish green	60.00		□□□□□
PR7	N3	25c dk carmine	80.00		□□□□□

1880 Soft porous paper White border

| PR8 | N1 | 5c dk blue | 135.00 | | □□□□□ |

1875 Thin hard paper

PR9	N4	2c black	12.50	11.00	□□□□□
PR10	N4	3c black	16.00	14.00	□□□□□
PR11	N4	4c black	14.00	12.50	□□□□□
PR12	N4	6c black	18.00	17.00	□□□□□
PR13	N4	8c black	25.00	22.50	□□□□□
PR14	N4	9c black	55.00	50.00	□□□□□
PR15	N4	10c black	25.00	20.00	□□□□□
PR16	N5	12c rose	55.00	40.00	□□□□□
PR17	N5	24c rose	67.50	45.00	□□□□□
PR18	N5	36c rose	72.50	50.00	□□□□□
PR19	N5	48c rose	135.00	85.00	□□□□□
PR20	N5	60c rose	65.00	45.00	□□□□□
PR21	N5	72c rose	165.00	110.00	□□□□□
PR22	N5	84c rose	250.00	135.00	□□□□□
PR23	N5	96c rose	135.00	100.00	□□□□□
PR24	N6	1.92 dk brown	175.00	125.00	□□□□□
PR25	N7	$3 vermilion	225.00	135.00	□□□□□
PR26	N8	$6 ultra	375.00	165.00	□□□□□
PR27	N9	$9 yellow	500.00	225.00	□□□□□
PR28	N10	$12 blue green	625.00	300.00	□□□□□
PR29	N11	$24 dk gray violet	625.00	325.00	□□□□□
PR30	N12	$36 brown rose	650.00	375.00	□□□□□
PR31	N13	$48 red brown	850.00	500.00	□□□□□
PR32	N14	$60 violet	850.00	450.00	□□□□□

Special printing Hard white paper, without gum

PR33	N4	2c gray black	70.00		□□□□□
PR34	N4	3c gray black	75.00		□□□□□
PR35	N4	4c gray black	90.00		□□□□□
PR36	N4	6c gray black	120.00		□□□□□
PR37	N4	8c gray black	140.00		□□□□□
PR38	N4	9c gray black	165.00		□□□□□

N15 N16

N17 N18 N19

N20 N21 N22

HOW TO USE THIS BOOK

The number in the first column is its Scott number or identifying number. The letter and number that come next (A41) indicate the design and refer to the illustration so designated. Following that is the denomination of the stamp and its color. Finally, the price, unused and used is shown.

Scott No.	Illus. No.	Description	Unused Price	Used Price	//////
PR39	N4	10c gray black	200.00		□□□□□
PR40	N5	12c pale rose	225.00		□□□□□
PR41	N5	24c pale rose	300.00		□□□□□
PR42	N5	36c pale rose	425.00		□□□□□
PR43	N5	48c pale rose	475.00		□□□□□
PR44	N5	60c pale rose	550.00		□□□□□
PR45	N5	72c pale rose	700.00		□□□□□
PR46	N5	84c pale rose	725.00		□□□□□
PR47	N5	96c pale rose	875.00		□□□□□
PR48	N6	$1.92 dk brown	*2400.00*		□□□□□
PR49	N7	$3 vermilion	*5000.00*		□□□□□
PR50	N8	$6 ultra	*6000.00*		□□□□□
PR51	N9	$9 yellow	*11000.00*		□□□□□
PR52	N10	$12 blue green	*10000.00*		□□□□□
PR53	N11	$24 dk gray violet	—		□□□□□
PR54	N12	$36 brown rose	—		□□□□□
PR55	N13	$48 red brown	—		□□□□□
PR56	N14	$60 violet	—		□□□□□
1879	**Soft porous paper**				
PR57	N4	2c black	6.00	4.50	□□□□□
PR58	N4	3c black	7.50	5.00	□□□□□
PR59	N4	4c black	7.50	5.00	□□□□□
PR60	N4	6c black	15.00	11.00	□□□□□
PR61	N4	8c black	15.00	11.00	□□□□□
PR62	N4	10c black	15.00	11.00	□□□□□
PR63	N5	12c red	42.50	25.00	□□□□□
PR64	N5	24c red	42.50	22.50	□□□□□
PR65	N5	36c red	150.00	95.00	□□□□□
PR66	N5	48c red	110.00	60.00	□□□□□
PR67	N5	60c red	80.00	60.00	□□□□□
PR68	N5	72c red	180.00	115.00	□□□□□
PR69	N5	84c red	135.00	85.00	□□□□□
PR70	N5	96c red	100.00	60.00	□□□□□
PR71	N6	$1.92 pale brown	80.00	55.00	□□□□□
PR72	N7	$3 red vermilion	80.00	55.00	□□□□□
PR73	N8	$6 blue	140.00	90.00	□□□□□
PR74	N9	$9 orange	90.00	60.00	□□□□□
PR75	N10	$12 yellow green	135.00	85.00	□□□□□
PR76	N11	$24 dk violet	185.00	110.00	□□□□□
PR77	N12	$36 indian red	225.00	135.00	□□□□□
PR78	N13	$48 yellow brown	300.00	165.00	□□□□□
PR79	N14	$60 purple	325.00	165.00	□□□□□
1883	**Special printing**				
PR80	N4	2c intense black	165.00		□□□□□
1885					
PR81	N4	1c black	8.50	5.00	□□□□□
PR82	N5	12c carmine	25.00	12.50	□□□□□

Scott No.	Illus. No.	Description	Unused Price	Used Price	//////
PR83	N5	24c carmine	27.50	15.00	☐☐☐☐☐
PR84	N5	36c carmine	40.00	17.50	☐☐☐☐☐
PR85	N5	48c carmine	55.00	30.00	☐☐☐☐☐
PR86	N5	60c carmine	80.00	40.00	☐☐☐☐☐
PR87	N5	72c carmine	90.00	45.00	☐☐☐☐☐
PR88	N5	84c carmine	190.00	110.00	☐☐☐☐☐
PR89	N5	96c carmine	135.00	85.00	☐☐☐☐☐

1894

Scott No.	Illus. No.	Description	Unused Price	Used Price	//////
PR90	N4	1c intense black	42.50		☐☐☐☐☐
PR91	N4	2c intense black	42.50		☐☐☐☐☐
PR92	N4	4c intense black	55.00		☐☐☐☐☐
PR93	N4	6c intense black	800.00		☐☐☐☐☐
PR94	N4	10c intense black	100.00		☐☐☐☐☐
PR95	N5	12c pink	450.00	–	☐☐☐☐☐
PR96	N5	24c pink	400.00		☐☐☐☐☐
PR97	N5	36c pink	*2500.00*		☐☐☐☐☐
PR98	N5	60c pink	*2500.00*	–	☐☐☐☐☐
PR99	N5	96c pink	*3750.00*		☐☐☐☐☐
PR100	N7	$3 scarlet	*5000.00*		☐☐☐☐☐
PR101	N8	$6 pale blue	*5750.00*	*3000.00*	☐☐☐☐☐

1895

Scott No.	Illus. No.	Description	Unused Price	Used Price	//////
PR102	N15	1c black	25.00	7.50	☐☐☐☐☐
PR103	N15	2c black	25.00	7.50	☐☐☐☐☐
PR104	N15	5c black	35.00	12.50	☐☐☐☐☐
PR105	N15	10c black	70.00	32.50	☐☐☐☐☐
PR106	N16	25c carmine	100.00	35.00	☐☐☐☐☐
PR107	N16	50c carmine	225.00	95.00	☐☐☐☐☐
PR108	N17	$2 scarlet	250.00	65.00	☐☐☐☐☐
PR109	N18	$5 ultra	350.00	150.00	☐☐☐☐☐
PR110	N19	$10 green	325.00	165.00	☐☐☐☐☐
PR111	N20	$20 slate	650.00	300.00	☐☐☐☐☐
PR112	N21	$50 dl rose	675.00	300.00	☐☐☐☐☐
PR113	N22	$100 purple	750.00	350.00	☐☐☐☐☐

1895-97 Watermark 191

Scott No.	Illus. No.	Description	Unused Price	Used Price	//////
PR114	N15	1c black ('96)	3.00	2.00	☐☐☐☐☐
PR115	N15	2c black	3.00	1.50	☐☐☐☐☐
PR116	N15	5c black ('96)	5.00	3.00	☐☐☐☐☐
PR117	N15	10c black	3.00	2.00	☐☐☐☐☐
PR118	N16	25c carmine	5.00	3.75	☐☐☐☐☐
PR119	N16	50c carmine	6.50	3.50	☐☐☐☐☐
PR120	N17	$2 scarlet ('97)	10.00	11.50	☐☐☐☐☐
PR121	N18	$5 dk blue ('96)	20.00	25.00	☐☐☐☐☐
PR121a		$5 lt blue	100.00	45.00	☐☐☐☐☐
PR122	N19	$10 green ('96)	18.00	25.00	☐☐☐☐☐
PR123	N20	$20 slate ('96)	20.00	27.50	☐☐☐☐☐
PR124	N21	$50 dl rose ('97)	25.00	30.00	☐☐☐☐☐
PR125	N22	$100 purple ('96)	30.00	37.50	☐☐☐☐☐

PP1

PP2

PP3

PP4

PP5

PP6

PP7

PP8

PP9

PP10

PP11

PP12

PP13

PPD1

OC1

OC2

Scott No.	Illus. No.	Description	Unused Price	Used Price	//////

PARCEL POST STAMPS
1912-13

Q1	PP1	1c carmine rose	4.00	.90	☐☐☐☐☐
Q2	PP2	2c carmine rose	4.50	.70	☐☐☐☐☐
Q3	PP3	3c carmine ('13)	10.00	5.00	☐☐☐☐☐
Q4	PP4	4c carmine rose	25.00	2.00	☐☐☐☐☐
Q5	PP5	5c carmine rose	25.00	1.25	☐☐☐☐☐
Q6	PP6	10c carmine rose	40.00	1.75	☐☐☐☐☐
Q7	PP7	15c carmine rose	65.00	9.00	☐☐☐☐☐
Q8	PP8	20c carmine rose	140.00	17.50	☐☐☐☐☐
Q9	PP9	25c carmine rose	80.00	4.50	☐☐☐☐☐
Q10	PP10	50c carmine rose ('13)	210.00	35.00	☐☐☐☐☐
Q11	PP11	75c carmine rose	80.00	30.00	☐☐☐☐☐
Q12	PP12	$1 carmine rose ('13)	400.00	20.00	☐☐☐☐☐

SPECIAL HANDLING STAMPS
1925-29

QE1	PP13	10c yellow green ('28)	1.50	.90	☐☐☐☐☐
QE2	PP13	15c yellow green ('28)	1.65	.90	☐☐☐☐☐
QE3	PP13	20c yellow green ('28)	2.00	1.75	☐☐☐☐☐
QE4	PP13	25c yellow green ('29)	20.00	7.50	☐☐☐☐☐
QE4a		25c dp green ('25)	25.00	4.50	☐☐☐☐☐

PARCEL POSTAGE DUE STAMPS
1912

JQ1	PPD1	1c dk green	9.00	3.00	☐☐☐☐☐
JQ2	PPD1	2c dk green	80.00	15.00	☐☐☐☐☐
JQ3	PPD1	5c dk green	11.50	3.50	☐☐☐☐☐
JQ4	PPD1	10c dk green	150.00	35.00	☐☐☐☐☐
JQ5	PPD1	25c dk green	85.00	3.50	☐☐☐☐☐

CARRIER'S STAMPS
1851

| LO1 | OC1 | (1c) dl blue, *rose* | *1500.00* | *2000.00* | ☐☐☐☐☐ |
| LO2 | OC2 | 1c blue | 20.00 | 20.00 | ☐☐☐☐☐ |

1875 GOVERNMENT REPRINTS

LO3	OC1	bl *rose*, imperf.	40.00		☐☐☐☐☐
LO4	OC1	bl perf. 12	*2500.00*		☐☐☐☐☐
LO5	OC2	1c blue imperf.	20.00		☐☐☐☐☐
LO6	OC2	1c blue perf. 12	120.00		☐☐☐☐☐

Scott No.	Illus. No.	Description	Unused Price	Used Price	//////
					□□□□□
					□□□□□
					□□□□□
					□□□□□
					□□□□□
					□□□□□
					□□□□□
					□□□□□
					□□□□□
					□□□□□
					□□□□□
					□□□□□
					□□□□□
					□□□□□
					□□□□□
					□□□□□
					□□□□□
					□□□□□
					⊓□□□□
					□□□□□
					□□□□□
					□□□□□
					□□□□□
					□□□□□
					□□□□□
					□□□□□
					□□□□□
					□□□□□
					□□□□□
					□□□□□
					□□□□□
					□□□□□

PLATE NUMBER BLOCK, SHEET AND FIRST DAY COVER PRICES

The Plate Block and First Day Cover prices have been derived from the 1988 edition of Scott's Specialized Catalogue of United States Stamps. The sheet prices were developed by the Editorial Staff of Scott Publishing Co. exclusively for this edition. Sheet prices start with the 1957 Flag Issue (Scott 1094), the beginning of contemporary multicolor and multiple plate number printing.

All plate blocks are blocks of four, unless otherwise indicated in parenthesis.

Scott No.		Pl. Blk.	Sheet	FDC	Scott No.		Pl. Blk.	Sheet	FDC
1893					282C	(6)	2,500.00		
230	(6)	350.00		3,000.00	283	(6)	1,500.00		
231	(6)	300.00		2,400.00	284	(6)	2,250.00		
232	(6)	650.00		6,000.00	**1898**				
233	(6)	950.00		6,000.00	285		225.00		4,500.00
234	(6)	1,350.00		6,250.00	286		210.00		4,000.00
235	(6)	1,050.00		6,750.00	287		1,100.00		
236	(6)	650.00			288		1,000.00		5,000.00
237	(6)	3,000.00		7,500.00	289		1,750.00		7,500.00
238	(6)	4,750.00			290		2,250.00		
239	(6)	7,000.00			291		13,500.00		9,000.00
240	(6)	9,500.00			292		40,000.00		10,000.00
241	(6)	20,000.00			293		80,000.00		
242	(6)	22,000.00		15,000.00	**1901**				
243	(6)	45,000.00			294	(6)	275.00		3,500.00
244	(6)	90,000.00			295	(6)	275.00		3,000.00
245	(6)	100,000.00			296	(6)	2,500.00		4,250.00
1894	**With Triangles**	**Unwatermarked**			297	(6)	2,750.00		4,500.00
246	(6)	300.00			298	(6)	4,750.00		
247	(6)	600.00			299	(6)	7,500.00		
248	(6)	200.00			**1902-03**				
249	(6)	1,250.00			300	(6)	185.00		
250	(6)	300.00			301	(6)	200.00		2,750.00
251	(6)	2,100.00			302	(6)	850.00		
252	(6)	1,200.00			303	(6)	850.00		
253	(6)	1,000.00			304	(6)	950.00		
254	(6)	1,250.00			305	(6)	1,000.00		
255	(6)	875.00			306	(6)	700.00		
256	(6)	1,500.00			307	(6)	1,150.00		
257	(6)	1,100.00			308	(6)	650.00		
258	(6)	2,400.00			309	(6)	3,000.00		
259	(6)	3,750.00			310	(6)	7,500.00		
260	(6)	6,000.00			311	(6)	16,500.00		
261	(6)	15,000.00			312	(6)	25,000.00		
261A	(6)	25,000.00			313	(6)	62,500.00		
262	(6)	35,000.00			**1906-08**	*Imperforate*			
263	(6)	— —			314	(6)	275.00		
1895	**With Triangles**	**Watermarked**			315	(6)	4,750.00		
264	(6)	185.00			**1903**				
265	(6)	350.00			319	(6)	100.00		
266	(6)	325.00			**1906**	*Imperforate*			
267	(6)	135.00			320	(6)	300.00		
268	(6)	575.00			**1904**				
269	(6)	600.00			323		180.00		3,000.00
270	(6)	600.00			324		180.00		2,750.00
271	(6)	1,100.00			325		625.00		3,250.00
272	(6)	700.00			326		750.00		5,500.00
273	(6)	1,150.00			327		1,600.00		7,500.00
274	(6)	3,000.00			**1907**				
275	(6)	6,000.00			328	(6)	300.00		3,750.00
276	(6)	10,000.00			329	(6)	425.00		5,500.00
276A	(6)	20,000.00			330	(6)	2,900.00		
277	(6)	18,500.00			**1908-09**				
278	(6)	60,000.00			331	(6)	80.00		
1898					332	(6)	75.00		
279	(6)	175.00			333	(6)	350.00		
279B	(6)	160.00			334	(6)	375.00		
280	(6)	600.00							
281	(6)	650.00							
282	(6)	900.00							

Scott No.		Pl. Blk.	Sheet	FDC
335	(6)	600.00		
336	(6)	900.00		
337	(6)	475.00		
338	(6)	1,000.00		
339	(6)	475.00		
340	(6)	650.00		
341	(6)	7,500.00		
342	(6)	12,500.00		

1908-09 Imperforate

Scott No.		Pl. Blk.	Sheet	FDC
343	(6)	80.00		
344	(6)	130.00		
345	(6)	300.00		
346	(6)	400.00		
347	(6)	650.00		

1909 Bluish Paper

Scott No.		Pl. Blk.	Sheet	FDC
357	(6)	1,150.00		
358	(6)	1,100.00		
359	(6)	16,500.00		
361	(6)	35,000.00		
362	(6)	11,000.00		
364	(6)	12,000.00		
365	(6)	17,500.00		
366	(6)	9,500.00		

1909

Scott No.		Pl. Blk.	Sheet	FDC
367	(6)	160.00		350.00
368	(6)	300.00		3,500.00
369	(6)	4,250.00		
370	(6)	300.00		1,800.00
371	(6)	400.00		
372	(6)	350.00		850.00
373	(6)	450.00		2,000.00

1910-11 Watermarked Single-Line USPS

Scott No.		Pl. Blk.	Sheet	FDC
374	(6)	85.00		
375	(6)	85.00		
376	(6)	175.00		
377	(6)	225.00		
378	(6)	265.00		
379	(6)	450.00		
380	(6)	1,250.00		
381	(6)	1,250.00		
382	(6)	2,750.00		

1911 Imperforate

Scott No.		Pl. Blk.	Sheet	FDC
383	(6)	65.00		
384	(6)	200.00		

1913

Scott No.		Pl. Blk.	Sheet	FDC
397	(6)	175.00		3,250.00
398	(6)	300.00		
399	(6)	2,250.00		4,000.00
400	(6)	3,000.00		
400A	(6)	9,500.00		

1914-15 Perforated 10

Scott No.		Pl. Blk.	Sheet	FDC
401	(6)	375.00		
402	(6)	1,850.00		
403	(6)	4,500.00		
404	(6)	15,000.00		

1912-14 Perforated 12

Scott No.		Pl. Blk.	Sheet	FDC
405	(6)	115.00		
406	(6)	140.00		
407	(6)	1,250.00		

1914 Imperforate

Scott No.		Pl. Blk.	Sheet	FDC
408	(6)	25.00		
409	(6)	50.00		

1912-14 Perforated 12

Scott No.		Pl. Blk.	Sheet	FDC
414	(6)	475.00		
415	(6)	750.00		
416	(6)	525.00		
417	(6)	550.00		
418	(6)	750.00		

Scott No.		Pl. Blk.	Sheet	FDC
419	(6)	2,000.00		
420	(6)	1,750.00		
421	(6)	9,000.00		

1914 Watermarked Double-Line USPS

Scott No.		Pl. Blk.	Sheet	FDC
422	(6)	5,500.00		
423	(6)	12,500.00		

1914-15 Perforated 10

Scott No.		Pl. Blk.	Sheet	FDC
424	(6)	45.00		
425	(6)	30.00		
426	(6)	135.00		
427	(6)	400.00		
428	(6)	285.00		
429	(6)	300.00		
430	(6)	850.00		
431	(6)	400.00		
432	(6)	550.00		
433	(6)	550.00		
434	(6)	200.00		
435	(6)	250.00		
437	(6)	850.00		
438	(6)	2,500.00		
439	(6)	3,500.00		
440	(6)	11,000.00		

1915

Scott No.		Pl. Blk.	Sheet	FDC
460	(6)	12,500.00		

1915 Perforated 11

Scott No.		Pl. Blk.	Sheet	FDC
461	(6)	950.00		

1916-17 Perforated 10 Unwatermarked

Scott No.		Pl. Blk.	Sheet	FDC
462	(6)	150.00		
463	(6)	120.00		
464	(6)	1,350.00		
465	(6)	650.00		
466	(6)	900.00		
468	(6)	1,150.00		
469	(6)	1,350.00		
470	(6)	525.00		
471	(6)	675.00		
472	(6)	1,350.00		
473	(6)	325.00		
474	(6)	550.00		
475	(6)	2,500.00		
476	(6)	3,500.00		
476A	(6)	— —		
477	(6)	25,000.00		
478	(6)	13,000.00		
479	(6)	6,000.00		
480	(6)	4,500.00		

1916-17 Imperforate

Scott No.		Pl. Blk.	Sheet	FDC
481	(6)	15.00		
482	(6)	25.00		
483	(6)	175.00		
484	(6)	135.00		

1917-19 Perforated 11

Scott No.		Pl. Blk.	Sheet	FDC
498	(6)	17.50		
499	(6)	14.00		
500	(6)	2,250.00		
501	(6)	175.00		
502	(6)	210.00		
503	(6)	185.00		
504	(6)	150.00		
506	(6)	210.00		
507	(6)	325.00		
508	(6)	200.00		
509	(6)	190.00		
510	(6)	250.00		
511	(6)	135.00		
512	(6)	150.00		
513	(6)	140.00		
514	(6)	675.00		
515	(6)	750.00		

Scott No.		Pl. Blk.	Sheet	FDC
516	(6)	600.00		
517	(6)	1,500.00		
518	(6)	1,200.00		

1917 Type of 1908-09 *Perforated 11*
519	(6)	2,500.00		

1918
523	(8)	*18,500.00*		
524	(8)	*6,000.00*		

1918-20 Offset Printing
525	(6)	30.00		
526	(6)	275.00		800.00
527	(6)	150.00		
528	(6)	65.00		
528A	(6)	400.00		
528B	(6)	165.00		
529	(6)	70.00		
530	(6)	12.00		

1918-20 Offset, *Imperforate*
531	(6)	100.00		
532	(6)	350.00		
533	(6)	2,000.00		
534	(6)	110.00		
534A	(6)	375.00		
534B	(6)	*12,500.00*		
535	(6)	70.00		

1919 Offset, *Perf. 12½*
536	(6)	200.00		

1919
537	(6)	150.00		700.00

1919 *Perforated 11x10*
538		100.00		
539		*15,000.00*		
540		110.00		
541		400.00		

1920 *Perforated 10x11*
542	(6)	175.00		700.00

1921 Rotary
543		20.00		
545		1,100.00		
546		850.00		

1920
547	(8)	7,000.00		
548	(6)	55.00		700.00
549	(6)	80.00		625.00
550	(6)	650.00		

1922-25 *Perforated 11*
551	(6)	7.00		22.50
552	(6)	25.00		32.50
553	(6)	40.00		35.00
554	(6)	25.00		45.00
555	(6)	210.00		37.50
556	(6)	225.00		50.00
557	(6)	250.00		125.00
558	(6)	425.00		200.00
559	(6)	90.00		100.00
560	(6)	725.00		100.00
561	(6)	210.00		100.00
562	(6)	300.00		100.00
563	(6)	35.00		550.00
564	(6)	90.00		135.00
565	(6)	60.00		300.00
566	(6)	300.00		350.00
567	(6)	300.00		*400.00*
568	(6)	250.00		*600.00*
569	(6)	450.00		*725.00*
570	(6)	900.00		*1,000.00*
571	(6)	500.00		*4,000.00*
572	(6)	1,650.00		*10,000.00*

Scott No.		Pl. Blk.	Sheet	FDC
573	(8)	5,750.00		*11,000.00*

1923-25 *Imperforate*
575	(6)	100.00		
576	(6)	30.00		45.00
577	(6)	30.00		

1923-26 *Perforated 11x10*
578		750.00		
579		450.00		

Perforated 10
581		125.00		*2,000.00*
582		45.00		47.50
583		30.00		
584		250.00		55.00
585		175.00		
586		165.00		55.00
587		70.00		70.00
588		110.00		70.00
589		250.00		72.50
590		45.00		75.00
591		675.00		100.00

Perforated 11 Rotary
595		1,500.00		

1923
610	(6)	30.00		22.50
611	(6)	140.00		100.00
612		375.00		110.00

1924
614	(6)	50.00		27.50
615	(6)	85.00		35.00
616	(6)	450.00		70.00

1925
617	(6)	50.00		27.50
618	(6)	95.00		35.00
619	(6)	400.00		50.00
620	(8)	225.00		25.00
621	(8)	750.00		45.00

1925-26
622	(6)	200.00		35.00
623	(6)	250.00		30.00

1926
627	(6)	50.00		14.00
628	(6)	110.00		22.50
629	(6)	50.00		6.25
631		70.00		35.00

1926-34 *Perforated 11x10½*
632		2.00		55.00
633		90.00		55.00
634		1.20		57.50
634A		2,100.00		
635		7.00		47.50
636		100.00		55.00
637		21.00		55.00
638		21.00		65.00
639		21.00		67.50
640		21.00		70.00
641		21.00		85.00
642		35.00		90.00

1927
643		40.00		6.00
644	(6)	65.00		16.50

1928
645	(6)	40.00		5.00
646		40.00		17.50
647		150.00		17.50
648		300.00		32.50
649	(6)	17.50		10.00
650	(6)	90.00		15.00

Scott No.		Pl. Blk.	Sheet	FDC
1929				
651	(6)	16.00		7.50
653		1.00		30.00
654	(6)	35.00		13.00
655		55.00		90.00
657	(6)	35.00		4.50
"Kansas"				
658		25.00		27.50
659		40.00		27.50
660		40.00		27.50
661		175.00		30.00
662		175.00		32.50
663		150.00		35.00
664		400.00		42.50
665		400.00		42.50
666		800.00		80.00
667		175.00		72.50
668		325.00		85.00
"Nebraska"				
669		25.00		27.50
670		40.00		25.00
671		25.00		25.00
672		150.00		32.50
673		200.00		37.50
674		210.00		37.50
675		500.00		55.00
676		275.00		57.50
677		375.00		60.00
678		400.00		62.50
679		900.00		70.00
1929				
680	(6)	40.00		5.00
681	(6)	32.50		4.50
1930				
682	(6)	40.00		5.25
683	(6)	65.00		5.50
684	(6)	1.50		6.25
685	(6)	10.00		10.00
688	(6)	55.00		6.00
689	(6)	35.00		6.00
1931				
690	(6)	17.50		5.00
Regular Issue				
692		19.00		80.00
693		35.00		80.00
694		18.00		85.00
695		25.00		85.00
696		60.00		100.00
697		30.00		1,750.00
698		65.00		185.00
699		62.50		1,750.00
700		100.00		275.00
701		300.00		425.00
1931				
702		2.25		4.00
703		3.50		5.00
1932				
704		4.00		5.00
705		5.00		5.50
706		22.50		5.50
707		1.50		5.50
708		16.00		5.75
709		5.00		5.75
710		24.00		6.00
711		75.00		6.75
712		6.00		6.75
713		70.00		6.75
714		45.00		7.75
715		150.00		10.00

Scott No.		Pl. Blk.	Sheet	FDC
1932				
716	(6)	17.50		7.50
717		12.50		5.00
718		25.00		7.50
719		40.00		9.50
720		1.50		10.00
724	(6)	18.50		3.00
725	(6)	30.00		3.00
1933				
726	(6)	20.00		3.00
727		6.50		3.50
728		2.50		3.00
729		3.50		3.00
732		2.00		3.25
733	(6)	25.00		6.00
734	(6)	45.00		5.50
1934				
736	(6)	13.50		1.60
737		1.75		1.60
738	(6)	7.25		1.60
739	(6)	7.00		1.60
740	(6)	1.50		2.25
741	(6)	2.00		2.25
742	(6)	3.00		2.50
743	(6)	11.00		3.25
744	(6)	16.00		3.25
745	(6)	30.00		4.00
746	(6)	20.00		4.00
747	(6)	30.00		4.25
748	(6)	30.00		4.50
749	(6)	50.00		10.00
1935				
752		16.00		10.00
753	(6)	25.00		12.00
754	(6)	35.00		12.00
755	(6)	35.00		12.00
756	(6)	5.50		12.00
757	(6)	6.50		12.00
758	(6)	20.00		13.00
759	(6)	27.50		13.00
760	(6)	35.00		13.00
761	(6)	47.50		13.00
762	(6)	42.50		13.00
763	(6)	55.00		15.00
764	(6)	60.00		15.00
765	(6)	72.50		15.00
771	(6)	65.00		25.00
772		2.00		8.00
773		2.00		8.00
774	(6)	2.75		10.00
775		2.00		8.00
1936				
776		2.00		12.50
777		2.00		8.00
782		2.00		8.00
783		2.00		8.00
784		.75		15.00
1936-37				
785		1.00		5.00
786		1.10		5.00
787		1.50		5.00
788		13.00		5.50
789		15.00		5.50
790		1.00		5.00
791		1.10		5.00
792		1.50		5.00
793		13.00		5.50
794		15.00		5.50
1937				
795		2.00		6.00

Scott No.		Pl. Blk.	Sheet	FDC	Scott No.	Pl. Blk.	Sheet	FDC
796	(6)	10.00		7.00	877	9.00		4.00
798		1.65		6.50	878	32.50		7.50
799		2.00		7.00	879	1.25		1.75
800		2.00		7.00	880	1.25		1.75
801		2.00		7.00	881	1.75		1.75
802		2.00		7.00	882	12.50		4.00
1938					883	50.00		7.00
803		.40		1.25	884	1.10		1.75
804		.25		2.00	885	1.10		1.75
805		.30		2.00	886	1.25		1.75
806		.35		2.00	887	11.50		3.50
807		.50		2.00	888	35.00		7.00
808		2.75		2.00	889	2.50		1.75
809		1.60		2.50	890	1.30		1.75
810		2.00		2.25	891	2.50		1.75
811		2.25		2.25	892	20.00		4.50
812		2.50		2.50	893	100.00		12.50
813		3.25		2.50	**1940**			
814		3.50		2.65	894	6.50		6.00
815		2.50		2.75	895	5.50		4.50
816		5.00		2.75	896	3.50		4.50
817		9.50		3.00	897	2.75		4.50
818		10.00		3.00	898	2.75		4.50
819		8.75		3.25	899	.70		4.25
820		3.75		3.25	900	.70		4.25
821		8.75		3.50	901	1.40		4.25
822		7.50		3.75	902	6.00		5.00
823		16.00		4.25	**1941–43**			
824		10.00		4.25	903	2.50		4.50
825		6.00		4.50	904	2.25		4.00
826		12.50		5.00	905	.60		3.75
827		11.50		5.25	906	18.50		5.75
828		35.00		5.25	907	.50		3.50
829		7.00		6.50	908	1.00		3.50
830		45.00		10.00	909	8.00		5.00
831		67.50		20.00	910	4.00		5.00
832		62.50		55.00	911	2.50		4.00
833		165.00		110.00	912	2.50		4.00
834		575.00		190.00	913	2.50		4.00
1938					914	2.50		4.00
835		5.50		6.50	915	2.50		4.00
836	(6)	6.00		6.00	916	20.00		4.00
837		15.00		6.00	917	7.50		4.00
838		9.00		6.00	918	7.50		4.00
1939					919	5.50		4.00
852		1.75		5.00	920	7.50		4.00
853		2.00		8.00	921	7.00		5.00
854	(6)	4.25		5.00	**1944**			
855		4.00		18.00	922	2.50		6.00
856	(6)	6.00		5.00	923	2.50		4.00
857		1.65		5.00	924	1.60		3.50
858		1.65		5.00	925	3.00		3.50
1940					926	2.00		3.50
859		1.10		1.75	**1945**			
860		1.25		1.75	927	1.00		3.50
861		2.00		1.75	928	.70		3.50
862		11.00		4.50	929	.50		5.25
863		50.00		7.50	**1945–46**			
864		1.75		1.75	930	.30		2.50
865		1.75		1.75	931	.40		2.50
866		3.50		1.75	932	.65		2.50
867		11.00		4.00	933	.75		3.00
868		45.00		7.50	**1945**			
869		1.75		1.75	934	.60		3.50
870		1.40		1.75	935	.60		3.50
871		3.25		1.75	936	.60		3.50
872		12.00		4.00	937	.50		2.50
873		32.50		7.50	938	.50		3.50
874		1.00		1.75	**1946**			
875		1.20		1.75	939	.50		2.50
876		1.75		2.75				

Scott No.	Pl. Blk.	Sheet	FDC	Scott No.	Pl. Blk.	Sheet	FDC
940	.55		2.50	1005	.60		1.25
941	.50		2.50	1006	.50		1.50
942	.50		2.50	1007	.60		.85
943	.50		2.50	1008	.55		.85
944	.50		2.50	1009	.50		.85
1947				1010	.50		.85
945	.50		2.50	1011	.60		.85
946	.50		2.50	1012	.50		.85
947	.50		2.50	1013	.50		.85
949	.50		1.50	1014	.50		.85
950	.50		1.50	1015	.50		.85
951	.50		1.50	1016	.50		.85
952	.50		1.50				
1948				**1953-54**			
953	.50		1.50	1017	.50		.85
954	.50		1.50	1018	.80		.85
955	.50		1.50	1019	.50		.85
956	.50		1.50	1020	.50		.85
957	.50		1.50	1021	1.40		.85
958	1.00		1.50	1022	.50		.85
959	.50		1.50	1023	.50		1.00
960	.60		1.50	1024	.50		.85
961	.50		1.50	1025	.50		.85
962	.50		1.50	1026	.60		.85
963	.50		1.50	1027	.60		.85
964	.90		1.50	1028	.50		.85
965	1.70		1.50	1029	.50		.85
966	2.50		1.50				
967	.60		1.25	**1954-68**			
968	.80		1.25	1030	.30		.85
969	.65		1.50	1031	.25		.85
970	.65		1.50	1031A	1.75		.85
971	.75		1.50	1032	7.50		.60
972	.75		1.25	1033	.25		.60
973	1.20		1.25	1034	2.00		.60
974	.65		1.25	1035	.40		.60
975	1.00		1.25	1036	.50		.60
976	1.50		1.25	1037	1.75		.60
977	.65		1.25	1038	.85		.60
978	.70		1.25	1039	2.00		.65
979	.55		1.25	1040	1.50		.70
980	.85		1.25	1041	5.00		.80
1949				1042	1.75		.60
981	.50		1.25	1042A	1.50		.60
982	.50		1.25	1043	1.50		1.50
983	.50		1.25	1044	1.65		.90
984	.50		1.25	1044A	1.50		.90
985	.50		1.25	1045	2.75		.90
986	.60		1.25	1046	4.25		1.00
1950				1047	4.50		1.20
987	.50		1.25	1048	13.75		1.30
988	.65		1.25	1049	10.00		1.50
989	.50		1.25	1050	17.50		1.75
990	.50		1.25	1051	16.00		6.00
991	.50		1.25	1052	50.00		13.00
992	.50		1.25	1053	500.00		75.00
993	.50		1.25				
994	.50		1.25	**1954**			
995	.55		2.00	1060	.50		.75
996	.50		1.25	1061	.50		.75
997	.50		1.25	1062	.60		.75
1951				1063	.50		.75
998	.50		1.25	**1955**			
999	.50		1.25	1064	.50		.75
1000	.50		1.25	1065	.50		.75
1001	.50		1.25	1066	1.50		.90
1002	.50		1.25	1067	.50		.75
1003	.50		1.25	1068	.50		.75
1952				1069	.50		.75
1004	.50		1.25	1070	.70		.75
				1071	.50		.75
				1072	.60		.75

Scott No.	Pl. Blk.	Sheet	FDC	Scott No.	Pl. Blk.	Sheet	FDC
1956				1140	1.00	9.50	1.00
1073	.50		.75	1141	1.00	9.50	1.00
1074	.50		.75	1142	1.00	9.50	1.25
1076	.50		.75	1143	1.00	9.50	1.25
1077	.65		1.10	1144	1.00	9.50	1.25
1078	.65		1.10	**1960**			
1079	.65		1.10	1145	.50	5.25	1.25
1080	.50		.80	1146	.50	5.25	.80
1081	.50		.80	1147	.60	7.25	.80
1082	.50		.80	1148	1.75	15.50	.80
1083	.50		.80	1149	.50	5.25	.80
1084	.50		.80	1150	.65	5.25	.80
1085	.50		.80	1151	.50	7.25	.80
1957				1152	.50	5.25	.80
1086	.50		.80	1153	.50	5.25	.80
1087	.50		.80	1154	.50	5.25	.80
1088	.50		.80	1155	.50	5.25	.80
1089	.50		.80	1156	.50	5.25	.80
1090	.50		.80	1157	.50	5.25	.80
1091	.50		.80	1158	.50	5.25	.80
1092	.60		.80	1159	.55	7.25	.80
1093	.50		.80	1160	1.75	15.50	.80
1094	.60	5.50	.80	1161	.50	7.25	.80
1095	.70	7.50	.80	1162	.50	5.25	.80
1096	1.75	11.50	.80	1163	.50	5.25	.80
1097	.50	5.25	.80	1164	.50	5.25	.80
1098	.65	5.25	1.00	1165	.55	7.25	.80
1099	.50	5.25	.80	1166	1.75	15.50	.80
1958				1167	.50	5.25	.80
1100	.50	5.25	.80	1168	.55	7.25	.80
1104	.50	5.25	.80	1169	1.75	15.50	.80
1105	.60	7.25	.80	1170	.50	7.25	.80
1106	.50	5.25	.80	1171	.50	7.25	.80
1107	.75	5.50	.80	1172	.55	7.25	.80
1108	.50	5.25	.80	1173	2.25	18.50	1.75
1109	.50	5.25	.80	**1961**			
1110	.60	7.25	.80	1174	.55	7.25	.80
1111	5.00	22.50	.80	1175	2.00	16.00	.80
1112	.50	5.25	.80	1176	.65	5.25	.75
1958-59				1177	.55	7.25	.75
1113	.40	2.75	.80	**1961-65**			
1114	.60	5.25	.80	1178	1.10	9.50	1.75
1115	.55	5.25	.80	1179	1.00	8.00	1.75
1116	.65	5.25	.80	1180	1.00	8.00	1.75
1958				1181	1.00	8.00	1.75
1117	.60	7.25	.80	1182	1.10	8.50	1.75
1118	3.50	18.50	.80	**1961**			
1119	.50	5.25	.80	1183	.55	5.25	.75
1120	.50	5.25	.80	1184	.55	5.25	.75
1121	.50	7.25	.80	1185	.55	5.25	.90
1122	.60	5.25	.80	1186	.55	5.25	.75
1123	.50	5.25	.80	1187	1.00	7.00	.75
1959				1188	.55	5.25	.75
1124	.50	5.25	.80	1189	.55	5.25	1.50
1125	.55	7.25	.80	1190	.70	5.50	.75
1126	1.75	15.50	.80	**1962**			
1127	.50	7.25	.80	1191	.55	5.25	.75
1128	.85	7.00	.80	1192	.65	5.50	.75
1129	1.50	10.75	.80	1193	.65	5.50	1.50
1130	.50	5.25	.80	1194	.55	5.25	.75
1131	.50	5.25	.80	1195	.55	5.25	.75
1132	.50	5.25	.80	1196	.65	5.25	.75
1133	.65	5.25	.80	1197	.55	5.25	.75
1134	.50	5.25	.80	1198	.55	5.25	.75
1135	.50	5.25	.80	1199	.55	5.25	1.00
1136	.60	7.25	.80	1200	.65	5.25	.75
1137	1.75	15.50	.80	1201	.55	5.25	.75
1138	.50	7.25	.80	1202	.55	5.25	.75
1960-61				1203	.70	5.50	.75
1139	1.00	9.50	1.25	1204	4.00	10.00	6.00
				1205	.50	10.50	.75

Scott No.	Pl. Blk.	Sheet	FDC	Scott No.	Pl. Blk.	Sheet	FDC
1206	.55	5.25	.75	1293	5.00	102.50	3.25
1207	1.00	8.00	.75	1294	10.50	245.00	7.50
1962-63				1295	50.00	1,250.00	60.00
1208	.55	12.50	.75	**1966**			
1209	.25	5.25	.75	1306	.75	6.50	.75
1213	.75	12.50	.75	1307	.90	6.50	.75
1963				1308	.75	6.50	.75
1230	.60	6.50	.75	1309	.90	6.50	.75
1231	.60	6.50	.75	1310	.90	6.50	.75
1232	.60	6.50	.75	1311	.75	6.50	.75
1233	.60	6.50	.75	1312	.90	6.50	.75
1234	.60	6.50	.75	1313	.75	6.50	.75
1235	.60	6.50	.75	1314	1.00	6.75	.75
1236	.60	6.50	.75	1315	1.00	6.75	.75
1237	.60	6.50	.75	1316	1.00	6.75	.75
1238	.60	6.50	.75	1317	1.00	6.75	.75
1239	.60	6.50	.75	1318	1.00	6.75	.75
1240	.60	13.00	.75	1319	1.00	6.75	.75
1241	.60	6.50	.75	1320	1.00	6.75	.75
1964				1321	.75	12.50	.75
1242	.60	6.50	.75	1322	2.75	12.50	.75
1243	.75	8.00	.75	**1967**			
1244	.60	6.50	.75	1323	.90	6.50	.75
1245	.60	6.50	.75	1324	.90	6.50	.75
1246	.60	6.50	.75	1325	.90	6.50	.75
1247	.60	6.50	.75	1326	.90	6.50	.75
1248	.60	6.50	.75	1327	.90	6.50	.75
1249	.60	6.50	.75	1328	.90	6.50	.75
1250	.60	6.50	.75	1329	1.00	6.75	.75
1251	.60	6.50	.75	1330	1.00	6.75	.75
1252	.60	6.50	.75	1331-1332	8.00	55.00	8.00
1253	.60	6.50	.75	1333	3.00	8.75	.75
1254-1257	3.25	70.00	.75ea.	1334	1.25	8.75	.75
1258	.60	6.50	.75	1335	1.50	10.00	.75
1259	.75	6.50	.75	1336	.60	6.50	.75
1260	.75	6.50	.75	1337	1.00	8.00	.75
1965				**1968-71**			
1261	.75	6.50	.75	1338	.60	12.50	.75
1262	.75	6.50	.75	1338D (20)	4.25	21.00	.75
1263	.75	6.50	.75	1338F (20)	4.25	21.00	.75
1264	.75	6.50	.75	**1968**			
1265	.75	6.50	.75	1339	1.00	9.50	.75
1266	.75	6.50	.75	1340	1.00	9.50	.75
1267	.75	6.50	.75	1341	25.00	260.00	6.50
1268	.75	6.50	.75	1342	1.00	9.50	.75
1269	.75	6.50	.75	1343	1.00	9.50	.75
1270	.75	6.50	.75	1344	1.00	9.50	.75
1271	1.00	6.75	.75	1345-1354 (20)	18.00	45.00	4.00 ea.
1272	1.00	6.75	.75	1355	1.25	11.00	1.00
1273	1.25	8.50	.75	1356	1.00	10.50	.75
1274	9.00	35.00	.75	1357	1.00	10.50	.75
1275	.75	6.50	.75	1358	1.00	10.50	.75
1276	.60	12.50	.75	1359	1.00	10.50	.75
1965-73				1360	1.00	10.50	.75
1278	.25	5.25	.60	1361	1.10	13.00	.75
1279	25.00	35.00	.60	1362	1.75	13.50	.75
1280	.30	5.25	.60	1363 (10)	2.75	10.75	.75
1281	.40	6.50	.60	1364	1.35	16.00	.75
1282	.40	8.25	.60	**1969**			
1283	.50	10.50	.60	1365-1368	7.50	60.00	2.00ea.
1283B	1.00	13.00	.45	1369	1.10	10.50	.75
1284	.90	18.50	.45	1370	1.35	13.00	.75
1285	1.25	26.00	.50	1371	1.50	16.00	2.00
1286	2.00	27.00	.60	1372	1.00	10.50	.75
1286A	1.50	31.00	.50	1373	1.00	10.50	.75
1287	1.65	31.00	.65	1374	1.00	10.50	.75
1288	1.50	31.00	.60	1375	1.00	10.50	.75
1289	2.50	56.00	.80	1376-1379	8.50	72.50	2.00ea.
1290	2.75	62.50	1.00	1380	1.35	11.00	.75
1291	3.50	77.50	1.20	1381	1.75	13.25	1.50
1292	4.25	96.50	1.60	1382	1.75	13.25	1.50
				1383	1.00	6.75	.75

Scott No.		Pl. Blk.	Sheet	FDC
1384	(10)	2.25	9.50	.75
1385		1.00	9.50	.75
1386		1.20	6.50	.75
1970				
1387-1390		1.75	9.00	2.00ea.
1391		1.10	9.50	.75
1392		1.10	9.50	1.00
1970-74				
1393		.60	12.50	.75
1393D		1.35	15.00	.75
1394		1.00	16.50	.75
1396	(12)	5.00	27.50	.75
1397		2.35	35.00	.85
1398		2.35	36.00	.75
1399		2.25	41.00	1.25
1400		2.25	46.00	1.00
1970				
1405		1.00	9.50	.75
1406		1.00	9.50	.75
1407		1.00	9.50	.75
1408		1.00	9.50	.75
1409		1.00	9.50	.75
1410-1413	(10)	6.00	30.00	1.40ea.
1414	(8)	2.25	11.00	1.40
1415-1418	(8)	8.50	50.00	1.40ea.
1419		1.25	10.00	.75
1420		1.25	10.00	.75
1421-1422		3.00	15.00	.75ea.
1971				
1423		1.00	9.50	.75
1424		1.00	9.50	.75
1425		1.00	9.50	.75
1426	(12)	3.50	11.75	.75
1427-1430		1.75	11.00	1.75ea.
1431		1.50	13.25	.75
1432		3.25	27.50	.75
1433		1.50	11.50	.75
1434-1435		1.75	13.50	1.75
1436		1.25	10.00	.75
1437		1.25	10.00	.75
1438	(6)	1.85	10.50	.75
1439	(8)	2.10	10.00	.75
1440-1443		1.85	10.50	1.50ea.
1444	(12)	2.50	9.75	.75
1445	(12)	2.50	9.75	.75
1972				
1446		1.00	9.75	.75
1447		1.50	9.75	.75
1448-1451		1.60	8.50	1.25
1452		1.25	8.75	.75
1453		1.00	6.50	.75
1454		2.75	20.00	.75
1455		1.00	8.50	.75
1456-1459		1.75	16.50	1.00ea.
1460	(10)	2.25	9.00	.75
1461	(10)	2.25	9.00	.85
1462	(10)	4.50	19.00	1.00
1463		1.00	8.50	.75
1464-1467		1.40	9.00	2.00ea.
1468	(12)	2.75	9.25	.75
1469	(6)	1.35	8.50	.75
1470		1.00	8.50	.75
1471	(12)	2.75	9.00	.75
1472	(12)	2.75	9.00	.75
1473		1.00	8.50	.75
1474		1.00	6.75	.75
1973				
1475		1.35	8.50	.75
1476		1.35	10.75	.75
1477		1.35	10.75	.75
1478		1.35	10.75	.75
1479		1.35	10.75	.75
1480-1483		1.35	11.75	1.75ea.
1484	(12)	2.75	7.50	.75
1485	(12)	2.75	7.50	.75
1486	(12)	2.75	7.50	.75
1487	(12)	2.75	7.50	.75
1488		1.00	8.50	.75
1489-1498	(20)	4.50	12.00	1.10ea.
1499		1.00	5.75	.75
1500		1.25	7.00	.75
1501		1.00	8.50	.75
1502		3.00	17.50	.80
1503	(12)	2.50	5.75	.75
1973-74				
1504		1.00	8.50	.75
1505		1.00	10.50	.75
1506		1.00	10.50	.75
1507	(12)	2.10	8.50	.75
1508	(12)	2.10	8.50	.75
1509	(20)	5.50	22.00	.75
1510		1.00	21.00	.75
1511	(8)	2.25	21.00	.75
1974				
1525		1.25	11.00	.75
1526		1.00	10.50	.75
1527	(12)	2.60	8.50	.75
1528	(12)	2.60	10.50	.75
1529		1.00	10.50	1.25
1530-1537	(10)	2.60	6.75	1.10ea.
1538-1541		1.50	10.50	1.50ea.
1542		1.20	10.75	.75
1543-1546		1.20	10.75	.90ea.
1547		1.00	10.50	.75
1548		1.00	11.00	.75
1549		1.00	10.50	.75
1550	(10)	2.25	10.50	.75
1551	(12)	2.60	10.50	.75
1552	(20)	5.50	11.75	.75
1975				
1553	(10)	2.20	10.50	.75
1554	(10)	2.20	10.50	.75
1555		1.00	10.50	.75
1556		1.00	10.50	1.25
1557		1.00	10.50	1.25
1558	(8)	1.80	10.50	.75
1559	(10)	2.00	8.75	.75
1560	(10)	2.50	11.00	.75
1561	(10)	2.50	11.00	.75
1562	(10)	5.00	20.00	.75
1563	(12)	2.60	8.50	.75
1564	(12)	2.60	8.50	.75
1565-1568	(12)	2.60	10.50	.90ea.
1569-1570	(12)	2.60	5.00	1.00ea.
1571	(6)	1.40	11.00	.75
1572-1575	(12)	2.60	10.50	.75ea.
1576		1.00	10.50	.75
1577-1578		1.00	9.00	.75ea.
1579	(12)	2.60	10.50	.75
1580	(12)	2.60	10.50	.75
1975-81				
1581		.25	5.25	.40
1582		.25	5.25	.40
1584		.30	6.25	.40
1585		.40	8.25	.40
1591		.90	18.50	.60
1592		1.00	21.00	.60
1593		1.10	23.00	.60
1594		1.15	25.00	.60
1596	(12)	3.50	26.50	.60
1597	(6)	2.10	31.00	.65

Scott No.		Pl. Blk.	Sheet	FDC	Scott No.		Pl. Blk.	Sheet	FDC
1599		2.25	33.50	.65	1783-1786	(12)	4.20	16.00	.75ea.
1603		2.75	50.00	.75	1787	(20)	6.50	16.00	.65
1604		3.25	58.00	1.20	1788	(10)	3.50	16.00	.65
1605		3.25	60.00	1.10	1789	(10)	3.50	16.00	.65
1606		3.00	62.00	1.10	1790	(12)	3.75	13.50	1.00
1608		5.00	105.00	1.50	1791-1794	(12)	4.75	20.00	.75ea.
1610		10.00	205.00	3.00	1795-1798	(12)	6.50	25.00	.75ea.
1611		22.50	450.00	5.00	1799	(12)	4.25	31.00	.65
1612		50.00	1,020.00	10.00	1800	(12)	4.25	31.00	.65
1622	(20)	5.50	26.50	.65	1801	(12)	4.25	16.00	.65
1976					1802	(10)	3.50	16.00	1.25
1629-1631	(12)	3.40	13.50	.65ea.	**1980**				
1632		1.30	13.75	.65	1803	(12)	4.25	16.00	.65
1633-1682	(50)	25.00	25.00	1.75ea.	1804	(12)	4.25	16.00	.65
1683		1.30	13.75	.65	1805-1810	(36)	11.10	19.00	.65ea.
1684	(10)	2.90	13.75	.65	1818		1.80	37.50	.75
1685	(12)	3.40	13.75	.65	1821		1.50	16.00	.65
1690		1.30	13.75	.65	1822		1.50	46.00	.65
1691-1694	(20)	5.50	14.00	.65ea.	1823		1.50	16.00	.65
1695-1698	(12)	3.40	14.00	.75ea.	1824		1.50	16.00	.80
1699	(12)	3.40	11.00	.65	1825		1.50	16.00	.65
1700		1.30	9.00	.65	1826		1.50	16.00	.65
1701	(12)	3.40	13.75	.65	1827-1830	(12)	4.50	16.50	.85ea.
1702	(10)	3.00	13.75	.65	1831	(12)	4.50	16.50	.65
1703	(20)	5.70	13.50	.65	1832		1.50	16.00	.65
1977					1833	(6)	2.25	16.00	.65
1704	(10)	2.90	11.00	.65	1834-1837	(10)	3.50	13.00	.75ea.
1705		1.30	13.75	.65	1838-1841		1.50	13.00	.75ea.
1706-1709	(10)	3.00	12.00	.75ea.	1842	(12)	4.25	16.50	.65
1710	(12)	3.65	14.00	.75	1843	(20)	6.50	16.00	.65
1711	(12)	3.65	14.00	.65	**1980-85**				
1712-1715	(12)	3.65	14.00	.75ea.	1844	(20)	1.00	5.10	.60
1716		1.30	11.00	.65	1845		.25	5.00	.60
1717-1720	(12)	3.65	14.00	.65ea.	1846		.40	8.25	.60
1721		1.30	13.50	.65	1847		.50	10.50	.60
1722	(10)	3.10	11.50	.65	1848		.60	12.50	.60
1723-1724	(12)	3.65	11.50	.65ea.	1849	(20)	2.75	12.50	.60
1725		1.30	13.75	.65	1850	(20)	3.00	14.25	.60
1726		1.30	13.75	.65	1851		.80	16.50	.60
1727		1.30	13.75	.75	1852	(20)	4.00	18.50	.60
1728	(10)	3.10	11.50	.65	1853	(20)	4.50	20.50	.65
1729	(20)	8.00	36.00	.65	1854		1.10	22.50	.65
1730	(10)	3.10	27.00	.65	1855		1.50	31.00	.65
1978					1856	(20)	7.00	33.00	.65
1731		1.30	13.75	.65	1857		2.00	41.00	.75
1732		1.30		.75	1858		2.20	45.00	.75
1733		1.30		.75	1859		2.00	39.50	.80
1732-1733	(20)	5.75	14.00		1860		2.50	51.00	.75
1734		3.25	44.00	1.00	1861		2.50	51.00	.75
1735		1.50	31.00	.65	1862		2.50	51.00	.75
1744	(12)	3.65	14.00	1.00	1862	(20)	8.50	41.00	.75
1745-1748	(12)	3.65	14.00	.75ea.	1863	(20)	9.25	44.50	.80
1749-1752	(12)	3.65	14.00	.75ea.	1864	(20)	12.50	60.50	.85
1753		1.30	11.00	.65	1865		3.50	72.00	1.00
1754		1.30	14.00	.65	1866		3.75	77.00	1.00
1755	(12)	3.65	14.00	.65	1867	(20)	20.00	81.50	1.00
1756	(12)	4.20	16.00	.65	1868	(20)	17.50	81.50	1.00
1758	(12)	4.20	13.00	.65	1869		5.00	102.00	1.25
1759		1.50	16.00	1.10	**1981**				
1760-1763		1.50	16.25	.75ea.	1874		1.50	16.00	.65
1764-1767	(12)	4.20	13.00	.75ea.	1875		1.50	16.00	.65
1768	(12)	4.20	32.00	.65	1876-1879		1.80	18.50	.75ea.
1769	(12)	4.20	32.00	.65	1890	(20)	10.00	36.50	.75
1979					1894	(20)	9.50	40.50	.75
1770		1.50	15.50	.65	1910		1.80	19.00	.75
1771	(21)	4.20	16.00	.65	1911		1.80	19.00	.75
1772		1.50	16.00	.65	1912-1919	(8)	3.50	19.00	.75ea.
1773		1.50	16.00	.65	1920		1.80	19.00	.75
1774		1.50	16.00	.65	1921-1924		1.80	19.50	.75ea.
1775-1778	(10)	3.50	13.00	.75ea.	1925		1.80	19.00	.75
1779-1782		1.50	16.00	.75ea.	1926		1.80	19.00	.75
					1927	(20)	30.00	38.50	.75
					1928-1931		1.80	15.50	.75ea.

Scott No.		Pl. Blk.	Sheet	FDC
1932		1.80	19.00	.75
1933		1.80	19.00	.75
1934		1.80	19.00	.75
1935		3.00	27.00	.75
1936		2.00	21.00	.75
1937-1938		1.80	19.00	.75ea.
1939		2.00	41.00	.75
1940		2.00	21.00	.75
1941		2.00	21.00	.75
1981				
1942-1945		2.00	17.00	.75ea.
1946		2.00	41.00	.75
1982				
1950		2.00	20.00	.75
1951		2.00	21.00	.75
1952		2.00	21.00	.75
1953-2002	(50)	20.00	20.00	1.00 ea.
2003	(20)	10.00	22.00	.75
2004		2.00	21.00	.75
2006-2009		2.00	21.00	.75ea.
2010		2.00	21.00	.75
2011		2.00	21.00	.75
2012		2.00	21.00	.75
2013		2.00	21.00	.75
2014		2.00	21.00	.75
2015		2.00	21.00	.75
2016		2.00	21.00	.75
2017	(20)	10.00	22.00	.85
2018		2.00	21.00	.75
2019-2022		2.00	16.75	.75ea.
2023		2.00	21.00	.75
2024	(20)	8.50	22.00	.75
2025		1.30	14.00	.75
2026	(20)	8.50	22.00	.75
2027-2030		2.00	21.00	.75ea.
1983				
2031		2.00	21.00	.75
2032-2035		2.00	16.75	.75ea.
2036		2.00	21.00	.75
2037		2.00	21.00	.75
2038		2.00	21.00	.75
2039	(20)	10.00	22.00	.75
2040		2.00	21.00	.75
2041		2.00	21.00	.75
2042	(20)	10.00	22.00	.75
2043	(20)	10.00	22.00	.75
2044		2.00	21.00	.75
2045		2.00	16.75	.75
2046		2.00	21.00	.75
2047		2.00	21.00	.75
2048-2051		1.30	14.00	.75 ea.
2052		2.00	16.75	.75
2053	(20)	10.00	22.00	.75
2054		2.00	21.00	.75
2055-2058		2.00	21.00	.75 ea.
2059-2062		2.00	21.00	.75 ea.
2063		2.00	21.00	.75
2064	(20)	10.00	22.00	.75
2065		2.00	21.00	.75
1984				
2066		2.00	21.00	.75
2067-2070		2.00	21.00	.75 ea.
2071		2.00	21.00	.75
2072	(20)	10.00	22.00	.75
2073		2.00	21.00	.75
2074		2.00	21.00	.75
2075		2.00	21.00	.75
2076-2079		2.00	21.00	.75ea.
2080		2.00	21.00	.75
2081		2.00	21.00	.75
2082-2085		2.00	21.00	.75ea.

Scott No.		Pl. Blk.	Sheet	FDC
2086		2.00	16.75	.75
2087		2.00	21.00	.75
2088	(20)	10.00	22.00	.75
2089		2.00	21.00	.75
2090		2.00	21.00	.75
2091		2.00	21.00	.75
2092		2.00	21.00	.75
2093		2.00	21.00	.75
2094		2.00	21.00	.75
2095	(20)	10.00	22.00	.75
2096		2.00	21.00	.75
2097		2.00	21.00	.75
2098-2101		2.00	16.75	.75ea.
2102		2.00	21.00	.75
2103		2.00	16.75	.75
2104	(20)	10.00	22.00	.75
2105		2.00	20.00	.75
2106		2.00	21.00	.75
2107		2.00	21.00	.75
2108		2.00	21.00	.75
2109		2.00	16.75	.75
1985				
2110		2.20	23.00	.80
2111	(20)	12.00	52.00	.80
2114		2.20	45.00	.80
2137		2.20	23.00	.80
2138-2141		2.20	23.00	.80ea.
2142		2.20	18.75	.80
2143		2.20	23.00	.80
2144	(20)	9.25	23.00	.80
2145		2.20	22.50	.80
2146		2.20	23.00	.80
2147		2.20	23.00	.80
2152		2.20	23.00	.80
2153		2.20	23.00	.80
2154		2.20	23.00	.80
2155-2158		2.20	18.75	.80ea.
2159		2.20	23.00	.80
2160-2163		2.20	23.00	.80ea.
2164		2.20	23.00	.80
2165		2.20	23.00	.80
2166		2.20	23.00	.80
1986				
2167		2.20	23.00	.80
1986-87				
2168		.25	5.25	.80
2169		.25	5.25	.80
2170		.30	6.25	.80
2171		.40	8.25	.80
2172		.50	10.25	.80
2176		1.00	20.50	.80
2177		1.40	29.00	.80
2179		1.75	35.00	.80
2183		2.50	51.00	.85
2191		5.50	115.00	1.25
2194		10.00	205.00	2.00
2195		20.00	410.00	4.00
2196		50.00	240.00	10.00
1986				
2202		2.20	23.00	.80
2203		2.20	23.00	.80
2204		2.20	23.00	.80
2210		2.20	23.00	.80
2211		2.20	23.00	.80
2220-2223		2.20	23.50	.80ea.
22224		2.20	23.00	.80
2235-2238		2.20	23.50	.80ea.
2239		2.20	23.00	.80
2240-2243		2.20	23.50	.80ea.
2244		2.20	45.00	.80
2245		2.20	45.00	.80

Scott No.	Pl. Blk.	Sheet	FDC	Scott No.	Pl. Blk.	Sheet	FDC
1987				2341	2.20	23.00	.80
2246	2.20	23.00	.80	2342	2.20	23.00	.80
2247	2.20	23.00	.80	**1987**			
2248	2.20	45.00	.80	2349	2.20	23.00	.80
2249	2.20	23.00	.80	2350	2.20	23.00	.80
2250	2.20	23.00	.80	2351-2354	2.20	18.75	.80ea.
2251	2.20	23.00	.80	2360	2.20	23.00	.80
2275	2.20	23.00	.80	2361	2.20	23.00	.80
2276	2.20	45.00	.80	2367	2.20	45.00	.80
2286-2335 (50)	22.00	22.00	.80ea.	2368	2.20	45.00	.80
1987-88				**1988**			
2336	2.20	23.00	.80	2369	2.20	23.00	.80
2337	2.20	23.00	.80	2370	2.20	18.75	.80
2338	2.20	23.00	.80	2371	2.20	23.00	.80
2339	2.20	23.00	.80	2372-2375	2.20	18.75	.80 ea.
2340	2.20	23.00	.80	2376	2.20	23.00	.80

_____ □□□□□
_____ □□□□□
_____ □□□□□
_____ □□□□□
_____ □□□□□
_____ □□□□□
_____ □□□□□
_____ □□□□□
_____ □□□□□
_____ □□□□□
_____ □□□□□
_____ □□□□□
_____ □□□□□
_____ □□□□□
_____ □□□□□
_____ □□□□□
_____ □□□□□
_____ □□□□□
_____ □□□□□
_____ □□□□□
_____ □□□□□
_____ □□□□□
_____ □□□□□
_____ □□□□□

Scott No.		Pl. Blk.	Sheet	FDC
Air Post				
1918				
C1	(6)	1,200.00		*17,500.00*
C2	(6)	2,250.00		*22,500.00*
C3	(12)	2600.00		*27,500.00*
1923				
C4	(6)	600.00		350.00
C5	(6)	3,250.00		750.00
C6	(6)	4,200.00		900.00
1926-28				
C7	(6)	55.00		65.00
C8	(6)	65.00		75.00
C9	(6)	165.00		115.00
C10	(6)	200.00		25.00
C11	(6)	65.00		50.00
C12	(6)	250.00		20.00
C13	(6)	3,850.00		1,850.00
C14	(6)	8,250.00		1,400.00
C15	(6)	13,000.00		2,000.00
1931-34				
C16		135.00		200.00
C17		45.00		20.00
C18	(6)	1,100.00		225.00
C19		27.50		*200.00*
1935-39				
C20	(6)	20.00		35.00
C21	(6)	150.00		40.00
C22	(6)	140.00		40.00
C23		11.00		15.00
C24	(6)	200.00		45.00
1941-44				
C25		1.00		2.25
C26		1.25		3.75
C27		12.50		7.00
C28		19.00		10.00
C29		16.50		10.00
C30		17.50		16.00
C31		100.00		40.00
1946-47				
C32		.75		2.00
C33		.75		2.00
C34		2.25		2.00
C35		2.50		2.75
C36		8.00		3.50
1948-49				
C38		20.00		1.75
C39		.90		1.50
C40		.85		1.25
C42		3.25		1.75
C43		2.75		2.25
C44		11.00		2.75
C45		.85		3.75
1952-54				
C46		55.00		17.50
C47		.85		1.50
C48		5.00		.75
1957-59				
C49		1.25	9.00	1.75
C50		5.00	26.50	.80
C51		1.30	22.50	.75
C53		1.50	13.25	.65
C54		1.50	13.25	1.10
C55		1.50	13.25	1.00
C56		5.00	24.00	.90
1959-62				
C57		15.00	155.00	1.50
C58		4.00	39.00	1.10
C59		4.00	39.00	1.50

Scott No.		Pl. Blk.	Sheet	FDC
C60		1.50	31.00	.70
C62		7.00	37.00	.80
C63		2.25	21.00	1.00
C64		1.10	22.50	.60
1963-64				
C66		7.00	67.50	1.35
C67		3.50	23.00	.50
C68		3.00	17.00	2.50
C69		5.00	47.50	2.75
1967-69				
C70		4.00	26.00	.70
C71		8.50	80.00	2.00
C72		2.25	32.00	.60
C74		5.00	35.00	1.50
C75		5.00	45.00	1.10
C76		2.50	11.50	3.50
1971-73				
C77		2.00	24.00	.50
C78		1.75	31.00	.50
C79		1.65	33.00	.55
C80		2.75	29.00	.60
C81		2.75	29.00	.75
C84		2.00	16.50	.65
C85	(10)	3.50	16.00	.50
C86		1.75	16.00	.50
1974-76				
C87		2.50	23.50	.65
C88		3.00	31.00	.85
C89		3.25	32.00	.85
C90		3.25	33.00	.85
1978-79				
C91-C92		4.50	95.00	1.15ea.
C93-C94		7.50	130.00	1.00ea.
C95-C96		8.00	152.50	1.00ea.
C97	(12)	12.00	47.00	1.15
1980				
C98	(12)	12.00	47.00	1.35
C99	(12)	9.25	37.00	1.10
C100	(12)	10.00	40.00	1.25
1983				
C101-C104		2.75	30.00	1.10ea.
C105-C108		4.00	44.00	1.35ea.
C109-C112		3.50	38.00	1.25ea.
1985				
C113		3.50	35.00	1.25
C114		4.00	41.00	1.35
C115		4.50	46.00	1.35
C116		4.50	46.00	1.35
Air Post Special Delivery				
1934-36				
CE1	(6)	20.00		25.00
CE2		8.50		17.50
Special Delivery				
1885-95				
E1	(8)	*12,000.00*		*8,000.00*
E2	(8)	*12,000.00*		
E3	(8)	*7,250.00*		
E4	(6)	*14,500.00*		
E5	(6)	*4,500.00*		
1902-17				
E6	(6)	*2,750.00*		
E7	(6)	*925.00*		
E8	(6)	*2,500.00*		
E9	(6)	*4,250.00*		
E10	(6)	*5,750.00*		
E11	(6)	200.00		

Scott No.		Pl. Blk.	Sheet	FDC
1922-25				
E12	(6)	375.00		550.00
E13	(6)	250.00		275.00
E14	(6)	37.50		150.00
1927-51				
E15		5.25		100.00
E16		6.50		1,000.00
E17		4.00		12.00
E18		28.50		12.00
E19		12.00		5.00
1954-57				
E20		4.00		3.00
E21		5.00		2.25
1969-71				
E22		11.00		3.50
E23		6.00		3.50
Registration				
F1	(6)	*1,850.00*		*9,000.00*
Certified Mail				
FA1		6.25		3.25
Postage Due				
1910-12				
J45	(6)	400.00		
J46	(6)	350.00		
J47	(6)	3,850.00		
J48	(6)	600.00		
J49	(6)	1,150.00		
J50	(6)	6,500.00		
1914-15				
J52	(6)	550.00		
J53	(6)	350.00		
J54	(6)	4,500.00		
J55	(6)	285.00		
J56	(6)	600.00		
J57	(6)	2,100.00		
J58	(6)	*36,000.00*		
1916				
J59	(6)	*7,750.00*		
J60	(6)	800.00		
1917-25				
J61	(6)	40.00		
J62	(6)	35.00		
J63	(6)	85.00		
J64	(6)	85.00		
J65	(6)	125.00		
J66	(6)	525.00		
J67	(6)	750.00		
J68	(6)	11.00		
1930-31	*Perforated 11*			
J69	(6)	35.00		
J70	(6)	27.50		
J71	(6)	40.00		
J72	(6)	250.00		
J73	(6)	225.00		
J74	(6)	425.00		
J75	(6)	1,000.00		
J76	(6)	1,250.00		
J77	(6)	275.00		
J78	(6)	375.00		

Scott No.		Pl. Blk.	Sheet	FDC
1931-56	*Perforated 11x10½*			
J79		22.50		
J80		2.00		
J81		2.00		
J82		3.00		
J83		4.00		
J84		8.50		
J85		45.00		
J86		57.50		
J87		300.00		
1959				
J88		125.00		
J89		.50		
J90		.60		
J91		.70		
J92		1.25		
J93		.75		
J94		1.40		
J95		1.60		
J96		1.75		
J97		1.25		
J98		5.50		
J99		6.50		
J100		10.00		
J101		40.00		
1978-85				
J102		1.10		
J103		1.30		
J104		1.70		
Offices in China				
1919-22				
K1	(6)	275.00		
K2	(6)	275.00		
K3	(6)	450.00		
K4	(6)	550.00		
K5	(6)	525.00		
K6	(6)	700.00		
K7	(6)	800.00		
K8	(6)	600.00		
K9	(6)	650.00		
K10	(6)	600.00		
K11	(6)	800.00		
K12	(6)	1,000.00		
K13	(6)	1,300.00		
K14	(6)	1,000.00		
K15	(6)	*10,000.00*		
K16	(6)	*7,500.00*		
K17	(6)	725.00		
K18	(6)	675.00		
Official Stamps				
1910-11				
O121	(6)	225.00		
O122	(6)	2,200.00		
O123	(6)	2,000.00		
O124	(6)	120.00		
O125	(6)	550.00		
O126	(6)	250.00		
1983-85				
O127		.25		.75
O128		.40		.75
O129		1.30		.60
O129A		1.40		.65
O130		1.70		.75
O132		10.00		2.25
O133		50.00		12.50
O138		1.40		.65

Scott No.	Illus. No.	Description	Unused Price	Used Price	//////
					☐☐☐☐☐
					☐☐☐☐☐
					☐☐☐☐☐
					☐☐☐☐☐
					☐☐☐☐☐
					☐☐☐☐☐
					☐☐☐☐☐
					☐☐☐☐☐
					☐☐☐☐☐
					☐☐☐☐☐
					☐☐☐☐☐
					☐☐☐☐☐
					☐☐☐☐☐
					☐☐☐☐☐
					☐☐☐☐☐
					☐☐☐☐☐
					☐☐☐☐☐
					☐☐☐☐☐
					☐☐☐☐☐
					☐☐☐☐☐
					☐☐☐☐☐
					☐☐☐☐☐
					☐☐☐☐☐
					☐☐☐☐☐
					☐☐☐☐☐
					☐☐☐☐☐
					☐☐☐☐☐
					☐☐☐☐☐
					☐☐☐☐☐
					☐☐☐☐☐
					☐☐☐☐☐
					☐☐☐☐☐
					☐☐☐☐☐
					☐☐☐☐☐

Scott No.	Illus. No.	Description	Unused Price	Used Price	//////
					☐☐☐☐☐
					☐☐☐☐☐
					☐☐☐☐☐
					☐☐☐☐☐
					☐☐☐☐☐
					☐☐☐☐☐
					☐☐☐☐☐
					☐☐☐☐☐
					☐☐☐☐☐
					☐☐☐☐☐
					☐☐☐☐☐
					☐☐☐☐☐
					☐☐☐☐☐
					☐☐☐☐☐
					☐☐☐☐☐
					☐☐☐☐☐
					☐☐☐☐☐
					☐☐☐☐☐
					☐☐☐☐☐
					☐☐☐☐☐
					☐☐☐☐☐
					☐☐☐☐☐
					☐☐☐☐☐
					☐☐☐☐☐
					☐☐☐☐☐
					☐☐☐☐☐
					☐☐☐☐☐
					☐☐☐☐☐
					☐☐☐☐☐
					☐☐☐☐☐
					☐☐☐☐☐
					☐☐☐☐☐
					☐☐☐☐☐

Scott No.	Illus. No.	Description	Unused Price	Used Price	//////
					□□□□□
					□□□□□
					□□□□□
					□□□□□
					□□□□□
					□□□□□
					□□□□□
					□□□□□
					□□□□□
					□□□□□
					□□□□□
					□□□□□
					□□□□□
					□□□□□
					□□□□□
					□□□□□
					□□□□□
					□□□□□
					□□□□□
					□□□□□
					□□□□□
					□□□□□
					□□□□□
					□□□□□
					□□□□□
					□□□□□
					□□□□□
					□□□□□
					□□□□□
					□□□□□
					□□□□□
					□□□□□
					□□□□□
					□□□□□

Scott No.	Illus. No.	Description	Unused Price	Used Price	//////
					☐☐☐☐☐
					☐☐☐☐☐
					☐☐☐☐☐
					☐☐☐☐☐
					☐☐☐☐☐
					☐☐☐☐☐
					☐☐☐☐☐
					☐☐☐☐☐
					☐☐☐☐☐
					☐☐☐☐☐
					☐☐☐☐☐
					☐☐☐☐☐
					☐☐☐☐☐
					☐☐☐☐☐
					☐☐☐☐☐
					☐☐☐☐☐
					☐☐☐☐☐
					☐☐☐☐☐
					☐☐☐☐☐
					☐☐☐☐☐
					☐☐☐☐☐
					☐☐☐☐☐
					☐☐☐☐☐
					☐☐☐☐☐
					☐☐☐☐☐
					☐☐☐☐☐
					☐☐☐☐☐
					☐☐☐☐☐
					☐☐☐☐☐
					☐☐☐☐☐
					☐☐☐☐☐
					☐☐☐☐☐
					☐☐☐☐☐

Scott No.	Illus. No.	Description	Unused Price	Used Price	//////
					□□□□□
					□□□□□
					□□□□□
					□□□□□
					□□□□□
					□□□□□
					□□□□□
					□□□□□
					□□□□□
					□□□□□
					□□□□□
					□□□□□
					□□□□□
					□□□□□
					□□□□□
					□□□□□
					□□□□□
					□□□□□
					□□□□□
					□□□□□
					□□□□□
					□□□□□
					□□□□□
					□□□□□
					□□□□□
					□□□□□
					□□□□□
					□□□□□
					□□□□□
					□□□□□
					□□□□□
					□□□□□
					□□□□□
					□□□□□

UNITED STATES
NATIONAL ALBUM

THE SCOTT UNITED STATES NATIONAL POSTAGE STAMP ALBUM is "The" Album demanded by serious collectors of United States material.

The SCOTT NATIONAL POSTAGE STAMP ALBUM provides spaces for commemoratives, definitives, air post, special delivery, registration, certified mail, postage due, parcel post, special handling, officials, newspapers, offices abroad, hunting permits, confederates and much more!

Available in U.S.A. and Canada from your favorite dealer, bookstore or stamp collecting accessory retailer or write:

Made in the USA
Lexington, KY
16 November 2019